The Eastern Yacht Club

For Louie Howland —
Esteemed old friend, editor
and counselor, with appreciation
for those flattering words and
your usual sound advice —
Affectionately,
Joe Garland

June 13, 1989

The Eastern Yacht Club

A History from 1870 to 1985   BY JOSEPH E. GARLAND

THE EASTERN YACHT CLUB   MARBLEHEAD, MASSACHUSETTS

Book and jacket design by David Ford

Distributed to the trade by Down East Books, Camden, Maine

ISBN 0-89272-263-0

This book is dedicated to Eugene T. Connolly,

an enthusiastic yachtsman

who realized the importance of this history

and whose leadership and perseverance

were an inspiration to the Historical Committee.

The Eastern Yacht Club is grateful to him

for his devotion to this project

and to the sport of yachting.

Contents

Foreword

It is a bit of a paradox that the nine founders of the Eastern Yacht Club, affluent blue-bloods of the 1870s, chose the westerly shore of Marblehead Neck as the site of their newly formed yacht club. These were the very shores where for generations fishermen had dried their fish in order to keep the smells away from the cozily nestled homes across the harbor in "old town." In retrospect, one could say that those visionary Yankees knew a good thing when they saw one. Here was a harbor of beauty that offered good holding ground, adequate depth, and superb accessibility to their favorite cruising grounds to the east.

The initial clubhouse was a modest structure built in 1880, and because places grow to serve their occupants and activities, the original physical plant grew substantially over the years to provide for the Club's changing membership. Today that plant offers the Club's yachting-oriented members superb waterfront facilities, fine onshore dining, comfortable and attractive public rooms, overnight guest rooms, six excellent tennis courts, two paddle courts, and a harborside swimming pool. In its early years, essentially all Eastern members claimed permanent residences in Boston, New York, and beyond. Nowadays, the vast majority of them live year round in Marblehead and the bordering communities, and the Eastern's facilities constitute the focal point of their summer enjoyment.

Inspired by the Club's centennial in 1970 and the nation's bicentennial in 1976, there was renewed interest in the Club's history and traditions. This spurred the notion that an updated history should be compiled and published to supplement the *Ditty Box*, written by C.H.W. Foster, which covered the Club's existence from 1870 to 1900. To accomplish that goal, the Eastern Council in 1977 made an excellent choice in appointing Eugene T. Connolly to chair the Historical Committee.

The committee's first two assignments were to inventory and catalog the Club's library and nautical collection and to research and write the history from 1900 to 1985. The committee members who assumed these responsibilities in varying degrees included Alice Blodgett, Eugene Connolly, Suzanne Connolly, Terrell Cooper, Nancy Godfrey, Henry Leonard, Priscilla Lord, George Page, Nancy Parker, Pemberton Pleasants, Joseph Roper, and Philip Tobey. Several current members were interviewed, as well as Elizabeth and Sherman Morss, past members, who willingly provided invaluable information and suggestions. Thanks in significant measure to Eugene Connolly's adept and persistent encouragement, this phase of the project was completed shortly before his death.

Under the successive chairmanships of Ronald N. Woodward and Suzanne Santry Connolly (married to Eugene Connolly's nephew), the committee struggled to devise a new format for the book, concluding finally that the wealth of information should be recast into a narrative history that would parallel the development of yachting as a sport. The committee began to seek an author. Most fortuitously for the success of the project, Joseph E. Garland accepted the challenge to breathe life into the assembled facts. He was ably assisted in further research by Matthew Widmer, a Harvard student chosen by the committee for a summer internship.

Subsequently, a photograph search committee was established, headed by Carole Benning and Beverly Stone, and including Ann Bullis, Judith Howe, Frank Jones, Joseph Santry,

Philip Seaver, and Arthur Strang. Their primary sources included the rich photographic archives preserved at the Peabody Museum of Salem (Massachusetts), the Hart Nautical Museum of Massachusetts Institute of Technology, Mystic Seaport Museum (Connecticut), The Essex Institute of Salem, in addition to the collections of the Club and some of its members.

Throughout the long and arduous process of creating the book, Llewellyn Howland, well-known maritime historian, expertly offered his services as an adviser, editor, and catalyst. He was particularly helpful to Joe Garland and the Publishing Committee.

We are also greatly indebted to a group of eighty-nine generous patrons, who provided the financial assistance that enabled us to retain such a respected author.

We expect that this ably written and interesting book will do for its readers what C.H.W. Foster in his own "introduction" anticipated the *Ditty Box* would do: inspire Club members to consider "'what a heritage of character, quality, and tradition we have!'. . . . No wonder that the 'spirit of the sea' still prevails on its vessels and that in its racing, true sportsmanship is the first consideration."

The Publishing Committee
Eastern Yacht Club

Suzanne S. Connolly, Chairman
Alice F. Blodgett
Nancy P. Parker
George A. Page, Jr.
Ronald N. Woodward

Patrons

Dr. and Mrs. F. Knight Alexander
Mrs. Frank G. Allen
James T. Baldwin
Commodore and Mrs. W. Gardner Barker
Mr. and Mrs. Thomas S. Barrows
Mr. and Mrs. Robert B.M. Barton
Mr. and Mrs. John A. Benning
Commodore and Mrs. Donald W. Blodgett
Mr. and Mrs. Archer L. Bolton, Jr.
Mr. and Mrs. James W. Bowers
Commodore and Mrs. Garrett D. Bowne III
Mr. and Mrs. F. Kent Bradford, Jr.
Mr. and Mrs. Edmund P. Bullis
Mr. and Mrs. Lawrence L. Burckmyer
William C. Burke, Jr.
Mr. and Mrs. William C. Burke III
Mr. and Mrs. Walter J. Cairns
Mr. and Mrs. Richard L. Case
Mr. and Mrs. E. Paul Casey
Mr. and Mrs. John P. Chase
Commodore and Mrs. Stephen J. Connolly III
Mr. and Mrs. Stephen J. Connolly IV
Mr. and Mrs. Henry W. Cook, Jr.
Commodore and Mrs. Henry E. Cooper III
Mr. and Mrs. Lewis C. Copeland

Mr. and Mrs. Lincoln Davis, Jr.
  Mr. Davis deceased
Mr. and Mrs. Thaddeus G. Driscoll
Mr. and Mrs. Charles Flather
Mr. and Mrs. Walter A. Friend
  Mr. Friend deceased
Mr. and Mrs. John N. Fulham, Jr.
Mr. and Mrs. Albert Goodhue, Jr.
Mr. and Mrs. James E. Grinnell
Mr. and Mrs. Ulf B. Heide
Mr. and Mrs. Richard D. Hill
Crosby Hitchcock
John Hitchcock, Jr.
Mr. and Mrs. Frederick E. Hood
Mr. and Mrs. Robert C. Hood
Mr. and Mrs. Charles R. Irving
Mr. and Mrs. Richard D. Jachney
Mr. and Mrs. H. Alden Johnson, Jr.
  Mr. Johnson deceased
Mr. and Mrs. Frank L. Jones
Mr. and Mrs. Erick Kauders
Mr. and Mrs. John P. Kehoe
Mr. and Mrs. James N. Krebs
Mr. and Mrs. Henry B. Leonard
Mr. and Mrs. Philip H. Lord

Mr. and Mrs. Joseph E. Lovejoy

Mr. and Mrs. Peter S. Lynch

Mrs. Robert C. Madden
 In memory of Capt. Eugene E. O'Donnell

Commander Francis H. Markey, USN Ret.

Dr. and Mrs. Frederic B. Mayo

Mr. and Mrs. John A. McCandless
 Mr. McCandless deceased

Vice Admiral and Mrs. John L. McCrea, USN Ret.

Mr. and Mrs. Edwin B. Morris III

Mrs. Garlan Morse

Commodore and Mrs. Wells Morss

Mr. and Mrs. Bradley P. Noyes

Mr. and Mrs. Eugene E. O'Donnell, Jr.
 In memory of Capt. Eugene E. O'Donnell

Mr. and Mrs. George A. Page, Jr.

Commodore and Mrs. Francis U. Paige

Commodore and Mrs. Albert C. Parker

Mr. and Mrs. Edward W. Parker

Mr. and Mrs. Joseph S.W. Parker

Mr. and Mrs. Lea B. Pendleton

Commodore and Mrs. Charles W. Pingree

Mr. and Mrs. Richard S. Robie, Jr.

Commodore and Mrs. Joseph C. Roper, Jr.

Mr. and Mrs. Arthur J. Santry, Jr.

Mr. and Mrs. Joseph R. Santry

Mr. and Mrs. Peter B. Seamans

Mr. and Mrs. Philip H. Seaver

Mr. and Mrs. Howard C. Smith, Jr.
 In memory of Frank M. Gring

Mr. and Mrs. Walter A. Smith, Jr.

Miss Ava Steenstrup

Mr. and Mrs. George H. Stephenson

Mr. and Mrs. P. Tapley Stephenson, Jr.

Mr. and Mrs. Ezra F. Stevens

Mrs. James J. Storrow

Dr. and Mrs. F. Howard Taggart, Jr.

Dr. and Mrs. Richard H. Thompson

Mr. and Mrs. Frank A. Thorn

Mr. and Mrs. Philip H. Tobey

Mr. and Mrs. G. Dudley Welch

Mr. and Mrs. William B. White

Mr. and Mrs. Albert G. Wigglesworth

Mr. and Mrs. Allen D. Willard

Mrs. John J. Wilson

Mr. and Mrs. Ronald N. Woodward

Introduction

My first memory of the Eastern Yacht Club is of watching Joseph Santry's schooner *Pleione* waft up Marblehead Harbor in an afternoon southerly. The year was 1947. I was going on eleven. How, I wondered, could there be so many boats in a single harbor, and how could any boat be more beautiful than *Pleione*?

In fact, the Club's fleet of my childhood was but a pale reflection of its prewar glory, and *Pleione* was herself an aging survivor. Gone before my time were the J- and M-boats, which had been such a commanding presence in the racing of the 1930s. Gone was the grand Edward Burgess–designed schooner *Constellation*, which had been the centerpiece of the Eastern fleet for half a century. No more did J.P. Morgan's last *Corsair* (324 feet), Vincent Astor's *Nourmahal* (232 feet), or Gerard B. Lambert's schooner *Atlantic* (185 feet, not counting jibboom) fly the Eastern burgee at the main truck. Not for decades would Marblehead Harbor approach the glory of the summer of 1937—a Depression year, lest we forget—when the Eastern Yacht Club started 390 boats on the first day of Race Week, 393 boats the second day, and 388 the third.

Yet I find myself thinking of the straitened years of the later 1940s and early 1950s as an enchanted time for the Eastern Yacht Club, when those members fortunate enough to own and sail boats did so with a special and hard-won regard for the human measure. This triumphant history of the Eastern Yacht Club has helped me understand why.

In the first place, American yachting—and Eastern in particular—has always been a family affair. No other sport or pastime affords so many opportunities for so many generations of a family to participate and compete. No child is too young, no grandparent too old to enjoy sailing. Come Race Week, nephews may crew for aunts, nieces for uncles, sons for fathers, and fathers for sons. Even the family mutt has enjoyed a cruise down east. And did not Starling Burgess, the most inventive and charming of the Eastern members, have a pet seal, Woo, which regularly and enthusiastically went yachting with its master?

It is true that the Eastern Yacht Club has sometimes been rather more attentive to "Yachting Families" than to family yachting; more concerned with the amenities of its clubhouse, its pool, its paddle courts than with the mandate of its charter, which is "to encourage yacht building and naval architecture, and the cultivation of nautical science." But as this book repeatedly demonstrates, the consanguinity of the Club, that lively fusion of Old and New Boston, speaks for its outreach as well as for its essential familiarity. Chary of change, the Club changes. Wary of strangers, it makes its strangers friends.

The Eastern was never more dependent on family support and family participation than after World War II, when, like yacht clubs up and down the coast, it found its treasury depleted, its membership rolls shrunken, and its fleet sorely diminished and largely obsolescent. No longer did the race results make sports-page headlines in the Boston press. The attention of the world had turned elsewhere.

These were slow times for the yacht business, too. One by one the great yacht builders—Herreshoff in Bristol, Lawley in Neponset, and Nevins at City Island—closed their doors for good. Then followed years of only modest demand, of confusion borne of changing demographics and technological innovation, and finally, of uncertain expansion into a mass market not contemplated by the founders of the Eastern Yacht Club.

The International and Cruising Club of America measurement rules for open-class and cruising-class boats were carryovers from the 1930s and favored traditional displacement hull forms and construction. Many who sailed most actively in the period, including some crack Eastern skippers, seemed not to care that American yachting was in development irons. For them, an old wooden boat with old cotton sails was infinitely to be preferred to twelve years of economic depression and growing international unrest, to five years of devastating world war, and . . . to having no boat at all to sail.

While the Club is today in most ways abreast of its times again, of more real and lasting significance is the fact that during all these decades since World War II, north of Cape Cod or south, coastwise or offshore, cruising and racing sailors from the Eastern have continued to add immeasurably to the pleasure and excitement of the sport. Mostly their boats have been of a size that a family could own, handle, and support at relatively small expense; all have been well maintained, well sailed, and much loved. Always their owners have been good sports, good teachers, good shipmates, good friends.

It is this tradition of kinship, friendship, good seamanship, and good sportsmanship to which the Eastern Yacht Club owes its survival during hard times and its prosperity in good ones. The tradition, a complex and arcane body of knowledge and values, is transmitted from generation to generation. Secure within it, the young sailor gains courage to move beyond his or her accustomed depth, to venture beyond home waters, to reach for the stars.

Sue Connolly and other members of the Eastern Yacht Club's Historical Committee spent years doing research in the Club's archives, interviewing senior members and longtime friends of the Club, and striving for a format for this book. The writing was another matter, until the committee turned to Joseph E. Garland, a Gloucester author and historian who for some thirty years has sounded the waters and marked the headlands of Massachusetts Bay. He has written with equal authority and style about the great days of the Gloucester fishery, the summer history of Boston's North Shore, and the life of the prodigious small-boat passagemaker Howard Blackburn. Although Joe was not, in his own estimation, a yachting historian, the committee reasoned that it would take only a single book to make him one.

What a fortunate choice Joe has proven to be. He has paid equal attention to the Club's nineteenth century origins and to its current activities. He has allowed the dominant figures from the Club's past and present to speak in their own words, even when their memories and viewpoints do not agree. He has revealed—tactfully but firmly—some of the Club's best-kept secrets. Above all, Joe Garland has written of the Club a serious and responsible history that is a pure delight to read.

Llewellyn Howland III

Preface

"We want the history of the Eastern Yacht Club, not of American yachting," were my instructions from its Historical Committee in the early spring of 1986. Fair enough. I countered, however, that on the strength of the little I then knew, the history of the one is in large measure the history of the other.

What follows, I submit almost three years later, takes the Club well beyond a passive place in the larger annals of the sport. For the first time we have a body of collective evidence suggesting the great extent to which the Eastern has in fact contributed to the development of yachting in this country.

And as one who has delved somewhat into the social history of the North Shore of Boston, I feel that in the process we have managed to elucidate, from the inside out as well as from the outside in, some intriguing insights into one of our unique maritime institutions.

Notwithstanding that this is a history commissioned by its subject, the discerning reader will observe that the author was given an entirely free hand. Yet the truth is an elusive prey. Misstatements that should be out are in, and who knows what elements that *should* be in are out? Yet how many members, how many yachts, how many races, how much interplay over 115 years? Anyone pretending to be a chronicler must begin with penance.

And then to Charles H.W. Foster's *The Eastern Yacht Club Ditty Box: 1870–1900*—just that, a ditty box of bare facts and miscellany not published until thirty-two years later. This remarkable senior member gathered some material for a se-

quel—including his personal correspondence with Nathanael Herreshoff, since found in a carton in the clubhouse—but it was never written. Not until 1977, seven years after the Club's centennial, was the Historical Committee organized, mainly on the initiative of the late Eugene Connolly. From Club records, the committee compiled annual reviews from 1900 into the 1980s and taped valuable interviews with older members.

Formidable as it was, such a mass of undigested information produced as many questions as answers. I am grateful for the additional investigations of the committee and other members, and of Matthew Widmer, a Harvard student who did excellent research to supplement my own. And I thank my old friends, Llewellyn Howland III, for his usual sound editorial advice and support, and David Ford for his usual superb design.

My special appreciation goes to Suzanne Santry Connolly. She chaired the Publishing Committee and piloted this long project around the shoals of research, writing, illustrating, financing, and publishing, with dedication to the Club and to the sport of yachting, while dishing up from her Valley Road galley an endless menu of patience, determination, sandwiches, and soup.

J.E.G.

Black Bess
Eastern Point
Gloucester, Massachusetts
November 1988

The Eastern Yacht Club

Ground Swell

The undercurrents of history may leave the surface seemingly undisturbed. They ebb and they flow, and what they bear away today they sometimes bring back another day. Thus the high water that bore the Eastern Yacht Club to these shores in 1870 flowed first in 1834, when it pitched up the two-skiff armada of the Boat Club on a Boston wharf. On the next season's tide, the Boat Clubbers bought the small schooner *Dream* and renamed themselves the Dream Club, the third yacht club in America after a couple of equally fleeting and practically fleetless efforts in the waters west of Long Island.

The Dream Club was hardly more than that, but very nearly all of its founders or their families founded its successor thirty-five years later. Tides and ground fogs be damned. The running lights never *were* doused. The crew stayed with the ship.

It was perhaps here that the distinction began to be made between pleasure boating in anything that would do and organized yachting in a craft built for speed or comfort, and on rare occasions both, around Massachusetts Bay. The nation was still young in 1834. It was fifty years younger in 1784 when Salem's diarist-pastor William Bentley made note that "only two Sail Boats had any claim to the name when their construction was considered in regard to amusement." Seventeen years elapsed before there was anything more in regard to such amusement to write about, when "Capt. G. [George] Crowninshield junr carried me in his remarkably fast sailing Boat from Salem into Beverly Harbour. We made the whole course in 15 minutes & returned in 34, wind fresh at S.W. We made no tack in going, & one in Salem Harbour upon our return. I never did sail so much at my ease in any other boat."

The year was 1801. The fast sailer was probably *Jefferson*, named after the nation's new president. She was originally a sloop-rigged fisherman type of 36 feet overall and a hefty 22 tons. Crowninshield, a flamboyant Salem bachelor-merchant scion of thirty-four, may have rerigged her, judging from the Reverend's elated entry of a couple of summers later when George and his two brothers took him "in their fast sailing two Mast Boat & this was the first time that I ever was 15 miles from land."

The Embargo Act of 1807 temporarily beached a slew of Yankee seafarers who, thus idled, turned—as observed the next summer by Dr. Bentley—to pleasure boats, which "have strangely multiplied . . . and upon every sudden gust some alarm is given." Two young men capsized and drowned in a squall in Marblehead Harbor. "The Seamen who are well qualified to navigate large vessels are found very inexpert in managing small craft & yet are often presumptuous from an ignorance of the principles on which dories with sails move."

Then came the War of 1812 and the conversion to patriotic privateering of diminutive *Jefferson*, so overmanned she looked like "so many goslings on a tray." War over, his father dead, George Crowninshield happily adopted the role of early American playboy and in 1816 built America's first large private yacht. This was the brigantine *Cleopatra's Barge*—83 feet on the waterline, all stripes and colors, gold lace and bird's-eye maple—which he sailed to the Mediterranean, where she made the expected splash. Back in Salem the next year, having achieved his special immortality, George unexpectedly died. His *Barge* was sold to King Kamehameha of Hawaii, whose royal sailors wrecked her.

Trade flourished with peace and freer seas, most lucratively

Cleopatra's Barge, America's first real yacht, painted by George Ropes in 1818.

---

with China, in which the merchant-shipowners of Boston and Salem took an enterprising lead under Colonel Thomas Handasyd Perkins. Two of Perkins's nephews, John Perkins Cushing and Robert Bennet (dubbed Black Ben for his youthful mane, now gray) Forbes—the one by land and the other by sea—secured a corner on traffic in fine goods, tea, spices, opium, and such high-density cargoes.

When the two returned home with fortunes made, pleasure beckoned. Forbes oversaw the construction of his cousin's 58-foot schooner yacht *Sylph* in the spring of 1834 up the Mystic River in Medford. Evidently boatless pro tem himself, Black Ben and a few Boston friends that summer launched the Boat Club: "no charter, no bylaws, no sailing directions, no flag, save the Stars and Stripes, and its only boats were row boats."

Next spring, with $200 in hand from each of the ten members, the Boat Club purchased the 40-foot, 30-ton schooner *Dream,* reconsecrated themselves the Dream Club under Forbes as commodore for a series of matches with *Sylph,* which was now measurably faster since her owner had her cut in half and lengthened her in the middle by eight and a half feet.

That July of 1835, when neither club was more than a twinkle in the eye, occurred the first chance encounter from which ultimately sprang the long and beneficial rivalry between the Eastern and the New York. Owner John Cushing and his cousins Commodore Forbes and Captain William Sturgis, Captain Daniel C. Bacon and Sam Cabot, Perkins's business partners, and shipowner R.D. Shepherd embarked in *Sylph* for a cruise around Cape Cod.

Off Nantucket they fell in with the rather larger schooner yacht *Wave,* 92 feet, owned by John Cox Stevens, future founding commodore of the New York Yacht Club, "and got handsomely beaten by her," as Cushing noted in his diary. Near Woods Hole, the tide carried them aground, and the owner, figuring his *Sylph* was a goner, sold her on the spot for a quarter of her cost to Forbes and Sam Cabot—a transaction that Cushing did not note in his diary. But with help from a government cutter, the wily Black Ben floated his prize. Homeward bound, they fell in again with *Wave* for a race down Vineyard Sound and were gaining when the rising wind made Stevens decide to give it up and bear away for Tarpaulin Cove on Naushon Island. Samuel Eliot Morison called this the first American yacht race of record, although one and possibly both of *Sylph*'s bouts with *Dream* might take precedence.

Sylph was sold as a Boston Harbor pilot boat, and in 1837 Commodore Forbes, Captain Dan Bacon, and William H. Boardman (called by one who knew him "as clever a specimen of human nature as ever sailed a boat in a stiff breeze") built the 30-ton schooner *Breeze,* 51 feet long, doubling the fleet of the Dream Club. That summer they raced to Marblehead. *Dream* arrived first and anchored. *Breeze* came up and tied alongside. Forbes hospitably invited the rival crew into his more spacious cabin for lunch, and when they were below, he slipped aboard *Dream* and induced their cook to pass his guests' own food and wine over and down his forehatch. Upon the conclusion of this deception, *Breeze* cast off first and got under way. Forbes hoisted a well-drained champagne bottle (one of *Dream*'s) to his main gaff and maintained his lead back to Boston (so he claimed) by tossing empty bottles and strawberry boxes overboard. This ruse allegedly caused the still-hungry Dreamers, who had unwittingly shared their lunch, to heave-to and pick up what they supposed, with astonishing naivete, was good wine and good fruit.

That first American yacht club and most of its humorous commodore's fortune evaporated in the financial crisis of

1837, and Forbes returned to China to recoup. Yet, though the shore east of New York remained clubless for thirty more years, the building of the fast little schooners (modeled after the speedy pilot boats that raced out to meet incoming ships and put a pilot aboard), the informal matches got up over a friendly glass, and the boisterous good times had had their effect. The sport of yachting, as distinct in a vague sort of way from messing about in boats, had caught the imagination of a slowly growing number of those who could afford to buy, man, and maintain their own private sailing vessels.

Robert Bennet Forbes was a superb sailor, where John Cox Stevens, the inventor-engineer-yachtsman, was merely first-rate, but when Stevens and friends celebrated the dawn of recovery from the 1837 depression by organizing the New York Yacht Club aboard his new schooner *Gimcrack*, anchored off the Battery on July 30, 1844, it stayed organized. A month later the New York squadron put in at Newport on its maiden cruise and rendezvoused with Captain Forbes in the chartered Boston pilot schooner *Belle* and Colonel William P. Winchester's 67-foot schooner yacht *Northern Light*. Along with David Sears of Nahant, they were enlisted on the spot as the club's first New England members; thus was sanctioned the long and frequently amiable rivalry between North Shore and New York yachtsmen.

The first regatta of the New Yorkers on July 17, 1845, must have motivated the Bostonians to follow swift suit. Two days later, in a brisk southeasterly, eleven small schooners sailed a twenty-mile triangle from Nahant around The Graves, Egg Rock, and back, regarded as the first formal yacht race east of Cape Cod. The winner on corrected time was shipowner Benjamin C. Clark's smart schooner *Raven*, successor to this early Nahant summerer's *Mermaid* of 1832, claimed to be the first decked-over "yacht" ever owned by a Bostonian.

The following season, four Boston schooners sailed to New York for the NYYC cruise and regatta: Winchester's *Northern Light*, James H. Perkins's *Coquette*, David Sears's *Brenda*, and Thomas Parsons's *Pet*. Parsons, Perkins, and Sears would all become familiar Eastern Yacht Club names and families. Sixty-six feet on deck and 74 tons, *Coquette* averaged 9 knots to New York, where her owner challenged any yacht to an autumn match for $500. He was taken up by Commodore Stevens in his new sloop *Maria*, more than 100 feet on deck. The race was held on October 10—twenty-five miles downwind from Sandy Hook and return in a northeaster. Part of *Maria*'s

Benjamin C. Clark's fast schooner yacht *Raven*, 1836.

centerboard broke off in the rough seas. The little Boston schooner won by five minutes, no time allowance. Coquette to the end, *Coquette* was next a Boston pilot boat and finished her career as a slave trader.

The greatest race of all was the outcome of a British suggestion in 1850 that a New York pilot schooner sail across for the Crystal Palace Exposition as a demonstration of Yankee know-how, the clippers then being in their heyday. Commodore Stevens and the New York Yacht Club responded with *America*, which to everyone's astonishment captured the Royal Yacht Squadron's Hundred Guineas Cup in 1851. In conjuring up his rakish underdog clad in tight-fitting sails that did *not* bag like bloomers, designer George Steers squeezed her shape aft and narrowed the traditional, bluff "cod's head" to a fine and hollow bow that reminded one historian of the Boston designer Louis Winde's *Northern Light*. Indeed, *America* drifted back through a lean and slippery run inescapably evocative of the most notable design departures of the period, the fast and beautiful Gloucester fishing schooners of the 1840s called "sharp-shooters."

There were yachting regattas off Marblehead and Swampscott at least as early as 1848. The fever reached Gloucester by

1855, when fifteen sundry craft tacked out of the harbor and back, regarded by the *Telegraph* as "a very fine, yet rather singular scene, scarcely any two being rigged alike, or carrying the same amount of sail. . . . It would be difficult to state the winning boat, as no measures were taken to make due allowance for tonnage, nor any rules laid down for guidance, and as far as we can learn no judges were appointed to decide." Nor any prizes given.

Black Ben Forbes dominated the next Gloucester regatta. The date was September 3, 1858, when four waterline classes of eighteen boats, with time allowances, raced over ocean courses of no less than eight miles outside Eastern Point. The best match was among the centerboard sloops, won by Forbes, then fifty-four, at the helm of his new 24-footer, *Grace Darling*.

Hardly had he pocketed his eight dollars from the centerboard sweepstakes when Forbes grabbed his New York Yacht Club cap and sailed from Boston for Buenos Aires—that November, if you will—in his 36-ton iron schooner *Edith*. Forty-seven days and a dismasting later, he wrote the NYYC that she was the first of its squadron to enter the Southern Hemisphere.

It is a matter of more than passing interest that the Burgess family of Boston took up summering on Beverly's Woodbury Point that season of 1858. Nearly thirty years later, at the height of his international fame as a yacht designer, Edward recalled those boyhood days in his introduction to *American and English Yachts*:

America, wung out, in a painting by Gloucester's Fitz Hugh Lane.

The only cabin yacht on the whole of that coast was a small schooner, the *Humming Bird*, about thirty-five feet long; and there were not more than three or four sail-boats. [There were many more; probably he meant "yachts."] What seemed to us then like a long cruise to Boston was made exciting by the rare glimpse of a few larger pleasure boats, the old *Mist*, *Tartar*, and *Scud*, all built by Smith of Stonington [Connecticut], the *Whip*, *Breeze*, and a few others, whose names I no longer recollect. A few years earlier, General Paine began his career as a yachtsman, in a small catboat, in these same waters of Salem Harbor.

Our own boat was a little sloop of about twenty-one feet, the *Cassie*, built by the same Stonington builder just mentioned. With enormous sails and lead ballast (even in those days), with a few sand-bags, *Cassie* was easily faster than the few boats we could find to try a tack or two with us. [Here Ned failed to mention—or had he forgotten?—the brushes the boys had in *Cassie* with a certain wily old Captain Forbes at the tiller of a certain *Grace Darling*.] The first race I sailed in was for a sweepstake, got up in Gloucester, in which, I think, six or eight boats entered. [It was. The date was August 17, 1850. There were four entries in the centerboard class. Ned was twelve, sailing with his older brother, Franklin, and the fishermen were up to their tricks.] We beat round the outer stake-boat so far ahead of the local boats that the patriotic keepers of the stake-boat cut her adrift, after we turned, so as to lessen the distance the other boats had to make! [The summer boys, of course, still won.]

With the end of the Civil War, yachts were discovered to be capital holes in the water for filling with both new and rejuvenated capital and the fruits thereof. And if derring-do be wanted, it was dished up that very first postwar season by the smashing transatlantic dash from Nahant to England of Thomas Gold Appleton's 48-foot-waterline sloop *Alice* in the record time (for a vessel of her modest size) of nineteen days. The well-known skipper and nautical writer Arthur H. Clark, son of Benjamin Clark of *Raven* fame, had her helm, and in her mixed crew of professionals and Corinthians was Charlie Longfellow, son of the poet, nephew of the owner, and a raffish character among Eastern members of the future. The year was topped off in December by a foolhardy winter race to Cowes under the burgee of the New York Yacht Club; James Gordon Bennett, Jr.'s schooner *Henrietta* won the $90,000 stake from *Vesta* and *Fleetwing*, from whose open cockpit six crew were swept to their deaths in a gale. But what a spur to the sport among the new breed of tycoons!

Boston's first try at a regatta on July 4, 1866, was a flop that so angered a participating trio of Dartmouth alumni that they

Robert Bennet Forbes

went to work in September to fill the organizational void with something "devoted to marine aesthetics."

Ninety were present at the formative meeting of the Boston Yacht Club, the first of permanence east of New York, on November 21. Among them was an eighteen-year-old freshman in the mechanical engineering course at Massachusetts Institute of Technology, Nathanael G. Herreshoff of Bristol, Rhode Island.

At this gathering, wrote L. Francis Herreshoff of his father in *Capt. Nat Herreshoff*:

He was elected a committee of one to formulate measurement and time allowance rules for rating the various sized yachts then owned by the members. . . . He dropped out of the club in 1869, but on January 30, 1877, was elected an honorary member because of his services, I believe, in formulating their first measurement rule and for making up the tables of allowance in minutes and seconds per mile that a yacht of one rating allows one of a smaller rating . . . still in use almost throughout the world with but few slight changes. . . . The tables have been the greatest boon to yacht racing of any one factor in the game. . . . The Boston Yacht Club deserves considerable credit for publishing these tables in their first club book, and few members today realize what an important contribution their club made to yachting at its start.

Yet, from this auspicious beginning the Boston Yacht Club had almost unsalvageably wrecked itself by the end of the decade and would be years more in recovering. What went wrong? In his history, *The Boston*, Paul Shanabrook cites the initial rejection by the Legislature of the club's act of incorporation in 1867 on the grounds that it "might lead to immoral and ungentlemanly conduct, detrimental to the public welfare." He attributes this extraordinary notion to rampant Victorian prejudice against good fun, whist, and drinking—although it sounds strictly political. Further, of the Boston's 158 members listed that year, only twenty-six owned or were part-owners of yachts, which must be closer to the mark, for, as he writes: "The specter of more ladies and gentlemen playing whist in sumptuous rooms at Tremont and Pemberton Square than gentlemen attending to the serious matters of yachts and racing rules made it evident that the club had missed its mark. . . . The club's early success attracted many hangers-on to its roster."

Whatever the causes, a promising start collapsed into bickering, a rumpus over racing rules, the scattering of fair-weather membership, and within two years the prospect of imminent demise.

Meanwhile, a vital, expanding, affluent circle of yachting enthusiasts who lived and sailed in and out of Boston were in those postwar years flocking to summer on its North Shore. They awaited with impatience a proper piazza, a proper landing, a proper committee, a committee boat, a commodore, and the satisfying sheen of well-won sterling on the mantelpiece.

Chapter 1

India Wharf to Marblehead   *1870–1885*

The Essex County Yacht Squadron had a rather grandiose name, a brief existence, a small but select membership that included Edward and Franklin Burgess, and a large role in the emergence of the Eastern Yacht Club. Years later, when he was a renowned designer, Edward recalled that there were scarcely any races and only about fifty yachts in the Boston Bay area when he and his brother and a few other Beverly yachtsmen ran some sweepstakes in 1868 under the burgee of their "squadron," which he identified as the nucleus of the Eastern.

On March 5, 1870, several of these Essex County Yacht Squadron members and their friends gathered at the Park Street home of John Heard in Boston and organized the Eastern Yacht Club.

An 1880 newspaper may be the source of the report that the Eastern sprang from a cabal of Boston Yacht Club malcontents. Anyway, an unattributed item in the *Ditty Box* claims that the Boston "did much to further the advancement of naval science for a year or two after its incorporation, but finally there was apparent a feeling of indifference, and the only results of the organization were the comfortable social gatherings which were afforded at the elegantly furnished rooms of the club, on the corner of Tremont Street and Pemberton Square. So a number of gentlemen who were averse to this order of things, and who seemed imbued with the true yachting spirit, seceded from the Boston Yacht Club and organized and incorporated under the name of the Eastern Yacht Club."

The Boston's ex-Commodore James R. Hodder amplified in his memoirs of several decades later that a fight over racing rules during his club's first Maine cruise in 1868 was responsible. He wrote that the secessionists never formally resigned, paid up their dues, or even said goodbye, and that one new Eastern member apparently said that they quit the Boston be-cause they were more interested in sailing and didn't regard anything under thirty feet as a yacht.

In fact, a comparison of the rosters of both clubs reveals that not one charter member of the Eastern in 1870 is listed as having belonged to the Boston, unless the names of those who jumped ship (if indeed there were any) were expunged from the rolls of the offended club.

There is no evidence that the founders ever heard of an Eastern Yacht Club, founded in 1835 in England and long since gone, which was cited without elaboration by an 1884 American yachting history as the world's fifth oldest. Coincidentally, the claim might rest equally with the Dream Club of exactly the same vintage; in fact, the heraldic connections between the Eastern of 1870 and the Dream of 1835 could be interpreted as giving America the genealogical edge:

Dream Club	*Eastern Yacht Club Founders*
Robert Bennet Forbes	Robert Bennet Forbes
Daniel C. and Francis Bacon	William B. Bacon
William F. Otis	William C. Otis
John Bryant, Jr.	
B. Bangs	
Samuel Hooper	Robert W. Hooper
John A. Lowell	
T.H. Perkins, Jr.	Augustus T. Perkins
Thomas G. Appleton	F.H., T.G. and W.S. Appleton
J.S. Copley Greene	
James Davis, Jr.	James Davis
W.H. Boardman	T. Dennie Boardman
E. Weston, Jr.	
P.C. Brooks, Jr.	P.C. Jr., and Francis Brooks
Edward and Samuel Austin	Edward Austin
T. Motley, Jr.	Thomas Motley

Other members of Dream Club families joined the Eastern later, and although only T. Dennie Boardman of Manchester and William C. Otis of Nahant were also enrolled in the Essex County Yacht Squadron at the time of the Eastern's founding, most of the rest followed along.

The Boston Yacht Club was Boston-based from the start. So was the Eastern, except that it drew its membership from the old Boston families who had joined in the postwar summer flight from the steaming city to the cool breezes and deepwater anchorages of the North Shore, where they were buying up the saltwater farms of the natives at prices that convinced buyer and seller the other was mad. The evidence shows that the Eastern was not the creation of a knot of dues-dodging dissidents from another yacht club, but an old Dream redreamed.

The dozen of "Boston's best citizens," as Charles Foster celebrated them in his *Ditty Box*, who met at John Heard's Boston home that evening with their host, were David Sears, Jr., John Jeffries, Jr., John G. Cushing, Augustus T. Perkins, Percival L. Everett, Jacob C. Rogers, Stanton Whitney, William D. Pickman, Richard D. Tucker, Edward Motley, and William C. Otis. Most were members of the Essex County Yacht Squadron.

These apostles of New England yachting went forth among about a hundred of their friends, and on March 31, 1870, their Eastern Yacht Club, as they decided to call it, borrowed the bylaws and racing regulations of the New York Yacht Club and dedicated itself to the organization of sailing in Massachusetts Bay. In truth, these first 110 salty yachtsmen listed in the *Ditty Box* owned only twenty-three yachts among them—not much better than the lamented proportion of Boston Yacht Club whist players to boats, 158 to twenty-six or less.

John Heard was elected the first commodore; Franklin Burgess, vice commodore; John Jeffries, Jr., secretary; Joseph P. Gardner, treasurer; George Z. Silsbee, measurer; Robert B. Forbes, S. Endicott Peabody, David Sears, Jr., William G. Saltonstall, and William C. Otis, Regatta Committee. The club signal, said to have been designed by T. Dennie Boardman, was adopted on April 26. The initiation fee was set at twenty dollars and the annual assessment at ten dollars, a level that, in the words of the commodore, "we were afraid to make too high." And a room was rented at 31 India Wharf, rather less pretentious than the Boston's, but nevertheless on the water, which bodes well for a yacht club.

Commodore Heard was a nephew of Augustine Heard, the China merchant. He had been the family firm's managing part-

Commodore Heard's flagship, the schooner *Rebecca*.

---

ner in Canton, where he raced, no doubt from the Canton Regatta Club started by Bostonians on the Pearl River in 1837. Returning with his fortune, he built a summer home on Ober's Point, east of Beverly Cove, and bought the schooner *Rebecca* of 77 tons, which he described as reasonably fast, going on to remark in a letter: "In her at first I won nearly all the races I sailed, but gradually faster boats were built. I was made the first commodore of the Club, but I ought to say that David Sears would have had the appointment only he had no yacht at the time." This gracious concession suggests that Sears, boatless after the wreck of his schooner *Actaea* on Chatham Bar in 1868, was the driving force behind the new club.

Commodore Heard and friends beat out the organizers of the Lynn Yacht Club by only two days and lost to them the honor of holding the North Shore's first club regatta, with a fleet of

---

John Heard, founding commodore.

India Wharf to Marblehead

fourteen over a seven-mile course on June 17, 1870. Twenty-five days later, the Eastern walked away from the Shoe City sailors by twenty-three miles. The first Annual Regatta, on time allowance, was sailed on July 12 from an anchor start off Marblehead Rock over a thirty-mile course to Minot's Ledge and back, in the company of a chartered steamer with the ladies and music. Philo S. Shelton's *Dawn* won the $150 prize for schooners and Vice Commodore Franklin Burgess's *Sadie*, the $100 for sloops.

The Eastern Yacht Club was incorporated by the General Court of the Commonwealth of Massachusetts on February 7, 1871, "for the purpose of encouraging yacht building and naval architecture, and the cultivation of nautical science." Overlooked were the dangers of immoral and ungentlemanly conduct. The aims were borrowed word for word from the charter of the New York Yacht Club, which didn't get down to such business until 1865, when it was twenty-one and of age.

Its second season put the new club on the chart with a membership of 207, "comprising men of wealth, high character, and who feel a vital interest in all matters pertaining to an organization of this kind," according to a newspaper report, and a fleet of twenty-three schooners, eleven sloops, and two steamers (including the *Minnehaha*, owned by Thomas Clark Durant of New York, builder of the Union Pacific Railroad).

For the first few seasons, the starting lines were off Marblehead Rock, off Swampscott's Great Pig Rocks, or between the Haste Rock and Coney Island stakes off Beverly. Starts were from anchor until a special regatta on September 7, 1872, when the flying start was adopted by the Regatta Committee and prevailed thereafter with the exception of 1879, when, for a single season and for reasons unknown, anchors again kept the steeds in check.

From the beginning, the founders had more than day racing in mind. Yankees with coasting in their blood, they institutionalized—if they did not quite invent—the down-east cruise. On July 25, 1870, five schooners and five sloops embarked on the first Annual Cruise of the Eastern Yacht Club, lasting a fortnight, with Bar Harbor its easternmost port of call.

The earliest documented pleasure cruise along the Maine coast was undertaken only twelve years earlier, in 1858, by the newspaperman Robert Carter and friends in the chartered sloop *Helen*. It was delightfully described in his classic book, *A Summer Cruise on the Coast of New England*. They sailed from Provincetown to Mount Desert, which, he reported, "has

become a favorite resort for artists and summer loungers." After the Civil War, wealthy men hewed vacation estates out of the wild country around Bar Harbor. Historian and yachtsman Samuel Eliot Morison, who summered at Northeast Harbor, wrote in *The Story of Mt. Desert Island* that "when Charles W. Eliot, the thirty-seven-year-old President of Harvard University, bought the sloop *Jessie* in 1871 and made the first of many cruises in these waters, he exchanged salutes with seven vessels of the Eastern Yacht Club off Schooner Head, but there were still no good charts of these waters and few buoys."

Young Dudley Pickman was on that cruise aboard Joseph Gardner's schooner *Belle* and wrote in the *Ditty Box* of those more primitive days:

> As Eastern yachtsmen were not inclined to make a prolonged stay at Bar Harbor on account of poor holding ground, lack of breakwaters and sudden squalls from the mountains, they generally made their headquarters in Southwest Harbor with flying visits only to points around the island. It was probably in the summer of 1871 that the fleet towards the end of its cruise was delayed at the latter port by one of those hopeless foggy spells that take the gimp out of every one on board. Conditions were becoming really serious, as fresh provisions were not to be had and canning had not yet been raised to a fine art; so it was decided at a council of war on the commodore's flagship [John Heard's *Rebecca*] to send a delegation on shore with instructions to scour the neighborhood for relief.
>
> As a result of their expedition the envoys returned with the welcome information that a farmer living near the village had agreed to kill a sheep and a lamb for our benefit, only it was understood that we must not sail away and leave him in the lurch.

The fog scaled up in a couple of days, and as the cruisers set sail, "they beheld the figure of a man holding up the slaughtered sheep and a boy holding a lamb, shouting and gesticulating wildly—the picture of despair." Luckily, Captain Gardner and Pickman had agreed to stay behind to settle up for the mutton. "Faith in a yachtsman's word was restored and the club burgee could fly once more in Southwest Harbor without the shadow of reproach."

The foragers were home just in time for the Eastern's inaugural joint regatta with the New York Yacht Club off Swampscott on August 11, 1871, in which the latter's first Boston members, David Sears and Robert B. Forbes, probably had a hand. Dudley Pickman was there:

The New York Yacht Club's fleet . . . hove in sight off Swampscott Bay, truly a noble assemblage of yachts: *Dauntless, Sappho, Columbia,* and others equally well-known. It was intended that our squadron should go out to meet the visitors, forming a dignified, though more modest, line, every movement to be carried out under strictest yachting regulations. Just before time for exchange of salutes between the squadrons a jaunty little sloop was observed coming out from under the lee of Nahant, an oddly decorated object, seen on nearer approach to have at masthead and on rigging a display of bottles with names of sundry popular concoctions inscribed on streamers attached to them. Our saucy craft—which proved to be *Daisy*—did not even slow up, but headed direct for Commodore Bennett's *Dauntless* and saluted by a shout of welcome from those on board, aided by very graphic gestures extending the Club's best hospitality to our guests.

Daisy's owner, Captain "Billy" Otis, having considered the reception as planned somewhat too formal, had decided to inject an element of frivolity and good fellowship to relieve any possible stiffness from the occasion. This plan of his proved eminently successful, for, after the first few moments of surprise, the joke was taken in good part all round and keenly enjoyed, dispelling at one stroke any risk of too much ceremonial.

Pickman was almost as early a member as William Otis and had little more use for ceremonial.

There was a time when yachting etiquette was still in its trial stage, and yachtsmen were allowed a good deal of latitude in regard to its application. One member of the club was most punctilious in its observance and endeavored to impress the importance of it on his fellow members. On one occasion, however, he fired a salute by some error of judgment in too close proximity to another passing yacht, the wad from the saluting gun burning a bad hole in this yacht's mainsail—a performance which, however well-intended, did not give the owner of the latter a very high opinion of etiquette requirements. This gentleman was afterwards quoted as saying that he had been under fire enough during his service in the Civil War, that he had bought a yacht for pleasure cruising, and damned if he'd stand being bombarded in Massachusetts Bay.

The evening of the grand rendezvous with New York there was a grand and gloriously dangerous display of fireworks from the Eastern yachts to a chorus of brass bands on the two towboats hired to attend the needs of the combined fleets.

The next day the steam tugs churned down from the Swampscott anchorage to Point Shirley with about a hundred jointly celebrating yachtsmen for one of the fish-and-game

dinners that had made Taft's Hotel world-famous (the menu included whitebait, frogs, black bass, owlets, eaglets, beetlehead plover, godwit, robin snipe, and peeps among seventeen species of wild game). Rounds of speeches broadly predicted a new era in yachting, if not in fowling.

Two days later, on August 14, the great race was on. The prizes were a $1,000 cup offered by the Eastern to the first schooner on corrected time and a $500 cup to the first sloop, and $800 to the schooner and $400 to the sloop making the best elapsed times, offered by the people of Swampscott. The course was from Swampscott around the Davis Ledge buoy off Minot's Light and back, twenty-seven miles. The New Yorkers made a clean sweep of it in a wind that increased to a fresh breeze, and it was said to be the largest yacht race held in American waters to that time.

From the beginning, the Club steamer was as essential to the regatta ritual as the committee boat. By 1875 the routine had been established: In the morning the chartered *John Romer* would depart Rowe's Wharf in Boston with the first contingent of members, families, and guests; take on more at the Nahant wharf; meet a tug from Beverly with even more from the Gold Coast; run into Marblehead for more; and then head off for the start, band playing, the 18-foot Club flag streaming aft from the masthead, wine and champagne (and cigars until the privilege was apparently abused and terminated) on the house; dinner at one.

Francis B. Crowninshield had purchased a large part of Peach's Point and built a summer home there in 1872. His grandson and namesake remembered how as a boy during the 1870s, Marblehead "was even then a favorite harbor for yachtsmen and Saturday afternoons many would find their way there, spend the night, and sail back the next day. . . . The non-yacht owners of the Club "got their money back on the steamer chartered for the annual regatta where a free lunch with champagne was served plus the noise of a brass band."

As stars cross in the firmament, the second yacht of any significance designed by Nathanael Herreshoff—the 25-foot-waterline sloop *Haidee*, later *Fanchon*, which he modeled in 1864 when he was sixteen—was acquired by Edward Burgess of the Essex County Yacht Squadron around 1869. *Fanchon* eludes the Eastern record book probably because she lacked the minimum 30 feet on the waterline. *Violet*, 32 feet, came out of the same model in 1866 for Eben Denton of Weymouth,

12   India Wharf to Marblehead

just in time for him to host the gam aboard her that resulted in the Boston Yacht Club, of which he was vice commodore in 1869–70. Denton was briefly an Eastern member from 1873 to 1874, when he resigned, leaving *Violet* behind. She was enrolled at least until 1880 and is said to have raced well until her final finish in the Chelsea fire of 1908.

The model for these two sloops that are of such interest in the early history of the Club, whittled by the budding designer, is the only one missing from his collection. His son explains the omission in *Capt. Nat Herreshoff*:

When the *Violet* was completed young Nat sailed her in a trial race against an older boat sailed by his father, and *Violet* was beaten. Nat was so disappointed that as soon as he got home he took an ax and chopped up the model from which *Violet* had been built so that no other boats would be built from it. Strange to say, all the boats built from this model turned out very well later and were much liked by their owners. This incident, Captain Nat told me, made him more patient in later life and taught him to wait until a boat was thoroughly tried out before he condemned her.

The Herreshoff-Burgess-Eastern connection produced some of the greatest designs in all of American yachting. Again, let Francis Herreshoff explain:

In the winter of 1866, when Captain Nat was a student at the Massachusetts Institute of Technology, he designed the sail plan and other drawings for the schooner *Sadie* which J.B. [John Brown Herreshoff, Nat's blind brother, the master boatbuilder] built for himself. *Sadie* was modeled by J.B. and his father and was fifty feet six inches O.A., forty-seven feet W.L., sixteen feet beam, five feet draft and of course, a centerboarder. *Sadie* was rerigged as a sloop in 1868 and had a large sail area—3,876 square feet. She was sold in 1869 to R. Franklin Burgess, an older brother of Edward Burgess. The Burgess and Herreshoff families, who were distantly related, kept up a friendship from that time on, so I will say something about the Burgess family.

The family consisted of six brothers of about the same age as the Herreshoff brothers; their father had been a wealthy Bostonian engaged in shipping and owning sugar plantations in Cuba. Besides their home in Boston, they had a summer residence at Sandwich on Cape Cod where the boys started sailing from their youth and, as they grew up, they owned several Herreshoff-built boats. Edward Burgess, who was to become the leading yacht designer of his time, was born the same year as

Captain Nat (1848) and, strange to say, there was a striking similarity in their appearance. They both attended college at the same time—Edward Burgess at Harvard and Captain Nat at M.I.T.

Edward Burgess had intended to devote his life to the study of natural history, and especially entomology, in which he was active the first ten or fifteen years after graduation from Harvard. On account of financial reverses, however, he was obliged to take up a more remunerative profession so that with his youthful love of sailing he decided to become a yacht designer.

Perhaps only weeks before they sold *Sadie* to Franklin Burgess, a few months prior to the organization of the Eastern, Nat and his brother J.B. almost lost her in the hurricane of September 8, 1869, while at anchor in the harbor of East Greenwich, Rhode Island. Francis described the event:

She dragged her anchors and fortunately just cleared the steamboat wharf when her crew succeeded in passing a line around a spile. She was the only boat in the harbor, and perhaps the neighborhood, that rode out the gale. Although they were just starting out on a cruise they returned to Bristol as soon as the wind went down to inform their parents of their safety. After

---

Overleaf: The joint dinner with the New York at the world-renowned Taft's Hotel on Point Shirley, Winthrop, August 12, 1871. 1. Admiral Steedman; 2. Commodore James Gordon Bennett, flagship *Dauntless*, NYYC; 3. Commodore John Heard, flagship *Rebecca*, EYC and NYYC; 4. Anson Livingston, *Vixen*, NYYC; 5. Philip Schuyler, NYYC; 6. Vice Commodore Franklin Burgess, *Sadie*, EYC and NYYC; 7. Laurence Jerome, NYYC; 9. Captain Samuel Samuels, *Dreadnaught*, NYYC; 10. J.S. Fay, Jr.; 11. Charles A. Longfellow, EYC; 13. F. Gordon Dexter, *Narragansett*, EYC and NYYC; 14. John Jeffries, Secretary, EYC; 15. William Amory, Jr., EYC; 16. William P. Fay, EYC; 19. T. Dennie Boardman, *Wivern*, EYC and NYYC; 20. Henry Steers, NYYC; 21. William Krebbs, *Gracie*, NYYC; 22. Robert Center, *Vindex*, NYYC; 24. Charles P. Horton, *Active*, EYC; 25. Frederick W. Bradlee, EYC; 26. Commodore Churchill, flagship *Ethel*, Portland Yacht Club; 27. Edward W. Codman, EYC; 29. Edwin A. Boardman, EYC; 33. Dr. B. Joy Jeffries, Chairman Regatta Committee, EYC; 34. John E. Atkins; 36. George H. Osgood, *Fleetwing*, NYYC; 37. J.E.C. Peterson, marine artist; 40. Henry B. Jackson, EYC; 46. Sheppard Homans, *Foam*, NYYC; 49. Henry S. Hovey, *Edith*, EYC and NYYC; 50. Stanton Whitney, *Julia*, EYC; 51. Richard D. Tucker, *Coming*, EYC; 52. Charles H. Walker, EYC; 53. S.V.R. Thayer, EYC; 54. Eben Dale, EYC; 55. Joseph C. Hovey, EYC; 56. Thomas Motley, EYC; 57. Ludlow Livingston, *Vixen*, NYYC; 58. Benjamin G. Boardman.

this, they sailed to Newport, not seeing another vessel afloat but counting between forty and fifty vessels and boats that had been driven ashore.

At least five other Herreshoff designs figured prominently in the Eastern's early fleet before Nat was twenty-five. *Clytie*, a 33-foot-waterline sloop built in 1867, was owned by four successive Eastern members between 1873, when A.A.H. Meredith bought her, and 1889. The 48-foot schooner *Ianthe* was designed for William D. Pickman in 1870, who followed her up with another Herreshoff schooner, *Latona*, 55 feet, in 1872. In 1873 the Herreshoffs launched the 74-foot schooner *Faustine* for George Peabody Russell, who sailed her to the Isle of Wight the following year.

The most noteworthy design of Herreshoff's youthful period—he was then twenty-three—was the fabled sloop *Shadow*, modeled in November 1870 and built for Dr. E.R. Sisson of New Bedford in 1871. *Shadow* foreshadowed a transatlantic revolution in yacht design under the burgee of the Eastern Yacht Club.

The problem in America was that builders unschooled in the dynamics of water and wind seemed to have cast all sense of perspective adrift in an obsessively wrongheaded craving for speed. Since the Civil War, yards had been turning out centerboard sloops that each spring were beamier, shallower, and more overcanvased. The ultimate caricature was attained in the New York sandbagger, whose peacock spread of sail was usually but not invariably counterbalanced by the ballast that brawny crews shifted from rail to rail, tack to tack, even shifting themselves overboard in light airs, if need be, to swim for the nearest channel buoy and hope to be picked up before dark. Capsizes and a drowning now and then were part of the fun. Schooner yachts, influenced by the swift pilot boats of the Atlantic ports, betrayed similar if slightly less lethal tendencies.

Across the Atlantic, the opposite trend held sway. The deep-ballasted, virtually uncapsizable hull with none of the initial stability and little of the speed of the American type was tending toward its own extreme in the blowy waters around Britain. Yawls and ketches gained favor over the schooner along the English coast (the yawl did not begin to catch on in America until the 1880s), while the cutter led all, a perfect wedge of a boat that heeled alarmingly and pitched nauseously but refused to quit in the briskest breeze. The deep, narrow hull and more conservative rig had advocates in America, and from the

The fabled *Shadow* shadows along for the camera of Nathaniel L. Stebbins.

---

early 1870s, these self-styled "cutter cranks" plumped for the importation of English common sense.

Along came young Nat Herreshoff, who cared for nothing but the elemental relationship of wood and duck to water and wind. Before sending his *Ditty Box* off to the printer in December of 1931, Charles Foster wrote the venerable designer, then eighty-three, requesting some recollections of the early days. Thus was launched a revealing correspondence from which he extracted two of Captain Nat's letters for inclusion in his Club history. A portion of the first, dated December 28, 1931, relates to *Shadow* and the first of the two occasions on which her designer recalled participating in Eastern races:

My first race under the E.Y.C. was in early Summer of 1872 [the Annual Regatta on June 12 from Marblehead Rock to Eastern Point, The Graves buoy and return, about 40 miles] when I sailed *Shadow* against Malcolm Forbes's *White Cap. Shadow* was designed by me and was of rather unusual type. She was 35½' on deck, 33½' w.l., 14'4" beam and 5'6" deep. Draft of water, without centreboard 4'9". Her midship section was something like this:

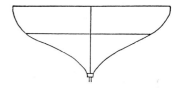

The freeboard quite low and nearly 6" hollow between bridge [probably bilge] and keel. The yacht was built for a Dr. Sisson of New Bedford in 1871 by John B. Herreshoff and at the time I sailed her was owned by Mr. Howland of New Bedford.*

---

* After reading the *Ditty Box*, Herreshoff wrote Foster on January 1, 1933: "I see I made a careless blunder in my first letter to you, in putting down Mr. Howland instead of Mr. (Charles S.) Randall (of New Bedford, an Eastern member) as owner of *Shadow*. I knew better." And the designer William P. Stephens, then 87, could not refrain from passing along the following hoarded scrap of gossip to Foster in a letter dated February 14, 1941: "I have no doubt that Nat actually designed the yacht (*Shadow*), but you know the New Bedford tradition? This runs to the effect that Dr. E.R. Sisson, for whom the yacht was built, cut a model and took it to John B., who refused to build it, saying that it was no good. He finally agreed to build it and, when she proved such a success, claimed it as his own."

India Wharf to Marblehead

White Cap was designed by "Bob" Fish [a well-known rule-o'-thumb designer of the day] and built for the Livingston brothers in 1867 or 1868, and like most of Bob Fish's designs was of quite shallow centreboard type and very fast. Her dimensions were very nearly the same as *Shadow* with a little more length on deck. The race started outside of Marblehead Rock in quite a moderate S.S.E. breeze which gave a beat to windward. *White Cap* was a little ahead and she began gaining slowly. Our club topsail was too large and could not be sheeted flat, so after getting sail needles and twine ready, we lowered it and sewed in a "reef" along the foot. By the time we had it reset *White Cap* was out to windward fully ⅛ mile, but we began gaining and had a very substantial lead at the weather mark, which we held to the finish. . . .

This race and a match race between the boats in Buzzards Bay later in the season, indicated an advantage by a hull that is deeper and of more displacement, even if the ballast is all stowed inside. The following year, *Shadow* was bought by Dr. John Bryant and under his handling was an unbeaten yacht for 15 years. . . .

Actually, *Shadow* was acquired by Charles Randall not long before the race with *White Cap*, because he became a member of the Eastern only a few weeks earlier, on April 3. From 1873 through 1875, she was owned by Caspar Crowninshield. In the September regatta of the latter year, she sailed a match race against the new sloop *Nimbus*, built and presumably designed by Edward Burgess in 1874 expressly to beat his friend Nat's creation—according to Tucker Daland, who bought *Shadow* from Crowninshield in 1876. *Nimbus*, of almost exactly the same above-water dimensions, did all right against the competition until she met the boat her owner was going after.

It was foggy at the start off Swampscott, Daland recalled for the *Ditty Box*, "and the two boats came out at Halfway Rock and met there and then sailed over to Harding's Ledge and turned the buoy almost together. The tide coming out of Boston Harbor made it rough which seemed to favor the *Shadow* who was very far ahead at the finish. The *Shadow* had a railroad for shifting ballast—wheels on rails across the cabin—which was used in races. This was not improper at that time."

In 1877 Daland sold *Shadow* to Dr. John Bryant of Cohasset, who had her from 1877 to 1896, during which reign she is said to have taken around 140 prizes. All four owners were Eastern members, and all but Crowninshield subsequently flew the Boston Yacht Club burgee as well.

The record of the part played by David Sears, Jr., in founding the Eastern Yacht Club is lamentably lacking, but he had a leading and senior role, judging from John Heard's statement that Sears would have been the first commodore had his *Actaea* not been lost in 1868, as well as his designation as Number One member by age from the start (he was Harvard Class of 1842, hence only about forty-nine in 1870). In 1871 Sears was back on the water with his new, 85-foot-waterline schooner *Caprice*. She did not fare well in her only recorded race, that summer's Annual Regatta, when she was last on corrected time among six schooners, several of them new. Heard stepped down at the annual meeting in March 1873, and David Sears was elected to succeed him as the second commodore.

A few days later, on March 14, Commodore Sears died. Out of respect to his memory, the office was left vacant for the rest of the year. Too little is known of this leading Bostonian who was either the driving or the inspirational force behind the founding of the Eastern Yacht Club. His namesake father had been one of Boston's eminent merchants. Immediately after his death, the commodore's house on upper Beacon Street became the home of the Somerset Club. This leading yachtsman of his day must have been a man of generosity as well as wealth: His charities in Boston alone were reckoned at $257,000 in the currency of the times. He followed his aged parents to the grave by only two years. The *Boston Transcript* eulogized on March 18, 1873:

> Of commanding stature and dignified presence, there was in him a modesty and gentleness of demeanor, which bespoke his true character, and which, though he had a warm temperament and quick feelings, never allowed him to depart from that perfect dignity of bearing which always distinguished him, and, with his genial manner and warm heart, so endeared him to his friends. . . .
>
> Born to the inheritance of wealth, he never lost sight of the obligations so imposed on him, but was ever ready to bestow of his abundance with a liberal hand, where he knew it to be truly needed. Fond of every manly exercise, it was a rare satisfaction to witness his accomplishment in all; whether on the deck of his favorite yacht, with the bearing and skill of a real sailor, or showing the keen enjoyment of the saddle with the grace and ardor of a thorough horseman.

In 1874 John Murray Forbes, younger brother of the Eastern's venerable grandfather, Captain Robert Bennet Forbes, was elected to succeed Sears as commodore. Like Ben and cousin John Perkins Cushing, he had climbed the family's Chinese ladder and descended, while almost precociously young, with a fortune. Unlike them, he turned westward from the Far East and the sea and put his money and energy to work building frontier railroads. One uncle was Colonel Perkins and another was his namesake, the diplomat John Murray Forbes; John and Black Ben each combined the drive, intelligence, and charm of both. The new commodore certainly had to get around, because his summer retreat from Boston was not the North Shore (though he owned Eagle Head at Manchester until 1869) but Naushon Island, all the way around Cape Cod in Buzzards Bay. He bought the island in 1857, and it remains today the unspoiled preserve of the Forbes family.

The flagship of the Club's third commodore was the centerboard schooner *Azalea*, built under his brother's supervision and "all bow and stern," as a grandson put it, until her owner cut her in half, as Cushing had done with *Sylph*, and improved her sailing immensely by adding 10 feet to her midriff.

So the story goes, but it must have been more like six feet. *Azalea's* first appearance in the annual regatta was in June 1873, when, at 54 feet waterline, she came in second on corrected time—not good enough for her owner, obviously, because in the Annual Regatta of 1874 she measured in at 60.6 on the water, 69.8 overall, and finished fourth out of five.

That 1874 regatta was distinguished by the unorthodox nonparticipation of a distinguished nonentry, to a chorus of gnashing teeth.

After her moment of glory, *America* had been reduced to blockade-running for the Confederacy during the Civil War, when she was sunk and ultimately salvaged by the Navy. She lay neglected at Annapolis until found by Benjamin F. Butler, Union general, Massachusetts governor, congressman, and prototype of the political wheeler-dealer. He acquired her in 1873 through the Navy's back door, so to speak, brought her to Gloucester (where he had a summer estate at Bay View on Ipswich Bay), and began what proved to be an admirable restoration. Butler joined the Boston Yacht Club, where he had friends, but not the Eastern, where he didn't, but that did not keep him away from its Annual Regatta on July 1, 1874. William U. Swan wrote in *The Yacht "America"*:

She did not come as a competitor, but much to General Butler's amusement and possibly at his direction, Captain [James H.] Reid sailed her up and down the starting line just as the fleet was preparing to get away. Several of the yacht owners, including Edward Burgess in the sloop *Nimbus*, complained to the judges, but the race officials were powerless to order the *Amer-*

David Sears, second commodore.

John Murray Forbes, third commodore.

ica off the line. The episode did not tend to distinguish General Butler as a sportsman among the owners of the competing yachts.

In the spring of 1875, Butler had Donald McKay, the East Boston clipper builder, modernize *America's* rig, and on June 25 he rejoined the Annual Regatta at Marblehead. This time he kept clear and sailed with the Eastern fleet around Cape Ann and into Ipswich Bay, where he eased sheets and ran down to his anchorage off Bay View.

There was no getting around the old charmer. By 1876 his caper on the line had been sufficiently forgiven that he was welcomed to the Annual Regatta on August 29. After a late start, *America* ran clean through the fleet of six schooners and two sloops but finished fourth. She showed up in 1878 but did not race.

"At times he was reluctantly permitted to enter regattas held by clubs whose members turned their backs on him socially when ashore," wrote Swan. "At other times he was barred altogether. Neither circumstance affected his good-natured enthusiasm for yachting, and eventually, it may be added, he broke down many social barriers in yachting circles."

Aboard *Dream*, around 1885. General Curtis and his children, Frances, Harry, and Greely, Jr.

Commodore John Murray Forbes was succeeded in 1878 by T. Dennie Boardman, who had designed the club signal and summered above Manchester's Black Cove Beach in a converted barn on the estate bought by his father from Robert Bennet Forbes in 1865. A newspaper article of later years described him as "a bluff and hearty sailor man . . . who preferred a blow to an afternoon breeze, a cruise to the east'ard to tea ashore, and, with a stout keel under him and boon companions aft, he was always ready for any weather—blow fair or blow foul." His flagship was the 76-foot centerboard schooner *Foam*. So handily rigged was *Foam*, and so ready was Commodore Boardman, that he required only three paid hands out of a crew of seven—leaving deckroom for four "boon companions."

A Manchester neighbor of Commodore Boardman was his fellow charter member General Greely S. Curtis, who bought the headland east of Dana's Beach and built "Sharksmouth," one of the North Shore's early summer mansions. He recorded his travails and small triumphs as one of the founders of the

Eastern Yacht Club in those primitive days in a hitherto-unpublished journal and account book that has been handed down in his family.

Probably in preparation for his contemplated summer life by the sea, General Curtis in August 1867 purchased a 42-foot sloop that he named *Dream*, perhaps for that earlier apparition. She was built the year before in New York for $6,000, and he paid $2,500. A few weeks later, in the hands of an unnamed helmsman, she struck the ledges trying to squeeze between Tinker's Island and Marblehead Neck and sank; it cost him $100 for a tug from Boston to raise her and tow her for repairs. And, almost exactly one year later: "Struck her on rocks between Tinkers Id. & mainland. sunk her. got tug boat & raised her."

Her owner moored *Dream* in "Crow Island Bay" at the mouth of Kettle Cove and wintered her up in the mud. She sailed in the new yacht club's second regatta on September 8, 1870, in the first-class sloops, but didn't finish. A year later she was among the seven sloops in the September 19 handicap whose times were not taken, and there is no further record of her in competition. General Curtis changed her over to a schooner in 1872, only to lose her in a southeast gale in November 1877, when her mooring parted and she broke up on Crow Island.

A.D. Frisbie of Salem built the general's second *Dream* as a centerboard schooner on lines by A. Cary Smith in 1878—49 feet overall, 42 feet 6 inches on the water, and 16 feet beam, cost $2,578 complete. On October 11 he noted that the designer "came from N.Y. to sail in *Dream* & was Sea Sick." This vessel was somewhat of a disappointment too, although she took the $50 first prize in the third class on July 9, 1879, and the third prize of $25 in the September handicap. Never content, Curtis converted her to a cutter and "raced" her once more in 1881, when she was the only entry in her class. Thereafter, the general seems to have kept clear of the line. He was finding the sport expensive and frustrating:

Sept. 24, 1883. Not a man as crew this summer who was not either incompetent or drunken except Marchant.

Dec. 31, 1885. Running Expenses for

Season of '85	$226	
G.W. Lawley's outrageous bill	317.25	$543.25

1886. John Anderson as crew—the best man I've had. Put on 4½ tons lead keel. Increased her stiffness & speed to windward. With a very smooth bottom she went at 4 pts 7.5 K—at 8 pts 9.5 knots.

In 1891 and 1893 she twice parted her mooring and drove ashore without much damage, and in 1896, after thirty years of service between his two *Dream*s, General Curtis sold her for $400.

At that, he came out well ahead of another member, Edward B. Robins, co-owner of the 34-foot-waterline schooner *Hermes* from 1879 through 1882, who recorded for one season:

A sleepy view of General Greely S. Curtis's sloop *Dream*.

Men (2)

Man	$182.98	
Steward	152.95	
		$335.93
Provisions		287.19
Yacht Club		70.00
Men's clothing		46.44
Wines and Liquors		44.25
Furniture		35.25
Washing		18.75
Insurance		18.00
Race Entrance fee		10.00
Ammunitions		7.95
Tobacco		4.63
Repairs		164.70
		$1043.09

In 1880, on the tenth anniversary of its founding, the Eastern Yacht Club listed 240 members, a fleet of sixty-nine yachts (including T. Wattson Merrill's *Edith* from an English design by Ratsey, the first yawl built in America), and no clubhouse—not a peg to hang a cap on, since the India Wharf room on Boston Harbor appears to have been used only for the first year. With each season, the North Shore increased its popularity as Boston's premier summer resort, and more members made the communities beyond the city their sailing base. By the late 1870s, Marblehead Rock had been established as the favored starting line, although races were still run off Swampscott as late as 1879.

Around Jack Point to the westward from the Rock lay Marblehead Harbor. The town's fishing industry was petering out. A few yachts lazed standoffishly at anchor. The isolated old place had hardly been discovered by the summer people. Plenty of room to pound a peg to hang a cap on. Late in the fall of 1879, an informal meeting was held in the home of Commodore Boardman, about which *The Yachts and Yachtsmen of America* (1894) tells us almost everything we know:

The matter of a Club House on the sea-shore was talked over, and it was decided to procure information as to site, etc., and have it considered at the next annual meeting, which would be February 10, 1880. At this meeting, Mr. B.W. Crowninshield [of Marblehead, who had joined the Club only the previous April 28] gave an interesting account of the various sites examined, especially those on Marblehead Harbor, and after a long discussion, during which it was evident that nearly all, if not all, there preferred a lot on Marblehead Neck, Messrs. Crowninshield,

John Jeffries and Daniel Appleton [of Marblehead] were appointed a committee with full power to purchase land and buildings, or a piece of land, and erect buildings thereon, at a cost of ten thousand dollars, which limit was increased to eighteen thousand dollars at a subsequent meeting, March 3d, and to twenty thousand at the second general meeting of the year, April 6, 1880.

Under this authority the Committee bought the site now occupied by the Club House on Marblehead Neck, about sixty thousand square feet, and built under their own supervision the present structure. [George Snell of Boston was the architect.]

According to the 1882 *Handbook of Marblehead Neck*, the Club repaired the Old Stone Wharf at the foot of the property and put a float off the end. Years earlier it had served boats taking on produce from the farm but was not included in the sale. Some friendly deal must have been made with the owner, since the Club did not take an option to buy the wharf until 1902.

It was all a canny stroke. Forty-five years earlier, the estate of Jesse Blanchard tried to auction off for recreational use his 130-acre farm on the 300-acre Neck as follows:

To the sportsman and angler it presents the greatest of facilities for the prosecution of their sports. In the summer season, pearch and tautog are caught from the rocks in abundance; plovers and curlews abound in the pastures. Persons disposed to obtain summer residences will find, in the Neck, capabilities equal to those of Nahant. . . . A Public House might be erected here, which would make the Neck a fashionable resort for people from all quarters, as soon as the beauty of its situation and its other attractions became more generally known.

But the Blanchard farm was sold to Ephraim Brown, who added it to his own 110 acres, and nothing further disturbed the pearch and the plovers until some men from Nashua, New Hampshire, bought and subdivided a harbor lot six ways in 1867, built summer cottages, and laid in a stock of dories, while a sea of summer tenters flooded the shore on the ocean side of the Neck. Meanwhile, the railroad had come to link Marblehead with the rest of the world, much to the sorrow of the old 'Headers.

The 240 acres of the Brown farm were sold by his executors to the Marblehead Great Neck Land Company in 1872 for $250,000. The developers laid out 250 lots, built Ocean Avenue, kicked off seasonal lessees who balked at buying, and went broke five years after the 1873 panic. The unsold land reverted to the Brown estate under foreclosure. The trustees finished the circumferential road and resumed land sales until the committee from the Eastern Yacht Club found its spot in 1880, when there were about seventy unpretentious summer cottages. Their lifeline to the town across the harbor was the steam ferry *Lillie May*, operated by Captain Allen Pitman, he of the timeless two-liner:

City feller: "Say, does this train stop in Marblehead?"
Conductor: "Wal, if it don't, there's gonna be one helluva splash."

The first reference in the Regatta Committee minutes to this contemplated abandonment of Boston notes that on May 24, 1880, Measurer George A. Goddard instructed all unmeasured yachts to rendezvous at the "Club Station" in Marblehead Harbor for measurement.

The clubhouse arose during the 1880 season, on the north side of the Samoset House for summer boarders, as a substantial stick-style, shingled, airy structure similar to the large cottages of the day, aproned with piazzas supported by posts rustically hatracked with the stubs of their lopped-off branches—pegs aplenty for every member to hang his cap on.

That winter of construction, a durable cap was tossed in the direction of its peg by Charles Henry Wheelwright Foster, who joined the Club on January 25, 1881. Foster was twenty-one and would graduate in June from Harvard, where he played football and lacrosse, rowed, boxed, wrestled, and held the "strongest-man-in-college" record. Most of all, however, he was crazy about boats, his absolute passion for the rest of his very long life when he was not running the family sugar business, the Brookline National Bank, and the Chickering piano factory, or serving as treasurer of the Massachusetts General Hospital and in a host of other civic and business capacities.

Foster would lose count and set a national record, as far as anyone knew, for private yacht-owning over the next sixty-five years, beginning with the first that he considered worthy of the designation back in 1875 when he was fifteen. With the acquisition of number 55 in 1933, he took inventory:

After several years of borrowing dories and other small boats in Marblehead, in 1875 through a serious process of saving I accumulated $40 with which I bought a Swampscott lapstreak boat, one of the type then used by all of the shore fishermen for lobstering and fishing. They were about 20 feet long on the waterline, and were partially decked over, and their sail spread consisted of a large foresail, a small mainsail and a jib which was carried in light weather. There was a step forward into which was placed the mainsail when it was desired to reduce sail in the heavy breezes. The foresail was rolled up on the sprit and lashed to the mast. This boat was called *Norwhoo*. What it meant, or who created the name, I have never known. The first noticeable characteristic of this boat was the fact that she could leak enough during the night to sink before morning unless I bailed her out at 9 p.m. and at 4 a.m., and, of course, with frequent bailings during the day. We did finally stop the leak, and thereafter I had a reasonably good boat in which to sail around the Bay.

Three years later, Charlie Foster replaced *Norwhoo* with another of the same type, *Faith*, and then in 1879 built his first boat, *Lola*, similarly rigged but carvel-planked, with flotation tanks. The town of Marblehead held Fourth of July races for these rigs, which came from all over Massachusetts Bay that year. They started from anchor, and *Lola* drew the number-one position at the Fort Sewall end of the line. Charlie was sailing with the family's professional skipper of long standing, Captain Samuel Dolliber, who took so long up forward taking in the rode as they worked to weather Point Neck that one of the officials called across the water from the fort: "Hey, Sam, are you going to get it up before you reach the Point?"

Lola won, and after the race one of Charlie's young crew, a Salem lad named Frank W. Benson, who was showing some promise as an artist, painted her picture for him. Foster sold *Lola* in 1880 and bought the 20-foot-waterline catboat *Anita*, which he owned when he joined the Eastern. About thirty-five years later, he crossed tacks with his old boat while cruising the Maine coast and was presented with her by her owner, Professor Charles Lanman, the Harvard Orientalist. Foster brought *Lola* back to Marblehead for harbor sailing and then hauled her out on his wharf in her old age.

An anecdote of the construction of the clubhouse that winter survives in Rebecca Benson Haskell's story of the uncle who told her late in life that he had supervised the job. "I said he couldn't possibly have been old enough. 'Ah, yes, Rebecca,' said he in his usual pontifical manner, and explained that the Bensons and the Kinsmans had hired the Samoset that summer, and the workmen were fed from a tent where a cook pro-

India Wharf to Marblehead

The new clubhouse of the Eastern Yacht Club. Note "Stick Style" porch pillars.

---

duced mouth-watering doughnuts which naturally attracted small supervisors."

The circumstances of the formal opening of the clubhouse on June 9, 1881, under the management of a Mr. Mortimer, confirmed the observation in the account of the site committee's proceedings that all was not quite unanimity. The party-crasher was a heavy, drenching northeaster. The ever-loyal author of the *Ditty Box* put the best possible face on the proceedings:

> The line officers of the Club gave a reception and dinner to the ladies and other friends at the clubhouse in the evening. At five o'clock in the afternoon a gun was fired from the Commodore's schooner *Rebecca* [Charles H. Joy had bought John Heard's flagship in 1877 and succeeded Commodore Boardman in 1880] whereupon the other yachts in the harbor "dressed ship" and repeated the signal, finishing in the evening with a display of fireworks and illumination. The members of the Beverly Yacht Club [founded in 1872 for boats *under* 30 feet waterline] were invited to be present as guests at the reception and at the clubhouse.

As the gale raged up the length of Marblehead Harbor, a stiff chop built to most uncomfortable proportions, boats dragged and fouled, sheets of rain and scud drove through the bedraggled fleet, and the Annual Regatta had to be postponed for five days. Dudley L. Pickman of Beverly, who already knew what a nor'easter could do to Marblehead, shook his head:

> Marblehead is certainly an ideal summer harbor, though at the time the club was planning to build, there was considerable discussion as to the desirability of selecting the present site. Probably a majority of yacht owners at that time lived on the northern side of Salem Bay, and many thought the entrance to Manchester Harbor, or even Misery Island, would be a more convenient location. The fact that occasionally a northeaster—being no respecter of "good old summer time"—cuts vicious capers on Marblehead waters, was an added objection urged to building there. When, therefore, at the opening of the new clubhouse . . . this unwelcome visitor from the northeast arrived and prevented guests on yachts from joining the festivities on shore, or gave them a good soaking if they ventured to do so, the remark: "Didn't I tell you?" was not infrequently heard from former northern shore advocates.

Benjamin Crowninshield, so instrumental in locating the Club on the Neck, was the son of the elder Francis, who had settled on Peach's Point for his family summer seat. Benjamin's son Francis (Frank, nicknamed Keno), born in 1869 with an even more abiding love of boats and the sea, would grow up to marry Louise Du Pont and thereby be able to cruise the coast in that reincarnation of the essence of Crowninshield, the lovely schooner *Cleopatra's Barge II*.

Keno was only eleven or twelve when the clubhouse was inaugurated, and he was just getting on what he called "intimate" terms with a yacht for the first time, the family's shallow centerboarder *Effie*, 40 feet on the water. The year was probably 1881, and Commodore Joy in his flagship *Rebecca* led the Club on a short, early-season cruise to the Isles of Shoals:

> The sail down was a pleasant one and so was the night. We started back the following morning in a fresh southwester—which kept freshening as the day wore on. This compelled us to put in reefs until ours were all in. But even so and with the bonnet out of the jib, it was a real man's job keeping her on her feet. By God's mercy only—at least so it seemed to me—we finally got in under the land and made Lanesville, and I didn't meet the watery grave I had anticipated all day. . . . The only boat in the fleet—the large schooner *Phantom* of Harry Hovey—the only one that even attempted to weather Cape Ann—broke her main boom and had to turn back.

The Eastern sketched from the rear.

Marblehead Harbor, 1882.

The lad was full of energy and enthusiasm, and nothing suited him better than the yachting protocol then approaching its heyday, the noisier the nicer:

It was considered the thing to do to fire a gun whenever you got under way, as well as when you came to an anchor. You also saluted all flag officers wherever you met them. It was likewise almost treason at "colors" in the morning and at sunset, to hoist or to lower your flags without the aid of a gun. If a Commodore's yacht was not at the anchorage the onus was on the eldest Captain (in seniority) to do the honors; all of which was simple enough when the yachts were all of the same club, but led to a certain amount of "unpleasantness" when yachts of different clubs were there together. We boasted a small yacht's cannon and to my father's great disgust, it was my greatest joy to fire it on every possible occasion.

And so, after eleven vagrant years, the Eastern Yacht Club had a home, a magnificent harbor out front, and an expansive desire to show them off. The regatta that fall of 1881 was open for the first time to yachts of not less than 30 feet waterline from the New York, Atlantic, New Bedford, Boston, and Seawanhaka clubs. The invitation was shifted to the Annual Regatta the next season and extended to Brooklyn, Dorchester, and Portland, and in 1883 to all yacht clubs, period.

"With increased facilities and improvements," in Charlie Foster's careful words, "the Club hoped to merit public favor."

It did, for by 1882, one year after the clubhouse opening, the membership had leaped from 237 in 1879 to 456, and the fleet from fifty-five to ninety-one, comprising forty-four schooners, twenty-nine sloops, eight cutters, one yawl, and nine steamers. And an eighty-room Victorian summer hotel, named after the local Indian chief Nanepashemet, had been built above the bluffs on the ocean side of the Neck in anticipation, obviously, of all the activity expected to be generated by the Club, described in an 1882 promotional handbook as having "one of the finest club-houses of the kind on the New England coast."

Then in 1885, the Regatta Committee invited Nathaniel L. Stebbins, Boston's soon-to-be-great maritime photographer, to lug his cumbersome camera and glass plates aboard the judges' steamer for the Annual Regatta, and in a magnanimous bid for public favor notified *Forest and Stream* and *Spirit* magazines, the *New York Herald*, and the Boston *Advertiser, Post, Herald, Journal, Transcript*, and *Globe* that their representatives would be permitted aboard the Club steamer.

By 1887 the membership stood at 548, the fleet at 113, and the Regatta Committee voted to oblige all yacht owners to have large numbers sewn on both sides of their mainsails.

The Cup and Burgess

Chapter 2   **The Cup and Burgess**   *1885–1891*

The story of American yachting is a rope of many strands, each made of innumerable yarns.
The "core" is the America Cup; about it twine many other subjects.

—William P. Stephens, *American Yachting*, 1904

And the story of the America's Cup in the 1880s is the story of yachting in Massachusetts Bay, at the core of which is the Eastern Yacht Club and its secretary and measurer, Edward Burgess, the brightest designer of them all during his meteoric transit of that glorious decade of sail. More than any other domestic factor, the deepwater traditions of the North Shore of Boston, responding to the emerging British challenge, shaped the course of American yachting. In only its second decade, New England's foremost sailing organization thrice defended the Cup and prevented it from recrossing the Atlantic.

The English had challenged twice with schooners, in 1870 and 1871, since *America* sailed through their fleet in 1851. Then the Canadians took up the cudgels with the schooner *Countess of Dufferin* in 1876, and in 1881 with *Atalanta* in the first match of the sloops, won by the New York Yacht Club's shoal centerboarder *Mischief*. A decade had elapsed since their last go at it; what mischief had the Limeys been up to?

Ominous hints arrived on shipboard, first in 1881 in the wedge-shaped form of the Scottish cutter *Madge*, built in 1879—38 feet 6 inches waterline, a mere 7 feet 9 inches of beam, 7 feet 10 inches draft, with 10 tons of lead on her keel. She split with the Eastern's pride, Herreshoff's centerboard sloop *Shadow*, off Newport. Then in 1882, George H. Warren of the Eastern imported the fast English cutter *Maggie*, 45 feet on the water and equally knifelike, and she outsailed *Shadow*

decisively. These brushes merely confirmed the blue-water Eastern members in their skepticism concerning the New York skimming-dish trend. Francis E. Peabody had already demonstrated the merits of depth with his moderate cutter *Enterprise*, designed and built in East Boston by Dennison J. Lawlor in 1878. J. Malcolm Forbes built the cutter *Lapwing* in 1882 from the plans of one English designer, Dixon Kemp, while Franklin Dexter had *Medusa*, the creation of another, John Beavor-Webb, racing the next year.

Twenty years later, William P. Stephens looked back on the cutter-centerboard controversy:

From the early days of yachting, New York has been the national centre of the sport, more prominent in many ways than Boston and claiming first attention from the historian; but yachting has always received a generous and hearty support from all classes about Massachusetts Bay, and in the matter of type the development has always been of a more healthy form. While the centre-board skimming-dish existed in considerable numbers and outrageous proportions, there has always been an appreciation of the value of depth and draft as factors of safety, even in centreboard boats. . . . While *Shadow* was deeper than most of her class, they in turn averaged much greater depth and draft than the New York yachts of similar classes. . . . At the time when the keel type was represented in New York only by half a dozen cutters, Boston could boast of a fine fleet of keel yachts, racing and cruising along the whole eastern coast. . . .

So far as the recapture of the America Cup was concerned,

the venture of *Madge* was a serious mistake, as it opened the eyes of American yachtsmen in a measure to the weakness of the national type and the real qualities of the cutter.

After thirteen years, the British dropped the other shoe when in December 1884 Beavor-Webb challenged on behalf of two cutters off his board: *Genesta*, 81 feet on the water (and only 15 feet beam!), owned by Sir Richard Sutton of the Royal Yacht Squadron, and *Galatea*, 86 feet, yet to be built for Royal Navy Lieutenant William R. Henn of the Royal Northern Yacht Club, the latter to race the next time around if the first failed. Both were 13 feet 6 inches deep and outsized anything in the New York fleet. New York announced that the defense would rest with a single-masted vessel of not less than 60 feet waterline fielded by a duly organized U.S. yacht club after a series of trials. It forthwith engaged A. Cary Smith to produce *Priscilla* as a matching edition of his 1881 defender *Mischief*, although even he was skeptical, calling her "a damned steel scow."

At this juncture, the Eastern entered the picture in a manner most evocatively described in the tribute of the City of Boston to the principals in the ensuing drama, Edward Burgess and Charles J. Paine:

In the early part of 1885, five gentlemen, members of the Eastern Yacht Club, consisting of Vice-Com. J. Malcolm Forbes, Gen. Charles J. Paine, Mr. Edward Burgess, Secretary, Mr. William Gray, Jr., and Mr. Francis H. Peabody, met at the office of Mr. Forbes to discuss matters pertaining to the Club. Allusion to the challenge of the *Genesta* was made there, and, after a discussion of the relative types of English and American yachts, it was agreed that none of the latter possessed the speed necessary to successfully defend the challenge. Mr. Peabody having withdrawn, the other gentlemen continued the conversation until the enthusiasm increased to the point of suggesting the building of an Eastern boat which would combine all the recent ideas in American yacht designing. The suggestion met with hearty approval, and plans were then made to secure the cooperation of other yachtsmen, the syndicate to assume the entire cost of designing, building, and fitting out the new boat.

At a subsequent meeting the syndicate was formed, the members being Gen. Charles J. Paine, Vice Com. J. Malcolm Forbes, Mr. William Gray, Jr., Com. Henry S. Hovey, Rear-Com. William F. Weld, Mr. Augustus Hemenway, Mr. W.H. Forbes, Mr. John L. Gardner, Mr. J. Montgomery Sears, Mr. F.L. Higginson, and one other, who desired that his name be not made public. The stock was divided into ten shares, one being divided between Messrs. Sears and Higginson. The entire responsibility of designing, building, and sailing the yacht was placed with

Messrs. Forbes, Paine, and Gray, the former being chosen chairman of the committee.

In their subsequent consultations the committee sought the advice of Mr. Edward Burgess, in whose ideas they had much faith. About this time it was learned that Messrs. James Gordon Bennett and W.P. Douglas, of the New York Yacht Club, had undertaken the building of an iron sloop, which was afterward named the *Priscilla*, to compete for the same honors. The Boston gentlemen, urged on by this intelligence, exerted themselves to combine in the Boston sloop the very best ideas obtainable, and, after a frequent exchange of views, Mr. Burgess handed to them the designs of a yacht which eventually brought renown to her designer, her owners, and to the city of Boston.

Messrs. George Lawley & Sons, of South Boston, secured the contract for the construction, and when the sloop left their hands their work was declared to have been well and faithfully performed. The keel was laid in March, and the new sloop, christened *Puritan*, was launched on May 26, 1885. The name was given by Mr. Forbes, and her coat of white, symbolic of purity, corresponded with the name. The rigging and fitting-out progressed rapidly, under the supervision of the committee.

The *Puritan* is a centre-board yacht, and built entirely of wood. Her keel was shaped from an oak stick, 56 feet long and 26 inches square. The lead keel is 45 feet long, 2 feet wide, and 16 inches deep. The frames are of the best white oak, spaced 22 inches on the centres. The centre-board, of hard pine, with upper and lower planks of oak, is 22 feet long, 11 feet deep, and 4 inches thick. The five lower strakes of the hull are of oak and are copper-fastened. Above the water-line the planking is of hard pine, 2¾ inches thick. On the deck, which is flush, the planking is of white pine, and runs the entire length of the yacht.

Her frames are double, except those about the stern-post and stem. The rudder-head is of locust, 10 inches in diameter; the backing is of oak, and tapers to 2½ inches. The after-companionway is 5 × 3 feet, and the forward one 3 feet square, and they, with the skylights, are of mahogany. Hackmatack was used for the twelve pairs of hanging knees, and yellow pine, 8 × 10 at the mast and 6½ and 5½ inches for the others, was used for the deck beams. The step of the mast is made of iron, which weighs 1,000 pounds, and is strongly bolted to the keel. Attached to the lower plank of the centre-board is an iron shoe weighing 900 pounds, and having a knife edge. The stanchions are made of locust, 16 inches forward and 14 inches aft, and the rail is of oak.

The interior finishing and furnishing are of the best. The main cabin, 16 × 12 feet, is finished in mahogany and pine, and has two mahogany sideboards, large lounges, and mahogany posts carved to resemble ships' cables. The ladies' cabin, abaft

General Charles J. Paine

Edward Burgess

the main saloon, is beautifully furnished and has every convenience. Two state-rooms, 10½ × 6½ feet, are forward of the cabin, and just forward of these is a lavatory. There is a room for the captain, two for the mates, a roomy galley, and a forecastle with iron swinging-berths, which will accommodate eighteen men. Crucible steel wire was used for the rigging. Messrs. H. Pigeon & Sons, of East Boston, furnished the spars, and Messrs. J. H. McManus & Son, of Boston, the sails, which are of Plymouth duck.

The maiden trip of the *Puritan* was made on the 17th of June, 1885, only, however, for the purpose of stretching her sails, and not to test her speed. On this occasion, as on all others during that season, she was under the command of Capt. Aubrey Crocker, of Cohasset, Mass., who was an adept at yacht sailing, and had attracted the attention of the *Puritan*'s owners by his skillful handling of the sloop *Shadow*, in which he won many victories. The trial trip of the *Puritan* was made on June 20, 1885, and on this and subsequent trials the result was most gratifying. On the 30th of June she was entered for her first race, in the regatta of the Eastern Yacht Club, off Marblehead; and over a triangular course of 30 miles she led the fleet, and easily defeated the fastest Eastern sloops and schooners. She showed remarkable speed during the cruise of the New York Yacht Club in July, and on August 3 she won the Goelet Cup, off Newport, R.I., defeating not only the crack yachts *Bedouin, Gracie, Mohican, Fortuna,* and *Montauk,* but the New York sloop *Pris-*

cilla, which had been built to contend with her for the America's Cup in September.

[The silver tankard won by *Puritan*—she beat *Priscilla* by almost twelve minutes—was presented to the Eastern and placed in competition in 1886 for the winner of the Annual Regatta as the Puritan Cup.]

With slight alterations in her ballast and main-boom she [*Puritan*] was ready to enter the contest which should decide which American sloop would be named to sail with the *Genesta* for the international trophy. Her official measurements, as given by her designer, were as follows: length over all, 94 feet; length on water-line, 81 feet 1½ inches; beam, 22 feet 7 inches; draught, 8 feet 8 inches; length of mast, from deck to hounds, 60 feet; length of top-mast, 44 feet; length of main-boom, 76 feet 6 inches; length of gaff, 47 feet; length of bowsprit, outboard, 38 feet; length of spinnaker boom, 62 feet; displacement, 105 tons; ballast, 48 tons; sail area (New York Yacht Club rules), 7,982 square feet; racing measurement (New York Yacht Club rules), 83.85.

In the high-technology context of a hundred years later, the speed with which *Puritan* materialized in the days of mainly wooden ships and absolutely iron men is wondrous. *Genesta*'s challenge was received in New York on December 29, 1884. Between January and March the Eastern group met, determined to build *Puritan*, organized, worked out the financing, and agreed to take their chances with an inexperienced designer, who, starting from scratch, drew up the plans for what they all dreamed would be the fastest sloop in the world. Contracts were let, yard and loft priorities were reshuffled, and an oak keel 56 feet long and 26 inches square was laid—all within two months!

Perhaps ten weeks later, the Eastern Yacht Club's 105-ton, 94-foot America's Cup defender was launched. By June 17, three more weeks, her sails had been made, a fifth of an acre of duck, every stitch by hand, and she was off and running on her first stretch.

Puritan's sweep of the Annual Regatta was tinged with irony: Ben Butler had challenged the Eastern schooners to a $100-apiece sweepstake in his restored *America* and trailed over the thirty-mile course by six minutes on corrected time. General Paine had served on General Butler's staff in Virginia during the Civil War.

Five months from a gleam in the eye to a bone in the teeth! Credit first the members of the Eastern syndicate:

General Paine, a lean, balding, hawk-eyed, down-to-earth Bostonian with a sweeping mustache, had commanded a division of black soldiers and been wounded in the Civil War. As a boy he had sailed a catboat in Salem Bay and was an avid yachtsman. Now he managed a family fortune in railroads and had two summer estates—one in the country town of Weston, west of Boston, and the other on Swallow's Cave Road at Nahant. Paine owned the centerboard schooner *Halcyon*, a slow boat that he had turned into a winner by alterations, whipping many of the New Yorkers; his dual membership in the Marblehead and New York clubs qualified the syndicate's entry.

Of the other members of the Boston group, Malcolm Forbes (son of J. Murray Forbes) had the new keel cutter *Lapwing*. His brother, William H. Forbes, sailed the keel sloop *Hesper*. Eastern Commodore Henry S. Hovey the previous year had launched his 109-foot *Fortuna*, which Captain R.F. Coffin, the leading yachting writer of the day, considered the fastest keel schooner in the world. Harry Hovey was the bachelor son of the late George O. Hovey, the Boston dry goods merchant. He wintered on Beacon Street and summered in his father's luxurious cottage on the bank above Gloucester's Freshwater Cove with his sister Marion. Rear Commodore William F. Weld, member of another Boston shipping family, had already cruised abroad in his handsome new keel schooner *Gitana*. The sixth of the syndicate, William Gray, Jr., was a good amateur sailor who had designed his own keel sloop, *Huron*. Augustus Hemenway of Manchester, a Boston merchant scion, owned the keel cutter *Beetle*. John L. (Jack) Gardner was the husband of "Mrs. Jack," Boston's flamboyant patroness of the arts, Isabella Stewart Gardner.

Credit the master yacht builder, George F. Lawley of South Boston, and the clocklike coordination of his gang of craftsmen; Pigeon the master sparmaker; and John McManus, artist in sailcloth, whose son Tom would be the most prolific designer of schooners in the history of the fisheries.

But the composer and conductor of this masterpiece was Edward Burgess. Entomology and sailing, as we have seen, were his passions from an early age. He was still a junior at Harvard in 1870 when he joined the Eastern within six weeks of its founding; his brother Franklin was vice commodore in 1871, and Ned was on the Regatta Committee the next year, rear commodore in 1875, and succeeded brother Sidney as secretary in 1884, when he was elected measurer as well.

Yet Burgess was too eclectic to confine himself to the big boats of the Eastern, and in 1872 he and a group of more active North Shore friends organized the complementary Beverly Yacht Club for the under-30s—most were considerably under. Within ten years, they had so successfully championed small-boat sailing that they had more members from the South Shore and Buzzards Bay than from north of Boston. In 1882 and 1883 they ran off Marblehead allegedly the biggest union regattas recorded in America up to that time—113 and 171 yachts, small and large, respectively. But the western tail was wagging the eastern dog; in 1895 the Beverly Yacht Club moved to Pocasset, and in 1913 to Marion, where it remains, name curiously unchanged.

Since his graduation in 1871, Ned had been working at Harvard as an instructor in entomology; in fact, the "bugologist," as his affectionate friends called him, was secretary of the Boston Society of Natural History for fifteen years. In 1883 he was spending the summer observing the yachting scene at Torquay and around the Isle of Wight, absorbing the virtues of the English cutter and thinking about boats, when he got the news that the family business had failed. On his return home, he had to go to work seriously; he more or less put the bugs behind him and started the felicitously named Eastern Yacht Agency with brother Sidney. There was not enough business for two, and Sid dropped out. Ned had designed a couple of keel sloops, both well under 30 feet on the water, and supervised the construction of several British designs for Boston owners. His most ambitious job, early in 1884, was the cruising cutter *Rondina*, 36 feet overall, for Dr. William F. Whitney of the Eastern Yacht Club. That was about the sum of his drafting-board experience when his Eastern friends put money on their bugologist of thirty-seven to cop the Big Cup in 1885.

To win, they decided, something was needed between the extremes of Cowes and New York. A compromise.

"The object in building the *Puritan*," as her designer summed it up less than three years later, "was not so much to get a vessel that would be particularly fast in light weather as to produce a good all-round yacht, and especially one that would give a good account of herself in a breeze of wind—at any rate, a boat that would not disgrace herself in heavy weather."

After her warm-up capture of the Goelet Cup off Newport, *Puritan* sailed on to sweep *Priscilla* out of the Cup trials off Sandy Hook, two out of three, on August 21, 22, and 24. Two weeks later, she was ready for *Genesta*, again off Sandy Hook.

The Cup and Burgess

Left: Puritan charges along in this early "instantaneous" photograph by David Mason Little.

Above: Shiny as a wet whale, *Priscilla* shows her stuff—but not enough. Edwin H. Lincoln photo.

The Puritan Cup

Under the direction of the professional Captain Crocker, *Puritan*'s veteran afterguard included, probably among others, Eastern Yacht Club members Paine, Burgess, J. Malcolm Forbes, Dr. John Bryant, Henry Bryant, and George H. Richards.

Maneuvering for the start on September 8, she fouled the challenger, carrying away *Genesta*'s bowsprit, and was disqualified—an unearned default refused with British sportsmanship by Sir Richard Sutton. W.P. Stephens was on the committee boat, and fifty-five years later, on August 20, 1940, wrote Charles Foster his own version of the foul:

> My recollection of the *Puritan-Genesta* foul is still quite clear, and it differs from all published accounts. I stood just outside the pilothouse of the *Luckenbach*, near enough to Fred Tams to touch him through the window as he stood inside with Charles H. Stebbins and Jules Montant [members of the NYYC America's Cup Committee for 1885]. As *Puritan* sailed up to us a big man in a white knitted jersey rushed about the deck with his arms in the air, in a great state of excitement; he called out, "They fouled us, we claim the race; we will sail the course." To this Fred Tams replied very quietly and coolly, "No you won't, not by a damned sight." The big man was Vice Commodore Forbes. Tams informed them that they were disqualified and they sailed away.

On September 14 and 16, light one day and blowy the other, the Eastern's defender defeated *Genesta*—albeit hard-pressed when it breezed up—and saved the Cup for America. As was his exuberant ritual aboard a winner when he had the deckroom, Ned Burgess turned a double somersault as his creation smashed across the finish.

"Human voices, cannons, and whistles sounded their applause, and excursionists danced with delight, embraced each other, and gave all sorts of evidence of joy," in the words of a chronicler.

About a hundred Eastern Yacht Club members gathered at Boston's Parker House for a celebratory banquet on October 28. "It is recorded as a great occasion and a noteworthy social event," according to the *Ditty Box*, "and it is said that there had never, perhaps, been a more enthusiastic dinner in Boston." His triumphant syndicate sold their winner for $13,500 to General Paine, who sold her to J. Malcolm Forbes, who put up the "Puritan Cup" in perpetuity and then proceeded to win it in its namesake for nominally the first (but actually the second) time in the Club's Annual Regatta the next season.

Was ever there more contrast between contenders? While they were virtually identical on the waterline, *Puritan* was three and a half feet longer on deck, with a beam of 22 feet 7 inches compared with *Genesta*'s 15 feet; their drafts were 8 feet 8 inches against 13 feet 6 inches, and sail areas 7,982 square feet and 7,150 square feet. The Burgess cutter carried 27 tons of ballast on the keel, 20 inside; the challenger had 70 on the bottom, only two inside. For all the controversy over the cutters, *Puritan* was closer to *Priscilla*, which was four feet longer on the water with the same beam, 22 feet 6 inches, though she drew only 7 feet 9 inches.

So the Eastern Yacht Club, only fifteen years old and a mere five in its own home, stood at the apex of the yachting world in 1885.

The crescendo in Marblehead that glorious season is attested to by the addition to the fleet, alongside plumb-stemmed *Puritan*, of the largest sailing yacht in the United States, the majestic schooner *Ambassadress*. At 130 feet on the water, 146 feet overall, weighing 232 tons and flying 28,000 square feet of sail, this stately vessel—a centerboarder until deepened to keel in 1881—had cruised the coast as William Astor's floating "Astor House" since her launching in 1877. In 1884 the New York magnate built the barque-rigged *Nourmahal*, the world's biggest steam yacht, and sold *Ambassadress* to Nathaniel Thayer of Boston. She presided over the Eastern anchorage until 1893.

On men and boys in Marblehead, the effects of Cup Fever were something to behold. Francis Crowninshield was sixteen that summer and could hardly restrain himself:

The first boat we boys ever owned "ourselves"—a keel boat 22 feet on the water line—called the *Witch* which some of our friends often referred to as if her name commenced with a B instead of a W—was rigged with two head sails and "to be in the swim" she naturally had to have a housing topmast as well as all the other gadgets of a cup defender.

Racing boats was about my only thought in those glorious days of yore and nothing was in any way allowed to interfere with it.

Genesta in 1885 made up in stateliness what she lacked for speed. Little photo.

Noting that in racing their full-rigged 22-footer they were allowed a crew of five but rarely had more than four, the master of *Witch* goes on to describe a typical Corinthian open race in the mid-1880s, wind strong from the east-northeast:

We started with our topmast housed for the beat to Half-Way Rock. Once around we sent up the topmast—a man-sized job I assure you when you consider the rigging which went up with it which had to be kept clear and then set up before the topmast could be made use of. We then set the club topsail with its "upper" and "lower" halyards, its "outer" and "inner" sheets as well as its "gob" line [the usage here is obscure; a gob line is a martingale backrope] and tack. The next event was the spinnaker, not of the ordinary variety but one with an "extension" spinnaker boom, a boom of two parts. The "outer" boom—which almost doubled its length—was hauled out once the "inner" boom was in place much the way a topmast was sent up from its housed position. The balloon jib was next in order—all for the run to the Pig Rocks Bell. This had not only to be "undone" but the topmast had to be re-housed before rounding the buoy for the beat home.

Five feet longer than *Genesta* and substantially heavier, *Galatea* challenged for 1886. This time, General Paine alone commissioned Ned Burgess to design what amounted to a bigger *Puritan*, making it essentially a rematch between Beavor-Webb's deep-keel extreme cutter and the Bostonian's compromise centerboard sloop. George Lawley's yard began work on *Mayflower*—85 feet 6 inches waterline, 100 feet overall, 23 feet 6 inches beam, drawing 9 feet 9 inches (20 feet with the board down)—on January 25, 1886. Her lead keel weighed a staggering 37 tons (and was added to later).

It was run in three moulds, to conform to the oak keel [two mortised oak timbers 60 feet long and 23 inches square], the forward piece being about fourteen feet long, the middle one about twenty-three feet long, and the after piece about twenty feet long. Along the centreboard box this enormous mass of lead measures forty inches wide at the top, and sixteen inches at the lowest part.

Mayflower had tuning problems in her trials and was defeated several times by *Puritan*, but after some alterations in sails, spars, and ballast, she romped through a fleet of seventy to lead the New York Yacht Club Cruise from New London to Newport.

Under Captain Martin V.B. Stone, General Paine's sailing master in *Halcyon* and one of a horny-handed elite of professional yachting skippers hailing from Swampscott, *Mayflower* sailed to New York in August and drubbed *Puritan*, an altered *Priscilla* under the burgee of the Seawanhaka Corinthian Yacht Club, and the new sloop *Atlantic*, built as a contender by members of the Atlantic Yacht Club of New York in an unsatisfactory attempt at incorporating Burgess's major design novelties.

On August 1, 1886, *Galatea* hove into Marblehead Harbor under jury rig from England, with Lieutenant and Mrs. Henn aboard, and was greeted with fireworks, bonfires, and salutes, a reception at the Eastern Yacht Club, more fireworks, and a serenade by the Salem Cadet Band. The mutual amiability survived *Galatea*'s one-sided defeat in frustratingly light airs off New York on September 7 and 11.

Britannia wasted no time with regrets. The old tonnage rule of yacht measurement, which had placed a premium on depth at the expense of breadth, was repealed after the defeats of *Genesta* and *Galatea*, and the leading English designer, George L. Watson, visited the United States in the autumn of 1886 to see what ideas he could discreetly borrow. That winter he returned home and drafted the steel cutter *Thistle* for a syndicate of Scots from the Royal Clyde Yacht Club. *Thistle* had more than the usual British beam for a cutter in ratio to depth and exchanged the plumb stem for a clipper bow with cutaway forefoot, a reduction in lateral plane that would have disastrous effects on her ability to claw to windward. But she was faster than anything afloat in her home waters, as she proved, and great things were expected.

As soon as *Thistle*'s dimensions were published (the New York Yacht Club had amended the Deed of Gift of the America's Cup to force the challenger to show something of his hand in advance), General Paine straightaway commissioned Burgess to outdesign her. *Volunteer* was rushed through construction and set maiden sail in July 1887. She, too, was steel and clipper-stemmed, continuing moderately the Burgess trend away from beam toward depth. Yet she was assuredly less cutterish than her Scottish rival, for the challengers still could not bring themselves to espouse the centerboard. She was 106 feet 3 inches overall, 85 feet 10 inches waterline, 23 feet 3 inches beam, 10 feet draft, 130 tons displacement, and carried 9,260 square feet of sail. She was built by Pusey and Jones in Wil-

Precarious perches don't bother the pros handing *Mayflower*'s jib and topsail, 1886. Little photo.

The Cup and Burgess

The Cup and Burgess

mington, Delaware. *Thistle* was 108 feet 6 inches overall, 86 feet 6 inches waterline, 20 feet 4 inches beam, 13 feet 9 inches draft, 138 tons displacement, with 8,968 square feet of sail. Mainly, Burgess's third defender carried less beam, more bilge, and a lower center of gravity than his second. General Paine sold *Mayflower*, incidentally, to E.D. Morgan of the New York Yacht Club that same July.

In her trials, the latest magic from the Burgess board left her parent *Mayflower* (as *Mayflower* had *Puritan*) far, far astern.

Thistle crossed the Atlantic with imperial hopes. Her design and construction had been shrouded in secrecy, and she had been a veritable terror among the British yachting fleet. The first Cup race was sailed through an armada of spectator boats on September 27 over the thirty-eight miles of the New York Yacht Club inside course. Under her professional sailing master, Captain Henry (Hank) Haff of Islip, Long Island, the stunning white *Volunteer* simply walked away from the gallant pretender, passed her in the opposite direction on the homeward run, and finished nineteen minutes ahead. The second race on September 30 was but a formality; the Burgess double somersault set off 11 minutes and 54 seconds of whistles and cannon fire before *Thistle* crossed the finish line. There would not be another challenge for six more years.

Volunteer sailed in triumph for Marblehead, and while a tugboat towed her the windless last few miles into the harbor on the evening of October 7, the City of Boston held a packed reception for her designer and owner in Faneuil Hall. The briefest of the panegyrics was the best, from the absent Dr. Oliver Wendell Holmes, who could not resist writing from Beverly Farms: "Proud as I am of their achievement, I own that the General is the only commander I ever heard of who made himself illustrious by running away from all his competitors."

Later in the evening, the half-encircling shore of Marblehead Harbor blazed with bonfires, and every yacht was illuminated. Into this eerie amphitheatre puffed the steamer *Brunette*, towing a serpentine procession of fifty dories strung with Chinese lanterns. As they completed their encirclement of *Volunteer*, the harbor exploded with skyrockets, Roman candles, and red fire. Then, on a toot from the steamer, every church bell in town pealed furiously, and the shores echoed with blasts of

Mayflower's deck. Ladies in black escape camera behind boom. Note array of reef points. Winch appears to lead from below.

cannon from the squadron. The Lynn Cadet Band burst into a medley of patriotic airs from *Brunette*'s deck, and Town Clerk Felton stepped aboard the third-in-a-row Marblehead defender of the America's Cup with congratulatory resolutions from the selectmen.

Three defenses of the world cup of yachting in three successive years by the same designer and owner, each boat brilliantly outsailing its predecessor, all under the burgee of a club founded only fifteen years earlier by a band of Bostonians weaned on salt water. Here was a tour de force unparalleled in the history of the America's Cup. In three years the Eastern had defended thrice—to New York's twice in the previous thirty-six—and catapulted Marblehead to the forefront of the American yachting scene.

His ecstatic fellow members presented Ned Burgess with a silver loving cup containing an extra measure of love—a check for $10,750. Their bugologist was on the top of his world.

Bill Stephens suggested that the story of American yachting is a rope of many strands and innumerable yarns of which the America's Cup is the core. Henry Howard would have enjoyed the metaphor but rejected the role of the Cup—more of that in a later chapter when, as Regatta Committee chairman, he would give some unique international twists to the Club's coil. First, however, a couple of yarns from this master spinner's autobiography, *Charting My Life*, concerning his admission to the Eastern Yacht Club at the age of twenty-one as co-owner of the old and leaky plumb-stemmed cruising sloop *Gracie* of 24 feet overall. Howard had just been graduated from M.I.T.

In 1888 [actually June 8, 1889] I became the youngest member of the Eastern Yacht Club at Marblehead and was proud of having been proposed by George Richards, once in the afterguard of the Cup Defenders *Puritan*, *Mayflower* and *Volunteer*.

Learning that there was always an annual club cruise, generally along the coast of Maine, I decided to join it with the *Gracie*, although most of the yachts were from 70 to 90 feet long on the waterline. As an extra hand or sailor I had hired a boy who was really about fifteen years old, but was undersized and looked about ten. Our first run was an easy one from Marblehead to Gloucester and we were in ample time to attend the captains' meeting at 8:30 P.M. on board the flagship, the schooner *Fortuna*, belonging to Commodore Harry Hovey. The next day was a long pull from Gloucester to Portland. We started at 4 A.M. while the rest of the fleet sailed about 9 A.M.

The Cup and Burgess

Hauling on the main sheet on the British challenger *Thistle*.
Little photo.

They overtook and passed us about noon and waved as they went by, but still we arrived in time for the captains' meeting. My sailor boy rowed me alongside the flagship in great style but he was so short he had to stand up to reach the oars, much to everyone's amusement. They all applauded as I came up the gangway steps. My sailor was a great diver and swimmer and was again applauded when the next morning he climbed to the cross trees and dove overboard from that considerable height. The next day was a seventy-mile run from Portland to Rockland, but by means of a very early start we were still able to attend the captains' meeting.

This ended the cruise for us because during the night a southeast gale came up and as soon as it was daylight we left the fleet and ran to Camden to get a smoother anchorage. The next day in a fresh nor'wester we ran over eighty miles back to Portland.

Around 1890 Henry Howard sold *Gracie* and bought the 30-footer *Elf*, Lawley-built and two years old, taking her to Halifax in 1893 on a fast and furious cruise that made the newspapers. In *Charting My Life*, he recalled its bachelor phase on *Elf*'s mooring off the Marblehead clubhouse.

I was working as a chemist for the Merrimac Chemical Company in North Woburn, Massachusetts, and had to take the train which left the North Station, Boston, at 8 A.M. This meant taking the 6:45 train from Marblehead to Boston, and in turn meant breakfast at 6 A.M., followed by a row across the harbor and a half-mile walk to the railroad station. I had to keep one paid man on board who would get my breakfast and row me across the harbor while I was completing my toilet. In the afternoon he would meet me about 6:20 P.M., on the arrival of my train, to row me back on board. I would then wash, dress and row myself ashore to dinner at the Eastern Yacht Club at 7 P.M., for a very pleasant two hours with a small group of interesting Boston men.

The young chemist's tablemates on such occasions were likely to include Charlie Longfellow, Ned Burgess, General Paine, Malcolm Forbes, the famous Captain Arthur Clark, and Richard Milton.

[Clark and Milton] took great interest in me as they had apparently both been in love with my mother before my father married her. . . . Then when the nine o'clock curfew bell rang on old Abbott Hall, across the harbor in Marblehead, it was the signal for me to go on board and go to bed to get a good night's sleep before my early breakfast.

Saturdays, as I was able to get off earlier, I would take the 2:30 P.M. train from Boston to Marblehead, with many other Marblehead yachtsmen. Sails would have been hoisted by our re-

Old 'Headers jaw over the race. *Harper's Weekly*.

Captain Hank Haff of *Volunteer*. *Harper's Weekly*.

The Cup and Burgess

spective boatmen and the weekly race to Gloucester would begin at the railroad station in Marblehead, and continue in our dinghies across the harbor to our boats where we would tumble on board, let go the moorings, break out the jib and forestays'l, which had been hoisted in stops for the occasion.

I learned much of seamanship and coastal navigation during these "scrub" races. . . . With my marriage in 1896 I had to sell *Elf*. I sold her in the autumn of 1896 for $1750 after seven years' use. So I felt the original $2000 had been well spent.

Young David Sears, son of the founder and second commodore who had died so unexpectedly in 1873, inherited his father's wealth and his love of sailing. After graduating from Harvard in 1874, he traveled in Europe for two years, returned to Boston, and joined the Eastern in 1876 when he was twenty-three. The next year he built the 43-foot-waterline sloop *Wayward* and in an evidently sentimental gesture was elected rear commodore, his first and last office in forty-seven years of membership, and bachelorhood. The same August he was off for the Himalayas to shoot ibex and see the Far East. By the time he returned home in 1879, his second year of absentee office was up.

Sears sold *Wayward* and built the schooner *Actaea*, 92 feet waterline, named for his father's wrecked yacht. In May 1881, he headed east in her on a 12,000-mile voyage that took him to the Welsh, Irish, and Scottish coasts as far north as the Orkneys, to England, France, Spain, Portugal, Morocco, Tangier, Madeira, Cape Verde, and back home by way of Trinidad and Cuba. Afflicted with arthritis, he remained in Boston until the lust for wander grew too strong to resist, and in 1887 he sailed down around South America.

In 1890 this restless semi-invalid relinquished *Actaea* and returned to *Wayward*, this time a keel cutter 60 feet on the water, designed by Edward Burgess and built by Lawley. It is recorded that in between frequent trips to Europe and recurrent bouts with illness, he embarked on at least one more major voyage under the Club burgee when he cruised the British and Norwegian coasts in 1896, yacht unknown (he had his second *Wayward* only through 1895). The Club's second David Sears lived abroad in declining health until his death in 1923, when it was revealed that some years earlier he had made up Harvard's deficit of $250,000 because of his esteem for President Charles W. Eliot.

In opposite style, Ben Butler's carte-less-than-blanche to yachting respectability, the icon *America*, wove her way as skillfully as her owner did through the 1880s and the fleets of the Eastern and New York yacht clubs. In August 1880, she sailed with the Eastern fleet to join the NYYC Cruise at New London, where, as William U. Swan wrote in *The Yacht "America"*, "as usual he drew about him a merry crowd that laughed at his breezy anecdotes, mostly about his yacht, then swinging at anchor off the dock. As in nearly every port she visited the *America* was surrounded nearly all the time by an admiring crowd of small craft."

In 1885 she came in far behind in the Annual Regatta and again sailed with the Eastern to rendezvous with New York at Newport. The following season, the first winner of the America's Cup served as a trial horse for Burgess's defender candidate *Mayflower* and his new schooner *Sachem*. *America* again in 1887 joined Eastern boats that cruised to Newport, where General Butler was seen on his afterdeck in a Panama hat and white gloves. She cruised back with the New York fleet to Marblehead, where, as Swan described it:

She flung to the breeze from her main topmast, a twenty-two-foot banner with "America" in the center in letters two feet high. The banner had a border of red, and on the hoist were a number of alternate red and blue triangular pennants about a foot in length. Some of the visiting New York yachting reporters described the banner as of "the East River excursion barge variety." Its display was a source of gratification to General Butler, to whom the unconventional always appealed.

A few weeks later—after hauling and having her bottom smeared with tallow and black lead—*America* on September 17, 1887, won a thirty-mile match race with William F. Weld's schooner *Gitana* for a $1,000 sweepstakes off the North Shore by five seconds, no handicap. To his everlasting regret, her owner was not aboard.

Ironically, it was one of the few wins in the almost forty years since the Big One. Swan eulogized him in *The Yacht "America"*:

For all his disregard of accepted yachting usages and customs, General Butler took his numerous defeats like a true sportsman, seldom offering excuses; and no matter how badly he was beaten, he was ready for another race. Often he was laughed at when the old yacht came trailing in at the finish, but he brought a touch of color and human interest to the sport, such as no other American yachtsman had offered up to that time. He kept before an interested public the representative vessel of

In her prime under Ben Butler, *America* close-reaches off Marblehead. Pity the foremastheadman straddling the rod spreader. Edwin H. Lincoln photo.

the American nation, in the best possible condition, for twenty years and gave thousands of her patriotic admirers every possible chance of seeing her.

No doubt the old general at one time had his hopes, but to the members of the Eastern Yacht Club he remained, for all his charm, a political and social anathema to the end of his yachting career, which came on a bright September morning in 1892. As he started for the quarter gangway to go over the side of his beloved *America*, he turned and said, "Good bye, old girl. God only knows whether I shall ever tread your decks again."

Ben Butler died the following January.

Opposite page, above: Saracen appears about to jibe around the mark and get out the ballooner for the downwind leg in the EYC Special Regatta on September 14, 1888.

Opposite page, below: The harbor from the ferry landing on Marblehead Neck in 1887.

The Cup and Burgess

The Cup and Burgess

Chapter 3 **Billowing Sails** *1890–1900*

Boston's one-two-three defense of the America's Cup a hundred years ago made waves in all directions. The whole impetus of yacht design responded to Edward Burgess's brilliantly simple compromise between beam and depth, and everybody had to have a boat off his board. His 40-footers took the lead and showed the way to the one-designs. The intense interest in the races gave a great spur to yachting. Waterlines stretched to the capacity of the deep pockets and contracted to within the capabilities of the Corinthians. Yacht clubs for every length and purse proliferated.

And surely it is more than coincidence that between 1885, when *Puritan* brought world fame to Marblehead, and 1888, the year after *Volunteer* made it three in a row, the roster of the Eastern Yacht Club escalated from 466 to 581 and the squadron from 94 to 128.

Volunteer was still in the works early in 1887 when Charlie Adams, a Harvard junior of twenty, knocked on the suddenly world-famous designer's door. The young descendant of presidents had been sailing since he was a child from the family's summer compound, "The Glades," on the west side of Cohasset Harbor, usually with older brother George as mate. Their father was a Boston lawyer, their uncles Charles Francis a railroad builder, Brooks and Henry men of letters. Fifty years later, the Secretary of the Navy recalled the day:

> Edward Burgess was just approaching the period when everything of importance in the racing fleet came from his designing board, when my timid and youthful steps took me to the simple establishment where nearly alone he was working out the lines of some one of his triumphs.
>
> Being a sympathetic soul, he was soon busy explaining what he could do to produce that long sought product, the perfect

combination of a race boat and a cruiser. Though it never had been done, he thought he could build a keel boat of approximately the speed of the well tried centreboard type of the time, and hoped to produce something faster than the *Shadow*, the best product of Herreshoff's earlier period. . . .

The result was *Papoose*, the first of a dynasty of fast Adams boats built for the brothers and dubbed with lucky seven letters that included a mysterious double "o" representing, for all anyone knows, a pair of snake eyes. A keel cutter 36 feet on the water, 44 feet overall, with plumb stem, graceful stern overhang, and powerful rig crowned with the characteristic club gaff topsail of the day, *Papoose* had a brush with the greying *Shadow* that summer while *Volunteer* was tuning up for *Thistle*, and, like the young buck challenging the old stag, emerged triumphant.

A decade later, W.E. Robinson appraised the brothers in the May 1898 issue of *The Rudder*, the new yachting magazine just founded by Thomas Fleming Day:

> George Caspar Adams is three years older than his brother Charles, but you would never think it to see them together in racing. Where Charles is cool, level-headed and masterful, George is impetuous, impulsive, and at times a bit hot-headed. Yet it is these very contrasting qualities that make the brothers such a hard team to beat. Strong, of stocky build, and very lively on his feet, George is a power in the work on board a racing yacht, and while the cooler head and steadier hand of his brother controls the boat and holds the tiller, George's strength, dash, and willingness to work, coupled with a rare knowledge of racing details, make him a right-hand man worthy the dependence of the most exacting skipper. There is no clash between the brothers in their racing work. Head and hand work

together in perfect harmony, so that although George is not himself a racing skipper, he is entitled to have a place very close to the fraternity, and would undoubtedly have been heard from had he not chosen to be his brother's mate.

Having made their point, the brothers sold *Papoose* and in 1888 asked Burgess to design a somewhat bigger version, *Babboon*, the first of several 40-footers he did that season, some with boards, some without. In September, at twenty-two, Charlie Adams joined the Eastern Yacht Club and began his practice of the next sixty years or so of sailing forth and back across Boston Bay to the Marblehead races from Cohasset. Burgess masterpieces and lucky sevens notwithstanding, it was the combination of his intuitive feel for the interaction among hull, water, and wind, his meticulous prerace tuning, the magic of his touch, his usually exemplary sportsmanship, and the cold cut of his competitiveness that was on the way to making Charles Francis Adams the top amateur helmsman of his day.

While Ned Burgess was designing his first 40-footer in 1888, his English opposite number, Will Fife, Jr., was creating the 40-foot cutter *Minerva* for Charles H. Tweed, a New York lawyer (not the Boss) who summered at Beverly Farms. *Minerva* was to succeed *Clara*, a Fife cutter of extreme lines (9-foot beam on a 53-foot 7-inch waterline) that Tweed and an associate had purchased in Britain. *Clara* had cleaned up everything in sight off the North Shore under the professional command of John Barr, the superb Scottish sailing master of *Thistle*, who had been induced by EYC members to settle in Marblehead. (Francis Herreshoff claimed Barr emigrated to Marblehead because his countrymen put so much blame on him, and that *Thistle* was superior to *Volunteer* except in the draft of her sails.) *Minerva* carried far less sail than her American rivals but had more grip on the water. She was brought across by Charles Barr, John's son and eventually the most famous of all the professional yacht skippers in the days when they reigned supreme. Under Charlie's touch the Fife cutter showed her wake to every 40-footer from Boston to New York until the whole yachting coast was crying, "Anything to stop *Minerva*!"

Minerva stormed the North American coast during the 1889 season while the Adams brothers barnstormed the British in one local yacht after another, and when they got home, it was back to Burgess, this time for *Gossoon*, a keel boat narrower and fuller than her sisters among the 40-footers, with a little less sail. Charlie Foster likewise went to Burgess for the deep centerboarder *Ventura*, which steered badly, while *Gossoon* rapidly established herself as the leader of the pack in 1890 and at least stopped *Minerva* in more or less of a dead heat of races, which in the view of Charlie Adams killed the class—but not before she won the Puritan Cup in 1891.

The Eastern Yacht Club was largely responsible for fostering the 40-footers, which W.P. Stephens considered "one of the best racing classes in American yachting. It numbered in all twenty-one yachts, all but five being designed by Mr. Burgess, of the same water-line length, in addition to such old boats as elected to race with the class. . . . They brought into racing many good yachtsmen, and they proved a good school for racing skippers."

Benjamin Crowninshield sold his first family sloop *Effie* in 1889 and the next spring sent Frank, who was twenty, with a gang down to City Island to sail Burgess's 40-footer *Tomahawk* back to Marblehead. *Tomahawk* and the new Burgess schooner *Constellation* had both been built for E.D. Morgan by the Piepgras yard at City Island; Morgan evidently sold the sloop to Crowninshield. The trip jogged Keno's memory:

The *Tomahawk*, while in no way remarkable for speed, is I think worthy of mention for three things. First, because she happened to be the smallest steel yacht ever built in this country. Secondly, because when George Atkinson and I and a crew of three went to New York and got her, we made the run from City Island . . . to Marblehead without tacking. A fresh southwester took us to Pollock Rip, where we jibed—and the port tack the rest of the way in. The tides were very considerate, changing at the most opportune times, which undoubtedly had much to do with the fast time we made—thirty-six hours—port to port.

And thirdly, because when she was sold in 1893, her new owner, who having first insured her for far more than she was worth, and under the pretense of using her as a yacht, operated her for smuggling phenacetin [an analgesic drug]. When she finally was far more than simply "suspected" and he was afraid to enter any port, he saw fit to scuttle her off the Peaked Hill Bars. When he and the crew finally made port, they gave a most graphic account of how, in the strong breeze then blowing, she suddenly began to sink, and of the awful time they had getting into their boat before she went down. I well remember how "queer" this sounded as that same Saturday afternoon our race at Marblehead was called off owing to the flattest of flat calms. The real story eventually came out when one of the crew feeling he had not received his "just" share of the spoils turned State's Evidence.

Two other 40-footers, *Alice* and *Helen*, were designed in 1889 by the amateur A.G. (Dolly) McVeigh, yachting editor of the *Boston Herald*, for Eastern members (and brothers-in-law) Philip Wheatland and Charles Prince. Crowninshield recalled:

The first race that year was sailed in a fresh summer northeaster with plenty of rain and a rough sea. I remember the race well as I sailed in it on the *Verena* [another Burgess 40-footer in the Eastern fleet] owned by J.A. Beebe. In the beat to windward it so happened that Phil Wheatland, heavy in rubber boots, oilskins and a sou'wester, fell overboard. Those on the *Alice* were powerless to help him. However, the one chance in a million turned up. He remained afloat long enough to be hauled aboard by one of the following yachts. A modern miracle truly.

The air was charged with change. "In 1891," wrote Charlie Foster of his tenth boat, "I ordered from Fife a design for a 46-footer which was supposed to be an enlarged *Minerva*, and this boat was built by Lawley from designs sent over. The sending for a Fife design of this sort stirred up yachting matters here, and there were a number of other boats built to meet her, some by Burgess. *Barbara* proved to be a very beautiful little vessel, said to be, even to this day, the handsomest craft ever to come into Marblehead."

Ever experimenting, Foster in 1897 made *Barbara* a schooner to cut down on crew, for the main drawback of these glorious sloops was their vast sail spreads, with splendidly overhanging booms and bowsprits, and club topsails that dwarfed the mains on many a respectable craft. The rig change was a great success, he decided. He kept her as a two-sticker for another three years before moving on to his next enthusiasm.

Thus came on the scene the exciting 46-footers, dominated by Burgess and including *Beatrix*, which the Adamses bought and renamed, for luck, *Harpoon*. And lucky she was, bringing home a shelfload of silver, including their second Puritan Cup in 1893.

Although the large sloops and cutters were gaining in popularity, a look at the Eastern's fleet of the late 1880s shows the schooner—grand old rig of Massachusetts coasting, fishing, and yachting—holding its own at about forty, around a third of the total. And the Burgess mark is everywhere.

Edward Burgess created the 40-footer *Gossoon* for Charles Francis Adams, and she took some of the wind out of *Minerva*'s sails in 1890.

One of the Boston designer's first schooners, produced in 1886 for Metcalf and Owen of Providence in the midst of the Cup race turmoil, was the 90-foot, deep centerboarder *Sachem*, which showed her heels to the New York Yacht Club fleet. The same year he overhauled and updated *America* for Ben Butler. Others were the smaller *Oenone* and *Quickstep*—winner of the Puritan Cup in 1889.

That year Ned Burgess wound it up with a pair of stunners. Of the lore was *Constellation*, 106 feet 6 inches on the water, an iron centerboarder drawing 12 feet, for E.D. Morgan, who named her after the 1855 corvette anchored on the other side of Newport Harbor from his summer home. Morgan was an Eastern member from New York who had bought *Mayflower* two years earlier and apparently couldn't wait to get his professional skipper's hands on another Burgess boat. But the Morgans ran through boats like banks, and in 1892 *Constellation* was returned to Boston and Marblehead by Bayard Thayer and remained the flagship, official and unofficial, of the Eastern fleet for another half a century.

His 90-footers (Burgess produced *Merlin*, a sister to *Sachem*, for William H. Forbes of Eastern in 1889, and the next year she won the Puritan) were big schooners whose owners delighted in racing the fishermen and pilot boats on a breezy afternoon offshore. In the course of winning the New York Yacht Club's Goelet Cup in 1892, as her owner's son, Ralph, relates in the *Ditty Box*, *Merlin* had rounded the windward mark, and they were running up the spinnaker—except that "when it was about twenty feet up, the Swede who was hoisting, said, 'Ho! Ho! Dat ain't the spinnaker, dat's the awning,' a proceeding which did not especially please my father who was steering."

For all his distaste for the math and engineering of it, in 1887, the year of *Volunteer*, Burgess launched the *Carrie E. Phillips* from the Arthur D. Story yard in Essex. She was a plumb-stemmed, deep-keeled, beautifully lined fishing schooner of 93 feet 6 inches on the water, only 3 feet longer than his yachts. She sailed in and out of Gloucester on a breath of fresh air for the industry, very fast and able, incorporating all kinds of technological advances and way ahead of her time.

The *Phillips* won the second Fishermen's Race against three other fishing schooners soon after her launch in 1887. The first of these great, salty brawls among the dory trawlers of Boston and Gloucester that gave rise to the famous international rivalry with Nova Scotia came off the previous year when Tom McManus—sailmaker's son, Boston fish dealer, and future designer—dreamed up the idea of giving the boys some fun during a fishermen's strike. He hit up Malcolm Forbes for prize money. The Eastern's vice commodore did him one better: He would put up a silver trophy if they would enter the Boston pilots' phenomenal flyer, the schooner *Hesper*. The wary fishermen balked until it was agreed that the purse would remain with them, the cup with the overall winner. Forbes put the arm on Commodore Henry Hovey, General Paine, and a few other Eastern members for $1,500. Ten working schooners raced off Boston on May 1, 1886; *Hesper* carried the cup back to the pilots, and the *John H. McManus* the purse. Such was the role of the Eastern Yacht Club in promoting a finny rivalry of fifty-two years that more than once outsailed the contention for the America's Cup, and outcussed it if it didn't quite outshine it.

If the Eastern had the bugologist, Malcolm Forbes had the bug, in all of which may be detected the fine hand of Commodore Hovey, who gazed from his summer house upon the immense fleet of Gloucester bankers and seiners slipping and surging past the anchorage where his splendid *Fortuna* graced the shore of Freshwater Cove. In 1889 Burgess designed the extremely pleasing and magically fast modified clipper schooner *Fredonia* for Forbes in partnership with Captain Charlie Harty of Gloucester, and her sister, the *Nellie Dixon*, both as fishermen. Well, the commodore first had to have a little race with *Hesper* for a little bet of $3,000 a side, which was sailed over a forty-mile course under the aegis of the Eastern Yacht Club on September 25.

Burgess's latest left the pilot far astern, but not without recriminations, as reported by Ralph Forbes in the *Ditty Box*, to the effect that when they heard the Boston pilots were pulling a fast one, sub rosa, with a new and much larger suit of sails, *Fredonia*'s quite as unscrupulous owners substituted the oversize mainsail from *Puritan*.

Nor was that the end of it. Forty-three years later, William S. Eaton, who was on the Regatta Committee in 1889, wrote Charles Foster his own version of the shenanigans of this famous contest after reading Ralph Forbes's account in the 1932 *Ditty Box*:

Although the Eastern Yacht Club Regatta Committee agreed to take charge, all arrangements, and the judging of the race itself, were attended to by me alone.

After the representatives of the vessels in conference in my office had reached an understanding I drew up an agreement, had it printed and signed by both parties. It was agreed that each

should inspect and approve the other's *light sails*. The inference is clear that the regular working sails were to be worn and the *Hesper* people never, to my knowledge, showed any inclination to be "sharp."

Until I just read Mr. F's [Forbes] letter, I never even heard the rumor that they wanted larger working sails, and, as they had to scrape East Boston to raise their $3000, I am confident the cost would have been prohibitive. *Hesper* used her regular sails.

If any such rumor reached *Fredonia* it appears to have served as a rather frivolous pretext for her use of *Puritan*'s mainsail, which seemed to me unfair, but which *Hesper* did not protest. No wonder unfriendly feelings were aroused!

The larger mainsail did not affect the result of the race because a large number of men, women and children roamed at will around *Hesper*'s deck while she tried to carry by the wind an enormous maintopmast-staysail, which dragged her bodily to leeward.

Having pulled it off, Commodore Forbes cruised *Fredonia* to the Azores that fall and turned her over to Captain Harty for fishing. Ten years later she went down with the loss of two men when she was swept; the giant sea loosened her great beam, and she filled. "The *Fredonia* model," wrote Howard I. Chapelle, the design historian, "became the fashionable type of fishing schooner with astonishing rapidity, utilized in not only the design of the fishing schooners but in small fishing craft—the 'Friendship sloop' for example." And she was the inspiration for the Commonwealth's promotional schooner *Spirit of Massachusetts* a hundred years later.

Edward Burgess died of typhoid fever on July 12, 1891. He was forty-three. The Council of the Eastern Yacht Club attended his funeral. Over a period of but seven years he designed 137 vessels and small craft in astonishing variety. Fresh from *Volunteer*'s crowning victory four years earlier, he had written in *American and English Yachts*:

As for the comparative merits of centreboard and keel, the question, I think, is more one of convenience and safety than of speed. For the smaller classes, where sufficient draught of water can be given without bringing the boat into constant danger of taking the ground, and rendering docking inconvenient, the keel boat has some advantages; but in the large boats, where the draught must be limited, the centreboard is a most desirable addition, and will come into universal use for cruising yachts as well as racers.

The present century will see the highest development of the sailing yacht; for it is probable that the ever-growing steam fleet will encroach more and more on the sailing yachts, until, in its turn, steam will succumb to electricity. But let us hope that we can at least continue the interest in sailing matches, even if we cruise in machine-propelled craft.

One thing, at least, is certain, that yachting is becoming more popular each year, and its pursuit is by no means confined to the rich. The three or four young men joint owners of some little cabin sloop find their craft quite as jolly and health-giving as an *Alva* or an *Atalanta*.

An expanding America, an expansive century. There remained the matter of the Eastern's new class of 46-footers (52 feet overall) up toward one end of the fleet, and no room for the little cabin sloop down at the other. Or, as Captain R.B. Forbes put it in the crustiness of his old age in 1888:

> In those days *when comfort was considered of more consequence than racing prizes*, yachts were not lumbered up as they are now, by spinnakers with long booms, club-topsails, jib-topsails and balloon sails. As yachts are sailed today I should consider it a great punishment to be obliged to take a sea cruise in one of them. Having saved the Queen's Cup by means of the fine sloops built by General Paine and Mr. Burgess, let us be content with their victories, and go back to the good old days when we were content to win by hard *seaman*'s work and good *seaboats*, and not mainly dependent on mere accidents for our victories.

Rejecting, finally, the vicarious joys of letting the pros do it, sailors of Long Island Sound had organized the Seawanhaka Yacht Club in 1871 to promote amateurism from mooring to mooring and the advancement of seamanship and design. ("Corinthian" was inserted after Seawanhaka at a later date, harking back to the amateur yachting aristocracy of ancient Corinth.) Ned Burgess and his friends put together the Beverly Yacht Club for much the same purpose in the wet-pants league in 1872, and the word spread that you did not have to be a plutocrat to be a weekend sailor. The Salem Bay Yacht Club followed in 1879, West Lynn and Cape Ann in 1880, Winthrop and Great Head in 1881, and Manchester, in a league by itself, in 1882.

The most significant result of the formation of the Seawanhaka Corinthian Yacht Club was the formulation in 1882 of its rule of measurement, namely, that a simple and reasonably fair method of handicapping could be derived by dividing by three the sum of the square root of the sail area and double the waterline.

The Seawanhaka Rule was adopted by the Eastern in 1885 and may have had something to do with inspiring Charles H.W. Foster, Benjamin W. Crowninshield, William S. Eaton, and a few others, who chafed under the Queen of the Waves's disdain of the under-30s, to organize on July 7 the Corinthian Yacht Club in Marblehead for sailing craft between 16 and 30 feet on the water. In 1888 Corinthian purchased part of Sparhawk Point toward the lighthouse on Marblehead Neck and opened its first clubhouse on July 14. In the same year, the Eastern amended the Seawanhaka formula by substituting the divisor "2" for "3" (New York finally adopted it in 1889) and extended the fleet classification, separating schooners into three waterline classes (30 to 50, 50 to 75, and 75 and over) and the sloops, cutters, and yawls into seven, from 30 to 75 and beyond.

Meanwhile, chafing under the Corinthian's disdain of the under-16-year-olds, a group of young men and teenagers founded the Pleon Yacht Club. And though it remained for more than sixty years as clubhouseless as the parent Eastern did during its first decade, the Pleon from the very beginning was recognized as the sire of junior yachting in the United States.

To promote smaller boat sailing, the Corinthian started its Midsummer Series on August 25, 1889, with nine boats in the first race. There was no big crowd afloat or ashore, but it was the first Midsummer Race Week in America, and it would grow to be the most populous yachting event in the world.

Ned and Nat had parted theoretical company when Burgess espoused the Seawanhaka notion of putting it all on the waterline over Herreshoff's old Boston Yacht Club formula that allowed for overall length by including one-third of the overhangs. Although preoccupied with steam during the 1880s, Nat was mulling over the vectors of a sailing hull, and the glorious result, *Gloriana*, burst on the yachting world almost precisely as his friend lay dying in 1891. Perhaps Herreshoff's work of sheerest genius, *Gloriana* was designed for the 46-foot class then dominated by Burgess productions, on order from NYYC Rear Commodore E.D. Morgan, and joined his Burgess schooner *Constellation* and 97-foot Herreshoff steam yacht *Javelin* in the Eastern fleet as well.

Nothing like *Gloriana*'s spoon bow had ever parted a wave. She was a sensation, winning her first eight races, and was put to pasture for a while to let the pack compete. Compared to her, mourned Charlie Foster, his beautiful *Barbara* was a toy.

Gloriana is the classic example of rule-beating advancing design. As she heeled, her dipping overhangs radically lengthened her waterline, which increased both her speed and her stability; the rule added a dividend of sail in the bargain. Technologically she was all breakthrough, with steamed and steel-angled frames, diagonal strapping, double planking, extra-light upper works, custom sail tracks, winches, turnbuckles, and other hardware since standard—the saved weight shifted to her outside lead below and huge sails aloft.

Gloriana had her first brush with the Eastern on August 5, 1892, in the New York Yacht Club's Goelet Cup race for sloops. In a freshening southwester off Newport, she and *Wasp*, sailed by the professional Barr brothers, John and his younger half-brother, Charlie, and *Gracie* lost to *Harpoon* and the amateur Adamses, inspiring the headline in the press: HURRAH FOR BEANTOWN AND THE BEANTOWN YACHTS. Bill Swan, the yachting writer, never tired of yarning about that one. It was a long beat to Block Island, and Charlie Adams, who was known to his intimates as "Deacon," sent George down to leeward to watch the headsails. "*Harpoon* was being driven hard, for *Wasp* was right astern, and before long there came a cry from the scuppers: 'It's getting kinda deep down here, Deacon!' To which was snapped back the reply: 'You stay there, damn you, until it's up to your neck!'"

Such rare defeats for the fabulous *Gloriana* say more about the Adams brothers than about their competition.

Meanwhile, Herreshoff had been fooling around with another of his radical ideas, the fin-keel boat, which Charlie Foster described as a large canoe with a metal blade for a keel and a bulb of lead on the bottom. After building the prototype *Dilemma* for himself in 1891, Nat created the 30-footer *Handsel* for James R. Hooper of the Eastern in 1892 and took the tiller that summer at Marblehead (he was finishing out a four-year term as rear commodore of the Boston Yacht Club) against a couple of Burgess 30-foot cutters with the full rig and about twice the displacement. *Handsel* beat them hollow, inducing her designer to crow to Foster decades later, at the very thought of it: "This race indicated the absurdity of the English cutter rig as compared to the small rig with few ropes aloft, requiring about one half the crew to race."

Nathanael Herreshoff's revolutionary, 46-footer class *Gloriana*, photographed by Henry G. Peabody on August 17, 1891.

Always *meanwhile*, Herreshoff launched from his imagination the next logical development, his first true bulb keel, the 46-footer *Wasp* for Archibald Rogers of the New York and the Eastern. She raced at Marblehead and points between, beat *Gloriana* with logical consistency, and won the Puritan Cup.

The great sport that summer of 1892, though—arguably the most exciting race ever to be sailed in Massachusetts Bay—was not out of Marblehead but out of Gloucester. The city was planning an all-out celebration of its 250th birthday that year and asked its leading yachtsman, ex-Commodore Henry Hovey, to head the Regatta Committee. The feature was to be a "flying fishermen's race," followed by an open small-boat regatta. Everything else about the anniversary dims alongside "The Race It Blew," and that lives on as *the* crashing classic of schooner-driving, right down to the hatches, played out in a near-hurricane.

Commodore Hovey, too, was in his element. He gave and raised money, put up a $300 silver cup for the big-schooner class winner, and turned over to the yacht race judges his *Fortuna*, from which he "entertained lavishly all day" those whose equilibria permitted the partaking thereof. Malcolm Forbes, who relished these rough-and-tumbles, was serving the first of his two years as commodore, and members were caught up in the fishy fever, although Marblehead was a caldron that day, and most of those few who stuck their bows out as spectators regretted it.

The entries were working fishermen, seven of them over 85 feet on the waterline, three under, which started a few minutes later. The course ran forty-five miles from between the Eastern Point whistler and the wildly pitching judges' tug, past Halfway Rock to a mark boat off Nahant, around the Davis Ledge buoy off Minot's Light, and back.

August 26 dawned to a near-hurricane of a northeaster driving fog and sheets of rain. Not one of the ten skippers would so much as tie a reef as they ran off at the start in tremendous and building seas. Inside Halfway Rock, the gale was pushing 50 knots. Approaching the invisible mark boat off Nahant in the lead, Captain Solomon Jacobs in the *Ethel B. Jacobs* came in too wide, had to jibe around standing for the next leg, and snapped his main gaff against the lee shrouds. Just the sight of it scared the *Grayling* and the *James S. Steele* out of the race.

Recklessly the rest rounded the leeward mark off Minot's Light and hit back for Gloucester in the teeth of it. "With every sheet hauled flat and every sail drawing," wrote Arthur Millett of the *Gloucester Times* in absolute awe, "they pounded and staggered into the heavy seas, burying their bowsprits and washing decks at every jump. Lee rails were buried and the water was up to the hatches as the schooners laid over before the strength of the fierce northeaster. Sea after sea they shipped and sometimes dove into them to their foremasts."

Maurice Whalen brought the *Harry L. Belden* first across the finish off Eastern Point, his jib in rags. Close astern, the *Joseph Rowe* lost both jibs, and, as the foresail started to go, was passed by the *Nannie C. Bohlin*, a lifeline rigged all around her deck. She was perilously light on ballast, Captain Tommie Bohlin having taken most of it out in anticipation of light air.

A veteran yachting writer who had covered every major race for the last quarter of a century had chartered a tug for the event. Still rolling ashore, he gulped that he'd never seen such savage starting conditions. Tom McManus told Charlie Foster that he was standing in the companionway of one of the schooners with his hands on the hatch combing when they jibed all standing around the Davis Ledge buoy. "Tom's fingers on the edge of the combing were in the water, and, as he vividly describes it, another quarter of an inch, and she would have been filled and sunk."

Lord Dunraven challenged for the America's Cup for the second time in the fall of 1892 with *Valkyrie II* (disagreement over conditions precluded a match in 1889), and four contenders for the defense were built, two of them from Boston, all about 85 feet on the waterline and 120 feet overall. Mourning the loss of Ned Burgess, his partner in magic, the general turned to his talented young son, John Paine, brother of the better-known Frank, who designed *Jubilee*, a steel, fin-keel centerboarder with a smaller auxiliary board in the bow, built by Lawley. Paine seems to have entered her under the New York's colors, since he resigned as chairman of the NYYC America's Cup Committee in January 1893, and she was not enrolled in the Eastern squadron until 1894.

The other Boston boat, *Pilgrim*, was designed by Stewart and Binney, Burgess's successors, for a syndicate headed by William Amory Gardner of Groton and including Bayard Thayer of Boston. Both were members of the Eastern, with which she was enrolled. She, too, was steel, with an extreme fin keel.

Jubilee's mast was stepped too far aft, among other faults, and although she was skippered by John Barr and showed spurts of liveliness, she was never in the running. *Pilgrim* fared even worse, steering so badly as to be uncontrollable at times.

After her early elimination, she was sold, her fin was removed, and she emerged as an acceptable steam yacht.

And so Boston's aspirants for the America's Cup of 1893 deservedly rest in the backwash, which probably explains why Foster gives them such a short rope end in the *Ditty Box*. History records that Nat Herreshoff—with the American yacht-design scene to himself now that his friend Ned was gone—came up with not one but two defenders for the NYYC. Neither was a fin-keeler, aware as Herreshoff was of that bizarre invention's unsuitability in sloops of large wetted surface. His *Vigilant* outsailed his *Colonia* and sailed on to win a great hairbreadth victory over *Valkyrie* and Lord Dunraven, who was elected an honorary member of the New York Yacht Club, to its subsequent regret. Ten years later W.P. Stephens wrote:

The formation of the several Cup-defending syndicates took from the regular class racing many good yachtsmen, who, though liberal in their support, soon tired of building a large yacht, or even a 40-footer, with the certainty that if she held together for more than one season she would be outclassed by a more extreme design, and outbuilt by still lighter construction, while from her extreme type she could not be sold for a cruiser. The result was that with the growing interest in the smaller racing classes even the wealthier yachtsmen abandoned the large for the small yachts, and, as the actual amount involved was but small, offered every inducement to designer and builder to produce the fastest possible racing machine....

As the building of freaks, large and small, became little less than an epidemic in yachting, a natural reaction followed on the part of the older and more conservative yachtsmen, and also some of the younger element, who demanded something more than continual outbuilding and match sailing.

One of the first evidences of this revolt was about Marblehead, where in 1892 the 21-foot length class was in existence, including some very extreme centre-board machines—for the time—and some expensively built fin keels.

The influence of the Corinthian and other clubs was surely there. Just as surely the weight of the Eastern, which up to that time had come right down to the line but not beyond with the 30-footers, did much to tip the scales toward what some yachting historians call a more "wholesome" bent in design. On July 28 of this remarkably productive year of 1892, the Eastern held a special invitation race for 21-footers and the since-forgotten

The 21-footers start inside on July 30, 1892. Henry G. Peabody photo.

Billowing Sails

Billowing Sails

25-foot raters. "Thus," wrote Foster, "we find it beginning to take a practical interest in the development of the boats under thirty feet measurement."

Not surprisingly, two of the fastest 21-footers in the fast-growing Marblehead fleet that season were Herreshoff fin-keelers joining his larger *Handsel—Vanessa* for Eastern member Albert S. Bigelow and *Reaper* for Henry P. Benson, a future member.

Far more significant, however, was the appearance among the 21-footers that same summer of what W.P. Stephens describes as "two peculiar little boats, in general type similar to the keel fishing boats of the coast, but with the symmetry of form and the finished construction of the yacht." This intriguing pair was designed by Stewart and Binney and can be regarded as atonement, and more, for their perpetration of *Pilgrim.*

Nancy and *Jane,* as straightforward in every respect as two characters from a first-grade reader, were the first two knockabouts, "being intended for sailing in the rough water of Massachusetts Bay in all weathers—a use which made the term 'knockabout' most natural and appropriate." They were built at Gloucester by Higgins and Gifford for Henry Taggard (who the following year was elected measurer for the first of many terms) and Herman Parker; both joined the Eastern only that May and also belonged to the Corinthian. As underlength foster children that would grow up to be progenitors of a race, these protoknockabouts were described by Stephens:

> On a waterline of 21 feet and a breadth of 7 feet 2 inches, the bow was carried out into a very easy and graceful overhang, making up most of the excess in the overall length of 24 feet 6 inches, there being no after overhang, except the small amount due to the moderate rake of the square transom. The draft was 4 feet 2 inches, of which about 18 inches was made up of an iron keel of 1070 pounds. The yacht was half-decked with an oval cockpit; the rudder was hung outside the transom; and beneath the foredeck was a cuddy, giving shelter in a sudden storm and dry stowage for gear. The rig was as peculiar as the hull: the total area of 400 square feet was distributed between a rather large mainsail and small jib, the latter with tack fast to the stem head, thus dispensing with a bowsprit. The hull was strongly constructed but neatly finished, and the complete

yacht ready for sailing cost but $450, as compared with $2000 for a racing 21-footer, fit only for sailing in moderate weather.

These two boats were seen outside Marblehead Harbor, sailed by one man at times, in weather when the larger yachts were glad to lie at their moorings. They were slow in light weather beside the racing 21-footers and some of the old catboats, but for real pleasure sailing at all times on such open waters they were unequalled.

(*Nancy* and *Jane* had a third sister, *Betsy,* launched at Gloucester in June 1893 for Eastern member Theodore Jones. Ninety-three years later, after generations on Long Island Sound and several name changes, she was back in Gloucester as Carl Brown's well-maintained cruising auxiliary *Edna.* Charles Foster in 1892 built a knockabout that he credited to Edward Burgess, who had died the previous July. Oddly enough, "she" was named *Carl* and was the only one with a clipper bow.)

Overnight the knockabouts became the rage, and then they had to be made faster and so "improved" from the original that in 1894 owners got together and agreed on restrictions, which led to the formation of the Knockabout Association in 1895.

That year was also the twenty-fifth birthday of the Eastern Yacht Club, which celebrated with sedate festivities ashore and a race dominated by Henry Lamb's 80-foot *Marguerite,* winner of the Puritan Cup. And it was the year Captain Nat himself came down with a bad case of typhoid fever.

The Great Leapfrogger was by now about through his fin-keel period, the epitaph for which was aptly penned by Foster, who had the 46-foot cruiser *Carmita,* with a 13½-foot fin keel, built for him in 1893 (not by Nat). He concluded that "there are few human stomachs which can stand the jumping of this kind of a boat.... Without any forefoot or after keel, they pivot on their fin and come to, or fall off on the slightest provocation. Of course, no real water ever came on deck, but the author wished many a time it would and keep her down."

The fin had served its purpose: it led Captain Nat to the bulb. Naturally, he had his eye on the knockabouts and in 1896 produced *Cock Robin,* a 21-footer with a bulb keel, for member Charles S. Eaton. She knocked 'em all about so thoroughly her first season (the Eastern ran several races for the knockabouts) that Eaton sold her to Charlie Foster, who found her so fast "that there was little fun to own and sail her, for she could run away from other boats of the class, and was considered by them as a nuisance in a race." Foster traded her back to Eaton for her

Speedy *Vanessa,* with her clubbed jib outreaching her bowsprit, joined the 21-footers in 1892.

Herreshoff successor *Cockatoo* and was glad to be rid of such an overachiever.

Cockatoo was what Bill Stephens derisively dubbed a "raceabout," the class of extreme and expensive racing machines into which he blamed Herreshoff for overdeveloping the knockabouts in 1898.

Always experimenting, Charlie Foster went to Stearns and McKay in 1899 for the raceabout *Persimmon*.

> In her I tried out, as far as I know, the first Marconi mainsail in Marblehead. The sail was 40 feet in hoist with 20 feet main boom. Inasmuch as at that time hollow spars had not been developed with any particular saving in weight, *Persimmon* was unable to carry this long solid spar in any except the lightest of breezes [on another occasion he said it comprised an upper spar lashed to the regular mast], but I found that in windward work, the theory which I had wished to determine, i.e., that the cutting edge of the sail was the vital force, was clearly demonstrated. After a few trials the old rig was substituted for practical convenience and racing.

The Crowninshields owned two fast raceabouts, *Jolly Roger* and *Pirate*, and Keno did very well racing the former in Buzzards Bay.

Designer Stephens underestimated the durability and good sense of the knockabouts, and it is a curious fact that just as he thought this sensible type was being fancified out of existence, it was intriguing the fishermen's designer Tom McManus of Boston, who in 1900 lined off the first knockabout fishing schooner, the *Helen B. Thomas*. She was built in 1902 without a bowsprit, the "widowmaker" from which so many good men had been washed while wrestling headsails.

The ink was fresh on the treaty formally ending the war with Spain and ceding Cuba and the Philippines to the victor when Frank McQuesten sailed from Marblehead for the Caribbean— it was Christmas morning, 1898—in his 93-foot-waterline schooner *Gitana*. One of the bigger two-stickers in the Eastern fleet, *Gitana* had been a prizewinner in her class on the Eastern and New York cruises. She had remained Marblehead-based since she was designed and built in 1882 by D.J. Lawlor at East Boston for William F. Weld, the Boston shipping magnate. McQuesten bought her from her second owner, Percival W. Clement. Years later, he wrote an account of this immediate postwar cruise for C.H.W. Foster:

> The weather was cold, and it grew constantly colder after we had rounded the Cape and headed into the Sound. The sails froze stiff as pine boards. . . . A northeast gale kept us hove to off Hatteras for a couple of days. Then the wind shifted to nor'west. The squaresail was set, and it drove us hard, with a heavy following sea. The wind continued blowing straight out. Now the *Gitana* would lose it down in the trough and then suddenly catch it full force on the crest with a tremendous snap of the squaresail. But she carried a deep draft, and we enjoyed such comfort as deep-water cruises on small ships generally afford. . . .
>
> After crossing the Gulf Stream a gale carried away one of the *Gitana*'s boats. A steamer sighting the boat reported to the *New York Herald* that the *Gitana* was probably in trouble, but the *Gitana* was then safe at Barbados and had already cabled home. . . .
>
> At Fort de France we fell in with a fleeing remnant of the once-proud Spanish navy. This small flotilla was going back to Spain to tell the dismal story. . . . At Santiago we saw the wrecks of Spain's ironclads, blistered, battered, stove up and sunk or beached, and on the wharves, the coffins of American soldiers were piled high for shipment home. . . .
>
> We looked in at Havana. This was before General Wood had taken charge. . . . It was still a Spanish city, and the battleship *Maine* still remained a sunken wreck in the harbor. And so from Havana to Charleston and to Marblehead.
>
> We came back in time to see the British steamer *Norseman* towed off Tom Moore's Rock. [She had gone ashore in a southeasterly gale on March 20, 1899. The Massachusetts Humane Society lifesavers took off thirteen by boat and eighty-eight by breeches buoy from the Neck.]
>
> The *Norseman* was probably the largest steamer that ever anchored in Marblehead Harbor. Alongside the *Gitana* she looked tremendous. We were forced to shift anchorage, for the *Norseman* took up more than her share of the bed. But then, she had known trouble; and the little *Gitana*, who had danced like a light-hearted gypsy to a safe return, was glad to move over and make room for the battered giant.

At the other extreme were those raceabouts, the subject of a good yarn of his youth from veteran Eastern member John S. Lawrence, in a letter to Foster too late for the *Ditty Box*:

> While at Harvard I saw quite a lot of my classmate, William Starling Burgess [Edward's son, future yacht and airplane designer, and Eastern member of note]. He then thought in terms of higher mathematics and aeroplanes and it was he who figured for me the details of the raceabout, *Indian*, in the fall of 1899.

A rainy day for Tucker's steam ferry *Blonde*, about to leave the Neck.

Billowing Sails

Start of the Raceabouts, August 6, 1898. Stebbins photo.

The clubhouse showing the 1891 addition on the right.

60   Billowing Sails

Billowing Sails

I well remember asking Starling if aeroplanes would be of value in war, to which he replied, "Yes, but how can the enemy be persuaded to go up in them?"

Indian was built of mahogany, with a large open cockpit, by Graves in Marblehead.

My father at that time owned the *Camilla*, a 30-foot sloop by Edward Burgess—long bowsprit, mainmast, separate topmast, boom, gaff, topsail, and two jibs. To me she seemed a very large boat. She was about the size of a Q-boat of today and weighed less. She carried two paid hands.

Camilla and *Indian* left Marblehead one early morning for Islesboro. The two paid hands on *Camilla*, and four Harvard juniors on *Indian*—Nathaniel Pride, J. Lothrop Motley, Charles Lovering, and John S. Lawrence. The four of us were lightly dressed and supplied with lunch, water, and beer. The two boats were to keep together. It was a beautiful day. At Thacher's we peeled off (except Pride who feared for his complexion) to tan our backs, and as the wind was light, *Indian* sailed about until *Camilla* came alongside.

By two o'clock, both boats were running along together inside of the Isles of Shoals before a nice southwesterly wind. We decided to go on. Off York, large white clouds appeared, coming nearer and nearer. The wind lightened. No use; we could not reach the shore for anchor to hold and water that would be smooth.

When the white cloud reached overhead and it was really black, to the west, sails were lowered and made fast, when suddenly a white spot appeared in the black cloud and grew into a great drooping feather, and the water under Cape Neddick turned black. A sure nasty squall was coming for us.

BIFF—and the hurricane rang in the rigging, and away we went, dragging our stern as if we had a line from an ocean steamer. The *Indian* had a wide stern and sharp bow, and she seemed to make better weather with the wind and wave on the quarter. Then came rain and hail. We were stripped, hoping to keep our clothes dry. God, how it hurt! But we could not quit our posts. It had shut in thick and we could see but a few yards around us. Hailstones drove holes in the water, while marbles bounced on the deck and off Lovering's red hair.

There was no choice but to keep her moving; no land ahead but Spain, and the waves getting larger and larger. Some slopped into the open cockpit. Her bow went through a wave that came aft by the mast and over the house. We had bulkheads in the *Indian*, but to accommodate the long spinnaker pole and the mop, openings had been cut and not repaired. If the *Indian* filled, her lead mine would soon find the nearest land.

The dinghy was filling; we were moving too fast for her. BANG went the painter and the little boat rolled over as if resting from her exertions.

"Gooder-bye," sang Pride.

"Bail for your lives now, boys."—The sea was getting higher; there seemed more wind, more rain, more waves came over the bow, and more slopped into the open cockpit to add to what the rain put in. Water was up to the cabin floor and slatting about—SWISH SWASH.

"Goodbye breakfast," said Pride with a whoop. "Wish I were dead."

"Bail, or I'll brain you," said I.

"Please do," was the reply as he lifted his foot to the cockpit seat, evidently preferring drowning. Motley pulled him down and tied both legs to the floor. "Bail, you!"—Lovering helped by kicking. Poor fellow. He lay on the floor and swashed about in the slop.

But the water came in faster than we could get it out. One great sea came over the bow all green, and filled us pretty badly. The rigging was singing a tune which only a sailor knows, and the mast was snapping a bit as the *Indian* jumped in the sea. She was getting quite waterlogged.

Lovering sung out, "Bet you a hundred dollars we never see land again, John."

"Take you," says I.

"Be damned if that's fair," says he. "You will not pay me if you lose."

"Bail, damn you, bail! I want my hundred!"

It did seem a bit hopeless; we had little buoyancy left and it was impossible to keep her before it so as to avoid every wave slopping into the open boat. The discipline was splendid. No one criticized. No one was scared. We were as calm as cucumbers in the sun. Great wales stood out on our backs from the hailstones, and poor Pride—not much of a yachtsman but the prince of fellows, sloshing about dead seasick.

It just stopped blowing. We kept on bailing. Our 22 inches of freeboard was down to eight. It cleared—but no land, no *Camilla*, no grub, no clothes. Sails were hoisted and we set our course N.W. It grew dark and we sighted Cape Porpoise Light, and made the narrow harbor by guessing and good luck, and put our hook on a mud flat.

No one seemed to be about. Pride recovered, so we jumped overboard and swam to shore. I had trunks and one sock; Pride, an old shirt, brown trousers, without shoes or socks; Lovering, a very long, red shirt and two socks; Motley, as I remember, had a shirt on his back and another upside down on his legs. We went for a light, over rocks and through a garden. The light grew into several lights, and then into "Porpoise Inn."

"Watch me," said Pride as he approached the service door. He knocked. It was opened. "May I play your piano?"

"A wonderful sight!" *Athene* pursues her jib. Probably by Stebbins.

Billowing Sails

"Who in hell are you?" was the reply.

"Sousa's band. We have a new march. How I love putting down food. Please be considerate!" said Pride.

"Shut up," said the young man at the telephone.—"Hullo, there.—No, ain't here. Awful storm, broke our gauge at 70 miles. Guess they must be drowned, Mr. Lawrence."

"To hell with ceremony," said I. "Hello, Dad. How are you? Where is *Camilla*?—Portsmouth!" (Damn those men for stopping fifteen miles back.)—"All's well, of course proceeding in the morning; send letters Dark Harbor. Nothing to worry about. Just a squall in a grand boat. Lost your tender. What fools those men were to worry you."

"Can we get some grub and covering?"— After dinner we did get to the piano, and Pride, a wonderful musician, made up the new march and most of the Hasty Pudding music for next winter attired in the cook's clothing, greatly to the pleasure of our new friends from Maine, their friends, and their friends' friends.

There could have been no better way to wind up the decade of yachting's renaissance, and the century, than with the hair-raising race for the Puritan Cup on June 30, 1900, between Nat Herreshoff's sleek new 70-foot-waterline sloop *Athene* and Ned Burgess's stately legacy, the 107-foot schooner *Constellation*. It blew nor'west so hard that *Athene*, built for William O. Gay in 1899, was the only starter in her class, and *Constellation*, recently purchased by Frank Skinner and the current holder of the Cup, was the only one in hers. So the Race Committee matched them. Gay submitted the account with which the Eastern Yacht Club's historian of its first thirty years closed his *Ditty Box*:

Captain Bill Gay had his old stand-bys aboard—Frank Gray, sometimes dubbed the Old Gray Mare; Ned Revere, commonly known as "Cop," due to his close association with the old Revere Copper Company; Jack (Bucko) Blanchard; and Llewellyn (Skipper) Howland. Also Captain Warren Haskell—a good man in a tight pinch.

With housed topmast, hatches well battened down, tender lashed securely to the deck amidships, but with whole sail and a determination to win that cup to the devil with the main mast, we left our anchorage and were at the starting line well before the gun fire. . . .

The race started about 10:30. We were first across the line, with *Constellation* a good second, our first leg being down to the can off Minot's Light, a broad reach in a northwester. *Constellation* soon had her foresail winged out, and passed us going like a racehorse. Her 107' water-line length was counting. She hauled around Minot's Ledge buoy with a handsome lead, but

it was now a dead muzzler up to Graves Whistler, and as soon as *Athene* hauled on the wind we began to eat her up, and rounded the Whistler several minutes to the good.

Our next course was about N.E. by E. to the turning mark off Marblehead, and here again on the reach we were outfooted. Twice around the course we went, thirty miles in a howling gale. *Constellation* carried away her main-halliards, we the jaws of our gaff, but we put her through just the same, and beat *Constellation* seventeen minutes boat to boat, and twenty-four minutes corrected time.

One most interesting moment occurred just as we were nearing the finish line off Cat Island. A particularly wicked puff came out of Salem Bay, one of those "green" ones that blow the tops right off the waves. It caught us at a bad moment, as we knew we had the race in hand, and had softened our main sheet a trifle to ease up a bit on our broken jaws. The result was when the puff hit us, it drove her head off, filled the mainsail hard full, and gave us immediately a bad lee helm, throwing the boat almost on her beam ends, so that we had green water right up to the main companionway. To add to the confusion, the Committee boat and others commenced blowing their sirens for all they were worth, evidently thinking we were purposely slamming it to her. Captain Gay, who had the helm, hollered to let go the headsails as she wouldn't luff. The cleats, of course, were four feet under water, and impossible to reach, so "Cop" Revere fished for his pocket knife, but found he had left it below. He then passed word to the mate, who pulled out a knife and cut the forestaysail whip, which immediately eased the head sail and allowed us to get her headed up on her course.

We were told afterwards that *Athene* was a wonderful sight when she got that knockdown, and I guess she was. "Windy" Watson [*Constellation*'s professional skipper] came alongside after the race, and congratulated us warmly, saying we had sailed a fine race. It was very nice of him, and showed good sportsmanship. One or two pictures of the *Athene* by [Nathaniel] Stebbins of that race still hang in the E.Y.C. at the head of the stairs.

When you look at the Stebbins photograph of *Athene* plowing across a feather-white stretch toward the fluttering mark off Marblehead, the foam whisking from that graceful bow and boiling along the rail to her quarter, headsails quivering in a breeze to house a topmast . . . and the master's *Constellation* simply smashing through it, triumphantly, joyfully, lee rail a gorgeous trail of suds, canvas towering, drumming, driving her, driving her through it . . . and a few dozen others that accelerate your pulse quite as instantly, why then, maybe the bugologist wasn't so far off when he wondered if his century wouldn't see the highest development of the sailing yacht.

Chapter 4   **Newport to Bar Harbor**   *1901–1903*

With three successive America's Cup defenses to its credit, an expanding membership and fleet, plans for enlarging the house, and a long and optimistic look at the dawning century, the Eastern Yacht Club crossed the line of 1901, everything flying and close to the weather mark.

The yearbooks tell the story: since 1880, when the new clubhouse was being built, the membership had increased by 258 percent, from 240 to 620, and the fleet had doubled from 69 to 140. The only further accommodation to growth had been the purchase in 1885 of 10,000 square feet of adjoining land for a stable and carriage sheds, and a modest addition on the southwest side of the original clubhouse around 1891.

So in 1901 the Council approved a $100,000 bond issue to retire outstanding indebtedness, to acquire four acres between the Club and Nanepashemet Street to the west, including the Samoset House and stable, and to build an addition. An option was taken on the Old Stone Pier that served as a ferry landing between the town and the Neck, future location of the Pleon Yacht Club and the swimming pool. The members were offered $65,000 of the bond issue for thirty years at four percent.

Nanepashemet Street memorialized an eighty-room summer hotel (named after a local Indian sagamore) built in 1882 at the corner of Ocean Avenue, where it dominated the scene until it burned in 1914. Though now owned by the Eastern, the Samoset continued for some years as a privately operated boarding house. A carpenter repairing sills around 1925 told Nathaniel Cushing Nash, Jr., that they were pegged and probably dated back to colonial times, bearing out the claim by Lord and Gamage in their history of Marblehead that it was built by John Andrews around the 1760s. "Perhaps the reason the Andrews home is still standing," they wrote, "was that,

unlike many Neck owners, he resided there year around and just may have held his ground when the few other permanent residents fled into town for safety at the onset of the Revolution."

The addition was finished in 1902. It gave the main house seventeen new chambers, a reading room, a new billiard room, and a private dining room and kitchen; the former billiard room was converted into a "ladies restaurant." Looking across as well as ahead, the Club arranged for the Hooper Wharf near the foot of State Street to be available as a townside landing for members and guests.

The Boston Yacht Club had been thinking in like vein. After a shaky start—helped not at all by the rise of the Eastern star—the Boston enjoyed a brief recovery of its fortunes, only to decline again in the mid-1880s as the yachting trend established itself away from Boston Harbor and along the North Shore. From its base at City Point in South Boston, New England's oldest yacht club had nevertheless been able to absorb as stations the Hull, Dorchester, and Massachusetts (Rowe's Wharf) clubs. Things were looking up again under the commodoreship of Benjamin P. Cheney, who thought his club should have a station at Marblehead, which was looking increasingly attractive to the yachtsmen of Boston. He bought the wharf at the foot of State Street for $5,000 and gave it to the Boston, which built its Marblehead Station thereon and opened it in 1902.

The Eastern's roster by 1902 had swollen to 663. It reached an all-time peak of 707 in 1906 before retreating to more manageable proportions. The practice of dual or even multiple memberships swelled the rolls of most clubs with absentee yachtsmen before the days of reciprocity and visitors' privi-

Steam ferry *Blonde* drops off passengers at the Old Stone Pier. A
3-master unloads across the harbor, probably coal.

The Samoset House in its heyday.

leges. More than thirty Eastern craft in 1902 hailed from beyond Massachusetts and as far away as Cowes, the Marblehead of Britain. Nor were fees a strain at fifty dollars entrance and annual dues of thirty. So it was voted that no candidate for membership who was not the owner of a yacht over 30 feet on the water was eligible for election while the club had 650 or more active members. This accomplished little if anything. The cutoff was raised to 700 the following year, and the fleet simply doubled from 143 in 1902 to 277 in 1906.

Founding Commodore John Heard is listed as the first Honorary Member of the Eastern in 1876; he died in 1894 at sixty-eight. Then in 1880, Frederick C. de Sumichrast, who had joined the Club only the previous September, was elected its second Honorary Member, continuing in that singular capacity only until 1887, and remained a regular member until 1895. Little is known of him. W.P. Stephens identified F.C. Sumicrast in *Traditions and Memories of American Yachting* as the long-time secretary of the Royal Nova Scotia Yacht Squadron and praised his work as a yachting writer under the nom de plume "Rouge-Croix." The America's Cup races produced Sir Richard Sutton, owner of *Genesta*, in 1886; Lieutenant William Henn, owner of *Galatea* in 1887 (*Thistle*'s owner, James Bell, for some reason was not elected in 1888); and the Earl of Dunraven, owner of *Valkyrie*, in 1894.

Following the practice of the New York Yacht Club, as in other matters of protocol, the Eastern—with an eye more to office and influence than to the holder—designated as ex officio Honorary Members the Secretary of the Navy, the Secretary of the Treasury, the Collector of the Port of Boston, the Justice of the Supreme Court of the United States for the First Circuit, the United States circuit judges and the District Judge, the Admiral of the Boston Station, the Commander of the Charlestown Navy Yard, the Superintendent of the U. S. Coast Survey, and the Inspector of the Second Lighthouse District.

But where New York extended its mantle to admirals, commodores, more judges, and assorted maritime functionaries, a few politicians including the President (nonpolitically ex officio, of course), and European royalty galore, the more conservative Yankees of the Eastern were more chary with their encomia all around and remained content with the bases touched pro forma. Indeed, Lord Dunraven, as the century opened, was the only private individual on the Honorary rolls.

Boston certainly took some perverse, if not grim, satisfaction in acknowledging New York's lead in spit and polish. A

special Eastern committee appointed in 1902 to look into matters sartorial reported that "uniforms of officers, captains and members now conform, except as regards cap devices and buttons, with those of the New York Yacht Club." Withal, the spirit of Billy Otis remained unquenchable. Henry Taggard, who was measurer at the time, recalled the matter of caps:

Early in the present century, a most popular racing member was appointed Fleet Captain by a worthy Commodore who carefully observed all the customs and ceremonies of yachting etiquette. Not so our F.C., who harbored a strong dislike for the trappings of office, but who had nevertheless burgeoned forth in gay uniform to do honor to the Flagship.

On the first day of the Cruise while beating to the eastward, the Commodore ordered Quartermaster "Long John" to come about, and curiously enough the F.C.'s bedizened cap was swept overboard by the mainboom.

It is vouched for that the F.C. heaved a hearty sigh of relief as he begged the Commodore not to turn back to pick up the cap.

Of course the nautical drill was not without its appeal. Nathaniel Cushing Nash, Sr., joined the Eastern in 1883 and owned the schooners *Breeze* and *Loyal* and the steamer *Adelita* at various times over the next twenty years. His namesake

Bristol fashion aboard Nathaniel Cushing Nash, Sr.'s, schooner *Loyal*, 1898.

Newport to Bar Harbor

son summered on the Neck with the family from 1892, when he was seven, until 1906. "Cush" Nash became a member in 1916, and sixty-one years later, as Number One, reminisced about the Club of his childhood when there was no club launch (it was available to members in 1902 for two dollars an hour, limit two hours):

To get to your yacht, you either rowed yourself out in your own tender, or if you had a yacht with paid hands, they came in to take you out. When Father had a schooner with four able-bodied seamen, it was a pretty sight to see them raise their oars at the command "oars," drop them smartly at the command "let off," and start rowing at the command "give way."

Yachting was largely confined to weekends. Most of the club members had their business offices in Boston. One way to get to the train was by the ferry and walking across the town to the railroad station. The other was to ride a horse-drawn barge, which made regular trips around the Neck scheduled more or less to meet the trains. [A third was by bicycle; a mechanic was engaged to clean machines in the Bicycle Room at the member's expense, no tips.]

Although the bylaws stated that a female yacht owner was eligible for a very limited membership while she owned her yacht, as yet there were none. The Eastern was a gentlemen's club. Properly accredited representatives of the other sex were permitted to use the main house on Ladies Day (Thursdays)

after 3 P.M., with the exception of the Ladies Restaurant, which served from 11 A.M. until 10 P.M. Cush Nash remembered:

During that period children were not expected to come into the clubhouse. Women did not come in either, except on Thursday nights, when they would come to dinner. After dinner the band from the 2nd Corps Cadets would give a concert. The young people were not invited, but they would listen from neighboring yards. It was especially fun to listen on the third Thursday in June. There were no telephones on the Neck, but someone would bring the word down from Boston, and if the band played "Fair Harvard," you knew that Harvard had won the boat race. Sometimes they played "Bright College Years."

Longtime member Robert E. Peabody summered with his family on Peach's Point, where his father kept the 19-foot-waterline sloop *Kathleen*, designed for him by Ned Burgess in 1888. In 1966 he looked back from his perspective as its oldest resident:

You had to row or sail if you wanted to go anywhere. The biggest event was to row around to the harbor on band nights when the Eastern Yacht Club gave a band concert on the lawn, and we sat in our rowboats to listen. Rowing back in the dark afterwards was always exciting on account of the danger of running on the Growler or other ledges off the end of the Point.

And the band played on. "There used to be a low fence across the front porch of the club," remembered Rebecca Benson Haskell, "with a swinging gate with a sign on it saying, WOMEN AND DOGS NOT ALLOWED BEYOND THIS POINT. When the rules were altered so that ladies could sit there during the band concerts, an uncle of mine [the *pontifical* uncle who supervised the building of the clubhouse] resigned from the club."

Another perspective on those days was provided forty years later by the Essex County historian James Duncan Phillips of Topsfield, who joined the Club in 1903:

The small gray Corinthian Yacht Club and the dull red Eastern Yacht Club were the most conspicuous buildings in sight, except possibly the Samoset House under its big elms. . . . Single men might go to the yacht clubs. The Eastern Yacht Club was the most select, and the oldest residents looked a bit askance at the Corinthian and said it was an excellent place for new people. There was a round table in the big bay window of the Eastern where a select group of gouty gentlemen gathered during the season to gossip and eat and discuss the affairs of the nation. There was little frivolity and only dignified liquidity around the club, and women were positively not admitted or cigarettes smoked, except Thursday evening when as a concession to the members who lived on the Neck, the club served a dinner at which members could reserve tables and entertain ladies and gentlemen and then sit on the piazza and listen to an elevating band concert. The ladies need not expect drinks on the piazza or dancing in the clubhouse and must go home as soon as the concert was over.

Some further inroads must have been made when Charles Foster, the patriarch of a large family, had something to say on the matter in his *Ditty Box*:

In all yacht clubs, there is a self-elected committee of great influence known as the "Piazza Committee." Their primary activity is to conduct a post mortem on the nautical conduct of members in regattas, cruises, and general nautical behavior; but they will, if nautical matters are dull, get up an argument on any subject, and the author remembers a vehement contention, in which money became involved, as to the proper way to carve a saddle of mutton. Elderly bachelors are apt to be predominant and in a wonderfully effective committee of the Eastern Yacht Club in its early days many a nautical reputation was made or unmade by these gentlemen. When the clubhouse was first opened, man was supreme but, as is usual, the fair sex began to win its way and finally some member under female domination offered a motion that would open the clubhouse to the general use of ladies. Our Piazza Committee was furious, but the motion was carried and what do you suppose happened? Three of the elderly bachelors soon became married! Ah, you sailor men know how it is: "Tis the old rope that is the easier spliced."

The old rope was spliced ashore, and the main brace afloat, where the water remained the domain of the gents, more or less, as explained by Kitty to her friend Molly in London on June 30, 1891. The writer had attended the Annual Regatta, when the wind was light and variable, as stated in the *Ditty Box* from which her still-tippy epistle is plucked, but there was a long, heavy roll with some cross sea.

My dearest Molly—

> "She who yachts and walks away
> May live to yacht another day."

I'm going to tell you all about the yacht race yesterday. . . . I was perfectly delighted when I was invited to go down on the new steamer *Mayflower* [probably the 184-foot S.S. *May Flower* built that year in Chelsea] to Marblehead with the other people asked by the Eastern Yacht Club. Uncle John took Jimmy and me, and Mr. Atherton came. . . . It was very gay at Rowe's Wharf; there were lots of girls in pretty new dresses. Most of them had blue veils, thin ones, of course, and I think they were not nearly as becoming as the white ones that several of the girls wore. . . .

Well, Uncle John and Mr. Atherton found me a nice place on deck, and by-and-by uncle went away to smoke, and "find Jimmy," he said, and he did not come back. Mr. Atherton stayed with me and told me the names of the islands and the lights as we went down the harbor. It was a bright, beautiful morning. The sky was blue, with just clouds enough; the sea looked very blue and deep, and other times sort of gray and shallow and tiresome. Boston looked beautiful behind us. I liked the tall buildings shooting up here and there. Mr. Atherton said they spoil the sky-line, but I couldn't see that the sky looked at all different because of the Ames Building.

The *New York* [there were four of that name in commission] started after we did and came bounding after us; there were lots of sails, and the shores looked a dozen shades of green. . . . You know if you look resolutely at the horizon you can ward off something I am not going to mention once in this letter, though almost everybody began to show symptoms of it.

There was a lovely girl sitting near us, with a really beautiful young man, one of those well-set-up, well-bred, clear-eyed, splendid youths of Hubland, and they had such a good time when we first started. They consulted the club book together; they looked at the paper they were going to keep the record of the race on, and marked things and talked so happily and merrily together. But, Molly, my dear, by the time we had passed the last lingering purple shadow of Nahant that girl had done what several others had done; she reposed peacefully upon her back on a bench in the middle of the deck, her pretty chin, her little boots sticking up (toeing out) to the skies, her eyes closed. On the other end of the bench, his feet toed in and downward, his face hidden from view, his broad back sadly shaken now and then, lay that beautiful, well-set-up young man! It was a sad sight.

Mr. Atherton asked me how I felt; for such sights multiplied about us, and I said—"All right, thank you." Mr. Atherton turned deadly pale, stood up and said he thought *he* would "go and find Jimmy," and *he* didn't come back. . . .

Oh! it was a beautiful day! I heard people say so, but I heard people say other things. A swell! Isn't there some other word to express a ship sticking her nose to the zenith, then down to the hidden haunts of mermaids? The *Mayflower* did her best, and there were times when the ocean took her in his arms with all her youth and all her charms, then tossed her towards heaven as if in sacrificial gratitude—and we all went along both ways, living sacrifices, and I forgot all about the purple shadows.

By-and-by I heard some men who were walking about (there were still men who could walk about) talking of the beauty of some yacht. I opened my eyes cautiously and peeped out, not turning my head. There was the most beautiful boat you ever saw. She looked so clean; so white-sailed, so poetic, proud and splendid that I longed to know all about her. Just then our steamer fled over a big billow with an up-and-downness indescribable, and that yacht I was looking at dipped and rose with so much poetry of motion that I clung to prose and closed my eyes.

"Six more hours of this!" I heard a woman near me groan to another woman, adding, "My poor husband hasn't shown his face since—. Of course he's a *man*, and he's ashamed."

Molly, can you imagine the utter bliss of hearing a voice of authority announcing, as a man with an official cap walked about—"We are going to put in to Gloucester, and all those who wish can go ashore."

Wish! Well, well, most of the people wished it with an ardor of wishing that people who dote on yachting can never dream of.

There was quiet water in Gloucester harbor when I sat up again. Jimmy (adorable boy!) stood by with a cup of hot bouillon. Uncle John and Mr. Atherton approached, Mr. Atherton still pale with emotion. He went ashore with me. Uncle and Jimmy stuck to the boat. Mr. Atherton remained pale during our ride up to town in the train with the great majority. The land looked uncommonly secure and stable.

"Terra is very firma," I said, trying to joke. Mr. Atherton did not smile.

"I often wonder," he said sadly, "that when it was written of 'those who go down to the sea in ships,' that nothing was said of those who go up *and* down *on* the sea in ships."

When I got home, and they all began to ask if it was a good race, I said, "Yes, it was beautiful."

I saw by the paper that the *Gossoon* won [the Puritan Cup]. I wonder if that was the beautiful yacht I had a peep at.

Just think of it, Molly! Think of going to a yacht race, and only having one peep at one yacht through one eye!

In future I'll just stay at home and never go to sea, and I'll get to be a yachter of braveree.

Your devoted
KITTY

P.S.—Jimmy says there was an elegant luncheon on board.

Edward Burgess predicted in 1888 that steam would continue to encroach on sail, though he failed to foresee that it would in turn succumb to electricity. Between 1890 and 1900, the number of Eastern Yacht Club schooners declined from forty to twenty-nine, while the steamers rose from thirty-four to forty-nine; together in 1900 they comprised 60 percent of the fleet. Most were in the medium range from 60 to 90 feet, although the grandest dwarfed the biggest of the schooners. A few day and cruising launches were not much above the 30-foot minimum.

Much has been made of the overdesigned, overpowered, overstuffed, and overbearing steam yacht as the most conspicuous of the rich citylubber's consumptions of the gilded age. J.P. Morgan, the one who advised that if you had to ask you couldn't afford, enrolled all three of his *Corsair*s with the Eastern (by turns 185, 238, and 304 feet overall). And James Gordon Bennett, E.D. Morgan, Lloyd Phoenix, John R. Drexel, Alexander Van Rensselaer, and a handful of other Newporters, New Yorkers, and Philadelphians added their floating palaces to the Marblehead fleet, in the main through the New York Yacht Club, whose steamers outnumbered its schooners 189 to 86 in 1900. But the great majority of EYC steamers were indigenous, and although they were manned by professionals, most of the owners knew an iron mainsail from a windy one.

No less a sailing man than Charles Foster co-owned the 85-footer *Hanniel* for thirteen years. Forbes, Sears, Pickman, Peabody, Weld, Cushing, Cabot, Amory, Ames, and Lawrence were sailing families who dabbled in steam; the Forbeses owned four big ones before the end of the century.

Others were devotees. Harry E. Converse of Boston started with the schooner *Caroline* in 1887 and then got steamed up

Commodore Henry S. Hovey

---

over *Edith, Eugenie, Calypso, Penelope,* and the *Mollie C.* over the next thirteen years, expanding from 79 to 186 feet on the water. Frank B. McQuesten of Marblehead Neck sailed his sloop *Thelma* in 1891 and 1892, abandoned her for the steamer *Random* in 1893, and ran through *Rajah, Chetolah,* and *Inca* before he returned to sail in 1899 with the fast and beautiful schooner *Gitana* (built by William F. Weld in 1882 and one of the queens of the fleet), only to revert to steam with *Valda* in 1900.

The only yacht Francis Lee Higginson is recorded as owning (and for only three seasons) in his twenty-two years of membership is the 109-foot steamer *Ibis,* which he took on the 1882 Annual Cruise to Bar Harbor, where he described to the *Mt. Desert Herald* his habit of bathing, dressing, and breakfasting aboard and steaming the two hours from his summer home in Beverly to work in Boston. "In the evening he returns in the same manner. He is a fortunate man."

Most members, for all the glamour and luxury associated with steam, were purists. Henry S. (Harry) Hovey of Glouces-

ter stuck with his fleet favorite—and the fleet favorite—the schooner *Fortuna,* from the day of her launch in 1883 until November 19, 1900, when at the age of fifty-five he was the first commodore to die in office. A charter member, he was elected rear commodore and then vice commodore in 1880 when he had the schooner *Phantom,* and commodore in 1884 for two years, declining reelection. Due to his unprecedented popularity, he was elected commodore again in 1889 and reelected in 1900, perhaps as a special mark of esteem in view of his failing health. His father and uncle, George and Charles Hovey, built the first summer homes on Cape Ann in the 1840s. Harry, a bachelor, was in the cotton business before retiring, living first with his father in Boston and then with his sister. At their annual meeting on February 13, 1901, the members of the Eastern Yacht Club declared of Henry S. Hovey:

> Both as Commodore and in his private capacity, he was unquestionably one of the most popular and best-loved members of the association. Well versed as to his duties, he was a model officer, and as a fellow member he was universally loved and respected.
>
> It was recognized when he consented to be Commodore for a second term that he had no new honors to gain, and it was felt that to accept the burden of the office for another term was a signal proof of the interest he felt in the welfare of the club and a generous wish to meet the desire of his fellow-members.

Albert S. Bigelow, a member since 1889, had been rear commodore since 1899, his first of two seasons as owner of the 137-foot-waterline steamer *Ituna.* He was elected to succeed Commodore Hovey in 1901, which may have had to do with his decision to replace *Ituna* with *Pantooset,* launched at the Bath Iron Works (Maine) in the spring of his second term in 1902. Another factor may have been his wealth, derived from his own and his inherited domination of the copper mining industry; in 1900 it was estimated at between twenty-five and thirty million dollars.

Commodore Bigelow's flagship was 175 feet on the water, 212 feet overall, 27 feet beam, 14 feet extreme draft, and 270 tons net. His sailing master, Captain Alexander C. Corkum, was responsible for her general design and supervised her con-

---

Broad off Marblehead Neck, Commodore Hovey's flagship *Fortuna* shakes the slack out of her enormous staysail, 1885. Little photo.

Newport to Bar Harbor

struction. She was said to be the largest steam yacht ever built for a Bostonian.

Pantooset was featured in *The Rudder* of May 1903 as "undoubtedly one of the finest steam yachts in the country." She was a typical hermaphrodite of the era, with pole masts for riding sails, signals, and sentiment; an immense stack; a stub bowsprit perched above ornate trailboards on a dignified clipper bow; a bit of sheer; an elegant fantail—a potpourri of features imported from the waters of the United Kingdom.

Pantooset's main deckhouse was topped with a pilothouse and chart room on which were perched a bridge worthy of a Cunarder. She was all steel, with five bulkheads, and a double bottom under the engine room. Topsides: lifeboats, owner's launch, smaller launch, and a brace of gigs. Single screw with a triple-expansion engine rated at 1,350 horsepower, 12½ knots normal, 14½ forced; a thousand pounds of coal an hour, with 150-ton bunker storage. Two dynamos ran a one-ton-capacity ice machine and 300 electric lights. Hot and cold fresh and salt running water.

Never will the world see her like again. The accommodations of the Eastern Yacht Club's flagship for 1902 were described in *The Rudder*:

Commencing at the forward end of the ship comes the forecastle. . . . There are eleven pipe berths in the room. Below this there is a bathroom for the crew and in this space is also the chain lockers. . . . A little abaft the forecastle, and on the main deck, is a companionway leading to the officers' quarters. These consist of a suite of three rooms, one each for the captain, steward and mate, finished in ash, with mahogany trimmings. . . .

At the forward end of the deck house is the owner's dining saloon, off of which is a vestibule, with winding staircase leading to the owner's quarters below. The dining saloon and vestibule are finished in burl mahogany. . . . At the foot of the winding staircase there is a stateroom on either side, each having its own bathroom. These are finished in bird's eye maple. . . . At the end of the little corridor are the owner's staterooms . . . finished in Hungarian ash, with panels of the same wood.

To the main deck again, and passing aft, the galley comes abaft the owner's pantry. . . . The officers' mess room is next, also on the port side. Twelve can be seated around this table. A passage leads to the galley. The mess room is finished in ash and mahogany. Next comes a passage through the deck house. On the port side of this is the quartermaster's stateroom. . . . Passing aft again, the upper engine room is entered from the port side. On the starboard side is the chief engineer's stateroom and on the port the assistant chief 's. Off the lower engine room space, the firemen sleep on the starboard side. . . . *Pantooset* carries four firemen and two oilers.

At the after end of the deck house is . . . a vestibule, off of which is the library, extending the full beam of the ship. They are finished in burl mahogany. . . . Over the center is a dome skylight with cathedral glass.

A winding staircase from the vestibule leads to the main saloon and the guests' quarters. The saloon extends the full beam of the vessel and is finished in white enamel, with mahogany trimmings. On each side there is a wide sofa, with buffets at either end. The furnishings are magnificent. There is an open grate as in the library. The guests' quarters are abaft the saloon. These consist of two staterooms on each side, with a bathroom between each pair, and are finished in white enamel, with green panellings. The bathrooms, as are those in the owner's quarters, are tiled and finished in white enamel.

Pantooset led the Annual Cruise to the eastward from Marblehead on June 28, 1902—accompanied by a tug, as was the custom—for the formal opening of the Eastern Yacht Club's Bar Harbor Station. A strong northwester fueled a race to the Isles of Shoals. Laurence Minot's 62-foot schooner *Hope Leslie*, the hopeless object of much punning during her quarter-century as a yacht, won the schooner class, and *Athene* the sloop. The fleet raced from there to Boothbay, Islesboro, and Bar Harbor.

The establishment of the Eastern's first and only station crowned thirty-three years of cruising, usually to the eastward except for those few occasions when the fleet rendezvoused with the New York Yacht Club west of Cape Cod. A ditty box indeed of stories was brought back from these coastal excursions.

Charlie Foster, probably in the 1880s, chartered a small cutter for the Annual Cruise down east with a couple of friends and signed on a first-rate steward, who, unfortunately, took one look at the galley on the eve of departure and backed out. A replacement was found, "so crippled with rheumatism and of such advanced age that it was considered unsafe that he should even appear on deck while the fleet was under way." They sailed a day late.

On a certain morning later, while the Eastern Fleet was at anchor in a down east harbor, there appeared a bedraggled looking little vessel, sails here and there tied with strings and the crew of three almost unrecognizable through lack of shaving and di-

Pantooset in her glory. Willard B. Jackson photo.

lapidated clothes. . . . Having anchored in a quiet spot in the early morning after a tempestuous career, the three were having a much needed sleep when all of a sudden there was a mighty splash. The E.Y.C. member, always fearful of the life of the cook, jumped out of his berth and looking over the side saw bubbles of air coming up through the water. With a yell to the other members, he plunged overboard and swam until his breath was no longer to be held when he came to the surface and was hauled aboard just able to cry out, "Dive for him he is down there." Over went a second member who was unable to find the corpse. Coming aboard, the third member dove over. Just about at that time, a head popped up out of the hatch with the remark, "What am de trouble, gentlemen?" And being informed, he said, "Why that splash was my ashes." And thus a near tragedy was avoided.

Dudley Pickman had as keen a sense of the droll as his friend Foster and passed on to him this cameo of the Annual Cruise's accustomed destination of a hundred years ago:

In its earlier days as a summer resort, Bar Harbor was colonized largely by young women from Philadelphia, deservedly reputed for their good looks and attraction. Even in that lovely spot, life at times was rather monotonous, and the prospective visit of our yacht squadron was a matter of decided interest to these charmers, who lost no time in planning a picnic in its honor. This invitation was, of course, enthusiastically accepted by us yacht owners and our guests in spite of ominous clouds still tenaciously clinging to the brow of Green Mountain. During the morning hours the event was an unqualified success with climbs over picturesque cliffs and rambling strolls through shady groves bordering on the blue waters of Frenchman's Bay.

Then came the time for placating the inner man, who was

beginning to claim attention. The sun had long been "over the yard arm." But where was the lunch hamper, carefully prepared early in the day—as only Philadelphians know how—with delicacies solid and liquid? There was no answer to this question, and, after diligent search, it was sadly admitted that no trace of the precious object had been found high or low. Pardonable consternation prevailed, for telephones did not exist in that vicinity at least, and the buckboards had gone back to the village. Evidently someone had blundered at the start, and both lunch baskets had been sent to another picnic at the northern end of Mount Desert Island. The situation was indeed a trying one: our own emptiness contrasted with the tantalizing picture of those rival picnickers revelling in extra portions from our missing luncheon. But soon gloom was in a measure relieved by a young woman of the party discovering a package of crackers with some sweet chocolates in an unclaimed overcoat pocket, probably provided for just such an emergency—and forgotten. . . . Under these unlooked-for conditions, our yachtsmen behaved nobly, doing their full share by song and story to maintain the morale of both sexes. Our hostesses, however, suffered, I fear, keenly from chagrin—responsibility for the lost hamper weighing heavily upon them, more especially as they had been given the tip by an experienced chaperon friend that Boston men, though awfully nice fellows and good company, were known as having a most profound regard for their stomachs.

After returning to Bar Harbor, the party was brought together again in the late afternoon by an invitation from us to our fair friends of the morning for a supper at Sproul's. Sproul's was a notable instance of local option in a bone dry state. The fare was always simple but choice. As a result of the mellowing influence of this entertainment, the tribulation of noonday soon faded as such, becoming merely an amusing episode of a summer pastime.

The descent of the young bucks from the Eastern fleet on Mount Desert must have seemed almost a mirage to the excitement-starved Philadelphia girls, whose mamas and papas may have felt justified in concluding that a more formal chaperonage than that provided by Sproul's was in order. The Oasis Club, organized by the males of the summer colony in 1874, was no help, nor was their formation in 1881 of the Mount Desert Reading Room for the promotion of literary and social culture among the manly membership: Vanderbilt, Morgan, Pulitzer, Drexel, Sears, Blaine, and that crowd. The Reading Room's bylaws excluded females not only from membership but from the premises, except for special receptions. Thanks in part to Maine's prohibition law, Samuel Eliot Morison speculated, "most of the 'reading' was done through the bottom of a glass."

In 1887 the Reading Room and the Oasis, which it appears to have absorbed in the process, built an expansive and attractive shingle-style clubhouse down on the water, designed by the eminent William Ralph Emerson, and ran out a wooden pier to a landing in the harbor. J. Pierpont Morgan was commodore of the New York Yacht Club ten years later and led the squadron in *Corsair* to his favored Mount Desert for the first time, in a race from Vineyard Haven. In 1899 the governors of the Reading Room extended the use of the float to members of the New York, Eastern, Seawanhaka, and Corinthian of Philadelphia yacht clubs, who received all the privileges of subscribers except voting, proposing and seconding candidates, and introducing strangers.

At about this time, the wooden pier to which the hospitable float was connected washed away in a storm. A new steel pier 236 feet long, with an upper deck for serving tea—ladies invited on special occasions—was built out over the ledge and finished in June 1902.

Commodore Bigelow's resplendent *Pantooset* brought the squadron of the Eastern Yacht Club to anchor at its Bar Harbor Station on July 1. It was all made official that same day in the shingle-style clubhouse, already a landmark:

> In accordance with an agreement made with the Mount Desert Reading-Room, dated July 1, 1902, under which a permanent pier and landing has been built at Bar Harbor by the two Clubs, any member of the Eastern Yacht Club present in Bar Harbor waters in a yacht which is owned by him shall be entitled, during the term of said agreement, to all the privileges which the members of the Reading-Room may enjoy or have in respect to its club-rooms (which includes the privilege of introducing strangers for one day under Club Rule No. 11 of the Reading-Room), grounds, and wharf in the village of Bar Harbor, except the right to vote, and of proposing and seconding candidates for membership. . . .

Eastern members had bargained for the right to introduce strangers for a day, but the doors of the Mount Desert Reading Room and their Bar Harbor Station remained closed to their

---

Those ashore during an 1875 cruise to Bar Harbor were identified in this photograph as, left to right, Mr. Boardman, "Ned" Haven, "Tom" Motley, "Bob" Stevenson, Allan Tucker, "Mr." Hovey, Griffith, George Whitney, Harry Hovey, T. Dennie Boardman, Henry Sullivan, C.A. Longfellow, Charles Whitney, E.F. Whitney, Eben Dale (?), Henry Fay.

Mount Desert Reading Room clubhouse

Mount Desert Reading Room pier. It looks like *Pantooset* at right and a brace of naval vessels in the distance.

ladies, except for special receptions, until 1921. This inaugural cruise of 1902 disbanded at Bar Harbor. Several boats continued east, and *Pantooset* steamed on to Labrador before returning to Marblehead. The Eastern's busiest season was in full swing under Regatta Chairman Henry Howard with a series of cruising races to Gloucester, a mid-July open regatta, and another series of special open races for 25-foot, 21-foot, and 18-foot cabin classes—a considerable concession to the under-30 advocates. All of this led up to the visit of the New York Yacht Club on August 9, the first in nine years.

William Randolph Hearst's Spanish-American War had been fought and won to no one's particular credit, the century had turned, President McKinley had been assassinated, Teddy Roosevelt was in the White House, and jingoism was in the driver's seat. The United States of America was feeling very muscular. The squadron of the New York Yacht Club, by order of Commodore Lewis Cass Ledyard aboard his flagship, the schooner *Corona* (ex-sloop *Colonia*, Herreshoff's unsuccessful 1893 Cup defense contender), assembled at New London on August 4, 1902. Eighty-six strong and growing by the hour, this great white fleet—precursor of the one TR would send around the world six years hence in a show of almost equal naval power—sailed on the first leg to Newport the next day. Frank Skinner's *Constellation*, representing the Eastern, won the big schooner race.

Off Newport, the fleet vied for the Astor Cups in a heavy wind and rough seas. (The cups had been presented as perpetual trophies for schooners, sloops, and yawls by John Jacob Astor in 1898 after Ogden Goelet died without providing for the future bestowal of his.) Of three men who fell overboard from as many yachts, two were picked up and one drowned. The next day's run to Vineyard Haven in a freshening southwester was led by *Constellation*, thirty-seven miles in three hours, 32 minutes, and 15 seconds—28 seconds ahead of *Corona*. From Martha's Vineyard, a series of close reaches in a stiff southeaster to Pollock Rip and spinnakers to Highland Light, where a squall struck, and it was lee rails under to Provincetown behind *Constellation*, seventy-nine miles for the day in 13 seconds short of seven hours, *Corona* a minute and a half in her wake.

The New York Yacht Club Cruise to Marblehead, August 11, 1902, looking out the harbor. Stebbins photo.

13654 Marblehead Harbor Aug. 11, 1902

Newport to Bar Harbor

Newport to Bar Harbor

Such winds had earned a rest, and the New York squadron of 118 yachts—thirty schooners, thirty-one sloops, fifty-one steamers, and six auxiliaries—drifted across the bay in light and baffling winds and was greeted by Eastern members at Halfway Rock and escorted into Marblehead. It had been Burgess's old *Constellation* all the way, with four firsts among the big schooners.

They kept rounding in for the rest of the afternoon and into the evening of August 9, long after the time limit had expired. Never had such a welcome been prepared—or been so necessary. Several days in advance, the Marblehead harbormaster had issued special anchoring rules—unique, surely, for the harbors of Massachusetts Bay:

1. A fairway, lengthwise of the harbor and about 300 feet wide, will be marked by flag buoys, red on the northwest and blue on the southeast side, and must be kept open.

2. All mooring privileges in water charted deeper than 18 feet will be suspended for the time stated.

3. Each vessel must anchor in the shoalest practicable water remaining unoccupied on the respective anchorage grounds.

4. Steamers over 125 feet waterline length must anchor northeast of a line drawn from the easternmost ferry landing to the first elm tree west of Fort Sewall. All other steamers and launches must anchor southwest of a line drawn from Boden's Rock buoy to the flagstaff on Crocker Park.

5. All sailing vessels less than 53 feet waterline length must anchor southwest of the line drawn from Boden's Rock buoy to the flagstaff on Crocker Park, except vessels less than 25 feet waterline length belonging in Marblehead, which may at the option of the owners, anchor as near shore as is practicable.

6. The space between these two lines, except the fairway, will be reserved for sailing vessels over 53 feet waterline length. Auxiliaries with power other than steam will be considered as sailing vessels.

7. Flagships of the Eastern and New York Yacht Clubs need not observe Rules 4, 5, and 6.

The next day, Sunday, August 10, the harbormaster counted 1,047 craft of all kinds in the harbor.

Monday was Regatta Day. The public came by the tens of thousands to catch a view from every vantage point on shore. The two clubs chartered the 200-foot excursion steamer *Gay Head* for nonsailing members and guests. It was a day of dra-

The NYYC Cruise, looking toward Marblehead Neck. The Club is seen over the stack of the black steam yacht *Colonia*.

matically changeable weather that opened brilliantly in the morning, as a reporter on board wrote, "the flashes of white canvas in the sunlight so numerous as to be positively dazzling," only to dump sudden downpours in which "young women with shirtwaists were pelted unmercifully before they could rush from the wide-open of the upper deck to shelter below"—and inspired the seagoing Cadet Band to tootle:

> Ain't it a shame, a measly shame,
> To keep yo' honey out in the rain?

Thirty-two started in ten classes in a southeast breeze that hauled into the south and then into the southwest after a hard rainsquall and finished south-southwest. Only Eastern members were scored for the Puritan Cup, which was won by Thomas McKee's schooner *Amorita*.

The old town turned itself inside out with vast entertaining by the Eastern and the Corinthian, in private homes and on yachts. James Duncan Phillips vividly remembered the to-and-fro of it all:

> Steam launches came smoking to the docks or little tenders rowed by the sailors. Ladies stood about the docks in long white dresses, picture hats and lovely white parasols, though how they ever climbed in and out and went up the ladders was one of the miracles of the summer. There was journeying to and from the yachts and the shore and the club with much good food and good wine so that by midnight on the closing day it was said you could walk across the harbor on the champagne corks!

The grand windup came at sundown on the evening of the regatta, with receptions at the two yacht clubs on the Neck. The spectacle as night fell was described in the *Boston Globe*:

> The great steam yachts were ablaze with electric lights from stem to stern and from truck to keel, and, to add to the effect which these decorations made, the color of the lights was changed every few moments from red to white and blue on several of the principal boats. The sailing craft of course could not make any such display as this, but these made up in red fire and bombs what they lacked in electric lights.
> Every cottage on the Neck was ablaze with lights, and red fire was burned on all the lawns. The fire alarm of the town was rung shortly after 8 o'clock. That was the signal to begin operations, and in about five minutes it seemed as if the shores all around the harbor had suddenly caught fire. The smoke from the red lights added to this feeling until it seemed like a vast conflagration.

Newport to Bar Harbor

The town did its part well on the cliff parks at Fort Sewall, Crocker's Park and Shirley's Point, and in addition every wharf and landing was illuminated. Then the bands on both sides of the harbor struck up, bombs were fired from the yachts and shores, and against the dark and clouded sky it certainly was a rare scene.

At the peak of these manmade pyrotechnics, just as a reminder from the Technician on High, a tremendous thunder-and-lightning storm roared down on the harbor with gusts of wind and a downpour that drove 20,000 drenched spectators from the rocks and other vantage points to houses, stalled streetcars, the overwhelmed railroad station, and wherever else they could find shelter. The Boston and Maine Railroad rolled sixty extra carloads out of town, and at one point 5,000 people were waiting. "There were a lot of fine millinery and imitation panamas ruined here during that storm," sympathized the *Globe* reporter, "to say nothing of shirt waists, negligee suits and white shoes."

As *The Rudder* opened its account, "There is no yachting event on the wide waters of the world like the annual cruise of the New York Yacht Club." And closed it: "There was a nice favoring breeze the morning the fleet disbanded [the next day, Tuesday], and by noon nearly the whole of the big fleet had left Marblehead, some going to the east and some west."

Commodore Bigelow was succeeded in office by Laurence Minot, and his *Pantooset* as the Eastern's flagship by the schooner *Hope Leslie*. Around the beginning of May 1903, *Pantooset* steamed out of Boston for Europe. *The Rudder* reported:

She will first go to Southampton, putting in at Fayal for coal. She will continue fitting out at Southampton and will then proceed to Cuxhaven, Germany, where Mr. Bigelow and party will join her. From there she will pass through the Kiel Channel and up the coast of Norway as far as North Cape, in the Land of the Midnight Sun. Returning, she will go up the Baltic as far as St. Petersburg. From there she will return to Cuxhaven, where Mr. Bigelow and party will leave her. She will then proceed to Boston, where she is expected to arrive about September 10.

And so she did, making Boston on the mark after a voyage of 14,500, miles, during which *Pantooset* flew the ensign of the Eastern Yacht Club in the Czar's window on the Baltic.

The clubhouse after the 1901 addition.

Eastern professionals at the ready.

Boarding the Club's steam launch, 1901.

Chapter 5

Blue Water Beckons

Ocean racing as an organized sport in America was first advanced by Thomas Fleming Day, the hard-sailing, tough-writing founder of *The Rudder* magazine and a genuine original. In 1904, Day rigged up an offshore spin for smaller cruising boats from Brooklyn out around the Nantucket Lightship to Marblehead under the back-to-back auspices of the Brooklyn and Boston yacht clubs for a cup put up by Sir Thomas Lipton. As usual, Day's rationale sounded apopletic:

I am sick of hearing that we are a lot of shore-skulkers, Central Park sailors; that while we can build racing machines and win with them, we have neither the craft nor the skill and pluck to sail on deep water, or even to go out of sight of land. . . .

Last season, when a yacht over 140 feet on top lay behind the Hook, her crew afraid to go out and race in a 35-mile breeze, a universal jeer went up from yachting-men the world over. What must the men, who thirty years ago started in a December gale to race across the Western Ocean, have thought of such cowardice? This was the last drop in the boiling bucket of my indignation, and I determined that we would show the world that we still had boats as seaworthy and men as skillful and plucky as those who crossed the Atlantic in sixty-six.

Here was a furiously thrown gauntlet, and Henry Morss and Regatta Committee Chairman Henry Howard picked it up. As the *Boston Globe* yachting writer Winfield Thompson put it later in *The Rudder*, they were "among the first to see that the idea was the beginning of a general movement toward blue water. The time was ripe for a change from harbor sailing, and the Eastern club showed its interest in the fresh deal by arranging a race for larger vessels, its own, and those of the New York club, over the same course as that sailed by the little fleet of Editor Day."

Howard had his hands full at the time with negotiations involving the Club in the coming international Sonderklasse matches and turned the promotion of the movement toward blue water over to Morss. As chairman/secretary of the Ocean Racing Committee (of which there is no official record), the equally busy wire manufacturer between April and July of 1904 wrote invitations to prominent East Coast yachtsmen urging them to enter the Eastern Yacht Club Ocean Race on July 6; it would be run from Sandy Hook to Marblehead Light, 331 miles in cruising trim, under EYC time allowance tables, with all accommodation fixtures in place below and no extreme racing sails. Prizes would be silver cups.

The inevitable resistance to a "fresh deal" had Morss writing a number of his candidates urging them to reconsider their decision not to enter, and on May 5 he had a fleet of seventeen on paper, including Commodore Minot's *Hope Leslie* and his own 37-foot cutter *Cossack*. A few more entries came in, but several withdrew before the race.

How to entice the great *Constellation*? "I have communicated with Mr. Charles F. Adams 2d who I think has considerable influence with Mr. Frank Skinner of the *Constellation*," Henry Taggard wrote Morss on June 21. "Mr. Adams suggests that the best course to pursue with Mr. Skinner is to communicate in some way with Capt. Nate Watson, who is fond of racing and who has a very pronounced influence in shaping Mr. Skinner's yachting plans." But no luck. Henry Morss's correspondence files at the Club lead one to conclude that this pioneering ocean yacht race was the work of a one-man committee.

Historic, yes, but it boiled down to only eight starters that made poor time in listless airs over practically the same course followed by the smaller Lipton Cuppers until they got past the Shoals, when the wind freshened enough for a decent run up the Cape and across the Massachusetts Bay to Marblehead. The winner on corrected time was the 75-foot Cary Smith schooner *Lasca* of New York, built in 1892. Not an especially notable demonstration of Yankee pluck and offshore seamanship. Nevertheless, as Winfield Thompson commented in *The Rudder*:

> The race was enough of a success to prompt a desire for something better in 1905, over a course freer from shoal water, and a course to Halifax was decided on. I first heard of the plan for the race to Halifax about the time the transatlantic race for the German Emperor's Cup started,* from Mr. Howard, who asked me to go give the idea as much publicity as I could, in order to attact entries; for, in keeping with the club's usual policy, the entry list was open to all. There was something attractive about the idea of sailing to Halifax, for Halifax, under the British flag, is to us as much a foreign port as Malta or Gibraltar; and in these times, when powers and potentates are busy cultivating each other's good will, it would be pleasant to fraternize with our Provincial cousins across the Gulf of Maine.
>
> It was not known at first whether our neighbors wanted to be fraternized with; but reports from Eastern Y.C. members who had passed summers in Nova Scotia agreed that the Nova Scotians were good hosts, and always proud to greet anybody with the slightest claim on their hospitality. This was encouraging, and when a committee went to feel out the ground at Halifax, they were ambushed, so to speak, and rushed into camp in such a hurry, amid such vigorous friendly acclaim, that they were quite taken from their feet, and came back to report that Halifax was O.K., and its people had declared they were anxious to entertain American yachtsmen.
>
> That the men of Halifax did not halt with hollow words in their mouths was shown by their offer to put up for competition their best trophy, the Prince of Wales Cup. The cup was a gift from the King, when he traveled on this side of the ocean in 1860. It is now venerable, as yachting trophies go, with 45 years of sport and good cheer, summer and winter, to mellow the memory of the Halifax yachtsmen's stewardship of it, as trustees for posterity. It is now a perpetual challenge trophy, and must always be sailed for at Halifax. The privilege of racing for the cup, and keeping it for nine months if won, had never before been accorded to yachts outside the Provinces.
>
> As a prize for the winner of the race to Halifax the Eastern

Y.C. put up a silver cup, to become the property of the winner; and other trophies were offered as prizes in each class.

Thus was hatched the first Halifax Race, run irregularly thereafter until taken hold of in 1939 by the Boston Yacht Club jointly with the Royal Nova Scotia Yacht Squadron.

In the opening paragraph of his detailed and colorful report on "Marblehead to Halifax" in the November 1905 issue of *The Rudder*, Thompson presents a jocular appraisal of the Eastern Yacht Club on the eve of its plunge into the blue water:

> Old enough to be dignified, and progressive enough, under the leadership of young men, to be a vital and respected force in American yachting, the Eastern Yacht Club of Marblehead has the reputation of doing things well. Its regatta committee, under the direction of Henry Howard, works for the good of yachting on broad lines, while yet serving the club, and promoting Marblehead, its home, as a yachting port. In some ways the Eastern Club reminds me of the older Clyde clubs in its sound

Commodore Laurence Minot's *Hope Leslie* shows her heels to photographer Nathaniel Stebbins on July 17, 1903.

attitude toward yachting, and its sane and honest way of doing things. Its Rocking Chair Council is smaller than in most clubs of its size, and men who know yachts are in a majority in its active membership. It has money, and spends it freely for races, giving liberal prizes, and sparing no expense. Its disbursements for a season, through the regatta committee, are about $6,500, which is far more than any other club, outside the New York club, invests in promoting racing.

The club's strongest bid for popularity, with yachting men at large, is in its policy of giving open races. Every year it has held a series of such regattas off Marblehead, to which every yacht in Massachusetts Bay or elsewhere was welcome, whether large or small, new or old, tight or leaky. Anything that could get over the course was timed, and the prize money was big enough to be hustled for.

Henry Howard and Henry Morss had grand plans when they arrived in Halifax on May 29, 1905, to work out the race details with the Royal Nova Scotia Yacht Squadron. The start would be August 21 in order to ring in entries from the New York Yacht Club Cruise to Marblehead that would be just winding up. The 360 miles should be covered in three days. They expected a fleet of twenty, including some fast 30-footers, and several big steam yachts as convoy. The commodore of the Shelburne (Nova Scotia) Yacht Club was on hand, urging a special race to Halifax on the way home.

A hopeful note aboard *Hope Leslie*, 1900.

This summer's was to be the first NYYC Cruise to Marblehead since the 1902 blast, and Stevens, the manager of the *Marblehead Messenger*, swore in an advance circular to "set the old town ablaze to show that we appreciate the coming of this fleet" with an illumination to beat all. His gimmick: everyone who had children should mail him ten or fifteen cents in their names, which he would print in his paper, all capped with a drawing for a five-dollar prize. As a small afterthought, he added: "NOTE—This plan is not to prevent older people from giving larger subscriptions."

Count on the weather not to be counted on.

The week of the NYYC Cruise was miserable from the northeast, with postponements, cancellations, and the inevitable black tempers; by the time the delayed and depleted fleet straggled into Marblehead, there was damp enthusiasm for pushing on to Halifax. Nothing dampened the Stevens pyrotechnics, however, as reported in the *Boston Herald*:

Three years ago a big crowd gathered, but that of last night [August 19] went beyond it, and the police estimates are that it was beyond it. Not an accident occurred on the cars or electrics, nor was a single arrest made. This speaks well for the immense crowd, which gave not the least trouble to the police. There were upward of 300 yachts of all kinds in the harbor this morning. . . . During the night a number of yachts of the New York Yacht Club joined the fleet.

[There was hardly a breath of air for Sunday's start on August 21.] Upon signal from the [NYYC Commodore Frederick G. Bourne's] flagship *Colonia*, all the yachts in the harbor "dressed ship" this morning at "colors." There were about one hundred in all, and they made an extremely pretty picture as they rolled gently on an easterly swell. Thousands of visitors from Salem, Lynn and other nearby towns dotted the rocky shores and occupied every available boat from noon until sundown.

Lieutenant Commander Holcomb, executive officer of the cruiser *Brooklyn*, and other officers of that ship paid a formal visit to Commodore Laurence Minot at the Eastern Yacht Club. Several officers and members of the club were entertained on board the steam yacht *Niagara* by her owner, Howard Gould.

Fifteen boats were on the entry list, but nine (four from the Eastern, three from the New York, and one each from the Larchmont and the Royal Cape Breton yacht clubs) dropped out at the last minute for various reasons that included the final blow of a flat calm, a jammed centerboard, and no competition in the class. Only five schooners and a sloop drifted or

Shorn of her mainmast and even her bowsprit, *Hope Leslie* wound up as a Gloucester dragger in 1904. William D. Hoyt photo.

were towed out to the line off Marblehead Rock. They were Commodore Minot's 66-foot-waterline schooner *Hope Leslie*, Arthur F. Luke's 85-foot 4-inch schooner *Corona*, W.S. Eaton's 45-foot 7-inch schooner *Agatha*, and Thornton K. Lothrop's 29-foot 5-inch sloop *Sauquoit*, all of the Eastern; Frederick F. Brewster's 87-foot schooner *Elmina* of the New York Yacht Club, designed by A. Cary Smith and just launched by Lawley in Boston; and Charles E. Gibbon's 42-foot schooner *Black Hawk*, a Norman L. Skene design also in her first season.

"So spiritless was the start," reported Thompson, "that the photographers who tried to make pictures of it got nothing worth reproducing. The boats barely drifted away from the line, and all the afternoon they remained within sight of the shore they were trying to leave behind."

Race Chairman Henry Morss, who had sent his sloop *Cossack* on ahead, Stephen S. Sleeper of the Regatta Committee,

William B. Revere of the House Committee, and Win Thompson went to Boston and took the steamer *Prince George* to Yarmouth, thence by train to Halifax, where they were met and escorted to their hotel in open barouches, "as important as aldermen on a junket." At the cottage-style house of the Royal Nova Scotia Yacht Squadron on the harbor shore the welcome was royal indeed and crowned in the upper-floor facility thereafter immortalized by one of the Eastern visitors as "The Fighting Top." Here, Thompson observed, "a youthful steward posted at an ice chest supplies the bottled bubbles needed as a wadding to highballs. . . ." He continued: "Before our visit was over the same visitor sketched on a wall, in soft pencil, a rude drawing of the burgees of the Eastern Y.C. and R.N.S.Y.S., with this line under them: 'One Speech, one Sport, one Thirst.' I am told that after the visit the house committee thought this a little strong, and decided to scrape it off the wall; but the thoughtful secretary caused the wood to be cut out, to be preserved . . ."

The Canadians bent over backward for the Marblehead visitors with a crowded week of receptions, smokers, watch meetings, house parties, a boat parade, fleet illuminations, and a ball. They were bound not to be put down by all those Yankee dollars in their harbor, a defensiveness perhaps justified by the remark of one of the American yachtsmen to Thompson: "If these Halifax chaps had the money for boats like ours they would be red hot yachting men. They have the real dogged spirit that means 'get there!'" The Royal Canadian Navy placed its new cruiser *Canada*, the patrol cutter *Petrel*, and the cable ship *Lady Laurier* at the disposal of the squadron, and they presented a grand sight in Halifax Harbor with the visiting steam yachts, Gould's great 272-foot *Niagara*, the *Hiawatha*, *Venetia*, *Felicia* and *Scionda*, all entertaining to beat the band.

On Wednesday morning, August 23, the NYYC schooner *Elmina* hove in out of the fog and "crossed the line [off the clubhouse between Morss's sloop *Cossack* and the RNSYS's cutter *Youla*, both flying large EYC burgees] with all canvas spread in a light breeze," as reported in the *Boston Herald*, "and presented a handsome spectacle as she sailed gracefully up the harbor and rounded to her anchorage, amid the cheers of the yachtsmen on the pier and the salute of Howard Gould's steam yacht *Niagara*."

Three hours later, the winner of the first Halifax Race was followed by Commodore Minot's *Hope Leslie*. *Elmina*'s rival,

Dressed to the nines, and in infinite variety, the New York and Eastern fleets comingle in Marblehead Harbor.

Winner of the first Halifax Race, the New York's *Elmina* displays a nigh- perfect set of her sails in this remarkable glass plate photograph by Marblehead's Willard B. Jackson. The gaff foresail has a loose-footed extension that overlaps the mainmast and sheets independently.

Blue Water Beckons

Corona, didn't finish until midafternoon, followed by *Black Hawk* next morning, and *Sauquoit* not far behind. The schooner *Agatha* had dropped out of the race off Cape Sable and turned back. The winner's notes were lost, but her rough log has survived:

Elmina crossed the starting line at 10:32 A.M. Monday, August 21, in light air from E.S.E. When off Cape Ann about 4 o'clock breeze came, fair and southerly, freshened up about 7 and we ran steadily about 9 knots.

Tuesday, light fog in the morning to clearing at noon. Passed Brazil Rock buoy about 3:25 P.M. Got soundings on German Bank. Set spinnaker about 4 o'clock. Sighted what we supposed to be *Corona* about 4 o'clock about five miles ahead. About 7 fog came in thick, and breeze stronger. Took in spinnaker about 9:30.

Wednesday, took in mainsail 1 o'clock A.M. on account of threatening squall. Picked up Sambro whistle 4:30 o'clock. Had a short squall which cleared the fog for about half an hour. Arrived Halifax about 9:30.

What happened to the Eastern's *Corona*? "She led to the Nova Scotia coast," in Win Thompson's postmortem, "but lost her lead, and the race, by failure to promptly pick up the automatic buoy off Sambro. With a Nova Scotia pilot aboard as *Elmina* had, she probably would have landed the cup."

The prize for gallantry, all agreed, belonged to Thornton Lothrop of the Eastern and his 1904 sloop *Sauquoit*, 29 feet 5 inches on the water, 47 feet 8 inches overall, 10 feet 4 inches beam, 6 feet 9 inches draft, designed by Burgess and Packard. Thompson told the crew's story in *The Rudder*:

The *Sauquoit* was never rated in her first and only racing season as anything but a light weather boat. Mr. Lothrop's yachting friends had chaffed him about her until he thought it time to show them what he could do with her. The first of this season he had caused her lead to be lowered, and other changes made in her keel. When he came out to the line to start for Halifax the jokers saw the point. He was going to show them his faith in the "*Sauerkraut*," as some of them called the boat, and in himself. He had a Nova Scotia pilot and a crew of four amateurs, and was out for a moral victory. He achieved it, at the expense of considerable discomfort, but not more serious damage to the boat than a burst balloon jib. This accident happened Tuesday night off Cape Sable. The sail was got off before it went to pieces entirely.

Through Tuesday night *Sauquoit* proceeded with four reefs in her mainsail. The wind came in heavy puffs of increasing strength from southwest. A confused cross sea sent solid water over her quarter, frequently flooding the cockpit. The scuppers in the cockpit carried the water off very slowly, and the helmsman had his feet in water most of the time. A bucket used for bailing was lost overboard. *Sauquoit* had made a landfall at Seal Rock at 10:15 P.M. Tuesday; at 1:25 A.M. Wednesday she was off Cape Sable. It was at this point the ballooner went and all hands were turned out to reef. *Sauquoit*'s log was fouled by seaweed, and registered short of the true distance sailed, so the boat failed at first to pick up the Sambro whistler. She was some distance off it at 4 P.M. Wednesday and could have finished that night had there been any wind.

Thompson continues with a period description of the post-race activities:

Mr. Gould entertained callers on board *Niagara*, and we looked over the splendors of that noble ship, listened to the orchestration in her music room, and pledged her owner's health, with considerable pleasure. When we left, with *Niagara*'s owner at the head of the gangway, his guests beside him, his officers close at hand, all very shipshape, our gasolene launch gave our sense of dignity a shock by refusing to start, and we drifted slowly astern of *Niagara*, while a square-head boatman in Mr. Gould's big mahogany steam launch presumed to smile a discreet little smile behind his hand.

That evening we all went around on *Petrel* to the Northwest Arm to see the boat parade. . . . The prize winner was a floating chapel, with stained glass windows and all that, a choir singing within, and a handsome angel in a white robe, and bare arms outstretched, outside. A military band played at the house of the rowing club, and thousands of people thronged the house and shore. . . . From the Arm we went to a great smoker given to a convention of doctors then being held in Halifax. The chief fixture was a demonstration of "physical culture," by two accomplished young gentlemen of the fisticuffs school.

[Friday night featured a second fleet illumination and a ball at the RNSYS clubhouse.] The rowboats were taken out of the boathouse, life-rings, ensigns and burgees were put up, and the floor was waxed. The windows were removed, a canvas pavilion was built outside for a military band, and on the lawn a markee tent was pitched for the caterer. By eight o'clock the ladies began to arrive, and when the first waltz struck up one of the best looking companies of young women that it has been my good fortune to see were ready for the dance. . . . It was late when the last dance had been played, the last carriage rattled out of the drive, and the old guard adjourned for a nightcap to the Fighting Top.

A mixed fleet of fourteen American and Canadian boats was lined up for the Prince of Wales Cup Race on Saturday, August

26, over a thirty-mile course from the clubhouse. Win Thompson was on Arthur Luke's EYC schooner *Corona*, no wind, whistling notwithstanding. George L. Batchelder of the Eastern broke out his ukulele for a chorus of "In the Shade of the Old Apple Tree." All hands joined in, and "scarcely was the song finished than a fine breeze began to darken the water, from the southeast. It came up so suddenly that it could be properly attributed to the music, and Batchelder swelled with a proper degree of professional pride."

All the while the crew was sweating at the windlass; *Corona*'s anchor seemed chained to the bottom. The start was 15 minutes away. The hook broke the surface with an ancient submarine telegraph cable. It took them 11 minutes to pass a sling under the cable, drop a slip rope over a fluke, catch the shank ring with a fishhook, slack the anchor clear, let the cable go, and trim the jib sheets. The big schooner filled away four minutes before the gun.

Once they got clear of the crowd at the start, it was head-to-head between *Corona* and *Elmina*, the Eastern and the New York, as the two schooners vied on every point in a freshening breeze with everything they had. But *Elmina* had the edge, as she had on the race to Halifax, for she was as smart a footer as her rival and tighter in the wind with her new sails. Win Thompson was exultant:

For the close reach home, No. 1 jib topsails were put on, and main topmast staysails, and the handsome pair came bowling up the harbor at a beautiful clip, just down to their bearings and rolling off the pure white foam from their lee bows in billowing waves with hearts of green.

As the winner went over the line the Imperial Garrison band, on the clubhouse pier, played "See the Conquering Hero Comes." Handkerchiefs were waved by most of the pretty girls in Halifax, assembled at the clubhouse; whistles were blown, people cheered, and, the strain of excitement over, the yachtsmen at the clubhouse made a break as one man for the Fighting Top. *Corona* was beaten four minutes eight seconds actual, and two minutes three seconds corrected time, but we also got guns, cheers and a tune from the band.

That night, the week of the first ocean yacht race from Marblehead to Halifax was topped off with a "hodge-podge" given by the squadron for the visiting yachtsmen on the grounds of the government quarantine station on Lawlor's Island. This peculiarly Bluenosed rite was preceded by a free-for-all baseball game fueled at third base by a bowl of Jamaica rum punch, the mere warm-up for the hodge-podge, which detonated an evening of speeches, toasts, songs around the bonfire, band music, orchestral offerings, comic routines, and Royal Garrison Corporal McNair's unparalleled imitation of a trombone solo.

Sunday, after more speeches and farewells and "a bathtub with cracked ice and what goes with it," the Americans set sail from Halifax for home on the heels of a gathering northeaster.

"When I told you several years ago that ocean sailing was the coming yachting," Editor Thomas Fleming Day berated the readers of *The Rudder*, "many laughed, some sneered, and few, very few believed. . . . The prevailing idea was that yachtsmen would not take part in them out of fear, want of skill and knowledge of ocean sailing."

Tom Day now had the two New York-to-Marblehead races of 1904 and the Marblehead-to-Halifax event in 1905 to his credit, two of them sponsored by the Eastern Yacht Club, and credit Henry Morss among his very few believers. The sneakered ones were capable of overcoming their fears, after all. The time had come to look the sea in the eye, all the way to a spot of coral called Bermuda.

In May of 1906, the first ocean race to Britain's little gem was sailed from New York over a 660-mile course for a cup donated by Sir Thomas Lipton and sponsored by the Brooklyn Yacht Club. The winner was Commodore Frank Maier's 38-foot yawl *Tamerlane*, skippered by Day himself, beating out the 28-foot sloop *Gauntlet* and the yawl *Lila*, which withdrew. Henry Morss was commodore of the Corinthian Yacht Club in 1906 and had a new boat, the schooner *Dervish*, which apparently was not ready for such an early-season workout.

Morss was no doubt active in organizing the donnybrook that was sailed from New London to Marblehead under the Eastern's aegis (it was his first year actually on the Regatta Committee) a few weeks later on July 1 and 2 in a northeast gale.

Three of the nine starters reached Marblehead. Arthur Luke's schooner *Corona* finished at dawn on July 2 and won the first-place $500 cup offered by Vice Commodore F. Lewis Clark. The schooners *Constellation*, Frank Skinner, and Clark's *Emerald* finished five and six hours later.

In the roaring seas off Cape Cod, Harold S. Vanderbilt, in his 33-foot Nat Herreshoff cutter *Trivia*, sought shelter at Block Island, then tried to continue but eventually telegraphed the committee that he had to withdraw to Newport. (*Trivia* enjoys a permanent calm now in the Herreshoff Museum at Bristol.) F.F. Brewster's *Elmina* ran into a fearful sea and wind in Pollock Rip and retired with a rip in her mainsail and one of her jibs dragging in the water. W.E. Iselin's former Cup defender *Vigilant*, rigged as a yawl, had to turn back and sail under jib alone from the Pollock Rip Lightship, her bow frames broken by the seas.

All three finishers had to put into port or heave-to until the brunt of the storm had passed—*Constellation* and *Emerald* at Hyannis, and *Corona* off Wellfleet. The schooners *Dervish*, H.A. Morss, *Taormina*, W.S. Eaton, made for Vineyard Haven and stayed there. At the height of it, *Emerald* was forced to bear off suddenly with all sails sheeted in to avoid a tugboat and tow of barges; her rigging was severely strained and had to be retuned and reset before she could continue.

All this could not have been in greater contrast to the Annual Cruise that departed east five days later and ran into such a doldrum of fog and flat in Ipswich Bay that the entire fleet had to be towed by its own accompanying steamers and the tugs *Portland* and *Mercury* clear to Portland, then on to Camden, Dark Harbor, and Gilkey's Harbor, where in desperation all went ashore for a dance while waiting for it to clear. It did, finally, in time for a couple of twenty-six-mile races approaching Mount Desert and a windup banquet at the Kebo Valley Club near Bar Harbor.

The second Bermuda Race, again sponsored mainly by the Brooklyn Yacht Club, was sailed on June 4, 1907, and won by Commodore Morss in his schooner *Dervish* for the glory of the Corinthian and the Eastern, Editor Day demurring:

> I am jubilant over Commodore Morss winning the Maier Cup not only because he and his crew deserve the victory, but because he hails from Boston. When I started these races it was expected that many New York yachtsmen would oppose and discourage them, but I had better hopes of Boston. I was foolish enough to think that the New England boys were the same old breed that years ago put the flag in every port of the world, and that sea-sailing would arouse the spirit of their ancestors, and appeal to their pluck and enterprise. I was disappointed: these men, whom I admired and trusted, with a few exceptions failed me. They either openly opposed the project or else what was worse, froze it with indifference. The Boston papers published interviews in which yachtsmen either sneered at or denounced the idea of sailing long distances; such races were foolhardy, nonsensical and proved nothing. . . . But there were a few who

stood by me from the start and fought my battle. Among these was Commodore Morss, who came forward and gave me help when I needed it badly. His entering this last race, which he was the first to enter, did much to encourage others to come in, and much of the success is due to his warm support. I think the Boston men who opposed this racing are today ashamed of their conduct—they certainly did not live up to the spirit of old New England; but let bygones be bygones, and that they may retrieve their honor and prestige in the future under the lead of the gallant owner of *Dervish* is my heartiest wish.

The scolding editor's wish was granted. The 1908 Bermuda Race, the third, would start from Marblehead, and Henry Morss went to work on it the previous fall. It was gunned off Marblehead on June 3, 1908, under the Corinthian's sponsorship, three days before *The Rudder*'s powerboat spree to Bermuda from New York, and was dominated by the chastised Bostonians. The overall winner was Elmer J. Bliss, flying the Eastern's colors, who took Class C in his 43-foot-waterline schooner *Venona* in 99 hours, 31 minutes. The Corinthian commodore's larger *Dervish* made it two-in-a-row in Class B by almost 24 hours, covering the 675 miles in 108 hours, 30 minutes.

Dervish's owner told the story to the *Queensboro, N.Y., Dispatch*:

> On the first night out, we ran into a southwest wind of considerable violence. The seas were fully twenty-five feet high. During the night we were compelled to take in the topsails. On Thursday the wind changed to the west some time before daylight, and Saturday had veered to the east. This east wind was fairly light at first, but it increased toward the middle of the day, and we were compelled to take in sail. We double-reefed the mainsail and later stowed it. All Saturday night and Sunday the wind blew a regular gale and the water was very rough.

In spite of losing her foretopmast the first night, *Venona* thrives on rough weather, Elmer Bliss valiantly declared, and always sails best when the winds are fresh.

Spoken like a New England boy of the old breed.

Three years out of Harvard and the owner of the new Her-

Henry Morss's great Bermuda winner *Dervish* hangs out the laundry on a sultry day in 1906. Jackson photo.

Blue Water Beckons

reshoff schooner *Vagrant,* 76 feet overall, Harold Vanderbilt joined the Eastern in May 1910 within a couple of weeks of Demarest Lloyd of Washington and Marblehead, who had the 75-foot schooner *Shyessa.* They were just in time to sail the only two schooners in the Bermuda Race that summer. In spite of the presence aboard of John Alden, future Bermuda great, *Shyessa* lost by a small margin.

Interest was on the wane, however, and the most fiercely fought of ocean races was not resumed until 1923, and then with a renewed ferocity indeed.

Chapter 6　　**The Sonders**　　*1902–1914*

In the course of a brilliant but ephemeral strategy to advance international amity through gentlemanly sailboat racing, the Eastern Yacht Club was drawn into the intrigues of the Great Powers that preceded World War I. How this came to pass is most revealingly told in the words of the *agent provocateur* of it all, Regatta Committee Chairman Henry Howard.

Howard had been on the committee since 1898, when he was thirty and already an industrial chemical engineer and entrepreneur both imaginative and bold. In 1902 he succeeded Henry H. Buck as chairman. Forty-six years later, in *Charting My Life*, he recalled his first official actions:

At that time racing in the Eastern Yacht Club had fallen to a very low ebb—partly as a result, I believe, of a mistaken policy on the part of the retiring Chairman in that he tried to avoid publicity for the club and repelled newspaper reporters to such an extent that they finally became unwilling to give an adequate space to the Eastern Yacht Club Races. This policy I immediately reversed, and my first act was to call upon the yachting editors of all the newspapers in Boston, and tell them that the policy had been reversed and ask them for their assistance and cooperation. This was enthusiastically given as I knew it would be.

My next step was to look around for some important race, or match, or series of races, in which the Eastern Yacht Club could take a leading part and which would bring it very much into the public eye. At that time, I think it was in 1902, Prince Henry of Prussia visited the United States ostensibly to attend the launching of his brother's yacht, the *Meteor*, but in my opinion the real reason was to try and use the occasion for bringing about a more friendly feeling between Germany and the United States.

Chairman Howard was correct. Prince Henry was sent over by his brother William, who was more than a keen yachtsman;

he was the Kaiser, and it was his intention to soothe America's sense of transatlantic detachment while pursuing the naval and colonial ambitions that were then just ruffling the waters of relations between his Fatherland and his cousinly neighbor across the Channel. "Our future is on the water," the Emperor told the Reichstag.

One of the newspapermen in line for cultivation by Howard was Winfield Thompson, the yachting editor of the *Boston Globe*, who wrote with striking prescience in *The Rudder* only four years later of the Kaiser's ambition "to make his young men sailors, and his nation a maritime people. Whatever the fate of this ambition—whether it will end, after centuries, as did the same dream of Peter the Great—none of us mortals, who may not read the book of fate, may say."

Kaiser Wilhelm's steel schooner *Meteor* was christened by President Theodore Roosevelt's young daughter Alice in February 1902. The next month Henry Howard ascended to the chairmanship of the Eastern's Regatta Committee.

It seemed to me that here was a chance ready for someone to seize and I could see no reason why the Eastern Yacht Club should not be the one to seize it. . . . The German Emperor, I believed, would look with much favor on any reasonable and dignified scheme which would provide for sending German gentlemen to mix with leading Americans in a natural way. An international yacht race between Germany and the United States appeared to me to provide a splendid means of carrying out this scheme.

At that time there was a good deal of dissatisfaction in the United States regarding various things that had happened in connection with America's Cup races. It was a sport limited to the very, very rich and the cost went into hundreds of thousands of dollars. It therefore seemed to me that an international race arranged with Germany, in which small boats should be used and in which helmsmen and crew on both sides should all be amateurs, would appeal to the public in both Germany and the United States and would also be very good for the yachting reputation of the Eastern Yacht Club.

And so the Chairman wrote Ambassador von Holleben in Washington, proposing that he convey to the Kaiser the Eastern's desire to offer a perpetual challenge cup for exclusive competition between Germany and the United States, and that he suggest to His Majesty that he appoint a committee for the purpose of arranging same.

The Council thought the plan was a little fantastic, in that I was using the German Emperor to boost racing in the Eastern Yacht Club! But they couldn't see that any harm would come of it, so our Commodore, A.S. Bigelow, signed the letter for the club, and asked his friend, John D. Long, then Secretary of the Navy, to deliver it in person to the ambassador.

The ambassador turned the proposition over to the German naval attaché, Commander Erwin Schaeffer, who turned it over to the Kaiserlicher (Imperial) Yacht Club at Kiel. Almost a year later, on February 24, 1903, von Holleben replied that the Kaiser was unable to accept the proposal because of two serious difficulties: "One of them was the fact that the Imperial Yacht Club and the other German yacht clubs could not yet afford enough yachts qualified for the purpose, and the other was the diversity of the American and German yacht measurement rules."

Howard responded on March 19 that the Universal Rule was then in the process of adoption, but that a race between boats of modest size the following year would make a good match while foreign designers were still on an even footing with American. After some further unproductive exchanges, Captain H.G. Hebbinghaus, the new German naval attaché, wrote Howard on December 14, 1904: "As His Majesty the Emperor intends to give an international cup to be sailed for across the Atlantic from Sandy Hook to the Lizard, and as further scarcely an individual or syndicate in my country can spend as much money on a pleasure yacht as would be required by the amiable proposition of the Eastern Yacht Club, I am very sorry to state that I see no hope to realize the kind and friendly plans of your club."

But Howard had already enlisted his friend from Hamilton, George von Lengerke Meyer, the ambassador to Italy, who cor-

nered the Kaiser at a court ball in Berlin. His Majesty was intrigued—if the races came as an aftermath of his big one.

The Kaiser's Cup race was set for May 1905, and the resourceful Regatta Committee chairman barged the line. The New York Yacht Club was in charge, and Captain Hebbinghaus, representing the Kaiser, invited Howard aboard the committee boat. During the two days they were stuck in fog, the German attaché got such an earful that he promised his guest that if he would travel to Kiel, he would be introduced to the officers of the Kaiserlicher Yacht Club, which was in fact no less than an arm of the German Imperial Navy.

Perfect. Howard had recently been made vice president of the Merrimac Chemical Company and had scheduled a trip to Europe the next month to promote sales of its arsenate of lead insecticide. He got a letter from the Council to the German club authorizing him to represent the Eastern. Ambassador Meyer, meanwhile, had been transferred to Russia. They met in St. Petersburg, where Meyer asked Howard to let him know promptly the results of his Kiel talks on September 7, since he would be lunching with the Kaiser in Berlin in a month.

Admiral von Arnim, President of the Kaiserlicher Yacht Club, greeted me cordially and introduced me to the other officials, after which he offered me his arm and we led the way to the dining room of the yacht club. As we walked along he said, "Mr. Howard, we admire your perseverance in this matter, but the difficulties seem to us too great to be overcome." However extraordinary as it may seem, before the evening was over I had converted them all to my plan with the result that then and there they appointed "The German-American Race Committee of the Kaiserlicher Yacht Club," consisting of Vice Admiral Barandon, Chairman, Rear Admiral Sarnow (also secretary of the club) and Baurat (naval constructor) Mueller. The proposition submitted to the dinner meeting I had drawn up in my room at the hotel as follows:
MAIN OBJECTS TO BE ATTAINED.
1st. To promote good feeling between the German and American people.
2nd. To increase public interest in yacht racing in Germany and America by bringing into it the spirit of international competition.
3rd. To enable yachtsmen of moderate means to participate by limiting the racing to small and inexpensive boats.
SUGGESTIONS AS TO REGULATIONS, ETC.
1st. Form as soon as possible a joint committee consisting of three members from the Kaiserlicher Yacht Club and three members from the Eastern Yacht Club, this to be a permanent

committee who will settle all questions which may arise and have charge of all contests.

2nd. A perpetual challenge cup to be given for a competition only by German and American yachts.

3rd. Yachts must be designed and built complete in every respect in their respective countries.

4th. Yachts must be owned, manned and sailed by native-born citizens of the country they represent.

5th. The challenging club may at its option send over one, two or three boats and the challenged club must defend with a number of boats not exceeding the number specified by the challenging club.

6th. Materials from which the boats are built should be limited to iron, steel, lead and wood for hull and spars (except that small fittings, etc., of bronze would be allowed).

7th. Size about 27-33 ft. rating or about 30 ft. (9 meters) water line length.

8th. *Measurement and classification to be that of the challenging club.*

9th. Challenge must be received before December 1 of the year preceding the race.

10th. Races to be commenced between September 1 and October 1.

11th. Race to consist of three out of five.

Howard's proposed rule 8 was his tour de force: "In the first match at Marblehead we would use the German system. This was so liberal and sportsmanlike that they simply could not refuse it." He forthwith notified Ambassador Meyer, who was as good as his word, replying on September 17 from Bad Homburg:

My dear Howard: I lunched with the Emperor yesterday and had a long talk with him, which gave me the opportunity to bring up your German-American Race and to explain everything in detail. This time he was much interested in it. He did not commit himself, but if the Admiral is able to assure him that there are German yachtsmen willing and able to go into it seriously, it would not surprise me that the matter became a *fait accompli.*

And so it did on October 14 when the Kaiser notified his Marine Cabinet that he approved the matches in principle. Five days later, Admiral Barandon counterproposed to Howard that it would be desirable for the Eastern Yacht Club to lodge the challenge; that the races be sailed in small boats easily transported, preferably the German Sonder, or special, class; and that helmsmen only need be members of recognized yacht clubs, namely, amateurs.

Howard returned from Europe in triumph and on November 13, 1905, the EYC Council met.

On motion of Mr. Jackson duly seconded, it was voted that the Commodore be authorized to appoint a German-American Race Committee to confer with the Committee of the Kaiserlicher Yacht Club appointed to arrange the terms for the proposed event.

In accordance with this vote, Messrs. Henry Howard, Charles F. Adams 2nd, and Louis M. Clark were appointed a Committee by the Commodore to serve jointly with the three members appointed by the Kaiserlicher Yacht Club as a German-American Race Committee.

At this juncture, Howard received a notice from the New York Yacht Club, of which he was a member, of a meeting four days hence "at which the announcement of a very important cup will be made."

I decided it must be a cup from some foreign ruler, probably from King Edward, to try and head off our German-American race, and if this announcement came first the Emperor would never be willing to follow along as an imitator. There was no time to communicate with Berlin and I felt that the German Embassy in Washington would probably not be able to act in time, so on my own responsibility, but with the approval of the Honorable Charles Francis Adams, a member of my committee, I immediately sent out through the Associated Press a statement to be released on Sunday, that His Majesty, the German Emperor, had given his approval and that the first race would be held at Marblehead in August 1906, and that in 1907 the Emperor would give a prize for a return match at Kiel. Great publicity was given to this all over the United States, and the Sunday newspaper carried headlines on the first page even as far away as San Francisco and New Orleans.

When it was too late to embarrass the German Embassy through having advance knowledge of this affair, I wrote my friend, Captain (in 1930 Vice Admiral) Hebbinghaus, naval attache, telling him my reasons. On Tuesday morning a small inconspicuous paragraph appeared in the papers, stating that at the meeting of the New York Yacht Club, held the evening before, the club accepted a cup presented by King Edward VII to be called the King's Cup, which would be raced for off Newport annually and awarded to the winner in a mixed class of sloops and schooners. The announcement fell perfectly flat and although it is still raced for, it has never had the importance of the Astor Cups.

John Parkinson put it somewhat differently in his history of the New York Yacht Club:

Certainly, this King's Cup has become one of the greatest trophies of American yachting, won by numerous famous yachts whose names will never be forgotten as long as men compete for sport in sailboats. In 1905, England's Royal Navy was still considered to rule the oceans of the world, and it was an honor for her King to present such a cup to the New York Yacht Club. . . . A special meeting of the New York Yacht Club was held on November 27, 1905, to discuss the acceptance of the King's Cup. The Minutes record that the Earl of Crawford, who raced his square-rigged *Valhalla* across the Atlantic that year, and who must have had the ear of King Edward, was the man who wrote the initial confidential letter concerning the offer of the King's Cup.

Who had the last word? "Several years later," wrote Howard, "an official of the New York Yacht Club told me it [the cup offer] had been sent by King Edward at the instigation of the British Foreign Office to try to head off the German-American races. In 1907, during the Kiel Races, I told this story to H.R.H. Prince Henry of Prussia, who said he had heard about it at the time and could tell me confidentially that the Emperor was much pleased at my action."

Countering the Eastern's offer of a perpetual challenge cup, the Kaiser preferred his own when the race was sailed in Germany and suggested that President Theodore Roosevelt do likewise when America was the host. Fleet Captain I. Tucker Burr approached TR, who balked, probably foreseeing the expense of an endless shelf of presidential trophies, but he agreed to "stand sponsor" (a novel notion in yachting circles) for a Roosevelt Cup offered by the Eastern Yacht Club.

The Emperor's desire to be challenged, notwithstanding the first race would be at Marblehead, elicited the formal hurling of the Eastern's gauntlet at the Kaiserlicher Yacht Club on February 16, 1906, which was promptly acknowledged.

Chairman Howard's insistence that crews must be "native-born citizens of the country in which the yacht was built" was questioned by some of his countrymen, and although his logic may not strike a later day and age as impeccable, it prevailed. ". . . Think how much it would take away from the interest of the contest if naturalized Germans were allowed to take part in the race against Germany. The foreigners would then say that we were unable to produce sufficiently good sailors in this country to represent us in any international contest and could point with justice to the case of the America's Cup races [where] Charles Barr, a Scotchman born and bred, has defended . . . for America in two or three races."

The decision of the Germans to defend in the Sonderklasse they had originated "caused almost as much excitement," in the whimsical words of Francis Herreshoff, "as a new girl in a mining camp." American yachtsmen and designers were intrigued by a measurement formula whose ingredients were almost infinitely variable. The class had originated in 1900 out of a challenge between England and Germany for a race to be sailed in relatively inexpensive and versatile boats that could be handled by a maximum crew of three. The matches had been the feature of the annual Kiel Week ever since. Several of the European nations had entered, including at one time or another Great Britain, France, Holland, Belgium, Denmark, and Sweden. Germany upheld the pride of its Kaiser every year but 1902, when an American entry, *Uncle Sam*, designed by B.B. Crowninshield, carried away his cup.

The Sonder rules were issued in March 1906. The formula: length plus breadth plus draft may not exceed 32 feet. (This produced a waterline of about 20.) Displacement at least 4,035

Program for first Sonder meet at Marblehead, 1906.

The Sonders

pounds; sail area not more than 550 square feet, or 51 square meters. Hull of cedar, mahogany, or heavier wood, copper-fastened. Double planking not allowed. Deck of any wood. Deck and planking not less than ⅝ inch thick. No diagonal or rib-band-carvel planking, no composite building and no center-boards or leeboards. Cockpit not to exceed eight feet in length. Metal plate for a fin and metals for interior trussing and braces allowed. Rig optional. No hollow or bamboo spars. Yachts to carry their entire outfit of spars and canvas on board during each race.

All appropriate American yacht clubs were invited to participate in the trials, which drew seven entries from the Eastern, namely, Francis Skinner's *Sumatra* and H.L. Bowden's *Hayseed III*, both designed by Crowninshield; C.H.W. Foster's *Caramba* and Charles B. Curtis, Jr.'s *Ellen*, both by Edwin A. (Coot) Boardman, a well-known Boston designer of light-displacement sloops and scows; Herbert M. Sears's *Skiddoo* by N.G. Herreshoff; F.G. Macomber's *Windrim Kid* by Small Brothers; and F. Lewis Clark's *Spokane* by Clinton H. Crane. Three more were from the Boston: Dr. Morton Prince's *Cod* by Crowninshield; E.W. Hodgson and R.L. Pond's *Alecto* by Hodgson; and Charles D. Lanning's *Lorelei* by Frank T. Wood. There were two from the Corinthian, Lawrence F. Percival's *Sally VIII* by Burgess and Packard and F.G. Macomber, Jr.'s *Chewink VI* by Herreshoff; one from the Hingham, George W. Wightman's *Bonidrei* by Crowninshield; one from the Quincy, Charles Francis Adams 2d's *Auk* by Boardman; one from the Manchester, Dr. J. Lewis Bremer's *Manchester II* by Boardman; one from the Southern of New Orleans, S.F. Heaslip et al.'s *New Orleans* by Small Brothers.

The seventeenth candidate was from New York, not the New York Yacht Club, which had been "headed off" by the Chairman, but the American of Rye, whose commodore, Trenor L. Park, engaged William Gardner of schooner *Atlantic* fame to design *Vim* for him on the condition that he serve no other masters on this one. The commodore's doctor, however, was *his* master and forbade the old gentleman to set foot in her, so *Vim* was raced by Clifford Bucknam, who had with him two pros for crew, the only ringers in the lot.

Crowninshield's success with *Uncle Sam* at Kiel brought him four commissions for moderate hulls. Another four went to Boardman, who had a reputation for fast scows. Burgess lined off a skimmer, and Nat Herreshoff produced two of the narrowest and shoalest. All were for Boston-area owners.

"Many if not most of the drawings for the Crowninshield Sonders," notes Gloucester designer Philip C. Bolger, "bear the initials J.G.A. for John G. Alden in the 'drawn by' space of the title block. I wouldn't say they averaged any less extreme than Boardman's except that the latter all had gaff cat rigs which were hurriedly changed to sloop after quick trials. The notable thing about the Herreshoff boats is that they were closer to the German designs than any of the other U.S. boats with the arguable exception of *Vim*."

One might speculate how much room there was left for competition within a rule so roomy as to admit boats that ranged in overall length from 31 feet 5 inches to 40 feet, from 19 feet 3 inches on the water to 22 feet, from 5 feet 6 inches of breadth to 7 feet 10 inches, 4 feet 5 inches to 5 feet 6 inches of draft, and from 2,100 to 2,400 pounds of lead. Most were planked in Spanish cedar on light oak frames ¾ inch by ¾ inch on six-inch centers, but one was described by Boardman as having a mahogany skin "highly polished by trained piano polishers."

The local Sonders were informally raced as they were launched in the spring and early summer of 1906. The airs during the trials were unusually light and fickle, even for August. Eight were sailed between August 13 and 17, and the conditions were frustrating for the seventeen entries and the committee, since boats that were clearly not strong contenders would be advanced by flukes, while others that had shown their mettle in a breeze had little chance to shine.

So the heat was on the committee, which sweated and narrowed the field to three scows, *Auk, Bonidrei* and *Caramba*, and three more conventional designs, *Spokane, Sumatra*, and *Vim*. They sailed three finals on August 18 in a light-to-moderate wind on a smooth sea. Close, but the mathematics selected *Auk, Caramba* and *Vim*. The Germans arrived. The official measurements:

AMERICAN

	Overall	Waterline	Breadth	Draft	Rating	Weight
Auk	37.77	19.87	6.90	5.12	31.89	4037
Caramba	37.00	19.25	7.18	5.50	31.93	4220
Vim	35.55	19.85	6.68	5.00	31.53	4485

GERMAN

	Overall	Waterline	Breadth	Draft	Rating	Weight
Gluckauf IV	32.41	20.51	6.00	4.90	31.41	4185
Tilly VI	32.80	21.10	5.94	4.55	31.59	4095
Wannsee	32.35	20.35	5.95	4.95	31.28	4290

The Sonders

The races were scheduled for September 3 through 10. Still to be settled was the course to follow. Again, the diplomacy of Chairman Henry Howard:

There were many pessimists around the Eastern Yacht Club who took great pleasure in telling me that the trouble experienced by the New York Yacht Club's America's Cup Committee would be as nothing compared with the arrogant attitude we were sure to encounter in the German officials. I gave the matter very careful consideration and with the approval of my colleague, Charles Francis Adams, waited until the arrival of Captain Hebbinghaus, the official representative of the Kaiserlicher Yacht Club, when I immediately took him out near Halfway Rock in Massachusetts Bay and said, "Here is Massachusetts Bay. We want you to select the course for the match and we also want you to do us the honor of serving as Chairman of our Joint Committee and to have in your hands the decision of postponing or calling a race off because of weather or any other conditions. We feel that any advantage this may give you will not offset the advantage we naturally have by sailing the match in our home waters."

This had the result I anticipated. It made it absolutely necessary for the German representative to lean over backwards to look after our interests because with the enormous amount of publicity these races were receiving throughout the world the German reputation for sportsmanship would have been seriously injured if they had not behaved properly.

Although he did not set hand to tiller during the international event he organized, Henry Howard emerged its top helmsman by barely steering clear, again, of another comic-opera waterspout. He had hardly intended to get pulled into the maneuvering behind the German throne that extended to the very North Shore of which the Eastern Yacht Club was a social magnet—the North Shore of the foreign embassies, most of which, including the Kaiser's, were wont to take up summer residence there in flight from the heat of Washington, and to keep an eye on each other.

The Affair Speck von Sternberg, as recounted by the Chairman, might have been composed by Sigmund Romberg:

It will be remembered that our first letter was handed by Secretary of the Navy Long of Massachusetts to Baron von Holleben, the German ambassador, in Washington. The ambassador evidently thought the matter of little importance and referred it to his naval attache, Commander Schaeffer. . . . Later, when

all arrangements had been completed and the races were an assured success, Baron von Holleben was replaced by Baron [Hermann] Speck von Sternberg, who was much disturbed to find that he would have nothing official to do with the arrangements but that they were still in the hands of his naval attache. He thereupon went out of his way to try to lessen the importance of this match. He was spending the summer at Beverly and took pains to spread rumors that the visiting German yachtsmen were men of doubtful social position and that it would not be necessary for the summer residents of the North Shore to show them any special courtesies.

We realized the ambassador's feelings but decided to treat him with the utmost cordiality and hospitality. Therefore, almost immediately after his arrival in Beverly, John Lawrence, then Fleet Captain of the Eastern Yacht Club, and I, Chairman of the German-American Race Committee, made quite a long trip from the Eastern Yacht Club to Beverly, and called on him about 5 P.M. After we sent in our cards there was a considerable wait and we were able to overhear his conversation with his butler, in which he informed the butler that he could not be bothered with seeing us and instructed him to tell us that he was not at home.

Naturally, Lawrence and I were furious as we had put ourselves to great trouble and inconvenience by the call, it having necessitated leaving Boston early and making the trip of twelve or fifteen miles before we got back to Marblehead. The result of this deliberate affront was that Lawrence passed the word along to his influential friends and relatives, who lived on the North Shore, to have nothing to do with Baron Speck von Sternberg, and as a consequence he was practically ostracized during the entire season.

The *Tilly VI*, although entered in the name of John T. Weitzman, was in reality jointly owned by Prince Henry of Prussia and Mr. Richard T. Krogmann of Hamburg. Mr. Weitzman was a close personal friend of Prince Eitel Fritz, and his crew, Baron von Riedesel and Lieutenant von Bories, were officers in the First Guard Regiment at Potsdam—the most aristocratic regiment in all Germany—and acted as the personal guard of the Emperor. These two young officers had been given leave of absence by special order of the Emperor.

When von Sternberg's disparaging remarks reached their ears you can readily imagine the result! With all this feeling in the background there appeared one night in the *Boston Evening Transcript* a paragraph, dated Washington, which stated that official Washington was very much disturbed at the attempt which had been made by the Eastern Yacht Club to get German warships to come to Marblehead, and that the races were a most unwelcome incident, which fortunately promised to be of small importance.

When this came to the attention of Captain Hebbinghaus he

was furious, saying that unquestionably Ambassador von Sternberg would clip it from the newspaper and send it in the next official packet to the Emperor as bearing out the previous unfavorable reports he had given regarding the whole scheme of the races, and that this would kill any chance of a return match in Kiel because with such conditions existing in Washington the Emperor would never be willing to offer a cup for a return match. The paragraph was a mystery to me because the *Boston Evening Transcript* had been extremely helpful in all our preliminary arrangements, and George Mandell, the owner of the paper, was an old member of the Eastern Yacht Club and a good personal friend of mine.

The first thing next morning I went to the office of the *Transcript*, saw Mandell, and asked him the history of the paragraph. He said, "What paragraph?" and knew nothing about it, saying he had never seen it, that it undoubtedly came from Washington and that we were in what they call the "silly season" when real news is very difficult to obtain. He said, "As a matter of fact our Washington correspondent, Mr. Williams, is here in Boston and I will go out and see if he can give any explanation." In a few minutes he returned and said, "Williams could not have written the article in Washington because he is here and as a matter of fact spent yesterday morning with Ambassador von Sternberg in Beverly."

This remark, of course, "spilled the beans" and it became clear that the paragraph had been inspired by von Sternberg with the direct object of having something which he could send to the Emperor to back up his previous unfavorable report. I persuaded Mandell to write an editorial, highly commending the races, and so far as possible offsetting the unfortunate paragraph. This was done, but Captain Hebbinghaus did not feel that it was sufficient because it did not specifically disprove the statements made in the paragraph.

I thereupon got hold of Charles Francis Adams, a member of my Committee, and got him to write a personal letter to President Theodore Roosevelt, whom he knew very well [Adams was treasurer of Harvard College among his other responsibilities], enclosing a clipping of the paragraph, asking if in reality this represented the feeling of "official Washington," and if not, if he, the President, would be kind enough to write a letter which we would be at liberty to show to the German Naval Attache, Captain Hebbinghaus.

We got the letter off by the mail that same evening and three days later received a splendid letter written in Roosevelt's characteristic forceful vein stating that the paragraph was absurd, that official Washington had not discussed the matter, that he himself was in hearty sympathy with the races and believed they would accomplish a great deal of good in the promotion of better feeling between the two peoples. The letter was in fact everything that we could have desired.

I received it from Adams late in the afternoon and immediately hunted up Hebbinghaus in his room where I found him in his underclothes dressing for dinner. As soon as he had read it he danced a regular jig around the room, put back his day clothes and said he was going at once to Washington, as he must get the letter in the same packet in which the unfavorable report was being sent by von Sternberg. As a matter of fact, Hebbinghaus, through underground channels in the German Chancellory, had learned that his worst fears were realized and the paragraph had actually been clipped out and was enclosed in a letter from the German ambassador to the Emperor. . . .

Captain Hebbinghaus reached Washington in time [the Kaiser had a standing rule that his naval and military attachés around the world were to report to him directly and not through the embassies or the Foreign Office], with the result that two weeks later we received a cable from Germany announcing that the Kaiserlicher Yacht Club invited the American yachts to a return match in Kiel in 1907, and that the Emperor would give the principal prize and present it in person to the winner.

What the Chairman did not know, it seems, was that the Kaiser had assigned Speck von Sternberg to Washington precisely because he was such a good friend of the President from the old days.

After all the preliminary intrigue, the races were almost anticlimactic. The German and American Sonders were decidedly different. Designed for the far more boisterous winds and seas of Kiel, the visitors were much shorter overall, somewhat so on the waterline, had less beam and draft, were lighter yet more heavily sparred and rigged. Their hardware was cruder, though they were fitted with English-type roller reefing, and their sails proved to have been cut too flat.

The first race was sailed off Marblehead on September 3 over a fifteen-mile triangular course in a westerly that rose to a squally 30 miles an hour at the finish. The U.S. revenue cutters *Dexter* and *Gresham* kept the course clear. *Auk* won, thanks to Charlie Adams, "whose skill in taking a boat to windward," as Win Thompson wrote, "would make a very ordinary performer appear fast." The Germans were outclassed from the start. The American boats were hauled for smoothing (the pounding had squeezed the putty from the seams of the overhanging bows of the scows *Auk* and *Caramba*).

More than 150 yachts followed the second race on September 5 over a windward course in a light to moderate southerly, three miles out and back, twice around. *Vim* won, *Wannsee* (from the Wannsee Yacht Club) was second, and *Caramba* nudged out *Auk*. *Vim* took the third on the sixth, a short triangle 2½ miles to a side in a whole-sail breeze, when *Auk*, overhauling her on the last leg, tried to luff across her stern and struck her boom, turning her around and causing her to jibe. Adams withdrew on the spot and sailed high of the finish to give *Vim* clear air, drawing praise for his sportsmanship.

The fourth race on September 8, three miles out and back twice in a moderate southeasterly, went to *Wannsee* after *Vim*, unable to luff without fouling the mark at the start, was struck by *Caramba* and withdrew rather than giving ground for a protest.

Vim took the fifth, and the match, on September 10 over a seven-and-a-half-mile triangle in and out of fog with an onshore breeze that collapsed into a thick calm at the finish.

Their hosts were observed by Francis Crowninshield to be more than obliging in solacing the visitors:

> During their stay here the Germans were "cared for" at the Eastern Yacht Club and by way of advice, they were told that whenever anyone invited you to have a drink it would be considered an insult almost not to take one. Not unnaturally, they met many men and just as naturally they consumed many drinks. When finally one of them who had already imbibed God knows how many, was asked to have another "Lonetree" [a popular gin cooler], he exclaimed, "My God. Must I then drink a whole forest?"

The presentation of the Roosevelt Cup was scheduled for September 14 aboard the presidential yacht *Mayflower* at Oyster Bay, Long Island, the presidential summer retreat. The Eastern's measurer, Henry Taggard, traveled with the contestants and committee on the night train to New York:

> We repaired to the Belmont for breakfast and preening. One of our German guests, who had slept not at all on the train on account of "those horrid noises," nearly broke up the party by giving his resplendent uniform to a valet and being unable to retrieve it.
>
> But we were off at long last by ferry to Long Island City where a special train waited to take us to Oyster Bay. On the platform we found members of the Cabinet standing about waiting for a train to take them to a hastily called meeting on the *Mayflower*. We at once extended the hospitality of our train, which was readily accepted, and off we started.
>
> Of the Cabinet members, those I remember best were [Secretary of War] William Howard Taft and [Assistant Secretary of State] Bob Bacon. I sat with Taft on the train and a wonderfully

The 1906 Roosevelt Cup.

> interesting ride it was. A great treat to listen to what he had to say about important matters and his ever-sparkling wit.
>
> Arriving at Oyster Bay, we were ferried to the *Mayflower* in small boats, and I recall the earnestness of the coxswain of our boat when he adjured Mr. Taft to "step into her *amidships*" and how Mr. Taft chuckled.
>
> When we boarded the *Mayflower*, we learned that naval etiquette forbad the President being on board to welcome guests, so he came a little later, and the Presidential launch waited alongside for the firing of the national salute [of twenty-one guns], TR standing, in a crash suit, holding his Panama hat over his heart. I regret to report that both suit and hat were very much in need of pressing. All in turn were introduced to the President, who had a few apt and interesting words for each of us.
>
> Luncheon was soon announced and was a jolly, almost informal meal. TR called his Cabinet by the first or nicknames, and as I remember there were no speeches, only the regulation toasts. Luncheon over, the President summoned his statesmen for the Cabinet meeting while we inspected his fine yacht. After the meeting TR came into the main cabin where we were

seated along the divans, sat down by each in turn and engaged in a short but interesting conversation.

Then the Roosevelt Cup was brought and presented to Captain Park by the donor with a speech eloquent of the sportsmanship of both Germans and Yankees, of "ties that bind," and of the skill and pluck of Captain Park for sailing the *Vim* to victory. I lived on Park's fine steam yacht during the whole week of racing and am obliged to say that it was from her deck that he watched the *Vim* win the Cup. This was no fault of his, for he was an elderly gentleman whose doctor had forbidden him to race his boat. But TR didn't know that, which gave an awkward moment to Park and the racing men.

Captain Park accepted the Cup with a few graceful and happy words, and our visit was over. But a most elaborate dinner given by the New York Yacht Club that evening at the Manhattan Club in New York, succeeded by some hours at the Brooke Club, sent us on our weary way to a celebration the next evening at the Manhasset Yacht Club, whence we Boston men left for home rather in need of rest and a change.

His Imperial Majesty, William II, Emperor of Germany, was voted the sixth Honorary Member of the Eastern Yacht Club on February 7, 1907. Five days later, Theodore Roosevelt, President of the United States of America, was elected the seventh.

Meanwhile, Henry Howard had invented the Howard Dust Chamber for the more efficient synthesis of the sulfuric acid that was both the basic product and the basic reagent of the Merrimac Chemical Company, of which he was vice president. An essential ingredient was crude pyrites ore, then in large supply in Spain but controlled for U.S. export by a London firm.

It occurred to the Chairman to visit Spain after the 1906 Marblehead races to see if he could make a deal directly with the mine owners, cutting out the British middlemen. How to get an inside track with them? The return Sonder match with the Germans was to be at Kiel the next summer. The Spanish monarch was an ardent sailor. Hmmm.

I thought if I could utilize the idea of my hobby of yacht races for getting an audience with King Alfonso, the whole situation might develop so that I could get such contacts and such introductions as I needed. . . . I felt so confident of my ability to accomplish something along this line that I took with me my evening dress uniform of the Eastern Yacht Club, a frock coat and silk hat to wear in a possible audience with King Alfonso, and, of course, my official letterheads in the Eastern Yacht Club, where I was Chairman of the Regatta Committee.

From Lloyd's Yacht Register and a map in the steamship library, he discovered that the young King (who was only twenty and had occupied the throne since he was sixteen) was honorary president of the Réal Club Nautico in San Sebastián, which was en route to Huelva, the Spanish pyrites port. So he wrote the club secretary, inviting himself to pause there with the proposition, as it were, of his Eastern Yacht Club committee that the three American Sonders racing in Germany the following August could easily be shipped to San Sebastián for a match with a Spanish team.

In Paris on Christmas Eve, the Chairman received a cordial invitation to San Sebastián, which he promptly accepted. Within a week he was conducted through the streets in the mayor's carriage; wined, dined, and toasted in his Eastern Yacht Club uniform and cap; made a *Member Merito* for life of the Réal Club Nautico; pressed to present his plan to the King in Madrid (for only the Honorary President could approve on behalf of the club); lined up for an immediate (in view of the emergency of his schedule) audience with Alfonso through high connections; and, finally, coached by his new friends in the proper etiquette at court, for Señor Howard did not speak Spanish.

In Madrid, clad in the full evening dress of the Eastern Yacht Club and with all the boldness of a Yankee in King Arthur's Court, Henry Howard presented himself at the palace. He bulled his way to the audience chamber and found the royal chamberlain, who, after a short wait, escorted him between a double line of functionaries who had obviously been cooling their heels and "had anything but friendly feelings," and presented him to Alfonso. The King immediately put his American visitor at ease, "smiled, one of his delightful friendly smiles, clicked his heels together and came up to a quick military salute, laughed and said, 'Mr. Howard, talk with me just as you would talk to any of your friends in America.'"

I found him not only interested and enthusiastic, but surprisingly familiar with the racing of small boats in the United States. He said that he had read about the Sonder Class Races at Marblehead during the previous summer and came to the conclusion that we won over the Germans rather because of the superior cut of our sails than by better models of the boat. This indeed had been the consensus of opinion at Marblehead and gave me an opening which I at once seized. I had learned at San Sebastian that the King had a Sonder boat of his own. I therefore replied that many of the experts at Marblehead were of his opinion and that it would give us great pleasure to present him

Prince Henry of Prussia at the helm of his Sonder *Tilly*, 1907.

with a suit of sails for his own Sonder boat for experimental purposes in Spanish waters. This pleased him very much and he replied that he would be delighted to have such an opportunity. I told him that we would need not only his spar plan and present sail plan of his boat but also the lines of the boat. All this information he promised to have sent forward promptly and asked my address which he wrote down in his pocket notebook, and a week or two after my return to America I received all the information, and the sails were duly made by Wilson and Silsby in Boston. They were, of course, paid for by the Eastern Yacht Club and were accompanied by a letter which I sent in the name of the Club.

The King said he would be glad to give the principal prize himself for the match the following September at San Sebastian, and assured me that he would personally see to it that the American yachtsmen were well entertained.

Thus ended the audience. It need hardly be added that the chemical engineer had nearly as smooth sailing in his efforts to secure a flow of Spanish pyrites to America at a bargain, enough by 1915 to last until 1920 and to enable his company to take advantage of sky-high wartime prices for sulfuric acid.

The light winds at Marblehead during the June trials for the 1907 races in Germany perforce revived Eastern Vice Commodore F. Lewis Clark's *Spokane* and advanced two new Sonders, Frank Macomber's *Chewink VIII* of the Corinthian and Sumner H. Foster's *Marblehead*, although boats fit for Kiel bluster were needed. The German finalists were *Wannsee*, the

only one to take a race at Marblehead, *Wittelsbach*, and Prince Henry's co-owned *Tilly X*.

For the 1907 season, Henry Howard was succeeded as chairman of the Eastern's Regatta Committee by Louis M. Clark, perhaps due to the former's required absence in Europe for the two sets of Sonder races during the Marblehead season. When he arrived at Kiel, he was chosen "president" of the Joint Race Committee. The Kaiserlicher Yacht Club banqueted the contestants while an orchestra played the national anthems of the two countries, eliciting the following embarrassing item in the Paris edition of the *New York Herald*:

> At the banquet given last evening at the Kaiserlicher Yacht Club in honor of the visiting American yachtsmen, the music was furnished by a German band, which played the "Star-Spangled Banner" so badly that the Americans present all burst out laughing.

Prince Henry had toasted Herr Howard from the head of the table and was furious at the insult. Through a journalist friend in Paris, Howard was able to expose what was said to have been a practical joke on the *Herald*'s man in Kiel, and through another connection to publisher James Gordon Bennett got a retraction printed—to the royal satisfaction.

The August blows of Kiel puffed the Germans home even as the zephyrs of Marblehead had wafted the Yanks to the cup the year before. The first race was sailed in what for the Americans was a two- or three-reef, pump-and-bail breeze over short, choppy seas—typical Kiel conditions described by Howard: "The wind comes off the land, hits the water, picks it up, breaks it into spray which goes dancing across the harbor." The Germans never even shortened sail, and they walked away with it from the start.

Edwin Boardman felt chagrined:

> The German boats having flat sails had a tremendous advantage, as the wind attained a velocity of forty miles an hour during some of the heavy squalls. The full sails of the American boats were all aback, while the flat sails of the Germans were carried full most of the time. Another surprising point was that on a broad reach in the heavy sea, the narrow, sharp boats carrying full sail were forced through the water at a greater speed than the scows with single reefs, which was all they could carry. . . .
>
> I looked over the German boats very carefully and they certainly have a great advantage in construction over anything that I have yet seen built in this country. The Spanish cedar

used by them has been drying out for years and many of them were built with flush seams, having no calking whatsoever.

The cocky Yanks arrived only two or three days in advance, and, to the frustration of the Chairman, ignored instructions to cover the knowledgeable Germans in their fluke-hunting:

In the first two races Prince Henry, sailing *Tilly*, did not do very well and our helmsmen were very contemptuous of his ability as a racing skipper, so in the third race when he was behind and went off by himself fluke-hunting they all let him go, only to wake up astounded when he crossed the finish line half a mile ahead of our leading boat.

The Americans actually led in the light airs at the start of the finale and would have won if it hadn't piped up. As it was, they had to watch the Germans fight it out for their Emperor's Cup, which went to *Wannsee*, owned by Otto Protzen, an artist. Henry Irving Dodge put the best face on it in *Yachting* after crediting the Eastern with promoting the international matches as an antidote to the "monopolistic attitude" that governed the America's Cup:

There is little doubt that every defeat suffered by either nation . . . will result in the further development of this type toward a perfect combination of wholesomeness, speed, seaworthiness and adaptability to all conditions. In this way *Sonderklasse* contests will prove a veritable boon to the science and sport of yachting.

After a farewell dinner at Kiel, the American yachtsmen were feted by the president and senate of the ancient Hanseatic free city of Lubeck, then by the burgomaster and the Hamburg-American Line at Hamburg on the invitation of the Norddeutscher Regatta Verein. Then on to Berlin for a tea with Crown Prince William and his princess at their castle on the Wannsee and a parade of 45,000 crack troops. After a climactic dinner at his palace in Hanover, the Kaiser awarded the prizes to his countrymen.

A "Court Circle" was formed around the Emperor in the center of the big ballroom on the second floor in the front of the palace—he standing alone in the center of the floor, and all the guests surrounding an invisible deadline which left an open space about thirty feet in diameter—a very brilliant sight! All the members of the General Staff, heads of the Navy, diplomats from all the countries represented in Germany—all in their full uniforms with all the orders they possessed pinned on their breasts. During this function the Emperor spoke with three people and I had the honor of being one of those.

Howard delivered a personal message from President Roosevelt to the Kaiser, who gave him a few words to take back to the White House. He had a few more of his own for TR.

It seems that while hobnobbing with the imperial brass on the committee boat, a German naval tug, Howard met Dr. Anschutz, inventor and manufacturer of a prototype gyrocompass then being tried out by the German, Austrian, and Russian navies; Anschutz even took it apart for him, explaining its nonmagnetic advantages on steel warships and submarines. Sailing around the harbor observing the Baltic squadron that Prince Henry, as commander of the Imperial Navy, had brought along to add interest to the races, the ubiquitous engineer discovered that his hosts had devised a way of signaling between ships in broad daylight with a narrow and intensely focused searchlight beam that defied oblique detection, much more private than the wireless.

The American Sonders had already been shipped from Germany to Spain when Howard arrived in Bilbao early in September 1907 for the next leap into all this international racing he had engineered on behalf of the Eastern. He found the Royal Sporting Club on a barge on the Nervion River inside the breakwater at Portugalate. On his heels arrived Alfonso XIII. The King pushed through the crowd, shook his hand, welcomed him to Spain, and was ferried out to the floating club, where he changed into oilskins for an informal and blowy race with the Americans within the harbor; His Majesty won, narrowly.

Francis Crowninshield had accompanied the American team to Europe and was asked by Vice Commodore Clark to skipper *Spokane* in the Spanish races. Forty years later, he recalled them in his introduction to the log of *Cleopatra's Barge II*.

Our first race, with the evident intention of making it spectacular, was from an anchor start. We were called upon to round a "preliminary" buoy, one third of a mile distant and from there sail the regular triangular course. The wind was way aft for that first leg and, as there was nothing against it in the rules, just before the gun we swung her round so that she was anchored by the stern, whereupon all the others did likewise. But where we outfoxed them all, and for keeps, was that instead of hoisting our mainsail first, as all the others did, which takes a certain amount of time, we had it all ready and in a very few seconds we had our spinnaker set and drawing. This pulled us well into the clear and we rounded the special buoy with a big lead.

One day it was blowing so hard that "the Jury"—their name for Regatta Committee—decided it was too rough outside and the race was called off. They, however, came in the afternoon with an invitation to sail in a special race for a cup offered by his Majesty, a three mile triangle, twice around, inside the breakwater, all the different classes to sail together. The first leg was a reach—the second a beat, and the third a spinnaker run. The King, who was sailing his English thirty-footer, had to allow us almost ten minutes. You can well imagine the mess on the line with some twenty to thirty boats starting together. We were fortunate in getting away in the clear. No one bothered us and we kept our lead all the way around. The King was close up at the first mark but as he was in our back wind all the time he was never able to get by. The second round was a dead ringer for the first and we finished well ahead. After bowing very politely to the King, we repaired on board the *Golden Eagle*, the English steam yacht chartered by Commodore Clark, on which we were living. Hardly were we there when the Jury reappeared with the information that his Majesty had offered another cup for another race and would we sail? We, not unnaturally, thought it very careless of his Majesty to belittle "our" King's cup by offering another, but we said we would be glad to.

This second race, funnily enough, was an exact duplication of the first—the only thing worth recording is that at the weather mark the second time around the King was right on top of us, so close in fact that unless we could put over something good, he was sure to pass us. Feeling confident he would do whatever we did, we purposely set our spinnaker on the wrong side. Our guess was a good one. We waited till his was on when we jibed over, and as we could handle our sails in a small fraction of the time it took him to do it, the race ended then and there.

And now another near-crisis. The King had long since received his new suit of Sonder sails at a cost to the Eastern of $160, and much appreciated. Except that only a few days earlier—as Don Enrique Careaga, His Majesty's old friend in charge of his yachting activities, informed Henry Howard—a bill for $600 had also been received, via the Crédit Lyonnaise in San Sebastián, sent from Cambridgeport, Massachusetts, addressed to "Dear Gents" and signed, "Yours truly, A. Crook." However, he had cautiously withheld payment until the arrival of Señor Howard, who assured him that a confidence artist, perhaps even the originator of the infamous Spanish trunk flimflam, must have been at work. Our usually triumphant snooper never did get to the bottom of it. Some

joker very nearly had an elaborate laugh on him at the expense of the King of Spain.

For Henry Howard, the high point of the race week at Bilbao prior to the Sonder matches was the royal attention. "Here I was, an American joining in sport with the King of one of the oldest kingdoms in Europe and being entertained by him with the utmost hospitality."

The low point, to his intense irritation, came at the conclusion of the preliminaries:

I was greatly disturbed by Commodore F. Lewis Clark telling me that he would not be at the official luncheon to which we were invited the next day at the club house of the Sporting Club, at which the Queen was to be present and be one of our hosts and personally deliver the prizes won during the racing week at Bilbao. Commodore Clark stated that he was very anxious to see a bull fight which was to take place at San Sebastian the following day and that he had invited all the American yachtsmen to go with him, and hoped I would go also, and he said that he was planning to tow their boats with the *Golden Eagle* from Bilbao to San Sebastian.

I pointed out to him that it was a very serious breach of etiquette—that when you were invited by the King and Queen, particularly when they had done much for you beforehand, it was in the nature of a command, and that unless some very good reason offered, the invitation must be accepted. No argument would prevail, however, and the entire party left early the following morning. I told Commodore Clark that under no consideration would I go with him, as I felt I must at least do the best I could to try and smooth over the difficulty. In the morning, after they had gone, I learned that the King had planned to invite all the American yachtsmen, including Commodore Clark and his party, to sail with him from Bilbao to San Sebastian on his magnificent yacht *Giralda*. This, of course, would have been a much greater attraction to the Americans than seeing a bull fight because bull fights can always be seen, but invitations of this sort from the King are not common occurrences. I naturally accepted for myself and was told that I could bring my baggage right on board, even a steamer trunk which I had with me. . . .

After lunch, the Queen presented all the prizes and I was much embarrassed at having to walk up and receive these prizes for each one of the American boats and to make the best apologies for their extremely rude action in being absent on this occasion.

Francis Crowninshield's version of the inter-race formalities and diversions differs slightly from Howard's, with not a word of bullfights:

As we wanted to have everything in perfect condition for the team match so soon to come, we left for San Sebastian the following day, too soon to be at the Clubhouse when the Queen presented the prizes of which we had won quite a few—money enough to buy us gold cigarette cases, field glasses, etc. However when she handed out the two King's cups we had won they were little larger than ladies' thimbles, too small in fact to be suitably inscribed.

The trio of American Sonders fared no better at San Sebastián than at Kiel. The winds had all the temperament of the people, flowing down from the Pyrenees offshore until late morning, taking a siesta in the hot sun, then returning onshore and climbing back up the mountains again. To accommodate them, Don Enrique Careaga in 1905 had developed an overlapping but flat version of the ballooner that turned Alfonso's Sonder into a winner to windward. By 1907, all the Spanish Sonders were flying what later became inappropriately (if Don Enrique was indeed the inventor) known as Genoa jibs. Howard described the results in the matches:

> The race would generally start with a fresh land breeze, then all the yachts would run into the calm streak and the fastest under these fluky conditions would get the sea breeze first and then be an almost sure winner. The American helmsmen thought the Spaniards were crazy to use their big jibs to windward, with the result that we were as badly beaten by the Spaniards at San Sebastian as we had been by the Germans at Kiel.

On the eve of the races, while the other Americans were taking in the bullfight, the young ruler was confiding to Howard that he hoped to wean his people somewhat away from bulls and casinos and toward yachting and ultimately a resurgence of Spain's maritime greatness. His guest on board the royal yacht invited a return match at Marblehead and reported this exchange:

> He said he was sure they would be glad to and that they would welcome an invitation from the Eastern Yacht Club. I then said, "Would it not be possible for you yourself to come in the capacity of a Sonder Class yachtsman, not as King of Spain, but incognito? To sail your own boat at Marblehead would appeal to the American people in a wonderful way and would greatly increase the friendship that now exists between Spain and the United States." He became very enthusiastic about the idea, saying that he had more or less planned to visit South America within the next few years, and perhaps he could arrange it so that he could come to Marblehead first for the races.

> After dinner was over, and I was strolling along alone on the deck, his Chamberlain came up to me and drew me to one side. "Mr. Howard, please don't say anything more to the King about going to Marblehead to the race. If he once makes up his mind that he is going, nothing that we can say will dissuade him. It might seriously jeopardize his crown to be absent so long from Spain while so many factions are working for his downfall and the downfall of the present form of government."
>
> I could not help thinking that it was quite an extraordinary incident that the Chamberlain of the King of Spain should be making a request of this sort of an ordinary chemical manufacturer of the United States. It showed that almost anything might happen as a result of a clean sport like yachting.

Back home again, Howard was invited to lunch at the White House, where he mentioned to President Roosevelt his invitation to Alfonso XIII to come sail sometime at Marblehead.

> This excited the President, who waved his hands and said, "For heaven's sake, don't ask him—we have had the greatest difficulty in keeping the King of Belgium from coming. The trouble is we have no appropriation available for their entertainment. It would need a special act of Congress, when some irresponsible Congressman in order to get a little publicity might oppose it on the ground that we should not tax the hard-earned wages of the workmen to entertain effete royalty. This would be regarded as an insult by Spain or Belgium and much harm might result. We had to tell King Leopold that he simply could not come."

Howard reported to TR on the German gyrocompass, which he told him was the most important aid to navigation since the chronometer, and on the new daytime signal searchlight. The President was impressed and sent for his naval aide, Commander (later Admiral) William S. Sims, to get the details from him. The fate of this intelligence would be another matter.

After the lapse of a year, the friendly yachting rivalry with Germany was resumed at Marblehead in 1909. Stephen Sleeper had succeeded Louis Clark as Regatta Committee chairman, but the Sonder matches remained the domain of Henry Howard and the crowned heads. Winfield Thompson rejoiced in *The Rudder* that the rules of the International Yacht Racing Union would apply, with a sideswipe at the New York and a bouquet to the Eastern and Howard: "It is no longer the fashion in international yachting to drive a hard bargain

Caleb Loring's Sonder *Wolf*, in ship's clothing, 1909.

The Sonders

The Sonders

when arranging a race; to impose terms more favorable to yourself than to the other fellow; to watch your opponent on his own boat and accuse him of making changes in her contrary to the terms of the match. These are relics of the good old days in international sport off Sandy Hook, when each side treated the other like a pickpocket."

Nineteen American entries, twelve of them new, from eight clubs and seven designers (nine by Boardman alone) embarked on the trials in three divisions in August. Seven flew EYC colors. C.H.W. Foster had *Bandit*, his twenty-ninth yacht, built in 1908 from Boardman's board, besides his *Caramba*, and the remaining five were new: Francis Crowninshield's *Demon*, Herbert M. Sears's *Eel*, F. Lewis Clark's *Spokane III*, all by Boardman; Rodolphe Agassiz's *Wag* by Herreshoff, and Caleb Loring's *Wolf* by Starling Burgess. Charles P. Curtis of the Eastern and the Boston also doubled his chances with *Ellen*, a revamped 1906 Boardman scow, and *Corinthian* by Lawley in 1907, both under the Boston burgee.

Ellen came out top boat, with *Wolf* and *Joyette*, a C.D. Mower design for Commodore William H. Childs of the Bensonhurst Yacht Club, Gravesend Bay, Brooklyn, completing the American team.

The Kaiserlicher men and their Sonders arrived in mid-August, *Seehund II* and *Margarethe*, and *Hevella*, to be sailed by Otto Protzen, Germany's top helmsman as already demonstrated. Two days later, he had the bad luck to slip and tear the ligaments in one leg, which seriously handicapped him.

In a repeat of 1906, the breezes still proved too light for the "Kiel-weather" Sonders, which remained less scowish and of greater displacement than the American boats. *Joyette*, with William U. Swan at the helm and designer Mower on the jib sheet, and *Ellen* took two races each, *Hevella* one, and *Joyette* broke the tie on September 7. Swan celebrated by jumping overboard.

In another of those quirks that a friendly fate bestowed all his life on Henry Howard, President Taft had chanced upon the mansion of Mrs. Robert Dawson Evans on Beverly's Woodbury Point as his summer White House. The mixture of the German yachtsmen, the races, the President (an Honorary Member of the Eastern since April 6), and all those foreign legations brewed something approaching excitement along the North Shore, which Win Thompson described as "a cottage colony much stiffer in the neck, in a social way, than that at Newport."

The presentation of the Taft Cup to *Joyette*, and the Governor Draper Cup for second place to *Ellen*, on September 9 aboard the 273-foot *Mayflower*—which the President had inherited from his predecessor along with the office—crowned the season of 1909. Though no yachtsman (golf drew him inland to the Myopia Hunt Club that summer), the Chief Executive viewed some of the Sonder racing anyway and congratulated the Germans on the style of their losing, which in sport is "a lesson in self-restraint and in everything that goes to make up what we call a gentleman." Very Edwardian—or, better—Taftian.

"I drink to the health of his Imperial Majesty, the Emperor of Germany," the President concluded his toast at the luncheon. "Long may he live to contribute to the peace of the world." Responded Henry Howard's opposite number, Admiral Barandon: "The good feeling which has been between the Germans and your countrymen has grown from day to day and I think it will continue to grow."

Secretary Henry Taggard was among the officers of the hosting Eastern Yacht Club invited aboard for the ceremonies and the luncheon. They were ferried on the naval yacht *Sylph* from the landing to the *Mayflower* off Beverly:

On being transshipped to the *Mayflower*, we found her decks already crowded by the great and near-great of the North Shore, including the governing officials of the towns and cities from Salem to Gloucester who had been invited to join the festivities.

I can tell you very little of the luncheon and presentation, for I was among the large number who could find no room in the yacht's saloon. I was fortunate, however, in being taken in charge by one of the ship's younger officers and introduced to the officers' mess, where I enjoyed an excellent meal in peace and comfort, in congenial company, and entertained by the antics of the President's young sons [Robert and Charles] and their Newfoundland dog.

On again reaching the deck, one of Boston's leading citizens, an elderly gentleman, implored me to get him ashore as he was completely fagged, not having found a place to sit or any food since coming on board. On appealing to my officer friend, he called away the President's launch and we were whisked ashore in regal style where I commandeered John Lawrence's car and dispatched the leading citizen to his home.

On returning to the ship alone in the gorgeous launch, I found many eyes peering over her rail, no doubt wondering why such elegance for a humble officer of the Club. However, I learned on such good authority as Harry Howard that there had been a luncheon, and I had heard cheers coming through the saloon skylight when the Cup was presented and accepted with becoming eloquence.

President Taft's elevation of George von L. Meyer from TR's Postmaster General to his own Secretary of the Navy in March of 1909 afforded Howard a chance to brief his friend on the fate of the intelligence concerning the German gyrocompass and signal searchlight that he had imparted to Commander Sims after the races two years earlier. As with most of the nonstoppable engineer's adventures in high places, one thing led to another. Suffice it to say that the famous naval reformer's report had been buried. Howard persuaded Admiral Barandon and Captain Retzmann, the German naval attaché in Washington, to demonstrate the gyrocompass on board the Secretary's personal dispatch boat *Dolphin* on an off-day during the Sonder races at Marblehead and wound up doing it himself, at their suggestion, for the Navy bureau chiefs whom Meyer had sent along for convincing. The next day, the Navy ordered its first Anschutz compass, and soon after, Howard introduced his old friend Elmer Sperry to the inventor in Kiel—but that is still another story. As for the signal searchlights, they weren't adopted by the Navy for years.

If the first Spanish-American Sonder match in Spanish waters in 1907 marked the beginning of the healing of the wounds from the Spanish-American War of 1898, the return meet in American waters at Marblehead in 1910 seems to have sealed the matter. Virtually decreed by the enthusiastic young Alfonso XIII, yachting was still new to the more Armada-conscious Spaniards, and in spite of their victory over the Yankee fleet in home waters, the Sonders they shipped over in August—*Chonta, Papoose* (shades of Charlie Adams), and *Mosquito II*—were not new, nor were they therefore designed for North Shore conditions, for all their advanced overlapping jibs.

Fourteen American Sonders began trials in two divisions off Marblehead on August 8. The 1909 team, *Joyette, Ellen,* and *Wolf,* was eliminated in the inexorable fashion of racing-machine progress. The all-new winners were all EYC boats: Charles Francis Adams's second *Harpoon,* with the tall, near-Marconi lug that he favored, designed by Boardman; Guy Lowell's *Cima* by Mower; and Charlie Foster's thirty-first yacht, *Beaver,* with a webbed mainsail that flew straight from the

inexhaustible imagination of Starling Burgess, with a lift from her owner, who wrote of her:

> In *Beaver* I placed a rig which consisted of a mainsail with long battens which became known and was quite a good deal copied as a "bat-wing sail." It consisted of a large curved leach, and I trimmed the battens down little by little so that when *Beaver* became overpowered these battens would curve over backwards and relieve the pressure on the sail. This made her steer very well under all circumstances.

Forty-six years later, writing Charlie Foster's eulogy in the *Boston Globe*, Leonard Fowle described the final minutes of a close one between *Beaver* and *Cima*:

> On the last leg of the crucial race, *Cima* was cutting *Beaver's* lead fast to the concern of Foster's crew, W. Starling Burgess, the yacht's designer, and Foster's son, Reggie. The latter, a famous Harvard quarter-miler, finally could stand it no longer and throwing off his cap, blurted out—"For Gawd's sake, Father, can't we do something?"
> "Yes, keep still!" was the quiet admonishment.
> A few minutes later, *Beaver* edged across the line with a 13-second lead.

Representing the recently organized Federation of Spanish Yacht Clubs, the visitors arrived seemingly prepared for defeat and did not bother to try out their boats before the races, which were sailed in the home team's favorite weather. One, Louis de Arana, was a handsome and amusing royal favorite with whom Crowninshield had struck up a friendship during the races in Spain; he stayed with Frank and Louise at Peach's Point, and his host recalled:

> My wife asked him if he had had any trouble getting into the country. He, in his broken English said, "Ze first question they ask me—'Are you a polygamist?' I answer, 'Alas, no.'"

Charlie Adams hurled *Harpoon* to four firsts for the Taft Cup between August 17 and 20, ceding the opener to *Beaver* after fouling the last mark. *Beaver* went on to eliminate *Cima* for the second-place Draper Cup.

Charlie Foster was the champion fleet owner and hurler of the entire series, and *Beaver* was his best, better than *Caramba* (1906), *Bandit* (1908), *Badger,* also by Burgess (1910), and *Otter* (1913), not to mention the best of the German Sonders, *Hevella,* which he bought so he could try out her roller reefing. How did he manage it all?

Even more intriguing, during the eight years of the international races between 1906 and 1913, Foster owned besides and at least, at one time or another, the knockabout *Lolita*, the 21-foot cutter *Porcupine*, the 48-foot schooner *Olivette*, the 51-foot ketch *Autocrat*, the 40-foot powerboat *Princess*, a 32-foot launch, and the three-masted merchant schooner *Lillian Woodruff*, which he bought in 1905 (of which more in chapter 7).

But to get back to the Sonder races of 1910, once again—this time before the start of one—Henry Taggard had to endure a test of his secretarial aplomb, as reported in the *Boston Herald* of August 28:

SURE ENOUGH, IT WAS THE SECRETARY

Secretary Henry Taggard of the Eastern Yacht Club was a central figure in an amusing incident occurring in connection with the recent Spanish-American races. The secretary viewed the contests from the deck of the *Androscoggin*, flagship of the squadron of revenue cutters detailed to prevent the pleasure fleet from hampering movements of the racing craft.

One morning he went aboard the *Androscoggin* shortly before 10 o'clock, at which hour the committee tugs *Orion* and *Confidence* were usually sent outside the harbor. Orders were given by the *Androscoggin*'s commander to display signals for the other cutters, the *Gresham* and *Acushnet*, to get under way. This order is represented by the code letters H I. Bunting fluttered from the *Androscoggin*'s signal yard but the other cutters did not hoist anchors.

Instead, boats were lowered and presently the captains of the *Gresham* and *Acushnet*, resplendent in full dress uniform they had not donned in several years, were being rowed smartly over to the *Androscoggin*. Officers on the flagship were dumbfounded, and persons aboard yachts in the vicinity gazed with awe at the gorgeous spectacle, the like of which had not been seen in quaint Marblehead these many moons. Everybody aboard the *Androscoggin* speculated as to what might happen. Nobody was more perplexed than Secretary Taggard.

Captain Uberroth of the *Gresham* was first to reach the cutter's deck. "Where is the secretary?" he inquired, as no one had sufficiently recovered from surprise to do much in the way of a welcome. An officer introduced Secretary Taggard, and the captain of the *Gresham* proceeded to salute that official of the yacht club in true service style.

While Secretary Taggard was pinching himself to be sure he was really awake, the captain of the *Acushnet* came over the side loaded down in blue and gilt. But explanations were bound to follow, much to the relief of the Eastern Yacht Club's representative.

Charlie Foster between *Beaver* crewmates Reginald Foster and designer Starling Burgess, 1910.

Charles Francis Adams (center) and the crew of his Sonder *Harpoon*, T. Nelson Perkins and Arthur Adams, 1910.

The signal snapping from the *Androscoggin*, it seems, was not what her commander had intended. Instead of ordering the cutters to get under way, it told their captains to report in full dress uniform to meet the Secretary of the Treasury, a function of considerable note and one that happens infrequently. The chap who picked out the flags had misunderstood instructions and instead of bending H I on the halyards, he bent H Y, sounding much the same, and caused all the flutter.

"The above is an account of an unusual incident," Secretary Howard wrote some years later, "no doubt amusing to the on-lookers, but highly provoking to the doughty Captains who had hastily released dress uniforms from a long repose among mothballs and donned epaulets, chapeaux, white gloves, and side-arms in honor of a grand occasion.

"I would have gladly sunk without trace as I met the wrathful glares of the Captains when they saluted me. However, I took special pains to promote the entente cordiale with Captain Uberroth, beside whom I sat at dinner that evening given in honor of the Officers of the Coast Guard, and I was overcome with pride when the gallant Captain insisted on placing his chapeau on my head and buckling his sword on my slender person."

President Taft was enjoying his second season in the summer White House he was renting from Mrs. Evans on the Beverly shore, and a few days later, on board the *Mayflower*, presented his namesake cup to Charlie Adams, helmsman of the lucky-seven Sonder *Harpoon* and future Republican Secretary of the Navy.

On October 25, His Most Catholic Majesty, Alfonso XIII, King of Spain and Duke of Toledo, was made an Honorary Member of the Eastern Yacht Club.

Neither team had been able to win on the other's water as Henry Howard prepared for their fourth meeting in 1911, their second at Kiel, when the Germans would have their chance to even it up. But perhaps some Teutonic thoroughness had rubbed off on the originator of the series. This time Howard was taking no chances. After the 1910 races with Spain at Marblehead, the trials for Kiel were moved at his insistence to Buzzards Bay, where the winds and shoal water had the feel of "Kiel weather." *Bibelot*, designed by Nat Herreshoff for Harry Payne Whitney and sailed by Robert Emmons II of the Eastern, and C.H.W. Foster's *Beaver*, now owned by Augustus H. Eustis—both old Buzzards Bay hands—and Guy Lowell's *Cima*, again for lighter airs, were selected.

The Kiel-tailored American Sonders were shipped to Germany in the spring of 1911, giving their crews three weeks of practice on the spot before the match, with the result that they knew the course and conditions better than their opponents, two of whom came from Berlin, the third from Hamburg.

Using the Eastern Yacht Club as his base, Henry Howard was as always playing two or three international games at once. Several months previously, he had persuaded Navy Secretary Meyer that the upcoming races might provide a unique chance to check out the Kaiser's formidably growing navy if Meyer were to send a U.S. squadron to Kiel from which Howard would name an expert to his Race Committee; this expert would then spend ten days with top German Navy brass and technicians on the German Navy tug that would again be serving as the committee boat.

And so it came to pass. Secretary Meyer ordered a three- or four-boat squadron to the races, and Captain R.H.M. Robinson occupied Kiel Week talking shop with his opposite numbers. And what he could not learn—the calibre of the guns going into the Kaiser's new battleships—Howard did, while chatting before the fire with a retired admiral who not only told him that they were of the high-velocity, 11-inch type, but also described in detail his navy's presumably secret new techniques of target practice.

This time, half an hour after the start of each race, it was between the Americans. *Bibelot* won the Kaiser's Cup. Francis Herreshoff claimed his father's only outstanding Sonder was the fastest ever built, "graceful as a whippet" due to the fairer curve of her sides and narrower stern that enhanced *Bibelot*'s speed, when heeled, over the more slab-sided scows.

The award of the cup to *Bibelot* provided the observant Harry Howard (the Emperor "always gave you the impression that he was afraid you would forget he was the Emperor") with another of his sidelights on history:

Mr. Emmons's father had been present with his yacht during the whole of Kiel Week and had been most courteous in inviting visiting Americans to follow the races on board his boat, which was a chartered steam yacht. Mr. Emmons, Sr., although well along in years, was full of fun and always seemed to be making amusing mistakes. Guy Lowell and I were talking together in the garden and noticed with much interest that Mr. Emmons, Sr., was apparently having a very pleasant time with the Emperor. They were both laughing heartily, apparently at one of Mr. Emmons's amusing stories and the conversation continued for some fifteen minutes. After leaving him, Mr. Emmons came up to me and said, "I had hoped that if I came here this afternoon, there might be some opportunity for me to get a chance to speak to the Emperor, but I am afraid it is hopeless."

Both Lowell and I looked at him in astonishment and I said, "Why, you have just been talking with him for the last fifteen minutes, and seemed to be having a very good time together." Mr. Emmons looked rather aghast and said, "Do you mean to say that that man over there in the yachting cap is the Em-

President Taft presents the Taft Cup aboard *Mayflower*, August 24, 1910.

peror?" I replied, "He most certainly is." Emmons replied, "Why, I took him for the captain of one of the German warships out here and I was telling him what a rotten harbor I thought Kiel was for small-boat racing." Mr. Emmons wandered off to gather his wits together and try and remember if he had made any other improper remarks.

During the final banquet at the Kaiserlicher Yacht Club, Howard was seated next to Ambassador David J. Hill and directly opposite the Kaiser, and it amused him "to see that old Mr. J.P. Morgan, who was there for the purpose of receiving a decoration from the Emperor, was given a place some fifteen

seats below me. But such are the rules of etiquette, an official position apparently takes precedence over private individuals, no matter how great their reputation."

After dinner, the Kaiser summoned Howard to the garden, where he complained to him about Ambassador Hill's impending recall, arguing that the American envoy, whom he had come to like, had learned the ropes and it would be a shame to replace him with a new man. A curious turnabout, since the Kaiser had let it be known after Hill's appointment in 1908 that he would have preferred a man of greater means, a lavish entertainer in the style of his predecessor. Obviously the Kaiser wanted Howard to intervene with President Taft, but it proved too late.

Never at a loss, the Chairman suggested to the Kaiser that he send Crown Prince William to sail his Sonder incognito in the next races scheduled for 1913 at Marblehead, and told him:

Of course everyone in the United States would know that it was really the Crown Prince, and his taking part in this way and sailing as one man against another would create a most favorable impression and be given enormous publicity in the United States. During the races he would be entertained by our best people in the neighborhood of Boston, particularly on the North Shore, and I believe that the contacts and friendships so formed would have a very far-reaching value. Of course the United States and Germany are friendly at the present time, but there is always the possibility that some incident may arise which would endanger this present state of affairs, and there is no knowing what effect the personal acquaintance of the Crown Prince with some of our leading citizens would have upon the trend of affairs.

The Kaiser liked the idea and sent for Reichschancellor Theobald von Bethmann-Hollweg, who worked out the details with Howard, and it was all but done. Three years hence, this "exceedingly interesting and kindly man," as Howard found the Chancellor, would dismiss the guarantee of Belgium's neutrality by the Great Powers as a "scrap of paper," and Germany would be on the march against France.

Two years passed. Woodrow Wilson and the Democrats defeated the Republicans, divided between Taft and Roosevelt, and the United States and Germany—as if reiterating their vows of innocence in a wicked world—resumed for the fifth time since 1906 their amiable yachting contests, again at Marblehead under the burgee of the Eastern.

Once again Guy Lowell's durable *Cima*, sailed by G.I. Edgerton, was matched against an *Ellen*, a new one designed by Starling Burgess for Charles P. Curtis and sailed by him and his sons, Charles, Jr., and Richard. They led the trials, joined by John L. Saltonstall's *Sprig*, Reginald Boardman at the helm. Everything was set for Crown Prince William to lead the German Sonder team on its third try for a win at Marblehead. His *Angela IV* had been shipped, and he was about to join her when the Imperial General Staff summarily required his presence in the army maneuvers that were about to begin. So the Crown Prince's friend Weitzmann was rushed across to take his place in the cockpit, joining *Serum* and *Wittelsbach X*.

Again, an American sweep, behind *Ellen* this time. Except

King Alfonso of Spain, autographed to Henry Howard.

for the final two of the six races, airs were so light and so far a cry from Kiel weather that "even the piazza yachtsmen could venture out without fear," as *The Rudder* put it. The Yanks treated their affable opponents to a lay-day Red Sox baseball game in Boston.

Ellen's crew of Curtises received the President Wilson Trophy in Washington on September 10. Governor Foss had awarded his namesake Cup to *Cima* at a dinner the previous evening.

If nothing else, the point had been proved time and again on both sides of the Atlantic, as put by Boston's excellent amateur designer of the Sonder scows, Edwin Boardman, in his *The Small Yacht*, published in 1909:

> From my own experience in the twelve boats I have designed, I believe it impossible to embody in one boat all the points that would make her successful under all conditions. . . . This being the case, it is necessary to build the boat to sail in the conditions of wind and water that prevail in that country where she is to be used.

The committee for the last of the International Sonder Races, for the Wilson Cup with Germany, gathers on the steps of the Eastern, September 5, 1913. Henry Howard is second from right, front row; Starling Burgess back row at left, Henry Morss third from left.

The lesson would be learned the hard way by all the contenders in the America's Cup races of the future.

War in the offing? Don't you believe it. Dinners and dances at the Eastern clubhouse and the Myopia Hunt Club and private homes on the North Shore, fireworks set off from a float nearly a quarter of a mile long in the middle of the harbor, culminating with whispers of larger bangs to come in the "big noise," a bomb containing seventy-five pounds of powder fired off on the grounds of the Eastern Yacht Club. Yes, with gold-braided insouciance the Eastern had launched these eight years of yachting light opera through the shark-infested waters of European intrigue into the gathering storm.

The Sonders

The Kiel Committee, 1911, Henry Howard center.

And although there had been speculation that the Germans thought they might have a better chance in Marblehead waters with their Six Meters against our R-boats, yachting's era of good feelings was capped off with the announcement during the dinner they hosted at the Club that Crown Prince William himself would accompany the Sonders to the next match at Marblehead in three years.

World War I erupted during the first week in August 1914. Three weeks later, the Eastern sponsored a series of seven races to select the Sonders to sail against the Germans at Kiel in 1915, on the assumption that the war would be over by then. For the record, they were again *Ellen, Cima* and *Sprig.*

La Belle Époque, c'était fini. "Little did I dream," Henry Taggard wrote so wistfully of the gentlemanly days, "that only a few years later, as Secretary of the Club it would become my painful duty to inform Emperor William II that his name had been removed from our list of honorary members."

Chapter 7

Rules, Ratings, and Regattas *1902–1913*

For all the international hoopla and glamour that surrounded the Sonder matches between 1906 and 1913, they sailed in an eddy that for eight years provided a mere diversion from the mainstream of the Eastern Yacht Club's preoccupation with matters of more substantial length, breadth, and depth.

To be sure, the under-30s were there to stay (eighty-eight in 1910), but the big boats (fifty schooners, sixty-four sloops and yawls, and forty-seven steamers) kept on crowding the channel. The Sonder Rule was a shapeless if momentarily intriguing diversion from the trend of measurement, foisted on American designers as Henry Howard's price for luring the Kaiser into competition.

The first attempt to bring law to the jungle, the flawed Seawanhaka Rule adopted by the Eastern in 1885, had imposed some order on handicapping and even on design, but only until the race for speed upended it and revealed for all to see its single egregious omission—the weighty element of displacement.

By the turn of the century, the bending of the Seawanhaka Rule threatened the very art of design by confining the science to the rule's two seesawing variables of sail area and centerline length on the water. The resulting scows eventually skimmed themselves out of the water, the weirdest being young Starling Burgess's first attention-getter, *Outlook*, designed to win, as she did, the 1902 Quincy Yacht Club Challenge Cup and her six other starts. At 52 feet overall, 21 feet on the water, 16 feet beam, and 8 inches draft, she more than doubled her waterline when she heeled.

Unhappiness with the Seawanhaka Rule was universal, and in early 1902 a committee of the New York Yacht Club importuned the leading designers to invent something to everybody's liking. Nathanael Herreshoff had, in 1867 as an M.I.T.

student, produced the first time allowance tables; now he responded with a formula that recognized the existence of displacement and the true shape of the waterline by measuring its quarter-beam length halfway between the center and the extreme breadth, instead of along the unidimensional midline. In another of his triumphs of intuition, he reduced the variables of area and weight to the linear by square-rooting sail and cube-rooting displacement:

$$\frac{L \sqrt{5A}}{5 \sqrt[3]{D}}$$

Here was the Eleventh Commandment of Measurement. The New York Yacht Club adopted Herreshoff's Universal Rule late in 1902 and embraced as an honorary member the Moses who carried the tablet down from the mountain. The ever-cautious Eastern fell into line on May 24, 1904, as proposed by a committee of Henry Howard, Louis M. Clark, and Charles Francis Adams. From here on, to a hitherto-unimagined degree, it would be helm-to-helm and hand-to-hand. (The Universal Rule used letters in place of numbers to denote waterline, a soup that had to be stirred until 1909 before it settled into an acceptable alphabet.)

On July 3, 1904, the Club ran the first race under the new rule in Massachusetts Bay with three classes—M (35 feet waterline) won by Herbert M. Sears in *Cricket*; N (30 feet); and O-P (18 to 25 feet), an amalgam in which competed Charles Francis Adams, H.S. Wheelock, and a twenty-one-year-old aspirant from Troy, New York, John G. Alden, who had apprenticed himself to the designer Bowdoin B. Crowninshield.

It is likely that young Alden's entry was the 22-foot-waterline yawl *Sea Fox*, designed and built by E.L. Williams in South

Outlook, young Starling Burgess's first daring design of 1902, was 52 feet overall and more than doubled her waterline when heeled. Jackson photo.

Boston around 1892. Alden bought her for $250 saved from the fifteen dollars a week that B.B. paid him, plus working nights and putting the arm on friends. "The most remarkable small craft of her time (or almost any time)," he wrote of her in a nostalgic letter to *Yachting* sixty years later:

> Her rig was large but it seemed very effective, and her hull form was a delight to the eye. I had no money to run the boat after I acquired her, and when placing her in commission was only able to paint one-half of her deck with the conventional buff, the other half being green.
>
> Her great speed was at once evident and I sailed her in the races at Marblehead under the Universal Rule. In the first race, by the Eastern Yacht Club, there were over forty entries, yet *Sea Fox* won both her races and, as cash prizes were then given by all the Marblehead clubs, the writer was the proud possessor of $87.50, which was promptly spent at the various clubhouses.

Herreshoff's immortal New York Yacht Club Thirty, incorporating the magic of his "mass" production technology and his first one-design built to this latest commandment of his devising, appeared in 1905, but there was no great rush by the Eastern to add new classes thereunder. In 1907 and 1908, the fleet included a few Ms, "N-Ps" (stretching the rule even further?), with the addition of some Qs as well as the foreign-born Sonders, which had quickly become mainstays of round-the-buoys racing as a sort of nursery and season-long conditioner for the international meets that Chairman Howard kept arranging.

Meanwhile, Europe had devised its International Rule using a more complex formula for arriving at displacement but a far simpler classification based on metric waterline length. In a bid for true universality of measurement, the Atlantic Coast Conference of yacht clubs had been invited to participate in the ratification conference for the International Rule in London in January 1906. Stuyvesant Wainwright of the New York and Henry A. Morss of the Eastern were all packed to sail as delegates when conference jingoists pulled the plug with protests that it was all too complicated to merge the rival rules. "Baloney," was the comment of Bill Stephens, convinced to the end that Herreshoff's worldwide reputation would have

calmed the waters and his rule would have been truly universalized, given half a chance.

Sir Thomas Lipton, who knew how to sell tea to the world, commissioned William Fife, Jr., to design the first of his *Shamrocks* to go after the Auld Mug in 1899. She lost to Herreshoff's third defender, *Columbia*, at the hands of the wily Captain Charlie Barr, and her owner turned to George Watson for *Shamrock II* for another try in 1901. A second New York syndicate had Herreshoff design and build *Constitution* along *Columbia*'s lines. Then along came a third contender that raised not a few eyebrows.

On May 18, the scowish sloop *Independence*, designed by B.B. Crowninshield, was launched by Lawley of Boston in what amounted to a publicity stunt for Thomas W. Lawson. This flamboyant and unpredictable stock market speculator was possessed of a spirit of adventurism so reminiscent of Ben Butler's that the Hull-Massachusetts Bay Yacht Club was the only one that would let him in. *Independence* did badly in the trials, from which *Columbia* emerged the winner over her two rivals, and it is a curious fact that although the New York Yacht Club barred her owner, Charlie Adams consented to be a member of the amateur board of strategy that managed her, and on occasion relieved her professional skipper, Captain Hank Haff, at the helm.

Although Adams did not sail *Independence*, according to a newspaper account of later years:

> He did what he could to improve her chances, which were never great, by reason of her defective construction. In her final race *Independence* made a great burst of speed, outreaching *Columbia*. As she tore along her hull swayed and twisted like a basket. The crew were ranged along the weather rail on the deck, and among them was Mr. Adams. With every wave the deck rose under them as if it would burst. All hands were speculating as to the yacht's holding together and whether they would be picked up if she did not, but the sailors near Mr. Adams noted that his manner was as serene as if he had a sound vessel under him. After that they would have followed him through thick and thin.

Sound or not, Lawson brought *Independence* back to Boston, had her broken up three months after her christening, and put B.B. Crowninshield to work designing the enormous steel schooner *Thomas W. Lawson*, the only seven-sticker ever, launched in 1902.

The persistent Sir Thomas turned again to Fife in 1903, for *Shamrock III*, which sent the New York syndicate under Cornelius Vanderbilt back to Herreshoff for *Reliance*, 145 feet of skimmer on an 89-foot waterline that stretched to 130 feet when heeled—the last pie plate built for the America's Cup under the old rules. It would be the last Cup race under the old regime, the last for seventeen years because of New York's reluctance to defend under the Universal Rule and the intervention of war, and it was fitting that the NYYC should return the previous summer's gala at Marblehead by inviting the Eastern to join its Annual Cruise.

Led by Commodore Minot's flagship *Hope Leslie*, the Eastern fleet raced on July 15 and 16 to Vineyard Haven, July 17 to Newport, and July 18 to New London for the rendezvous with the NYYC. The combined squadron of more than 130 sail and steam vessels included *Reliance* and six former Cup defenders and aspirants—*Volunteer* and Vice Commodore C.H.W. Foster's *Puritan* rerigged as a schooner from the Eastern, and *Columbia*, *Vigilant*, *Mayflower*, and *Constitution* from the New York. After some leisurely racing between Newport and the Vineyard, the fleet disbanded on July 25. *Shamrock III*, unfortunately, proved no match for *Reliance* that fall.

This does not sound like Commodore Foster's cruise around Cape Cod in *Puritan* when he experienced his worst storm ever in a sailboat:

> It was a heavy northeast gale, and we were obliged to heave to for 36 hours off Highland Light because her long bowsprit was whipping about. During one of the nights while she was jumping about, I heard a terrific banging in the two connecting staterooms, one occupied by Governor Charles H. Allen and the other by the late Judge L.M. Clark. We tried to open the stateroom door but for a long time were unable to do so, but finally found upon entrance, Allen and Clark squeezed in under the deck with a couple of bureaus which had worked loose, banging back and forth. It took some time, strength and ingenuity to relieve the situation. *Puritan* behaved beautifully and justified her later reputation on her trips between Cape Verde Islands and New Bedford in which she carried Bravas [descendants of Cape Verde immigrants] back and forth.

Charlie Foster sold *Puritan* in 1905 and, always doing the unexpected (with the excuse of a growing family), purchased the 419-ton net (or so she was when he got through building a 30- by 70-foot deckhouse on her), three-masted lumber schooner *Lillian Woodruff*. This latest addition to the Foster fleet was 133 feet on the waterline, built in 1889 in Boothbay to carry salt fish to Europe, later bringing mahogany and other woods up from South America. Below, the athwartships dining saloon seated sixteen in office swivel chairs screwed to the floor, and the new owner turned the captain's quarters into the main saloon, with an upright piano and a Franklin stove. Captain Sam Dolliber, the old Marbleheader who had sailed before the mast around Cape Horn as a boy and been skipper for the Fosters for forty years, had a mate, two quartermasters (one on deck night and day lest a child slip overboard), an engineer (though he had nothing but a sail-hoisting donkey to tinker with), a cook, a steward, and four hands.

For five summers her irrepressible owner cruised with his family in the *Woodruff*, "and I had some real navigation stunts to sail her into the small places on the coast, but luckily, never with any serious adventure. Without any power it is not easy to navigate such a large vessel up through the thoroughfares and into the small harbors, as you find them on the Maine coast."

One such occasion was vividly re-created by one of his four daughters, Edith Foster Farwell, in an article in *Yankee* magazine:

We had been becalmed off Burnt Island in Maine. All night long the tide made us go backwards, and as we towed a twenty-one-foot knockabout, it meant that one man had to stay in the stern with a boat hook to keep the knockabout pushed off. The foghorn from the lighthouse blew and blew, each blast seemed more dismal than the last, only to be answered by the still more dismal blast of our own foghorn. The sea was calm as a millpond with oh, such a swell! . . . The two Irish maids below decks were telling their beads frantically. "Sure, good Lord, have mercy on me; Lord, why can't I die?" The youngest children were miserably seasick, but nobody could help them. . . .

At last we reached Penobscot Bay and made our way through Fox Island Thorofare to North Haven, the favorite port of the entire family. It is a difficult piece of navigating to get a big ship between those two islands, and I marvel at my father's courage in even attempting it.

Whistles began to blow from on shore, auto horns honked, flags were raised and dipped, bath towels were waved out the windows to greet us. Captain Sam [Dolliber] used to say that Admiral Dewey himself never got a more royal welcome than we did on the *Lillian Woodruff* coming down Fox Island Thorofare. As soon as we dropped anchor, veritable fleets of small craft pushed out from shore in our direction, and soon there

was a call for "gangway." Children of all ages tied their small rowboats astern, and we were a gala party. The phonograph, complete with horn, was brought up on deck, and in the evening the dew on the decks made a wonderful surface for dancing with rubber-soled shoes—and dance we did until all hours of the night.

The Fosters' good friends, the Charles Francis Adamses, came aboard one summer, and Mrs. Adams spent the night in Edith Foster's stateroom:

She was so intrigued with the bulge made by Mr. Adams in the berth above her that she could not resist pushing a hatpin up through the mattress. Mr. Adams jumped at such length that he bruised his bald head against the beams. After that he thumbtacked a pillow across the beam to prevent any further blows on the head.

The wide availability of the relatively compact, if not reliable, gasoline internal-combustion engine after 1900 sparked a landslide of launches of every description and aroused in cruising men a certain amount of cautious curiosity as to whether the coughing one-lunger could be squeezed under the cockpit. The rivalry hung on longer under the hoods of the new automobiles, but it was the last gasp of steam as a pusher of small boats (after the brief flirtation with naphtha), harbinger of new depths of spluttering profanity in the reeking bilges afloat. Suddenly everyone on every body of water—salt, fresh, or brackish—with three or four hundred dollars to spare, had to have a launch or a speedboat, and the makers were swamped.

Henry Howard thought of himself as a modern man and took pride in having driven the first automobile from Boston to Marblehead, and indeed the Eastern Yacht Club, one day in July of 1897, when he took the tiller of a steam carriage made by George E. Whitney of South Boston and made the trip after a single instructional drive around a city square. He liked this prototype so much that he ordered a replica, which took another year to build.

By 1902, however, when Howard had become chairman of the Regatta Committee, "young men were buying automobiles instead of racing yachts, which left yachting in a very bad way," as he wrote in *Charting My Life*. "Fast motorboats were just coming into existence and were equally unreliable. Here, I thought, was a chance to get young men back to sea. The development of the fast motorboats is something that ought to appeal to them, and moreover is something that ought to be encouraged by the United States Navy."

"Autoboats," they were called by their fans, who were crazy to see how fast one of the powerful European engines coming out of the Mercedes and Fiat plants would drive anything that floats through the water. Starling Burgess, always *au courant*, and Appleton Packard turned out *Mercedes U.S.A.* and *Macaroni* among a few others at this time.

Early in 1904, Howard wrote Secretary of the Navy William H. Moody, a Massachusetts man, telling him of his plan to run autoboat races under the auspices of the Eastern Yacht Club. Would the secretary get behind the idea by sending an old torpedo boat to Marblehead to police the course and lend the presence of the Navy to the occasion?

You may judge of my excitement and delight when a few days later he wrote that he had ordered a flotilla of four of our most modern destroyers to be present and asked the exact date when we would need them! . . . This was, I think, the first motorboat race held in New England waters. There were no precedents to go by, except some races the year before at Monte Carlo, but none of their circulars were available.

I decided to make the results as reliable as possible and laid out a triangular course, three nautical miles to each side, and had the marks set with great care by professional surveyors, and at the same time had an accurate measured nautical mile marked off. [Probably the measured course of one and a quarter nautical miles, actually, north thirty-three degrees east, set up in May 1904 from range poles on Tinker's Island to Marblehead Lighthouse bearing on the Marblehead Rock beacon, and marked by white spar buoys flying the club burgee.] I then engaged three men who were professional timers for automobile races, which were much in vogue at that time. With their watches synchronized, I stationed one at each of the marks to take the times of each boat on each side of the triangle. In addition, I had an expert photographer photograph each boat at full speed, when it was abreast him, to show the wave formation.

The instigator had a great time feeding developments to the newspapers, so that as the event approached, even though he had very few entries, what he laughingly called the "spontaneous" interest was full blown, "much to the disgust of the nearby yacht clubs, who had the wind taken completely out of their sails."

"Most uninteresting to watch," in the rather curious assessment of Chairman Howard, "these races accomplished what they were started for—they brought the young men of that period back into racing sailing yachts, which they found to be infinitely better sport than racing motorboats." It was an odd rationale, considering his representations to Secretary Moody that it would greatly benefit the Navy to get behind speedboating.

All the same, the Eastern ran an autoboat race on the Fourth of July, 1905, twelve miles and only six entries, which disappointed the press but evidently not everyone connected with the event, because six more races were held that season. Two power races were run off in 1906. And on July 18, 1908, possibly inspired by Thomas Fleming Day's first ocean power race from New York to Bermuda on June 6, the Club sponsored a race from Marblehead to New Rochelle; J.E. Peabody's *Chud* was the only Eastern entry and was forced to withdraw off Highland Light.

Fast speedboats were one thing; Gray and Palmer make-and-break-powered launches were another. The Eastern Yacht Club in 1903 listed (although it did not officially enroll) eighty-five craft between 17 and 30 feet waterline, including six launches. By 1905 the Club admitted to eighty-five sailboats and twenty-nine launches (power unspecified) under 30 feet, most if not all serving as tenders, runabouts, or plain playthings for the owners of something more substantial.

The stinkbug had bit. The next season there were thirty-eight launches.

These were years of keen competition as hot new boats emerged under the Universal Rule. One was the 39-foot-waterline sloop *Dorello*, designed by George Owen and launched in 1908 for George Batchelder, whose ukulele knew whence the winds blew for the Prince of Wales Cup Race at Halifax. "This yacht was to win many races," wrote John Parkinson in his New York Yacht Club history, "because her designer had conceived a radically new type of rig for her, high and narrow, with her sails well inboard in contrast to those of other racing yachts of that era."

A greater winner yet was the 53-foot K-class sloop *Avenger*, which Robert W. Emmons 2d of the Eastern gave Captain Nat carte blanche to design and build in 1907; this was after he had to return the New York Yacht Club's Astor Cup in 1906 when

The K-class sloop *Avenger* by Captain Nat, for Robert W. Emmons of the Eastern in 1907, was "the finest all around sailing yacht ever built," in the decided opinion of the designer's son Francis. Jackson photo.

Rules, Ratings, and Regattas

Rules, Ratings, and Regattas

it was discovered, to his annoyance, that his *Humma* had been mishandicapped. *Avenger* cleaned up east and west of the Cape. Her spars were hollow, in contrast to the solid sticks of the rest of her class, and Francis Herreshoff credited her owner with inventing what amounted to a Genoa jib in the shape of a flat-cut, overlapping ballooner that won many races to windward in light airs.

Francis Herreshoff averred, with excusable filial pride, that *Avenger* was

> the finest all around sailing yacht ever built. She was not excessively lofty or deep but was a fine yacht in which to cruise and a most successful cup winner. I happened to race on *Avenger* in most of her races in the first two or three years of her life. Not only did she win most of the races she started in, but several times on New York Yacht Club cruises she would win two cups in a race—one, the cup for her class, and the other the cup for the whole fleet under time allowance. I remember one morning her owner, Robert Emmons, came aboard and said, "Boys, we won two cups yesterday and one of them is most big enough to use for a dinghy."

Another multicup winner was William S. Eaton's Eastern schooner *Taormina*. With *Avenger* and *Dorello* she formed an ad hoc silver cartel that ruled the 1908 Annual Cruise down east and the splendid New York Yacht Club Cruise to Marblehead, more than complete with the now-traditional illumination, fireworks, band concerts, and protocol. (All were humbled in the light-aired Annual Regatta when *Onda II*, owned by John Greenough of Gloucester and just over 30 feet on the water, became the smallest yacht to date to win the Puritan Cup taken by *Avenger* the previous season.) *Onda II*, designed by Starling Burgess, was one of the popular P class (25 to 31 feet on the water), regarded by Devereux Barker as providing the most interesting racing out of the Eastern until about 1920, when the smaller Qs took over.

When it was all over that summer, *Taormina*'s owner wrote the Race Committee requesting that he receive his awards in cash so that he could go out and buy prizes that did not duplicate the cups she had already won.

The committee obligingly agreed to mail him a check in a week or so.

The first notable Q-boat in Marblehead was *Orestes*, designed by Starling Burgess in 1906 for Caleb Loring, who was then eighteen. She was the latest in a fleet of small sloops for the family (the Burgesses and Lorings had been summer neighbors in Beverly Farms for many years) and at least one launch dating back to 1901, the lines for which are the earliest of Starling's that survive. *Orestes* won every race she entered in 1906, including a silver cup intercity match for Q-boats between Boston and New York with Charles Francis Adams as skipper at the request of the young owner to ensure that she be sailed to the hilt. In 1908 Burgess designed the Q *Achilles* for Loring.

Chester C. Rumrill's new Herreshoff 46-rater cutter *Adventuress* was the Eastern's most promising addition in 1909 (along with a new Regatta Committee launch custom-built by Stearns and McKay). With no competition in her class in the Annual Regatta, she hoisted the L flag and challenged and outran the schooner *Taormina* in faint breezes for the Puritan Cup. The cruise was marked by a very fast run on a southwester that carried the old Cup defender *Vigilant*, now a yawl, six minutes ahead of *Constellation* the ninety miles from Marblehead to Portland in about seven and a half hours. *Adventuress* won the Puritan Cup again in 1910, showing herself a consistently good if not exactly brilliant performer both east and west of the Cape.

Mindful of the ever-increasing value and prestige of the Club's crown jewel, the Regatta Committee commissioned the Boston silversmiths Bigelow and Kennard to make sectional plaster casts of the Puritan Cup "so that in case of loss the cup could be reproduced."

Alexander Cochran of the New York Yacht Club had bought Robert Emmons's superlative sloop *Avenger* in 1909, only to be convinced by Charlie Barr, his skipper, to commission Nathanael Herreshoff to build him the big steel schooner *Westward* in 1910 so that they could sail across and clean up on the Europeans even more effectively than had Morton F. Plant's 1903 Herreshoff schooner *Ingomar*. They did, and Captain Barr, the greatest of the professionals, died aboard, of a heart attack while she was laid up the next winter in England.

As these things go, *Westward*'s easting merely sent Plant back to the well again for *Elena*. *Westward* was 136 feet overall, 96 feet on the water, 26 feet 8 inches beam, 17 feet draft. She was built to the European measure with less girth and more drag to her keel than her near-sister, which Captain Nat

---

William S. Eaton's full-blown *Taormina* leaves not a breath for the opposition. Jackson photo.

Rules, Ratings, and Regattas

126

designed to the Universal Rule. Francis Herreshoff described his father's method of doing business:

Plant used swear words when talking to men (although he was a most kindly man to children). At any rate, one evening after a good dinner he called Captain Nat on the telephone, and their short and sweet conversation was about as follows:
  Plant speaking: Is this N.G. Herreshoff?
  Capt. Nat: Yes, I think so.
  Plant: I want a —— —— schooner for Class B, and I want her to be —— —— good.
  Capt. Nat: Humph, all right.

Elena turned out to be —— —— good indeed. Eleven schooners and three sloops competed in the invitational 200-mile, New London-Marblehead Race at the beginning of July, and she won the gold cup offered by Commodore F. Lewis Clark as an incentive for yachts attending the Harvard-Yale crew race on the Thames River. Two days later (Morton Plant had established eligibility by joining the Eastern in May), she won the Puritan Cup in the Annual Regatta.

Then off on the Annual Cruise to the eastward. Six times in six races since her launching, *Elena* had beaten E. Walter Clark's 126-foot schooner *Irolita*, but she lost to her on a twenty-six-mile race in Penobscot Bay on July 10, although at the dinner at the Mount Desert Reading Room in Bar Harbor, *Elena* was awarded the prize in the first division schooners for fastest total corrected time on all the racing runs. To round out her first season, *Elena* carried home the schooner cup in the annual New York Yacht Club Cruise against *Irolita*, the *Westward*, and William E. Iselin's new *Enchantress*, 136 feet, designed by Cary Smith.

Devereux Barker, in *The Eastern Yacht Club Story*, gives Walter Clark, a Philadelphia member of the Eastern, major credit for the gradual takeover of the helm by the amateurs from the pros, remarking that "many of the owners, in fact, I think most of them, although enjoying yachting and life afloat, were not really sailors as we know the word today and were probably incapable of handling their yachts in rough weather and, much less, of racing them." Clark took up yachting when he was about forty and always sailed his own boats, according to Barker. He had several *Irolitas* and a professional skipper his

---

Irolita, Walter Clark's 126-foot overall schooner, one of the quartet of glorious ones. Jackson photo.

crew called "Captain Gunpowder" because he had a way of exploding without warning. Nevertheless, Barker was Clark's guest around 1911 on the schooner *Irolita*, ex-*Emerald*, with a professional crew of twenty-two, when the owner raced her himself against three other big ones with pro skippers.

It was the sunset glow of the years before World War I, and the income tax, the last sail-off of the great schooner yachts, and this quartet of the glorious ones (in which *Elena* usually enjoyed the edge) had at it for fair as the pride of the Eastern and the New York yacht clubs, of which all the owners but Cochran were joint members. Compare their dimensions with those of the great but ill-fated *Columbia*, one of the biggest Gloucester fishing schooners, claimed to have sailed at 16 knots, built in 1923 in a bid to defeat the Canadian *Bluenose* in the International Fishermen's Races.

	Overall	Waterline	Breadth	Draft
Elena	136'	96'	26'8"	17'
Columbia	143'	110'	25'8"	15'8"

Again in 1912, and in a gale of wind this time, *Elena* won the Clark Cup in the Eastern's invitational race, this time from Newport to Marblehead, and although she led the fleet and beat *Irolita* in the big schooner division in the Annual Regatta, the Puritan Cup was won for the second time by the sloop *Avenger*, which had passed from Robert Emmons to Alexander Cochran and now to Henry L. Maxwell.

The Annual Cruise of 1912 was not only one of the most successful in recent years but was the last one to the east before World War I. It was, in a sense, the swan song of an era. Forty-eight made up the squadron at Marblehead, including sixteen schooners, nine sloops, six yawls, and sixteen under steam or gasoline, aggregating 3,102 tons. The sloop *Dorello*, now owned by Barclay Henry of Philadelphia, joined by invitation. Commodore Robert Treat Paine 2d was aboard his flagship, the 125-foot schooner *Constance*, but he had his sloop *Shimna* in the racing division.

The fleet left Marblehead early in the morning of the Fourth of July for a good downwind sail in a light to moderate southerly and southwesterly to the finish at the Portland Lightship, coming to anchor at Peaks Island in the late afternoon. On July 5, the racers ran the twenty-eight miles from Portland to Boothbay Harbor in favorable and increasing winds, while the more leisurely cruised there through the Casco Bay islands.

The Guy Norman Cup, 1910.

On July 6, the run was thirty-three miles to Whitehead, and although the smaller boats finished late in light air, with a long run up Penobscot Bay, the fleet anchored at Camden in plenty of time for an evening dance at the Camden Yacht Club.

On Sunday the fleet proceeded at will to North Haven and the next day raced to Billings Cove, where all hands were entertained aboard the *Irolita*. On Tuesday morning, July 9, soon after morning colors, *Elena* reported three cases of diphtheria and was taken in tow by the committee tug to Portland for possible quarantine of yacht and crew and treatment of the sick men. The fleet moved on at will in very light airs to Swan's Island Harbor for the gig and dinghy races, of which the winners were: Gentlemen's Pairs, William Homans and George Denny; Crew Singles, *Taormina*; and Crew Pairs, *Muriel*.

The run to Northeast Harbor on July 10 was eighteen miles in light and favoring winds. By evening, the roadstead was a crowd of yachts, including *Elena*, back from Portland at the end of a towline. There was much back-and-forth with shore, "the music boxes were brought on deck, and grand opera and ragtime fought for supremacy."

Lack of wind killed the race to Frenchman's Bay on Thursday at noon, and the fleet made its way to Bar Harbor, where it dressed ship. During the Annual Cruise dinner at the Mount Desert Reading Room, Commodore Paine's cup was awarded to *Irolita* in the first-division schooners; Captain Plant's to *Princess* in the second-division schooners; Captain Winslow's to *Dorello* in the second-division sloops; Fleet Captain Emmons's to *Vagrant* in the third-division schooners; and a special prize was given by Vice Commodore Herbert Sears to *Irolita* for the schooner making the fastest total corrected time on all the racing runs from Boothbay to Bar Harbor. During the dinner, John C. Cobb, a guest on *Irolita*, offered a prize to the yacht winning the 161-mile race back to Marblehead; it went on corrected time to Commodore Paine's sloop *Shimna*.

For the third year, *Elena* ruled the upper levels of yachting in 1913. Morton Plant's schooner won the invitational race, again from Newport to Marblehead, for the third time, thus retaining permanent possession of the Clark Cup. In the Annual Regatta she won the Puritan Cup for the second time, again as the nemesis of the slightly smaller but ever-game *Irolita*, consistently her closest rival. *Elena* beat *Irolita* again to win the New York Yacht Club Regatta, and then the Astor Cup. Predictably, she prevailed over her in the Eastern's Annual Cruise, which was foreshortened by a southeast gale at Swan's Island and was otherwise memorable for the appearance (though she did not race) of Regatta Chairman Henry Morss's latest, *Halcyon*, a three-masted caravel modeled more or less after the little ships of Columbus's time, 70 feet on the water and equipped with an auxiliary.

The most attention-getting feature of the New York Yacht Club's Cruise to Marblehead in August 1913 was the appearance for the first time of the big sisters to the New York Thirties, the New York Yacht Club Fifties, nine of which had been built by Herreshoff the previous winter. The biggest class of large one-design daysailers ever created—72 feet overall, 50 feet waterline, over 9 feet draft—and foot-for-foot no doubt the least expensive, cost the lucky buyer a mere $17,000 complete with sails. The Eastern's *Elena*, *Taormina*, *Irolita*, and *Avenger* all distinguished themselves, but the icing on the cake was provided by the special complimentary race sponsored by the Club on August 15 for the Fifties over a 24½-mile course, starting and finishing at Marblehead Rock. It was won by Ralph Ellis's *Iroquois*.

Elena, another breathtaking example of the Wizard's wizardry. At 136 feet one of the largest and certainly handsomest schooner yachts ever built. Could that be *Irolita* astern? Jackson photo.

Rules, Ratings, and Regattas

Rules, Ratings, and Regattas

Rules, Ratings, and Regattas

Joining the Eastern fleet later was W. Earl Dodge's *Samuri*, renamed *Andiamo* by Walter Shaw, who moored her near her sister, *Pleione*, close off the Rockmere Hotel. Very fast in light air, she was called "The White Ghost" during her Marblehead racing days up to about 1925. Around 1930 the professional skipper of her five-man crew was the well-known Herbert (Herbie) Jackson. "*Andiamo* was a vision sailing down the harbor in the usual southerly," wrote one who cherished vivid memories. "As she tacked over near Frazier's boat yard, she took down the headsail and then off Skinner's Head dropped her main from the top of her 108-foot mast. With a thundering clatter the slides came down the track, and the echoes were heard all over the harbor as she silently glided to her mooring."

Of this great and lively class of New York Yacht Club Fifties, the greatest and longest-lived was *Pleione*, built for Eastern member Chester C. Rumrill and E.T. Ervin. She won five Astor Cups and a King's Cup and was owned for most of her fifty-year career by Joseph V. Santry, when as a schooner she and *Constellation* were the Eastern's sentimental favorites.

Under Regatta Chairman Stephen Sleeper in 1911, the Club made an unaccustomed effort to give a boost to small craft in open, round-the-buoys competition at the beginning of what was then called Corinthian Midsummer Week. Fog postponed this second of the Club's two efforts by three days, when fifty-two boats in seven classes started, including the A and B Interclubs, Cape Cod cats, and 18-foot knockabouts, all newly recognized by the EYC. The Corinthian started 147 in twenty-two classes.

The 1912 season was an improvement, with twenty-one of the popular new 17-footers designed by Edwin Boardman for Marblehead, and 1913 was more successful still. Three regattas instead of two were held, in June, July, and on August 4, the Monday of Race Week, when sixty-two boats in twelve classes turned up: M-and-Ns, Ps, Qs, Bar Harbor 31-footers, Sonders, Boston Yacht Club Second-Raters, Marblehead 17-footers, Corinthian 15-footers, A and B Interclubs, Cape Cod cats, 18-foot knockabouts, and Manchester 17s.

Wearing the mantle of his late father even as he wove his own, Starling Burgess was already making a splash with his imaginative and frequently brilliantly successful designs. He

Neck-and-neck, a trio of New York Fifties off Marblehead, August 13, 1913—*Pleione, Iroquois II* and *Barbara*. Stebbins photo.

had been the Club's measurer since 1907 but since 1910 had been preoccupied with designing and building aircraft for the Navy. His prior obligations must have suffered, judging from the dissatisfaction of the Regatta Committee, which met in Chairman Sleeper's Boston office on January 25, 1911, to review the 1910 races and "the results as figured," as reported by Secretary Henry A. Morss:

> As nearly as could be determined, the Measurer, Mr. Burgess, has not furnished proper rating for yawls and sloops, which has led to one error, and the Committee has made another error in rating yawls at 93% and schooners at 90% of the ratings given when sailing in mixed classes. The discussion came up through the fact that it was found that in the case of *Iris*, we got her rating from her New York Yacht Club certificate, and this was as it should be 90% of her measurement, so in all the races during the Cruise she sailed 10% less rating than the other boats in the Fleet.
>
> It was decided to determine finally by inspection of the Measurer's book just what figures should be furnished, then to employ Mr. L.M. Fowle to refigure the results of all races of last season according to the ratings which should be determined as right.
>
> There was some discussion concerning the general inefficiency of the Measurer.

Nonetheless, in March the Regatta Committee reappointed Burgess as measurer without further official comment; and it decided, incidentally, that the Club was not in a position to follow the suggestion of the Hollis Burgess Yacht Agency that it buy a steam yacht to replace the towboat usually hired for the Annual Regatta.

In January 1912, however, the Regatta Committee "decided not to appoint a Measurer at this meeting," and on March 14 replaced Starling Burgess with Professor Harold A. Everett of M.I.T. Or Burgess may simply have succumbed to the lure of flight and resigned.

Forever the optimist, Sir Thomas Lipton challenged for the America's Cup for the fourth time in 1913, the match to be sailed the following year. After much controversy with the New York Yacht Club over measurement, he was permitted to go ahead with *Shamrock IV*, 75 feet on the water, built to the Universal Rule.

A New York syndicate was quickly formed to have Nathanael Herreshoff design and build *Resolute*. E.W. Clark organized a second syndicate to build *Defiance*, and Alexander Cochran went along on his own with his aptly named *Vanitie*, a

Rules, Ratings, and Regattas

No wind, the 22-footers try to start on July 24, 1905. A brigantine is at anchor behind them. Jackson photo.

A bouncy day for the start of the 18-footers. Jackson photo.

glorious J-class designed by William Gardner, bronze-plated from keel to railcap. The power was with the *Resolute* men, among whom were Arthur Curtiss James, J.P. Morgan, and Cornelius Vanderbilt, and it is a mark of New York's sometimes grudging respect for Boston's prowess that they asked that outstanding Eastern helmsman Robert W. Emmons 2d to manage their syndicate.

That December, Charles Francis Adams was proposed by Emmons and elected to the New York Yacht Club. In the 1914 trials, Adams would be the first amateur skipper of an America's Cup candidate in the history of the series. His assistant helmsman would be Emmons's brother-in-law, John Parkinson, Jr.

All three—Adams, Emmons, and Parkinson—were good friends and members of the same club at Harvard. And all three, with their backers, seem to have shared Sir Thomas's assumption that nothing was about to interfere with business as usual on the North Atlantic.

Chapter 8

The War Years

Europe might rumble, but America was as aloof from such alien quarrels in 1914 as three thousand miles of salt water could make her. The style that took its name from England's rotund monarch carried on of its own substantial momentum, even though Edward had been in his grave for four years.

Perhaps because *Resolute, Defiance,* and *Vanitie* would be testing their mettle west of the Cape that summer, the Eastern's now-almost-usual ocean race from New London or Newport to Marblehead was forgone, and the club took the unusual step of scheduling the Annual Regatta to coincide with the Annual Cruise, which was directed to Newport, where the trio of contenders for the defense of the America's Cup would be vying to take on Sir Thomas Lipton's *Shamrock IV*, due to cross from Britain in a few weeks.

Herbert Mason Sears had succeeded Robert Treat Paine 2d as commodore for the 1914 season and led the Eastern squadron in his flagship *Cristabel*. Commodore Sears had been vice commodore since 1912, rear commodore from 1910. A Harvard graduate of 1889, a widower, and the father of two daughters, a trustee by profession, he was long active in the Club, a devotee of the sport of yachting regardless of waterline (an avid racer in his Sonder *Mingo*), and a warm host aboard and from his estate at Pride's Crossing in Beverly (now the nucleus of Endicott College).

For the first time since 1903, the Annual Cruise sailed south around Cape Cod, rendezvousing off Newport on July 3. Fog and heavy weather delayed the regatta until July 8, when only four yachts entered. Ex-Commodore Paine's *Shimna* won the Puritan Cup. More spectacularly, *Vanitie* lost on time allowance to *Resolute*, steered by Charles Francis Adams, after leading her across the finish by 30 seconds. *Defiance* broke down

before the start, never did get in the running, was withdrawn by her backers before the season was over, and was broken up as a bad job.

Momentously, the waters of Massachusetts and Buzzards bays commingled for the first time on July 4, 1914, while the fleet was commingling on the far side. But even if the Annual Cruise had been delayed by a few days for a maiden passage through, the newly completed Cape Cod Canal would not be officially open to navigation (and then only to vessels drawing 15 feet or less) until July 30.

Charlie Foster, meanwhile, had turned his restless curiosity to the ever-elusive debate between the technocrat and the humanist as it applied to the objects of his own dichotomous passion: how to compare with some degree of accuracy the performance of two class boats under various conditions. In 1914 he commissioned his friend Starling Burgess to design and build for him a pair of knockabouts, which he named with classical logic *Alpha* and *Beta*, his thirty-seventh and thirty-eighth, so alike that they weighed within 30 pounds of each other.

My idea was to try with them various experiments with sails and other things. Curiously enough the human factor destroyed the possibility of accuracy in these matters, although we did learn some things. I found that the ability to sail a boat on Monday night might be quite different on Tuesday, and the chap sailing the other boat was equally different on different days. It was an interesting fact that during the first year *Alpha* was the consistent winner under various rigs and conditions, while in the second year *Beta* seemed to do the better work. The lesson to be learned was that it takes very little to make a difference of quite a number of seconds over a given course even though the two boats are supposed to be alike.

One of the little differences was an average of a minute gained over the average Marblehead course by the boat that was hauled and scrubbed every week for every week the other remained in the water. And Foster fooled around unsuccessfully with the curve of the mainsail along the foot, a notion that is said to have influenced Burgess to experiment with the J-boat *Enterprise*'s boardwalk boom in 1930. After he had satisfied his curiosity for the moment, C.H.W. Foster altered his twins to R-boats.

Germany declared war on Russia August 1, and two days later on France, as the Eastern opened Midsummer Race Week with the second of its three round-the-buoys regattas, followed by the Boston's and the Corinthian's. The three clubs, with

---

Commodore Sears by the mainmast of *Constellation*. Water color by John Singer Sargent, 1924.

136

Manchester, arranged a North Shore Championship on a percentage basis among the small classes.

Britain declared war on Germany on August 4, and President Woodrow Wilson affirmed America's neutrality. In two more weeks, *Shamrock IV* arrived in New York after a passage of horizon-scanning lest she be captured by the Eastern's Honorary Member number six. She would be holed up there for the duration. During the last week of the month, the Club, as already noted, held trials for the Sonder races scheduled for Kiel in 1915.

The owner of the schooner *Constellation*, Frank Skinner, had died, and in the autumn of 1914, Commodore Sears purchased her from the estate and "had her interior cut-up entirely changed to suit my needs, and I also put in an engine." Thus began the golden era of the grand old 134-foot schooner designed by Edward Burgess and built in 1889 for E.D. Morgan, from whom she passed to Bayard Thayer for ten years until she was purchased by Skinner in 1899. And thus, too, it may be said, unfolded the golden years of Commodore Sears.

With Sears at the helm and Henry Morss in his second season as Regatta Chairman, participation in smaller-boat racing took a leap forward when the Eastern agreed with the Corinthian, Boston, and Manchester clubs on a North Shore Championship. It was arranged on a percentage basis for classes P, R, BYC Second-Raters, Marblehead and Manchester 17-foot One-Designs, CYC 15-foot One-Design, and Sonders. The Club's three open races would be counted, and its June 27 race would include draft from all these classes and from class L and the Bar Harbor 31s.

The Eastern's race on Monday, August 3, opened the 1914 Midsummer Race Week with all the agreed-on classes except L, plus six primarily Boston Bay classes, and was followed by the Boston's on Tuesday and then the Corinthian's. Although the process occurred over several seasons, the impetus given by Commodore Sears to interclub racing, and his encouragement of youthful sailors, mark the metamorphosis from Corinthian Midsummer Week to Marblehead Race Week.

The ocean race from New London to Marblehead was resumed in 1915, on June 26. Although Harold S. Vanderbilt offered a gold cup for the first-division schooner winning three times under one owner, there were only three entries: *Irolita*, the winner; *Constellation*; and the sloop *Avenger*. Was the distant war provoking caution? In 1916 only two schooners

competed for the Vanderbilt Cup from Newport to Marblehead—*Virginia*, which carried away her topmasts near Vineyard Haven, and the donor's *Vagrant*, which then withdrew.

Just ten yachts competed in the Annual Regatta off Marblehead in 1915; George L. Batchelder's *Dorello II* won the Puritan Cup. The Annual Cruise again pushed eastward, on July 1,
into the worst weather in years, with fog, rain, no wind, and a
near-hurricane followed by a 30-knot nor'wester.

The fun was provided this year by the New York Yacht Club,
which on August 2, 1915, embarked on its first cruise through
the Cape Cod Canal. Most of the fleet of ninety-two was powerless; twenty-one steam yachts and chartered tugs did the
towing; auxiliaries were under orders to stay clear and bring
up the rear.

This armada arrived at Marblehead on August 7, raced on to
Gloucester, and then back on August 10. Nearly two hundred
yachts dressed ship in Marblehead Harbor, with the traditional
illumination, fireworks, and band concert in the evening. On
August 11 the New Yorkers raced for the King's Cup for the
first time off Marblehead, in light and fluky airs, before head-
ing for home, some of them no doubt renegotiating the new
canal.

Having refitted the schooner *Constellation* to his satisfaction, Commodore Sears was anxious to see how his twenty-
six-year-old flagship would perform offshore. So he planned a
cruise to the West Indies in February of 1916—a little reminiscent of Frank McQuesten's in *Gitana* after the War of 1898—
taking along his pals John Lawrence, Parkman (Parkie) B. Haven, and Henry (Harry) Dalton (who would join them in Bermuda via the S.S. *Bermudian*). Sears was then forty-eight. His
journal of the cruise is a window, curtains carefully parted, on
a departing era of the Eastern Yacht Club:

> I went to my sailing master and told him to get the yacht ready
> for the cruise. She was painted black, but thinking that she
> would be much cooler white, I had her painted over. I also had
> a new winter rig made which was very much smaller than my
> summer rig and instead of taking a spinnaker I had a squaresail
> made. I also had a lifeboat built which I carried on deck and two
> Swampscott dories and my regular gasoline launch.

They departed from East Boston under power on February 1,

George Batchelder's lovely *Dorello II* won the Puritan Cup in
1915.

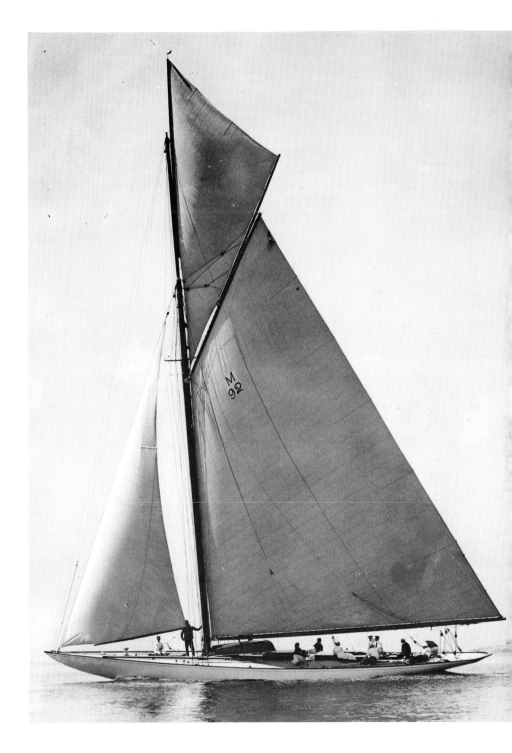

but got only as far as Hull, where they ran in when it began to snow. Next morning they sent the dory in for the newspapers and the weather report, which they learned would not be due in from the weather bureau in Washington until the afternoon. So the dory was sent in again at 3:30 and brought back the prediction of a northeast snowstorm. Early on February 4, *Constellation* departed Hull.

We passed the Boston Light Ship at 9:50 A.M. and John Lawrence and I took an observation just for practice for me and I was pleased that I practically agreed with what he got. We reached the Gulf Stream the next day in the morning, and the rigging that had been covered with ice soon got all melted out and was once more soft and workable.

On Sunday morning at four o'clock it began to blow really hard from the west, and we took in the foresail which we had left up all night and set the fore-trysail in its place and took the bonnet out of the main-trysail. She did not make much headway under this canvas in the ugly sea but behaved finely. At twelve o'clock the wind and sea were both increasing, and we took in the jib and went under the two trysails only. It blew a moderate gale all that afternoon, increasing at night.

At four in the morning of February 7th we hove the *Constellation* to under both trysails and got out the oil and filled the bags and put them out over the side. We soon took in the fore-trysail as the boat was fore-reaching a little too fast. We kept the oil going all the time, and we used over seventy gallons of it and had to use a little of the machine oil.

At about noon on this day, Monday, February 7th, the gale was at its height and blowing harder than I had ever seen wind blow before. Funnily enough, it was raining hard all the time. The boat behaved splendidly and took on no dangerous water, although, while I was standing near the wheel, hanging on to the after companionway, we did get a green sea over the quarter which gave me an idea of how hot the Gulf Stream was.

This was my first experience on a small sailing yacht on the Atlantic Ocean in a heavy gale of wind, and it was really exciting. The old "sea dogs" on the boat said they had seen nothing harder for many years. The good ship *Constellation* behaved really beautifully, I thought. The same sea that ducked me took the sailing master off his feet, but he too was holding on to a life rope and no harm was done. Nobody could stand on deck without holding on to something. Early in the afternoon the wind began to go further to the north, the barometer began to rise, and at 5 P.M. we had signs of better weather with the clouds breaking in the west.

Constellation and the steamship *Bermudian* arrived at Bermuda simultaneously on February 10.

I could see through the glasses Harry [Dalton] on deck. He hailed us through the megaphone. We anchored in Hamilton Harbor at 9:35 A.M. and found the *Vagrant*, Commodore H.S. Vanderbilt's yacht, there. She had started from New London a day earlier than we left Boston and her course was quite a good deal shorter than ours. Commodore Vanderbilt was also on the *Bermudian* and he came right aboard the *Constellation* as soon as he had left his bags on his own yacht. We had hoped to cruise in company through the West Indies, but his party [including Herbert Sears's brother, Philip] were to meet him at Porto Rico and their steamer had started a day earlier than originally scheduled so he told me that he wanted to get away as soon as possible to join them at Porto Rico, and we both hoped to join forces there.

Rainy weather decreed otherwise, delaying *Constellation*'s departure from Bermuda. When they arrived in San Juan, *Vagrant* was gone. So on to St. Thomas, and then to St. Kitts, Guadeloupe, and Dominica. On March 4 they reached Fort de France, Martinique, where, "at 4:30 P.M. I was surprised to see a very good looking gig come along to the port gangway (which is like coming to a back door of a house) and the harbor master and a friend came on deck. . . . I had their gig called to the starboard gang when they left!"

St. Lucia, St. Vincent, Bequia, Grenada, Trinidad, and on March 11, La Guaira, Venezuela, where the officers and sailors all bought parrots, and one of the sailors a small monkey, which "was either very feeble or seasick on the way up to Jamaica, and when we arrived there [he] traded him for two boxes of very poor cigars."

It was Curacao on March 14, and on to Jamaica in a good breeze of wind that put *Constellation*'s rail under, with the result that a sea carried away a dory in the lee davits—fortunately empty of the eight or ten parrots that a few minutes earlier had taken refuge therein. Indeed, so good a breeze that "I think the *Constellation* made the best time she has ever recorded. For the first 24 hours we averaged eleven and a half knots, and we arrived at Kingston, Jamaica, on Friday, March 17th. We had made a fine run from Curacao, making the 585 nautical miles, and this was all under sail, with no power, in 54 hours."

Business called John Lawrence home, and he was lucky at Kingston to get in the captain's quarters on a United Fruit Company banana boat for New York, "as she was very full and nothing else was left."

We left Kingston at 1:30 on Monday morning, March 20th, bound for Santiago, Cuba. We arrived off Santiago Light at nine in the evening but had to wait overnight just at the entrance to Santiago Harbor. The pilot came aboard at six o'clock the next morning, and we immediately began to get the anchor. It did not come up very easily, and finally the pilot told us that we had caught in what was left of the *Merrimac* which Hobson sank in the Spanish War across the mouth of the harbor to "bottle up" Cervera's fleet. [Lieutenant Richmond P. Hobson on June 3, 1898, tried to scuttle the old Navy collier in the channel, but she drifted out of it and was sunk by a combination of Spanish fire and his own torpedoes. He and his men were captured briefly by Admiral Cervera.]

As soon as we got the anchor free, we proceeded up to the harbor of Santiago. That finished our cruise of nearly 3,500 miles, as we all had to leave and come home by steamer or rail.

Constellation was back at Marblehead in ample time to lead the Eastern through its last yachting season of the war. *Irolita* won the 1916 Puritan Cup in the Annual Regatta, of which the main feature must have been the appearance of three of Herreshoff's New York Yacht Club Forties just built the previous winter. The Club again ran three open races for small classes participating in the North Shore Championship; the last led off Race Week on August 8 in a 50-knot squall at the start that left the survivors looking for the finish in the fog.

Nearly thirty yachts sailed east in the Annual Cruise, which was distinguished by the return of Henry Morss's anachronistic caravel *Halcyon* and by the appearance of Charlie Foster's fortieth boat in forty-two years—the biggest he ever built, and in his estimation, his best—the huge ketch *Finback*, of which her owner wrote:

In 1916 I happened to be present at the launching of a fine fisherman at Essex, and after the launching casually asked [Arthur D.] Story, her builder at what price he would deliver to me another boat like her—hull, spars, and ironwork—at Gloucester. I had at the moment no idea of building such a boat, but had always dreamed of the joy there must be in owning a real deep sea-going vessel of that type. Story, at the time, was without any work for the winter and said it would be an act of charity if I would give him an order. Within two days he named a price of $9200 for such a boat delivered in Gloucester, and I made the deal. As a result, I was possessor of the best boat that I ever owned or had been aboard.

The launching Foster witnessed from the Story yard may have been of the fishing schooner *Catherine* the previous fall.

The caravel *Halcyon*, Henry Morss's bit of fun, ploughs along in one direction—another flight of fancy, likely Starling Burgess's, in the other.

Autocrat, C.H.W. Foster's ketch, 51 feet waterline, was built in 1911 on the lines of fishing schooner designer Thomas McManus. Stebbins photo.

Navy trainees line up in front of the clubhouse, April 26, 1917.

Finback was built on her model and that of her predecessor, *Knickerbocker*, and at 136 feet overall was the largest yacht ever turned out by A.D. Story in his long career. The builder's son, Dana, wrote of *Finback*'s debut on May 4, 1916, in his book *Frame-up!*: "On launching day a caterer was brought in and a big spread laid amongst the chips and piles of lumber. When she finally slid down the ways she almost didn't make it, her keel digging into the mud so that she nearly stopped."

The majestic fisherman hull was her owner's second ketch after *Autocrat*, 51 feet on the water, which he built in 1911 from plans by fishing schooner designer Tom McManus. Foster cruised and liked *Autocrat* so much that he had to have another twice as big. Hence *Finback*, of which he wrote many years later: "Weather made no difference to her, and while I never made any foreign trips in her, we never stopped through stress of circumstances to go anywhere on the coast we desired at any time. When we entered the war, I sold her to carry foodstuffs to foreign ports. Later she was sold to a moving picture outfit to go to the far north, and was finally lost on an uncharted reef in Hudson's Bay."

One more memorable encounter awaited the Eastern's last peacetime Annual Cruise for three years. Coming to anchor in Northeast Harbor on July 12 after the run from Billings Cove, the cruisers were greeted by none other than the old Boston pilot schooner *Hesper*, which had won the first Fishermen's Race back in 1886 and was defeated three years later in a match with Commodore Forbes's new *Fredonia*. *Hesper* had been converted into a yacht now owned by Mrs. Andrew C. Wheelwright, a "Flag Member" of the Club since the death of her husband, a charter member, in 1908. The other Flag Member in 1916 was Mrs. Charles G. Weld, who continued to keep the 151-foot schooner-rigged steam yacht *Malay* in commission after the death in 1911 of her doctor-husband, a wealthy benefactor of the Massachusetts General Hospital.

The bylaws provided that a woman owning a yacht could be elected a Flag Member with annual dues of forty dollars and no initiation fee. She had the privileges of flying the Club flag and her private signal, entering the yacht in Club races, using Club stations and floats, and using the clubhouse as prescribed for ladies, but she was not allowed to vote.

The coda to the 1916 cruise was a 162-mile ocean race back from Bar Harbor to Marblehead for the Norman Cup among four schooners. It was won by Harold Vanderbilt's new *Vagrant*. Each contestant was to take its own time at the finish "when the beacon on Halfway Rock bears NNW distant not over ¼ mile" and report the result in writing to the Regatta Committee.

That cruise was the last until 1919, and very likely the last accompanied by chartered steam tugs, of which there were three with plenty of towline. And 1916 was the last year, or close to it, that a towboat was hired as the committee boat for the Annual Regatta. The Regatta Committee in 1911 had de-

clined the offer of a local brokerage to sell it a yacht for its exclusive use; two years later, it sold its launch for $150 but was still budgeted for $5,000, some of which was tugboat charter money.

The year 1916 was the first of fifty-three seasons for M.I.T. Professor Evers Burtner as fleet measurer for the three Marblehead clubs. He followed Professor Harold A. Everett, who had replaced Starling Burgess in 1911. From the vantage of 1963, Professor Burtner looked back on the Marblehead scene a few months before America was drawn into the war:

Yachtsmen and summer residents didn't depend on the automobile so much for transportation but could count upon fairly good train and ferry service. Two little steam ferries, *Queen* and *Blonde*, with the motor ferry *Delta* left Tucker's Wharf, stopped if necessary at the Corinthian float and at the ferry's own floats at the foot of Ferry Lane and also at the present Pleon pier [the Eastern's Old Stone Wharf].

Coal was delivered to Marblehead by large coastwise coal barges, one wharf, Martin's, being near the Marblehead Power Plant, the other the site of Charles Foster's Ship's Cabin, now the Marblehead Station of the Boston.

Off Beacon Street, at Little Harbor, James Graves's yard was active in hauling and building yachts. Stearns and McKay's yard was very busy, having perhaps the best hauling railway; it is now the Marblehead Yacht Yard operated by Graves. The Boston Yacht Club Station was just south of this yard and north of Tucker's Wharf. Frazier ran a yard off Gregory Street. The fin keel America's Cup aspirant *Jubilee* was hauled out just north

of the Power Plant at a yard formerly run by Starling Burgess, who at this time was interested in seaplanes and had a plant near where Ted Hood's sail loft is. The harbormaster kept a "free channel" cleared of yacht moorings for the seaplanes and coal barges.

One of Burtner's first recommendations to the three clubs in 1916 was that the Q and R boats be weighed to determine displacement, with the result that Graves installed the first platform scales in place of the yard scales suspended from a derrick or shears that had been used to heft the Sonders.

The rejection by the Allies of the Kaiser's peace overtures through President Wilson forced the showdown between the German civilian and military that resulted in the resumption of unrestricted submarine warfare. On April 6, 1917, after the sinking of several American ships, Congress declared war, and it became the painful duty of EYC Secretary Henry Taggard to declare His Imperial Majesty, William II, Emperor of Germany, no longer on the roll of Honorary Members of the Eastern Yacht Club. The New York Yacht Club was similarly embarrassed and struck the Kaiser and Prince Henry, who had been likewise honored after the launching of the imperial schooner *Meteor* in 1903.

B. Devereux Barker was chairman of the House Committee and recalled that the commodore telephoned Assistant Secretary of the Navy Franklin D. Roosevelt, offered the clubhouse gratis as a naval base, and was almost immediately accepted.

"We turned the Club House over to the Navy, I think on April 19th, for I remember distinctly going to the Boston Navy Yard and then motoring to Marblehead and turning the Club House over to R.F. Herrick, Jr., [a member] who was in command of the Naval Detail sent down for that purpose. I also remember that it was a very cheerless day with flurries of snow. . . . James O. Porter was at first in command, and Charles K. Cummings was his Chief of Staff."

During the relatively brief period that first year of America's entry into the war, when the Club served as a naval training station, Cummings wrote to Henry Taggard that it was alive with activity.

Men were quartered throughout the house, and hammocks were swung under the verandahs and in the hitching sheds; also huge open barracks were built as shelters for additional hammocks on the tennis courts. At times I believe there were over eight hundred officers and enlisted men quartered at the station. The personnel was trained as well as the time at our disposal and the very limited abilities of our amateur officers allowed, and then were sent off in groups as they were needed for battleships, converted yachts, destroyers, etc.

Unfortunately, the record of the Club's role as a naval training station is elusive. Henry Taggard wrote proudly that "our members took great satisfaction in the knowledge that a large number of men received training while quartered at our club house." In 1932, in preparation for Foster's planned second volume of the *Ditty Box*, Taggard requested members who had seen service during World War I to send him their records and recollections.

Daniel R. Sortwell, for example, wrote:

I enlisted on April 3, 1917, as Ensign in command of our yacht *Shada*. I did patrol work on this boat from Boston and Cape Cod to Eastport until August 1917. From this time I was connected to the Boston district in the Communication Service. This meant having an eight hour watch in charge of every kind of message in or out of this District by wire, cable or radio, doing the coding and deciphering when necessary. During the raids at Cape Cod by the German submarines and during the passage of the German subs across the Atlantic this was of course most interesting, as their position was accurately wired to us in advance. So accurate, in fact, that I could never understand why we did not sink some on this coast.

In September 1918 I was attached to the old *Yanckton* then at the New York Navy Yard for repairs and due to return to the Mediterranean. But before sailing I was transferred to the de-

stroyer *Dent*, the service I had been requesting for some time. The Armistice kept this ship at New York, however, and I was discharged there on January 20, 1919.

Service of a different sort was undertaken by Alexander S. Porter, a widower with the responsibility for two small daughters that kept him in Boston, where he drove an ambulance based at the Commonwealth Armory, was postmaster at the Red Cross Mailing Bureau, pitched in making surgical dressings, and became a "Four-Minute Man" pitching Victory Bonds in movie houses:

I think the hardest job I had was one night going onto the stage at the Colonial Theatre between the first and second acts of the Follies, with Will Rogers, and selling Victory Bonds. However, we managed to sell that night more bonds than all the Shubert theatres together. Eleonora Sears was on the runway with Al Jolson at the Opera House, but they did not begin to sell as many as we did.

Charles Francis Adams was treasurer of Harvard, among numerous other responsibilities, and going on fifty when his country entered the war:

I have no war record worth speaking of. I did serve in some secret service organization and on a committee or two of minor importance, but I had to choose between the College and the war and felt it my duty to turn towards the College.

On the other hand, Henry Howard just kept juggling, as might be expected, only substituting one ball for another. To the dismay of the ever-alert Sonder chairman, the legislation creating the United States Shipping Board in January 1917 for the purpose of building up the inadequate merchant marine made little or no provision for manpower. So he worked out a recruiting and training plan and presented it to the new board, which, not surprisingly, accepted it. Howard accepted appointment as director of the Recruiting Service of the U.S. Shipping Board at a salary of five dollars a month—provided he could stay in Boston and remain on as vice president of the Merrimac Chemical Company.

Director Howard rolled up his sleeves, organized the Recruiting Service, and set up navigation and engineering schools around the entire coastline. In a typical enveloping operation, he got Louis K. Liggett of Boston, head of the United Drug Company, to establish every one of his 6,870 Rexall corner drugstores nationwide as merchant marine recruiting stations at a cost of $6,870, or a dollar a year per manager. After the war, Liggett was put up for the Eastern and joined.

Lifeboat drill was an essential, and Harry Howard was a congenital recruiter, if he did say so himself in *Charting My Life*:

In one case I invited all of the members of the Eastern Yacht Club to take a trip on one of our training ships from Boston to Marblehead. On their arrival we put all the lifeboats overboard and sent all the members ashore after which we brought them on board again and returned to Boston. This made a pleasant excursion for the members but most important it gave a realistic opportunity for training our crew how to act when it was necessary to abandon ship.

If details are few on the role of the clubhouse as a naval training station, they are no more than clues that a part may have been played by some members at sea—as tossed out by John Parkinson in his *History of the New York Yacht Club*: "A group of Boston yachtsmen, which included some NYYC members, built a one-design division of fast patrol boats at their own expense before their country entered the war. They were about 50 feet long and proved useful."

The 1917 EYC *Yearbook* lists eight powerboats, all 62 feet overall, 61 feet waterline, and 11 feet beam, except one 58 feet overall, 57 feet waterline and 11 feet beam. All were under construction for single and multiple owners, including Maximilian Agassiz, John S. Lawrence, Herbert M. Sears, Oliver Ames, Charles F. Ayer, Francis S. Eaton, Charles P. Curtis, and Charles A. and Henry A. Morss. Nathaniel F. Ayer was building the 58-footer. There is no further reference to them. Philip Bolger heard that Ralph Winslow claimed to have designed them while working as Loring Swazey's draftsman. On the other hand, one wonders whether these or the fast patrol boats mentioned by Parkinson—considerably elongated—are the same as those alluded to by Devereux Barker in *The Eastern Yacht Club Story* many years later:

Shortly after the Declaration of War, the Government asked yachtsmen to subscribe for power boats to be used for submarine patrol. They were to be built by Herreshoff, be about 40 feet long, and cost $18,000. The added inducement was that the owner would be commissioned as an ensign and command his own vessel. This inducement was shortly annulled, but in any event, the delays in the yard were so great that few, if any, of the craft were delivered in time to be of any use.

Try as he might, Barker was not quite able to suppress a mixture of disappointment and resentment when he wrote a little tartly in response to Henry Taggard's request for war memoirs:

Although it had been expected in the beginning to use the Club as a Base for water activities, it developed almost entirely into a land situation. [And here Foster crossed out "land" from Barker's letter to Taggard and penciled in "aviation."] Towards the end of the season, Mr. Godfrey Cabot replaced Lieutenant Porter in command.

Enter Godfrey L. Cabot, Bostonian extraordinaire, producer of possibly the world's largest supply of carbon black, patriarch plenipotentiary of the Cabot clan until his reluctant relinquishment of the role at the age of 101 in 1962, and pioneering aviator. Cabot related to Henry Taggard how he got to the Eastern that spring of 1917:

From January, 1904, to the beginning of the World War in 1914, I was greatly interested in trying to induce the United States Government to increase its military power in the air. Confident that the country would be ill prepared in case of war, and wishing to do what I personally could do, I began in October, 1915, to learn to fly, and ordered a seaplane and built a hangar.

The seaplane, or hydroplane, Cabot bought was a Burgess-Dunne open-air flying machine of struts and cloth developed by Starling Burgess under the patents of the English designer J.W. Dunne. The Navy began ordering them in 1913. The hangar was on the western end of Misery Island, offshore of Cabot's Beverly Farms estate. He continued:

In June, 1916, I joined the Massachusetts Naval Volunteer Militia with a rank of Ensign for Aeronautical duties only. I practised flying at Pensacola in April, 1916, and in January, 1917, and was very active in the winter recruiting pupils for the Squantum Flying School. In the fall of 1916, I gave a seaplane, which I named for Norman Prince, to the State of Massachusetts in behalf of the Aero Club of New England, of which I was for six years the President, and on this seaplane many volunteers were trained.

Norman Prince was about the only male member of the Prince family—all keen yachtsmen and Myopia horsemen—who was not a member of the Eastern. He never really had the chance. Deeply involved with Starling Burgess's earliest flying projects, young Prince and the older Greely S. Curtis, Jr., of another stalwart Eastern sailing family, conceived the idea of a volunteer squadron to fight the Germans late in 1914. Curtis was over-age, but Norman Prince went on to France to found the Lafayette Escadrille and was killed in a crash on October 12, 1916. Hence Godfrey Cabot's memorial. Cabot again:

In 1917 I was appointed a Lieutenant, Senior Grade, in the U.S. Naval Reserve Force, and on the 14th of April I was assigned to active duty, taking charge on the 16th of a contingent of volunteer flying men at the Eastern Yacht Club at Marblehead, where I remained until the middle of August, when the Camp was dissolved and I became the Aide for Aviation of the First Naval District.

Besides training (and financing the training of) some of the pioneer Navy pilots, Lieutenant Cabot invented and patented an "apparatus for picking up burdens in flight," worked out a technique for in-flight refueling between aircraft, experimented with camouflage, came up with a plan for converting twenty-four warships into aircraft carriers, flew a number of sub-spotting missions off the New England coast, and in October 1918 was awarded the gold wings of a naval aviator, "being 12 years 355 days older than any other man to whom these wings were ever granted," as he proclaimed to Taggard.

On July 25, 1917, three months after Godfrey Cabot took charge for the Navy of the small flight training program at the Eastern Yacht Club that he had started so informally and with his own resources, he became a Club member. He was more the airman than the yachtsman, however, and resigned in 1919.

Looking back from 1962, Devereux Barker had a little more to add:

Of course, we all expected the Navy would use the floats and facilities of the harbor, so we induced Jim Porter, the first commandant, to close the road in front of the Clubhouse. This road had been and still is a nuisance, and since everyone thought the war would last for years, we hoped that by the time it was over the existence of the road would be forgotten. Large, tall posts were sunk in the roadway at Nanepashemet Street and just in from Harbor Avenue with space enough for a person on foot to go through, but not enough space for vehicles of any sort. Unfortunately, the Navy never used the float or harbor but only drilled incessantly in the field across the way. When Godfrey Cabot succeeded in command, he said the posts were unnecessary, refused to listen to pleas, and took them up.

The clubhouse was not intended for winter occupancy, and at the end of the summer of 1917, the Navy withdrew and turned it back to its owners. That fall, at a dinner at the Algon-

quin Club in Boston, Assistant Secretary Roosevelt was a speaker and thanked the members for the loan.

For the first time in forty-seven years, all racing was suspended by the Club for the 1917 season. Members were leaving for the service, many yachts were not placed in commission, U-boats were out there, and yachting was not considered an appropriate activity with wartime strictures on and belt-tightening all round as the order of the day.

Following Ben Butler's death in 1893, the schooner *America* had passed to his son Paul, who was more partial to canoeing than to yachting and turned her over to Butler Ames, his nephew. The general's grandson recommissioned her, joined the Corinthian in addition to the Boston, and in 1898 was elected to the New York Yacht Club, which of course reinstalled its queen immediately. She even defeated *Mayflower* during the NYYC Cruise of 1899. In 1901 she engaged in the last race of her career, from Vineyard Haven to Newport, when she lost to the New York flagship *Corona*.

From 1901 until 1912, *America* lay at her old winter berth by the Chelsea Bridge in the Mystic River with a caretaker aboard. Then she was shifted to Fort Point Channel alongside the Summer Street Bridge. In 1917, her owners sold her to the Cape Verde trade, but when the marathon collector C.H.W. Foster heard about it, he stepped in and made an offer. Title had not yet passed; the Cape Verdeans graciously accepted another schooner, and the Ameses accepted the Foster offer.

The new owner had George Lawley remove the lead from *America*'s keel, and Foster patriotically sold it to a munitions factory, which covered most of her cost to him. He formed a holding company of Eastern members to take title, with Secretary Taggard as secretary and titleholder, and Charlie Foster's forty-first was moored in Lawley's basin for the duration.

The Navy's return of the clubhouse to the Club after one season provided some limited options for the summer of 1918, and Chairman Henry Morss of the Regatta Committee made a significant report to the members on the results:

Owing to the War the Annual Cruise, Annual Regatta and all racing in the larger classes were omitted during the season of 1918.

At the April meeting the Club voted to encourage yachting through the racing of small boats and the Regatta Committee was instructed to study the question of the purchase of a class for the members to race. After considerable investigation and with the approval of the Council five 15-foot, one-design sloops were purchased [at a cost of $970, plus $357.91 for fitting-out and repairs] and put in commission for the use of members.

During the season six races were held, for regular classes P, Q and R, the 15-foot one-design class, a handicap class, Beach-comber dories, Pleon Yacht Club boats and a class of 12-foot catboats [evidently Brutal Beasts]. In these races there was a to-tal of 169 starters. Many of the boats were sailed by boys and girls and the Committee feels that the races were most success-ful in encouraging a yachting spirit.

At the present time [January 14, 1919] it looks as if the An-nual Cruise and the racing of large yachts could be resumed in 1919, but even so the Committee believes that the Club should encourage small boat racing as well, and suggests that this mat-ter be given serious consideration and that for the guidance of the Regatta Committee the Club express its opinion at the next meeting in April.

The races that wartime summer of 1918 were held jointly with the Corinthian, and the committee's announcement to members dated July 26 set rental charges of thirty cents an hour for sailing, two dollars for the afternoon on race days, and advised: "In these war times the Club cannot furnish boatmen and members must assume all responsibility for the handling of these boats. . . . For all races held by the Eastern Yacht Club the starts and finishes will be in the harbor in front of the Club House. This will be an attractive feature to members who visit the Club even if they do not want to sail."

After the season, the Council met in the Boston office of Commodore Sears at 53 State Street and voted to recommend to the members the following course of action for 1919:

First, that for patriotic reasons the Club house be closed for the duration of the war.

Second, that while the Club house is closed the annual dues be reduced to twenty-five dollars which will be sufficient to pay interest, insurance, taxes and other expenses necessary to conserve the property of the Club.

Third, that members be urged to retain their membership for the maintenance of the organization through the war, thereby showing their loyalty to the Club, its history and its traditions.

The date was October 10, 1918. It had proved to be a harder time for the boys over there, making the world safe for democ-racy, than anyone had figured on. Probably another winter in the trenches anyway, maybe more. None of those present could have dreamed that in a month it would all be over.

Chapter 9

Changing Tacks

On November 11, 1918—the end of what was, with hopeful finality, called The Great War— sneakers, sloops, and schooners were back in, salutes and sub-chasers were out. The following spring, the Eastern Yacht Club, now an honorably discharged veteran of the home front, donned civvies and resumed peaceful pastimes with its first Annual Regatta since 1916, gunned off on the Fourth of July, 1919.

If for no other reason, the first postwar season at Marblehead would have been noteworthy for the introduction of the Marconi rig.

There were but nine entries, and the Puritan Cup was won by George Lee's P-class sloop *Valiant* over three schooners, two New York Forties, and three other Ps, including Devereux Barker's *Olympian* and Herbert L. Bowden's *Hayseed IV*. In *The Eastern Yacht Club Story*, Barker credited Bowden with being among the first to take the great step: He changed *Hayseed IV* from gaff to Marconi so successfully that "the rig was quickly adopted for all classes of sloops and for the mainsail on schooners. At first, the Marconi masts were curved at the top and immensely high, but the curve was soon abandoned and ruled out and the mast height limited."

Though popular before the war, the P-boats were big (37 feet waterline) and expensive and required crews of seven, and they gave way after the armistice to the smaller Rs, led by the phalanx of Charles Francis Adams, Devereux Barker, and Charles Curtis. (Most of the Sonders, which had inaugurated open-class racing in Marblehead, were sold to the new Eastern Point Yacht Club at Gloucester.) Two of the Ps, however, as noted by Evers Burtner, continued racing into the 1920s—Bowden's *Hayseed IV* and Harold Wheelock's *Britomart* (dismasted during a 50-knot squall in August 1916):

One day *Britomart* on the first leg of the course worked out a fairly good lead and just got by a long tow of laden coal barges headed north. Seagoing tugs normally towed three 200-foot barges at six knots in tandem. With 800-foot hawsers between barges, such a tow would be over a half mile long.

Unfortunately, *Hayseed IV* didn't make it and was held up. Harold Wheelock saw the situation and, sport that he always was, luffed until the tow passed so that he had not increased his lead due to the string of coal barges.

Actually, the changeover to the Marconi did not come all that easily. Charlie Foster had tried it back in 1899 with his raceabout *Persimmon*, the sixteenth in his lifetime armada, only to find his solid spar too much weight aloft. Now he tried again with the cutter *Winsome*, his forty-third, built for Henry F. Lippitt in 1907 by Herreshoff as one of only three of her class of New York Yacht Club 57-footers (so rated, but actually 62 feet waterline, and called "65-footers" after their draft and sail area were later increased). Foster bought her in 1919 and as usual began experimenting, first by changing her from gaff- to jib-headed with the same sail area.

This made a very tall mast and was too much sail for comfort. I cut it down somewhat, and then a squall took the rest of it, so that when I finally had her properly rigged as a Marconi there was about seventy-five per cent as much sail as she carried originally. She was much faster even then, and of course was more easily handled by a smaller crew. Later, to cut down the number of crew and for further experimentation, I changed her into a Marconi ketch rig which she still carries [about 1933]. Her reduction in speed and general ability was astonishing, although of course she still is a fine cruising boat. This change convinced me that the Marconi rig ketch or yawl is the slowest prevailing rig that we have, and today we know the reason why this is so.

Foster owned *Winsome* until 1925 and claimed she was the first large, jibheaded boat in New England waters. In 1950 she was a yawl, and Francis Herreshoff thought her the handsomest yacht to visit Marblehead all season.

After a wartime lapse of two years, the Eastern's Annual Cruise was resumed on July 5 behind Commodore Herbert Sears's flagship *Constellation*. The New York Yacht Club did not race in 1919, but some members joined the Eastern at its invitation. Eight schooners, three New York 40s, and five sloops and yawls made their way to the eastward, and Harold Vanderbilt's *Vagrant* won the big schooner cup put up by the commodore.

It may have been on this occasion that Secretary Henry Taggard's sense of the ludicrous was again aroused:

The fleet was cruising among the Islands of the Blest, off the Maine coast, during some pretty warm weather, and a hot sun was proving too much for the complexion of our handsome Fleet Captain. Another member of the afterguard of the Flagship had found a vanishing cream that had proved efficient in saving his face from sun blisters, so urged the F.C. to apply some early in the day when it would soon disappear but would protect his face until sundown.

At breakfast the next morning we were startled by the appearance of our F.C., his face smeared with a sticky white substance that gave it a most ghastly effect. After our merriment subsided, it was discovered that the F.C. had visited his fellow voyager's stateroom to borrow his vanishing cream, but by mistake had taken his tube of toothpaste!

The fleet captain's chagrin couldn't have exceeded Measurer Burtner's during an Annual Regatta when he was preparing himself for a day of figuring handicaps on board the Race Committee boat and had a run-in with his zipper, just then being sewn into men's pants. "Inquiry of the staff at the Club desk produced no thread or needle. Thus, while aboard among the mixed company, an imitation of the Scotchman's kilt had to be followed; luckily, a sweater served."

The Volstead Act became the looniest law of the land in January 1920. In May, deflation swept the country as a delayed aftermath of the war boom, touching off a business recession that would hang on through the following year. Perhaps as a result, only two entries marked the resumption of the New London-Marblehead ocean race on July 31, and only two crossed the line in the Annual Regatta three days later. The Annual Cruise did not do much better, with just two sloops and six schooners racing from the rendezvous at Mattapoisett on to Newport, where they were joined by a sizable fleet that included six New York 40s. With six victories, the schooner *Queen Mab*, owned by Reginald C. Robbins, won a cup put up by Commodore Sears.

The high point of the immediate postwar years with respect to design was probably the appearance of Nathanael Herreshoff's S-class sloops in 1919. Members ordered eleven of these one-designs, which raced at Marblehead for the first time in 1920. About 150 were built. The S was 27 feet 10 inches overall, 20 feet 6 inches waterline, 7 feet 2 inches beam, and 4 feet 9 inches draft, carrying 425 square feet of sail in a large main and small working jib, with a single-luff spinnaker, and displacing about 6,000 pounds. With a large, open cockpit and a cuddy, the basic model sold for $2,450 complete; another thousand dollars got you a cruising model with a smaller, self-draining cockpit. The sponsors of the class wanted the short overhangs and full bows and sterns that Francis Herreshoff thought "made them rather queer-looking Universal Rule boats, and consequently they are not particularly fast for their rating."

The hollow, tapered, octagonal mast was bowed slightly forward from the deck and curved until the masthead was abaft the partners; it was held aloft by plenty of wire that included running backstays, because the boom overhung the stern. Other Herreshoff features were the molded and varnished sheerstrakes, cabin sides that curved aft into the cockpit coamings, and custom bronze hardware.

Twenty or more of the S-class sailed in the Saturday Series and Race Week and in certain of the matches with Canada, and they attracted some of the Eastern's top skippers. Probably the best documented and among the longest-lived was Herreshoff hull number 871, purchased in 1922 for $2,800 by Franklin Remington of Oyster Bay and named *Perneb*. Robert E. Peabody and Alexander Wheeler bought her in 1927 and with their wives sailed her in two days to Manchester, where they renamed her *Sturdy Beggar*. In 1931 the Peabodys bought out Wheeler when he acquired his own S-boat.

The prerace regimen of the Peabodys began with a leisurely lunch in their hilltop home off Beacon Street in Marblehead. When they spotted Harold Chalifoux raising the sail of his S-boat across Salem Bay on the Beverly shore, they gathered up their guests as crew and drove to the Club, knowing they had plenty of time to get out and underway for the start.

Changing Tacks

For several years, the S-boats rounded out the season with a race to Gloucester and back, often convoyed by the 260-foot schooner-rigged steam yacht *Aztec*, one of the ten biggest in America, owned by Chalifoux's father-in-law, Albert C. Burrage, the copper king. Robert Peabody recalled:

> After finishing the morning race at the mouth of Gloucester Harbor, the S boats would anchor inside the breakwater, with skippers and crews being ferried to the *Aztec* for lunch with the spectators on board the yacht. Afterwards, the sailors weighed anchor and raced back to Marblehead.
>
> On one occasion Francis Cummings ran away from the fleet by picking his way through the ledge-infested waters between the North and South Gooseberry islands, while more cautious skippers stuck to the deeper Pope's Head Channel near Baker's Island.
>
> In addition to being a crack helmsman, Cummings proved his seamanship on another occasion. Rounding the offshore leeward mark in a heavy northwest blow, his S boat was rammed just below the waterline on the starboard quarter by the heavy stem of an S boat sailed by a younger skipper who mistakenly tried to get buoy room at the last second. Since the damaged part of the boat would have been well below water if he had tacked back for Marblehead, Cummings sailed on into Boston Harbor while attempting to fix a canvas patch over the hole. Soon after a power boat offered assistance his mainsail split from leech to luff. They were taken in tow, and a temporary patch was secured over the hole before too much water had entered the boat. The Coast Guard towed Cummings and the S boat back to Marblehead for repairs, while his crew traveled back by land.
>
> Mr. and Mrs. Guy Lowell were the hosts for a traditional dinner banquet at their Marblehead Neck home which topped off a season of congenial competition as most S class skippers and crews repaired to the Club porch for a generally friendly rehash of the day's racing. The Eastern also served as a repair base for the S boats, as two or three of their unique curved masts were stored under the porch to facilitate the quick return of dismasting casualties to competition.

The decades unfolded, and by the 1950s, *Sturdy Beggar* was the sole S-boat remaining in Marblehead. She was kept by the Peabodys on a mooring in Fluen Point Cove. On August 31, 1954, Hurricane Carol's southeast fury ripped the *Beggar*'s mushroom anchor from the bottom and hurled her broadside toward the rocks of the Point, heeling until her cockpit was

The S-boats were still sailing strong in 1929.

awash. A hundred yards from shore, the mushroom snagged another anchor, and she fetched up. The Peabodys took her out of commission in 1972. *Sturdy Beggar* was refinished, sold to Don Kuhlman of Salem, and returned to the harbor.

The 1920 America's Cup races were going to be sailed between amateur helmsmen for the first time in history. In preparation for New York's defense against Sir Thomas Lipton's *Shamrock IV*, which had been laid up in New York during the war, Alexander Cochran turned his *Vanitie* over to the NYYC group that had commissioned Nathanael Herreshoff to build *Resolute*. The syndicate chose George Nichols to manage *Vanitie*; he had been in *Resolute*'s afterguard during the prewar trials under the management of Robert Emmons and the helmsmanship of Charles Francis Adams (both of the Eastern), and he got his old friend Starling Burgess to redesign more speed into his new charge. *Resolute* had already outsailed *Vanitie*, but because Captain Nat had designed her to a smaller rating under the Universal Rule than *Shamrock IV*, her owners—concerned about the public reaction if *Resolute* won on a heavy time allowance—asked him to beef up her rating with more sail. This he reluctantly did, substituting for her steel

Samuel Eliot, skipper Caleb Loring and Samuel Vaughan were the Eastern's winning S-boat crew in 1924.

spar a higher, hollow, wooden stick that incorporated the topmast in a combination of sophisticated staying and below-decks winching that represented literally the pinnacle of the gaff-headed rig.

Though hard-pressed by *Vanitie*, which some thought the faster, *Resolute* prevailed in the 1920 trials after losing her new mast while jibing around the mark—perhaps due to poor co-ordination on the running backstays. Then she had to with-draw from her first race with *Shamrock IV* when her throat halyard went aloft and the sail came down. Always defensive of his father, Francis Herreshoff blamed in part the "lack of mechanical sense" of Charlie Adams and Bob Emmons—their inability to grasp the technical sophistication of *Resolute* and hence to communicate intelligently with the genius who designed her.

In the July 20 race, *Shamrock IV* performed beautifully and made it two up on the defender. The public in general, the younger Herreshoff convinced himself, "wanted to see *Resolute* beaten as she had never been a popular boat, perhaps because she had a Boston afterguard but was New York owned, and thus was not a thoroughbred but rather some sort of mongrel, or worse." Adams was vice commodore, and he and Emmons were Bostonians and longtime members of the Eastern; John Parkinson was Emmons's brother-in-law; George Nichols and George F. Baker, Jr., were NYYC and EYC members; and George Cormack was secretary of the New York Yacht Club. *Resolute*'s fate surely was in the hands of members of the Eastern Yacht Club.

The challenger lost the third race on corrected time; *Resolute* evened it up in the squally fourth. A 36-knot gale canceled the fifth, which was finally sailed on July 27. For two hours they were neck-and-neck. According to one newspaper report:

> This was the time that Charlie Adams's nerve in yacht racing stood by him. Tack for tack, the *Shamrock* met the *Resolute* every time, keeping between the turning mark and the defender. But finally they met on opposite tacks, the *Shamrock* carrying boom out to port having the right of way. Instead of trying to cross the bows of the *Shamrock* with the *Resolute*, Charlie Adams tacked the defender on the lee bow of the challenger in just the right position.
>
> Giving the Lipton sloop a fine dose of back wind, the *Resolute* drew away in great style to a fine lead and to win her third and deciding race. This was as fine an exhibition of handling a big sloop up the wind with a close-fighting competitor as ever had been seen in American waters.

After it was over, EYC member Parker H. Kemble memorialized an incident in this first successful defense of the Cup by an amateur helmsman in "Lines Inspired by *Boston Herald*'s Account of Great Daring on the Part of Charles Adams: 'And as a Final Test, Just Before Entering the Harbor, the Mainsail was Jibbed [sic] Without Mishap.'"

> Charles Adams on the Resolute
> Stood by the straining wheel,
> Through which he felt in worriment
> The thrill along her keel.
>
> The time had come when he must set
> All precedent aside,
> Regardless of all consequence
> Attempt the fatal jibe.
>
> With courage of an ancient race,
> He calls the fearsome crew,
> And bids them strap the life belts on.
> With prayers his will they do.
>
> With hasty glance once more he views
> The beauties of the world,
> And then in desperate anguish gives
> The fatal wheel a whirl.
>
> She starts, she turns, she shivers
> As she turns tail to the blast.
> No chance to dodge the coming crash
> They see their end at last!
>
> They hold their breath in wonderment,
> Then shouts ring o'er the sea.
> The deed is done, the victory won,
> They've dodged eternity.

There was one wild and wonderful aftermath: the fifth race—wisely postponed in the face of a gale and rough seas (the contenders were afraid of losing men overboard, not to mention damage to gear)—provoked the publisher of the *Halifax Herald and Mail* to proclaim loudly that no *Canadian* would be afraid to race in a little breeze, least of all a salty salt banker from Lunenburg. And he flung the challenge to Gloucester, for a $5,000 stake and a silver cup, that started off the series of International Fishermen's Races between the fishing schooners of both ports that were fought over so colorfully, if with frequent rancor, from that October until the last one in 1938.

Well, when it came to yachting anyway, you had to rise mighty early to get to windward of Mr. Adams, as Measurer

Evers Burtner discovered in 1919, the year before the America's Cup Race:

Yachts with fairly long overhangs of small rake, and having rather full transverse sections at bow and stern, increase in actual water line length when heeled. This naturally improves a yacht's speed when under sail and laying over. To discourage the undue adoption of the scow form, the authors of the Universal Rule provided for the measurement of the quarter beam length, in a sense the assessment of the yacht's fullness in the bow and stern overhangs, the fore and aft distance between the quarter beam points.

In 1919 Charlie Adams purchased the *Sumaki* of William Harcourt, the actor who summered in Gloucester. He renamed her *Gossoon*. She was an Owen-designed R built by Hodgdon Brothers that took a quarter beam length penalty of smaller sail area for a given load water line length. Through study or probably in conference with George Owen, Charlie decided to shorten *Gossoon*'s stern overhang.

The Club's Measurer recalls being present at Lawley's Neponset Yard when Charlie, saw in hand, started the cut in her beautiful mahogany covering board. The saw cut just deep enough so that Lawley's had to finish off with a new stern at this point. This cut, appreciably forward of the aft quarter beam point, abolished her quarter penalty. The days of taxing a man for something he didn't have had not arrived.

The schooner *America* had been laid up at Boston for twenty years, four of them as the phantom flagship of the Eastern Yacht Club, when in the spring of 1921 it occurred to Elmer J. Bliss, winner of the 1908 Bermuda race for the Eastern in his schooner *Venona*, and William U. Swan, the Boston yachting writer for The Associated Press, that the place for her was with the United States Naval Academy at Annapolis. Secretary of the Navy Edwin Denby was agreeable but pointed out that regulations required that transfer be by sale, for which he proposed the sum of one dollar. Charles Foster, who had saved her from sale into the Cape Verde trade in 1917, was agreeable and invited the Club to finance the project.

On May 2 the Council voted to accept *America* from Foster "when put in suitable condition" for turning over to the Navy, for one dollar, "provided no expense to the Club be incurred thereby." Since there was nothing in the budget, a committee of members was got up consisting of Harvard Treasurer Charles Francis Adams, State Treasurer James Jackson, T. Nelson Perkins, Charles K. Cummings, and Bill Swan. Their efforts were oversubscribed.

With her lead gone and unballasted, her spars were laid on deck, the Eastern Yacht Club burgee was raised at her bow, and *America* was taken in tow on her final voyage by Navy subchaser number 408 from Lawley's yard on September 10, 1921. From Swan's log:

At Long Wharf in Boston the yacht took on board some eighty girls and boys, all members of the Pleon Yacht Club of Marblehead, a juvenile organization whose team two weeks before had won the first Massachusetts Junior Yacht Championship. The Pleon club colors supplanted the Eastern club's at the bow and the command of the yacht was turned over to the club's commodore, Richard S. Thayer. Under the leadership of Arthur G. Wood of the Corinthian Yacht Club and with the assistance of a bugler from the Charlestown Navy Yard, all hands joined in singing "America" amid salutes along the Boston waterfront, from shore and shipping alike.

The youngsters owned the yacht on the run to Marblehead—a detour to show the yacht in the largest American yachting port—and there was not a dull moment during the trip. On rounding into the ancient New England haven, the *America* was saluted by church bells in the town and cannon on Marblehead Neck.

From Marblehead down the coast, the relic was handed along from club to club, to the Beverly at the Cape Cod Canal and then to the Fall River, the Rhode Island, the New Haven, the Stamford, the Seawanhaka-Corinthian, the Larchmont, the Marine and Field of Brooklyn, and the Philadelphia-Corinthian. On September 29, after a couple of groundings and some extra towing help, *America* was brought up the Severn River and docked at the Naval Academy.

America under tow for Annapolis from Boston, 1921.

Charles Francis Adams transfers *America* to Rear Admiral Henry B. Wilson, Commandant of the Naval Academy, for $1.

On October 1, before 2,500 cheering midshipmen, Charles Francis Adams presented *America* to the Academy and on behalf of the Eastern Yacht Club accepted in payment a one-dollar bill from Rear Admiral Henry B. Wilson, the superintendent.

Later, a brass tablet with the following inscription was fixed to the starboard side of her cabin:

TO COMMEMORATE
THE RESTORATION
OCTOBER 1, 1921
AFTER 48 YEARS OF PRIVATE OWNERSHIP
OF THE
SCHOONER YACHT *AMERICA*
TO THE
UNITED STATES NAVAL ACADEMY
BY THE
EASTERN YACHT CLUB
ON BEHALF OF
CHARLES H.W. FOSTER
AND IN COOPERATION WITH

Charles Francis Adams, Elmer Jared Bliss, Harry F. Bradford, S. Parker Bremer, William H. Brownson, Arthur H. Clark, Albert W. Finlay, Sydney A. Friede, James B. Ford, Louis A. Frothingham, John Good, Roger Griswold, James Jackson, Arthur Curtiss James, Demarest Lloyd, Frank B. McQuesten, Edgar Palmer, Thomas Nelson Perkins, Robert M. Thompson, Henry Walters, John W. Weeks, and the Cohasset Yacht Club, Corinthian Yacht Club of Marblehead, Corinthian Yacht Club of Philadelphia, Fall River Yacht Club, Larchmont Yacht Club, Manchester Yacht Club, Marine & Field Club, New Bedford Yacht Club, New Haven Yacht Club, New London Chamber of Commerce, Newport, R.I., Chamber of Commerce, Pleon Yacht Club, Quincy Yacht Club, Rhode Island Yacht Club, Seawanhaka-Corinthian Yacht Club, Stamford Yacht Club.

AMERICA RESTORATION COMMITTEE, Charles Francis Adams, Chairman, James Jackson, Treasurer, William U. Swan, Secretary, T. Nelson Perkins, Charles K. Cummings.

Thus ended what old Ben Butler was never able to achieve in his lifetime, the enrollment of the schooner *America* in the squadron of the Eastern Yacht Club.

And there she lay.

The Depression descended upon land and sea, and in the early 1930s Charles Foster embarked upon correspondence with Nathanael Herreshoff, which has since been rediscovered (and is being published for the first time in this book). Foster had made some reference to *America* in a letter that elicited this reaction from Captain Nat, then eighty-six, dated at Bristol, December 22, 1934:

In reply to your kind letter about *America*—the memory of the public to the good old ship would be just as strong if the hulk is kept in sight or *not*. She did her part very many years ago, and it's quite time she was put to rest, with proper ceremonys, as did Elbridge Gerry with *Electra*. I certainly don't approve of rebuilding. Sailing old yachts is not the correct training for the Naval School. Manning completely up-to-date sub-chasers would be more proper.

The original *America* has been re-built over and over and there is a false feeling in trying to copy these replacements. However if anything is to be done to preserve the present hulk, I would recommend hauling out and propping her up where she probably would be viewed by one in one hundred thousand of our inhabitence. . . .

By 1941, some limited restoration was undertaken on the hulk where it was stored in a shed. On Palm Sunday, 1942, a freak blizzard dumped such a load of snow on the shed roof that it collapsed on what remained of the schooner *America*, age ninety-one, and she was crushed to pieces.

The Pleon's stewardship of the most famous yacht in the world for the run from Boston to Marblehead was a gesture of official recognition that the late war had irrevocably altered the world and its ways, that out of the horror of a generation lost, out of weariness and cynicism, youth might as well have its day.

That forward-looking yachtsman Herbert M. Sears sealed the bargain with the new generation in this season of 1921 when, in his eighth year as commodore, he placed in competition under the Eastern the trophy that has ever since been the most sought-after in junior sailing. The Sears Cup was to be competed for annually by 15- to 18-year-olds whose parents or guardians were members of the yacht clubs of Massachusetts tidal waters; crews would sail in unfamiliar boats and exchange them after each race. His aim was to promote the interests of yachting, sportsmanlike racing, and skill in seamanship among junior sailors.

Richard S. Thayer, the commodore of the Pleon who skippered *America* on her last trip out of Boston Harbor, was the first winner. Overnight, the unprecedented game of "musical boats" caught on in other areas, and the event became a national championship.

Opposite the commodore's pull was the push of the Regatta Committee, which on January 27, 1921, recorded this historic vote establishing the junior sailing program:

That Mr. Philip P. Chase investigate the advisability and the probable cost of acquiring the services of a person suitable to instruct the children of the members of the Club in sailing, and also conduct morning classes for them, and also help the Regatta Committee in running their races, and to report to the Committee at its next meeting.

If the Sears Cup and the junior program supplied motivation to youth in the early stages of a postwar era when incentives for excellence and sportsmanship were surely in demand, the means was supplied by the homely but serviceable Brutal Beast and Fish class boats and the more comely Alden O-boat.

The Brutal Beast, a hard-chine, V-bottomed open catboat of 14 feet overall, with a beam of 6 feet 2 inches, was the creation of Starling Burgess for his children around 1916, the story

The original gaff-rigged Brutal Beast as conceived by Starling Burgess, photographed around 1921.

One division of the later, Marconi-rigged Brutals starts off the Corinthian as the next approaches the line, 1929.

goes—at first gaff-rigged but soon converted to Marconi. The family is said to have owned a Great Dane nicknamed "The Brutal Beast" by the neighbors. After the war, the stout and steady little craft was adopted as *the* trainer for the youngsters of Marblehead and farther afield. Many outstanding helmsmen first put hand to tiller in the Beast. (So, incidentally, did the author, on the Annisquam River in the 1930s in a second-hander acquired from the renowned Boston restaurateur Jake Wirth and renamed—what else?—*Pig's Knuckle*.)

The Fish of about the same size was designed by Gloucester boatbuilder Nicholas Montgomery and yachtsman Harry Friend and turned out by the Montgomery yard on the Annisquam River from 1921 on. Monty soon got into unique mass production by filling an early model with concrete. Out of this indestructible mold, bottomed-up, schools of Fishes unto a

thousand have taken flight to this day from the hands of Monty, son Herb, and now grandson Dave, and taught generations of 'Squam youngsters how to let go the sheet in a squall, or else.

John Alden's 18-foot centerboard sloop, originally designated the Marblehead One-Design but always known as the O-boat, also appeared in Marblehead in 1921 as a trainer for teenagers and sharpened up Dick Thayer for the first Sears Cup.

The Brutal Beast and Fish classes first raced at Marblehead in 1921, under the auspices of the Corinthian, and the following season were included in the Eastern's small-boat events. Devereux Barker recalled some sideplay of the period:

One very amusing episode occurred when a match race was arranged for a Sunday morning between three children and three of our older and better skippers in a new and thoroughly undesirable type of boat called the Fish class, about 15 feet long. There was a fresh northwest wind, and the senior skippers fared

154

very badly. Only Charlie Adams was able to finish; Guy Lowell and Herbert Sears both capsized.

Youth, which since long before anybody could remember had been under orders to be seen and not heard, was finally having its day. For a generation or two, the Brutals would be able to do all their racing inside the harbor, cavorting through the openings kept clear by the wide mooring scope of the large yachts in the last days of the big ones.

The year after making his unique contribution to the wellsprings of sailing with the cup that bears his name, Commodore Sears in 1922 chaired a committee that organized the Junior Eastern Yacht Club, with its own house in a small, portable building on the property, from which it moved in 1925 to a room under the new veranda for several years. Forty-seven children, age twelve to eighteen, of Club members were selected. David C. Percival, Jr., was the first commodore.

It was planned that membership would subsequently be open to the public, subject to approval by the admission committees of the parent and the junior clubs. Privileges would include the right to fly the Club burgee and to use the floats, tennis courts, and other Club facilities—subject to the rules of the House Committee. Annual dues were ten dollars.

The Junior Eastern Yacht Club's activities centered on sailing, racing, tennis tournaments, and swimming meets, and an instructor was employed to take charge and give sailing and swimming lessons. The new club was entirely separate from the Pleon Yacht Club, and its appearance created a friendly competition that ultimately was resolved by their consolidation, as such rivalries occasionally are.

After only one season, eligibility was extended beyond Massachusetts, and the 1922 Junior Sailing Championship and the Sears Cup Races were sailed off Marblehead under the sponsorship of the Eastern, with members from three New York clubs—Cedarhurst, Larchmont, and Seawanhaka-Corinthian—participating by invitation as well.

Even as the youngsters were being readied for a leg up the yachting ladder, the self-styled bluewater men at the other end, who scorned formal racing and for whom "nowhere is too far," were splintering off from more traditional east coast yacht clubs of the day and organizing themselves in the winter of 1921–22 as The Cruising Club of America. Seven of the thirty-four charter members were also members of the Eastern

Yacht Club: John G. Alden, George P.P. Bonnell, C.H.W. Foster, Roger Griswold, Henry S. Howard, Samuel S. Pierce, and Samuel P. Wetherill. This dual allegiance among Eastern members who are strongly pulled to deep water and distant places continues to this day.

S.S. Pierce of the Boston importing firm, a family long active in the Eastern, claimed to have caught the germinal idea for the CCA while cruising the Baltic in 1913 with Erskine Childers in the latter's ketch *Asgard*, when the author of *Riddle of the Sands* told him about the Royal Cruising Club of which he was a member. Pierce wanted to get up such an organization in America and made common cause with William Washburn Nutting, editor of *Motor Boat*, who would be the CCA's first commodore. Nutting ignited Herbert Stone, editor of *Yachting*, who brought in Roger Griswold in 1921, and the idea had caught on.

Fifty years later, George Bonnell recalled that although the Cruising Club was headquartered in New York, about half of the founders were Bostonians. "It was a practice in the early days of the club, every certain number of years we would elect a commodore from Boston. We considered Boston one half of the Cruising Club in effect. . . . They were a substantial membership, and they were fine people and great sailors."

Of the Eastern's three prewar ventures into internationalism—the Halifax Race and the series of Sonder meets with Germany and Spain—only the Canadian connection survived, although the honorary status of Alfonso XIII remained undisturbed as long as his kingdom did. Henry Morss, having been responsible for the cosponsorship of the Halifax Race with the Royal Nova Scotia Yacht Squadron, after the war struck inland for fresh water and arranged a series of match races with the Royal Canadian Yacht Club of Toronto, the boats being supplied by the host club. Devereux Barker recalled his involvement not long after.

The first series of six races was sailed at Toronto in August, 1922, in P boats with Charlie Adams representing us but winning only two of the races. The races at Marblehead in 1924 were sailed in S boats by two crews from each club, and this series we won. In 1926 I took a crew to Toronto to race in P boats. I was accompanied by Caleb Loring with a crew to race in R boats, for the Royal Canadian Yacht Club did not have four boats of either class. I won one race and lost one, but Caleb proved the better sailor, for he won both of his races. The third and final race could not be sailed, for a howling easterly kicked up such a sea on Lake Ontario that I was not willing to race someone else's boat in such weather. It was really bad. In 1928, racing at Marblehead in Q boats with two crews from each club, the Canadians won. Again, in 1930, I took a crew to Toronto and raced in 8 Meters but was beaten two races to one. The Canadians were fine sailors, delightful guests and gracious hosts who gave us wonderful welcomes at Toronto.

For the first time since 1915, the New York Yacht Club in 1922 cruised around Cape Cod to Marblehead. En route, the squadron had rendezvoused at Newport, where on August 2 Commodore Vanderbilt's schooner *Vagrant* won the Astor Cup for schooners, hard pressed by Eastern Rear Commodore Nathaniel Ayer's *Queen Mab*, followed by E.W. Clark's familiar *Irolita*, Carll Tucker's *Ohonkara* and Winthrop Aldrich's *Flying Cloud*, which had won the Vanderbilt Cup a month earlier in the Eastern's ocean race from New London to Marblehead.

All five owners were members of the Eastern as well, and it is of interest as a preview of things to come that the four runners-up were smaller schooners than *Vagrant* and than the great *Elena* and her rivals, which got and gave such sport before the war.

Yet none could compare with Commodore Sears's magnificent *Constellation* in her shining black, her regal clipper bow adorned with carved, gilded trailboards, at the very head of the fleet whether underway or moored in her customary place of honor at the mouth of the harbor. Nathaniel Cushing Nash, Jr., remembered vividly the routine followed in raising sail:

When ready to hoist the mainsail, three sailors would climb each set of the main shrouds, reach through the ratlines and grasp the halyard that was on their side of the mast. When the other sailors began hoisting from their position on the deck, those on the shrouds hauled down on their halyards. At the appropriate moment, the upper shroud-man and his opposite each seized hold of his halyard, and while he was descending to the deck his weight added to the hoisting of the mainsail. At appropriate times the other pairs of shroud-men followed suit.

Not one to push an old-timer too far, the commodore raced *Constellation* for the last time in the 1920 Annual Cruise, filling out the auxiliaries, when she ran well ahead from Mattapoisett to Newport; he declined to have her time figured, however, and the race went to *Queen Mab*. That was

Constellation's last season with her full complement of twenty-five. In 1921 Sears had ten feet taken off her masts, reduced her bowsprit and main boom accordingly, and cut her complement back to fifteen. During his long term of office, the Council held its regular meetings during the season, preceded by dinner, aboard his flagship at the commodore's invitation, a memorable custom that took its place in the lore of the Club. On one such occasion, Secretary Taggard noted as an afterthought to the minutes:

It may be of interest to record that immediately after dinner, the Commodore took the Council to the Corinthian Yacht Club house, where a reception to Vice President and Mrs. Coolidge was being held. After the Commodore and his staff had been presented, they returned to the flagship and the meeting was held as reported above.

Eugene Stetson, later a well-known New York yachtsman, was a member of the Pequot Yacht Club crew that came up from Long Island with another from Larchmont in 1928 for the Sears Cup Races:

We stayed at the Eastern, and one afternoon of a semi-lay day we were taken out to *Constellation*. We'd never seen anything like her in our lives. Mr. Sears was as nice as could be, but I remember that his crew—or maybe they were the stewards— all wore white gloves and watched us as if we were going to steal everything that wasn't tied down. I couldn't believe it.

A veteran staff member observed the commodore for years: "All dressed up, he'd come in his beautiful mahogany launch with his two launchmen, one dressed in dark clothes, and the other like a sailor, up front. And he'd walk up from the dock, get into his car, a beautiful car, and take off with his chauffeur. And go out the same way."

By contrast, the old yacht *Vashti* and her merry crew stirred the wake of the 1923 Annual Cruise with such alcoholic abandon that the member who chartered her supplied an account on condition he remain anonymous, as he has for fifty years.

To begin with, the cruise of the *Vashti* was conceived amid a flock of cocktails and I think it may be fair to say it was carried through with that stimulus.

The Eastern's queen, *Constellation*, in all her majesty. Morris Rosenfeld photo, 1939.

Changing Tacks

The scarcity of coin obliged the chartering of a very old-fashioned and antiquated ark, but the *Vashti* even exceeded our expectations in this respect. She was decrepit from every angle. When it got too rough, she leaked badly. Her gear parted continually, fair weather and foul, and her engine worked on state occasions only. She was one of [Edward] Burgess's boats.

I had heard that it was etiquette, in taking a chartered yacht on a cruise, to ask the Commodore for permission to have her accompany the fleet. Considering the antiquity and general make-up of the yacht in question, it took some nerve to write a letter requesting this permission. I wrote Commodore Sears, suggesting that we would be very gratified should he grant his permission to accompany the cruise, and by way of not being too serious about it, I advised him that I regretted that the *Vashti* was not quite as long on the water line as the *Constellation*, but that in the matter of age she took precedence, and by virtue of her age was entitled to some consideration.

Knowing the situation, he replied with an amusing letter to the effect that he regretted very much to advise me that the *Constellation* in the matter of age also took precedence over our "yacht," but nevertheless, he would be very glad to have her accompany the cruise. It seemed possible that I might be required to attend a meeting of captains on board the Flagship, so I went so far as to purchase a cap with the proper insignia. I think that was the only important expense in connection with keeping up standards.

A difficulty arose in the acquiring of a steward. A great number of men looked at her, shook their heads and went their sundry ways. She was too much for them, and it appears that they were more foresighted than we were, as she eventually appeared too much even for us. Finally, the ever-useful Jimmy at the Club floats secured—it was suggested from one of the graveyards in Marblehead—a very antiquated specimen of humanity, probably, without doubt, the oldest man that ever proclaimed his ability to still function. He belonged, in every sense of the word, to the Great Unwashed. Soap and other cleansing compounds he kept at a distance, but he had two or three redeeming virtues. He was as faithful as Old Dog Tray and always anxious to please. When in port he never wanted any leave of absence, and he thoroughly entered into the atmosphere of the etiquette which should surround the formalities of a fleet cruise.

He was so old that he actually tottered in the cabin when we were lying at anchor, and it became evident that we would lose our one and only helpmate if we ever allowed him on deck while we were under way. Consequently, his head and shoulders appearing through the forward hatch were the only signs of his existence when the sails were up. I truly believe he thoroughly enjoyed himself and, to our great delight, was never seasick.

We started that cruise about eleven o'clock in the morning from Marblehead, the fleet leaving shortly before sundown. The smallest boat had passed us by two o'clock in the morning, and we arrived in Rockland hours after the last anchor had been dropped. We were always the last to anchor everywhere, even by cutting all the corners that could be discovered.

One of the rules of the cruise was that since the four of us were all coastal sailors and knew the general layout of buoys, etc., the boat could be safely turned over by lot to one of us while the rest indulged themselves, if they pleased, in various libations. This caused a tremendous argument, even including the helmsman, as we were running up the Muscle Ridge Channel to Rockland. It appeared that where a red buoy showed on the chart a white buoy had suddenly loomed up, and, whether this sudden change in color was due to Barbados rum or not, further complicated the situation. The helmsman himself was not sure, so we approached the buoy carefully, and in truth it was white, the paint having been entirely worn off, and it was bleached by the sun.

Going into Rockland Harbor we got a few puffs in the way of a small squall which carried away one or two sheets, but finally anchored safely.

There was no privacy in such a small craft. In the middle of a cocktail party in the cockpit one of our members decided that it was an opportune time to slip into the washroom and polish up some "dining room furniture" that had been supplied him by his dentist. It slipped through his fingers and disappeared down the bowl. That broke up the cocktail party and almost the cruise since he could not appear without these additions to his anatomy. But we had everything on board, plumbers and carpenters, and a complete job of plumbing having been performed, the lost articles were recovered amid great rejoicing, shined up and embalmed in a glass of pure alcohol.

At Islesboro there were so many visits to other yachts and visitors on board ours which preceded a dinner we were to attend on shore that everyone was in a cheerful mood. The launch of our host, which took us on shore, was so crowded that one of our members was obliged to sit on the forward deck, which was turtleback in shape. As we approached the float at high speed, the launch swung suddenly to port, and overboard went our member. He disappeared completely and came up alongside of the float, and all his respectable clothes were quite ruined for the occasion.

At Burnt Coat Harbor it was quite rough when we put out, and our "yacht" leaked so badly that we were busily engaged bailing and repairing part of the gear which, true to form, kept carrying away.

Vashti in better days. Jackson photo.

Changing Tacks

Changing Tacks

We finally reached Bar Harbor, and the Committee Boat, objecting to where we were anchored, had us towed out some distance. We all suspected that secret orders had been issued to keep the *Vashti* as far from the fleet as possible so that onlookers might not be led to believe that she was included as a member of the Eastern Yacht Club.

While lying at anchor, another cocktail party for some reason or other occurred just as the sunset gun was fired. Nobody was interested excepting our steward. He rushed from the cockpit to haul down our pennant, fell over two or three ropes and almost went overboard. I yelled at him to ask what the matter was, and he replied, "My God, sir, didn't you hear the Admiral's gun?" He was filled with the idea of admirals, commodores, commanders and captains, and he could think of nothing else but doing the correct thing on all occasions.

At Bar Harbor we suffered a terrific loss. Our steward, having washed up what he called the "silverware," dumped overboard the pan of dish water, at the bottom of which were all our knives, spoons and forks. He was so upset by this accident that he offered to give one of our members $10 to replace the lost "silver," with the understanding that he was not to tell me, and he was much upset for fear he would be discharged then and there. Of that there was no chance because he could boil water and fry an egg. I think the "silver" was replaced at the Five and Ten Cent Store for about $1.50.

The engine which theoretically was installed back in the Dark Ages with the idea that it would propel the "Yacht," was only an engine in form. A down east Yankee looked at it and remarked, "when them engines go, 'taint nawthin' but an ac-cident." I had taken it apart and cleaned it at least five or six times before the cruise was over, and no one, until we reached Boothbay on the return, was ever able to discover that a pinhole admitting water to the cylinders was the cause of our difficulty. After cleaning, it would run from fifteen minutes to a couple of hours, and then it had to be cleaned again.

On the return, we put out from York Harbor in a heavy sea kicked up by an easterly, and a light air, and fog covering the water. The fog finally shut in so thick, and the wind disappeared completely, that just off the coast a few miles east of Portsmouth we had to let go both our anchors and wait for some wind or clear weather. She dragged and at times swung stern to the sea so that plenty of water came over into the cockpit. We were so close to the shore that it was only a question of time when we should bring up there, stern-first or bow-first.

Many consultations took place. The engine refused to budge, of course. We had a rifle on board, and that was fired, hoping to attract some fisherman that would tow us out. Our flag was sent to masthead theoretically upside down, but in the excitement it flew right side up. The fog had lifted temporarily by this time, but no breeze, and we still continued toward the shore, which we could see at no great distance, white water breaking over the ledges.

Our relief was great when a good breeze from the southeast came in, and the fog again lifted for a few moments, and we set our course for Portsmouth. And there, as far as most of us were concerned, the cruise was ended, and I think it is fair to say that a more tired crew never finished what started out to be a restful vacation.

Chapter 10   # Under Full Sail   *1924–1926*

America had recovered from the postwar recession by 1924, and the Twenties were in high gear. In the wake of the automobile, the yacht was undergoing democratization. The Eastern, now in its fifty-fifth year, remained the last bastion east of Newport of the big ones built before the income tax, yet the Club showed it could move with the times by starting 950 in the smaller classes that season in nine regular races around the buoys.

Herbert M. Sears had been commodore since 1914, vice commodore and rear commodore back to 1910. His flag service had spanned the war and carried the Club, with continuity and grace, across the chasm from the days of Edwardian yachting splendor to the Corinthian world of the Model-T Ford and the S-class sloop. Who else could have slid with such aplomb from the helm of his flagship *Constellation*—Marblehead's *Constitution*, almost, riding out there in stellar majesty off Fort Sewall—into the harbor from the tiller of a capsized Brutal Beast?

After ten years as commodore, the longest term in the history of the Club, Sears stepped down at the January meeting in 1924. He was succeeded by Vice Commodore Nathaniel F. Ayer, who had purchased the successful 77-foot *Queen Mab*, first schooner in Massachusetts Bay to carry a Marconi mainsail, from Harold Vanderbilt.

The new flagship kept it in the family by beating off her old rivals, *Irolita*, *Shawna*, and *Flying Cloud* (which went aground for four hours in Vineyard Sound after their luffing match), to win the annual ocean race from New London to Marblehead for the third time. Thus *Queen Mab* brought home for good the gold Vanderbilt Cup put up by her former owner as successor to the Clark trophy captured before the war by Morton Plant's *Elena*.

The same annual meeting in January that marked the official end of the Sears era institutionalized the most significant legacy of the commodore by voting to admit to junior membership young men between the ages of fifteen and twenty-one. They were given the privilege of flying the Club burgee and the use of the clubhouse, floats, and grounds—with the exception of such rooms as the House Committee might designate—but were denied voting, officeholding, and Club property rights. Only sons of members were eligible while the roster exceeded fifty. Dues were twenty dollars the first year, ten thereafter. Five were elected that spring. James C. (Bunkie) Gray, Jr., was Number One.

The election of James C. Gray, Sr., to head the Regatta Committee in 1923 assured the Club's commitment to the cause of junior and small-class sailing that had been so energetically advanced by Commodore Sears. Gray worked closely with William L. Carlton, chairman of the Corinthian Race Committee for several years, and later with his counterparts at the Boston, on behalf of interclub relationships that reached ultimate fruition in the founding of the Marblehead Racing Association in 1969.

The distance the Eastern Yacht Club had traveled since 1903, when boats under 30 feet waterline were first listed in the yearbook (but not regularly enrolled), can be measured by the 485 yachts the Race Committee started in the Club's three championship Race Week races in 1924 and the 465 that crossed its line in the six others for the small classes—a total of 950 that does not include the Sunday Series and other special events. Crews from eighteen clubs were enrolled in the Sears Cup and Junior Championship. Three crews led by

Under Full Sail   161

Under Full Sail

Charles Francis Adams raced and won in an S-class series sponsored by the Seawanhaka-Corinthian at Oyster Bay. John Lawrence lost to Adams in the Quincy Yacht Club Challenge Cup series, and then Eastern crews took the international match with the Royal Canadian Yacht Club.

In addition to all this, the Annual Regatta had six big schooners, three New York Fifties, three New York Forties (joined by three more in a special race), and a pair of Bar Harbor 31s. The Puritan Cup went to P.H. Mallory's 50-footer *Mystic*.

The Annual Cruise was confined to a foggy rendezvous off Newport with the New York Yacht Club, in view of the latter's plan to cruise in August to Maine for the first time since 1910—and the Eastern's disinclination to sail east twice in one season. A survey to determine how many of the fleet of about thirty were equipped to tow their sisters through the fog and calms revealed one sign of the times, as reported by yachting writer William Swan: A good half of them were equipped with auxiliary power.

It was said that Bill Swan, unfazed by the frugality of his employers, slept in his Model-T Ford while covering the yachting circuit, a signal devotion to the sport that seems to be borne out in the records of the Race Committee for 1924. The committee concluded that it would be desirable to grant Mr. Swan's request to accompany the Annual Cruise on the condition that he understand clearly that although he would be welcome aboard the committee boat during the day, and even be given lunch and a rowboat with which to deliver his reports, he should expect to provide his own quarters ashore, except when invited to reside on a yacht; that he should not ask favors of new members and strangers; and that he should conform to the hours and convenience of the committee. The committee also decided that Leonard M. Fowle, the yachting writer for the *Boston Globe*, should be invited on the cruise if Swan was.

The 1924 season was one of the most active in the annals of Marblehead as a yachting center, and it was almost concluded with what was believed to be the worst storm, a northeast gale that swept the coast with sheets of rain and winds of near-hurricane force on August 26. About two dozen larger yachts were driven ashore around the harbor and on the causeway. Small craft and tenders littered the beach in front of the Eastern, and numerous others swamped at their moorings.

Queen Mab, first schooner in Massachusetts to carry a Marconi mainsail. Jackson photo.

Robert Bridge, the owner of the Old Stone Wharf property on which the Eastern had held an option at least since 1902, died in 1921. This gave some urgency to the question of picking it up and more generally, now that a new era was being entered upon, to the adequacy of the Club's house and facilities for the future. A committee under Francis A. Seamans, the former house chairman, was appointed to make recommendations. Its report, dated October 15, 1923, commenced as follows:

> The Clubhouse is an old wooden building of considerable extent, standing close to salt water, unoccupied for about eight months every year, and consequently subject to rapid deterioration, necessitating excessive expenditures for repairs. Extensive repairs, including reshingling of the roof and painting of the building, must be made at once at considerable expense unless some plan is adopted for general changes.

A good breeze, and Commodore Nathaniel F. Ayer holds *Queen Mab* to it.

Starting with the original Clubhouse, additions have been made from time to time without any definite plan as to what a clubhouse should comprise, with the result that it is now unsuited to the use of members, and at the same time its physical arrangement is such as to cause extra cost of operation over a properly arranged house. Another cause of excessive cost of operation is the lack of patronage by the members, and all house committees of recent years have stressed this very strongly. This committee feels that this lack of patronage is partly because the house is dark, gloomy and unattractive and partly because the part of the Clubhouse reserved for members only and the part opened to members and their families are not divided into right proportions.

For several years the Club has lived along without increasing its floating debt while paying off some of its bonded debt, and this policy might be followed for some years longer; but this committee concludes that as the membership is regularly, even if slowly, growing smaller, and many members are dissatisfied with existing conditions, this policy should not be adopted but that the time has come to make real changes and improvements.

The committee engaged architect Arthur H. Bowditch to study the possibilities, and proposed two alternatives. The first called for razing and replacing the old clubhouse with a new one located toward the Samoset House, which would be moved behind it for servants' quarters, abandoning the existing pier for the Old Stone Wharf for landing purposes, and eventually selling off the easterly part of the Club property to help pay for the project. Estimated cost: at least $150,000.

The committee's second alternative, which it recommended, was to remodel the clubhouse. "A slate roof would replace the shingle roof, and stucco walls the present wooden-covered. A complete rearrangement of the entrance floor would afford a suitable distribution of space for members and their families. While the bedrooms should be repainted and repapered, there would be no great change except that some of the present bedrooms should be cut up for bathrooms." Estimated cost: $50,000 to $75,000, to be borne by a 4 percent second mortgage and sale of a large part of the Samoset property.

But somebody must have been doing some politicking. The general meeting on January 8, 1924, at the Union Club in Boston voted to borrow $25,000 to buy the Old Stone Wharf, and nine days later the Council overturned its Building Committee and told it to draw up plans for a new $275,000 clubhouse to be built on the site and in turn to establish a fund-raising committee.

Obviously, this grand vision evaporated.

This was the year of Frances Gilliland's investiture behind the front desk.

I worked for a private automobile club in Boston, and my boss there was Ken Skylar. He got the position here as Manager. When all the girls would get their vacation I'd go home, and he said, "Frances, how about coming down to the Eastern Yacht Club to work for me for the summer?" "Oh no," I said, "I'm not interested." "Come down," he said. "You'll like it." So I came down.

It was my first day on the job and the very first call I took as the switchboard operator. No one had told me a thing about how to operate that switchboard, and I was all alone when it started to ring. I took a chance and plugged it in and heard this man on the other end start telling me about this jib and that sail, and I said to him, "Now, you're going to have to go slower because I don't know a canoe from nothing."

Come to find out, it was Mr. Walter K. Shaw from the boat *Andiamo*. He came right up to the desk to find out who it was that was so honest. I said, "It was me, sir, and if I ever come back here again, you can shoot me!"

I was the first woman in the office. There was a partition, and one side was for the ladies, and the other side was for the men. If a lady came across, Mr. Randolph Frothingham would come into the office and say, "Frances, send the bellboy out. There's a lady in the men's department." And they'd have to go over to the other side.

Invasions of this sort, intentional or not, were not to be tolerated and were considered sufficiently grave to be brought to the attention of the Club's highest authorities. Mrs. Henry A. Morss, Jr., writes of one such that shook the ad hoc Piazza Committee to the soles of its sneakers:

A lady never, never, never went into the men's section of the Club and its bar nor onto the men's portion of the porch. Very small nephew escaped from my mother, who had taken him to the ladies' room in the days of many buttons. Before she could catch him and fasten the rear hatch, he toddled onto the men's porch and backed up to a very crusty senior member and asked to be buttoned up.

The member was furious when Mother appeared on the porch to gather up the little boy and not only lectured her but wrote a stern complaint to the Commodore and House Committee, delightedly shared with Mother! One can say now that the Club did not come to an end as the letter stated it was doing.

Not long after the appearance of Frances Gilliland, George B. Henderson arrived on the Eastern scene and many years later, as its "oldest living inhabitant," recalled a certain day during this time of heated debate about the future of the club-house:

I noticed from the tennis court that several shingles on the roof were ablaze. Evidently some sparks from the chimney had started it. So I yelled to Frances to call the Fire Department. They came and soon had the fire out. I was all set to bask in my new role as a big hero, when I realized that my "popularity curve" among my Eastern friends had dipped sharply. It took me several years to live that episode down!

The piazza debate on the subject that summer of 1924 must have rivaled the racing, because in November the vote was rescinded, and Commodore Ayer was instructed to implement Architect Bowditch's more conservative remodeling scheme. Work began in December. The results, described by William Swan in the *Boston Transcript* in 1925, suggest more extensive changes than originally planned, as is usually the case:

The facilities of the club have been increased 30 per cent but its attractiveness has been more than doubled. As one of the older members remarked after roaming through the rejuvenated structure, "Thank heaven, the Eastern Yacht Club has now a comfortable club house, not a barrack."

The almost somber exterior has been brightened by a light gray hue and light green blinds, so that the big building commands attention even from the town side of the harbor. Interiorly the club house has been decorated artistically, and the members have today one of the most convenient, up-to-date and sumptuous club stations on the coast and are on all fours with Larchmont, Indian Harbor and with their neighbors and friendly rivals the Corinthians. . . .

[After the war] came the project for an entirely new club house directly on the water front but it was soon decided that the older building was capable of improvement and Mr. Bowditch, who had drawn plans for a new building, was asked to evolve another wing. The result has been in the form of an angular crescent, for the addition has been southwest instead of west. This addition has been devoted to a main dining room, outside of which is a broad veranda canopied by a broad green and white striped awning, an ideal space for afternoon teas or supper parties.

This dining room with the lounge in the main building are the gems of the new club station both architecturally and artistically. The dining room with its light blue furnishings is greatly enhanced by its specially painted window shades, which show in greens and reds old ships and ancient maps of the country, New England and Massachusetts Bay. Incidentally, behind the swinging doors is one of the best equipped serving rooms on the North Shore, while below stairs the old kitchen has been brought up to date with nearly every known culinary appliance.

The lounge is a symphony in greenish blue, with hangings of linen damask and chairs of inviting proportions dressed in figured textiles. Its quaint quietness is most appealing, while the whole effect is one of comfortable beauty.

The well-known library on the east side has not been neglected, for it has been hung with printed linens of old Jacobean patterns.

Not the least among the features of the new club house are the new pictures which have been hung in the main hall, the lounge, the hall leading into the dining room and in the dining room itself. The most striking of these effects is an oil painting of a ship under full sail running down the Trades, by Frederick Vining Smith. This picture is the gift of Mrs. "Commodore" Nathaniel F. Ayer.

Over the fireplace in the main living room is an unusually large photograph of the first *Shamrock*, donated by Edwin A. Boardman. It is said that immediately after this picture was snapped in the British Channel in 1899, and the plate had been removed, the camera, which was one of the largest ever constructed, was knocked overboard and lost.

On the wall just outside the main dining room is a panelled sail fish which Commodore Ayer killed in Florida last winter, while over the sideboard in the dining room Mrs. James C. Gray has set up a beautiful flower panel.

Many years ago, even before the first club house was built, an enterprising hotel man erected a two-story structure a hundred yards up the Neck, as a boarding house, which the club subsequently acquired in order to protect its property. This boarding house, known familiarly as the Samoset, was taken over last winter by the club, completely renovated and thrown open to club members and their families. The Samoset has also been modernized with two, three and four-room suites, and before April 1 every room had been taken. The guests there take their meals at the club dining room a few steps away, and are thus relieved of many of the household cares of a summer villa.

There are few more extensive views on the coast than that from the dining room veranda at the Eastern Yacht Club. The harbor is in the foreground, Salem Bay stretches out beyond, while in the distance is the Beverly shore dotted with residences. The race is over, the yachtsmen stroll up the long pier and seek this veranda to discuss the contest and drink their tea, for this English custom has taken a strong hold in yachting circles. The modern Eastern Yacht Club now spells rest.

Numerous unplanned improvements emerged as well. A room for the Junior Eastern Yacht Club was built under the veranda, the office was upgraded, fire escapes were added to the third floor, a refrigeration plant was installed, and garage accommodations were created for twelve cars. Most of the old plumbing was replaced, the cold-storage room was rebuilt, landscaping and drainage were undertaken, and repairs of structural damage caused by leaks and rot were carried out. George Henderson recalled:

The zealous House Committee decided to clean out a lot of junk which had accumulated over the years in the attic. It consisted largely of assorted bedroom crockery—pitchers, washbowls, etc. I particularly remember about a dozen king-sized thunderjugs. All this stuff was colored a beautiful pastel blue, and every piece had a gold stripe and a colorful reproduction of the E.Y.C. burgee! I have no idea what became of all this. Undoubtedly it ended up in the town dump. But I have a feeling that today some of these items would fetch big prices among antiques collectors and others!

All this redoing after some lean postwar years required a $100 assessment in 1925 and in 1926 an increase in dues to eighty-five dollars.

Possibly the most significant aesthetic improvement followed the vote in 1921 by the Council, after lengthy debate, "that the House Committee arrange for one or two evenings for dancing at the club house in addition to the Thursday evening concerts." Now, four years later, there was ample floor for such unproscribed mixing of the sexes and more. Devereux Barker wrote that "the rule regarding the admission of ladies, although little changed in the club book, was, in fact, relaxed. This change came about because the original ladies' dining room was in the new construction, and the main dining room was now used by members and ladies alike."

It is at least possible that the new order had something to do with the relatively liberated status of women following World War I. As further evidence, this was the maiden year of the renowned Ladies Plate, donated through subscriptions under the leadership of Mrs. Charles Francis Adams, Mrs. C.H.W.

Foster, and Mrs. Frank C. Paine. It was originally for the R-class, thirteen of which—including two from Long Island Sound and one from Buzzards Bay—raced in the inaugural series August 3, 4, 6, and 7. On top of that, Mrs. B. Devereux Barker donated a cup for the Q-class Sunday morning races, and Mrs. Guy Lowell the Lowell Cup for the S-class.

As for Bill Swan's straight-faced reference to the members' shoreside partiality to their postmortem "tea," the wary reader should bear in mind Vashti's vagaries afloat; evidence, or hearsay, as to the vigor with which the mariners of Massachusetts Bay made free with the Eighteenth Amendment is plentiful. The House Committee on at least one occasion found the quantity of soda water dispensed in the dining room worth reporting. And it posted a notice at the start of the 1929 season advising that the attitude of the Club regarding the observance of Prohibition on the premises was well known to all members, admonishing: "Servants in the main Club House and dining room must not under any circumstances be asked to depart from the letter and spirit of this policy."

The authors of Marblehead: The Spirit of '76 Lives Here said no more than they needed to in citing the townie who was asked during this exciting period, when the "isolated, dark coves once more found themselves popularized by twentieth-century smugglers," why his nose was so red. His retort: "My nose ain't red, it's just blushing with pride that it ain't been stuck in anybody else's business."

Or maybe Mr. Swan was only having a little fun in print with his yachting friends. There is tea, and there is tea.

Six years after the run-in with the squall in the raceabout Indian that he described in an earlier chapter, John S. Lawrence joined the Eastern Yacht Club. It was 1905. Commodore Minot thought well enough of his seamanship to appoint him fleet captain on the spot. Subsequently, "Johnny" joined the New York Yacht Club and for several years did most of his racing on Long Island Sound, notably in his New York-Forty Squaw as one of the class sponsors in 1916. He won one race when the wind died by unobtrusively anchoring and waiting for some air. Back at Marblehead after World War I, he raced in S-boats and the R-boat Quiver, with which he engaged in a friendly but sometimes heated rivalry with Charlie Adams. In 1923 he won the Puritan Cup in Squaw and the next year was elected vice commodore.

While Commodore Ayer was trying out his prototype jib-headed mainsail on the schooner *Queen Mab*, Lawrence and his Harvard classmate W. (Bill to friends) Starling Burgess were experimenting on sail aerodynamics with some experts at M.I.T. Out of this project at some time in 1924 emerged Burgess's design of the 63-foot-waterline schooner *Advance*, with jibheaded mainsail *and* foresail, as well as revolutionary staysails between the masts first proposed by Eastern pioneer Robert Bennet Forbes some fifty years earlier.

Advance was built that winter at the yard of designer/builder Johan Anker in Asker, Norway. Her owner planned to take her on trial in one of the fjords and inspect the Q and R boats at Asker; Anker had shipped several to Eastern members and was building the R-boat *Norsman* for Charles Foster—C.H.W.'s forty-eighth. Thence he would check up on the new 16-foot-waterline Rainbows at Copenhagen; these light, straight-stemmed racing machines were making their debut that season at the Eastern, and Lawrence had ordered one for his children. He returned to the States by steamer.

Advance sailed from Oslo for Marblehead on May 13, 1925, under jury rig consisting of storm trysail on the main, staysail on the fore, and headsail from the stem (all of brown hemp duck). The crew was nine Norwegians. The upper portion of her mainmast and her bowsprit were shipped by steamer.

Calvin Coolidge was renting "White Court" in Swampscott for his summer White House, and the presidential yacht *Mayflower* was back at anchor in Marblehead Harbor. The ubiquitous Leonard Fowle was there, too, when *Advance* emerged from the fog on June 27, forty-five days out of Oslo. He wrote in the *Boston Globe*:

As the *Advance* came into the harbor she dipped the large American flag on her mainmast to the Presidential steam yacht *Mayflower*, which salute was returned by the dipping of the colors aboard the big yacht. She also received cannon salutes from the Corinthian and Eastern yacht clubs as she was towed up the harbor. . . .

The *Advance* had rather a hard passage, encountering much head wind from the north and west. For 12 days in a heavy westerly gale not a single mile of westing was made, the schooner being laid to for eight days. In the other four she ran before the heavy wind and seas. . . . For practically the entire voyage until well in toward the coast of the United States, winter temperatures were with the schooner, and all the crew had to keep warm and dry out their wet clothes before a Primus stove. The deck fittings of the boat were covered by heavy wooden boxes to protect them from the ravages of the seas.

After a week of refit at Lawley's, *Advance* returned to Marblehead with her unique racing rig and finished first in the Annual Regatta on the Fourth of July, though she lost to *Queen Mab* on corrected time. Fowle was impressed:

She is the first of the larger two-masters to have jib-headed rig on both fore and main masts. In the first leg of the course, a beat to windward, the schooner carried a jib-headed mainsail, the usual three head sails, a "queen" maintopmast staysail, and a main staysail between the main and fore masts. On the wind the regular jib-headed foresail was brailed up on the foremast,

---

Advance under short-rigged stormsails on her arrival at Marblehead May 13, 1925, after her maiden voyage from Oslo. Jackson photo.

but off the wind when this was broken out there was much added canvas.

So it was that in *Advance*'s first race the experimental jib-headed foresail, designed in combination with a staysail to replace the sagging gaff foresail, gave way to the double staysails trimmed flat on the wind. The new foresail did not survive the test, but the staysails (not to be confused with the "fisherman" slung between the maintopmasthead and the fore top of the Gloucester fishing schooners for many years) revolutionized the rig.

Calvin Coolidge had been voted an Honorary Member of the Eastern Yacht Club on April 7, 1925, not because he was a sailor, which he was not, but because he was President of the United States. Had he been as consummate a yachtsman as he was a politician, Silent Cal would not have returned the compliment to a harborful of Republicans in the manner that he unwittingly did. The problem was his perquisite, his yacht *Mayflower*, at Marblehead ten days before the commander-in-chief set foot on her. She was 273 feet on deck, 36 feet beam, 2,690 tons displacement, with a complement of 200—and moored so close to the outside starting buoy of the Corinthian line that in many races, as Bill Swan complained mildly in the *Boston Transcript*, she split the breeze and crowded the starters:

But the most conspicuous incident in the *Mayflower*'s two-month sojourn in Marblehead was her memorable run through the racing fleet at the start of the Eastern Yacht Club's opening race week regatta, August 8. Few will forget the hair-raising dash of the big 250-foot steam yacht across the starting line, with nearly a hundred almost helpless small boats making frantic efforts in a light air to prevent being run down. The incident seemed inexcusable at the time.

Phil Lewis, the author's uncle, was crewing for Eastern member Alfred Chase that day and remembered the charge of the *Mayflower* quite vividly sixty years later. There was the President, sitting on deck up in the bow in his yachting cap, entirely alone and apparently oblivious to the havoc in his wake. Chase and Lewis were lucky. "Fact is, we rode her bow wave, got a head start across the line, and it was the only race we won all season."

John Lawrence shows off *Advance*'s radical staysail rig off Marblehead in late July, 1925.

Continued Swan:

Yet it afterwards transpired that Captain [Adolphus] Andrews gave official notification to the Eastern Yacht Club of his intention of leaving the harbor at the hour scheduled for the start of the race, and it would have been possible for the regatta committee to have hoisted a postponement flag, and waited a few minutes. The fleet, however, would have been well bunched about Marblehead Rock.

It would have seemed as if the commander of the *Mayflower* might have been a trifle more cautious in running out into the bay, knowing, as he must have at the time, that the yachts were outside. He did not touch a boat, but there were some very narrow escapes, and the incident was a lively topic for the rest of the season.

Nevertheless, the *Mayflower* was proceeding on her lawful occasions. The Eastern Yacht Club's starting line for the championship races for a greater part of the season was plumb in the fairway, officially designated on the Government chart as the Marblehead Channel. The *Mayflower* might have headed over into Salem Bay and threaded the ledges, but she chose the deepest and most direct route into open water. In the absence of any Government supervision or patrol, any vessel, Government, commercial or for-pleasure craft has a perfect right to use this channel and crash a starting line at any time. A tow of barges can break up a start off Marblehead Rock and leave a regatta committee angry but helpless. It is quite true that most towboat captains are good sports and usually give the yachtsmen plenty of room. A starting line located farther up the channel, off Lighthouse Point, might not be so threatened.

Only the Eastern and the Cohasset, of all the clubs in Massachusetts, failed to give their members a clear view of the racing from their verandas, Swan noted by way of an aside. Various suggestions for relocating the starting line in the long wake of the *Mayflower* were tendered as the season progressed, including the leasing of Marblehead Rock by the Eastern and the Corinthian and building a judges box on it. In October, Commodore Ayer appointed a committee of joint membership to study the problem. Perhaps in penance, the President received the three Sears Cup finalist crews at White Court. Duxbury was the winner, its skipper a lad named C. Raymond Hunt.

In spite of Mr. Coolidge's decision not to return to the North Shore the next summer, the Corinthian line was moved to the mouth of the harbor, directly under the lighthouse, and beyond that in 1927. Out of deference to the piazza crowd, however, it was returned in 1928 to its 1926 position. The President re-

The Presidential yacht *Mayflower* dominates Marblehead Harbor in the summer of 1925.

mained an Honorary Member of the Eastern ex-officio and in absentia. The status of his presidential yacht with respect to the fleet and the line it had so mightily fractured remained moot, as did the in-absentia flotilla of six, ranging from a 30-foot cutter to a 222-foot steamer, attached to the honorary membership of King Alfonso.

Both the President and the Spanish monarch were outclassed in the category of the Club's distant heavyweights in 1925 by J.P. Morgan's *Corsair* at 304 feet, with Arthur Curtiss James's stately square-rigged auxiliary barque *Aloha*, 218 feet, a close runner-up. Though an NYYC member, Harold Vanderbilt and his 109-foot *Vagrant* were a familiar sight on the Eastern line. Mrs. Mary Weld's 176-foot steam yacht *Malay II*, 25

feet longer than the 1899 *Malay*, dominated the locally owned fleet, while Commodore Sears's *Constellation* led the big schooners at 134 feet overall, followed by (among others) Charles Harding's *Wildfire*, 95 feet, built by Herreshoff in 1923; John Lawrence's new *Advance*, 88 feet; Mary Wheelwright's *Liria*, 84 feet; Gordon Dexter's *Mystic*, 80 feet; and Commodore Ayer's *Queen Mab*, 77 feet. The challenges facing the Regatta Committee are attested by the numbers: 159 yachts of more than 30 feet on the water, ninety-four under, with more small classes coming along every season.

Among the latter was the popular but ill-fated O-class of 15-footers from the productive John Alden in 1921; eleven began racing at the Eastern the following year. Then, in 1925, his office conceived the Marblehead 18½s (known as Triangles), of 28 feet 5 inches overall, somewhat similar to the S-class and built by Graves. A dozen first raced at the Eastern in 1926,

Under Full Sail

when their designer was chairman of the Committee on Models. In 1928, the Triangles began replacing the fleet of old Sonders that had been racing for three or four years at the Eastern Point Yacht Club, and two years later they were adopted as well by the Annisquam Yacht Club. The author owned the Triangle *Goblin* in the early 1970s and found her a joy to sail.

"John o' Boston" was less interested in racing than in ocean-going, however, and his fame during the 1920s and later rests mainly on his series of Malabars—all but one of them schooners—and hundreds of other cruising boats. The Malabars were the successors to the Long Island Sound "Schoonerettes," of only 40 feet overall, designed in 1912 by Crowninshield, Alden's early mentor. The first *Malabar* appeared in 1921—a compact, all-around cruising boat fashioned after the Gloucestermen so much admired by their creator, who adopted the "*Advance* staysail" when it proved itself but otherwise stuck with the tried-and-true gaff rig he had been brought up on.

The Bermuda Race was resurrected in 1923 by Herbert Stone, editor of *Yachting*, coming under the sponsorship of the Cruising Club of America in 1926. The 1923 race was won by Alden in *Malabar IV*; in fact, his *Malabars* took three of the first five places among twenty-three starters, and his hand at the helm won two more. His friend William H. Taylor, Stone's successor, described the master's style:

> It was an education to watch John come on deck during a race. He'd stand there and look around, alow and aloft, for a few minutes, then quietly start adjusting the trim: six inches in on the mainsheet, perhaps; a slight easing of the vang on the fore gaff; hardening down the tack downhaul of the fisherman and an easing of an inch or two of jibsheet. The difference in the set of the sails was almost imperceptible, but inch by inch the schooner would start to draw ahead or to windward of that other craft—usually a bigger one—that had been holding even with you for an hour or two. Whereupon John would sit down and relax.

Malabar VI won her division on the 1925 Annual Cruise, which was led by Commodore Ayer's *Queen Mab*, on board of which all hands gathered at Rockland on the way home for the annual rowing races between the Corinthians and the professionals at about teatime. The next day, July 11, was the last long run to Portland, won by *Advance*. Measurer Evers Burtner, who was aboard the 1907, 56-foot-waterline Lawley schooner *Mistral*, owned by Howard E. Perry of Falmouth Foreside (not to be confused with John Blodgett's 1938

schooner), recalled that Perry, confident he knew the channel, decided to sail her home without an auxiliary and a chart:

> She ran aground at high tide and resisted moderate attempts to pull her off. Naturally, the entire Eastern fleet witnessed her grounding. *Mistral* lay way over but didn't fill and righted, working off at next high tide. However, sleeping that night in the high side berth was impossible. My stateroom mate, a portly, elderly guest, Alexander Lincoln, a nephew of the poet Longfellow, had a safe starboard berth and slept, snoring, through the night, observed by inquiring fish through the portholes.
>
> A thorough check-up showed no damage except to our dignities. Sailing master was Captain Sommers, a friendly, good looking, capable skipper, perhaps a bit pompous, who had never taken *Mistral* to Falmouth Foreside since she was generally hauled and moored at Marblehead. Imagine his being ribbed by other professional skippers later, although he was in no way responsible.

Commodore Ayer sold *Queen Mab* to Easterner Horace Binney and took over from another member of the Club the contract to build on the Dalmatian coast (in the Adriatic) a 68-foot-waterline steel schooner designed by George Owen of Boston that he named *Lynx V*. In late May of 1926, she set sail

President and Mrs. Coolidge, with Captain Adolphus Andrews, head down the Eastern's pier for the launch and a cruise on *Mayflower*.

under short rig, under Captain Martinolich of the family yard that built her, arriving after sixty-one days in Bristol (Rhode Island), where the Herreshoffs refitted her after their style in time to win her maiden race from New London to Newport in the New York Yacht Club Cruise.

The sensational Lawrence–Burgess *Advance* staysail had effected such a mass conversion of schooner owners that the NYYC actually amended its rules to substitute "sails between the masts" for "foresails." Among them were the owners of the Cup defender *Resolute* and her old rival *Vanitie*, rigged as staysail schooners for the 1926 season. On the first day of the New York regatta, they joined *Vagrant, Advance, Flying Cloud, Wildfire, Queen Mab,* and *Shawna* on the starting line. "This was the last but great era of big schooner racing in the

history of the New York Yacht Club," wrote John Parkinson, "and the author can say these yachts were a sight to see."

And it might be added that of the eight, all but *Resolute* were owned by members of the Eastern, half of them in Boston. Six of the great schooners, except for *Queen Mab* and *Shawna*, with a considerable fleet of New Yorkers, joined the Eastern cruise led by *Lynx V* in July, for which the NYYC postponed its own in deference to the cordiality that prevailed between the two clubs and the large role played by the New Englanders in its own activities. Historian Parkinson noted that on this joint cruise, all the racing sloops and schooners carried Marconi mainsails—most of the latter rigged with staysails as well. Only the New York Forties and Thirties flew gaff mainsails.

On a cruise loaded with sensations, one of the more brilliant was created by *Pleione*, the famous New York Fifty rerigged by Francis Herreshoff as a Marconi staysail auxiliary schooner for Joseph V. Santry, a flag officer of the Corinthian and former Marblehead summer resident whose business was in New York. That year, however, he bought "Red Gate," a harborside estate on the Neck, and joined the Eastern. After winning the second of her four Astor Cups (she won the first as a sloop in 1914), she cleaned up in her unfamiliar two-sticker class, winning the Vice Commodore's Cup for schooners on the run from Vineyard Haven to Mattapoisett over the big ones on corrected time, vying with *Advance* for the top honors down east.

Joe Santry was born in 1884 and learned to sail with his brother Arthur at Cotuit before the family shifted to Marblehead for summers beginning around 1909. In 1915, while a member of the Corinthian, he bought the Bar Harbor 31 (on the water—49 feet overall) *Flight*, in which he won the class the same year and swept the field in 1917. Then came the P-boat *Ahmeek*, bought from C.F. Adams, and in 1925 the 46-foot Q-boat *Spindrift*, purchased from J.P. Morgan. Outclassed by the newer, longer Qs, *Spindrift* was replaced by the Alden 50-footer *Taygeta*. Then, in 1926, Santry joined the Eastern and acquired *Pleione*, originally sloop-rigged, now changed over to schooner from a gaff yawl by her designer's son.

With an almost-overflowing schedule of round-the-buoys racing, 1926 was hailed by many as the busiest season ever in America's yachting capital.

Success on the water notwithstanding, matters ashore were different. Delinquent house accounts contributed $308.63 to

Euellan II, Number One of John Alden's Marblehead One-design, popularly known as the Triangle class, leads the fleet on the run, around 1926. Jackson photo.

Under Full Sail

a deficit of $731.90 at the end of November 1926. House Chairman Frederick Flood wrote Commodore Ayer:

I dislike very much indeed to go to the Treasurer for any more funds, for the showing is quite bad enough as it is. With this in mind I stand ready personally to assume one half the outstanding deficit of $731.90 if you can see your way clear to provide the other half. I feel a little reluctant about suggesting this disposition of our obligations, but still less inclined to pass the hat among the Council and so prefer to assess myself in order to get our bills cleaned up and the books closed. . . .

The commodore had no choice but to reply on December 7: "Here is $365.95 for my half. You are more than fair. Am off for the South for ten days."

The Adams Administration

Chapter 11

The Adams Administration *1927–1929*

By the middle of the 1920s, the International Rule was coming more or less into favor in the New York Yacht Club, although not with the son of the man who had devised the Universal Rule that still dominated American yachting. Francis Herreshoff grumbled that the European measure produced expensive, sharp, homely, and wet boats. New York Commodore George Nichols steered a middle course, leading a movement to convert New York Fifties to the M-class in 1927, including *Chiora* (ex-*Iroquois II*) and *Andiamo* by Charles L. Harding and Walter K. Shaw of the Boston and the Eastern, even as a dozen Ten Meters designed to the International Rule by Starling Burgess and built in Germany joined the New York fleet.

Was it to some extent in response that Charles Francis Adams, now sixty, was elected commodore of the Eastern for the 1927 season? He had been rear commodore in 1892 and 1893 and vice commodore in 1894 and again in 1918 and 1920, and he held strong opinions about matters of measurement. The elevation of "the Deacon" was hailed by a Boston yachting writer:

This is Marblehead's answer to the clique of Long Island Sound yachtsmen who are so anxious to put aside the American rating rule and substitute in its place the international rule, which has not proved at all satisfactory to European yachtsmen.

Marblehead yachtsmen, with the P Class in years past and with the R's and Q's of the last few seasons, have advanced far beyond all other yachting localities in development of the smaller craft under the rating rule, and thus naturally do not wish to change to another rule, which they are not sure would produce as fine racing yachts.

In the selection of Charles Francis Adams as commodore for 1927 the Eastern Yacht Club has named the leading and best-known Corinthian in the United States, a yachtsman that is sure to lead the organization in the right way through the troubled waters that are liable to come by the monkeying with rules by those that have had experience only with one-design classes.

Adams began racing in the R-class in 1918 and tried an S-boat in 1920. But he found the one-design too confining for his independent style and returned to the Rs, launching his latest—another *Gossoon*, by Burgess—in time to serve as his flagship. In his first season, he and *Gossoon* won the Manhasset Bay Challenge Cup for the Eastern and the R-Boat Race Week Ladies Plate. And when the America's Cup candidate *Vanitie* took her third straight defeat by the defender *Resolute* in the New York Yacht Club Cruise, a hurried phone call to Boston had him at the helm the next day, and she won the Astor Cup.

Frequently it's the little things about a celebrated figure that stick in one's mind. Herbert Baldwin, house chairman in 1950 and 1951, and bachelor resident of the clubhouse between 1938 and 1953, wintered on Arlington Street for several years. He was crossing the Public Garden one day when he overheard Adams, who happened to come up behind him, remark to a companion, "Five dollars is enough to pay for a felt hat."

For Adams, however, a yacht was another matter. Joseph Santry, much his junior, once gave way to his intimidating helmsmanship, although Joe clearly had the starboard right-of-way. Back at the clubhouse, Santry summoned the outrage to declare to this icon that he could have rammed him. "Young man," was the tight-lipped reply, "the next time you have that opportunity, you go ahead and ram."

A picture of a competitive but perhaps less combative commodore was drawn by his nephew, George C. Homans, who crewed for him with Charles Francis Adams, Jr., later president of Raytheon, most summers from 1923 to 1940. They raced in the Rs, with the addition of a third, usually George's other cousin, Thomas Boylston Adams, in the larger boats. A decade after the death of his uncle, Homans was professor of sociology at Harvard when he reminisced about those days in "Sailing with Uncle Charlie," before the Massachusetts Historical Society, of which Tom Adams was then president. The profile was published in *The Atlantic Monthly* of July 1965.

The Adams boats were moored behind "the Glades," a tribal compound of few amenities that resembled a latter-day Brook Farm on Scituate Neck, the eastern shore of Cohasset Harbor, eighteen miles from Marblehead. Almost every Saturday, every season, Uncle Charlie commuted across the bay to the Eastern in whatever boat he was going to race. Observed his nephew:

> The result was that we got more experience in handling ship and sails than did the others, who only went out for the afternoon race, and far more experience in keeping her going in light airs. . . . In all my years with Uncle Charlie we always reached Marblehead in time for the race, and almost always in time for lunch before it; and as for getting home, I spent only one full night aboard, when fog, blowing in before an easterly, surprised us halfway across and made it doubtful that we should find the entrance through the Cohasset Ledges. We ran in under the old Boston Light and then anchored in Hull Gut till morning, when the weather cleared. . . . For the record, our fastest run across the bay was made in *Bat* from Marblehead in one hour and three quarters under trysail and small jib before a fresh northwester. Our average run was, I suppose, somewhere between four and five hours.

(As soon as she saw her husband off, Mrs. Adams would phone Frances Gilliland that he was on his way; Frances would return the alert when he started back, and his wife would confirm to the always concerned EYC receptionist his safe arrival home.)

> When people tried to explain Uncle Charlie's racing record, they spoke of his touch at the helm. That was what they could see; what they could not see was his tireless obsession with anything that would help the boat sail faster. . . . He was, above all, death on superfluous weights. When he bought a boat secondhand he went over her with a screwdriver taking off useless gadgets and dumping them unceremoniously overboard. A whole stove once went overboard in this fashion—and with it any suggestion of hot coffee. All cushions and mattresses went the same way; should anyone want to lie down, there were always the sail bags, which were in fact much more comfortable.

> He would have been glad to get rid of the heads, and the boats he had built for himself never had one. Even for crowded waters a canvas bucket was just as good. . . .

> He never shined brass. He seldom coiled a line. When we hoisted the mainsail below deck, we let the halyard lie where it dropped. If it came in all right, he argued, it would, left undisturbed, run out all right again. Our furls had only to be good enough to let the sail cover be put on. . . . The appearance of the vessel was nothing to him as long as the paint in contact with the water was smooth. . . .

> At night we ran, quite illegally, without lights, for lights prevented the helmsman's seeing what he ought to see. In the days of Prohibition this suspicious feature of our behavior led Coast Guard cutters to overhaul and hail us, until, I suspect, they got used to our presence in the bay on Saturday nights. Finally, Uncle Charlie never insured his boats, and never lost one, though the moorings off the Glades were pretty well exposed to northeasters. The loss of a vessel would, in his mind, have paid him off fairly for being a damned fool. . . .

> At Marblehead we came to our moorings, took off the working sails, put on the racing sails—we were always heaving sails up on deck—and went ashore for lunch at the Eastern Yacht Club. Uncle Charlie's approach to the clubhouse was in some ways his finest moment, and the only one when I ever suspected him of self-consciously acting the reverse of self-consciousness. An old navy seaman's duck cap, its brim reversed, might be pulled down over his noble beak; then came a pullover sweater, and finally a pair of knickerbockers, left unbuckled perhaps and drooping below the knees, held up by a sail stop instead of a belt, a stop passed not through the belt straps but below them so as to hitch the knickerbockers up. The effect was as little nautical as possible, and put Uncle Charlie at once one up on the gentlemen in white flannels and yachting caps on the piazza.

> How shall I reproduce the smells of an old-time yacht club before it became just another country club: smells of tarred marline, manila rope, and new cotton duck, of large, dark highstudded rooms fitted with varnished woodwork and straw matting, of the sea breeze blowing through open transoms and slatted doors, of clam chowder and blueberry pie?

> After lunch we dumped our spare sails into the dinghy and went to the starting line off Marblehead Rock. . . . He was never very bold or skillful at getting the best berth at the windward end of the line. Indeed, I never felt he liked, as so many racing skippers do, maneuvering at close quarters. In starting, at any rate, Uncle Charlie seemed to be content if at the gun he was somewhere near the line with his wind clear. . . .

> He counted on getting ahead on the windward leg and holding his lead on the run or reach that followed. . . . Nor was he at his best in strong breezes, which demanded crude methods. His

supreme expertise lay in coaxing a ship to windward in light airs—and at Marblehead in summer the winds are light; the place fitted the man. . . .

Uncle Charlie never sailed any extreme course on the mere gamble of picking up a favorable slant. Even when he was, for once, behind, he seldom went off wind-hunting. . . . Since he ought to be able to beat any boat sailing under the same conditions as his was, the best strategy was to stay with the rest of the fleet, and especially his chief rivals, rather than leave them and look for a breeze. To the usual maxim "Stay between the leading boat and the mark," he added the rule "Stay with a boat you're beating."

And he did beat them. Besides what I have called his rationality, his only gift was a superb sensitivity to the helm and the trim of the sails, as if he were a delicate machine that could register to ten decimal places when the ship was doing her best. Characteristically he sat to leeward watching the jib, the tiller over his shoulder, holding it, as he could in these beautifully balanced yachts, between thumb and forefinger, as if to pick up and read its least vibration. Occasionally he would say in a low voice: "Ease the jib a hair," or something of the sort. And however bad our start—and it was seldom really good—we found ourselves before long well up in the fleet or leading it.

Professor Homans acknowledged that his uncle was known as a pretty hard cusser under stress when he was younger, but he never swore at his son and nephew. There were times, just the same, when he got excited:

They were likely to come when we had rounded the weather mark for the run to the finish, and another boat was close astern. As one of us went forward to struggle with the spinnaker, he would appear to jump up and down in the cockpit, not shouting so much as passionately exclaiming: "Hurry, boys! Hurry up! Oh, hurry!" These vivid comments did nothing to speed the setting of the spinnaker. . . .

His preoccupation [on the run to the finish] was not to pass but to avoid being passed. He would sight astern, holding at arm's length his thumb erect, with his index finger against it, to measure the angle subtended by our nearest pursuer's mainmast, and so determine, by comparing two successive observations, whether she was gaining. I never found out how he remembered where against his thumb his finger stood on the previous occasion. Under these circumstances the finish line came as a blessed relief.

With the end of the race our opponents' work was done. Ours had barely begun: we had to work the ship back across the bay. We returned to Marblehead Harbor, bent on once more our working sails, and got under way again. By this time our late rivals were sitting on their piazzas, knocking back the first of many cocktails. Toward them our attitudes had all the ambivalence of working stiffs eyeing the fat cats of the bourgeoisie. No doubt they were to be envied their costly pleasures. On the other hand the moral superiority was unquestionably ours. Ours was

all that beauty
Born of a manly life and bitter duty.

In the fall of 1927, Francis B. Crowninshield of Peach's Point, whose sailing adventures have figured earlier in this narrative, and his spouse, the formidable North Shore dowager Louise Du Pont Crowninshield, bought the exceedingly handsome steel schooner *Mariette*, "owing," as Keno manfully stated, "to my good fortune in having such a wife—who luckily for me was fond of the water." Eighty feet on the waterline, 109 feet overall, with fine overhangs and a towering rig, *Mariette* was designed and built by Nathanael Herreshoff in 1917 for Frederick Jacob Brown along the lines of Harold Vanderbilt's phenomenal *Vagrant*. Her proud new owner renamed her *Cleopatra's Barge II*, after the first American yacht built by his ancestor, gave her a coat of black with a gold stripe, and signed on a captain and twelve crew. (The Cleopatra's Barge Cup offered in the Annual Regatta, incidentally and coincidentally, was put up the year before for the Annual Regatta and was first won in 1926 by Harry Payne Whitney's *Vanitie*; it may, of course, have been Crowninshield's inspiration.)

The *Barge* took a mooring just inside the harbor and, with *Constellation*, until the war ended it all, kept alive the last glory days of American yachting. For thirteen seasons, her owner, two or three close friends—who might include Charlie Adams and Fleet Surgeon Hugh (Old Doctor Bones) Milliken—and her regular crew traveled to City Island to sail her up the coast, take on Louise and guests, pause at New London for the Harvard-Yale crew races, and then continue to Marblehead for the Annual Regatta and subsequent Annual Cruise, for which they were frequently on hand but in which they never raced. Always there was the midseason haulout for scraping and a fresh coat of bottom paint.

Her owner maintained an entertaining log that he published in 1948 when he was seventy-nine, only two years before his death. In it he chronicled the comings and goings of the ever-more-famous *Cleopatra's Barge II* between the Chesapeake and the Penobscot: their excursions ashore for legendary "antiquing" by Louise and "movieing" by the males; his "mudslinging" with his watercolors and the resorts perforce to passagemaking in a "gasoline breeze." And always there was his obsessive and losing battle with the flies from shore ("An enormous quantity of flies kept coming on board all day. All hands and cook busily employed in swatting them 'to keep the Barge afloat.' I hate the G.D. things!"), the Maine fog, and, from 1932 on, Franklin Delano Roosevelt.

On the Fourth of July of 1928, the *Barge*'s maiden season with the Crowninshields, the Marblehead fleet of Alden O-boats, sent on a course to Pig's Rock bell, was hit by a thundersquall and swamped en masse. The hero of the day was Captain Eugene O'Donnell, a former Boston-New York steamer skipper, then president of the Eastern Steamship Company, who commandeered the Corinthian launch and plucked twenty or so of the flailing O-boat sailors from the ocean. The centerboarders were thereafter banned from competition at Marblehead. "Until a man knows how to sail an easily capsized boat," was Keno's wise caveat, "I don't consider him a real boat sailor."

Five weeks later, the *Barge* joined the New York Yacht Club cruise at Newport, and Frank Crowninshield and a guest "visited the *Nourmahal*, the new German-built flagship of the NYYC, and paid our respects to Commodore Astor. Finding the going there dull and uninteresting and the whiskey very ordinary we soon left."

Another five weeks, and during the last cruise of their first season, the breeze gave out on them abreast of Monhegan: "The lightness of the wind plus the strength of the head tide forced us into Tenants Harbor at 5 P.M. L.B. [Louise] thinks it would be well to record a necking party on one of the Sound Schooners. We are of the opinion that the crew and some lady friends were having a good time."

And then, after the usual spell of fogbound, it was all worth it as the yacht owner confided to his seagoing diary the exhilaration of renewed discovery:

Saturday, September 22nd, Castine. A beautiful morning truly. As it was a flat calm we got under power at 6:45 with real sun shining through the ports. Once abeam of Dark Harbor the S.W. breeze freshened enough to warrant setting our sails. For several hours it seemed unable to decide where it wanted to come

---

Cleopatra's Barge II, designed and built by Nathanael Herreshoff in 1916. Starboard launch and a pair of port gigs attest to the amphibious proclivities of the Crowninshields.

from. Went through the Musselridge. On the other side we found quite a swell coming in from the southward. As we were far from home and the wind dead ahead, we gave her the Queen staysail and the baby jib topsail (to cheer her up a bit).

Just as she began to go some, we parted the main topsail sheet (wire) and hardly had we repaired the damage and reset the sail when our S.W. wind hauled into the N.W. and breezed and breezed until it was blowing like Hell. We doused the light stuff as fast as we could and put her on the course again. That, however, was not enough. It kept coming harder and harder, so we put her in the wind again and took in our mainsail, but even so she was going considerably faster than any of us thought we could swim. After lunch we had to haul up a bit, so we gave her the main trysail, really to see what it looked like. I might say it looked good, but awfully small. Let go off Peaks Island at 6 P.M.

When Lloyd Bergeson visited his grandparents in Marblehead as a boy in the late 1920s, he made a beeline for the rocky prominence of Fort Sewall, where the whole busy panorama of

Francis B. Crowninshield at the wheel of *Cleopatra's Barge II.*

America's yachting capital was spread out below him. *Cleopatra's Barge* was moored right off the fort.

The *Barge*, if not cruising, was sailed on practically every good day just as if she were a small knockabout day sailer. *Constellation* left her mooring under sail less often, but when she did, with her perfectly cut Egyptian cotton sails, she was a sight to behold.

Well up in the harbor lay two of Herreshoff's New York-50 class, *Andiamo*, rerigged as a Class-M sloop and owned by Walter K. Shaw, and Joe Santry's *Pleione* for which L. Francis Herreshoff had provided a modern staysail schooner rig.

All maneuvered under sail alone, as did the racing fleet, and when making their moorings in the fresh afternoon sou'wester which always drew through the harbor, it was routine to drop the jib and shoot for the mooring, dropping the main when head to wind and stopping the vessel dead in the water with the bow exactly over the buoy, the pendant of which was then picked up and secured to the bitt. On the better managed yachts, the main was off the boom and bagged by the time the buoy was reached.

Early in Commodore Adams's second season of 1928, Henry Howard, who had recently retired from business, arranged through his old Sonder connections with King Alfonso to have the New York Yacht Club, of which he was a member, sponsor a two-class ocean race from Sandy Hook to Santander, Spain, for the King's and Queen's cups for yachts of over and under 55 feet waterline. Although Charlie Adams was with Gerard B. Lambert on his famed three-master *Atlantic*, the winds were light, and the great *Elena* ghosted across to win the big class. The small class was left in shambles by *Niña*, the immortal Marconi mainsail/staysail schooner designed by Starling Burgess for Paul Hammond (of the NYYC) and this very event. It was the first transatlantic race since 1905, and the last in large yachts with professional crews, thanks to the first of the 59-foot *Niña*'s numerous brilliant performances over a long career.

As if this were not enough for one season, two more new international one-designs from the Burgess board arrived in New York—Eight Meters and Twelves—and were represented for the first time in the Eastern's Annual Regatta. Countering the trend to uniformity, Commodore Adams forsook his familiar R-class and took up with the Qs, purchasing the *Sally XIV* from Lawrence Percival and stripping her of her numeral and some other weight he considered unnecessary in preparation for his return from the Spanish race.

The Adams Administration

After owning five Rs since 1921, Charlie Foster followed Charlie Adams for his fifty-first and fifty-second yachts:

In 1928 the gang seemed inclined to a larger type of boat with a little more accommodation, and I purchased *Hawk*, a 32-feet-waterline class Q boat, and after a summer in her I built *Questa*, another Q boat the same length and class from a design by Francis Herreshoff. I think she is acknowledged to be the fastest and best heavy-weather boat in the fleet. . . . In her I incorporated my plan of a double cockpit with a bridge deck between the two on which the main sheet and runners are fastened.

Interest in the Rs (20-raters), however, remained undiminished in spite of the commodore's abandonment of them. Chandler Hovey brought the New York Forty *Pampero* with him when he transferred his racing from Marion and Buzzards Bay to Marblehead in 1926. In 1927 he bought the New York Fifty *Chiora* and the R-boat *Gypsy*, designed by Frank Paine, in which he won the Paine Cup.

Herreshoff considered the R a development class, as indeed he and Foster did all classes, and there was no telling what the two might come up with when they got their heads together. Foster was experimenting with a curved boom on an R in 1924; the sail was bent to mast hoops on the spar, bellying the foot and evidently slowing the boat because of increased downdraft, which set the Skipper to thinking about a better boom.

In her *Yankee* magazine memoir of her father, Edith Foster Farwell was struck by the reciprocal relationship of these two originals:

Father was always working out new theories as to sails and rigs and studied sailing rigs all winter on land, preparing to put them into practice when summer came. Never shall I forget the day I came home from school and saw a high pole in the field, a sail hoisted up this impromptu mast, and Father sitting on the lawn holding the main sheet with a mirror placed behind him to see "how she filled." We children felt a bit embarrassed and carefully explained to guests, "No, Pa is not crazy, he is merely working out some new wrinkle for his boat."

He and Mr. Herreshoff were always having heated arguments about sails. One winter's day they were both seated in the library at a card table. On the card table was a model of a sailboat,

Walter K. Shaw converted *Andiamo* from a New York Fifty to an M-class in 1927. Jackson photo.

sails all set, and the electric fan blowing on the sails while the two men argued and argued as to this "fill" and that "fill" and when "you luffed her up she would do thus and so, what about the back fill," etc., etc.

Herreshoff achieved an epochal design breakthrough via the Rs in 1925 with *Yankee* for Charles A. Welch of the Eastern. "This boat was a portent," wrote Gloucester designer Philip C. Bolger in a profile of Herreshoff in *Nautical Quarterly*. "If I had to point to a single ancestor of the present generation of racing (and most cruising) boats, it would have to be this *Yankee*."

What the Skipper did, Bolger pointed out, was to come up with the structural backup to make it possible to incorporate the rule-beating device of enlarging the spinnaker by increasing the foretriangle at the expense of the main. To stiffen *Yankee*'s rig for the bigger jib and to reduce windage, he hung the shrouds from tangs instead of splicing the ends around the mast over chocks, likewise the halyard blocks. The stick he designed as a hollow rectangular box curved slightly aft at the head, and he planked the hull diagonally over longitudinal stringers on web frames, giving great strength-for-weight, the forerunner of modern cold-molding. *Yankee* dropped in on the Manhasset Bay Challenge on Long Island Sound her first September and brought back the cup.

The heat of competition in the Rs may be gauged from a multiple protest lodged with the Regatta Committee against B.B. Crowninshield, who had acquired *Norsman* from Charlie Foster. Foster himself in *Mary*, Charles Welch in *Yankee*, and Sherman Hoyt in *Bob Kat* apparently were spitting mad over port-starboard violations by the designer on four occasions in three races during August of 1926:

The letters of protest having been read, Mr. Crowninshield made a statement as to his view of the three cases and the protestants also stated their views. After some discussion Mr. Crowninshield and the protestants withdrew and upon full consideration of the matters in dispute it was the unanimous decision of the Committee that *Norsman* should be disqualified in all three races and the owner notified of this decision

Charles Welch's 1927 R-boat *Live Yankee* demonstrated the lively genius of L. Francis Herreshoff, always ahead of his time. Snub nose, canoe stern, straight sheer, swivelled and whipped mast, swivelling luff spar among an array of other breakthroughs. Jackson photo.

The Adams Administration

and warned that further flagrant violations of the racing rules, particularly of the Port and Starboard tack, would result in his disqualification from all future races of the Eastern Yacht Club.

As if *Yankee* weren't lively enough, Welch had his good friend follow his own act in 1927 with the radical, canoe-stern, straight-sheer R-boat *Live Yankee*, described by Bolger:

She had 80% of her displacement devoted to ballast. She had no rudder in the usual sense, the trailing edge of her keel being flexed in a curve to steer her. Her deck edges and the tips of her overhangs were rounded off to reduce drag when the lead-mine [10,400 pounds] hull put its ends and rails under. She had a luff spar in place of a wire stay for her jib, but it revolved and the sail had a double luff; the mainmast also swiveled and that sail was double-luffed as well. She had a broad tee-boom to form an end plate for the mainsail. As conceived this was much the cleanest rig, aerodynamically, ever put into a boat up to that time or for 40 years after.

After an understandably slow start due to technical problems, *Live Yankee* swept the New York Yacht Club's R Series. She effectively put her class out of business, in Phil Bolger's opinion, and contributed mightily to the crippling of the Universal Rule—aided and abetted by *Bonnie Lassie*, which the Skipper created for Dr. Morton Prince in 1928. She, too, was mahogany planked diagonally over sugar pine on web frames. Her shrouds led through the deck to turnbuckles above chainplates on the inside of the hull. Her mast was radically hooked along the top four or five feet, with a sort of conforming headboard or curved gaff at the head of the mainsail intended in theory to sharpen her windward ability, and a curved jibboom for her big jib.

Evers Burtner, the Eastern's longtime measurer, contributes a postscript to the story of *Live Yankee* that adds to the mystery of the rudder that wasn't a rudder:

By mid-January previous to actual construction, Francis Herreshoff sent a print of *Live Yankee*'s construction plan to the Measurer. The scantlings of the principal members were checked as being OK and so reported. After construction by Britt Brothers in Lynn, she arrived in Marblehead.

To ensure smooth water it was agreed that hull measuring would begin at 7 A.M. The Measurer picked up his 13-foot tender at the Eastern float and rowed across harbor to *Live Yankee*, reaching there about 6:50 A.M. and before the owner and others reported.

On looking at the rudder, his jaw dropped. The rudder blade

was parallel to and about one-half inch above the load water line. Thus this construction had the effect of increasing the load water line length from stem to rudder stock by about ten inches. To the Measurer, the load water line length should include the rudder length.

When this proposal was advanced, Herreshoff and Welch strongly objected, stating that when first seen by the Measurer the yacht was down by the head; with the proper trim, the rudder edge would be submerged about one half-inch. To support the designer's position of neglecting the rudder length, Frank Paine produced the published figure of an International Meter Yacht which showed that with that Rule the rudder was omitted in measuring LWL.

The Measurer reversed his procedure and has omitted rudder when LWL length is measured for all yachts, although logically it seems wrong.

Of further interest in this yacht, the designer and owner tried the experiment of introducing several small streams of kerosene through the planking forward to see if it would reduce resistance and help the yacht's speed.

At the 1929 annual meeting, Henry Taggard retired as secretary after twenty-two years. He was succeeded by Boston lawyer Caleb Loring, a summer resident of Beverly Farms who had been in the forefront of Eastern yachting even before he was old enough for membership in 1909—from the old 18-footers through the Qs, Sonders, Rs, S-class, Eight Meters, M-Bs, and International One-Designs. "Of course I am prejudiced," writes Caleb Loring, Jr., who crewed for his father, "but I will always consider him among the all-time best of American racing skippers and without a peer when it came to tuning a racing boat."

Charles P. Curtis, another Boston attorney who had been a member since 1906, succeeded Charles Francis Adams as commodore at the same 1929 annual meeting; on March 5, 1930, the Number One helmsman in the United States was sworn in as the newly elected President Hoover's Secretary of the Navy.

Charlie Foster took the occasion of the elevation of Charlie Adams to pen a whimsical (and useful) insight in his *Ditty Box*:

And now, my dear Mr. Secretary of the Navy, assuming your permission, I will create a hypothetical case, picturing you in the simple nautical life that we older members like to recall, and which we hope may be of inspiration and profit to our younger readers.

Two boats are built just alike, and Jones challenges Adams to a series of races. The conditions having been concluded in the late evening, Jones makes arrangements to have an early breakfast, in order that he may have a look at his boat soon thereafter. Upon arising, Jones looks out of his window and, "By Gosh," what does he see? Adams already at work on the boat he is to sail—been up an hour or two already studying over details of rigging and sails. Yes, and there he goes lugging a jib or something over to the sail maker to be cut over or adjusted to a better lead. Hullo, and what is this? It is the power-boat from the boatyard hitching on to the Adams boat to haul her out for a cleaning. No, siree, no dirty boat for Adams. And so it goes in preparation for the race, with Jones just about a lap behind in recognition of the importance of these details. Meantime, Adams has sailed three miles to one for Jones in his practice spins, and has the better feel of his boat.

White-capped in the cockpit of his 8-meter *Ellen*, Commodore Curtis must not have noticed the unforgivable, right there for the camera to immortalize.

Commodore Charles P. Curtis

And now for the race. Jones is a good boat sailor, and his helmsmanship is equal to that of Adams for a while, but, after a bit, one can see the angle of heel of the Jones boat change. Not so with the Adams boat, and it gains a few feet. Then no change for a while, then another few feet for Adams, and so it goes, with the steady pressure all the time on the Adams boat and most of the time on the Jones boat. The little niceties of trim of sail and balance of boat, too, are in favor of Adams, and he wins as usual.

As a boy, Commodore Curtis had sailed out of Swampscott on the family schooner *Bessie*. One day she was in the lead when their dog mistook a lobster buoy for a duck and leaped overboard; coming about and retrieving the retriever cost them the race. Curtis was a noted stroke oar in his Harvard class of 1883 and made his mark as a big-game hunter in Africa, a helmsman in the Sonder series; and later as a six-time winner

The Adams Administration

of the Quincy Challenge Cup. All his boats were named *Ellen* for his wife (including the 65-foot Herreshoff patrol boat he commissioned at his own expense and commanded for a while during World War I, as well as his latest, an R-boat by Burgess).

The Twenties raced from roar to bellow in 1929. The stock market was out of sight, money flowed like honey, and the yachting world was in ecstasy. The Eastern was overflowing with 616 members and 225 yachts over 30 feet on the water, including forty-seven schooners; sixty-eight sloops, yawls, and ketches; ninety-six powerboats; 11 steamers; one barque; one brig, and one houseboat. There were 129 boats under 30 feet, including 112 sloops, yawls, and ketches; one cat; and sixteen powerboats. The Council considered building a swimming pool on the Old Stone Wharf property.

And *Cleopatra's Barge II* was sailing north early in the season from Du Pont country and the Chesapeake—concerning which, the Crowninshield log: "It is a very interesting place to one whose mind can think of other things than jazz, cigarettes, flappers, etc. There is much to see, the country is beautiful as well as interesting. The objectionable features are, first of all, flies—and Oh God how they bite—and fish nets. The whole Bay, alas, is infested with them—*both of them.*"

Thirty-one yachts in eight classes raced in the Annual Regatta, which was remarkable for the maiden appearance of the J-class of 65-to-76-feet waterline, one year after the debut of the Twelves that outlived and ultimately replaced it. (The Royal Ulster Yacht Club had challenged once again for the America's Cup in 1930 on behalf of Sir Thomas Lipton with his Shamrock V. For the first time in Cup history, the races

Eastern T-boat skippers in 1929 are Barbara Eustis, Peggy Turner, Marion Leeson, Catherine Tappan and Ruth Edmands.

would be off Newport instead of Sandy Hook, boat-for-boat according to the Universal Rule. The old days of the gaff rig and time allowances were gone forever.) Gerard Lambert's *Vanitie* and *Resolute* were re-rerigged jibheaded sloops and used as trial horses. *Vanitie* was outstanding in the regatta, as was R.B. Metcalf's Alden schooner Sachem.

Commodore Curtis, whose racing preference was for the smaller classes, had chartered the 250-foot steam yacht *Surf* for his flagship. It was a glorious Fourth. The Regatta Committee arranged with the Coast Guard to have the cutter *Mojave* on hand, and, having more than a little pull with the Navy, a destroyer as well. In fact, permission was obtained for members and their families to go aboard both vessels as spectators, with box lunches gratis from the House Committee.

In ten years, the world—and the world of yachting—had made nothing short of a spectacular recovery from the effects of the most devastating war in history, and in the summer of 1929 the future looked up, and up, and up.

Chapter 12   *Yankee* Comes Close   *1930–1934*

America rode the crest of the wave that summer of 1929, and Sir Thomas Lipton's challenge with *Shamrock V* enticed even conservative Boston back into The Race for the first time in a generation. Of the four J-boat syndicates that were formed for the 1930 races, one, though nominally belonging to the New York Yacht Club in order to qualify, was strictly Yankee and the Eastern.

Harold S. Vanderbilt would skipper and manage *Enterprise*, to be designed by Starling Burgess. Clinton Crane was to create *Weetamoe* for Junius S. Morgan, with George Nichols as skipper. Both were to be built by Herreshoff in Bristol. Francis Herreshoff would spin off *Whirlwind* for a syndicate headed by manager/skipper Landon K. Thorne. All were New York boats.

The decision to form the Boston-Marblehead Syndicate (also known as the Eastern Yacht Club Syndicate) to build *Yankee* was reached on Chandler Hovey's Marblehead Neck porch right after the Labor Day race. Since Burgess was already committed to Vanderbilt, *Yankee* would be designed by Frank C. Paine and built by Lawley at Neponset, after *Whirlwind*. Secretary of the Navy Charles Francis Adams would be skipper and John S. Lawrence manager. Those four were the core of her afterguard. Edwin S. Webster and W. Cameron Forbes were also members.

A few weeks later, on October 24, the stock market crashed. All four syndicates had already announced their plans prior to the general meeting of the New York Yacht Club, and none flinched. Construction started that winter.

After racing his R-boat *Robin* in 1929, Chandler Hovey switched to Q-boats and bought B. Devereux Barker's light-air *Hornet*; he sailed her that summer and in 1934, when he passed her on to Ray Hunt. In 1930, he bought the Q-boat *Norn*

from Isaac Edmands after watching him slip through his lee one day. He renamed her *Robin*, and she won the season's championships in 1931, 1932, and 1933, when in the Annual Regatta she beat *Weetamoe* for the Puritan Cup on corrected time by one second. Hovey's constant sailing companions were his sons Chandler, Jr. (Buss), and Charles, and his daughter Elizabeth (Sis).

Frank Paine designed Yankee much on the model of his successful Q *Cara Mia*, full and rounded forward, with heavy-weather lines; she was the beamiest of the four Js, measuring 125.6 feet overall, 84 feet waterline, 22.33 feet beam, 15.08 feet draft. She had 148 tons displacement, 7,550 square feet of sail, a triple-head rig, and a small centerboard fitted just ahead of the rudderpost. Her mast shot 152 feet into the sky from deck to top of sheave. Next to *Whirlwind*, *Yankee* was the biggest of the four Js, outdisplacing *Enterprise*, the smallest, by 20 tons, though she carried 33 fewer square feet of canvas.

Yankee, *Enterprise* and *Weetamoe* were built with steel frames and deck beams, wooden decks, and bronze shell plating. Skipper Herreshoff's double-ended *Whirlwind* was an advanced composite with steel frames, wood planking, and five cockpits, the first with a double-head rig and no jib topsail; she would prove a great disappointment to him. *Yankee*'s hull plating was carried completely around the keel to form a trough in which the ballast was stowed. Starling Burgess came up with the most radical innovations, not in the hull but topsides. Borrowing from aeronautics, he got his brother Charles to design a stick of Duralumin for *Enterprise* that was held together with 80,000 rivets, thus saving 1,200 of the standard spruce mast's 6,000 pounds. And from that he swung his immortal elliptical "Park Avenue boom" that two men could march along abreast and that allowed the foot of his towering sail to follow the slant of the wind on either tack.

That winter of 1929–30 was a busy one for Frank Paine. While his contender for the America's Cup defense was building at Neponset, another of his designs, the *Gertrude L. Thebaud*—last of the full-rigged fishing schooners and Gloucester's final bid to take the International Fishermen's Cup from the Canadians' too-formidable *Bluenose*—was rising on the stocks at the Story yard in Essex. Chandler Hovey was a *Thebaud* backer, too, and his daughter Sis christened the last of the Gloucestermen on March 17. In point-counterpoint through the thirties, the Js and the "flying fishermen" would usher out the Great Age of Sail in sensational style.

Yankee was late launching. By June 23, 1930, when the Eastern was to sponsor a J-boat series off Newport, *Enterprise, Weetamoe,* and *Whirlwind* had been mixing it up since June 11;

Chandler Hovey's fast Q-boat *Robin*, 1932.

the latter, heavy and sluggish, was back with the trial nags, *Resolute* and *Vanitie*. *Weetamoe* withdrew the first day after failing to give *Enterprise* the right-of-way at the start, and Vanderbilt's boat won the next two, with *Yankee* and *Weetamoe* splitting second and third. For the Boston boat, good weather—that is, anything under about 16 knots—was proving bad.

Among *Yankee*'s afterguard in several of the races that summer was the former junior champion C. Raymond Hunt, who in 1928 had switched from Duxbury to Marblehead, looking for deepwater racing. He attracted such attention from Frank Paine, first in the R-class and then in Paine's Eight Meter *Gypsy*, that he woke up one day and found himself at the age of twenty-two crewing for the Secretary of the Navy.

When the speculative wave of the Twenties broke that fateful day in October, the momentum of prosperity swept many a financial mariner over the shoals of the Crash and into what seemed to be safe haven beyond. The membership of the Eastern actually rose by eight to 624 in 1930, and the fleet by eight to 362.

Not content merely to be racing or cruising a New York Forty, a New York Fifty, a Q, an R, and a J, the Hoveys got interested in the Thirty Square Meter. Near the end of the 1928 season, *Gluckauf*, a German example of one of this sail-rated Swedish *Scharenkreuzer* class, was demonstrated at Marblehead. She excited some interest among the avant garde, including the Hoveys and L. Francis Herreshoff, who was commissioned to design one of this so-called X-class for Sis. *Oriole*, a typically Herreshoff double-ender, was the first American Thirty Square, smaller but fast.

The following August, the Corinthian Yacht Club revived international racing at Marblehead in response to a German and Swedish challenge. Alfred Chase, Arthur Shuman, and Charles and Sohier Welch from the Eastern, with a couple of others, built their own Thirties. *Gluckauf*, from the Kaiserlicher Yacht Club, won the President Hoover Cup in the German-American match; *Bacchant*, carrying a high, short-footed main and a long-footed, overlapping jib not familiar in America, won the Marblehead Cup in the series with Sweden, which built larger boats to a simpler version of the German rule.

(By the late 1930s, the Thirty Squares racing at Marblehead were virtually all imports from Sweden, as attested by George Poor, whose family abandoned their winning S-boat *Woodcock* in 1934 for *Skjold VII*, Swedish-built and German-raced.

Yankee Comes Close

The class, he notes, was remarkably open, varying from about 38 feet to as much as 45 feet overall.)

Sis Hovey (Mrs. Sherman Morss), at the helm of *Oriole*, had the distinction of being the first woman ever to skipper an international race. Six American boats were taken to Europe for the 1930 internationals. There were three Six Meters and, from the Eastern, three Thirty Square Meters—*Oriole II*, the second double-ended version designed by Herreshoff for Sis to race; Alfred Chase's *Michl*; and the Welches' *Yankee*. During the fortnight at Kiel, it blew hard. The three weeks of lighter airs at Sweden's Sandhamn are vividly remembered by Mrs. Morss:

We had a long, long day because the nights were very short in June. It never got dark. At midnight you could still see daylight, and we had no time limit on our races. We would be towed out to the line around 8 a.m. after a large smorgasbord breakfast, and sometimes we would not get home until 8 or 9 at night because of the very light air.

Mr. Herreshoff had designed for *Oriole II* the first jib which has become known since as the Genoa jib. The other boats that went over in our team did not have big jibs, and at that time we called it our "biggest, biggest" jib. It lapped so far aft that it led almost out to the stern. On the one we used in light air, the clew was aft of the main boom.

We had twenty-one different nations racing in Sweden, and when the Italians and some of the others saw our jib they all tried to get dimensions and learn all they could about it because no other boat had anything like it outside of large, high-cut jibs.

So each night we took the jib home and hid it. We never let them see any more of it than we possibly could except when we were racing. Just about a year later the Italians came out with the jib which has been known ever since as the Genoa jib, which was a complete copy of the one Mr. Herreshoff designed for *Oriole II*. He often said it should have been called the "Hovey jib."

Another thing he did for us that summer was to design what is known as a ventilated spinnaker. This was the first one. The International Rule said that your spinnaker pole had to be the length of your forward triangle, on deck between the mast and the headstay. It was a silly little, short pole, and he thought that if the spinnaker had holes in it letting some of the air get through, making a vacuum on the other side, it would hold out better without a pole. The Rule didn't say anywhere that you had to use a pole, and he picked this up.

Two Q's clip close under Lighthouse Point approaching the Inside Finish, August 1929.

On *Oriole II* we didn't use our pole at all when we were dead before the wind, and our spinnaker spread way out, and we flew it like a kite. One of my crew would stand on the stern, and we had this enormous spinnaker, and there wasn't a boat that could touch us downwind.

After we had had two days of the windward-leeward course there was no question but that we went away from everybody, and we went away from everybody with our Genoa jib in light air. So they gave us triangular courses from then on, with one beat and two reaches. We could carry a spinnaker sometimes, but it was just like any other spinnaker when we had to use a pole, not having a dead-to-leeward leg.

When we got home, the J-Boats tried to use the ventilated spinnaker with the pole, and some thought it helped, that it steadied it a little bit, but not enough to continue using it.

This was the thing about Francis Herreshoff—way ahead. I used to go over to see him in his "Castle" in Marblehead. He didn't see many people, and I felt very privileged to be one of his friends. He came over for lunch quite often.

When the races were over, or if we had a day off on Sunday, we went into Stockholm, which was about a three-hour boat ride from Sandhamn, where we all lived and raced. It was the first big regatta, the Royal Regatta, after World War I, and King Gustav, who was quite a sportsman, tennis player and yachtsman in his own right, had this tremendous dinner one evening with over two thousand people.

All the women had to wear white, and all the men wore their yachting jackets, seated at these long, long tables in the Rathaus, the town hall. We sang the national anthem of all twenty-one nations represented; the dinner went on for about four hours, and there was dancing afterwards. I had the pleasure of meeting King Gustav because we were lucky enough to win the "Best American Boat" and other prizes. King Olaf of Norway—he was Prince Olaf at the time—raced a Six-Meter, and I got to know him very well, a most delightful person.

Back at Marblehead, twenty-six boats started in the 1930 Annual Regatta on July 4. Walter K. Shaw's old *Andiamo*, a New York Fifty now rigged as an M-boat, won the Puritan Cup (and a month later the NYYC's King's Cup); R.B. Metcalf's fast schooner *Sachem* won the Cleopatra's Barge Cup. The following day, nineteen were off on the Annual Cruise as far as Block Island, behind Commodore Curtis in his chartered schooner *Ingomar*. The Midsummer Series was as full as ever, with 260 boats finishing on the last day.

This season, his second in office, Commodore Curtis donated the Curtis Cup, a silver bowl, as a perpetual trophy for the North Shore Junior Championship at the suggestion of yachting writer Bill Swan. Catherine H. Tappan, C.H.W. Fos-

ter's granddaughter, representing the Club, was the first winner of the new cup and the first girl to be North Shore Junior Champion. However, a House Committee rule, since abolished, barred her from the clubhouse for the presentation, though her two crew, Albert Goodhue and James Hunnewell, were admitted. (Fifty-seven years later, the former Miss Tappan, now Mrs. John Farlow, laid eyes on the (her) cup for the first time in her life at an Eastern dinner.)

The young women were forcing recognition of their skills on the water. Catherine Tappan and Marion Leeson first attracted attention in 1929 when they won the Marblehead T-class 15-footer championship in *Oolong*. Marion, who was thirteen, also won the Pleon's Snail Cup in the family Brutal Beast *Black Cat* in 1929 and in 1930, when they repeated the sweep in *Oolong*, leading Leonard Fowle to write on July 2 that the T-class "seems to be predominated by young yachtswomen. Of the seven racing this afternoon, five young girls were at the tiller and the best the boys could do was a fourth place. . . ."

In 1933 Marion Leeson was captain of the Eastern crew that tied with the Corinthian for second place in the Curtis Cup; then in 1936 she and her Eastern crew of Mrs. Lincoln Davis, Jr., and Ann Upton won the George Lee Memorial Trophy, earning the right to represent the North Shore in the national women's Adams Cup championship.

Nancy Leiter of Beverly Farms was right behind Leeson and Tappan, graduating when she was eighteen in 1935 from the 15-footers to the S-boat *Venture*, which she bought from Mrs. George S. Patton, Jr., of Hamilton, whose husband had been assigned to Hawaii. His neighbor, fellow Eastern and Myopia member Gordon C. Prince, found the 52-foot schooner *Arcturus* for Colonel Patton, who had it shipped to California, whence the Pattons, the Princes, and a fifth crew member sailed to Honolulu in a month. Nancy Leiter sailed on too, to distinguish herself later in the 1930s in *Venture*, an Eight Meter of the same name.

Joining the 1930 New York Yacht Club Cruise for a look at the penultimate Cup trials off Newport, *Cleopatra's Barge* sailed into a mix-up on August 4 that skirted disaster, as logged by a shaken Frank Crowninshield:

The Cup boats had a close race and a close finish—*Yankee*, *Enterprise*, and *Whirlwind*, in that order. *Weetamoe* lost a man overboard at the Hens and Chickens Lightship and gave up the race, or so it seemed to us. Later on, when reaching in to Nyes

Ledge, the first three yachts having already finished, she apparently thought she was still racing, with the result that she ran all over us and for several minutes it was 50-50 whether we collided or not. (It was blowing hard. We were on the port tack with wind on the end of our main boom. She was converging on us on the starboard tack. She had the entire Bay to luff in. We could only keep clear by jibing, and as we were beam and beam and not twenty feet apart, it would have meant an inevitable collision with disastrous results to both of us. Just why we were able to keep from jibing, God only knows.) Which goes to show it doesn't pay to be too polite.

The final trials started on August 20. Since the rules did not yet require accommodations (though *Yankee* had two staterooms), she and her rivals were almost wide open below decks, with space for an array of winches and stress gauges; the professional crew of twenty and afterguard of from four to six lived on a barge anchored in Newport's Brenton Cove and commuted to work.

The results were scarcely a test as far as *Yankee* was concerned. In a 16-knot easterly the first day, she raced *Whirlwind*, which split her mainsail and withdrew while *Enterprise* defeated *Weetamoe* by a mere minute. In 24 knots the next day, *Yankee* ran away from *Whirlwind* and set an all-time record for the thirty-mile triangle, while *Enterprise* bested *Weetamoe* by three minutes. After several days of adverse weather, the third series was called for lack of wind, and the New York committee picked *Enterprise* to defend the Cup without pitting her against the Eastern's J—chiefly, it was claimed, because she was clearly a light-weather match against *Shamrock V*. Commented *The Rudder* editorially:

Many have considered the selection committee a bit hasty in picking *Enterprise*. Perhaps it was. Until recently *Weetamoe* had made the best showing but *Enterprise*'s steady improvement and her marked superiority in heavy weather finally shifted the balance in favor of the Aldrich-Vanderbilt sloop. If any boat was put at a disadvantage by the early selection it was *Yankee*.

It is generally conceded that *Yankee* was a boat with latent possibilities that had not been brought out at the time of the selection of the defender. It is distinctly unfortunate that she was not allowed to race a little longer for she showed marked improvement toward the end of the trials.

Here was a craft that might have shown us something.

An intriguing postmortem was offered by Phil Bolger in his

Nautical Quarterly article on Francis Herreshoff's problem-plagued, double-ended, water-going spaceship *Whirlwind*:

Paul Hammond was not able to make her go, or rather he wasn't able to control her; he was seen to be thrown over the top of her wheel once as she luffed to a squall, suggesting that she didn't lend herself to subtleties of handling. He had her mast moved three times, two feet each time. She pulled the headboard out of her mainsail at least twice. The sheet winches couldn't handle her overpowering headsails (she had the largest and highest foretriangle of any J ever built). After the disastrous season of 1930 she never sailed again, but speculation about her has continued because the invincible *Ranger* of 1937 looked very much like her, including all the most visible characteristics like the huge headsails and the long stern overhang. William H. Taylor said in a private letter that in his opinion a lot of patient work and a little luck would have made her the Cup defender in 1934 and a strong contender in 1937.

Catherine H. Tappan, first of her sex to win the Curtis Cup, poses in 1930 with her Eastern crew, Albert Goodhue, Jr., and James F. Hunnewell, Jr.

The outcome of the 1930 Cup races was almost boringly anticlimactic. *Shamrock V* was out of her class against Burgess and Vanderbilt and *Enterprise.* "I canna' win, I canna' win," Sir Thomas moaned after three decades of trying, and in another year the gallant old sportsman was dead.

But not before he put up another special Lipton Cup for the winner of a renewed series between the Gloucester and Lunenburg racing fishing schooners. The new *Gertrude L. Thebaud* was reaching along the westerly off the North Shore on September 25 when the *Barge* fell in with her: "She with everything on," exulted Keno, "and we bare all except the main topsail, finally got by us to windward whereupon we gave her the fisherman [staysail] and the No. 1 which did the trick." Twice more they brushed, when on September 30, "we observed the *Thebaud* coming out of Gloucester. With the idea of helping her all we could (in her coming race with the *Bluenose*) we put about and ran down alongside her." Captain Ben Pine was rowed over in a dory and challenged the *Barge* to a test on October 2:

At 9 A.M. F.B.C., Emily Davis, Louis Bacon, Commodore [Herbert] Sears, and Gordon Dexter came on board. The wind was fresh from the north and east so we took the launch and longboat on deck and beat to Eastern Point. There we met the *Thebaud* coming out of Gloucester and took her on over the Fisherman's Course. A triangle—five miles to a leg—the windward one first. We let her start well ahead (45 seconds actually). She led us all the way (almost) to the first mark. We, however, had our chance and took the lead just before rounding. We added another minute down the wind and about as much more reaching home. We finished about 3¾ minutes ahead.

Pretty good going for a fishing schooner. Warmed up by yachting, the *Gertrude L. Thebaud* beat *Bluenose* two straight in the October races for the Lipton Cup in the only series she ever took from the big Lunenburger.

Nineteen thirty-one was the year of the Aldriches. Charles Curtis was succeeded as commodore of the Eastern by William T. Aldrich of Brookline and Peach's Point, an architect and owner of the Eight Meter *Armida,* which won the championship in her new class in 1930. Almost simultaneously, his

Starling Burgess, designer of the great J-boat and Cup defender *Enterprise,* gazes balefully into Morris Rosenfeld's lens during fitting-out at the Herreshoff yard in Bristol, R.I., 1930.

brother Winthrop, a leading New York lawyer and banker, was elected commodore of the New York Yacht Club.

It was also the year that the flood tide of the Twenties receded into the dreary ebb of the Great Depression. The membership fell 10 percent from 624 to 562. The fleet at first was less affected: Nineteen of the big boats disappeared from the rolls, while the under-30s increased by one, only to follow the doleful trend in 1932. Charlie Foster was gathering material for the sequel to his *Ditty Box*, which was in preparation for the press, and tried to put the best face on it:

In the year 1930, there began a period in which matters other than the winds and waves affected yachting to a marked degree. While there was some water connected with them, yet it was not of a navigable type. We will sum up in a short verse composed by some wit of the day:

> He searched throughout his pocket
> And at last he found a quarter.
> From that he knew he'd been in stocks
> And bought when he hadn't oughter.

Nevertheless, twenty-three yachts sailed east on the Annual Cruise to rendezvous at North Haven on July 7. The feature attractions were *Weetamoe*—now owned by Frederick H. Prince of Boston and the only one of the Js of 1930 in commission—plus *Vanitie* and *Resolute*. From the financial doldrums the fleet drifted into the meteorological ones and was fogbound in Fox Islands Thorofare for five straight days, besting the old record set in 1909 in Burnt Coat Harbor, it was said, by three days. E.B. Schriftgiesser caught the feel of it in the *Boston Transcript*:

So dense was the mist that during the forenoon not a single yacht was visible from the wharves along the shore although more than forty of them lay at anchor in the harbor. . . . Many of the captains took advantage of the continued delay to bring their craft to the wharves for water, fuel and supplies, and the waterfront was crowded with boats all day, despite the blinding fog. The island steamer *J.T. Morse* has made her way through the harbor each morning and evening since the fleet has been here, avoiding collision with the anchored yachts by what seems miraculous navigation on the part of her officers. . . .

Some have been glad of the enforced rest. North Haven offers little in the way of amusement, but last night one of the few remaining road companies staged a vaudeville show at the local auditorium at which were seen as many yacht owners as members of their crews. . . .

Some yachts have yet to be visible from certain others. The committee boat, the M's and the *Resolute* are at the eastern end of the Thorofare; some of the big cruising schooners, such as the *Michabo*, the *Blue Dolphin* and the *Malabar X*, are opposite the steamship landing; the racing schooners, such as F. Haven Clark's *Joan II* and the Q boats, are farther west, and the *Vanitie* towers over still more boats almost out to the Sugar Loaves.

As a diversion, the North Haven Yacht Club came up with a race or two (as fog permitted) for the visitors in its famous old sailing dinghies. But Commodore Aldrich, under schedule pressures, could delay no longer and finally had to hoist the flags on his flagship *Wayfarer*: PROCEED AT WILL TO GILKEY'S HARBOR, ISLESBORO. Many proceeded by auxiliary or under tow, in time for the dinner dance Mr. and Mrs. Aldrich had on for the night of July 11 at the Dark Harbor Club. And even that festivity was nearly fogged out, as the *Boston Herald* correspondent reported: "Most of the yachtsmen found their dinner jackets and boiled shirts much too wet to don, and some of them tried dancing in sneakers."

Not until July 18, with the cruise disbanding the next day at Rockland, could anything resembling a race be started. They left from off Duck Trap Harbor and went out into the bay and back—nineteen miles for the big boats, ten for the smaller. And that, as the *Transcript* man ruefully conceded, served mainly to dry out sails threatened with mildew.

Most of the fleet was back in Marblehead in time for the arrival of the U.S.S. *Constitution* in July 1931. Newly restored, the historic frigate had just got under tow of the minesweeper *Grebe* on the first leg of her three-year, 22,000-mile voyage to the west coast and back to Boston. During that time, she would visit ninety ports and be visited by 4,614,792 Americans. Having gone as far east as Bar Harbor, stopping at Portsmouth, then Gloucester, now she towed into Marblehead for her first visit since 1814, when she had found shelter from British warships under the guns of the fort in the War of 1812.

Cleopatra's Barge was in Marblehead too, and her owner dropped a famous name in her log:

All of us, and a lot more, were on board at 9.30 to see the old frigate *Constitution* enter the harbor. She passed us soon after eleven amid a great booming of guns, much cheering, etc. She was a great sight. F.B.C. lunched at the E.Y.C. to meet her officers. At six o'clock by special invitation we inspected the ship. I presented her with letters to my great-grandfather, Benjamin W. Crowninshield, from Isaac Hull, William Bainbridge, and

Charles Stewart, her best-known commanders. Captain [Louis J.] Gulliver gave us a special photograph of the ship. We had a stand-up dinner of twenty afterwards on board.

Emphasis on small-boat racing in Marblehead generally and at the Eastern in particular intensified in the summer of 1931, as might be expected in the worsening economic conditions. In the ten years it had been in competition, the Sears Cup for juniors had evolved into such a de facto national institution under the sponsorship of the Club that it was decided to bring the Deed of Gift into line with reality. The Eastern deeded the Cup to the North American Yacht Racing Union (renamed the United States Yacht Racing Union) as the more-encompassing sponsor of the competition, which was to be open to crews of three boys or girls from the ages of thirteen to eighteen who were members, or whose parents were, of a recognized yacht club in North America.

Harry K. Noyes, who started out as a farm boy in Haverhill, New Hampshire, started the New England Buick distributorship (Stanley Steamers too) in Lowell with such success that by 1914 he was the proprietor of a small private power fleet. The flagship was the 130-foot steam yacht *Seyon*, a name that requires a double-take. This led to the ownership of a boatyard in Quincy founded by his friend Fred Lawley (son of the famed George), which had gone broke; they named the resurrection the Quincy Adams Yacht Yard. Noyes joined the Eastern in 1921.

Harry K.'s son, Harry E. Noyes, by 1929 not only had the Buick distributorship but also was New England distributor for Chris-Craft and ACF Cruisers as well. He also owned marine centers near Frazier's (later Oxner's) boatyard in Marblehead, at Danversport, and on Fort Point Channel in Boston across from South Station, where they lifted big doors and you drove your boat right inside the building to be worked on. He had three sons—Harry K. II, E. Pike, and Bradley, the youngest—and around this time became interested in sail, when they were living on Galloupe's Point in Swampscott. Brad recalls:

My father's first sailboat was a 16-footer like a Town Class, and he had it right off the beach on a mooring. He took Pike out for

Gypsy, Harry E. Noyes's 8-meter, won the Chandler Hovey Gold Bowl in 1933, 1934 and 1935. Jackson photo.

Yankee Comes Close

a sail and went on the rocks. He figured there was something wrong with the boat, so he bought a bigger one, an 18-footer, thinking that would solve the problem. They went on the rocks again, trimming the jib to weather.

Enter Frank Blaney (of Blaney's Beach in Swampscott), who was a former Swampscott dory champion. He volunteered to teach my father the basics in sailboat handling and was so effective that three years later Dad had leapfrogged to his 50-foot sloop, the Eight-Meter *Gypsy* and the 57-foot Francis Herreshoff ketch *Tioga* ("Beautiful Wife" in American Indian).

Gypsy was phenomenal, culminating her career in 1935 by retiring the Hovey Gold Bowl and winning the Ladies Plate for the second time, "establishing herself as the outstanding Eight Meter on the coast," in the words of one yachting writer. Noyes bought *Tioga* from member Waldo Brown, who had commissioned Francis Herreshoff in 1924 to design the 50-foot schooner *Joann* after a painting of a ship his grandfather had built in 1850. The larger *Tioga*, intended as a cruising auxiliary, incorporated some of *Joann*'s lines. Her designer wrote of her: "Strange to say, she acquired the habit of winning ocean races and particularly ones where power and sail were allowed."

(While a Navy pilot shortly before the war, notes Bradley Noyes, Brown lost an engine over Boston. To avoid crashing into the city, he flew his dying plane out over the harbor and was killed.)

Prior to publication of *The Eastern Yacht Club Ditty Box* in 1932, Charles H.W. Foster wrote Nathanael Herreshoff, who was then eighty-three, seeking a few words from the oracle of Bristol about design changes and his part in them before 1900, when this first history of the Club ended. He received two full responses from Captain Nat that he eagerly included in the volume, dated December 28, 1931 (pages 39 to 41) and March 6, 1932 (pages 139 to 141). At about that time, Foster and his wife paid a visit to Bristol, and he told Herreshoff about the staysail ketch rig he was experimenting with on the old dory *Utility*, his fifty-third yacht of record (of which more in the next chapter). While perusing his copy of the *Ditty Box* soon afterward, the designer made a number of marginal comments, and the subsequent correspondence of the two was aimed at another gam in Bristol, which may or may not have come off.

In the interim between his first two letters from Herreshoff, Foster addressed the following suggestion to Commodore William Aldrich, dated January 29, 1932:

My dear Commodore:

In looking over the yachting matters of the past six years, one is tremendously impressed with what Nathanael G. Herreshoff has meant to the advancement of the science of boat building and sailing.

In appreciation of his position in the yachting world, the New York Yacht Club has elected him to Honorary Membership [in 1902] and it occurred to me that possibly the Eastern Yacht Club would like to honor him likewise, and I believe that it would be very acceptable to him in his retirement to have us express some appreciation of what he has done.

I do not know the exact method of procedure in such a matter, but would presume that a nomination by the Club from the floor at our next meeting would express the feelings more forcibly than in any other way.

What do you think about it?

Yours very truly,
C.H.W. Foster

No record of a reply from Commodore Aldrich can be found, nor of any action on Foster's proposal by the Council. The great yacht designer had six years to live and never was elected as an Honorary Member of the Eastern. Ironically, the following year a figure whose very name was anathema to a considerable bloc of members, Franklin Delano Roosevelt, assumed honorary status by virtue of his election as President of the United States.

With the effects of the Depression permeating every stratum of American society except the uppermost, the high point of 1932 was the appearance of *The Eastern Yacht Club Ditty Box: 1870–1900*. This chatty, "all-sorts compilation," as the ever-cheerful Charlie Foster, then seventy-two, called the latest addition to his fleet, was launched with the approval but without the financial participation of the hard-pressed Council in a private printing by the Plimpton Press of Norwood. The author assembled some of the early yachting background and his anecdotal overview of the Club's first thirty years essentially for the edification of his fellow members, and no doubt as an antidote to the times as well. In the fifty-five years since its appearance, the *Ditty Box*—with its all-sorts compilation, its roster of members and their boats, its numerous yarns and reminiscences, and its splendid photographs—has taken its place in the literature of yachting.

Inspired by his old friend, Secretary Henry Taggard, Foster explained in his introduction, the challenge was "how to invent a scheme of curtailment." Hence "the idea . . . of asking you readers to imagine that all these matters of the Eastern Yacht Club were as papers and records in its Ditty Box, from which certain ones had been extracted, more or less at random, and published herein." Marking the author's embarkation on his second half-century of membership (he joined on January 25, 1881), this pleasant task gave him the occasion to sum up his well-seasoned philosophy of yachting:

The first and most impressive thought that should come to a present-day member from an examination of these papers is "what a heritage of character, quality, and tradition we have!" Look at the list of members of the past, not only as individuals but as families, even now in some cases to the fourth generation, who have been the making of the Club. No wonder that the "spirit of the sea" still prevails on its vessels and that, in its racing, true sportsmanship is the first consideration. Let us hope that our Club officials will continue to appreciate, extol and perpetuate this heritage.

As for C.H.W. Foster's feelings about the long and cordial relationship with the New York Yacht Club:

It is of record that, in its first years, the Eastern patterned its career upon the rules, regulations and experiences of the New York Yacht Club and, ever since, it has sought the friendly advice and cooperation of that club in all important yachting questions. Many members in each club have held membership in the other. We have enjoyed many a joint cruise and race, and friendly and keen competition has been encouraged. While we here have striven always to "beat the New Yorkers" yet the underlying feeling in our minds is akin to that of the little girl who, in her composition on the subject of "Mother," concluded her thesis with the sentence: "If I had never had her, dear me, how I would have missed her!"

Among the papers, now in the Club archives, that Foster collected in anticipation of a sequel to the *Ditty Box*—which never, unfortunately, materialized—is a job application directed to him by an unemployed Cambridge professional sailor of obvious competence that poignantly illustrates the despair gripping America.

July 15, 1932

Dear Sir:

As an efficient, capable, sober and trustworthy mariner with a wide range of yachting experience in both power and sail craft, I am taking the liberty of writing you in the hope of securing a berth. I am a native American, well recommended, 32 years old, and have been a professional seafarer since the age of fourteen.

Although you do not know me personally, I am intruding upon you in this manner because of extreme necessity due to an aggravating financial plight, the result of being without a position for a year.

The problem of securing a berth is so serious to me that I am prepared to work for a small wage, particularly so if some degree of permanency may be expected. However, I would not care to displace any one whom you may already have engaged.

I am a thoroughly skilled navigator, quite capable and efficient in all the problems of yacht upkeep and personnel, and I have a thorough knowledge of gas and diesel engines, and am equally "at home" in large or small craft. Further, I have driven and repaired many types of American and foreign automobiles.

While I present myself as a captain, I should highly appreciate the opportunity of serving you in any subordinate capacity, and would be deeply obliged if you will consider me for either immediate or future employment. You may be assured that I would exert every endeavor to give the utmost satisfaction.

May I request the kindness of a reply, and, if you should need a man, the opportunity of a personal interview?

I am,

Respectfully yours,

To which Foster could only reply on July 19: "I shall be glad to keep your letter in case I hear of any position to which I can refer you, but at present I do not know of any place of the nature that you ask for."

In the light of such pleas from those who had served him and his father and grandfather so faithfully, the plight of the yachtsman paled. Be that as it may, each season found fewer familiar faces around the clubhouse and more open water in the anchorage. From the high of 624 in 1930 the membership dipped to 489 in 1932 and then plummeted to a Depression low of 386 in 1933. The fleet dropped from 362 (236 over 30 feet waterline and 126 under) in 1930 to 269 in 1933 (167 over 30 feet and 102 under) and bottomed out at 255 (167 over 30 feet and 88 under) in 1935.

The big-boat racing figures are equally bleak. Sixteen yachts entered the Annual Regatta in 1932, compared to forty-seven the previous season, and there were only eleven in a single handicap class on the Annual Cruise, which limped along as far as Kittery, Maine, and back in a total of but four runs.

A crisis of attrition. In February 1933, the Council appointed a committee "to consider the matter of dues and the general finances of the Club" and directed the secretary to "omit publishing the names of those members that either resigned or were dropped for non-payment of dues in his Annual Report, if in his discretion it seemed best." And the possibility even of closing down the clubhouse as an economy must have been raised, because the secretary reported it to be the sense of the meeting "that the large Club House should be kept open during the current year."

At the end of the 1933 season, the House Committee reported that stringent cost control had reduced its deficit, despite membership losses. To reverse this slide, it suggested that members obliged to resign during the previous three years be allowed to rejoin without incurring another initiation fee and that dues be reduced in conjunction with a membership drive.

The Twenty-first Amendment repealing Prohibition was ratified on December 5, and the committee urged application for a liquor license for 1934 as a draw for the house.

A revised dues schedule aimed at attracting new younger members was adopted for 1934. While the levy remained at eighty-five dollars for those with boats over thirty feet, it was dropped to fifty dollars for those under, and the initiation fee for the latter was waived.

From 1934 on, membership began a slow climb back, until it was again depleted by war. An even more extraordinary accomplishment was the financial solvency maintained during the Depression, as reviewed in the Council minutes of September 18, 1940:

Accountant shows income from dues in 1928 = $51,000; rose to a high of $54,000 in 1930 and fell to a low of $32,000 in 1935 and then in each year through 1939 rose to about $35,000, a drop of 44% since 1928. Expenses in 1928 = $42,000, rose to $51,000 in 1930 and fell to $28,000 in 1935, $35,000 in 1938 and $32,000 in 1939. Income exceeded expenses in every year except 1938, the largest excess being $12,000 in 1929 and the smallest $300 in 1933. Net result for the past twelve years was that cash on hand rose from $4,669 on 12/31/28 to $18,795 on 12/31/39 while debt *fell* from $162,900 to $125,000.

Much of the Club's remarkable vitality during the Depression can be credited to the tendency of boatowners to find their own level when times are hard, trading in the Rolls-Royces of the sea for the Chevys and the Model A's. The number of boats started by the Eastern during Race Week rose almost without interruption during the 1930s in line with the aggregate of all four Marblehead clubs—from 1,938 in 1930 to 3,009 in 1940.

The 1934 round-the-buoys season illustrates the concentration of activity in the small classes at a time when an abbreviated Annual Cruise to Mattapoisett featured a racing division of three Qs and two Eight Meters, combined with a thirteen-boat regatta off Newport.

Still under the chairmanship of James C. Gray, the Race Committee held seven races on twenty-six days in the First and Second Series between June 16 and September 9; eight Sunday Series for Qs, Eight Meters, S's, and M-Bs (in the S and M-B classes for cups donated in memory of Guy Lowell by Mrs. Lowell); four days of racing by the Eights for the Ladies Plate; three days by them for the Eastern Challenge Cup, offered in 1933 for international entries; and three days during Midsummer Week, as well as resails and sail-offs of ties. Eight classes were entered in the First and Second Series, the Brutal Beasts the largest with twenty-six, followed by the M-Bs with twelve and the Thirty Square Meters with ten, plus the S's, the Triangles, and the Ts. The total of entries for 1934, including the cruise and the regatta, was 1,570, bettering the 1933 count by 137.

The Depression was imposing a new pattern on American yachting. Thirty-three classes sailed in the 1934 Marblehead Race Week, and they included twenty-three from at least twenty other ports.

Franklin D. Roosevelt was inaugurated on March 4, 1933, and ex-Secretary of the Navy Charles Francis Adams and ex-President Herbert Hoover went home. One of just plain Charlie's first, and characteristic, moves as a civilian was to commission Starling Burgess to design a new Q-boat, which he called *Bat*. Professor Evers Burtner remembered quite vividly the day of her launching:

Normally the P, Q and R sloops were measured well up Marblehead Harbor toward the electric power plant where smoother water could be expected. Under very favorable conditions and early in the season these yachts might be measured near the Eastern or Corinthian floats.

Charles Adams, Starling Burgess and Evers Burtner had just finished measuring the former's Q sloop *Bat*, which lay at a mooring off the Eastern float. At this period, the quarter beam length was measured by a caliper made of thick mahogany arms weighing about thirty pounds.

Charlie Adams had a very lightweight, clinker, cedar dinghy built by Lawley. With Burgess in the stern, Burtner forward

holding the quarter beam rig, Charlie rowed to the float. Out of respect to him, Burgess and Burtner suggested that he disembark first.

Normally Starling was a most gracious and exceptionally polite man. This time he hopped out right after Charlie, leaving Burtner with the quarter beam rig to put the bow of the tender under water. The Professor was partly immersed and lost part of his dignity.

It happened that a heavy rainstorm swept the course during one of the Race Week days, the wind died, and a thick-o'-fog rolled in. A big Coast Guard cutter on hand for the week had steamed out for the start but retreated to the harbor when the weather fell apart. When the former secretary of the Navy felt his way home through the fog in *Bat*, there was the cutter looming up, more or less across the entrance to *his* harbor.

"In no uncertain terms, and using very 'salty' language," according to one who was there, "Mr. Adams conveyed his thoughts in a booming voice. All listeners were amused and in agreement with him."

Back in Washington, the Club's leading Honorary Member, President Roosevelt, was swinging into action against the Depression with his New Deal for America, translated by Congress into the "Hundred Days" of nation-shaking legislation that ended on June 16, 1933. Treating himself to a vacation, FDR chartered the 46-foot ocean-racing schooner *Amberjack II* from EYC member Paul D. Rust, Jr., for a cruise to his family summer retreat on Campobello Island in New Brunswick. He signed on Rust and another member, George Briggs, plus son James Roosevelt, Amyas Ames, and a U.S. Navy bos'ns mate. The skipper was to join them at Marion (Massachusetts).

On the evening of June 14, their Navy escort, the 125-foot radio communications ship *Cuyahoga*, anchored at the entrance to the harbor. As they were about to sail, word arrived that Jimmy's New Hampshire house had burned down. He rushed ashore, and *Amberjack* got under way without him, advising *Cuyahoga* that light airs would stretch the run to the canal to as long as ten hours.

But a quartering breeze sprang up. They made it in six hours. No sign of their escort, so they took a fair tide through to Buz-

---

Charlie Adams was no sooner ex-Secretary of the Navy in 1933 when he commissioned Starling Burgess to design his new Q-boat *Bat*, another magical flyer in the hands of the Deacon. Jackson photo.

Yankee Comes Close

zards Bay and sailed on to Marion, where the destroyers *Ellis* and *Bernadou* informed them that the *Cuyahoga* was looking all over Massachusetts Bay for them.

Paul Rust and James Roosevelt, in their excerpts from *Amberjack*'s log published that August in *Yachting*, described FDR's arrival by automobile from Groton with Jimmy on June 17:

The engine was running. Each member of the crew had some particular job; two were on the bow and stern lines, one on the main signal halliards, ready to hoist the President's flag as soon as he stepped on board, and Rust was at the wheel prepared to get underway as soon as the gangplank had been removed. [They had been joined at Marion by John Cutter, described as a Roosevelt friend and an excellent cook.]

All went smoothly and we shoved off amidst a burst of applause and cheering, took a short spin around the harbor and then picked up our mooring. As the little *Amberjack* settled back on her chain in the quiet water, and the sun went down behind the old sail lofts on shore, it seemed as though the world had been left behind. The President gave a sigh of contentment and said nothing for a few moments while he sat taking in that peaceful scene. . . .

Just before nine [on Sunday, June 18], our scheduled hour of departure, when the skipper's anxiety to get underway could be held in check no longer, he asked the photographers to leave and gave the order to hoist sail. With a beautiful nor'west breeze and all our kites flying, we ran out of Marion, across Buzzards Bay for Naushon Island. How many who see this, whether casual readers, old-time racing men or deep sea cruisers, can picture a President of the United States sitting at the wheel of a small boat, quietly giving orders in a manner that stamped him as a real sailor. From the moment we weighed anchor, every one of us knew that he was, in reality, the skipper.

In Woods Hole Passage, they were met by another Eastern member, W. Cameron Forbes, who escorted *Amberjack* to Hadley's Harbor, where he came aboard for a gam with the skipper while the crew had a horseback ride ashore. Then on to Nantucket, except that the weather ahead looked so dirty that FDR decided to put into Edgartown for the night. The next day was spent at Nantucket, amid intense excitement and hoopla.

On June 20, the nation's Number One Yacht embarked for Provincetown in light airs; Assistant Secretary of State Raymond Moley dropped in, literally, by plane from Washington. He came aboard for a two-hour conference with The Boss, then departed the same way he had arrived.

Originally the plan had been to put in at Provincetown for at least one night, but, as the sun sank below the precipitous dunes of Cape Cod, a beautiful quartering breeze overtook us and it was decided to push on to Gloucester. With the skipper at the wheel, and after a wonderful evening sail, we rounded up just under the lee of Gloucester breakwater, lowered our canvas, dropped anchor and turned in.

The morning of June 21st found Mr. Roosevelt returning the call of those hardy men of the "Banks," the Gloucester fishermen who had visited him in Washington scarcely two months before. That was a pleasant and memorable day for everyone. Early that morning, small boats, crowded with people, appeared from every nook in the harbor and by nine o'clock nearly every craft in Gloucester swarmed about the *Amberjack*. The climax of the visit occurred when the veteran sea captains of Gloucester came aboard and presented Mr. Roosevelt with an oil painting of the *Gertrude L. Thebaud*, the schooner in which they had made their voyage to Washington [to dramatize the Depression plight of the fisheries].

The next day they powered through the Annisquam River shortcut to Ipswich Bay, where the end-run Navy was standing by nervously, and into Little Harbor at Portsmouth for the night. Then Maine, Casco Bay, and Chandler's Cove at Great Chebeague Island.

That little spot was picked out for its apparent solitude, but, upon approaching our anchorage, what should greet us but one of Portland's fire boats which laid down an exquisite barrage of sea water.

Early the next morning, the number of our crew was increased by three when Franklin, Jr., John Roosevelt, and one of their schoolmates, Drexel Paul, joined the ship. Probably the hardest and most exciting day's sail followed. It was blowing a fresh breeze out of the northwest and, with full sail, plus the fisherman staysail, we logged nearly eight knots all the way to Pulpit Harbor, a tiny landlocked indentation on the northwestern side of North Haven.

En route the skipper gave his escorts the slip again, taking *Amberjack* inside Seguin Island, where they enjoyed a little impromptu excitement not mentioned in their *Yachting* write-up. They were pounding along under the brisk nor'wester when William E. Stanwood, a self-styled, dyed-in-the-wool Republican who summered on Squirrel Island, fell in with the President in his 50-foot ketch *Kidnapper* (with fifteen passengers, including daughter Mary Elizabeth Crockett, the teller of the tale). Stanwood hailed: "Sir, would you like a race to the bell off Cuckolds?"

FDR was at the helm, the familiar cigarette holder set at a jaunty angle from his mouth and a wide grin on his face. "You bet!" was his response. It was very exciting to see Mr. Roosevelt at such close range. He and Father were both dressed in white, long-sleeved shirts open at the neck. The President, wearing a floppy white duck yachtsman's hat, looked happy as any sailor out on a blue bay on this most perfect of days.

Off the Sheepscot, the *Ellis* and the *Bernadou*, forced by their wayward charge to keep outside, steamed toward the racers; a signalman on the bridge of the closest was semaphoring purposefully.

Since no one aboard the *Kidnapper* could read the flags, we in our ignorance waved gaily in response. . . . At this point we were closehauled and gaining on *Amberjack* when the Navy decided to take serious action. The first ship put on speed and bore down on us, a gun trained directly at our stern. Then came a message over a bullhorn. "Stay a mile from the President's boat. Repeat. Stay a mile from the President's boat."

Just short of our finish line which would have made us winners in this informal race, we now had no option but to fall off and head away. As we left, we attempted to express our regrets by gestures.

FDR leaned from the wheel and, taking his hat from his head, threw it down on the deck in apparent disgust. One of his sons dipped the Presidential flag, conceding victory to us.

We all stood and cheered, having been privileged to witness an extraordinary display of sportsmanship from a man too important to our country to be allowed the prerogatives of ordinary sailors.

From Pulpit the skipper took *Amberjack* through Deer Island Thorofare to Southwest Harbor in their last day of June weather. They made Roque Island just ahead of the fog, which he enjoyed so much—because of the complete rest it afforded—that he declared it made to order. The Roosevelt-Rust log:

The date set for the termination of the cruise was Thursday, June 29th, and fog or no fog, the skipper had to be at Campobello. By eight bells that morning we were underway. Our small detachment of the Navy was most apprehensive as to the advisability of the President setting out in such miserably thick weather. However, under his skillful handling and clever piloting we got away from the anchorage and worked through the maze of little channels formed by the surrounding islands, along the coast, and out of the fog into Lubec Narrows.

Just twelve years had slipped away since Mr. Roosevelt's last visit to Campobello. The setting for the return to his boyhood home was perfect. The tide and wind were fair and the sun was shining brightly overhead as we sailed up the Narrows, past the quaint little town of Lubec. Upon rounding Quoddy Light a most impressive spectacle came in to view. There, just ahead, in the middle of the bay which was filled with boats of every size and type, were the new 10,000-ton cruiser *Indianapolis* and our two destroyers. As we sailed quietly along, thousands of people rushed to the waterfront, whistles blew, and on the deck of the *Indianapolis*, the "Star Spangled Banner" was struck up, while the entire crew manned the rail. Then there was the roar of the twenty-one gun salute. When going by the docks and piers at Eastport, a whole fishing fleet of some fifty boats, dressed for the occasion, paraded past. . . .

Promptly at four o'clock, as he had promised, our skipper took the *Amberjack* alongside the dock at Welch Pool [Welshpool] on Campobello Island and disembarked.

One of the most interesting and pleasing cruises of all time had ended, and we, the crew, were mighty sad at seeing the skipper go over the side.

As an enduring remembrance of the cruise and his send-off at Marion, the skipper presented the Beverly Yacht Club with a perpetual trophy that was placed in competition for Thirty Square Meters as the President Franklin D. Roosevelt Bowl. Lincoln Davis, Jr., of the Eastern won it for the first time in 1934 in his season's champion, *Starling*, a German heavy-weather Thirty Square built by Abeking and Rasmussen that he had difficulty getting Measurer Evers Burtner to pass. He won the bowl twice more in Buzzards Bay.

Thomas Octave Murdoch Sopwith, the prominent British aviator and airplane manufacturer whose Sopwith Camel carried many an ace over the Western Front in World War I, challenged for the America's Cup in November 1933, through the Royal Yacht Squadron. His J would be *Endeavour*, designed by Charles Nicholson, and it was agreed with the New York Yacht Club that the match would be in September 1934. The contenders would be required to have living quarters for crew below.

New York responded with only one candidate for the defense, *Rainbow*, like *Enterprise* designed by Starling Burgess for Harold Vanderbilt and his syndicate. She was launched on May 15, 1934, from the Herreshoff yard; everyone agreed she was a beauty and looked fearsomely fast.

The Eastern this time put forward two contenders—*Yankee*

under the management of Vice Commodore Hovey, and *Wee-tamoe*, now owned by Frederick H. Prince. Frank Paine had been working on making *Yankee* more of a light-weather boat, and she entered the trials with a smaller keel, a new bow, and more sail under a double-head rig with quadrilateral jib, an improved Genoa, a bigger mainsail, and parachute spinnakers. Hovey's three children—Buss, Charlie, and Sis—would rotate through her afterguard in the trials. Charles recalled that the sharpening of *Yankee*'s bow was prompted by the fact that, ironically, Paine's Q-boat *Cara Mia*, designed to beat the Hoveys' *Robin* and the rough model for *Yankee*, had failed to do so; hence the finer entrance.

Skippered as in 1930 by Charles Francis Adams, *Yankee* had for her afterguard Chandler Hovey and one or another of his children, his nephew Morgan Harris, Frank Paine, and Professor Richard D. Fay of M.I.T. as navigator, along with a professional crew of twenty-two, all living aboard. Paine had worked wonders, and the first spins revealed a brand-new J with a hitherto-undreamed-of turn of speed. *Weetamoe* was left at the gate pretty much from the start but continued in the running, with Gerard Lambert's *Vanitie* as a trial horse in all but name.

Yankee beat *Rainbow* (whose afterguard included the Eastern's Caleb Loring) on the one occasion when they raced in the preliminaries off Newport, June 16 to 24. A fortnight later, the Boston J-boat took eight of the observation races, four of them against the new Burgess/Vanderbilt creation. *Rainbow* won four, including only one—not finished within the time limit—over *Yankee* by eleven seconds.

Then came the New York Yacht Club Cruise in mid-August. *Yankee* won all the racing runs, and there was one jubilant day when she had beaten *Rainbow* in ten consecutive matches. Then Burgess and Vanderbilt added five tons of ballast to their slumping boat and sailed away from the competition to win both the Astor and King's cups.

The final trials were held off Newport in moderate to fresh breezes from August 22 to 31. *Weetamoe* was officially eliminated. One very close race between the remaining pair was called when *Yankee* carried away her jumper strut in a squall, and *Rainbow* was sent home. *Rainbow* then won three in a row. The final and decisive match was recalled fifty years later

The Olympian power of the Js. *Yankee*, designed by Frank C. Paine for Chandler Hovey's Eastern Yacht Club Syndicate in 1930, dwarfs her crew.

Yankee Comes Close

Always in control of the smallest or the largest, Charles Francis Adams exudes concentration and mastery at the wheel of the express-training *Yankee* in 1934. "Why don't you come aboard, Rosie?" he called over in irritation to the famed yachting photographer, who had been close aboard indeed for five minutes in his speedboat *Foto*, waiting for this moment. Morris Rosenfeld photo.

---

by Mrs. Sherman Morss, the former Sis Hovey, who was in the afterguard that day:

> We had Mr. Charles Francis Adams as skipper. He sailed her beautifully, as you can imagine. We had a very, very close summer all summer long with *Yankee* and *Rainbow*. It came to the last day, and they said it was so late this was going to be the last race. We went out, and we raced thirty-five miles, and when we crossed the finish line with our spinnakers before the wind, neither *Rainbow* nor *Yankee* knew who had won that race, we were so close. When we went ashore we found out that *Yankee* had lost to *Rainbow* by one split second. It was about the toughest summer that any of us had ever had. . . . I think that New England felt very badly, and people used to call down there at Newport and ask how *Yankee* came out instead of how did the race come out. It was a very sad story.

Sad indeed. After the heartbreaker, poker-faced Charlie Adams, the epitome of Yankee self-control, took Sis Hovey in his arms and cried. Weeping did not come easily to the Deacon.

Tom Sopwith had fired most of his professionals, who had struck for higher pay just before *Endeavour* sailed for the United States in July, and replaced them with less-trained amateurs; yet the fastest and most competitive challenger the British had ever sent over took the first two races from *Rainbow*.

Endeavour's bad luck in running into a soft spot, and the helmsmanship of Sherman Hoyt, recouped the third race for *Rainbow*. Frank Paine was invited to replace Starling Burgess in *Rainbow*'s afterguard; he brought a *Yankee* parachute aboard, and Mike Vanderbilt credited Paine's spinnaker-handling and morale-building skills with playing the key part in winning the next three races (the last of which was marred by protests and bruised feelings) and saving the Cup.

The winner's masterful skipper made no secret of his belief that *Endeavour* was the faster boat, and you couldn't convince anyone in New England that *Yankee* wasn't, too.

After *Rainbow*'s split-second selection over *Yankee*, but before her match with *Endeavour*, John Lawrence wrote the *Boston Globe* on September 2, 1934:

> In 1930 I was manager of the *Yankee* and although very much disappointed that the trial races were cut short and that the smaller boat, the *Enterprise*, was selected, I was aware that the English challenger was a light-weather boat but that it was not likely that the committee would select a larger boat like *Yankee* to defend the cup, unless she had clearly proven her superiority in all points of sailing. This she had not done.
>
> I am writing this to the newspapers of New England as one who ought to know, is not now connected with either boat, is interested in and loves the sport, and also one who knows that New Englanders do not care to be unfair in their criticisms of a sincere committee.

And that about summed it up as far as the Eastern Yacht Club syndicate was concerned.

Chapter 13

Resurgence and the J-Boats

Having steered the Eastern around four of the reef years of the Depression, William T. Aldrich turned over the helm for the 1935 season to Gerard B. Lambert, who gained the quarterdeck in one of the more rapid ascensions in the annals of the Club. That was the way of the new commodore, and just what was needed in the sagging mid-Thirties.

Lambert came from St. Louis, was graduated from Princeton in 1908, and inherited the Lambert Pharmical Company (later Warner-Lambert) from his father, the founder. In 1927 he helped finance Charles A. Lindbergh's solo flight across the Atlantic. The next year he sold out ahead of the Crash and got serious about sailing. He took his celebrated 185-foot, three-masted schooner *Atlantic* on Henry Howard's race to Spain, sharing the wheel with Charles Francis Adams. She lost to *Elena*, but her owner gained the enduring friendship of the Deacon.

Atlantic in 1905 set a transatlantic sailing record of twelve days, four hours, one minute, and nineteen seconds that stood for seventy-five years—until 1980, when it was broken by the fabulous Frenchman Eric Tabarly in the 54-foot trimaran *Paul Ricard (II)* in ten days, five hours, fourteen minutes, and twenty seconds.

But the seconds did not count that much to Commodore Lambert, who in 1929 bought the fifteen-year-old, 1920 Cup contender *Vanitie*, *Resolute*'s old rival, from Harry Paine Whitney. He had Starling Burgess, who had made a staysail schooner of her in 1920, rig her back to sloop, Marconi this time, as a horse for the 1930 trials of the Js. Secretary Adams had sailed her frequently over the years and "came with the boat," as it were.

In 1931 Lambert was elected president of the troubled Gil-

lette Safety Razor Company, taking his pay in stock pegged to earnings. He moved to Boston from Princeton, New Jersey, and joined the Eastern. *Vanitie* continued to pile up one of the more impressive records on the coast, often as a pacer for the Js, with *Atlantic* in the offing housing her afterguard. In 1934 he was elected rear commodore. At the end of the season, he bought the J-boat *Yankee* and was elected commodore.

Commodore Lambert jury-rigged *Yankee* as a yawl and on April 25, 1935, started her off against his *Atlantic*, under his own command, on a private race from Boston to England. Her designer, Frank Paine, skippered *Yankee*, with John Parkinson and Alfred Loomis, the editor of *Yachting*, as his afterguard. The J won the windy crossing to Bishop's Rock in fifteen days and twenty hours, fifteen hours ahead of *Atlantic*. Under Lambert and Paine, *Yankee* in her racing rig mastered strange waters to take eight firsts, four seconds, and two thirds in thirty-two contests off the British and French coasts, in the Solent, and during Cowes Week against Sopwith's *Endeavour*, *Shamrock*, the great old *Westward*, and *Britannia*, royal yacht of King George V. Lambert dined with His Majesty at Cowes, and in turn entertained. The King sent him a wire of condolence when *Yankee* lost her steel mast in a squall during her last race off Dartmouth.

"*Yankee*'s British campaign created great good feeling among English yachtsmen," John Parkinson, Jr., wrote in his *History of the New York Yacht Club*, "and restored friendship that had been badly strained by the Sopwith protest in the America's Cup match of the previous year. It has been suggested that it caused Sopwith to challenge again for the America's Cup."

Back at Marblehead, having broken bread with a king, Commodore Lambert had no problem bending protocol to share it with a little girl, as remembered by Mrs. Henry A. (Elizabeth) Morss, Jr.:

When Mr. Lambert became Commodore, he was often at the house my parents rented for the summer at Peach's Point. In return, he invited them, and to my great excitement, me for a day's sail with other Marblehead guests on the *Atlantic*. I was very young at the time and about the age of one of his daughters. Mother and Dad had to leave for a dinner engagement when the *Atlantic* returned to the harbor entrance. Mr. Lambert said, "Why not let me keep Betty for supper?" And friends who were staying on promised to take me home.

Mr. Lambert had a formal seated dinner and placed me on his left. I noticed that the steward came and said something to him in a very low voice and then went away again as dinner began to be served.

Much later, Mother told me the reason, having heard it from the friends who took me home. "Mr. Lambert, Sir, the crew are worried because there are thirteen at the table." Mr. Lambert's reply was, "Not thirteen, but," looking at me, "twelve and a half."

On one occasion Commodore Lambert put on such a bash at the Club that Frances Gilliland still reels with the memory. "We had so many telegrams back and forth that they put in a Western Union machine."

The commodore revived the 171-mile New London-Marblehead ocean race after an eleven-year lapse and offered a cup for the yacht making the best corrected time in Classes A, B, C, and D. Cups were also offered for the winners in each class and for second place in each class with at least four entries, a requirement met by all four. There was a Universal Rule class, too. Boats were required to be between 32 and 75 feet overall. Thirty-one started from New London on June 22, and all but one finished at Marblehead the next day after passing through a violent thunderstorm rounding Cape Cod. D.S. Berger's schooner *Mandoo* won the first Lambert Cup.

The Annual Cruise of 1935 was again to the southward and incorporated the Annual Regatta in Buzzards Bay on July 4. No Js, but two Ms, five Twelve and Ten meters, five first and second-division schooners, and three cruising yachts, besides four Qs and Eight Meters and a power fleet led by Theodore Hollander's 154-foot *Seapine* and William S. Eaton's 120-foot *Taormina*. After the regatta (Ray Hunt won his second Puritan Cup, this time in his Q-class *Hornet*), the fleet raced from Mattapoisett to Edgartown, the first visit of a large yacht club to

the old whaling port since 1858. The event was celebrated with a dance given by the Edgartown Yacht Club.

In fact, the Eastern was southward-tending in the 1930s. The traditional preference for the Maine coast had generally prevailed through 1931, except for 1928 and 1930, when it was beyond the Cape for the rest of the decade save for 1938. New York, Newport, and the Js may have had something to do with this unfamiliar swing of the cruising pendulum.

In 1935, the Club lost three longtime loyalists.

Leonard M. Fowle, Sr., had been yachting editor of the *Boston Globe* for many years and was one of the leading writers on the subject in the country—a veritable encyclopedia of the sport. A member since 1924, he had served on the Race Committee and was one of the originators of the National Junior Sailing championship for the Sears Cup. The Leonard Munn Fowle Memorial Trophy for Race Week's outstanding yacht was put up in 1936. Fortunately, Leonard, Jr., succeeded his late sire at the *Globe* and would carry on in the same high tradition.

James McNeil, head boatman, died in March after thirty years of service with the Club that began at the helm of a rather lethargic naphtha launch. Stanton Deland wrote of him in the *Boston Transcript*:

Jimmy, whose diminutive size immediately attracted attention and whose ever-sunburnt face arrested it, had come to be regarded as an almost permanent fixture in Marblehead, along with his famous boat, "the covered wagon." Together these two weathered the successive years and seemed to understand each other perfectly, for no one else has ever been able to manage the difficult wagon. Since lameness forced Jimmy, protected from the elements by a straw hat of incredible dimensions, to direct affairs from his booth on the dock, the wagon has been the object of much abusive language from all acquainted with her; but, although her seams opened and motor faltered, Jimmy alone remained loyal. It would seem that a sea burial would be a most fitting tribute to her only master.

They pulled Frances Gilliland's leg about Jimmy. "He used to be gone for two or three days, and I said, 'Where's Jimmy, anyhow?' 'Oh, he's to the Saugus Navy Yard.' And I thought there was a Saugus Navy Yard instead of that he was gone for two or three days of drinking for himself. That's how much I knew."

Henry Taggard, whose service to the Eastern began in 1893, the year after he joined, when he was appointed measurer, died

Resurgence and the J-Boats

at seventy-four on December 27 in Brookline. He was secretary from 1907 until he retired in 1929 and was elected an Honorary Member. His influence permeated and provided continuity to forty-two years of the Club's history, and beyond, for his yachting immortality would forever lie with *Nancy*, previously described, one of the first two knockabouts to part the wave in 1892.

While the rest of the world was exclaiming over Park Avenue booms and parachute spinnakers, Charles H.W. Foster was trying to figure out why he couldn't drive a ketch to windward. He concluded that the gap between the mainsail and the mizzen caused the one to backwind the other in the ketch and the yawl. This theory was given some credence by the M.I.T. aeronautical experiments on the Charles River Basin demonstrating that the leeward side of the main was the source of propulsion to windward and benefited from the slotted draft of the headsails.

Perhaps a staysail set close to the leech of the main on a permanent backstay from the masthead to a stump mizzenmast, Foster mused, would clear the air and serve in the same relation to the main as the main to the jib. He tried this out with some success in 1931 on his old keel dory *Utility*. Then, he recalled:

> In the late summer of 1933 I purchased a Down East–built schooner named the *Harvard*. She is of heavy construction, and as a schooner was one of the worst I have ever sailed. Slow and unhandy. I put on her the staysail ketch rig, and on her first sail thereafter she won the chowder race of the Corinthian Yacht Club against some twenty-seven competitors. Her speed and handiness under this rig have astonished me and my friends who have been out in her.

After the 1934 season, Charlie Foster, seventy-five, resumed his correspondence with Nathanael Herreshoff, eighty-six, with high enthusiasm over the experimental rig he had given his fifty-fifth yacht, for he enclosed a photograph. Three more letters to him in the hand of Captain Nat have been found among the papers Foster was gathering for the second *Ditty Box*, which never came to pass. Because of the significance of any substantive unpublished correspondence from Herre-

Nathanael G. Herreshoff at 85.

shoff, they are offered here verbatim as of special interest to devotees of the divided rig.

December 22, 1934

Dear Mr. Foster.

[Reference to Foster's rescue of *America* appears in an earlier chapter.]

I thank you for the very interesting photo of your experimental rig, in your staysail ketch. It is an interesting rig and I wish others could go into experimenting in perfecting sailing yachts as you have. Up to date, the Bermudian, or jib-headed jib & mainsail rig has proved fastest, and most convenient [sic] in the smaller yachts. To try out experiments properly of rigs, there should be two hulls built exactly alike, and one rigged with the most up to date sails of limited size, and the other with the experimental rig of same size.

I am a firm believer in having a small sail aft that is only large enough to keep the vessel head to the wind when needed, and will make her managable with forstaysail set and mainsail off in a squall. Its driving power when mainsail is set, I have proved

---

Commodore Lambert's flagship *Atlantic*, the grandest schooner yacht of all. Morris Rosenfeld photo.

is worthless and such a sail might be neglected in measuring racing yachts. I have no use for what is called ketch-rig, or even a schooner in the smaller craft.

Sail areas equal, I am doubtful if your staysail-ketch would compare favorably with the standard jib & mainsail rig if compared as suggested. With Christmas Greetings

Sincerely yours—Nathl. G. Herreshoff

Foster went ahead anyway with *Oceana*, his fifty-sixth yacht, a 43-foot- waterline staysail ketch, and broke the heretical news to Herreshoff, then eighty-seven, who replied:

Nov. 16, 1935

C.H.W. Foster, Esqr.
791 Tremont St, Boston.

Dear Mr. Foster.

I thank you for your kind and interesting letter with the inclosures of photo. of your yacht *Oceana* and the clever little pictures showing how you would rig *Belisarius* and *Thistle* [Herreshoff yawls].

I suppose I may be thick-headed but I fail to see any advantage in your new rig. There is a little less windage as compared to the ordinary yawl & ketch and much less than a schooner rig. But the latter has so very much oppirtunity [sic] to set light, or balloon sails, it cannot be ignored.

From my own experiance [sic] in cruising and pleasure sailing at home, I very much prefer the yawl rig, and the mizzen about as diminutive as will insure the yacht to lay-to well in a gale and to keep head to the wind when at mooring with sails set for airing &c. Of course, the mizzen sheeted hard and other sails flowing.

My many trials with mizzen set and with mizzen lowered, has shown me the sail is of no use on the wind unless the vessel has lee-helm when off. In reaching the yawl is quite as good, or better, in my yacht that was rigged both ways with equal sail area. When broad off enough for the mizzen to break true wind to mainsail it had better be lowered and then sloop rig is faster. I think these statements will apply even more directly to your rig.

Of course your rig causes more stress on the jib stay, which experiance [sic] has shown makes the jib efficient. It gives the mast (and bowsprit if there is one) much greater load to carry, and must be more robust than in the usual rig. Compairing [sic] weight moments I think the rig with mizzen mast would be least, and windage moment about the same. Your mainsail and backstay mizzen are so very narrow for height, they would be very inefficient when sheets are lifted for reaching and running. But this defect could be avoided by having higher clued [sic] sails fitted with sprit booms.

I notice you have a big double clued jib on *Oceana* and have also shown the same on the re-rig of *Belisarius* & *Thistle*. This being essentially a racing sail I am wondering why you use it on your cruiser. Mr. Rockwell [Charles B. Rockwell, owner of the 41-foot-waterline yawl] has used one on *Belisarius* in racing and said it appeared to be of little advantage.

It may be alright when racing and with racing crew, but in a cruiser?

To my observation—In all moderately sized cruising yachts, yawl rig is best, and far better than a ketch, or schooner, and I think you will find it so if you will try it out. Your back-stay mizzen rig can be a yawl as easily as ketch if so planned.

I have just heard the old *Athene*, Wm O. Gay's sloop of 1899, has recently had a new owner, turned her back to a yacht and restored her original name. He is fitting her out for a long cruise to China and the Orient from a California port. I hope he will have her surveyed and properly repaired—for the lower part of steel frames must be rusted away by this time.

I would be pleased to have your criticism of my remarks on your rig, and hope to hear from you again.

Very sincerely yours—
Nathanael G. Herreshoff

Foster prefaced his response to this lesson from the master, dated December 31, 1935, "As we grow older and winter sets in [he had another twenty to go], the yachtsman gets his fun in life through nautical discussions, and this is one reason for continuing our letters. Then, too, I always learn something from you as for instance, it had not occurred to me to keep my tall narrow sails down when off the wind by having sprit booms." But he held his ground, defending his staysail ketch to the end. Who else would argue yachts with Nathanael Herreshoff? And who else but Captain Nat, now approaching eighty-eight, would invite criticism of his remarks on an amateur's experimental rig? The Eastern's historian drew a quick reply.

Jan'y 13, 1936

Dear Mr Foster.

Your kind letter of 31st ult is much appreciated and is full of thoughts on cruising yacht rigs.

As you state, the sloop rig has proven the fastest for racing. And may I add—about three-fourths the time is also easiest to handle and pleasantest to sail.

For conditions of making sail or picking up moorings and in squally weather she is like Longfellow's little girl with a curl, and can be very very naughty.

A little story of my later day experiance [sic] may be interesting to you. In 1924 when at 76 years and passing winters in southern Florida, I designed and had built a small cruiser, to use in Biscayne Bay and about the Keys. This boat, *Pleasure*, was 30' oa, 24' wl, 8'5" beam, 31" draft, ballasted by lead, which was part of keel & centreboard legs, and some stowed inside. Rig— jib & leg-o-mutton mainsail with no bowsprit, of about 445 sq ft. She appeared to be a good sailer and a real "ghoster" in light airs, and was easily the fastest boat about Biscayne Bay. My ordinary sailing was generally alone, and cruising, with my wife only, and the boat had a comfortable cabin for it. I was sometimes bothered at moorings, or to reef if overtaken by strong wind. With this rig, the boat appeared to do her best windward work in tacking in about 7 points. The second year I changed the rig to yawl, by cutting off boom and aft part of mainsail and adding mizzen mast with sail ½ hoist & boom as cut down mainsail. The total sail area a very little increased by change. Not having a standard to go by I could not gauge the speed efficiency of the boat but the loss was small and not apparent in sailing alone. After getting sails in correct condition she was almost as close winded, and I usually tacked in very near to 7 points. In reaching she may have been a trifle faster, and in running, I had learned very many years before in my cat yawls the boat was faster with the mizzen lowered. This change of rig made the boat a much better single-hander. At both leaving and picking up moorings and specially in negotiating [sic] the unpleasant trade wind rain squalls, which were never too much for jib & mizzen, and mainsail could be lowered into its lazy-jacks in an instant. All halyards & downhauls lead to cockpit, and in reach.

In stiff breezes and with 2 reefed ms [mainsail], jib & mizzen, the boat proved to be very close winded and fast. Due to the shallow water the seas would not make up large to pitch the boat, and so could sheet in very close, and so to tack in 6½ to 7 points, and do fine windward work and a pleasure to sail the boat as with very little spray. In these conditions the reefed mainsail was enough removed from the mizzen, so the latter didn't have to be sheeted almost fore & aft and could give wearer its share of driving power it would [have] if in perfectly free wind. With the yawl rig, reefing the mainsail was very easy for me. I had occasions to [reef], several times while sailing on Biscayne Bay or below among the Keys. While the mainsail was lowered to be reefed, the boat would sail herself by jib & mizzen at fully ½ speed to windward, and the time from lowering away mainsail to have it set reefed varied from 13 to 15 minutes.

Of course I had my reefing stops and lace line properly fitted and kept where I could lay my hands on.

Due to the position—in trailing the mainsail—I cannot believe the mizzen of your staysail ketch can have any driving power, and the craft will be as fast, or faster without the sail if balanced properly on helm. Also, the sail being so high & narrow, it would not be so good, as would a lower sail attached to a mizzen mast, when laying-to in bad weather. Of course, this is only my opinion at present, and after thought I hope you will write me wherein I am wrong.

> With kindest regards,
> Sincerely yours,
> Nathanael G. Herreshoff

Yankee set sail for home in April 1936 and arrived at Boston on May 5, twenty-two days from Bishop's Rock. Chandler Hovey had purchased *Weetamoe*, so the Eastern had two Js in its anchorage, albeit they did most of their racing off Newport.

The first major event of the season was the second annual revival of the New London-Marblehead ocean race on June 20, made the more exciting by the encounter of all but one of the leaders with a tug and a tow of barges near the Cross Rip Lightship. There were seventeen in the fleet. Brothers Henry and Sherman Morss had to crank up the engine of their schooner *Grenadier* to avoid tangling with the hawser at nine knots.

Henry A. Morss, the brothers' father, had died only the previous month at the age of sixty-five. A member since 1897, he was the leading spirit in organizing the run from New London in 1906 and a prime mover behind the sport of ocean racing. Beginning with *Aspenet*, he made a habit of naming his yachts alphabetically—*Brigand, Cossack, Dervish*, and so on. No one had a more distinguished record of service to the Club and devotion to yachting than the wire manufacturer, a loyal alumnus of M.I.T. and a life member of its corporation. He had served as assistant treasurer (his brother Everett was treasurer) and led the development of the Tech dinghy sailing program on the Charles River. The Morss Bowl for intercollegiate racing was given in his memory.

Young Harry and Sherman (their brother, Wells, was five years their junior) learned to sail in the Fish class under the guidance of Harry Fitzpatrick, the Club's sailing instructor, and they attended a model-building class in a barn, racing their miniature productions on Redd's Pond. In 1929 their father considered them salted enough to buy them a cruising boat, *Vagabond*, which he and they sailed up from Stamford, Connecticut.

The boys mastered *Vagabond* so rapidly that their father went to John Alden, then at the height of his schoonerdom, for the next jump-up. Aage Nielsen was drafting for him then and helped design *Grenadier*, 59 feet 10 inches by 41 feet 8 inches

Resurgence and the J-Boats

The Morss brothers' schooner *Grenadier* in 1932, designed by John Alden with the help of Aage Nielsen, and built by Lawley the previous year.

by 13 feet 8 inches by 7 feet 5 inches, built by Lawley in 1931. After a season of practice racing and cruising along the coast, they entered her in the 1932 Bermuda Race. Alden's *Malabar X*, with the designer at the helm, beat *Grenadier* on corrected time by three minutes and thirteen seconds. Third on time was his *Water Gypsy*, and fourth was his *Teragram*. Four Alden schooners within an hour and fifteen minutes of each other!

"So-called ocean racing is a farce when looked on as yacht racing," grunted L. Francis Herreshoff years later, denying sour grapes, "for in a long race the competitors are often so widely spaced that one may have a rail-down breeze while another is becalmed." The competition between the two designers was described by Alden's biographer as being "as sticky as fresh varnish on a dank day."

In 1933 the Morss brothers sailed *Grenadier* to England in three weeks and came in second in the Fastnet Race behind Olin Stephens's fabled *Dorade*, only to see the wind and tide carry a vagabond ferry down on them at Cowes, causing enough damage that they had to ship her home in time to make it back to school. The next year this great schooner was third in her class of twenty-three in the Bermuda run. She was less successful in the 1938 race, but in 1939 they won the Halifax Race in *Grenadier*, "thanks partly," explains Sherman Morss, "to the acquisition, during the interval of a delayed start due to lack of wind and a dense fog, of a primitive radio direction finder; no other boat had such a novel instrument."

During World War II, *Grenadier* was on Coast Guard patrol, after which the brothers sold her. Converted to a knockabout ketch in 1949, she was seen in Majorca, then at Fort Lauderdale around 1973 as *British Grenadier*, and last reported in Honolulu.

For all his crankiness on the subject of ocean racing, Francis Herreshoff had no objections to taking commissions for boats that were both seaworthy and fast. He designed the 57-foot clipper-bowed, keel ketch *Bounty* for Edward Dane of the Eastern in 1933 (rebuilt, refitted, and in elegant condition in Cali-

The elegant ketch *Bounty*, by L. Francis Herreshoff for Edward Dane in 1933. Jackson photo.

fornia in 1987). A couple of years later, he redrew her for Harry E. Noyes, who had the bug for fair now and wanted an even bigger successor to the Herreshoff *Tioga* he had only just acquired from Waldo Brown.

This new ketch *Tioga* was 72 feet overall and very close to *Bounty* in hull form, though with a different layout. She could hardly have been less auspiciously launched at her owner's Quincy Adams yard on August 10, 1936. The starboard side of the cradle collapsed just as she cleared (fortunately) the building shed, and *Tioga* careened one way, tossing Johnny Rhyn, her sailing master, the other, in an infamous photograph caught by a news photographer. His second *Tioga* remained a lifetime favorite of Francis Herreshoff, who compared her with his 87-foot M-boat *Istalena*, boasting mildly of her most famous feat two years later in 1938:

> As for maximum speed, *Tioga* sailed from New London to Marblehead, a distance of 180 miles, in 18 hours [and 37 minutes]. *Istalena* never could have done this in her palmiest days with all her sloop rig, draft and sail area, so you see our short waterline, pot bellied racers are a joke, and our rules radically wrong

Sailing Master Johnny Rhyn, in his brand new uniform for the occasion, is launched one way as *Tioga* goes the other when the starboard side of the cradle collapses at the Quincy Adams Yard in Quincy August 9, 1936. Nothing damaged but dignity.

when they develop a racing yacht slower for the sail area than a useful cruiser.

That was an hour and eighteen minutes faster than the previous mark set by the designer's father's 135-foot schooner *Elena* in 1911, a course record that still stands, even though—irony of ironies—*Tioga* failed to make up enough of her time to win the Lambert Trophy. And she broke the course record in the Lightship Race.

Out of an encouragingly expanding Annual Cruise of forty-five yachts, twenty-two in eight classes participated in the 1936 Annual Regatta after the rendezvous at Mattapoisett on July 8. The glamour was provided by *Rainbow*, *Weetamoe*, and *Yankee*, which won the J-class and the fiftieth-anniversary Puritan Cup, to which Commodore Lambert added the New York Yacht Club's King's Cup for the third time in his still-young racing career. Two grace notes of optimism were provided by Vice Commodore Malcolm Greenough's cruising/racing cutter *White Lady*, one of the first U.S.-built boats to be added to the Marblehead fleet since the Crash, and D. Spencer Berger's big new yawl *Mandoo II* (later *Royono*), regarded by many as John Alden's fastest ocean racer to date. The cruise fleet lowered burgees on learning of the death of Rear Commodore F. Haven Clark.

A heavy northeast gale, the backlash of a hurricane that devastated the Atlantic coast, swept through during the night of September 18, 1936, sank a number of boats at their moorings, and drove many more ashore. The 88-foot schooner *Freedom* dragged on a rampage the length of the harbor, making free with several yachts, under suspicion of sinking two. Among the total losses were two S-boats and Walter McKim's ketch *Houqua*. The Club's committee boat stove a side when it fetched up on the rocks.

Cleopatra's Barge was wisely shifted to anchor behind the Gloucester breakwater, where she rode out a storm that may have struck her owner as bearing out his forebodings at the beginning of the season, when he logged at City Island: "There was quite a fleet of yachts getting ready to go in commission, a few medium sized but most of them small. The last year of yachting in all probability unless the people vote right in November and defeat Roosevelt."

The three Js—two of which, astonishingly, were outright Eastern boats—had been put into commission in anticipation of the Royal Yacht Squadron's Cup challenge on behalf of T.O.M. Sopwith and his *Endeavour II*, which was received by the New York Yacht Club in late August 1936. (The previous year the Royal London Yacht Club had challenged with the smaller, 65-foot-waterline *Windflower*, pleading expense—it cost about half a million dollars to build a J and race it for a season—but withdrew when the NYYC balked at starting a new class.) So it must have seemed foreordained that Chandler Hovey, *Weetamoe*'s owner, should succeed Gerard Lambert, *Yankee*'s, as commodore for 1937—and almost beyond the wildest dream that Hovey should buy *Rainbow* from Harold Vanderbilt for his flagship.

After all, *Endeavour II* had spent the summer of 1936 out-endeavoring *Endeavour I*, which all agreed was faster than *Rainbow*, if she had not been as well sailed. It wouldn't do for New York not to have a defender quite a lot faster than *Rainbow*. A syndicate was formed, and Starling Burgess and Olin Stephens were commissioned to design *Ranger*, but even the NYYC members were having money troubles. Vanderbilt wound up with the bill and Chandler Hovey with two Js.

A Brookline native, grandson of the founder of the well-known Hovey's department store in Boston and son of W.A. Hovey, editor of the *Boston Transcript*, the new commodore was fifty-seven, a graduate of M.I.T., the first commissioner of the Massachusetts Aeronautic Commission and an investment banker with Kidder, Peabody & Company. His vice Commodore was B. Devereux Barker, owner of the 63-foot cruising cutter *Good Hope*, who had been secretary since succeeding Caleb Loring in 1934.

Marblehead's cup of racing in 1937 overflowed for the first time since the beginning of the Depression. Perhaps the busiest season in the entire history of the Eastern Yacht Club, it was dominated by the magnificent fleet of Js competing up and down the New England coast in a queenly seagoing road show, a beehive that buzzed all the way down to the busy working fleet of forty-eight Brutal Beasts. During the summer, 2,366 boats started in Eastern races, compared to 1,879 in 1936 and 1,592 in 1935.

The Beasts, incidentally, were true trainers, perhaps the most durable and effective ever designed. And what work-

A favorite of Francis Herreshoff was his ketch *Tioga*, created for Harry E. Noyes along *Bounty*'s lines in 1936. Morris Rosenfeld photo.

horses! Tuesdays and Thursdays this swarm of broad-bottomed cats banged and brawled through the "Ice Cream Races" (named for the postrace reward for all at the Hotel Rockmere); Fridays the Pleon Races; and Wednesdays, Saturdays, and Sundays the Eastern and Corinthian Races, leaving only Monday for boredom ashore.

Could there be any doubt that the bad times had bottomed out and that a new wave of yachting was making up?

The year 1937 opened with great expectations as ex-Commodore Lambert established his New London-Marblehead Race cup as a perpetual challenge, and the classes were re-arranged by rig to give the schooners and ketches a break against the growing dominance of the cutters and yawls in ocean racing. But the wind and sixteen of the twenty-five starters pooped out on June 26, and the race was won by Charles F. (Bubbles) Havemeyer in his New York Yacht Club Thirty-two *Apache*.

Both Starling Burgess and Olin Stephens produced models for *Ranger* that were tank-tested, and Burgess's was chosen, a result never officially revealed, but confirmed twenty years later by Stephens. *Ranger* and *Endeavour II* were both built to the class limit, 135 feet-plus overall, 87 feet waterline. *Ranger*'s 166 tons were 25 more than *Rainbow*'s, and she was nearly ten feet longer, with about the same sail area and the same unique, dynamically bending boom—Burgess's refinement of the Park Avenue boom that Sopwith stayed with for his second challenger. Commenting on *Ranger*'s unusual "snub nose," Stephens said, "We could have provided more graceful lines, but we felt certain that they weren't necessary. We were able to build a well [the famous "coal chute"] in the bow that enabled Art Knapp or myself to keep a close watch on the headsails." She was launched from the Bath (Maine) Iron Works on May 11. Her 165-foot mast was hurriedly stepped, mainly so the workmen could see what it looked like upright, and *Ranger* was taken in tow for Newport. In a seaway the rigging parted, the towering stick snapped 35 feet above the deck, and they had to put into Marblehead before resuming.

At Newport, *Ranger* borrowed *Rainbow*'s 1934 mast, and on June 2 beat *Yankee* in the first of four straight trial wins. On June 15, she had her new mast, and from her next race on, there was never a doubt. *Ranger* was a super-J. A new breed of yacht had burst on the scene. Wrote Llewellyn Howland III in his intriguing profile of Burgess in *WoodenBoat* magazine:

With *Ranger*, tank-testing of sailing yachts came of age. In *Ranger* the maritime applications of aerodynamics found their most complete pre-World War II expression. Thanks to Starling's genius and the skill of Olin and Roderick Stephens, . . . *Ranger* came physically to embody those abstractions of speed, beauty, grace, power, and function that it is the yacht designer's grandest dream to achieve.

The week before the Cup races, on July 24, the Annual Regatta was sailed by twenty-eight boats in a light southwesterly over a thirty-mile triangular course. Frank Paine's great Q-boat *Robin*, owned now by Francis E. Waterman and sailed by Richard S. Thayer, former National Junior champion, won the Puritan Cup for the fourth time, a remarkable record. As *Norn*, owned by I.R. Edmands, she had won in 1928 and 1929, and then as *Robin*, owned by Chandler Hovey, in 1933.

The following day, the Annual Cruise raised anchor for Mattapoisett, Newport, and the 1937 America's Cup. The accompanying flotilla of yachts, which brought more than a twinge of nostalgia, was led, as almost always, by ex-Commodore Sears's apparently immortal *Constellation*. With her were *Cleopatra's Barge*, the great Santry schooner *Pleione*, the schooner *Wildfire*, *Yankee Girl III*, and Tom Sopwith's steam yacht *Philante*.

At Mattapoisett the fleet was joined by *Ranger*, *Rainbow*, *Yankee*, and *Endeavour I*, which Sopwith brought over as his trial horse, for the run to Vineyard Haven, followed by a special race of the Js (minus *Ranger*) off Newport, won by *Endeavour I*.

The 1937 Cup races were an anti-climactic, four-straight rollick for the magnificent *Ranger* and the climax to the career of Mike Vanderbilt. They would be the last for twenty-one years—to be resumed on the other side of the chasm when all the world, for the second time in a generation, had been changed forever by war. And yet, there was always continuity, for, as Howland observed, "*Ranger* brought to a triumphant conclusion one entire line in the evolution of yacht design—and thus gave birth to another."

For Sis Hovey, whose marriage to Sherman Morss would

In a godlike duel, *Rainbow* crosses the bow of the Eastern's furiously frothing *Yankee* in the foreground during a tacking tiff preceding the 1934 trials dominated but not won by the Eastern J-boat. Morris Rosenfeld photo.

Resurgence and the J-Boats

unite two of the Eastern's most distinguished racing dynasties, the Js represented the Everest of her family's sailing experience—first in *Yankee*, then in *Weetamoe*, finally peaking in 1937 when *Rainbow* was her father's flagship and the afterguard included the commodore, her brothers Charlie and Buss, their cousin, Eastern Fleet Captain Morgan Harris, and Henry Morss as navigator.

On *Rainbow* we had twenty-two crew and eight in the afterguard, thirty of us living on board all the time. These were the rules at the time, because the British, when they came over to challenge, had to sail their boat over with a jury rig, so they obviously lived on board.

In those days we had canvas sails which were very heavy and very difficult to maneuver. When you came about, it took about five minutes to get under way again, so you didn't do all this short tacking that you do today in Twelve-Meters. We had what we called a quadrilateral jib that had two clews, because canvas sails stretched, and there was no way, with the heavy material and the stretching, to be able to use a real Genoa jib. We had one high-cut jib that we used reaching and in very, very light air; it was a pretty good-sized jib.

[*Ranger* flew a huge, overlapping quad with more area aloft, strictly speaking, than a Genoa, of a type first developed by Gerard Lambert for *Yankee*, except that it was rayon. Our "Mysterious Montague," Sherman Hoyt dubbed it. *Ranger*'s main was a hand-me-down from *Enterprise* in 1930 via *Rainbow* in 1934.]

We had a triple head rig in 1930 and a double head rig in 1934 and 1937. The spinnakers were perfectly enormous, a third of an acre, if you can visualize that. [*Ranger*'s was 18,000 square feet, 41 percent of an acre!] The mast was 165 feet tall, and the boats about 130, and it was a real thrill when you would get up to fifteen and sixteen knots on waves, which was about maximum speed, and they would get up there quite often.

The Twelve-Meters, which are the America's Cup defenders today, have about half the length of the J's, a quarter the sail area and an eighth the displacement.

The crew was rather interesting. They were all Norwegians and Swedes. They didn't speak English except for the captain and first and second mates. The captain was the one who took the orders and passed them along to the first mate, who communicated with all the crew. They were very, very good sailors. They'd all been brought up on the water. A lot of them were oyster fishermen, and their hands were just as tough and calloused as could be, which of course worked out well with the type of work they had on board.

Jibing the spinnaker, you had the cup on the mast. The length between the headstay and the mast was not enough to swing your pole through, so you had to detach it from the mast and shift your sheet, make your sheet your guy and vice versa—the guy turned into the spinnaker sheet—and you pushed the pole across, or sometimes we used two poles. It was a very, very heavy pole, hung on a boom lift that held it up, and it just had to be balanced. We also had a pole that went out from the bow. It looked like a bowsprit, and in light air we had that out because the spinnaker, being so large, hung down in light air and would get caught under the bow, so this would hold it from getting down into the water.

In a season of record-setting, the 1937 Race Week beginning August 7 would be by far the most populated to date and for another ten years. "Nowhere in this nation," wrote Leonard Fowle, Jr., "and probably only at Sandhamn in Sweden, can racing fleets the equal of Marblehead's during Race Week be approached." He captured hints of the coming excitement in *New England Yachtsman*:

The trek towards Marblehead will begin with a few early comers by midweek, and on Friday the steady procession commences. That afternoon one standing in the shadow of the Lighthouse and watching yacht after yacht being sailed or towed past the Point, and then casting an eye seaward towards the Graves or Cape Ann for a break in the endless chain of approaching small boats, will shake his head and wonder where they can all find mooring space as one views a seemingly already over-crowded harbor.

Yet the procession into port will be renewed and even intensified all Saturday morning as into port sweep Indians from Newburyport and Boston, Cats, Birds, and Fishes from Conomo and Annisquam, Triangles and Stars from Cape Ann, "O" boats from Sandy Bay and Hingham, Baby Knockabouts from Gloucester, more Stars from Nahant, Boston Bay, and even South of Cape Cod, little Yankee Clippers manned by the Sea Scouts, Snipes and Winabouts from half a dozen ports, Yankee Dories from Swampscott and Squantum, Snow Birds from Wollaston, Sea Birds from Hingham, 17-footers from Cohasset, Cats and Bantams from Quincy, Skimmers and Comets from the lakes of the Mystic Valley, Radios and Hustlers from Winthrop, Dinghies from M.I.T. on the Charles, and a scattering of boats from more distant waters as far away as Narragansett Bay and the Sound.

On the other hand, the fleet of five Alden Triangles sailed off the Eastern scene after eleven years of good one-design racing (although fourteen remained at the Eastern Point Yacht Club, along with five elderly Sonders), and an equal handful of Herreshoff S-boats barely hung on. The M-B (Marblehead-Buzzards

Bay) Knockabouts, 17-footers originally intended for both waters (featuring Caleb Loring, E. Sohier Welch, and Francis H. Cummings), and Thirty Square Meters (Lincoln Davis, Jr., E. Arthur Shuman, Jr., Alfred E. Chase, and John S. Lawrence) continued strong. The 25-rater Qs had to move over in the limelight for the International Eight Meters, which got a big lift with the entry into the class of former Secretary of the Navy Adams, who won the Eastern Yacht Club Challenge Cup and the three major championships. Fowle doffed his cap in *New England Yachting News*:

> It is a long time since a yachting observer has been able to write the once common phrase "Charles Francis Adams won the championship of his class as might be expected." Through the season of 1928, it was the unusual year when the nation's No. 1 skipper did not top his class, but that remark ceased to be apt when "Charlie Ad" left the 20-raters nine years ago and entered Class Q with *Bat*. The combination of *Bat*, a very mediocre boat in a class where stiff competition existed, and the years devoted to official duties in Washington and to Boston's *Yankee* brought a drought in the succession of Adams championships which came to an end when he brought *Thisbe* out of the West [Lake Erie] last winter.

Realizing from the first day that *Ranger* was an absolute breakthrough and that extended trials would merely be postponement of the inevitable, according to Sis Hovey Morss, her father suggested to the NYYC committee that the Cup races be moved ahead to the end of July and that the rest of the season be given over to cruising and racing all the Js up and down the coast for pure pleasure and public appreciation.

And so, due appreciably to Commodore Hovey's sporting initiative, after the Cup races the five J-boats—the all-white Americans *Ranger*, *Rainbow*, and *Yankee* and the two royal-blue British *Endeavours*—joined the New York Yacht Club Cruise to Buzzards Bay, the Vanderbilt boat sweeping up everything in sight, including the Astor and King's cups. George Poor had just joined the Eastern and was cruising south of the Cape in *Tinavire*:

> The Js were down there, and Chandler Hovey had the whole cruise aboard *Rainbow* for cocktails on deck, she was that big, and a buffet supper. Sherman Hoyt was sailing *Endeavour I*. I think they'd been in Vineyard Haven and were racing to Newport in very little air, but they were moving and we were powering. All of a sudden Hoyt started to pull ahead from the rest, and then we realized he'd put his anchor down, and they were

all going backward with the tide. Earlier we were anchored in Brenton Cove, and I watched Rod Stephens in those long red pants that everybody wears now go up to the masthead of a J hand-over-hand without a bos'n's chair.

From there, the flotilla of Js sailed on to Marblehead at the invitation of Commodore Hovey to wind up the season, and indeed the era, of the tallest and swiftest sloops—cutters, actually—the world has ever seen, with five races between August 28 and September 2 under the auspices of the Eastern Yacht Club.

Coincidentally, the occasion would exactly mark the fiftieth anniversary of the last meeting of America's Cup contenders off Marblehead, and there were a few around who remembered. It was on August 11, 1887, two weeks before *Volunteer*'s match with *Thistle*, that the New York Yacht Club had arrived for a special joint regatta with the Eastern featuring no less than Ben Butler's schooner *America* herself, and Edward Burgess's trio of defenders, *Volunteer*, *Puritan*, and *Mayflower*.

And here, half a century later, were his son Starling's *Rainbow*, and right with her his *Ranger*, the all-time fastest winner in the history of the Cup, preparing to do final friendly battle with their remaining American rival and the two gallant challengers from overseas. All five were anchored at the harbor entrance under Fort Sewall, masts higher and with plenty to spare than Marblehead Light, which stands 130 feet above sea level.

An Eastern member's memories of the wonder and excitement of the sight remain undimmed after fifty years:

> Even to circle the Js at their moorings was a thrill. I can picture now the clean lines of those incredibly long and graceful hulls, their towering masts, the immense sweep of their decks. We saw them only in light air, when under sail they moved with uncanny silence through water that was without a ripple. While all around them lesser boats were becalmed, the queenly Js ghosted over the glassy sea, picking up speed, making scarcely a whisker of bow wave and hardly any wake, propelled by the air aloft that they alone could capture. The crews in their immaculate whites worked with wondrous precision hoisting and trimming sails and spinnakers so absolutely vast that I can hardly believe they really existed. This is a memory that lives with me as fresh as the day I first laid eyes on these greatest of all sloops.

The newspapers were quite as wild with enthusiasm. "Sight

of a Life-Time for Yachtsmen and Landlubbers," headlined the *Boston Transcript*. "May Never Happen Again."

The J Boats are coming to town, not one of them but five of them, and right in our back yard—to the historic sailing port of Marblehead where the largest racing sloops in the world, representing about two and one-half million dollars of shipbuilding and sailmaking art, will sail through the waters of Massachusetts Bay for the express benefit of thousands of John Q. Publics who will watch from advantageous spots along the shore-line and from hundreds of yachts which will make a spectacle the like of which has never been seen before in these waters and may never be seen again.

Much was made of the inshore courses laid out between Marblehead, the Boston Lightship, and the Eastern Point, Minot's and The Graves whistlers—far closer than the Cup courses at least nine miles off Newport—"which will put the shore line from Gloucester to Cohasset within view of the sloops. But bring your field glasses." When sea buoys were lacking for a proper course, Harry E. Noyes's 100-foot power yacht *Seyon* would serve as a turning mark. The spectator fleet would be patrolled by two Coast Guard cutters and an 80-footer, and the 1,400-passenger excursion steamer *Steel Pier* would leave Long Wharf in Boston each morning for Marblehead, where tenders from the Eastern and the Corinthian and the town landing would ferry the lucky ones aboard for the show.

The opening day, Saturday, was disappointingly flat, and the next was the day off for the professional crews. Some wag dreamed up a Sunday race of the J skippers in the smallest class in the harbor. Thus was placed in competition the Brutal Beast Challenge Cup, donated on the spot by Morgan Harris of *Rainbow*'s afterguard and Arthur Knapp of *Ranger*'s. There would be two go-rounds in five 14-footers borrowed from Peter and Barbara Connolly, Janet Harwood, George O'Day, and Hope Noyes. It is of interest that the Brutals and three of the Js were the creations of Starling Burgess. Fessenden S. Blanchard wrote up the results in his section on the Brutal Beast in *The Sailboat Classes of America*:

On August 29, 1937, a pretty fifteen-year-old girl, "Janny" Harwood, the proud owner of a new Brutal Beast, the *Rip Tide*, brought her boat to the dock of the Eastern Yacht Club at Marblehead and waited. She was one of five skippers of these wicked-sounding boats who had been asked to meet at the dock with their craft.

. . . A tall figure approached and explained that he had drawn *Rip Tide* for the first race.

"How close will she point?" Mike Vanderbilt inquired of Janny. "About five points, I'd imagine?"

Janny didn't quite know where five points would be but she took a chance and said that she guessed that was about right. But she failed to remind the new skipper that in Brutal Beasts it was important to keep a proper balance of weight between bow and stern. Vanderbilt hadn't worried much about this when he was on the *Ranger*, at least so far as the distribution of his own weight was concerned. He sat too near the stern, I am told, and came in last in the first race of the Brutal Beasts. Tom Sopwith was first in a boat [*Kraken*] belonging to Barbara Connolly.

For the second race Sopwith had drawn *Rip Tide* and asked Janny for instructions. Again he won. Obviously there had been nothing wrong with the boat in the first race. Vanderbilt, in another boat, was again last. [He had centerboard problems, too.] The final results were in this order: Sopwith, Hovey, Sigrist [Frederick Sigrist, Sopwith's business partner], Lambert and Vanderbilt. The winner was so pleased with his success that he invited the owners of the two Brutal Beasts on which he had raced to be his guests on *Endeavour II*.

"Did you and Barbara accept the invitation?" I asked Janny (now Mrs. John C. White, Jr.), as she reminisced about Brutal Beast days.

"You bet," was her answer.

Not only did the girls sail on *Endeavour II* the next day, but they took tea with the Sopwiths aboard their steamer *Philante* after the race and were invited back to the British J for the windup on September 2 with Pleon members Peter Connolly, Clark Shepard, and Peter Langmaid. George O'Day circled *Yankee* so persistently in his Brutal that he was finally invited aboard, too.

The grand finale of the Big Ones? Lack of wind dogged the Labor Day weekend, but they managed five races. The last, on Thursday, September 2, 1937, was a proper curtain-dropper. The course was twenty-eight miles to The Graves and return, twice around, and there was enough of a breeze from the southwest to make it a contest.

Ranger led *Yankee* by 90 seconds rounding The Graves on the first leg, *Rainbow* was third by another minute, as reported by Richard P. Waters in the *Boston Transcript*:

A tiny figure at the helm, Charles Francis Adams guides *Yankee*, supreme missile of the wind, into sailing history in a moment of power and beauty never to be duplicated. Morris Rosenfeld photo.

Then the duel started between *Ranger* and *Yankee*. The seven-year-old sloop thrashed her way down the wind in all her old-time form and had five seconds short of two minutes on the America's Cup defender as they turned to repeat the course. The question was whether *Yankee* could hold that lead on the beat or not. *Ranger* came about behind *Yankee* and then started to catch up relentlessly, edging to windward and slowly eating up the space between the two yachts.

Yankee fought her off, but the course was just long enough for ground-gaining *Ranger* to tack in front of *Yankee* as they hitched for the mark and round almost two minutes in the lead. . . . *Yankee* at one point about half-way home was ahead of *Ranger*, and followers of the Lambert boat had their hopes high, but she was nearly a half a mile to windward of the course, and when she headed onto it and jibed she dropped back.

The wind had hauled into the eastward a bit, and the boats doused spinnakers for reaching Genoas, with *Yankee* performing the maneuver first in her last-minute attempt. But *Ranger* was not to be denied and had about a minute and a half on *Yankee* as she swept grandly across the line which marked the finish of the race and the finish of racing for the J boats this summer.

As for the Hoveys' *Rainbow*, she turned in a good performance, as Stanton Deland described it in the *Transcript*, "but fate just seemed against her."

Sis was at her helm up the wind the first round and held onto *Ranger* tenaciously, while down wind *Rainbow* gained on *Ranger*. Buss sailed her on the next windward leg and turned in another good job, but misfortune hit hard when the crew was in too much of a hurry and hoisted her parachute before turning the Graves with the inevitable result that the stops broke and the chute became torn, tangling on the lower spreader. Left with only a smaller spinnaker, the Hovey craft lost out to *Endeavour II*, with whom she had enjoyed keen competition.

The incomparable *Ranger* had swept the last of the J-boat races, winning the last silver she or any other J would ever win, five Eastern Yacht Club cups, and the Town of Marblehead Trophy, for which the official scoring in points was: *Ranger* 30, *Endeavour II* 22, *Rainbow* 18, *Yankee* 18, and *Endeavour I* 11.

After it was over, and their most glamorous of all yachts were back at their moorings, Mike Vanderbilt and Tom Sopwith and their wives were taken ashore in their evening clothes for the award dinner at Marblehead's Fox and Hounds.

And then the J-boats, 60 feet higher than Marblehead Light, sailed off . . . towering Dutchmen flying forever across the seas of memory.

The Winds of War Again

An ominous note crept into the *New England Yachting News* at the end of 1937: "Because of the international aspect of the 8-Meter and 30-Square Meter racing for the Ladies' Plate and Eastern Challenge Cup no plans will be made for these races until the situation abroad clears up."

The following year, on June 2, Nathanael Herreshoff died at the age of ninety. He had outlived his friend and rival Edward Burgess by forty-seven years. Between the marks of the Eastern Yacht Club, his boats had won eighteen of the forty-two Puritan Cups since 1890.

Shortly thereafter, Ned's splendid creation, Herbert Sears's schooner *Constellation*, had a birthday party off Newport. The date was June 20, and the Crowninshields and their guests on *Cleopatra's Barge II* were there, for the morrow was the start of the Bermuda Race. How often had Keno twitted the *Barge*'s bigger and older cousin when there wasn't much stirring—"a regular *Constellation* day, if you know what I mean." But this *was* the Eastern's honorary flagship's day:

> Went on board the *Constellation* (Commodore Sears), and paid my respects. She was dressed in honor of her fiftieth birthday. I also had lunch on her later. . . . Under the heading of what other people think of us, let me record what a lady said to me today. "She didn't understand why we didn't go into the Bermuda Race in the *Barge*, as she felt sure that if the wind was light we might do very well." Sweet of her, wasn't it?

The Herreshoffs sailed on. Three weeks after the Wizard's death, the 72-foot ketch *Tioga*, designed by his quite-as-extraordinary son Francis, beat the course record from New London to Marblehead set by his 135-foot schooner *Elena* in 1911. Then his great M-sloop *Andiamo*, owned by Walter L. Shaw,

captured the Puritan Cup for the second time since 1930 and dominated the Annual Cruise, headed eastward for the first season since 1931.

Leonard Fowle sailed with Harry Noyes on that 1938 cruise and sent back a story headlined in the *Boston Globe*'s sport pages of July 4: "Globe Yachting Editor, Aboard *Tioga*, Uses Radio Telephone." He wrote: "In sending this first newspaper description of a long distance, overnight yacht race ever attempted by radio telephone from one of the contestants in the middle of the Gulf of Maine to the Globe, your correspondent is seated comfortably in the roomy main cabin of the racing yacht *Tioga* and the call to Boston has been put through with practically the same ease as a toll call between two shore stations."

By contrast, the financially troubled New York Yacht Club confined its 1938 racing to its first cruise in several years as far as Marblehead, where a joint regatta with the Eastern and the King's Cup Race came off on August 15.

It is unclear when the Club officially adopted the Cruising Club of America Rule, which the CCA had devised specifically for the Bermuda Race in 1934, except that in 1938 about twenty Eastern boats were measured to it, in contrast to but one the year before. New York would not make it official until 1946.

Former Commodore Charles P. Curtis was seventy-six in 1937 when Francis Markey, then twenty, first crewed on his Thirty Square Meter *Ellen*, as all his yachts were named. Markey:

> The Thirties were all brought over from Sweden, all mahogany finished bright, and most had a professional. They were called

"Squeaks" because they were so fluid; when you shot the mooring in ten knots of breeze you'd better be sure you were well down because they'd really come up. Every Wednesday and Saturday morning as soon as the dew was off the grass the professionals would be out there to stop the spinnakers with rotten twine [which snapped when the sail broke out and filled].

The captain would usually stay in the hatch forward of the mast and yell out "It's light!" or whatever. After I got the jibs set I'd usually stay there and say it looks like it's a little light

---

Ernest Fay's sleek 30-meter *Roulette II*, hard on the wind.

or a little heavy. Mr. Curtis had a tremendous feel for the boat, but it was scary if we had a port-starboard situation; we lost a couple of races because he couldn't see that well and didn't know where the other boat was and fell off too soon.

One time we were coming up on the mark in *Ellen*, had starboard and felt we could make it. We were number two from the bottom of the series, and the boat we had covered was number two from the top with a good chance of being number one. He wanted to know who it was, and we said, Mr. Sohier Welch and maybe someone else. "Are we close?" "Yes, but I'm sure we can make it and should hold our course." "No," said Mr. Curtis. "He has a good chance of being a deciding factor in the series. We will not interfere." I said, "But we're gonna lose our position!" "Mr. Markey," said he, "there are times when it's more fun to be sporting than to win." He was that type of man. A gentleman.

Not quite so, the veteran skipper known up and down the coast for his competitiveness. He was drifting toward the finish of the Triangles one day during Race Week, neck-and-neck with a doctor. Frustrated beyond bearing, he worked alongside his rival, took out his knife, leaped across, cut the astonished physician's main halyard in one furious slash, jumped back as the offending sail collapsed, and floated first across the line by an inch or two.

No tale of the fabled Thirty Squares or of the prowess of those who rode these slim steeds of the sea surpasses James T. Connolly's account of his astonishing part in the New London-Marblehead Race of 1938—during which *Tioga* was blown to the all-time course record—and the events immediately preceding it. Connolly was finishing Harvard, had joined the Club in March, and owned *Valiant*.

We had perhaps the hottest class in the country. Arthur Knapp came up to race and did not do nearly as well as he did in the Long Island Sound International class. Ernest B. Fay of Six-Meter fame, came up to race for one summer and did much worse than he did in the international racing. Bob Bavier, then a *Yachting* reporter and later a successful America's Cup defender in *Constellation*, came up to crew for me in *Valiant* for one Race Week because, as he said, we had the hottest class at the time. I did not run away with the class, although I did win four or five championships.

Each year at the end of July we went down to Marion to race three days for the Roosevelt Bowl. We organized the "Deep Soda Water Cruising Club of North America," every skipper a commodore. Our burgee was a silver soda siphon on a blue field. The crews formed the "Bilge Boys Union" in retaliation.

We then raced to Edgartown and then in the Edgartown Regatta for two days.

In '38 we won all the "ocean" races to Edgartown, and as a result I fancied the *Valiant* as an ocean racer. Three of my Harvard classmates and I decided we would enter the then annual New London-to-Marblehead Ocean Race. Of course there was no class that we could measure well in, but Professor Burtner measured us in the Universal Class and gave us a certificate. We sailed the boat to New London. This meant that we missed our Class Day at college, and also my crew and I on the Harvard Sailing Team missed the final race of the college season in the Wianno Seniors. This was just as well, because Jack Kennedy took my place and was instrumental in Harvard's winning.

Came the day of the race, and the wind was practically nonexistent. Our competition was two identical 60-foot schooners built to the Universal Rule. Their rigs were tall enough to catch whatever breeze there was aloft, and before the wind finally reached us they were both practically out of sight. As they gave us only three and a half hours, because they measured so much better under the rule, things looked very dismal.

However, the wind was fair and was steadily increasing. By the time we reached Cuttyhunk in the evening we were surfing and averaged eight and a half knots down Vineyard Sound. The strong southwesterly pushed us through Nantucket Sound at a great clip, and by the time we reached the Slough I was afraid that the suction of our speed would pull us down in the trough and let a sea break over us.

One of my crew had just been married and thought we should put into Stage Harbor to save his wife from widowhood. We convinced him, however, that to attempt an unfamiliar harbor in the pitch black would be more dangerous than to sail up the back of the Cape, where we would have a lee in the southwest gale. Accordingly, we took in the main and put up a small jib on the main halyard, which I figured would slow us to a safer speed.

At this point a Coast Guard boat signaled us for our name, as we had no racing number on the jib. I signaled *Valiant* several times, but because we were out of sight in the troughs half the time, they did not pick it up and told the Race Committee that we were unreported. The Committee was not much help when they telephoned my mother in the small hours of the night to tell her that we had not been reported, but not to worry.

We turned the buoy at the easterly end of the Slough to save distance, although I heard later that our competition went out to the Lightship. We put up the main with a reef and skated up the back of the Cape, then, as the wind was easing, shook out the reef and headed for Marblehead.

There was fog, and we saw nothing until we were about a mile or so from the finish. As we crossed the line we asked the Committee when our competition had finished, but they did

The yawl *Fright* took frightened flight in the '38 Hurricane and fetched up at Fort Sewall a total loss.

not know. Later we learned that one of them had withdrawn, and the other finished seven hours or so after we did. So the ill wind had blown us some good.

Three months later, about five hundred yachts were still on their moorings when the wild hurricane of September 21, 1938, roared unheralded up the coast, leaving historic havoc in its trail, but they were mainly saved in the lee of the Neck. Had the brunt of the blast come from the northeast, the wholesale destruction would have cleaned out the harbor. Of the forty that drove ashore or sank, only about ten were regarded as total losses. The force of the wind raised the jib on A.L. Loomis, Jr.'s *Lands End*, which sailed across the harbor and piled up. The captain had already disembarked from *Rose*, G. Peabody Gardner, Jr.'s schooner, and the steward barely jumped ship as she careened by a float; she sailed herself out the harbor, lights on and radio full blast, and wrecked herself on Baker's Island. The 40-foot sloop *Lady Hawk* soloed by the Neck and vanished.

Thomas Shepard's captain rowed out to *Celeritas* off Peach's Point as the storm was building, put out an extra anchor and chain, and came ashore, to his boss's displeasure. She was soon dragging with celerity across Salem Bay until the extra anchor fetched her up in the shoal water off Beverly's Hospital Point.

A day or so later, they went around and got her, undamaged.

Vice Commodore B. Devereux Barker followed Chandler Hovey as commodore in 1939. A 1901 Harvard graduate and a lawyer, Dev Barker was a lifelong sailor who won the Puritan Cup in 1920 with his P-class *Olympian*, pioneered in the Qs and retired the class trophy in 1928 with *Hornet* (sold to Hovey in 1929), and was on the Eastern team that raced in the series with the Royal Canadian Yacht Club. He turned to cruising, first with his Seawanhaka schooner *Flytie*, then in 1937 with the Frank Paine sloop *Good Hope*, his flagship.

At seventy-three, former Navy Secretary Charles Francis Adams was back in his old form in the last peacetime season of 1939. He took the Puritan Cup for the third time, in his Eight Meter *Thisbe*, and skippered F.T. Bedford's Olin Stephens Twelve Meter *Nyala* on the NYYC Cruise to win both the Astor Cup for sloops and the King's Cup.

But the Deacon couldn't win them all. It was so thick on the line in the Challenge Cup race on July 29 that the windward boats were unable to make out the bell buoy at the other end. Charlie Adams, sailing *Thisbe*, and Richard Thayer in *Robin*, in the Eight Meter/Q-class, split tacks and didn't see each other again until the Newcomb's Ledge buoy loomed up. A luffing match toward the finish took them high of the course. Both were jibing in when Nelson Aldrich's *Armida* materialized out of the thick; he saw *Robin*, jibed, located the bell buoy dead ahead, and won. Swore Aldrich: "You could have knocked me over with a feather when I saw that bell buoy."

Hazards enough that summer. In the August 8 race, a pair of squalls off Lighthouse Point dumped six Townies and disabled twenty more, while several Thirty Squares and M-Bs had the temerity to jump the line between a tug and a tow of barges.

The year 1939 marked the appearance at Marblehead of the possibly immortal International One-Design class. Twenty-one feet on the water, 33 feet 6 inches overall, they were designed by Bjarne Aas of Norway at the behest of Cornelius Shields, Sr., who formed a syndicate to create the prototype, so smitten was he with the new Six-Meter *Saga* while racing at Bermuda in 1935. In 1937, twenty-five IODs were racing on Long Island Sound. Stanton Deland, in the *Boston Transcript* of July 26, 1939, described the manner of their arrival:

First suggestion of introducing the class at Marblehead was inspired by a cocktail on the piazza of the Eastern Yacht Club during the visit of the America's Cup sloops [in 1937] when young Arthur Knapp, member of Harold S. Vanderbilt's afterguard, strongly boosted the cause of the Internationals as the answer to Marblehead's need for a smart one-design class.

Efforts were made during the following winter to arouse sufficient interest in the formulation of this class at the Head but though the need for some such class was apparent, the campaign was washed out with the March slush. One enterprising yacht broker, however, had realized the possibilities of this craft and continued to bear it in mind and when another winter rolled around once again brought up the idea of bringing the International to Marblehead, and this time the idea carried with the result that six of these racing craft are now enrolled in the Marblehead flotilla.

All sorts of opposition were encountered in the formation of this class, the chief argument being the support of home naval architects and yacht yards. And this argument was a considerable factor in delaying the appearance of the International in Marblehead waters, but though local architects did produce designs which well matched the Norwegian product, the local yards could not match the price despite a sizeable protective tariff....

Original fleet members include: Caleb Loring's *Pompano*, which has been sailed to date by Caleb Loring, Jr., and whose record thus far is top notch; Arthur Poor's *Woodcock II*, whose skipper dominated the S Class with the original *Woodcock* for several seasons; *Gone Away*, owned by Mrs. George Patton, another S Boat skipper boasting a successful record; *Periwinkle*, owned by Mrs. Frances Copeland, whose green-hulled Triangle of the same name was long a Marblehead champion; Alexander Putnam's *Kungsornen*, whose captain, though a newcomer to Marblehead racing, has established himself a serious contender; and *Oomiak*, owned by Miss Marion Leeson, who has buffaloed the fleet more than once.

Marblehead's class troubles that gave rise to the Internationals were reviewed at about the same time by the *Transcript* yachting writer: the Os, the Ts, the Ss, the Eight Meters, the Qs, the Triangles, the Thirty Squares—all virtually gone or departed, diminished, or endangered. Guessed Deland:

If there is an answer, a good hunch is that it lies in the fickleness of the Marblehead yachtsman himself, who for some unknown reason is of a different breed than most of his neighbors and is more easily dissatisfied.... The International is at any rate secure for several years, but the fate of the now top-notch "squeaks" is more problematical. And what's to supplant the Qs and Eights? ... Classes will come, and classes will go, but who cares? Certainly not the yacht broker.

About the time Harry E. Noyes graduated (with Frank Blaney's tutoring) from his 18-footer to his first *Tioga* around 1932, he bought his older boys, Harry K. II and Pike, the M-B *Hapi*, and himself the Eight Meter *Gypsy*, from Frank Paine. He even tried starting up a couple of local classes in his boatyard—the Adams Interclub, which didn't succeed in Marblehead, and the 22-foot Sophomore, designed in 1937 by Arthur Shuman and built by George Gulliford of Lynn for $850 (spinnaker ten dollars extra).

By 1938 it was definite that the Boston Yacht Club the next year was going to revive the Marblehead-Halifax Race, founded by the Eastern back in 1905. Pike and Harry were in their late teens and confident and accomplished sailors. Their father commissioned John Alden to design for his two eldest sons the yawl *Tioga Too*, 53 feet 6 inches overall, 37 feet 6 inches waterline, 13 feet beam, and 7 feet 5 inches draft. Double-planked in bright mahogany, teak deck, with her natural spoon bow flared out into the *Tioga* clipper, she was built at his Quincy Adams yard and launched early in 1939, when the boys were eighteen and sixteen.

His inspiration, Alden wrote years later, was *Sea Fox*, a little gaff-rigged yawl half her size, that had won him his first prize money in the initial Eastern races under the Universal Rule thirty-five years earlier. According to Richard Henderson's account in *John G. Alden and His Yacht Designs*, the Buick distributor "could always locate a new car for John Alden to buy on short notice. Chet Sawtelle, Alden's son-in-law [and an Eastern member], recalls that John had a habit of watching sailboats instead of the road while driving alongside the Charles River on regatta days, and he used to rear-end the cars ahead of him with regularity. He wrecked four cars in one five-year span, and his family sometimes hoped he'd lose his driver's license before a serious accident occurred."

Tioga Too had no such propensity, for there was rarely another boat in front of her. She won sixteen of her twenty-two starts, including three firsts and two seconds in the EYC Annual Cruise and much of whatever else was up for grabs at Marblehead, including the Boston's Spring Cruising Race, top honors in the NYYC Cruise, the Edgartown Regatta, and, to clinch her reputation as the outstanding boat of the season, the revived Halifax Race in late August.

Periwinkle was among the fastest International One-designs, owner Frances Copeland a top IOD skipper.

Sailing much of the 350 miles to Halifax in fog and against light-to-moderate winds that remained with her alone in the end, *Tioga Too* beat out a fleet of fourteen by nine hours without using any of her time allowance. These included such veterans as Frank Paine in his *Gypsy*, Arthur Shuman sailing C.E. Stevens's *Essex V*, and the precocious Morss boys—Henry, Sherman, and Wells—in the schooner *Grenadier*, which won Class A. The fog and the Bay of Fundy tides were the worst, or almost. *Pirouette* grounded on Mud Island and had to power to Yarmouth, while *Kirawan II* bounced her centerboard so hard and so many times on Seal Island's rocks that it ruptured, spilled out half a ton of lead shot, and served as a sea anchor for the rest of the race.

In the thick-o'-fog, *Joy Two* was almost struck by a steamer, and George Poor's 41-foot cutter *Tinavire* of the Eastern was very nearly cut down by the cruiser *Tuscaloosa*, rushing President Roosevelt—who had hoped to be on hand for the finish August 22—back to Washington from Halifax as Hitler prepared to rush into Poland.

Harry K. and Pike Noyes, Stephen Connolly, John O'Day, Eric Shepard, all eighteen or under, and navigator Jeff Smith, with her professional skipper, R. Nelson Porter, sailed *Tioga Too* on the voyage that crowned a brilliant maiden season. In Halifax they were welcomed aboard the German liner *St. Louis*, only to be unceremoniously ushered ashore when an insistent gong called all hands, as Steve Connolly very vividly remembers his first contact with the far-off war, to get her under way for the Fatherland.

Editorializing in October on the subject of the Star World Championships sailed in August at Kiel, the *New England Yachtsman* had only praise for the German hosts:

> Although all outside communication was shut off, consulates, time tables and travel agencies were being hurriedly looked up and the contestants of many countries were being called to arms almost every hour, the Star championships went on to a successful and happy conclusion. Parties, receptions, banquets and friendly gossip all went on between the racing unmarred by the ugly war being cooked up by politicians.

Shades of another friendly, prewar German-American yachting rivalry marked by toasts to international amity.

The yawl *Tioga Too*, 53 feet overall, designed by John Alden for Harry and Pike Noyes and launched in 1939, capped a brilliant maiden season with the Halifax Race.

While his older brothers were polishing their seamanship, Bradley Noyes was just getting the feel of it under the influence of his new friend from Danvers, a kid named Frederick E. Hood, who was already a pretty good summer sailor in Marblehead. Brad had a 12-foot spritsail Dyer dinghy; they made a mast for it in the Noyes garage. The Hood boy had designed and strip-built a mahogany dinghy he called *Doohdet* (play with that one). Noyes recounted:

> Before that, Ted's first boat was a little eight-footer. He was off sailing it one winter, got into a northwester and had to sit back on the transom to keep from pitchpoling. No lifejacket. Just barreling, planing out to sea. The mast broke and probably saved his life. He jury-rigged his little boat and made it back to Marblehead Harbor. I'll bet he didn't tell you about that.

No, but the usually taciturn helmsman, sailmaker, designer, builder, broker, businessman, and Eastern member since 1951 talked about quite a lot else one morning in the office over-

Winning crew of *Tioga Too* in the 1939 Halifax Race: Sailing Master Johnny Rhyn, Steve Connolly, John O'Day, Eric Shepard (rear), Harry K. Noyes and Pike Noyes.

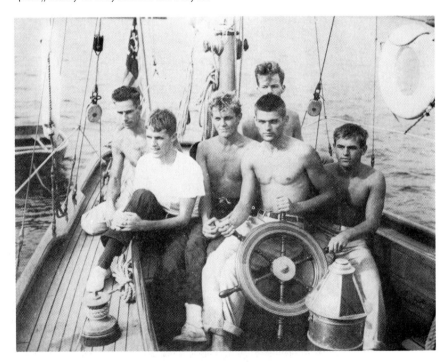

looking his new layout in Bristol, Rhode Island, the home base of an earlier Renaissance man of yachting.

I started sailing when I was a year old [Hood and Noyes were both born in 1927] at Salem Willows in a 40-foot Friendship sloop with my father and grandfather. They joined the Corinthian in 1935, and the next year my father [Stedman Hood] bought an R-Boat, the *Shrew*, which we raced, though I was just a little kid and don't know how much help I was. Three generations in one boat, I listened to them yell at each other—my grandfather was the spinnaker man—and I learned a lot.

Then they decided to get cruising and in 1938 bought Bob Leeson's 40-foot cutter *Narwhal* that had just returned from the Bermuda Race and been wrecked in the hurricane. We fixed it all up, raced in Marblehead, cruised it and lived on it summers until 1942, when we moved ashore to Marblehead from Danvers, which was only twenty minutes away anyway. My brother was younger, didn't sail as much, had a Brutal. I raced with Johnny Marvin in his Brutal, crewed with other people.

I built my first little boat that I sailed, not a racing boat, when I was thirteen or fourteen. Took an old rowboat and decked it, with centerboard trunk, seats. When I was fifteen I one-designed my own racing dinghy, round bottom, mahogany, double-spreader rig, nice-looking and sailed fine. I picked it up trial and error, living in the same household with my father and grandfather, who were electrical, chemical, and mechanical engineers, all three. All my grandfather did was invent things and go broke. He invented the first electric starter and generator and headlights for an automobile, sold it to General Electric, and with the money started building the Hoodmobile and went broke.

Then I went out and raced 110s and things like that. I think you learn a lot more racing with other good skippers than you do with your own boat. Johnny and I were the first young people to go out and race 110s. We were kids and would beat people like Linc Davis, and they'd say, "Who are these guys?" It was a big-deal boat for kids of fifteen to be in in those days. With Gus Seamans we got in an M-B once in a while, and we used to race the cruising-racing Eight Meter that his father had.

Among the visitors to Marblehead in that distant earthquake year of 1939 was Crown Prince Olaf of Norway, who sailed John Lawrence's Thirty Square *Moose* to a class triumph on July 4 and was the guest of honor on Vice Commodore Malcolm Greenough's cutter *White Lady*. Another was the U.S.S.

John Lawrence's Moose wins the Roosevelt Bowl for the Eastern, 1936.

Texas on her summer training cruise, disembarking several hundred Annapolis middies for a colorful dance in the clubhouse.

The presence in the harbor of the battleship, and the dire news from abroad, signaled that another prewar era—the finale this time of yachting even faintly reminiscent of the years before World War I—was drawing precipitously to its close. Robert Barton had joined the Eastern in the 1930s and in 1977 gave an account of his and his wife's invitation to tea aboard one of the Club's grandest yachts in that twilight of the grand style. It may be whispered discreetly that the yacht was the schooner *Constellation*, and their hosts were former Commodore Herbert Sears, a widower of many years, and a lady of his acquaintance. Barton:

She was maintained beautifully—seventeen in the crew, a captain and, I think, two mates. I was in seventh heaven. I had always wanted to go aboard. We were invited at four in the afternoon. The starboard launch was to meet us at the float at a quarter to four. My wife, in white gloves and white shoes, properly attired, walked down with me to the float. I had white flannels and white shoes, full regalia.

The starboard launch drew up with the first mate, and we were taken out, and the owner met us at the top of the ladder. Taken down to the grand saloon which went all the way across the ship, not a baby grand but a concert grand piano on one side of it, and a tea was produced for the four of us which could easily have taken care of twenty, beautifully done.

When it was over, the owner, who was very shy, said, "Barton, would you like to see the ship?" I said, "Sir, I don't want to inconvenience you, but nothing would give me greater pleasure." "Very well, come with me."

So we went down to his quarters. They were magnificent. Next, we came up, and he began to show me the various staterooms. Then he went on to the motor, which had been a late installation in the ship. We worked our way back to the grand saloon, and I saw him look at the door going out to the galley and the crew's quarters. And he took a deep breath and said, "Would you like to see the galley?" "Well," I said, "I don't know whether that would be convenient or not, but there's not a part of this lovely vessel that isn't fascinating to me." "Very well,"" he said, "let's go."

With that he opened the door. I strode out right behind him. The chef was sitting up on the counter. His mouth fell open, he gave one look and fell off. The owner then turned and walked up to the crew's quarters. Some of them were lying in their bunks. They gasped. All of them got up and stood at attention. We walked all the way up to the forepeak, looking over the whole thing like a child going to Disneyland. We came back through the galley, the chef leaning up against the stove in a state of near-collapse.

We went up into the cockpit, which was enormous, with wicker chairs and so forth. "Sir," I said, "it must be wonderful to sit out here on a nice evening and, you know, you're up high and see everything."

"Oh yes," he said. "Very interesting, Barton, sitting out here. You're high up off the water, and you hear everything. People coming in on boats, particularly with the motor running, don't understand how far their voices carry over the water. And you can't imagine the things that I hear. Just the other night some people were coming in on a small yacht with the motor running, and I heard the owner say, 'Oh, there's one of the largest yachts, you know, and owned, you know, by a real plutocrat, oh yes, and there's the old bastard sitting up there now!' The lady who was sitting beside him said, 'Oh dear! Such language!'"

I can imagine him sitting up there each evening, and of course he heard everything. I said, "Sir, at least you know what the fleet thinks about you, don't you?"

He replied, "I certainly do, Barton. I certainly do."

On another occasion, so the story goes, two young girls were rowing around *Constellation*, descanting audibly on her beauty to the delight of Commodore Sears, who hailed them to come aboard for a better look. "Oh, no!" they demurred. "We know you yachtsmen!"

Ray Hunt had been in the afterguard of *Yankee* in the 1934 trials, occasionally taking the helm, while understudying Frank Paine at the drawing board until 1938, when he was on his own. His first outstanding design, *Java*, was the prototype of the classic Concordia yawl for Llewellyn Howland of South Dartmouth, who had lost his previous boat in the hurricane.

Giving an inkling of his versatility, Hunt the same year took advantage of the new marine plywood (four by eight feet) and conceived the futuristic, flat-bottomed, fin-keeled, 24-foot (three sheets to the wind), double-ended wedge of the 110 (square feet of sail) class. With its 300-pound cast iron fin keel, the 110 was the first of the semiplaning hulls and destined to be one of the most popular and long-lived learning and racing classes in the world. George Lawley built them for $350 each, and they beat everything in sight except the Stars in the 1939 Race Week.

A dozen 110s were entered in the 1940 Midsummer Series, which was officially but mistakenly identified as the Fiftieth Anniversary Race Week; it should have been 1939, since the Corinthian's first Midsummer Series was in 1889. There could

have been no more appropriate winner of the Fowle Memorial Trophy for the outstanding performance of the week than Charles Francis Adams, who at seventy-four took seven straight in the Eight Meter class with *Thisbe*.

A new feature of North Shore racing was the first Guy Lowell Memorial Cup Race on August 18, conceived by the new Race Committee chairman, John R.C. McBeath, in honor of the late architect and avid EYC sailor. (This new trophy seems to have been offered in addition to the cups put up for several years by Mrs. Lowell in memory of her husband.) Sixteen started in Class A over 30 feet waterline and twenty-two in Class B under 30.

The final full season of sailing before America's entry into World War II was in 1940, and it was plagued by fluky breezes or none at all.

Frank Crowninshield was obsessed with FDR. He peppered the *Barge*'s log, as the New Deal wore on, with "Regular Roosevelt weather" (always the worst kind), and when he found the new Deer Isle Bridge barring his progress through "Egamoggin" Reach the previous season, he was beside himself:

> Now, alas! it is no longer possible to have that pleasure, thanks to our beloved President, who, in order to assist his re-election, in the good American way, has seen fit to spend some millions of other people's money building a bridge across it, which no one wants and very few use. A regular ROOSEVELT proceeding.

And then in Newport, in June 1940, "there were practically no yachts there last week and the same is true today. Roosevelt and his cursed war have seen to that."

Charles L. Harding's Twelve Meter *Anitra* was the first to round what was apparently the Club's erroneously located turning mark for the first leg of the Annual Regatta that final year of American peace. She sailed several miles on the windward leg before the rest of the pack had located the spar and turned. A hauling but dying breeze helped her home, and a feather from the southeast wafted her across the line to the Puritan Cup while the rest were becalmed and then had to beat to the finish.

The 1940 Annual Cruise to Northeast Harbor, the last cruise before the war, was marked by forgettable light airs and an unforgettable parade on July 7 from Kittery to Boothbay Harbor, led by the schooner *Constellation*. The fleet reorganized itself into a cocktail party aboard, hosted by ex-Commodore

The Winds of War Again

The 110s, Ray Hunt's double-ended invention of plywood that revolutionized one-design sailing, off to a flying start on the Inside Line.

Sears. Had anyone but known, an era breathed its last then and there on the sweeping deck of the venerable Queen of the Fleet.

After *Tioga's* triumphal if less than winning sprint from New London to Marblehead in 1938, that prototypical ocean race ran into the 1940 doldrums, and only two of the five schooners and seven of the thirteen in Class B finished. Frank Paine's *Gypsy* won the Lambert Trophy just before the wind gave out altogether. The following year's race ended the revived classic (before Pearl Harbor changed everything) and was sailed mainly in the fog and even slower; the cup went to Arthur W. Page's New York Forty *Rampage II* in anything but that.

Robert Barton got in on the last legs of the Eastern's brief Lambert Trophy ocean-racing revival and treasured his memories:

This race was always held rather early in June. The start was on the Saturday after the Harvard-Yale crew race at New London so the captains and crews could leave their offices at noon, get to New London in time to take in the Varsity crew race in the late afternoon, enjoy the night-long celebrations over all New London and hopefully have enough stamina left to get their boats over the starting line Saturday morning.

Many a race was started in a dense fog. The current at Race Point was invariably against the fleet, and woe betide any boat that was more than twenty feet away from the buoy at the Point, since if it was, its captain and crew need only wave goodbye to the rest of the fleet, as they were carried at six miles an hour towards New York.

Fog in Vineyard Sound and among the constantly changing sand bars on the back of the Cape was practically always present at night. Heavy commercial traffic came through the Slough at full speed. A few toylike radio-telephones had come into use, but the rules precluded talking over them.

Before one race [according to Barton's version] Walter Rothschild had acquired one of the first radio direction finders. His lovely yawl *Avanti* had come down on the sand bars at the time of a full moon and high tide. There were no turning point buoys down there since no one in his right senses would cut across the bars at night. Rothschild, with his direction finder and high tide, took a chance, went right across and found himself out in front of the fleet by about three hours. He thought the situation over for a few minutes, turned on his radio-telephone, and reported to the Race Committee that he was giving up the race and returning to New York.

Europe was in shambles, and the draft was tooling up. The roster had dropped from 442 to 409 as young members joined the armed services when the January 1941 meeting empowered the Council to remit, suspend, or modify dues of men going off to what looked more each day like a fighting war. The April general meeting created service memberships for commissioned officers, who could be elected for a season upon ap-

plication in writing by two members and without the usual notification of the entire membership: no entrance fee, ten dollar dues, and no voting, officeholding, or equity rights.

The deepening world crisis at first affected the fleet, that sensitive barometer of change, even more dramatically than it did the membership. The number of yachts over 30 feet waterline in 1941 dropped from 197 to 157; under 30, from 110 to 83. There were other signs. So few members indicated an interest in the Annual Cruise that it was scratched. The new class of 110s nearly doubled, but Cape Cod Shipbuilding in Wareham was appointed class builder for the east because Lawley's in Neponset was committed to defense work.

And the Council approved a Committee on Nautical Instruction comprised of Gordon Abbott, Leonard Fowle, and John McBeath—an innovation that may be traced back to a concern expressed by Fowle in a 1938 issue of *New England Yachting News*:

> Marblehead is falling steadily behind other Atlantic Coast racing ports in developing racing yachtsmen. Since the early 1920 era that produced the Thayers, Gray, Shuman, and Davis, almost no first-class helmsmen have come up from the junior ranks except "Buss" Hovey, who received his early training on Buzzards Bay. . . . Marblehead is the only major racing port on the Atlantic Coast without regular nautical instruction for junior yachtsmen. . . . The consequences may be grave indeed, in the opinion of a considerable body of prominent yachtsmen, if steps are not taken soon to mend this situation.

In 1942, seventy-five pupils enrolled in the Eastern's new nautical instruction course.

Nevertheless, all this straw and even debris in the wind was but chaff before the day former Commodore Gerard Lambert turned his flagship, the great three-masted schooner *Atlantic*, and his power yacht *Utilitie* over to the Coast Guard for patrol work. And when he ordered his—the Eastern's own—J-boat *Yankee* broken up for scrap and then donated the proceeds toward the purchase of a warplane for Britain—and had a section cut from her mast as the base for a coffee table in the Club's living room—that day his fellow members knew it was all too real.

From the *North Shore Breeze*, April 4, 1941:

> We regret to report that owing to uncertain conditions next summer, as well as the loss of his sailing master, Captain Shofus Larson, former Commodore Herbert M. Sears has decided

Officers of the Eastern Yacht Club in 1941: Rear Commodore Henry A. Morss, Jr., Race Committee Chairman J.R.C. McBeath, Secretary J. Amory Jeffries, Commodore B. Devereux Barker, Treasurer Stephen W. Sleeper, retiring Secretary Morgan H. Harris, and House Committee Chairman George E. Stephenson.

The Winds of War Again

not to put the grand fifty-two-year-old schooner *Constellation* into commission the coming season. *Constellation* will remain at Lawley's in charge of the mate, while her engineer will run the launch with its dog house, between Beverly and Marblehead.

The Japanese bombed Pearl Harbor, and Herbert Sears knew the time of parting was at hand. But he could not bear to think of her abused or neglected on patrol or on duty as a dirty lighter. *Constellation* was iron, desperately needed in the war effort to make up for the scrap we had been sending to Japan for years.

And so the commodore had her broken up and melted down. His action sounded the knell of the gentleman's sport as irreversibly as if Herbert Sears had sailed his big black schooner off soundings and scuttled her, which was reportedly his first impulse as war descended on land and sea. He saved *Constellation*'s wheel and transom and gave them to his Club. Within two months, on February 19, 1942, he was dead at the age of seventy-four.

The Council decided to open the clubhouse in May of 1942, partly on the assumption that there would be no wartime restrictions on travel to Marblehead Neck, and with the determination to run in the black. Travelers to the Neck after dark, however, soon were required to identify themselves; members and guests were issued passes; and the Town of Marblehead borrowed the Club's tennis house and moved it to the causeway as a guard station. Everything was cloaked in the coastal blackout against the prowling German submarines, and more or less stalled by the rationing of gasoline.

Notwithstanding ever harsher strictures, careful management under Commodore Barker's direction produced a profit of nearly $4,000 in the first year of the war—this in the face of dues abatements for fifty-six members in the service, leaving 306 to carry on. Helping the situation was the decision to invite members of the Corinthian to use the dining and other public rooms in exchange for access to their house, pool and tennis courts (a reciprocation of Corinthian hospitality when the Navy occupied the Eastern during World War I). Hoping to forestall resignations among the assessment-shy, the Council broadcast the bottom line in mid-September. As a further economy, the usual listing of yachts (many were not in commission), the full-color display of owners' private signals, the racing rules, signal code, and some other sections were omitted from the 1942 Yearbook.

The Battle of Britain was at its climax when Frank Crown-

inshield saw the hated handwriting on September 5, 1940, while daysailing from Marblehead in the *Barge*. They passed four of the President's Lend-Lease destroyers bound for Canada, "to be given over," as the old Anglophobe jabbed in his log, "to the only country on this earth which has ever abused us . . . all done really to make a smoke screen for a Roosevelt third term, an act of war itself. And what made it some hundred per cent more horrible was that one of the four was named *Crowninshield*. The vessel that dear little Emily Davis, now Mrs. Eugene Record, christened not so many years ago."

Keno fell ill the following day and was hospitalized, so it turned out to be their last sail in *Cleopatra's Barge II*. The Coast Guard drafted her for offshore patrol and submarine watch duty, along with the Noyeses' *Tioga*, William T. Aldrich's converted M-sloop *Valiant*, and other large yachts.

Model of *Constellation* in the Eastern clubhouse evokes the genius of Edward Burgess. Note length of bowsprit, fine ends, relatively shoal draft, centerboard, maintopsail jackyard, and spinnaker pole nearly the length of the foremast above deck. Clive Russ photo.

(Harry E. Noyes, *Tioga*'s superenergetic owner, like Waldo Brown from whom he bought her predecessor, died in an airplane crash in 1940 during a snowstorm over Hartford in a Stinson Reliant. Although trained as a pilot, he was not at the controls at the time.)

Even the committee boat was commandeered by the Coast Guard Academy as its race committee boat at New London, leaving only one launch in service. (Commodore Barker convinced the War Shipping Board to pay $2,512 for it; the Club bought it back in 1944 for $1,100.)

Yacht skippers returning from a tour of sub patrol were supposed to report in at a small shed on the Corinthian pier. The story is told of the practical joker who rigged a signal cannon with a string to the door. When the first poor patriot checked in from an all-night stint on the black, U-boat-infested Atlantic and grabbed the door handle in the wee hours, he was damned near blasted back into the harbor.

In spite of cannons and enemies lurking underwater, small-boat racing continued on a reduced scale. Pleasure craft were banned beyond certain points without sparingly granted Coast Guard permits that required photographs and fingerprints. The 1942 season did not get going until June 20, when the Coast Guard established the outer limits as a line from the Neck to Children's Island to Baker's Island. The inside line was moved inshore to start from the porch of the Corinthian—to the delight of spectators at Lighthouse Point and Fort Sewall—not to revert to Marblehead Rock until 1946. Largely on the insistence of Race Committee Chairman McBeath, the Saturday Series and Race Week were allowed to come off. The Coast Guard granted permits for the Boston Bay and Cape Ann boats to be towed in for Race Week under its protection and assigned its Auxiliary to patrol each event.

Brad Noyes and Ted Hood, both fifteen that summer, made traps and went lobstering. "I really started liking sail when I bought my 110 *Hapi* in 1942," says Noyes. "I had good luck racing her and won the New Englands in 1944. In the summer we sailed all the time during the war, toward Manchester, staying inside the bell off Marblehead Rock and Baker's. There were the 110s, Town class, and Brutal Beasts."

That year, 1942, the Fowle Trophy was awarded to former Commodore Curtis, still going strong at eighty-one, for his lifelong competitive skill and sportsmanship.

By 1943 the manpower shortage eliminated the Sunday night suppers and movies, although the clubhouse and the Sa-moset were kept open. The balance sheet continued in the black despite the dues abatement of seventy-two members in the service and a heavy repair bill after the collapse of a piazza roof, which alerted town officials, in the words of a Club officer, "to condemn everything in sight." Gas rationing kept the one launch at the float and members in their dinghies until late in August.

The tide of the Battle of the Atlantic had turned, and German U-boats were so rarely reported along the coast that the Coast Guard allowed the outside racing mark to be extended off Halfway Rock, although it would not authorize towing the Boston Bay fleet to Race Week, when only 798 boats crossed the line.

While the land war in Europe finally was looking up with the Normandy invasion, the hard-pressed U-boats were keeping so clear of the coast by the spring of 1944 that the Coast Guard lifted all restrictions on sailing and allowed racing on the prewar lines, with no limits to seaward. Yachtsmen were cautioned, however, to "report anything unusual and be careful not to contact any floating object"—namely, stray mines. Several large yachts, such as *Tioga* and *Cleopatra's Barge II*, were released from war service to their old moorings—some still in grey, some service-disabled beyond the redemptive capabilities of putty, white paint, and spar varnish.

Before he signed up in the Navy, Brad Noyes would row out to the mooring and pump out his late father's last boat. But it was too much for the family to cope with; a tug towed her back to the Quincy Adams yard. In 1946 they sold her—but not her name—to Allan P. Carlisle, who ingeniously rechristened her *Ticonderoga*. As "Big Ti," she sailed the seas to glories ever greater, and when last heard from was in Palm Beach undergoing a thorough rebuild.

Frank Crowninshield was told that the *Barge*, the love of *his* life next to Louise, had spent only a few weeks at sea. "In the fall of '43 she was returned to us, what was left of her, I mean. The Captain said it would have made you cry could you have seen her. What they hadn't done to her never was done to a boat."

By then Keno was seventy-five and no longer had the heart for it. He and Louise were awarded $25,041 in damages, and in November 1944, they sold the *Barge* to a man who renamed her *Gee Gee*—and kept her in Marblehead. Names, hails, owners, and years later, she was in the Caribbean under the Panamanian flag.

With the virtual departure of the U-boats, the blackout had been relieved, but not the manpower shortage, so there was insufficient help to oblige members who requested a resumption of the Sunday suppers and cinema. For the same reason, the House Committee discontinued the cooperative arrangement with the Corinthian because it could no longer provide the extra food and service. An additional rationale was footnoted some years later by Commodore Barker: "Since longtime guests tend to consider themselves members, two years proved to be enough."

And still the Club profited in these reef-taking times, and looked to the future. The New York Yacht Club had broken with its long tradition of independence in finally joining the North American Yacht Racing Union in 1942, and on January 11, 1944, the membership of the Eastern followed, on recommendation of the Council. According to John Parkinson, Clinton Crane, president of the NAYRU, wrote that "he was very happy when Charles Francis Adams helped him to persuade the conservative Eastern Yacht Club of Marblehead to join the organization too."

Another watershed was in process. That anemometer of the times, Race Week, was winding up again. There was an average of 166 daily starters in 1944, compared with a hundred in 1943. Lincoln Davis, Jr.'s *Javelin* and Francis Copeland's *Periwinkle* were tied in the International One-Designs; Davis came out the winner, not by a match race as the committee proposed, but by a toss of a coin by telephone. The 110 and Town classes took off with the younger generation; George O'Day, Bradley Noyes, John Marvin, and Barbara and Ellen Connolly starred in Ray Hunt's startling creations; Lars Anderson and his *Avant* led the Townies. After an enrollment dip in 1943, the nautical training program resurged in 1944, encouraging Commodore Barker to predict that the Club would come out of the war in a strong and vital condition.

With the end of the fighting in sight, talk returned to the future, to the resumption of full-scale yachting activity in the postwar period, to sailors returning from service, to the new generation coming along, to old boats and possibly outmoded classes, and to the direction the one-designs would take when it was all over and the recent past had again become prologue.

An effort by Homer M. Clark to inoculate Marblehead with the Star-class virus failed. Race Committee Chairman McBeath commissioned John Alden to sketch a 22-foot sloop with a large cockpit and wide beam as an intermediate racer for juniors who had outgrown the Brutal Beast. He unveiled the plans at the October general meeting, contending that the M-B knockabout was too expensive and too difficult for young sailors to handle, while the 110s, as far as he was concerned, were "probably the most uncomfortable boats ever built and most impractical for sailing by older people"—leading one observer to comment that that may have had something to do with their popularity with the younger set.

Not only did the McBeath-Alden boat never get off the ground, but the 110s continued to dominate youthful racing and in fact grew in the fertile brain of Ray Hunt into the full-size, 30-foot, plywood International 210, which he would unveil in July 1945. Meanwhile, in 1944, a group of owners of M-Bs and other prewar classes, including Eugene Connolly and Lincoln Davis, commissioned Carl Alberg of Alden's office to line off a more traditional, open-cockpit sequel that would combine the best points of the Thirty Square Meter rig with those of the International One-Design hull. This was the U.S. One-Design. Recalled Gene Connolly:

We told Carl what we wanted, he drew up the plans, and we sat down on the floor and went over the designs to tell him what we wanted changed and what we thought was great. He got hold of the Quincy Adams Yard in Quincy to build the boat, but they couldn't do it until after the war.

Perhaps the most significant war-induced change at the Club was more symptomatic than substantive at the time—a change suggestive of deep and far-reaching social and economic currents that would affect the entire course of yachting and of the Eastern's future. As a reaction to the exodus of two-home families from Boston to take up year-round residence in Marblehead and on the North Shore generally, the bylaws were amended in 1944 to hold the second general meeting at the clubhouse in Marblehead between June 15 and July 31 rather than in Boston on the second Tuesday in April. Accordingly, the first general meeting of the Eastern Yacht Club ever held on the Neck instead of in Boston was on July 10, 1945. That year a further amendment provided that the second and third general meetings be held on the last Tuesdays in June and August in the clubhouse.

The available members of the New York Yacht Club and their guests celebrated its centennial on December 14, 1944, at a breast-of-chicken dinner. The Eastern was represented at this austere (except for the champagne) birthday party by

Commodore Barker and Charles Francis Adams, the speaker, who addressed his remarks to the part yachtsmen were playing in the war.

The part that one Eastern yachtsman had played in the war came to an end on April 12, 1945. FDR was the second Roosevelt to be an Honorary Member by virtue of his office, dating back to the beginning of his first term in 1933 when he cruised east in fellow member Paul Rust's schooner *Amberjack II*. The Club, of course, was a lonely bastion of Republicanism, and it is amusing to note that until 1942 "That Man in the White House" headed the list of Honorary Members in the Yearbook as "President Franklin D. Roosevelt." Thereafter he was simply "Honorable Franklin D. Roosevelt"—almost as if the mere utterance of the office was too much to take. At his death in 1945, his name was stricken from the rolls, and no President has been so honored since.

And so came V-E Day on May 7, 1945, and the end of World War II in Europe. Even as members returning from the service were recommissioning their hibernating boats, a surprise squall of near-hurricane strength in late June tore several large cruising yachts from their moorings and swept away numerous floats, tenders, and racing marks. Still, Race Week was the biggest since 1941. It was dampened by another blow that canceled the Eastern's third day, but enlivened by a twenty-mile cruising class race to the Boston Lightship won by Thomas L. Shepard's 61-foot Alden-designed *Irondequoit II*—named sentimentally by her owner after his first, and favorite, and launched by Lawley in 1940.

Having cosponsored the U.S. One-Designs, Lincoln Davis changed his mind and bought one of the 210s that were racing in their maiden season. He was elected the Club's representative to the 210 Class Committee, which picked Graves of Marblehead as one of the three official builders.

The New London-Marblehead race and the Annual Regatta and Annual Cruise were still in mothballs, but there were stirrings. Commodore Barker bought the Twelve Meter *Gleam* from NAYRU President Crane, and John H. Blodgett bought the 64-foot schooner *Mistral*, designed by Francis Herreshoff in 1938, and had her reconditioned after Coast Guard service. She would be a jewel in the harbor's crown for many years to come.

Was the war bringing a tidal wave of change, seemingly distant but all too discernible? Several members at a late August 1945 special meeting hoped that the membership could be restored to former levels without compromising standards, and that the Club would be able to attract more junior members and children of regulars, for it was noticed that youngsters had used the facilities only rarely during the season.

Marblehead was rapidly becoming a bedroom community for Boston, and, like it or not, the Eastern would never again be *the* sanctuary of wealthy male summer residents who sailed large yachts and ruled their quarterdecks afloat and their porches at home.

The first breath of a change quite as profound in its way was whispered in an article in the July 1945 issue of *Yachting* entitled "The First All-Plastic Sail Boat Hull." The Columbian Rope Company was producing a 16-foot one-design, centerboard sloop designed by Sparkman & Stephens and constructed—if one could give credence to such nonsense—of sisal fiber in a plastic binder patented as "Co-Ro-Lite." This creation was rigged with Du Pont nylon sails, of all things, by Ratsey & Lapthorn.

It was claimed that four men could produce two of these plastic hulls in an hour.

The Old Order Changeth

Chapter 15   **The Old Order Changeth**   *1946–1949*

It is well to recall, as the Eastern Yacht Club ghosts through the blackout of World War II into modern times, that it was founded after the Civil War by men of "wealth and high character" (and lofty spars) for the purpose, as their charter of 1871 set forth, "of encouraging yacht building and naval architecture, and the cultivation of nautical science."

Could a club of such rarefied rationale and roster survive such a boat-rocking as the world had just barely survived, and thrive? Whether fully recognized or not, the leveling effects of the income tax, the Depression, the attempts of the New Deal to cope with it, the war, and the ebb and flow of history were rearranging the foundations of American life.

Gone from the top stratum, as if torpedoed, were the great yachts of yore with their protocol and professionals. The North Shore's Georgian estates were being sold off, and the next generation was setting up housekeeping in the gate lodge. Labor-intensive production, conspicuous consumption, and male dominance were on the wane; war-born technology, built-in obsolescence, informality, and women and children were the new wave.

The young men were coming home, eager to make up for lost time. Outwardly, things didn't look so different. But the breeze was piping up, and there was a new message borne on the wind: Pile on sail or be left behind.

Commodore Barker's seven years of leadership had spanned the war and kept the breath of life in the Club; he turned over the helm to Rufus C. Cushman in 1946. The House Committee, under its new chairman, John Blodgett, raised more than $13,000 for an improvement fund to renovate the interior of the clubhouse, with the goal of attracting younger members. Paradoxically, although it had run in the black through the

war, and dues income was up with the return of veterans, the resumption of regular activities was tipping the Club into the red.

After four years of limitations that verged on suspension of competitive sailing in Marblehead, racing came back like a squall out of Salem Bay. John McBeath's Race Committee, beefed up from five to eight members, ran the first Annual Regatta since 1941 on the Fourth of July. Joseph Santry's Class Q sloop *Taygeta* shook off ex-Commodore Barker's Twelve Meter *Gleam*, the scratch boat, for the Puritan Cup. The resumed Annual Cruise to Provincetown and the islands featured Ray Hunt's latest attention-getter, his 38-foot plywood 510 sloop *Diana*, which dominated Class B (over 30 feet).

However, all was not as it had been. In late-season meetings, it was suggested that nonracing yachts be better accommodated in the future, that ports of call be notified in advance of the fleet's arrival, that evening social events be more extensive and better organized, and that cruising as well as racing boats be notified about them. The membership recommended that the Council appoint a cruising committee to achieve these ends.

The most exciting immediate postwar development was the unveiling of the first fleet of U.S. One-Designs, contracted for (a minimum of a dozen at $3,500 each, complete; cabintop $250 extra) by representatives of the three Marblehead clubs with the Quincy Adams Yacht Yard in November 1945. Dimensions were: length overall 37 feet 9 inches, length on the waterline 24 feet, beam 7 feet, draft 5 feet 4 inches, displacement 6,450 pounds, sail area 378 square feet, mahogany-planked and bronze-fastened.

Quincy Adams was still owned by the Noyes family. "We

The Old Order Changeth

took a bath on those," remembers Brad Noyes. "We sold them for $3,300 less sails, and they cost us over $6,000." He bought one anyway. He really wanted an International One-Design, but Norway obviously hadn't been building any for export for some time.

Eugene Connolly's *Leenane* (traditionally a family boat name, after the coastal town northwest of Galway, seat of the Connollys) was assigned sail Number 1. Number 12 went to Charles H.W. Foster, going strong at eighty-six. *Jennifer* was his fifty-ninth boat, give or take one or two, and, one may tentatively venture, his last. He promptly converted her to staysail ketch, and under her "Foster rig," *Jennifer* and Charlie were a familiar and sentimental sight on the water.

Six U.S. Ones raced for the first time, in the Eastern's series, on July 20, 1946, then competed in a lively Race Week (during which the historic battleship *Missouri* lay outside the harbor; the officers were entertained at a cocktail party in the clubhouse), and *Leenane* won the Club championship for the year.

The sleek, fine-ended U.S. One-Design was probably about as racy a boat as John Alden was willing to be associated with. Editor William H. Taylor put it in a nutshell in his 1962 *Yachting* series on his old friend:

> As so often happens, the apostle of a new type of yacht of the 1920's had become the conservative designer of the 1945–55 decade. There was little "fisherman style" in the lines or rigs of most post-World War II Alden boats, but neither were there any of the radical features in looks or performance that characterized many new boats. If you wanted something on the "freakish" side, you found a cool reception around 131 State Street.
>
> Many owners who wanted "a ship as is like a ship" came to John, and they were by no means all old-time shellbacks. Alden boats—old and new—kept right on winning races, besides cruising happily from port to port and—in a few cases—around the world.

Evers Burtner extolled what he called the Golden Age of open class racing at Marblehead—from the rage for the Sonders in 1906 until the outbreak of the war in 1940—in a talk at the winter meeting of the Eastern in 1966 (subsequently published in a small pamphlet). By "open class," Marblehead's long-time

---

Everything pulling, the U.S. One-designs—the first postwar class—show their class (all but one, that is). Lawrence Lowry photo.

measurer meant yachts, often by different designers, with specifications within the latitude allowed by the Universal and International rules and boiling down to load waterline, or in certain cases other parameters such as sail area.

Was development ashore over these thirty-four-odd years advanced at the expense of competition afloat? Professor Burtner didn't see it quite that way, but then his professional interests and loyalties were involved—and why not? His comment:

> Although the New York Yacht Club first adopted the Universal Rule and used it during Club Cruises and for important Cup contests, its members did not support open class racing as Marblehead and members of some clubs at other centers did. They often preferred to go to Nat Herreshoff as a group and order a class of one-design yachts, all of which were built at the Bristol, R.I., plant to Nat's design.
>
> Possibly, they thought this procedure would provide them a finer yacht for a given investment; furthermore, it would produce more even racing. (Could they have wanted to deter those skilled Massachusetts Bay boys from annexing too much silverware?) It did give the New York Yacht Club the option of setting up races for their one-design classes alone or races which would include their one-design classes and non-one-design yachts of equivalent rating. . . .
>
> World War II, higher income taxes, coupled with more expense for yacht building and maintenance, combined to greatly reduce open class racing after 1940.

The objective of the founding fathers of the Eastern to encourage yacht building and naval architecture was matched by their determination to promote the cultivation of nautical science. And so the nautical instruction program for the juniors, which had been suspended between 1943 and 1945, was reinstituted under Yale student Raymond Young. In the morning, there were classes in "elementary and marlinspike seamanship, boat maintenance, coastwise navigation or piloting, racing tactics and yacht etiquette," and in the afternoon, sailing and racing tactics on the water. Twelve dollars for the season.

And the North Shore Junior Championship Races were revived. Gene Connolly, Jr., won the Curtis Cup—twice—when an accident prevented the committee boat from reaching the finish line the first time.

W. Starling Burgess, that genius son of genius—the very walls of the Eastern Yacht Club had pulsed with the souls of the two for sixty years—died of a heart attack on March 19, 1947, at sixty-eight. As fascinated with the "freakish" as ever,

The general alarm fire of June 9, 1947, heavily damaged the southwest wing before it was brought under control.

he had designed, under contract with Alcoa and even before the war, a high-speed aluminum destroyer that for various unfortunate reasons should have been but never was built. Swallowing his disappointment, he threw himself into anti-submarine research for the Navy. His last years were crowned with domestic happiness.

A few weeks after Burgess's untimely death, the House Committee's refurbishing plans got a rude setback. Early in the morning of June 9, a few days before the opening, a general-alarm fire swept from the kitchen through the main dining room in the southwest wing, the quarters of the Pleon Yacht Club below, guest rooms, the tower, and the piazza before it was stopped by the Marblehead, Lynn, Salem, and Swampscott fire departments. Damage was estimated at $50,000.

The blaze was discovered by Police Captain Howard McGee, who was cruising by and called in the alarm. Employees and member Francis Cummings of Prides Crossing, who was staying overnight, evidently did not awake until the arrival of the apparatus. Firemen helped a waitress, a desk clerk, and telephone operator Frances Gilliland through the smoke and down fire escapes.

Cummings, head waiter William Samuelson, and a chef were asleep in another part of the clubhouse and escaped. According to Frances Gilliland, Cummings tossed a couple of sailbags (doubtless belonging to his new 210 *Janet*, in which he was destined to win the Massachusetts Bay class championship in September) out his window before taking to the front stairs in blue pajamas and a straw hat, with a third sailbag slung over his shoulder.

When it looked as if the fire might spread, Manager Nicholas F. Shea, his staff, along with Vice Commodore James J. Storrow and member James C. Gray and his sons Pete and Billy, who lived nearby, evacuated models and trophies, including *Constellation*'s wheel, from the trophy room. Smoke and water damage to most of the rest of the clubhouse was extensive, and the Corinthian offered access to its dining facilities. Thus was urgency imparted to the postwar course of the Club, and the

The main dining room gutted by the fire of June 9, 1947.

The Old Order Changeth

direction reconstruction should take was warmly discussed for the rest of the year.

Fascination with sailing was reaching chain-reaction proportions nationally. One spark was the popularization of "freakish" but furiously fast boats like Ray Hunt's 110s and 210s designed for simple plywood construction. Another was the appearance of synthetics such as nylon, used in the war for parachutes and clothing and now adapted for spinnakers and line, finishes, seam compound, glue, and hardware. Given added impetus by aeronautical science, the technological avalanche, so long held at bay by conservative yachtsmen and builders, was overtaking the sport and the industry.

One of the leaders of the new breed was Lincoln Davis, Jr., a top Thirty Square helmsman who had jumped into the 210 championship in his *Amourette*—and into the debate about the merits of nylon, from which some lofts had been cutting sails right after the war when they were unable to obtain cotton. Some who tried the tough but stretchable fabric thought it wouldn't hold its shape in a mainsail or jib, but Linc flew a whole suit on *Amourette* and swore that was what made her fly.

Ted Hood, out of the Navy in the fall of 1946 at nineteen, went back to finish high school. When they were seventeen, he and Brad Noyes had gone to Salem with their mothers one day in 1945 and signed up—Ted because "I was behind in school from fiddling with boats instead of studying." Before the service, Hood had been buying the cloth and making the sails for the little boats he built. Now, in his spare time and that first summer or two, he made cotton sails for Brutal Beasts and 110s, which worked well, and a whole suit with bigger roaches than the others for Johnny Marvin's 110, which worked even better. Why? "Dunno. Put a little more roach in them, made them a little fuller. Just observed. The other sails didn't look right, and I thought I could make 'em better, and I did."

After high school, young Hood went for a year to Bryant and Stratton Business School, then for two years to "good old Wentworth Institute" in Boston.

That was why I ended up in construction. Not that I used what I learned there too much, but it's all helpful. I can still lay a brick faster than a union guy can do it. Took design, the whole works. A lot who went there were sons of big contractors like John Volpe. We did the whole thing, built a whole house right inside the building, plastered it, laid the brick, made chimneys.

Later, that's why we did all our own contracting in building the loft in Marblehead.

We bought the IOD *Princess* around 1947. I made sails for her, and we did well, and then all the IODs bought them. But when I got out of Wentworth I couldn't get a job as a sailmaker. Went down to Marion Cooney's loft in Gloucester, and they said you gotta belong to the union.

So I started building houses. My first house—up on Bubier Road between John Newhall's and the water—I had it all designed and started building, and the next-door neighbor went to the owner and said, "Anything you got in it, plus five thousand dollars, if you don't keep building it." Well, five thousand was a lot back then. So the guy took the five thousand and what he had in it, and that was the end of my contracting business.

Race Week in the second war-free season of 1947 started more than fifty 210s, fifty-nine 110s and four divisions of Brutal Beasts. Practically every record was smashed: 3,637 boats in forty-five classes; 522 on August 6 alone, (first time ever over 500 in one day). The Eastern gunned off its own record

---

The swift, double-ended 210s were among the first to window the jib. Robert Sides photo.

total of 126 for the Saturday Series on August 12. As many as fifteen U.S. Ones were on the line all summer. The temporarily burned-out Pleon celebrated its sixtieth birthday as the nation's oldest junior club with two successive record-breaking Sunday afternoons.

Former Commodore Barker won his second Puritan Cup in twenty-seven years, this time with his Twelve Meter *Gleam*; in 1920 he did it in his 31-rater *Olympian*. The Manhasset Bay Challenge Cup Regatta, resumed under the sponsorship of the Cohasset Yacht Club, was won by Linc Davis, and Barbara Connolly sailed to her second straight North Shore Women's Championship. In late August, the M.I.T. Nautical Association sailed its fourth annual 110 championship out of the Club with thirteen fleets from as far off as Honolulu.

And in an inspired act of civic sportsmanship, former Commodore Chandler Hovey gave the Town of Marblehead $5,000 with which to purchase what was ultimately known as Hovey Park on Lighthouse Point so that the public could view the races forever and ever.

Through snowfall and into next spring drove the uncapped head of steam, with the revival of winter dinghy racing after a ten-year lapse. Ray Hunt, Charles Pickering, and George O'Day started the Marblehead Frostbite Club with 12-foot "Waterbugs" designed by and chartered from the ever-inventive Hunt.

In a to-hell-with-the-mines gesture, the Cruising Club in 1946 had taken the lead in resuming blue-water competition with the first Bermuda Race since 1938, even as the New York Yacht Club relinquished another increment of cherished autonomy and adopted the CCA Rule of measurement. In 1947 the Boston Yacht Club and the Royal Nova Scotia Yacht Squadron sponsored the Halifax Race, the first since 1939.

But the Club held the New London-Marblehead Ocean Race in abeyance for another season, although it scheduled the first postwar Annual Cruise to the eastward as far as Penobscot Bay. Frank Paine's 53-foot *Gypsy*, his last yacht, danced ahead most of the time; she was a unique double-ender, strip-planked over five bulkheads, no frames. Hunt's mentor would race her until his death and chalk up a remarkable record. Early in August, Eastern members joined the New York Yacht Club Cruise at Mattapoisett and raced back to Marblehead, where, just out of mothballs, Joseph Santry's *Pleione* was the first schooner since 1926 to win the King's Cup.

What to do about the clubhouse? That was the big question at the general meeting in late August. Some wanted merely to rebuild the destroyed southwest wing; others wanted to sell the entire building and lot and erect a new house on the old stone wharf with the proceeds. Architect/member Nelson Aldrich pointed out that no rational decision could be reached until they decided whether they wanted a yacht club or a country club.

Not a new question. A building committee under Harold D. Hodgkinson was appointed to grapple with it. Demolition of the damaged wing was completed that fall.

The Hodgkinson committee leaned heavily toward the waterfront, and on January 13, 1948, the annual meeting accepted its recommendation to stay put and rebuild. The first-floor ladies' lounge and powder room would become a new kitchen and dining room; a new and smaller powder room would be built; the piazza would be continued around the house as if the wing had never been there; and below it would be installed a small snack bar for cold drinks, coffee, and sandwiches—later known as the Galley Grille—designed to attract more Club use by informally attired younger members.

The meeting also voted to offer the use of the Old Stone Wharf to the Pleon, whose directors set about planning a separate clubhouse thereon to replace their burned-out quarters.

Nelson Aldrich designed the Eastern's nonelective facelift. The insurance was insufficient, and the new commodore, James J. Storrow, asked for contributions, which ultimately came to almost $30,000. On May 29 an informal dinner dance celebrated the noontime commissioning of the rebuilding project.

Part of the new, or reasserted, direction for the Club, however, involved a slight lean away from the waterfront, recognized by Commodore Storrow when he appointed a committee to study whether or not a swimming pool should be built, since some had been agitating for it for several years, and how to finance it, as another service—and attraction—for youth. Robert Barton had recently moved to the Neck and joined the committee as secretary, with Storrow, Rufus Cushman, Devereux Barker, and George McQuesten:

> The Club was suffering terribly then because young, married couples with children naturally wanted to have a pool. The Corinthian had built a pool, and they were all flocking down there and wouldn't join the Eastern because we had no pool. We were losing members, and we were in bad shape financially.

The location was established down between the old pier and the Club pier. To build the whole pool [75 by 35 feet], the fence, the locker room and the filtration and pumps would cost about $50,000. Dev said, "Well, let's sell more bonds than that because there are a lot of other things that need doing. So we determined to sell $70,000 worth of pool bonds.

In Boston at the Union Club one day after lunch we were getting closer and closer to the committee leading off. These old Bostonians had been putting it off and putting it off, and finally Dev turned to the others and said, "Well, I guess we've got to start. I'll put up $5,000." And then he looked at George, and George, who was very shy, said, "Helen and I will each put up $5,000." Rufe immediately came in and said, "All right, five is my absolute limit!" And Jack said, "I'll go along with five too." And I said, "I have a little money in the savings bank. I'm going to get $500 out. I want to be part of it."

We raised $70,000 [with ten-year notes at 3 percent]. The members came through very handsomely. But the interesting thing is, as the pool got towards the end, Dev Barker, without any by-your-leave from the rest of the committee or the Council, proceeded to put in the present parking lot. He just had it done. Next Rufe Cushman—I think he had a tennis court redone—and he never asked anybody anything about that. Then George McQuesten wanted some planting, and he went ahead and had it done.

Barton's turn came, and he was worried about the big pier, especially about the adequacy of the footings at the end and the rot in the main beams. He got the go-ahead from the rest and had the work done for around $2,000.

I am quite certain that had we not done it, in the next big storm the whole thing would have gone, and the Club might have been out $35,000 to $45,000. That pool turned the Eastern around overnight. We had a waiting list for members right away. We had a pool membership and a charge per diem, and it saved the Eastern Yacht Club without any doubt at all.

The New London-Marblehead Ocean Race was run in June 1948 for the first time since 1941. Ray Hunt won the Lambert Trophy on corrected time by almost two hours in his prototype round-form, 36-foot cruising/racer 410 *Et Toi.*

In the Annual Regatta, Morris LaCroix's 59-foot schooner *Mariann* won her second Cleopatra's Barge Cup since 1946. The Annual Cruise rendezvoused at Mattapoisett, where Dr. Seth Milliken's lovely 102-foot yawl *Thistle,* said to be the largest American yacht then racing, won in the Universal Rule class. A bad squall struck the race to Newport, moving the Race Committee to append to the cruise list of twenty-one

yachts: "Any omissions from this list will be found floating off Brenton Reef." It was the last season of "Old Doctor Bones" as fleet surgeon before declining reappointment in 1949; Dr. Milliken had attended the Club since 1925, when he had succeeded Dr. Hugh Williams.

A fortnight after the Annual Cruise, the Eastern and the Scituate clubs sponsored a weekender to Scituate, where Commodore W. Marriott Welch offered the prize that bears his name for the cruising boat making the best time on the race.

Philip Lord had dreamed of going a-voyaging since he was six years old and learning to handle a sailing dory with a chum at Duxbury. In September of 1948, he and Priscilla made the dream come true when they embarked from Portland (Maine) with their daughters, eight and nine, in the 45-foot diesel ketch *Argo Navis* and a revolving crew of two that included Phil's old fellow dreamer for one shift. An early postwar experience in long-distance family cruising.

Following the Inland Waterway, they arrived at Havana via the Bahamas on Christmas morning. After a few weeks in Cuba, on to Costa Rica, three weeks at San Blas Islands and through the Panama Canal to the Galapagos for five more weeks. Return by way of Ecuador, the Canal, Jamaica, Cuba, Miami, the outside route to Norfolk, and back to Portland in August 1949. Lowest point: burning out the starter motor in the Galapagos and learning how to kick the kicker with a rope.

Rex Smithwick, at seventeen the youngest skipper ever awarded the Fowle Trophy to date, sacrificed a probable qualifying spot in the eliminations for the New England International 110 Championship when he went to the aid of the crew of a boat capsized in the heavy westerly of the Eastern's first day of Race Week.

Former Commodore Charles P. Curtis died in April 1948 in Beverly Farms, at eighty-seven. He was still racing his old Thirty Square *Ellen* as late as 1944. Then, after he reluctantly gave up competition, he bought a kayak that Francis Herreshoff had designed, and the two paddled all around the bay in their tight-fitting craft.

The Club also lost William Storer Eaton, who joined in March 1880 and had been Number One member since succeeding Dudley L. Pickman on that patriarchal pedestal in 1939. The Eastern's new Number One (as well as at the Corinthian and the Beverly in Marion) was Charles Henry Wheelwright Foster, now in his ninetieth year and still at the helm.

Tom Shepard was not about to relinquish the helm either, although of course he was the Number One's junior. Still, he acquitted himself well enough as a future candidate for the top of the Club ladder one summer day in 1948. They were out for a Sunday sail in *Irondequoit II* when a severe thundersquall struck as they passed three people in a small boat between Eagle and Baker's islands. Visibility dropped to zero, and when it cleared, the waters astern were empty. Something told Shepard to put back, and they found and rescued the trio clinging

---

Winners of the 1950 Prince of Wales Trophy for match racing in Bermuda are Ted Hood, Ray Hunt, and Brad Noyes.

to their overturned boat. Later they learned that the wind had registered 98 miles an hour at Salem.

The old order was changing indeed. To the groans of the Old Guard, the annual meeting in January 1949 followed the lead of the New York Yacht Club that winter and amended the by-laws to lower from 30 feet to 25 the minimum waterline required of yacht owners for eligibility to vote for flag officers and members of the Race Committee. For seventy-nine years, 30 feet had separated the yachts from the sailboats in the Eastern's book. But in fact, as the 1950 Yearbook revealed, the fleet not only had increased from 117 to 144 in two years but also was in the ratio of sixty-three over 30 feet to eighty-one under, and most of them were one-designs.

At the opening on May 28, Frances Gilliland, the receptionist dubbed "Miss Information Please" by Leonard Fowle, was feted on her first twenty-five years with the Club. She received a gold watch and a purse. "Frances not only answers all the questions," Fowle wrote in the *Boston Globe*, "but also is the personification of tact and accommodation. How many wives, whose husbands still were sitting at the bar, have been told, 'Mr. Smith just left the clubhouse.' And she quickly sent them homeward, unsuspecting what her tact had accomplished."

The pool and its pavilion, crowning symbol of decadence to those ancients who decried the descent to 25-foot waterlines, was dedicated with a ribbon-cutting on June 30. Leonard Fowle, however, shared Bob Barton's feelings of relief, writing that many of the younger members were greatly concerned about the Club's future after the fire. Now, he wrote, with the pool and locker rooms, the rising interest in tennis, and the revitalization of the nautical instruction program (two instructors were to be on hand for the first time), "the Eastern will offer its younger elements and juniors of Marblehead facilities and a program for sailing and sports which no club on the Massachusetts coast can rival."

Without further ado, the Pleon began raising funds for its planned new clubhouse, floats, and launching facilities, which were started in August and finished in October.

A committee of the North American Yacht Racing Union drew up the "Optional Right of Way Rules," which the Eastern tried applying to its 1947 Sunday Morning 210 Races for the Guy Lowell Cup (at the request of the class) and to the Curtis Cup. The Pleon did likewise with its Sunday Afternoon Series. The new mast line luffing rule, for instance, was regarded as

The Old Order Changeth

more accurate than the old one, which was to the effect that a lee boat could not luff up a windward one if it would strike it aft of the main shrouds—if it struck at all, of course, the conjecture being, how can you tell without trying?

The racing scene had become so cosmopolitan so rapidly in the welter of change brought on by the postwar explosion of national pride and self-consciousnesss that even so staid a club as the New York by 1948 was falling in line with the rules of the NAYRU. Although most of the clubs in Massachusetts Bay belonged to the NAYRU, it was the only major American yachting center without a governing authority, obviously required if the rules reform of 1947 was to apply across the board.

With that objective, representatives from the Eastern, the Corinthian, the Boston, and the Eastern Point clubs gathered at the invitation of former Race Chairman John R.C. McBeath in the Boston office of Eugene Connolly of the Eastern on April 27, 1949. The result was the organizational meeting of the Yacht Racing Union of Massachusetts Bay (YRUMB) at the Boston's Rowe's Wharf Station on May 24. Eighteen clubs (twenty-one by the year's end) joined, and their emissaries adopted a constitution and elected officers and an executive committee. Gene Connolly was the first president.

The first regional appeals committee was appointed in June, with McBeath (concurrently on the NAYRU executive committee) in the chair. The North Shore Junior Yacht Racing Association, formed in 1934 under Leonard Fowle to take over the responsibility from the Eastern, disbanded and turned over the Curtis Cup to the YRUMB. The new group then petitioned the parent organization for more equitable representation of local young skippers in eliminations for the Sears Cup by discontinuing the previously required alternate sailoff between winners of the North and South Shore eliminations and the winners from Maine; as a result, the NAYRU reorganized the Sears Cup Atlantic Coast eliminations.

Meanwhile, the creative geniuses behind it all were fueling the boating boom with their postwar midnight oil.

Arthur Martin, whose designs would stroke the recreational rowing revival, was doing detail work for Ray Hunt after the war and recalled that during Hunt's highly productive years in the 1940s and 1950s, the boss "had a tremendous concentration on what he was doing; he'd come into the office [at Graves Yacht Yard] on Monday morning, get out some plans, and say, 'Let's try this; look what would happen if we did this.'"

And there was no end to what this extraordinary designer, virtually lacking in formal technological training, would try.

Hunt produced a new, 23-foot 5 inches one-design class, the Javelin, that proved in its maiden season of 1949 to be about as fast as a 210; he won the Corinthian Chowder Race by more than four minutes.

Of greater significance for the future was the "Huntform" powerboat, precursor of the deep V-bottom, which occurred to him while lobstering out of Cohasset early in the war. While in the Coast Guard, he was borrowed by the Navy and adapted his Huntform to a 20-foot tank-test model of a destroyer that Charles Francis Adams persuaded the Bureau of Ships to test. Beamier, it was said to be as fast as the conventional "can," and probably incomparably more comfortable. But the Navy did not wish to inflict Hunt's comfort on the boys any more than Burgess's aluminum, and nothing came of it.

Ahead of the power squadron as with everything else that floated, Hunt in 1948 designed and Graves built the 54-foot Huntform *Yankee D*, which cruised at 30 knots and topped out at 45. A year later, he bettered that with the 42-foot cabin cruiser *Sea Blitz* for Brad Noyes, built by Quincy Adams in 1950; it cruised at 40 knots—and hit 60. They put a 1500-horsepower Packard PT-boat engine in her.

Fooling around with planing hulls, Ray Hunt came up in 1949 with one of the first catamarans ever to astonish Massachusetts Bay—a 42-foot plywood job with a cat-rigged rotating mast for Arthur W. Stevens of the Eastern. "She had no cabin and didn't tack too well, but she did prove to be fast," wrote B. Devereux Barker III in a 1964 article on the designer in *Yachting*. "They didn't know too much about engineering or sailing this type of boat at the time, however, and she didn't hold up long. It is unfortunate that, because of this failure, Ray became discouraged and didn't go any further with catamaran designs, for he was ahead of his time."

While creating the first Concordias with Llewellyn and Waldo Howland, Hunt fooled briefly with sailcloth at the Wamsutta Mills in New Bedford, but then came the war, and it would not be won by sailboats. Afterward, he was back in Marblehead, where his 210s were hot, and Arthur Martin had one. Martin told *Nautical Quarterly* of "a kid named Ted Hood who showed up and asked to make 210 sails."

"Ray wanted to give this kid a chance," Martin recalls, and he also remembers thinking that it was ridiculous to let a local kid

Brad Noyes at the throttle of *Sea Blitz*, his 42-foot Huntform cruiser designed by Ray Hunt in 1950 and driven by a 1500-horse Packard PT boat engine. Ronald E. Stroud photo.

make sails when two established sailmakers were on the job. Ted Hood made some sails, and Arthur Martin got the first set for his own 210. "It was like sitting in a motorboat and riding through the fleet," he says, when he sailed his first race with them. Hunt's business stationery in 1947–48 lists Frederick E. Hood as Associate Sailmaker, and those who were close to both men in those years give Hunt equal credit with Hood for the development of the modern spinnaker.

(After bombing out, or being bought out, as a housebuilder up on Bubier Road, Ted found himself with no interesting alternative but to try serious sailmaking. He recalls that he was associated with Ray Hunt, designing and cutting sails for him to sell, from about 1950 to 1952, but evidently it was earlier.)

The day after Ted and brother Bruce sailed their IOD *Princess* on June 18 to break the winning streak of Don Mackintosh's *Kungsornen*, Leonard Fowle wrote in the *Boston Globe* that "the sail which Ted Hood used in *Princess* this afternoon is the fourth this young man has made. . . . Ted laid this one

down in the dining room of Corinthian less than ten days ago. He figures it cost him about $100 against $500 for a commercially made International Class mainsail." *Princess* won race after race with what Fowle called her "home-made sails," until losing to Caleb Loring's *Pompano* on July 16. The press was already at work fashioning Ted, who was rather more than a simple scissors-snipper, into a folk hero out of whole cloth.

The 1949 Race Week ended as it began, with a bang, but of a different sort—not from the starter's gun but one reminiscent of the salute that blew the hole in that Eastern member's sail eighty years earlier. It was August 13, the last day, at the start of the Corinthian's 210s. Former Sears Cup winner Robert Coulson of the Eastern, with crew Thacher Loring and John Newman, were on the line when Sears (Nick) Winslow of the Eastern Point Yacht Club tossed a friendly cherry bomb in the direction of Bobby's *Willow Wand*. Instead of a harmless hole in the air, the missile landed in the water and blew a foot-square hole in their bow.

"Hey, you've sunk my boat!" yelled Bobby, as he headed for the harbor. Their attempts to stuff the hole were to no avail, and as they approached Lighthouse Point, they swamped. Vance Smith's powerboat *Panther* came up and pulled his crew out of the water as Coulson swam around to secure a towline before joining them aboard.

"Funniest thing that ever happened to me," laughed the Yale senior to reporters back ashore. "I guess Nick didn't know what had happened at first, and he turned white as a sheet when he apparently realized we weren't kidding. Gee, he must have gun ports in that boat of his. Wait until he gets the bill for this!" Winslow finished eighteenth and offered—and Coulson accepted—his *Windblow* for the Eastern's defense the following week of the Manhasset Bay Challenge Cup in the 210s.

As a lesson in arms control, however, the incident seems only to have imbued the older generation with notions of proliferation. A year or so later, it is said, a certain crew on a certain boat in a certain anchorage at cocktail time on the Annual Cruise gleefully placed cherry bombs on paper plates, lit them, and set them adrift downstream, much to the annoyance of Fleet Captain Nelson Aldrich, the object of the caper.

And of course there was the day some prankster fired an open can of baked beans out of the cannon from the clubhouse.

In like vein is the occurrence, long deserving to be immortalized in print, in which the late J. Amory Jeffries was the star performer. Jeffries had been a club stalwart since he joined in 1929, Race Committee chairman from 1935 to 1939, and secretary since 1941. When Stephen Sleeper resigned in 1943 after twenty-seven years as treasurer (and before that, regatta chairman from 1908 to 1912), he was made the Eastern's only Honorary Member, and Secretary Jeffries took over the treasury until former Commodore Barker accepted the job in 1947.

Jeffries almost always participated in the Annual Cruise, and he imparted to its more leisurely proceedings a special touch of class—he was the epitome of the distinguished yachtsman in his spotless white flannels, Eastern blazer, and braided cap. In 1949, the fleet had put into Boothbay Harbor, whence the members were ferried by launch to Southport, where Mr. and Mrs. Alfred Moses gave a memorable cocktail party at their summer home. Don Blodgett was with his father on the schooner *Mistral*:

That was a party. Joe Parker [the hostess's son] was pouring the drinks. Father asked for a bourbon and water. Joe gave him a bourbon, and Father grabbed a pitcher of martinis and poured it on top. Joe's eyes were bugging right out of his head, and Father drank it down. That was the kind of party it was.

As parties must, the party wound down, and Messrs. Amory Jeffries, John Blodgett, Benjamin Tower, and one or two others wound down to the float. Coming to the ramp, Jeffries and Tower walked abreast and in lockstep down to the landing, caught up in animated conversation. Through the blackness of the night they strode, and across the float, and as Benny marched straight out the diving board, he was aware of a mighty splash, which stopped him just short of the end.

"Amory's cap bobbed up before he did," muses Albie Parker, Joe's brother, "and they got a boathook and gaffed it, which I think was more humiliating for him than walking off the end of the float."

The Roaring Fifties

Chapter 16   **The Roaring Fifties**   *1950–1958*

In 1940, membership stood at 442 and the fleet at 307, of which 197 were over 30 feet waterline. A decade and a world war later, there were 400 members and 144 boats, only sixty-three over 30 feet. The annual meeting in January 1950 lowered the ceiling beyond which only yacht owners were to be accepted as new members from 700 to 500.

How to keep the salt from losing its savor? Back in 1902, the membership had decreed that candidates must own boats of more than 30 feet to be eligible while the Club had more than 650 on the rolls; but the rush could not be stemmed, and the next year the limit was raised to 700.

Brookline banker Edward Dane, owner of the Francis Herreshoff ketch *Bounty* for fifteen years, followed Commodore Storrow in 1950. One innovation of his regime was Ladies Day early in the season, which led to the weekly Tuesday ladies' luncheons, popular for years to come, at the suggestion of the unrelated Mrs. William H. Dane. In 1951 there were eighteen women associates.

Some of the bigger yachts familiar on the prewar scene still dominated the major Eastern races during the early and middle 1950s. Joseph Santry, who had won the Puritan Cup in his Q-class *Taygeta* in 1947, won it again in 1953 in his ageless *Pleione*, originally Captain Nat's New York Fifty of 1913—the first schooner to top the Annual Regatta since 1927. (Taygeta, by the way, was one of the Pleiades, the seven daughters of Atlas and Pleione, herself the daughter of Oceanus.)

And then in 1956, *Pleione* won the Cleopatra's Barge Cup for the sixth time since 1935 and the Norman Cup for the Universal Rule yachts for the third time. Right on her shapely heels was Morris LaCroix's Seawanhaka schooner *Mariann*, taking the Lambert Cup in 1949 in the Eastern's round-the-

Cape ocean classic (which was getting to be known in hard-sailing quarters as "The American Fastnet") and the Cleopatra's Barge Cup in 1952 for the sixth time since 1937. Frank Paine and his old *Gypsy* won the Puritan Cup in 1941 and 1952 (when it was raced for the first time under the CCA Rule instead of the Universal Rule) and the Norman in 1947, 1950, and 1951. And G.D. Haskell's Eight Meter *Navigo* won four straight Puritans between 1948 and 1951.

Ray Hunt won the Lambert Cup with *Et Toi* in 1948, then twice again in 1950 and 1951 with the 53-foot ketch *Zara*, which he bought in 1950 for his family to live aboard and cruise in. In April 1952, with his wife Barbara, son James, and members Bill White and Brad Noyes, he sailed from Nassau to Bermuda and home to Marblehead—a voyage of more than 1,500 miles by dead reckoning—with only a compass and taffrail log. Their error worked out to less than one percent, in spite of the fact that *Zara* was hove-to at one point for twenty-one hours, and they learned that they had passed less than five miles south of the Nantucket Lightship, their destination, obscured by rain.

In 1955 the Hunt family raced the Concordia sloop *Harrier* in the Cowes Week Regatta, winning six out of seven starts. One very proper English skipper was unable to refrain from expressing his belief that such brilliance could only be the result of too low a rating. Hunt met the challenge with a smile, and a remeasurement lowered *Harrier*'s rating by a tenth—and raised the rating of her crew with the Brits no end.

New York had to swallow hard on occasion, too. On the New York Yacht Club Cruise from Provincetown to Marblehead in August 1951, *Pleione* lost the Clucas Trophy for the best elapsed time to Marblehead to John Matthews's Twelve Meter

Vim when she missed the finish line in the fog but beat out DeCoursey Fales's great Starling Burgess schooner *Niña* of 1928 for the NYYC Challenge Cup for schooners and ketches.

Two years later, in 1953, New York was back. Philip Benson's *Wassail* (ex-*Shoaler*, New London-Marblehead winner in 1952, and designed by Hunt), chartered by Lincoln Davis and William Kip, Robert Coulson's *Finn McCumhaill*, and Edward Kelley's *Departure* among them took six firsts, four seconds, four thirds, and three fourths out of fifteen in Class C. Among the schooners and ketches, *Pleione* had two firsts, a second, and two thirds, winning the Navy Challenge Cup, was the first schooner in the Queen's Cup. In 1954 she won the Clucas Trophy after all.

The Beverly Yacht Club returned the Franklin D. Roosevelt Bowl to competition. Originally put up in 1934 for international racing in the Thirty Square Meters, it was reoffered after the war for team racing in the Yankee class at Marion and the 210s at Marblehead. Now the Eastern team of Lincoln Davis, Robert Coulson, and Francis Cummings challenged in the 210s at Marion and brought the trophy back to Marblehead. The Manhasset Bay Challenge Cup was defended by the Boston at Marblehead and was won by Cornelius Wood in a sailoff after tying Morton Bromfield of the South Boston. Wood successfully defended against twelve challengers in 210s at Marblehead the next season, only to lose to the Long Islanders in 1952, the first time the cup had left Massachusetts Bay since Ray Hunt carried it away in 1934.

The same season, the Eastern held the first National Senior Sailing Championship for men for the Mallory Cup, honoring Clifford D. Mallory, founder of the sponsoring USYRU. Its history is unique: The large silver soup tureen was originally presented by Sultan Selim III to the family of Lord Nelson in 1812 as a token of gratitude for his victory over the French in the Battle of the Nile in 1798, which relieved Turkey and Egypt from the threat of Napoleon.

Having made less than a splash at housebuilding (fortunately for the yachting world), Ted Hood at twenty-three took up sailmaking in 1950—full time when he and his brother weren't rapidly making a name as hot IOD sailors.

I was in Martin's dairy barn first, then a summer in Oxner's boat yard in the spar loft, then behind Maddie's Sail Loft, where I had to go up to the high school floor to make the big sails. The first synthetic was Nylon. I didn't get involved; it wasn't too good. But when Orlon first came out, we worked on developing sails from that. Then Dacron, which was invented by the English and called Terylene; Du Pont called it Fiber B, and we made a mainsail for Frank Paine's *Gypsy* around 1952, the first real Dacron sail probably; that was for Ray Hunt, who was friendly with Paine, and we made an Orlon jib for him and a crosscut spinnaker.

With the appearance of the first synthetics, his initial experiments convinced Hood that the inconsistent quality—the varying tightness of the weave of the commercially available mill fabrics—was a critically compromising factor in his aim to achieve the ultimate airfoil with every sail. The alternative? Weave your own. And here the expertise of his father, known familiarly by one and all around the shop as "The Professor," played a key part.

I didn't start making cloth until 1952. The main thing in sailmaking is to get consistently good fabric. I found that out in my early years when I'd pick out the cotton and test it and stretch it and pick out each bolt, and the same with each bolt rope. I got help from my father, who didn't know anything about weaving but did know about applying chemicals to textiles. We had four looms down in back of Maddie's from 1952 to 1954. I kept them running all day long and fixed them roughly, the best I could, and the loom fixer came in on Saturdays and tuned them up and did the stuff I couldn't.

We had a lot of flaws and imperfections in the fabric, but at least it was woven tight. One reason for the imperfections was that the yarn would break because we were weaving to the limit, narrow on a wide loom, so you had only half the load. We wove it tight and learned to have the fibers go in the direction of the load on the sail, which stretches up the leech of the main; so we made the extra-strong fibers go that way, which no one did before, when all the cloth stretched the same in all directions. Finishing, we held it sideways while it was being calendered so it wouldn't shrink. We'd stretch it under heat.

Synthetics being new, the experience of the old cotton manufacturers didn't mean much any more, and it was a good time to get into the business with the new fibers.

Meanwhile, Hood had joined the Eastern in June of 1951. The brothers' IOD *Princess*, with his sails, was beaten only four times out of twenty-one starts in the 1951 Saturday Series run by the Club and the Corinthian. At one point, she ran up a string of twelve straight wins. The next season, Ted won the Eastern, the Corinthian, and the season's championships in the Internationals; piled up the greatest number of points for the seven 210 races during Race Week; won the Norman Cup (offered to the Internationals for the first time) with three firsts in *Princess*; won the Lipton Trophy with a first, second, and fourth in the U.S. One-Design *Evanthia*; and, to wrap it all up, dominated the Frostbite sailing. In 1953, sailing for Corinthian, he brought the Manhasset Bay Challenge Cup back to Marblehead once more.

Although the smaller one-designs were beginning to proliferate, they were kept at bay by the Eastern, where the planing hull of the Raven was considered pretty "radical" in 1950; the established Towns and the 19-foot Lightnings that Sparkman & Stephens brought out in 1938 were considered more acceptable. A handful of Brutal Beasts, the first since the war, were built by Lowell in Amesbury (cedar-planked with mahogany seats and transoms), but the class that belied its name and was gentle to generations of tyros was on the way up the creek. Harold Turner's cocky 9-foot Turnabouts were just turning up here and there, and soon would be everywhere.

The 1950 season opened with the dedication of the new Pleon clubhouse on the Stone Wharf. It closed on September 11 and 12 with thirty hours of winds up to 60 knots and extra high-course tides that broke sixty boats from their moorings in the harbor. Thirty-five to forty suffered severe damage. Ray Hunt's new *Javelin* was a total loss on Skinner's Head. Gene Connolly's U.S. One-Design *Leenane* sank on Bowditch Rock but was raised. The LaCroix schooner *Mariann* broke away toward Skinner's Head but was rescued by the harbor taxi. The havoc refueled breakwater talk, but with the usual absence of outcome.

Then on July 27, 1952, a Sunday squall with gusts to 60 roared out of Salem Bay. Thirty-two boats swamped or capsized. All but two 110s swamped. Fourteen of the twenty Townies and all five Lightnings capsized. Forty boats were in the Guy Lowell Cup race, which was canceled just in time to keep the U.S. Ones from starting. Seventy sailors were in the water, but by the quick action of the launches, lobstermen, the police boat, and the Power Squadron, no lives were lost.

Head Boatman George Simmons, in the Club launch with three members of the House Committee, rescued a 19-year-old M.I.T. student from near-drowning when he was swept from the deck of a rented 110. Dr. and Mrs. George Nichols plucked six from the water after the historic Massachusetts Bay 18-footer *Dorchen II* swamped between Tinker's Island

and Tom Moore's *Rock*, sinking just as their rescuers got the last person aboard the Nichols's 210 *Jimmy*.

Gifford K. Simonds, Jr., succeeded Ned Dane, becoming the youngest commodore in Club history to date in 1953, and the winds of change piped up. At the January annual meeting, the bylaws were amended to move the election of officers from the winter to the late summer, and to provide for the election of female associate members who were neither yacht owners nor unmarried members of a deceased member's family. And an end-of-the-season awards dinner was inaugurated.

The clubhouse was painted grey instead of the old green. A room cost four dollars a day, a suite in the Samoset five hundred for the season. The regular family dinner was a dollar sixty-five, the Fourth of July dinner dance was four, a family tennis membership set you back all of fifteen, pool twenty, and a tennis lesson cost but three.

The clubs agreed to shift Race Week from August 8 to August 15, in the hope of getting by the light airs at the beginning of the month. The Eastern and the Corinthian moved the regular starting line from Marblehead Rock bell to the Four-Fathom Gong. A new perpetual trophy, the Guy Lowell Memorial Bowl, to take the place of the Guy Lowell Cup (Mrs. Lowell died in April) was given by Mr. and Mrs. Harold Hodgkinson; it was offered in competition to the International One Designs as being closest to the S-class in which Lowell last raced one of his *Cima*s. The Manchester Yacht Club held its first George S. Patton Bowl along the lines of the off-soundings races; due to bad weather, there was only one race instead of the two-day series planned, Ray Hunt and Bobby Coulson placing one and two in Class A.

Although the 1953 New London-Marblehead Ocean Race drew a strong list of entrants that included *Pleione* and Ray Hunt in the old sloop *Janet*, Talcott Banks won the Lambert Trophy with *Sparhawk* in the dawdling time of seventy-six hours. Indeed, she was the only boat to finish, besting several Bermuda Race veterans. There was talk of racing through the Cape Cod Canal the next year, but only talk.

Along about this time, Boston was being linked with the North Shore by the new Mystic River Bridge and the Northeast

Joseph Santry's ageless *Pleione*, winsome daughter of Oceanus, 1954.

Expressway, and the driving public was being importuned on numerous four-by-eight-foot signs over the signature of Governor Paul A. Dever to "Pardon the Inconvenience." One night toward the end of Race Week, Don Blodgett, Albie Parker, and Hoppy Damon set forth in a pickup truck with a saw, found one of these roadside signs, cut it down, hove it in back under partial cover of a torn awning, carted it home to Marblehead, lugged it down to the Eastern landing, dumped it in the harbor, and rowed out to Blodgett's powerboat.

The contraband proved too cumbersome to load, so they towed it all the way out to the Four-Fathom Gong, which they boarded in the darkness. The fog was now coming in. Amid the rolling and the clanging, and to the counterpoint of their own expostulations, the roisterers succeeded in strapping the great sign upright to the buoy. Then they inched their way harborward through the thick. The boat's compass was not working as it should, nor were their internal bearings, and they made their landfall near Orne Island. But no matter. Blodgett:

Next day Albie and I went out and raced with my brother Jack in the U.S. One-Designs. He wanted to try out the sails, and we sailed down to Baker's Island. Didn't go anywhere near the Four-Fathom Gong until the start of the race, when Albie and I are looking at it and saying, "Oh, look at that, Jack!" and trying to call attention to the sign. He could care less. He went off and raced and never noticed it. There was a picture of it on the front page of the *Globe* the next morning.

In an almost equal feat of modesty, the culprits kept the whole thing under their hats for years.

For the third time since its revival in 1950, the Eastern defeated the Beverly for the Roosevelt Bowl. The Beverly won the race in 1955, when it lapsed. In 1958 it was revived for junior sectional team racing.

"I will not listen to mere reason," Commodore Simonds announced to the annual meeting. "This year we go south." And to the southward sailed the 1953 Annual Cruise for the first time since 1948, behind his schooner *Trade Wind*. At least twenty-five boats raced to Provincetown on July 5, the next day through the Canal for a race in Buzzards Bay to Marion, then to Padanaram, Edgartown, and Nantucket, back to the Vineyard, disbanding in Marion. It was the best since the war, everyone agreed.

Conviviality had traditionally marked the annual cruises of the Eastern. "Explosive" is the word for the eastward cruise resumed in Commodore Simonds's second year of 1954, as described by Jim Connolly, who was not along but believes what he heard to be true:

The story goes that the commodore of the yacht club at Dark Harbor got wind of the fact that the Eastern planned a night in his harbor, so he got hold of Giff and extended to him and the fleet an invitation for them all to be the Islesboro club's guests ashore for chowder. Giff accepted, and on the appointed day the Eastern fleet had chowder at the Dark Harbor club. Much was Giff's surprise when the Islesboro commodore presented him with a bill at $5.00 a head for the chowder as Giff was leaving the pier.

Giff went back to his schooner and thought things over. Then he proceeded to wreak his vengeance by firing his loud saluting cannon every hour on the hour all night long.

I understand that he became persona non grata at Islesboro as a result.

Charles Francis Adams died in Boston on June 10, 1954, at the age of eighty-seven. He had been a member for sixty seasons, since September 17, 1888. He was commodore in 1927 and 1928, served in other flag positions and on the Council for many years. His membership in the New York Yacht Club, which made him an Honorary Member in 1953, dated back to 1913. The *Boston Globe* eulogized:

Of him it can be truly said that he preserved to the full the qualities of "patriotism, perseverance, integrity and diligence" for which Congress officially commended his ancestor, the first John Adams.

That left Charlie Foster Number One at ninety-four and Tom Shepard, the irascible Squire of Peach's Point, the heir apparent at eighty-seven. Shepard won the Cleopatra's Barge Cup in 1946 and 1948 in his 61-foot Alden sloop *Irondequoit*, built for him by Lawley in 1940, and the Welch Trophy in 1950 and 1952, and displayed no signs of flagging. He sailed her on the overnight race to Boothbay Harbor in the Annual Cruise of 1954, which featured, for the first time since 1936 and the second in history, the Annual Regatta away from home. Edmund Kelley's *Departure*, one of a trio of Owens cutters, won the Puritan Cup, while Chandler Hovey's *Robin*, four-time holder of the Puritan Cup and regarded as the fastest Q-boat ever built, won the Norman Cup for Universal Rule boats.

That race to Boothbay, incidentally, was won by Henry

Sears's new 40-foot Concordia sloop *Actaea*, skippered by Ray Hunt. She was the latest in a succession of Sears *Actaeas* beginning with the schooner yacht that her owner's great-grandfather David sailed to England in 1830. Harry's grandfather, David Sears, Jr., was a founder of the Eastern and its shortest-lived commodore three years later in 1873; his older cousin was the late Commodore Herbert Sears. Dual membership was a family tradition, and that December of 1954, Henry Sears was elected commodore of the New York Yacht Club.

With the resumption of their education after their Navy service, Brad Noyes and Ted Hood had met up again:

Ted and I would get in the car on weekends and go look at boats when the other guys were going to football games. One time we slept in my mother's convertible. It was freezing cold. We went to a gas station to borrow some pliers to pull the seats apart so we could put them down; we were too cheap to spend the money on a motel. We found this Hinckley 28 in Mamaroneck, and I bought it. Named it *Piranha*, supposed to be the lucky seven letters. Ted made a jib for me in his bedroom for a hundred and fifty dollars.

I only had it for one or two summers. It was up for sale with my U.S. One-Design when I found a boat called *Solution*, a 48-footer designed by Aage Nielsen when he was with Sparkman & Stephens. I went to Fred Wakelin at Alden and said I wanted a masthead rig for it. He told me to go across the street and talk with the designer. Aage fooled around with it for a while and then said he could really come up with a better boat than that, and that's what happened.

Nielsen was working in a yard in his native Denmark when, at twenty-one—so the story goes—he won a design contest in *Yachting* for which the position with Alden in America was the prize. He told Brad that later he worked for Francis Herreshoff designing Brad's father's *Tioga* for sixty cents an hour and a bottle of wine with lunch.

Hoping to get around the rising costs of custom-built yachts—accelerated by the postwar closing of the Herreshoff, Lawley, Nevins, and Quincy Adams yards, Noyes took his plans in hand and headed for Europe.

Junius Beebe and I sailed transatlantic with Howard Fuller on *Gesture*, which had been built at Quincy Adams in 1940, and raced in the Fastnet and won our fair share with her at Cowes Week. Then I took some time off and found a yard in Varazze, Italy, and they started building my first *Tioga* from Aage's plans in 1952. My first choice was Abeking & Rasmussen, but they

were so booked up that they were going to almost double their price if they built a boat for you. The Italian yard did a nice job.

This latest *Tioga* was a 50-foot keel-centerboard wooden yawl, the bronze board boxed entirely below the cabin floor, designed to the CCA Rule as an ocean racer. Sails by Ted Hood. She arrived from Genoa and was launched on May 27. Her owner took her on the New York Yacht Club Cruise in August, and in her maiden race she won the first of three consecutive Una Cups from a fleet of forty. "They didn't pay much attention to us when we first joined up," her proud and somewhat surprised owner said, "but after the first day's racing we had plenty of visitors." Her starting record: two wins and three seconds.

Something new, something old: in winning the NYYC Cruise's Clucas Cup for the best elapsed time on the longest

K. Aage Nielsen

run from Block Island to Newport, *Pleione* passed *Vim* off Point Judith and worked up such a lead over the rest of the pack, including *Bolero* and *Baruna*, that she was at anchor in Brenton's Cove with her sails furled before they finished. New York Commodore John Nicholas Brown, owner of *Bolero*, visited *Pleione* to congratulate Commodore Santry.

Pleione, it might be noted, had won the Puritan Cup in 1953 although severely penalized by the CCA Rule. In 1954, her rig was modified under the rule, and although she rated higher than most of the fleet, she continued to win.

The extremely unsettled and unpredictable weather that had characterized the 1950s hit 1954 with a triple whammy. On August 12, a thundersquall struck the Boston's day of Race Week with hail and a 30-mile-an-hour wind upsetting forty boats and a hundred sailors; the Salem Coast Guard and patrol boats rescued all, and no one was lost.

Then, on September 1, Hurricane Carol smashed across with winds of eighty, providentially from the southeast, although it inflicted great damage on land and sea, leaving the Neck without power for a day or more, and many phoneless for several. Broken spars, stove planks, and missing equipment kept fifty-two of the usual eighty-five boats from showing on the inside line for the September 5 race. They were still trying to find the pieces when in blew Hurricane Edna on September 11, with less wind but torrential rains.

Providential again for Thomas Shepard, whose *Celeritas* had broken loose from his mooring off Peach's Point in the 1938 hurricane after his skipper put an extra anchor overboard and fetched up off Hospital Point. This time, another skipper was aboard *Irondequoit II*; he put out an extra anchor and chain and stayed with the ship. Repeat performance: The mooring broke and she dragged to Corn Point, where the anchor caught just in time. All she suffered was a boom broken by the banging and a rudder chewed by the rocks. Family and neighbors rushed to Corn Point, while Linc Davis rescued the captain, who couldn't swim.

And providential too, where Ted Hood was concerned. Following in the family tradition established after the 1938 hurricane, he bought a 44-foot yawl off the rocks at Padanaram,

Tioga, Bradley Noyes's 50-foot, keel-centerboard yawl, was designed by Aage Nielsen and built in Italy. She won the first of her three straight NYYC Una Cups in 1954. Richard Veit photo.

The Roaring Fifties

The Eastern launch, an IOD, and an unidentified ketch on the rocks during the storm of September 12, 1950.

fixed her up, called her *Princess*, honeymooned on her with Sue, and even raced her a little.

Rear Commodore Neil W. Rice succeeded Commodore Gifford Simonds in 1955, and Devereux Barker wanted to step down after eight years as treasurer. Barker's immediate legacy was the forehanded provision in the 1953 budget for the re-roofing of the clubhouse and the Samoset, a project for 1955 to which the 1954 hurricanes gave timely urgency. This left the Club with but the $500 expense of removing fallen trees, and enough to activate the Galley Grille under the northwest porch, with tables on the lawn. The Grille served sandwiches, hamburgers, frappes, and such to the sailing-duds-and-bathing suit crowd.

Robert B.M. Barton was elected to succeed Devereux Barker as treasurer. A number of members were in arrears, costs were rising with inflation, and dues were insufficient, although the Club was $10,000 in the black for 1955 on an income of $135,476. To raise money, a new classification of Life Membership at a thousand dollars was created; eleven signed up in 1954. Barton recalls:

> Neil Rice ran U.S. Smelting with an iron hand. He told his board exactly what it would do and what it wouldn't do, and he proposed to run the Eastern Yacht Club the same way. I told him the first thing we had to do was get the dues up, which every commodore hates to do. He said, "It'll be opposed by the Council, you know. What I want you to do when we have the Council meeting is to howl and make all the noise you want to get the dues up, and I'll just sit there, saying nothing, and when the time comes I'll just say, 'It's a vote,' and the dues will go up."
>
> We met in the Race Committee Room, and I can remember it to this day. Jim Parker [Rear Commodore James P. Parker], a lovely fellow and very gracious and soft-spoken, said, "No, wait." A few others objected. Neil let this go on for ten minutes and finally banged on the table and said, "I think we've had a very helpful discussion, and now the time has come to end it. We've got other business. All in favor . . . those opposed." Bang. "It's a vote. All right now, next order of business." That was how the dues went up under Neil.

Hurricane Carol, Marblehead Harbor, winds of 80 MPH, September 1, 1954.

On one occasion, an ad hoc committee looking for new sources of operating income proposed selling the two corner tennis lots, according to Barton, for $10,000. Foreseeing the ultimate need for parking if nothing else, he threatened to resign as treasurer and carry the issue to the membership. He prevailed. "I think that was perhaps my greatest contribution as treasurer, saving that corner. I think today [1977] it is easily worth $200,000."

On the water, because 1955 was an off-year for the Bermuda Race and there were big plans for a combined August cruise with the NYYC, the Eastern cosponsored with the Storm Trysail Club the Mount Desert Ocean Race from New London and back, 418 miles, on July 23, and awarded the Lambert Trophy to the first boat, A.L. Loomis's *Good News*. But this year's version of the ill wind, Hurricane Connie, dumped such a mess of weather that only sixteen boats turned up for the big cruise, half of whose racing runs were canceled.

Withal, her second season was a blast for *Tioga* and Brad Noyes. Beginning in Florida with the Southern Ocean Racing Circuit, she won Class B and placed third in the Miami-Nassau Race, second in the Lipton Cup, and third in the Nassau Cup, to finish second to *Finisterre* in the overall standings. Back north, she won the two-day Patton Bowl series, scoring two firsts over Lincoln Davis in *Merlin* while *Gelouba* placed third. She won the Puritan Cup, and did it over every boat except *Pleione* on elapsed time, and the C.F. Adams Trophy (the first year outside the Star class) for the Scituate-to-Marblehead race. On the New York Cruise, *Tioga* won Class B on the first two runs and also beat four Class A boats on elapsed time on the third, led her class for the Astor Cup, and won the Una Cup by 90 minutes over thirty miles.

In her third season, 1956, *Tioga* again beat the first-to-finish *Pleione* on corrected time for the Puritan Cup. The New York fleet arrived in Marblehead on August 4 from Gloucester. The next day was a lay day, celebrated by a huge concourse of EYC and NYYC members over cocktails under a vast tent spread across the lawn of Joseph Santry's harborfront home, "Red Gate." Then, for the first time, the Astor and Queen's cup races were held in Massachusetts Bay. Forty-two yachts competed for the Astor in a good breeze. *Tioga* won and sailed on to capture her third successive Una Cup for Class B. *Pleione*, four-time Astor winner (thrice as a schooner and once as a

sloop), won the New York Yacht Club Cup for Schooners and Ketches. *Tioga*'s record, after only three seasons, was exceeded only by *Finisterre*'s.

Still more honors were brought back to the Club by Ted Hood, with Brad Noyes and Charlie Pingree crewing—cross-country this time—when they won the Mallory Cup for the National Senior Sailing Championship in Seattle, sailed in a local class similar to a Star but with bunks and a head. It fell to the Club, as defender, to host the 1957 Men's Championship with the YRUMB at Marblehead September 9 through 14, this time in borrowed Thistles, which just about weeded out of the finals all but the intercollegiate dinghy sailors. Thus were eliminated big-boat helmsmen Hood and Bus Mosbacher. George O'Day, who had been North American Firefly and Jolly champion and New England Senior champion, won the Mallory Cup for the Marblehead Frostbite Sailors.

Rounding out his Diamond Jubilee as a member of the Eastern Yacht Club, Charles Henry Wheelwright Foster—Number One—had died in Boston at the age of ninety-five on September 22, 1955. He was also Number One in the Beverly Yacht Club, which he had joined in 1880, after which he was admitted to the Eastern on January 25, 1881, the year of his graduation from Harvard, of which he was the fifth oldest alumnus at the time of his death, having led the academic procession only the previous June.

Accepting the *Boston Post* cane in 1954 when he became, at ninety-four, the oldest resident of Marblehead and thereby entitled to this badge of longevity, Charlie Foster observed that everybody takes you for granted until you turn ninety, at which time you become a curiosity. Yes, he had sailed his curious, staysail-ketch-rigged U.S. One-Design in the Corinthian's (of which he was the last surviving founder) Chowder Race in 1950 when he was ninety—against all the advice to the contrary about his pet rig from his nonagenarian friend, Nat Herreshoff. And he achieved the probable lifetime record for a private Yankee yachtsman of fifty-nine boats of all sizes and types, sailed through a lifetime of curiosity about what makes them go. The *Boston Globe*'s Leonard Fowle, Jr., had dropped in during the summer for a reminiscent chat with Mr. Foster, who was assisting a Spanish writer with a history of the Sonder racing in the Bay of Biscay. Shortly after, under a dateline of September 10 and only a few days before his death, C.H.W. Foster wrote the yachting reporter from his characteristically long view:

I hope in anything you write about our talk the stress will be along the line of encouraging international small boat racing—with any mention of me incidental—for at the moment it would seem to me most appropriate as furthering goodwill between nations.

In 1927 Foster had bought a former coal wharf at Number One Front Street, on the town side of the harbor. Evers Burtner wondered "how bulky coal barges of say 150 feet in length were towed or maneuvered through the huge fleet of yachts even in those days." Maybe in the off-season. The new owner built "The Ship's Cabin" on the property, a landmark inn for selected paying guests. In his will, he left it to Harvard College, which had no use for it and put it up for sale. The Boston Yacht Club, getting crowded out of its old quarters, merged with the Marblehead Harbor Yacht Club, which had been founded in 1946, and purchased Charles Foster's Ship's Cabin in 1956 for its new home.

A quarter of a century before he died, the Grand Old Man of the Eastern told a story on himself in the third person in his *Ditty Box* that said something about his vigorous attitude toward life. Years earlier, during a run from Newport through Vineyard Sound in an overpowering southwester, Foster was trying to slack the spinnaker halyard when he lost the belaying pin from the pinrail:

His left hand was grasping the halyard and before he could let go he was carried aloft and had just time to let go before his head struck the heavy oak crosstree. This meant a fall of some forty feet to the deck with the halyard going at great speed through his left hand. Why his legs were not broken is a wonder, but the inside of his left hand was cut almost to the bone by the halyard's passage through it. Meantime, the spinnaker pole was broken and a piece about twelve feet long came flying through the air and struck the man at the wheel across the back, "laying him out."

Charlie Foster was loath to let go.

Less than a year following the demise of its remarkable Number One, the Eastern lost its only Honorary Member of long standing, Stephen W. Sleeper, chairman of the Race Committee 1908–12 and treasurer 1916–43. He died on July 21, 1956, at eighty-two. Sleeper was a Boston real estate broker who summered at "Black Bess" (since 1959 the home of the author), on Eastern Point in Gloucester.

With C.H.W. Foster's passing, Thomas H. Shepard succeeded to Number One at the age of eighty-nine in 1956, sixty-eight years a member since he joined in 1889. Long the *vieux terrible* of his hearth and his office—he ran the Shepard and Morse Lumber and Shepard Steamship companies of Boston—the tall, muscular old man ruled establishments in Brookline and Marblehead, where his 61-foot sloop *Irondequoit II* was the queen of the Peach's Point fleet. His first yacht of note was his favorite, *Irondequoit I*, a fast gaff sloop of about 65 feet that had won the Canada Cup around 1900; he bought her in 1911 or so and sold her some time prior to the 1920s, then owned and raced the New York Forty *Catherine*, with a club topsail, when there was a class of them at Marblehead.

A grandson, Timothy Shepard, drew a salty, semifictionalized portrait of the old tyrant, doughty tennis player, and terror at the helms of his Pierce Arrow and his yacht, in *Peaches Point: The Summer World of the Irascible T.H. Shepard and His Clan*, published in 1976.

A driving competitor was the new Number One, undaunted by deafness and failing eyesight, which, according to one member who observed with horror more than one near-collision, rendered him "a menace on the water." *Irondequoit* won the Norman Cup in 1946 and 1948; the Welch Trophy in 1950, 1952, 1955, and 1956; the Boston Lightship Race and Albert Gould Memorial Bowl on the 1954 Annual Cruise; and the Fleet Captain's Cup in 1956.

"When he was ninety or ninety-one," recalls Herbert Baldwin, "he had to hire a new captain, as I heard the story, but the man wouldn't sign on for three years, so Mr. Shepard wouldn't take him."

During the 1951 Annual Cruise, when he was eighty-three, Tom Shepard was one of the very, very few to take a dip one cold, foggy day, inspiring an awed grandchild to call with clarion voice that rang from shore to shore: "Grandfather, you look like a walrus!"

Everyone who sailed with or against The Irascible T.H. Shepard seems to have a Shepard story or two. Robert Barton in *Sally II* was on the Annual Cruise that put into Morgan Bay beyond Blue Hill when John B. Whitmore was Race Committee chairman, which must have been 1957—thus making T.H. about ninety:

His children gave him up. They wouldn't race with him, so he raced with his grandchildren. And *Irondequoit* was an ageless vessel. No matter how they changed the rules, his rating remained about the same, so he could do very well. But as he got

older, whether he thought that rank has its privileges or not, he would start every race by barging. No matter what happened, he would barge down.

So we were up at Morgan Bay, and we had had a lot of barging. Jack Whitmore, as the Race Committee chairman, said, "All right, we'll start tomorrow's race off normal in every respect, except *Irondequoit* will go on the final gun. The rest of you will go two minutes later on a big horn. The old man doesn't hear anything. He doesn't see anything. He'll never know the difference. We'll correct the two minutes very easily, and he won't upset the start by barging."

Who was the first man to see the Race Committee that evening but Mr. Shepard, and he wanted to know what was going on, and why, and whether they were going to insult him. He laid down the law to the Race Committee. He had both seen and heard it. So they finally decided after that, if you were that old, you had to be allowed to barge.

[In fact, recalls Chairman Whitmore, he let Mr. Shepard's family crew in on his scheme in advance, and the double start was the order of the day for the rest of the cruise. The old gentleman thought the competition was getting poor starts and never did catch on.]

Another thing happened up there with him. We'd gotten in early and were anchored, and he was up off our port bow just ahead. It's the finest swimming there when you get up to Morgan Bay, the only warm water on the coast. The party was to start about six or a little later [the Seth Millikens and Fred Camps had made a tradition of entertaining the fleet at cocktails ashore]. Shortly after four o'clock, Sally and I were in the cockpit when we heard a great deal of splashing and commotion up ahead.

There was the old man going up the ladder of *Irondequoit*, and following after him were three fully clothed grandchildren. I remember they were in their late teens. I couldn't imagine what was wrong. We got in to Mrs. Camp's, and Mr. Shepard came up to me immediately and said, "Mr. Barton, very sorry that you and your afterguard were disturbed. Children are not well brought up in this day and age."

The old man, it seems, had decided he wanted to go swimming. He had gone below, put on a pair of trunks, never said anything to the grandchildren, and just jumped over. They gave one horrified look and went in after him.

Barton went on to relate to a Shepard granddaughter, after

In white yachting hat, Thomas H. Shepard can be discerned at the helm of *Irondequoit II*.

The Roaring Fifties

Attired for a brisk day, Tom Shepard handles his beloved *Irondequoit II* with his usual look of purpose.

fetching her a gin and tonic, what may have been a secret or two of the old gentleman's vigorous longevity:

> "I know how dry Grandpa is, because a few years ago we had a meeting at the Tennis and Racquet Club, and I was smoking in those days. I went up to Mr. Shepard. He looked a little lonesome because his generation had died, and he didn't know the younger members.
>
> "I said, 'Mr. Shepard, Bob Barton of *Sally II.*' 'Oh, yes! Mr. Barton! Oh yes! Nice to see you!' I said, 'Won't you have a cigarette?' 'No! No! No! I never use it. Never use tobacco.!' A little while later I said, 'Mr. Shepard, can't I get you a drink?' 'No! No! No! I never use alcohol!'
>
> "And being a brash young man, I immediately said, 'Good heavens, Mr. Shepard, what do you do for a good time?'
>
> "And your Grandfather looked me in the eye, very straight, very, and he said, 'Young man, that's a question one gentleman doesn't ask another in a gentlemen's club!'"

Three weeks before a 1957 Annual Regatta swelled by Halifax Race entries, Brad Noyes sold *Tioga* to Charles Pingree; as *Sonora*, with an unfamiliar hand at the helm, she simply won the Puritan Cup for the third time, a performance she would make four-in-a-row in 1958. "Perhaps the fastest ocean racer of her size yet produced," in the opinion of Leonard Fowle.

A highlight of the Annual Cruise was the maiden win by George Batchelder's *Gelouba* of the MacPherson Bowl given by Warren MacPherson for the best overall corrected time in the cruising division. This was matched in 1958 by the Shepard Trophy, a silver bowl and tray donated by the Number One for the best overall corrected time in the racing division. The first winner was Wells Morss's new *Legend*, a German-built Sparkman & Stephens boat with a good racing record, owned in England by a Swede. (Mrs. Frances P. Copeland's *Periwinkle* qualified for perpetual custody with her third win in 1964, and the Shepard family presented a second bowl the next year. Subsequently, *Tioga* won it three times and *Taygeta* five, retiring it in 1985.)

The effort to move Race Week out of the early August doldrums, first into mid-August, then back into late July, was paying off superabundantly in these blowy fifties. On the Eastern's second day of 1957, July 22, a buildup of squalls to 45 knots with hail and rain knocked down or out eighty-three boats, mostly Jollys, 110s, Lightnings, Towns, and Fireflies, leaving 150 occupants in the water, some for two hours, all rescued. In 1958, more squalls the first day, sixty-three boats variously disabled, twenty sailors in the drink, all rescued.

Such small-boat vulnerability to the vagaries of the weather was hardly in the Eastern tradition. On the initiative of B. Devereux Barker, Jr., and George Nichols, the Eastern, the Corinthian, and the Boston agreed to underwrite for three years the junior sailing program in the Pleon. Such instructional priming paid off, and has to the present day. At the same time there was, during the 1950s, a growing emphasis in the Club on the uses of cruising and ocean racing and all they imply for wholesomeness, ableness, and seamanship in the face of the popularization of the increasingly fragile and fine-tuned little one-designs.

The incentives added to the Annual Cruise by the MacPherson and Shepard trophies are one example. Another is the metamorphosis of the traditional New London-Marblehead Ocean Race into the less arduous but more widely challenging Mount Desert Race, sponsored with the Storm Trysail Club,

in 1958 (when several Bermuda Race entries used it as a tune-up), its further evolution and broadening into a Marblehead-Portland Lightship (and return) Race, and finally an overnighter in Massachusetts Bay, retaining the Lambert Trophy as the prize throughout. A third example is the addition of a cruising division to Race Week in 1958.

One summer day in 1957, Dr. Henry Stebbins provoked a stir of nostalgia when he chugged into Marblehead in his *Zephyr*, a 26-foot Navy whaleboat built in 1943, with a 1908 steam engine and 1954 boiler. At a cruising speed of 7 or 8 knots, *Zephyr* had steamed from Stony Creek, Connecticut, with pauses for more coal at Mystic Seaport and a piston problem off Point Judith that was taken care of by the engineer of a towboat at Sakonnet, where *Zephyr* convalesced until the following weekend, when her voyage was concluded.

Zephyr graced Marblehead with something very special for many years, and with special emphasis when she slid silently alongside a soulless modern craft equipped only with an air horn and "blew her tubes." When the Stebbins family abandoned Marblehead for Seal Harbor in the 1970s, *Zephyr* made the voyage with them.

After a lapse of twenty years, the longest in the history of the America's Cup, the Royal Yacht Squadron challenged again in May 1957 in the Twelve Meters, the biggest class then racing, for a revival in September 1958. The receptive New York Yacht Club agreed that changing times and stratospheric costs ruled out the Js and secured a court-approved amendment to the Deed of Gift lowering the minimum waterline to 44 feet and dropping the requirement that the challenger sail over on her own bottom. The match was on.

By the end of the year, John N. Matthews's nineteen-year-old *Vim*, a veteran Sparkman & Stephens winner then under facelifting, was in the contention, and three others were in the design stage: *Columbia*, also by Sparkman & Stephens for a syndicate headed by ex-New York Commodore Henry Sears; *Weatherly*, by Philip Rhodes for Henry Mercer's group; and

Right: An Eastern gam at Padanaram, 1958. Norman Fortier photo.

The Roaring Fifties

Easterner, by Raymond Hunt for Chandler Hovey of the Eastern.

In view of the vast publicity surrounding resumption of the world's greatest yacht race, the reentry of the Hoveys, and of course the Eastern, in the Cup competition after so many years, and with a Hunt boat, created great excitement in Marblehead and New England sailing circles and indeed among the general public.

The beautiful, bright mahogany *Easterner* was built by Graves and launched into Little Harbor at high water one May evening of 1958 to the accompaniment of horns, whistles, shouts, and a generally glorious uproar from the invited, who were entertained at cocktails and dinner under tents and canopies. Well-wishers crowded around in skiffs, outboards, and whatever conveyance could get them there by water.

Following her fitting-out, *Easterner* joined the Annual Cruise at Newport on July 9, just after a race run by the Club for the Twelves competing for defender. She had been delayed at the Massachusetts Bay end of the Canal, closed overnight by fog and high winds, but got a big compensatory welcome of cannon, whistles, and cherry bombs from the thirty-five Eastern yachts anchored in Brenton's Cove.

That day's race off Newport was special in more ways than one: the Charles Francis Adams Memorial Trophy was put up for the first time by the Club and was won by the new contender *Columbia* in a race that developed into three reaches due to a wind shift thirty minutes after the start. The trophy, a handsome sterling silver bowl and tray, was purchased from a fund raised in Adams's memory by an Eastern committee headed by Asa E. Phillips, Jr., owner of the 62-foot schooner *Arbella*, Cleopatra's Barge Cup winner in 1941 and 1947. The seal of the Secretary of the Navy is engraved on the bowl, and the names of the 192 donors on the tray. The originals were to remain in the Club, a silver replica of the tray going to each year's winner under circumstances to be determined by the Race Committee.

Against her competition on the NYYC Cruise, *Easterner* was a disappointment. The ancient *Vim*, on which both Ted Hood and Brad Noyes were representing Marblehead, won all five races, although the Hovey boat showed possibilities when

Chandler Hovey was back in the America's Cup competition with Ray Hunt's handsome, bright Twelve-meter *Easterner* in 1958.

The Roaring Fifties

she finished second several times. In one close match with *Vim*, the lead switched at least twice, and the Hoveys dared to take their beauty, which drew more than 9 feet, over Middle Ground Shoal in Vineyard Sound with only 6 to 8 feet at low water. *Vim* declined the dare, and *Easterner* led when they met again. On another occasion, the Marblehead Twelve beat clear up into Hadley's Harbor while the competition called for their tenders to tow them.

Before one of the races in Marblehead against *Weatherly*, the man on the committee boat in charge of the cannon was so mesmerized by the tight circling of the two Twelves jockeying for the start that he forgot to pull the lanyard.

There was a feeling that *Easterner* never reached her potential, although the Hoveys have steadfastly argued that as a light-weather boat she never had it. She lacked her rivals' backlog of sails, for one thing. Ted Hood cut probably the majority of them for the four contenders, *Columbia* being the last holdout until early August, when *Vim*'s success with his cloth brought her into line for a spinnaker at least. Eugene Stetson, who worked in *Easterner*'s afterguard, admired the way the Hoveys raced her as a family, yet:

> It was a sailmaker's race, but Mr. Hovey wasn't built that way. It was sort of a downfall for poor Ray Hunt, a perfectionist who'd be promised a mainsail and be way up in the clouds, and the next day Mr. Hovey'd say, "I don't think we need it. Cancel it."

And *Easterner*'s crew work appeared to some to be outclassed, especially by *Vim*'s with Hood and Noyes aboard and some magic with the spinnakers. They broke out 'chutes within 15 seconds of rounding a mark, when it took *Easterner* sometimes more than two minutes, although her captain invented a fitting—later adopted by the competition—that Sis Hovey Morss says enabled them to set in 10 seconds. The Hoveys raced superbly, individually and as a family, but they were not the athletic supermachine that the crew of the typical Twelve has since become. Reflects Mrs. Morss:

> Ray Hunt designed us a heavy-weather boat when my father asked for a light-weather Twelve for Newport, having studied conditions there. We had no complaints except that *Easterner* was not good in Newport waters in light air with the turmoil and seas and cross chop. Bus Mosbacher and others couldn't make her go in light air under ten knots; she hobbyhorsed. Olin Stephens did the best with all his Twelve Meters. He seemed to be able to figure out the lines, both below water and above, which would help the boat in very, very light air, and I think the hulls of all the foreign boats and ours are pretty much the same now, and almost all the same speed.

> Our family—my two brothers, my father, my husband, and one nephew and I—were aboard. Later on in other years, our son was also on board. We raced all that summer, had a lot of very light air, and in fact it was supposed to be the lightest summer they had had. We knew she could go whenever we had a breeze. She was a lovely boat; we all thought she was the prettiest of them all, and most people felt that too.

> Of course it was all volunteer crew, and it seemed as if we were awfully crowded—ten or eleven of us on board boats that ordinarily you would put five or six on. But with the competition, the tacking duels, the quick spinnaker and jib changes, you had to have more on board, so it was very different from the great, big, enormous J-boat.

> We had coffee grinders, and each year you would have more complicated equipment. In recent years it became so computerized that it took the fun out of it, because you do everything by dials, computers, instruments, and so forth. A lot of the real challenge for the individual has gone. It is a matter of trying to understand all those gadgets and instruments, and it is very difficult for skippers who have always sailed by the jib to change, much harder for some than for others.

With Chandler Hovey at the wheel of *Easterner* during the trials are family members and designer Ray Hunt in cap, standing.

The Roaring Fifties

Smoking *Easterner* dips her jenny and wets her rail in this smashing photograph by Norman Fortier.

No one could do anything with *Easterner* in light air, but we could win in heavy air. Somehow no one ever wanted to admit that, especially the news media, so we just said nothing.

In his *Yachting* interview with Ray Hunt in 1964, a couple of years after *Easterner*'s equally disappointing showing in the 1962 Cup trials, B. Devereux Barker III had this to say about a lovely yacht whose promise nobody could quite get a handle on:

She has done well only in fits and starts, even with Ray at the helm, as he was for the latter part of the 1962 trials. In answer to the question of why she has not done better, Ray is frank to admit that part of the fault lies in the design, specifically her overweight hull scantlings. Also in '62 Ray made a keel change, which he is now convinced was not the right thing to do. When Hovey decided to build the boat late in the fall of 1957, precious little time was left before building had to start for a June launching. Thus there wasn't much time for experimental tank testing, and Ray is sure that with more time she would have been a different and better boat. He is definitely not in agreement with those who believe that all of *Easterner*'s troubles have stemmed from her management.

Easterner never did get going during those 1958 trials. In the pinches, *Weatherly* was unable to follow up on her early press notices, and it came down to *Columbia* and old *Vim* in an exciting back-and-forth that gave the edge to the newer of the Sparkman & Stephens productions. *Columbia* and Briggs Cunningham put down the British *Sceptre* in an anticlimactic four straight.

Four years later, Devereux Barker looked over the current Twelves and observed that there had been no advance in yacht design in more than nineteen years: "*Vim*, built by Mike Vanderbilt in 1939, was almost chosen to defend the Cup in 1958. In that year she was rated as a better boat than *Weatherly*, which, improved by a few changes, was the successful defender in 1962."

Chapter 17

The Early Birds

Old *Vim*'s performance against *Columbia*, *Weatherly*, and the unaccountably disappointing *Easterner* in the 1958 Cup trials did indeed suggest that not much had happened in yacht design in two decades. Even more so did the unflagging brilliance of Joseph Santry's 1913 New York-Fifty-turned-schooner *Pleione*. Had the Burgesses and the Herreshoffs and their peers already laid down the sweetest lines, leaving their postwar imitators in their wake? Was technology backwinding aesthetics?

Captain Nat's jackknife had given way to the tank test, but perhaps the element of creative intuition remained, more challenged and better armed than ever by the postwar popularization of all-around sailing and seamanship, by the explosion of new materials and techniques, and by the resultant pressures of competition, afloat and at the drawing board.

Brad Noyes believed so, and with sufficient confidence that after only three super seasons with his 50-foot yawl *Tioga*, he sold her in 1957 to Charlie Pingree and returned to Aage Nielsen for more—and, if possible, even better. From now on, it would be a single stick.... "Sailing the yawl, ninety per cent of the time you never put the mizzen up, and I thought, why have the thing?" So this *Tioga* was a 39-foot sloop built in Copenhagen at the Walsted yard, regarded by some as the best in the world.

Like her predecessor, the *Tioga* that was slung off the boat from Denmark early in 1959 was keel-centerboard, favored by Nielsen. In spite of a penalizing rule change, she won her maiden race for the Southern Circuit's Lipton Cup in Florida in a very light air against some of the best in the nation.

All the while, across from the Neck at his growing Little Harbor complex, Ted Hood had been ruminating about what makes a boat go. Looking to the 1956 Olympics, Ray Hunt had sketched the radical 5.5 Meter *Quixotic* on the back of a manila envelope for Hood and Don McNamara; Ted built her and they sailed her, only to see *Quixotic* live up to her name, as related by Dev Barker III in his *Yachting* article on Hunt:

She was far and away the fastest boat in the trials, but it may be recalled that she missed going to Australia because of an incredible series of circumstances in the last two races. In spite of being disqualified in the next to last race, *Quixotic* still had only to beat *one* boat in the final, while her closest rival was winning. When she was well up in the fleet, the main halyard shackle opened, the sail came down, and she finished last. Her closest rival did win the race and thus the trip to the Olympics.

Three more years of mulling it over, and Ted Hood was ready to break into the design end of the game on his own:

The first boat I really designed seriously was the first *Robin* [not to be confused with Chandler Hovey's classic Q-boat of the same species] in 1959, a 40-foot ocean racer of planked wood. I worked on her for quite a few years. She was sort of a take-off on Carleton Mitchell's *Finisterre*, which was the closest I could think of, though I never sailed on her. *Robin* was beamy, much shallower, longer, more extreme, with a much taller rig, a little bigger than *Finisterre*.

I wanted a shallow-draft boat to go in shallow water. I thought centerboards were more efficient than keels, and I wanted a tall rig and a comfortable cruising boat at the same time. She was fairly heavy but only twenty-five per cent ballast, which was almost unheard of, because you were supposed to have at least fifty per cent to make a decent boat. She had more room inside with the beam. Her best was to windward in a breeze, so it was her form stability, not ballast, that did it.

Funny how many designers, their first boat's their best boat because they've spent quite a bit of time working on it. They've been researching it, put a lot more effort into it. It's been germinating for a long while, and later on you don't have the time to put that much effort into any one design.

Some may have called her "fat," but *Robin*, built in her designer's Little Harbor yard, proved the early bird and won the 1959 Patton Bowl. Then came the Annual Regatta on July 4. A year from the day she first sailed, *Easterner* carried off the Puritan Cup, though she rated 64.6 under the Cruising Club Rule, beating the new *Tioga* by three and a half minutes, *Finn Mc-Cumhaill*, and *Robin*.

A month later, on August 4, fifty-seven yachts in the New York Yacht Club Cruise hove into Marblehead in a spinnaker race from Farnham Rock. *Sonora*, ex-*Tioga*, was second in Class II on the run, but *Robin*, though having won three races, including the Corsair Cup, placed only fifth in Class IV, with *Tioga* sixth. Again Joseph Santry hosted a Camelot-style cocktail party at his "Red Gate" on the Neck, followed by a dinner dance at the Club.

(The Council in 1956 had distributed the models from the middle of the Model Room around the Club to make the room available for small meetings and private parties. On the eve of the New York Cruise, one of the flag officers proposed to remodel the Model Room into a $25,000 cocktail lounge for the entertainment of the visiting opposite numbers. Treasurer Barton put his foot down.)

The next day, Hood in *Robin* won the Astor Cup off Marblehead from a field of sixty-one in a 7-to-16-knot northeaster over a seventeen-mile, leeward-windward course. The press praised her beat home as outstanding. Noyes in *Tioga* was right behind for second. *Robin* defeated all eleven boats in her Class III, the smallest, turned in the best elapsed time in Class II except for two boats, and even beat four in the big Class I.

Chandler Hovey had presented the New York Yacht Club with the Chandler Hovey Gold Bowl, to be awarded annually to the Twelve with the highest percentage in the races for the class in its Annual Cruise and others sponsored by the club after July 1, for as long as the Twelves competed. The first winner was *Weatherly*, seventeen points to ten over the donor's own *Easterner* in ten races.

On the first leg of the returning New York race to Provincetown, Frances Copeland joined the fleet in her new, 35-foot Ohlsen yawl *Periwinkle*, which won the LaCroix Trophy in the Eastern's Chowder Race on the last day of Race Week and had the lasting satisfaction of dominating the class, leaving *Tioga* second and *Robin* ninth.

The end of the 1950s saw technology catch up with the Eastern and Corinthian race committees. Chairmen Jack Whitmore and Doug Nystedt issued a joint circular with a single set of starting times and equipped their committee boats with two-way radios beamed boat-to-boat and to the Corinthian booth ashore.

And finances began to catch up. As commodore, Wells Morss had the distasteful task of again raising the entrance fee and dues under pressure from Treasurer Barton. During his regime, the four at-large members of the Council were given overlapping four-year terms to provide continuity, and an advisory committee was created to review the budget and the bylaws and to consider long-range plans.

Chief upholder of the family tradition, Commodore Morss had been ocean racing for twenty-five years when he bought the 52-foot, bright-finished, Sparkman & Stephens yawl *Legend* in 1958 and embarked on what was for him the well-worn route to Bermuda. With Jim Connolly navigating; Jim Carroll, J. Amory Jeffries, and Bob and Frank Scully crew; and Sarge Goodchild paid student hand, they finished seventeenth out of 110 and won Class A.

The 1960s opened on a wider-than-ever yachting front for Marblehead, which was picked for the Olympic trials in the International 5.5 Meters (hosted by the Club) and the Finns, because of the similarity of Marblehead weather conditions to those anticipated on the Bay of Naples later in the summer. Then, after the trials, the 110 Worlds were held August 15 to 19, and the Raven Nationals August 23 to 25. The choice in the 5.5s fell on George O'Day and his *Wistful*, which right after her selection was rammed and badly damaged at another club's float. He shifted boats and sailed to victory for America.

Brad Noyes won his third Puritan Cup, the first with his second *Tioga*, which romped in seven minutes ahead of the pack and also won Class C. At the other end of the stick, Thomas Shepard, Number One at ninety-three, had the helm of *Irondequoit* over most of the Annual Regatta's twenty-mile course to Boston Lightship and back in a rising southerly and won Class B.

Ted Hood had sold *Robin* to Lee Loomis and Emil (Bus) Mosbacher, Jr., *Vim*'s helmsman during the 1958 Cup trials. As

Fun, she won Class III in the New York Yacht Club Regatta. Her success prompted such demand for clones that Hood arranged for a yard in Taura, Japan, to build his second *Robin*, a 40-foot centerboard yawl, in 1960. Straightaway she won the Astor Cup in the New York Cruise, while Pingree's *Sonora*, ex-*Tioga*, was taking the Una Cup and Brad's current *Tioga* the Corsair Cup.

There is a time to race and a time to retire from the race, and as 1960 came up, and her fifty-eighth season (her thirty-fifth under his ownership and his seventy-seventh), Joseph Santry reluctantly decided to put his beloved *Pleione* out to pasture.

Although his career as head of Combustion Engineering based him in New York, he disliked Long Island Sound, preferring to daysail in Marblehead, with its smoother water and usually better breezes. *Pleione* had a new and taller foremast going into one New York Cruise in the 1950s—heavy winds and a big sea running—and a nephew (Santry didn't marry until he was fifty-two) suggested that they not jeopardize a new rig on such an old boat. "We didn't come down here to show these people we're quitters," was the comeback. "If we lose the stick we lose it, but we're going to race."

Santry's hospitality at "Red Gate" was famous, embracing more than once the entire New York fleet. When Francis Herreshoff gave him the bow and stern of the immortal *Shona*, he mounted them on his boathouse and threw a long-to-be-remembered party to the tune of the bagpipes.

So if there were curves on the chart of yachting history to plot the courses of the new and the old, they crossed somewhere off the float of the Eastern Yacht Club that Labor Day of 1960 with the end of the first season of the decade. It is hard to imagine any single event more symbolically closing the age of wooden boats, if not of iron men, leaving the field to the driven and hard-driving prophets of high tech. The owner's niece, Suzanne Santry Connolly, was there to bid farewell:

Labor Day, September 3, 1960, at the first stroke of nine from Abbot Hall, Captain Avard (Pat) Morris of *Pleione* cast off her mooring in Marblehead Harbor for the last time. She fell off on the port tack and then rapidly picked up speed, although there were no obvious ripples in the water.

The original plan had been to leave the harbor under power and set sail at the mouth, but it was learned at the dance at the Club the prior Friday night that there was to be a big celebration as *Pleione* left her homeport of thirty-four years to go to the Mystic Seaport in Mystic, Connecticut. She had been given

by Commodore Joseph V. Santry to Mystic as an addition to its museum of sailing ships.

Consequently, without spoiling the surprise, family members urged Commodore Santry to sail from the mooring as he had done on so many occasions, and she left under main, mainstaysail, jib, and topsail. The race committee boats of the three main clubs, all dress ship, along with many privately owned boats, escorted her down the harbor, and people on board moored yachts gave their best wishes as she sailed by.

Horns and whistles blew, and the Eastern, Corinthian, and Boston yacht clubs saluted with their cannons as the old New York Fifty swiftly glided by, her owner at the helm with tears streaming down his face.

Her speed in the light air was amazing to many, and as a result there was a near-collision in the middle of the harbor. The Boston's committee boat was to leeward running parallel when someone on board decided to cross *Pleione*'s bow. They sped up, but not realizing how fast *Pleione* was sailing, did not leave enough clearance. Uncle had to throw the wheel hard over to swing *Pleione*'s bow off to avoid a collision. His grand-nephew, ten-year-old David Connolly, was out on the bowsprit at the time and had a thrilling experience as the two boats came close.

By the time *Pleione*, still followed by a few faithful escorts, reached Marblehead Rock, the wind had died completely, and she had to start up her engine as she headed toward the Boston Lightship on the way to the Canal and her last voyage.

Unable to resist the call, her owner was soon dividing his sailing between Marblehead and Florida on the 68-foot Trumpy-built *Pleione II*.

The Australians embarked officially on their all-out campaign to wrest the America's Cup from New York with a challenge from the Royal Sydney Yacht Squadron in 1960 for two years hence, although Sir Frank Packer's charter of *Vim* for four years the previous fall should have been the tip-off. Without *Vim*, the familiar three were back at it again as the trials got under way in 1961. The Hoveys were as eager as ever with *Easterner* and a new helmsman, Bus Mosbacher, who had not been part of the *Vim* deal with the Aussies. *Weatherly* was back, with Arthur Knapp skippering, while the 1958 defender, *Columbia*, was bought by Paul V. Shields and sailed by his nephew, Cornelius (Glit) Shields, Jr.

With a new hand at the helm, *Easterner* at first almost held her own. She placed third out of fifty-five for New York's Astor Cup (won by *Weatherly*), actually leading on the first leg to windward until her spinnaker fouled as she fell off the wind.

Steve Wales and *Duquesita*, winners of the 1961 Sears Cup for the Pleon Yacht Club.

More encouraging still, she came out of a series off Newport on August 12 and 13 in a three-way tie with the other two Twelves. But then, in a runoff on August 28, *Columbia* found her old form.

The Yacht Racing Union of Massachusetts Bay conferred its fifth annual Distinguished Service to Yachting Award on Chandler Hovey.

Continuing their cooperative efforts to bring order to the increasingly complicated and crowded round-the-buoys racing, the Eastern and the Corinthian agreed to abandon the old inside line off the Corinthian for most championship events, commencing with Memorial Day, 1961. The fleets were growing, the harbor was more crowded than ever, and besides, the air was better outside. It was a major break with tradition, requiring two committee boats for starting and finishing lines—generally one in the vicinity of Four-Fathom Gong between Marblehead Rock and Cat Island for the larger boats, the other for most of the smaller boats between Peach's Point and Cat Island.

It was decided that each club would give individual prizes for each championship race and for the season, with joint season prizes based on the combined standings in the championship series of eight races of both. By now at least seventeen classes were racing in the series, including the U.S. One-Designs, Internationals, Ravens, 210s, Day Sailers, Rhodes 19s, Explorers, Townies, Interclub Dinghies, Bullseyes, Herreshoff 12½s, Jollys, Lightnings, 110s, Brutal Beasts, and Turnabouts. The average number of starters in each of the Eastern's seven races was about 140.

Mrs. Robert K. Bell (captain), Mrs. George Poor, and Ann Pevear, the Club's women's crew, won the Wakeman and Commodore Colt trophies for the Massachusetts Bay and New England championships and qualified as New England representatives for the Women's National Sailing finals at Balboa, California, where they finished around the middle.

Commodore Parker ("Mr. Eastern" because he was also president of the Eastern Dog Club) was succeeded by Vice Com-

The Widgeons proved an excellent class for the learners and juniors.

modore Henry B. Kingman as 1961 closed, and Robert Barton decided to step down as treasurer after six years, summing it all up:

> When Jim left as Commodore in 1962 I think we were a real, old-time yacht club in the true sense of the word. The racing was fine. The restaurant was excellent. Dues were reasonable. We were not borrowing any money. We were completely out of debt, and contrary to what Dev Barker had thought possible, the pool bonds came due. He wanted them extended, and I said, "That's defaulting in my language, and there's no need for it." We paid off every one of the bonds except those that were given to us, refinanced everything on a mortgage of about five and a quarter per cent. I left the Club without anything but this long-term mortgage, no short-term debt at all.

Frederick J. Shepard, Jr., succeeded Barton as treasurer in 1962, and after two years turned the job over to John McCandless, who handled the finances until 1975.

The sensational flights of Ted Hood's first *Robin* in 1959 had flushed a springful of them, and in 1961 the Japanese yard turned out about thirty other 36- and 40-foot centerboarders for eager customers before going broke. One 40-footer was for their designer. Among the two 36-footers were the centerboarder *Robin Too* and, to thoroughly confuse things, *Robin Too II* with a keel, which turned around and beat her sister.

Commodore E. Ross Anderson of the Boston Yacht Club announced in January 1962 that he would head a syndicate with Robert W. Purcell to go after the defense of the America's Cup with the Twelve Meter *Nefertiti*, to be built at the Graves yard. The idea had been born aboard Anderson's 72-foot schooner *Lord Jim* at the finish of the Halifax Race of 1961, in which she was first to finish, beating DeCoursey Fales's *Niña* but not Hood's winning *Robin Too II* on corrected time. Ray Hunt would design her. Hood would cut her cloth. *Lord Jim*'s skipper, John J. (Don) McNamara, a national winner in the 210s and Olympic medalist, and Hood would be co-skippers.

But Ted's fat and fast *Robin*s appealed to Anderson, and he wound up with the design job. He worked fast, and so did Graves. Three months in the building, *Nefertiti* was launched on May 19, 1962. Australia's *Gretel* had been sailing against *Vim* for more than two months, not brilliantly.

By July, Ray Hunt had altered *Easterner*'s trim and moved her mast forward, among other changes, and had the helm; Mosbacher had moved over to *Weatherly*, and Glit Shields still

skippered *Columbia*, both boats variously redone. In a series off Newport between July 2 and 14, in winds varying from 8 to 22 knots, the Boston's *Nefertiti* won eleven, *Weatherly* six, *Columbia* four and the Eastern's *Easterner* only one. 'Titi was hot and looked like the choice.

That was the apex of her pyramid. The morning of July 15, *King Tut* took the empress-presumptive in tow. Don McNamara evoked a mysterious image of her ghosting in around the Neck that Sunday evening:

> *Nefertiti* gently moved up-harbor, when from around the point came a milling horde of launches and "whalers," tooting, buzzing, and waving. We gave back in kind on our foghorn, waving with eyes slightly misty and grins to our ears. The boats fell in, in echelon, on our quarters as we glided on toward our mooring. The docks and porches of the Corinthian Yacht Club were jammed with waving people, down for the Sunday night movies. So was the lawn of the Eastern. Then a strange thing happened; in the apricot twilight, across the tranquil harbor, people started to clap. At first it was barely audible above the muffled rumble of the engines astern, but it grew. As we drew abeam of Eastern it became a roar, like a fall day in the stadium. The cannons started, first Boston, then joined by Eastern and Corinthian. The harbor became a din of horns and bells and cannons, flares and people. *Nefertiti* had returned. She was the yacht of the people in a town that loves yachts.

But from that moving moment on, it was almost all downhill. Maybe *Nefertiti* was overtuned: her mainsail was reduced, ballast was added, and she emerged more of a heavy-weather boat. Perhaps her crew was overtuned: Ross Anderson fired McNamara. Hood stayed on as skipper. Brad Noyes joined his old buddy on this Cup contender as he had on *Vim*. "A whole summer of that was not for me, getting up at six in the morning and going out and changing sails all day for that one day of glory." But *Columbia* and *Easterner* were eliminated, and *Weatherly* nosed out the Marblehead Twelve in winds that never exceeded 11 knots. The rest is history. *Gretel* took only one out of five, and 'Titi took her place among the might-have-beens and if-onlys.

Twenty-five years later, Ted Hood looked back:

> In *Nefertiti* we added more beam to get form stability, which was a good thing, and to get a wider sheeting angle, and a big jib

A regal evening launching for Marblehead's Twelve-meter *Nefertiti* from the Graves Yard, May 19, 1962.

The Early Birds

The Early Birds

Charles Pingree's *Sonora*, cast up on Mason's Rocks by the storm of September 27 and 28, 1962.

because the rule was telling us jibs were more efficient than mainsails. But the keel was all screwed up. The tank kept telling us, make the keel bigger, bigger, bigger, and every time we added, it told us we were faster. That was our inexperience in the tank. We had the first boat with the rudder long on the bottom because the tank said it was better to extend the keel—and it was, slightly—but the wetted surface they gave you credit for in the formula was more than it should have been, so it negated the advantages. If we hadn't tank-tested we'd have had a better boat because the tank was giving us credit for wetted surface it shouldn't have. She did well in a breeze.

It is of some significance that the Lambert Ocean Race for 1962 (from Tinker's Bell around Peaked Hill Bar and Cape Ann whistler buoys and back to the lighted bell at the entrance to Marblehead Harbor) was specifically restricted to *single-hulled* yachts. So was the Annual Regatta. Perhaps not entirely coincidentally, the same year Henry Morss, Jr., introduced the multihull to the Eastern:

I took a lot of physics in school. It was natural that I should wish to apply this both to sailing and to the oceans. After World

War II this led, along with other things, to a curiosity about multihulls, mostly because it didn't seem altogether sensible to have to carry around a heavy keel to keep right side up. My wife and I worked over plans for catamarans and trimarans, finally settled on a trimaran.

We acquired one in 1962, the *Charade*, the first trimaran in the Eastern fleet to the best of my knowledge. She was designed by Arthur Piver, 32 feet overall and about 18 feet wide. In many ways she was a very comfortable and attractive cruising boat. Because she was pretty heavy, she did not have the overadvertised speeds that multihulls are thought to have, but we found her an interesting boat to sail. Along the way we learned a bit about the inadequacies of design. Those early boats were not designed by people who understood sailing very well.

She was built for us in Maine. The designer lived across the bay from San Francisco. It was difficult to make major changes. Most of those I made were in the rig. The rigging did not permit trimming the jib properly. Rather than the diversified sailing we do, Piver was primarily interested in broad reaching, the best course for real speed. One of his objectives, late in his brief life, was to ride one wave, surfing, all the way around the world in the Roaring Forties. One of the things he didn't know was that no one wave rides around the world, no single wave lasts forever.

A severe northeaster with winds up to 55 struck the coast on September 27 and 28, 1962, sweeping nearly eighty yachts, lobsterboats, and other craft ashore. Many were broken loose by others drifting or dragging down on them, and casualties were heavy, including Charles Pingree's ocean racer *Sonora* (ex-*Tioga*), so badly hurt when she was slammed onto Mason's Rocks off Gregory Street that he sold her for rebuilding.

This latest in a series of devastating storms and hurricanes of the 1950s was another reminder of the vulnerability of the anchorage from the northeast that had prompted the Council only the previous year to publicly favor construction of the perennially debated but never realized Marblehead breakwater.

The storm broke an outstanding ocean-racing record chalked up by Charlie Pingree since he acquired *Sonora* in 1957, when she took first in Class A in the West Penobscot Bay Race, as she would again in 1960 and 1962. In 1958 she won the Boston's Gould Bowl, and in 1958 and 1959 the Patton Bowl. She won the Monhegan Race (under brother Sumner Pingree) and the NYYC's Una Cup in 1960, and the following year a NYYC Cup for third place in the Block Island-Vineyard Haven run.

The Early Birds

Thomas H. Shepard, the dry and doughty owner of *Irondequoit*, died on February 19, 1963, at ninety-six, having been a member since 1889, the year following his graduation from Harvard, and a charter member of the Corinthian. He was replaced as Number One by former commodore and treasurer B. Devereux Barker, who was admitted to membership on July 28, 1898. At the request of the officers, he had been compiling with ex-Commodore Parker a brief review of the Club's history since 1900, the last year covered in the *Ditty Box*, which he concluded in October with these observations:

Of course, the exclusion of ladies from the main clubhouse is long since a thing of the past. From the bridgehead in the new dining room in the Twenties they surged along the piazza and into the house, while the males retreated to the bar and adjoining reading room, where they are sometimes free from intrusion. [At the time of writing, there were thirty-two women associate members out of 456.]

Before World War I [1914 to 1918, actually], as Chairman of the House Committee, I sat on the Council. Whenever a change was suggested, the invariable question was, "Do you want a yacht club or a casino?" Well, now we have a casino and a good one; but the hard core of interest is in boats and life afloat. This perhaps is due to the Nautical Instruction introduced some twenty years ago. Whatever the reason, we are today a group of better sailors than the worthy gentlemen who so cherished their "Yacht Club."

The Historical Committee's account of the 1962 Annual Cruise may be appended as a forceful postscript:

After a captains' meeting at the clubhouse at 1800 on July 4, an overnight race from Marblehead to Boothbay Harbor on July 5 was sailed. The next day was a lay day at West Boothbay Harbor during which cocktail parties were given by Commodore and Mrs. Henry E. Kingman aboard the flagship *Capella* and Fleet Captain Stanley R. James and Mrs. James aboard the *Bonanza*. Then followed races on successive days to Tenants Harbor, Pulpit Harbor (with a cocktail party by Vice Commodore and Mrs. Maynard Ford and Rear Commodore and Mrs. John Wilson), Mackerel Cove, Northeast Harbor (with cocktails by John H. Simonds), Morgan Bay where a cocktail party was given by Mrs. Frederick Camp in her home at Webber Cove, East Blue Hill, Buck Harbor, and finally to Camden. There the Race Committee served cocktails for all captains and crews. There the cruise disbanded.

After the Japanese yard that had turned out so many *Robins* and their fledglings went broke at the end of 1961, Ted Hood went halfway around the world before he stumbled on a candidate worth considering:

We found a little yard in Holland—way out in the sticks, practically in Belgium—building North Sea pilot boats out of steel, and I said, if it's good enough for them, why can't we make a yacht out of it? I'll pay the money for the research for the first boat. We gave them very nice plans how to do it, and it made that yard into one of the best over there by giving them the new American way of building a yacht. We started building all our boats there in 1962, steel hulls covered with glass, with wood decks.

One of the earliest of these Hood boats to be built by Maas Brothers in Breskens was another *Robin*, a 45-foot centerboard yawl of glass over steel with boiler punchings in cement for inside ballast. She zipped through the 1963 Annual Regatta and emerged with her designer's second Puritan Cup and the Charles Francis Adams Memorial Trophy. Then, on the New York Yacht Club Cruise in Buzzards Bay on July 28, she won Ted's third Astor Cup, finishing fifth in a field of sixty-one, first on corrected time in a fresh southwester, and took the Southern Circuit for dessert.

Around 1965, Hood's research paid off with the first Airex-core sailboat, as far as he knows—a 36-foot ocean racer of this expensive and extremely tough PVC foam, most of it manufactured in Switzerland, under fiberglass, that was the prototype at the Netherlands yard for the next ten years. Meanwhile, back in the States, he was producing his first conventional fiberglass boat, a 37-footer molded by Graves at Marblehead and finished off with wood deck and trim in his Little Harbor shop.

Maynard Ford followed Henry Kingman as commodore in 1964, a year marked by the challenge of the British Twelve Meter *Sovereign* for the America's Cup and the decision of Chandler Hovey to retire *Easterner* from active competition. A group of members presented the Club a perpetual trophy to honor the distinguished former commodore, to be raced for annually as determined by the Council and the Race Committee.

And it was a sign of the times that the bylaws again were amended, reducing the minimum waterline length of yachts from the 25 feet that had prevailed since 1949 to 16.

The Chandler Hovey Trophy was the occasion for a new ocean race for cruising yachts between 30 and 73 feet overall with valid CCA measurement certificates. Seven of the twelve entries started the inaugural Chandler Hovey Ocean Race in the fog on August 23. The course was from Tinker's to Cape Porpoise and back to Marblehead Rock, a time-allowance distance of 117 miles. Four finished.

The first of twelve replicas of the Chandler Hovey Trophy was won on corrected time by Bradley Noyes's third *Tioga*, a Nielsen 43-footer again built by Walsted in Denmark in 1962. She had started the season in the Annual Cruise by winning the race to Falmouth Foreside, the race across Casco Bay to The Basin the next day, and to Boothbay Harbor the next. (Mrs. Frances Copeland's *Periwinkle* won the Race Committee Run, and, as noted earlier, the Shepard Trophy for the third time, retiring the family's first bowl.)

Tioga then fell in with the New York Yacht Club Cruise at New London on July 24 and won the Cygnet Cup and Commodore's, Vice Commodore's, Rear Commodore's, and NYYC cups, as she had Vice Commodore's and NYYC cups on the 1963 Annual Cruise. As Brad Noyes certainly should know,

> Aage Nielsen liked centerboards and didn't get into too many new ideas. But he was a wonderful person who produced wholesome boats. He would draw every bolt, its size, and exactly where it should go, and in all my sailing days in his boats, there was never any metal fatigue, no structural problems. I never even parted a jib sheet. The rules would fluctuate, and his boats always came out pretty well, never outstanding [the Noyes racing record raises some questions there], never down around the bottom. If you sailed it well, you could usually do well, whereas today [1987] you build a boat for the rule, and six months later it's obsolete.

The Annual Regatta (Arthur J. Santry, Jr.'s Nielsen-designed *Temptation* won the Puritan Cup in 1964, as she had in 1962) and the Lambert and Chandler Hovey ocean races, all open to yachts of any recognized club, were accepted in 1964 as three of the seven races in the Ocean Racing Circuit of Massachusetts Bay—a substantial contribution by the Club to area yachting.

Gear failure didn't help, and *Easterner* couldn't score in any of the five preliminary Cup trials that year. She won the Queen's Cup in the New York cruise on July 26, however, over *Gesture*, *Windigo*, *Bolero*, *Cotton Blossom IV*, *Nina*, and *Katuna*, in that order. But the rest of the Twelves had outrun her, and she was not entered in the final trials, which saw the elim-

ination of *Columbia* and *Nefertiti* and a surprising turnabout that brought *Constellation* to the fore over the favored *American Eagle*. Once again, the finale was no contest, and *Sovereign* failed of sovereignty four straight.

The 1964 season marked the seventy-fourth Race Week and the Seventy-Fifth Anniversary of the institution that started in 1889, and 459 started in the Eastern's opening series in spite of a chilly northwester. The regular Marblehead classes were augmented from other ports by Manchester I's, Yankee One-Designs, Shearwater catamarans, Thunderbirds, Thistles, Crocker 20s, Hustlers, Merry Macs, and Aqua Cats.

For the rest of the decade, the familiar names and boats dominated the Club's ocean racing. Ted Hood's Dutch yard turned out *Robins* at the rate of a couple per year. He won the Lambert Trophy in 1967, as he had in 1963, and took the Puritan Cup in 1965, 1966, and 1968 (his fifth). Brad Noyes's newest *Tioga*, 43 feet, won the Norman Cup for the race back to Marblehead from Bar Harbor at the end of the Annual Cruise in 1964, 1965, and 1967, and the Shepard Trophy in 1965 and 1969. In 1966 she won her class and came in third in the Bermuda Race.

Important as it was for the handicapping of serious ocean racing, the CCA Rule by 1965 was seen as defeating its own purpose for cruising. It was complex and required weighing,

---

Winning 5.5-meter sailors in 1964 were Frank Scully, John J. (Don) McNamara, and Joe Batchelder.

and the bother and expense of obtaining a CCA rating was definitely inhibiting participation in the Annual Cruise. Under the initiative of Chairman Garrett Bowne, the Race Committee and Measurer Burtner devised the simplified Eastern Yacht Club Special Measurement Rule, based on the individual boat's plans, which was applied for the first time to the 1965 Annual Cruise. The result was a dramatic increase in entries, with about fifty starting in the race from Padanaram to Sakonnet. The EYC Rule prevailed until 1972, when adoption of the New England Rating Rule stimulated further participation in ocean racing.

The same season, the Puritan-Genesta Cup was put back into competition for the first time in eighty years at the discretion of the Council, which offered it, in a reciprocal gesture, during the New York Yacht Club Cruise to Marblehead in August. The "Captain's Decanter" had been presented by the New York to the owners of *Puritan* to commemorate her America's Cup victory over *Genesta* in 1885, and by them in turn to the Eastern in 1887.

The Astor Cup Race was sailed by fifty-three yachts on August 7. A.E. (Bill) Luders, Jr.'s 40-foot sloop *Storm* won both trophies. Arthur Santry's yawl *Temptation* led Division I over such big names as *Niña*, *Impala*, *Gesture*, *Ondine*, and *Legend*. She was proudly claimed by Leonard Fowle as a Marblehead craft, since she spent at least half of each season in North Shore waters—as well she might, for although her owner was secretary of the NYYC, his roots were in Boston, and his Uncle Joe Santry kept *Pleione* the pride of the Eastern for decades.

At the other end of the racing scale, the durable Widgeons replaced the Sprites and Turnabouts, which had replaced the Brutal Beasts, as the starting class for juniors. The Pleon acquired a fleet of them, still in service twenty-two years later.

John Wilson was elected commodore in 1966. His flagship was the 42.6-foot-overall, double-planked mahogany cruising ketch *Holger Danske*, designed by Aage Nielsen and built in his native Denmark by Walsted in 1964. Named for a Danish folk hero, she won the third Chandler Hovey Ocean Race in airs so light that ten of the thirteen entries withdrew. An early protocol of Commodore Wilson's was the tradition thereafter of standing to colors before dinner.

That year, to celebrate his golden anniversary as measurer, Professor Evers Burtner was elevated to a rare Honorary Membership.

One-design racing at Marblehead advanced another step with the appearance of the Shields class on the Club's opening day of Race Week, which saw 462 boats start with fair skies, a 15-knot south-southeaster, and whitecaps.

To promote his handsome namesake fiberglass keel sloops, 30 feet 2 inches overall, Cornelius Shields, Sr., a notable skipper who had founded the International One-Designs back in 1936, gave them to the Merchant Marine Academy, the Naval War College, and the New York, Massachusetts, and Maine Maritime academies. The Eastern's Frank Scully—who won the 110 and 210 National Championships in 1943 and 1948, the National Intercollegiate Dinghy Championship, the gold in the 1958 Pan American Games, and the bronze in the 1964 Olympics crewing in 5.5s—brought the Shields class to Marblehead with his *Aeolus* and scored over Henry Cooper's *Finesse*.

On the third day of Race Week, the wind was southerly, and

The Eastern's Race Committee in 1964: (front) Thomas Welch, Chairman Garrett D. Bowne III, Robert Reardon; (rear) Henry Duane, Pendleton Keiler, Henry Watson, Denton Cook, John Nichols

the good racing weather held. Captain Arthur Shuman, U.S.N. (Ret.), and John Whitmore, president of the Yacht Racing Union of Massachusetts Bay and ex-Race Committee chairman—old cronies from the Eight Meters and Thirty Squares of the 1930s—lunched together on the Club lawn and had to admit the presence of a few prerace gastric butterflies. But the one got out there and won in the Shields class by 32 seconds, and the other in the Day Sailers by 58.

The Race Committee donated the Eugene T. Connolly Trophy, a silver bowl, to the Shields class in honor of this outstanding helmsman and member, and Frank Scully's *Aeolus* won first honors in the championship series for 1967, again in 1968 and in 1970.

At season's end, the YRUMB reelected President Whitmore and bestowed its award for Distinguished Service to Yachting on Ted Hood. Ray Hunt was the 1963 recipient, and the 1967 awardee was J. Amory Jeffries, whose contributions to the Eastern alone (twenty years as chairman of the Race Committee, secretary, and treasurer) would have earned him the honor.

Hood was busy hatching his latest *Robin*, which joined the 1967 New York Cruise and collected the Una, Navy Challenge, and Cygnet cups. A seeming paradox, she was a displacement sloop of 47,000 pounds on 49 feet overall, very fast, yet drew but 4 feet 3 inches with an 8-foot airfoil-shaped daggerboard housed in a trunk that went up to the cabintop. Hood altered her to a yawl and won the 1968 Bermuda Race.

Brad Noyes was on the New York Cruise too, with *Tioga*, and was given the coveted Nathanael Greene Herreshoff Medal, first presented by Captain Nat in 1926 for the most points in the largest NYYC class during the season. It had lapsed since its award in 1937 to the J-boat *Ranger*. Duck soup for Noyes, who had just won his fourth Puritan Cup, now neck-and-neck with Hood.

Ted also had other things on his mind. Australia had challenged with *Dame Pattie*, and Olin Stephens was much more than matching with *Intrepid*, which, with Hood sails, was proving to be the fastest Twelve yet. So the designer/builder/sailmaker/racer was busy aboard, smoothing the wrinkles out of his cloth during the trials, grabbing a day off here and there to put his own youngest prodigy through her paces. Bus Mosbacher steered *Intrepid* through a brilliant sweep.

The Eastern's Annual Cruise was to the east, with the MacPherson Bowl for the best overall corrected time in the cruising division going to the commodore's *Holger Danske* for

the second time since 1965 and the Shepard Trophy for the best overall corrected time in the racing division to Lincoln Davis's *Swan*. At Maple Juice Cove, downriver from his native Thomaston, John H. Blodgett of the schooner *Mistral* was presented a special trophy for his many years of contributions to the Annual Cruise.

Distaff sailing was continuing to gain recognition. The crew of Katherine (Katums) Copeland (captain), Marjorie Burke, Jane Danforth, and Ann Copeland Pingree won the North Shore Women's Sailing Championship and the Lee Cup that went with it. Mrs. Frances Copeland, the mother of Katherine and Ann and one of Marblehead's outstanding women sailors, had won the championship for the Corinthian in 1936, and it was the first time one daughter, let alone two, had earned the title previously held by her/their mother. They also finished second in the New England elimination trials for the national Adams Cup Races.

The 1967 season opened on a tempestuous note and closed on a poignant one. A severe northeaster on May 25 and 26 wrought such havoc that the May 30 races had to be postponed. Richard Hill's U.S. One-Design *Flair* and Secretary Nichols's 38-foot sloop *Katahdin* were among the many victims, shattered beyond salvage by the surf on the Club beach. The pier runway was destroyed and the floats severely damaged.

On September 28, 1967, the old schooner *Pleione* was taken under tow from Mystic Seaport—where she had been a floating exhibit since 1960 in front of the gingerbread station given by the New York Yacht Club—to be scuttled according to the last instructions of her owner, Joseph V. Santry. Originally he ordered that this last of the nine New York Fifties—one of the longest-lived prizewinners in American yachting—be destroyed after a year. That year stretched until his death at eighty-three. He funded her maintenance at Mystic year by year but stipulated in his will that it cease upon his death and that she be given a fitting burial at sea, for he could not bear to have her fall into other hands and not be kept up as he had done for forty years.

Hatches, skylights, interior paneling, her winches, wheel, binnacle, and transom were removed, along with her spars and lead keel. She was ballasted with 52,000 pounds of concrete and towed by the Seaport tug through 3-to-4-foot seas in a south-southeasterly breeze to a 50-fathom hole in Long Island Sound, a little over three miles south of the eastern end of Fishers Island.

The tug stood by dress ship. *Pleione*'s anchor was let go. The old schooner *Brilliant* was in the offing, flying the code flags "Bon Voyage." The seacocks were opened. A wreath was cast upon the sea. Beautiful *Pleione* settled in ten minutes, and in half an hour she was gone beneath the surface.

Vice Commodore B. Devereux Barker, Jr., owner of *Owl*, succeeded John Wilson as commodore in 1968. His father, the ex-commodore, was Number One; the third generation, B. Devereux Barker III, had been a member of the New York Yacht Club Race Committee since 1966 and would be chairman from 1969 through 1971.

Facing a duty-free season for the first time in two years, Commodore Wilson rounded up a crew of four and faced his ketch *Holger Danske* in the general direction of the Azores on June 15, 1968. In the Cruising Club's compilation *Far Horizons*, he described "Flirting with Brenda":

> The Eastern Yacht Club Committee lined up with a final salute at Newcomb's Whistler and made a long slow turn back to the harbor. Our log was streamed and we were on our way. It was to be the first "transatlantic" for each of us and we were surely excited.

Their first week, in nigh-perfect conditions, *Holger* carried them 1,072 miles, averaging 6.4 knots. Not until then did they hear about Brenda from a chance gam with a radio ham:

> Although some 800 miles west of us, [Hurricane] Brenda was within half a degree of our latitude. Making three to four times our speed, she would clearly be down on us in about 48 hours. So—not knowing anything better to do—we changed course to the north northeast to make more northing.
>
> Hoping for the best, but preparing for the worst, we bagged our mainsail and packed it in the cabin. We removed our heaviest genoa from the lazarette and parked it alongside the main, and transferred another heavy jib from the lazarette to the cockpit. Our weather cloths and spray hood were removed. Our life raft was brought from its position on the cabin trunk by the mast and parked in the cockpit. The ends of our 60 fathom 3/4" diameter nylon rode were led through the stern hawsepipes and secured around our No. 30 Barient winch aft of the lazarette hatch, coiled and ready to let go if we got going too fast. By late afternoon, after a lot of heavy work, especially tiring in the big sea that was running, our crew was pretty well done in—but *Holger Danske* was ready for Brenda. Windage had been reduced, the ends had been lightened and much weight brought below.
>
> Sooner than anticipated, these proved to be worthwhile precautions, for the wind that evening progressively increased from Force 6 to 9 and at 0500 hours on Tuesday, the 25th, we logged in Force 10, the highest of our entire trip. . . . This storm was not associated with the hurricane.
>
> We spent two and a half days trying to outmaneuver Brenda. We sailed northeast, then north and later when it appeared that she was clearly going to pass us to the south, we tacked to northwest and then southwest so that she would surely pass to the east. We were happy to learn on the evening of the 25th when we were sailing southwest that Brenda was heading northeast approximately 150 miles abeam to port. When there was no longer any question of her getting to us, we returned to our northeasterly course knowing that, although Brenda had not yet crossed our projected track, she soon would and well enough ahead to cause no problem. We spent 55 hours and sailed 200 extra miles in the outmaneuvering process, but we had won out.

Back at Marblehead in this season of 1968, *Tara*, in which Charles Hovey won the Norman and Shepard trophies as a charter in 1966, brought BYC member Don McNamara the Hovey and the Lambert. And Jonathan Wales took the first of six consecutive Guy Lowell Cups in his IOD *Duquesa*. Jon and brother Stephen were the sons of John W. Wales, ten years a member of the Race Committee and house chairman from 1961 to 1967. They started sailing when they were ten. Jon won the Curtis Cup for the Eastern at sixteen in 1956 and the Manhasset Bay Challenge in 1961, when he was on the Olympic trial team. Stephen won the Curtis for the Pleon in 1960

True to her owner to the end, *Pleione* sinks beneath the waves on September 28, 1967.

and 1961, then the Boardman Trophy in 1962, while his older brother, as a Boston University undergraduate, was picked for the crew of *Nefertiti* during the trials.

But the big day for Jon Wales was to come as the climax of the first world championship of the Internationals to be held in Marblehead, the eighth since their designer and builder donated the Bjarne Aas Perpetual Trophy for the event in 1959. The worlds were hosted from August 26 to 30 by the Eastern, the Corinthian, the Boston, and the Pleon, and Jon capped a brilliant season by defeating the defending champion, William S. Widnall, also of Marblehead.

As the first century of the Eastern Yacht Club and the troubled decade of the sixties draws to a close, stocktaking is in order.

There were 477 members as of March 15, 1969, including twelve life, thirty-nine women associates (of whom two were life), and six juniors. Professor Evers Burtner was the sole Honorary Member besides the various ex officio governmental officers. He retired from the post he had held as measurer since 1916 and was succeeded by Damon Cummings.

Of the 259 craft in the fleet, the thirty-seven of 30 feet waterline or over included four schooners; twenty-two sloops, yawls, and ketches; ten powerboats; and one motorsailer. The 222 of less than 30 feet on the water included 185 sloops, yawls, and ketches; one catamaran; two catboats; thirty-one powerboats; and two motorsailers.

Twelve entries (among them several midget ocean racers) sailed the Lambert Cup Race on June 15 and 16 over a hundred-mile course from Tinker's around buoys at Manomet, Race Point, and Cape Ann and back. Robert Brockhurst's CCA class *Comet II* won on corrected time.

Thirty yachts in three classes found light airs and smooth seas for the Annual Regatta on July 4, twenty-one miles from Tinker's south-southeast to the Atomic Buoy and return. Lincoln Davis's *Cherry Bomb* won the Puritan Cup, Walter Adams's *Sally Tiger* the Adams Memorial Trophy. Next day, the Annual Cruise was off for Boothbay Harbor, Tenants Harbor, North Haven, Camden, Castine, Gilkey's Harbor, and Harpswell. James A. Carroll, Jr.'s *Glide* won the MacPherson Bowl. Bradley Noyes's fourth *Tioga* by Aage Nielsen, 46 feet overall and built in this year by Walsted in Denmark, won the

Ted Hood's 49-foot *Robin*, altered to a yawl, wins the 1968 Bermuda Race.

The Early Birds

Shepard Trophy. Again keel-centerboard, she featured the new separated skeg/rudder; Ted Hood supplied her sails and the aluminum spars to hang them from.

This was the first year of the Marblehead Racing Association of the Eastern, the Corinthian, and the Boston, formed for joint planning and supervision of the local races. The conduct of six season championship series and its own portion of Race Week was assigned to each club, with three starting lines: an outside line for the IODs and others of comparable size; a high-performance line for the Tempests and others; and an inside line for the Day Sailer and similar classes. The total number of starters in the Club's six championship races was 1,441.

Under the new association, Race Week ran from July 26 through August 2. The Eastern was assigned the first three days, but the Race Committee canceled the third due to a bad-weather forecast, only to see the sun smile and the wind blow too late to cancel the cancellation. The Eastern started 436 its first day, 428 its second, in thirty-two classes. The Fowle Memorial Trophy for the outstanding performance of the week was awarded to Jonathan Wales and his IOD Duquesa.

Most significantly for one-design racing, 1969 was the summer the Etchells 22s and Solings made their first slippery appearance in Marblehead following their debut at the Olympic

Robin's triumphant crew grouped around skipper Ted Hood includes old friend Brad Noyes, at left.

trials in Europe. The E-22s initially came up from Long Island Sound for Race Week for a couple of seasons, while a small fleet of Solings took tentative root locally. Dave Curtis was among the first to buy a Soling:

Both classes were formed about the same time for the Olympic trials. The criteria were that they had to be keel boats under 30 feet six inches and sailed by three people. So Skip Etchells decided he'd build the fastest he could according to the specs, and he did, but it turned out to be too big or too heavy for trailing around Europe, though they had two ten-race series, and his boat won over the 5.5's, Dragons and lots of others designed for it. The Solings did very well, though they were a smaller boat. But the Europeans packed the meeting, decided they wanted a European boat and eventually picked the Soling.

The New York Yacht Club Cruise was cut short on August 7 by the sudden death of Commodore W. Mahlon Dickerson aboard his flagship Mustang in Pocasset Harbor. Ted Hood's most recent Robin, however, had already won the Commodore's and Una cups, and the 36-foot yawl Shearwater of his design, built in Japan in 1961, won the Navy Challenge and Corsair cups. Although the Annual Cruise was officially disbanded, a number of boats continued on to Marblehead, where the party at the Club was held as scheduled.

The Chandler Hovey Races were held on August 23 and 24, and it was decided to split them into the CCA division—28 to 73 feet having CCA certificates, racing over a twenty-mile course from Tinker's to The Graves Whistler to Boston Lightship and return—and the MORC division—23 to 30 feet with MORC ratings, eighteen miles from Tinker's to Boston Lightship and back. In the CCA division of twenty-three starters, William C. Brewer, Jr.'s Jeanne d'Arc of Manchester won the Hovey Trophy over Ted Hood's Robin Too, which won Class A and finished second in the fleet, beating Dana Atchley's Appledore and Brad Noyes's Tioga.

Representing the Club, David Curtis won the Match Racing Trophy of the Yacht Racing Union of Massachusetts Bay, which elected Vice Commodore James A. Carroll, Jr., president and gave Eugene Connolly—the fifth Eastern member so honored since 1961—its Distinguished Service to Yachting Award.

And to round out the season, the decade, and the first century, the Eastern Yacht Club's annual Chowder Race was held on September 7, 1969, in three divisions—keel, centerboard, and cruising—104 starters in all. When it was all over, free chowder was served at the Club to the skippers and crews.

Chapter 18   **Yacht Club or Casino?**   *1970–1975*

On the eve of its centennial, the Eastern was caught in the backlash of the turbulent 1960s. The issues involved private clubs and the right of assembly, common purpose and standards of admission, racial and ethnic discrimination or accommodation, compatibility, covenants, constitutional guarantees, liquor licenses, and the role of government in such matters, but had nothing to do with sailing.

Some claimed that the start was lost but the race was won. The course, however, remains enshrouded in fog, and the finish is not in sight. It may never be, as long as clubbishness is a human trait and boats cruise in company.

Several weeks before Christmas of 1969, Marblehead school officials had advised teachers to be sensitive to the ethnic backgrounds of their pupils in planning holiday programs, a caveat that touched off an anti-Semitic eruption among some parents and children. The issue seems to have smoldered until the election to the school committee the following spring of John K.P. Stone III, who had mentioned in a campaign interview with the *Marblehead Messenger* that he belonged to the Eastern and another club.

Public notice of the Club's routine annual application to the selectmen for renewal of its seasonal liquor license appeared in the *Messenger* of April 9, 1970, as did a letter from Norma and Paul Warren questioning whether elected town officials could represent all the people without bias if they were members of clubs "which have institutionalized bias as an official policy and way of life."

A week later, the newspaper ran a letter, among others on the subject, from Louis K. Brin of Clifton, an editorial writer for the *Jewish Advocate* of Boston, criticizing the *Messenger*'s editorial position that club membership was a "private value

judgment," by which "curious illogic" Stone, "who belongs to two such clubs (which he has failed to extricate from persistent and substantial allegations of prejudice), is supposed to himself be free of the implicit racism that such memberships make inevitable. . . . Any candidate for such a critically important office who is willing to defend his exclusivist private club memberships and at the same time cry out for relief for educationally disadvantaged children in this town, as Committeeman Stone did in a recent *Messenger* statement, is unsensitive, kidding himself and insulting my children and the children of many of my friends and dear ones. . . ."

Brin said that he and Attorney Carl K. King would oppose granting the Eastern's liquor license on the grounds that the Club was "obviously racially and ethnically exclusivist."

In the same issue, Club Secretary George H. Stephenson called Brin's accusation unfounded. Members could propose anyone, without regard to creed or color, to the Club's five-member Admissions Committee, which must unanimously approve the candidate. The bylaws contained no restrictive clauses. There were some Jewish members. The prime criterion was compatibility. "You have to have people that get along with people," explained Stephenson. "If they do that, they'll make good club members."

In a crowded hearing on April 22, the selectmen unanimously approved the license after Attorney King conceded that he had no proof of discrimination in the Club's admissions but questioned whether it was in the public interest for such a license to be granted if discrimination is "quite likely." Selectman Arnold Alexander responded that "we are not here to discuss moral issues. . . . We are an administrative body, not a judicial one." The next day the *Messenger* editorialized:

... What is really happening in Marblehead these days is that those protesting the clubs are being categorized as misfits who wouldn't want to join even if they could, and that members of these organizations are being willy-nilly branded as callous racists without regard to their individual merits or defects. . . .

We find it surprising that no Eastern Yacht Club official deigned to answer contentions last night that his group had exhibited a "pattern" of discrimination in selecting members. With a membership of .6% Jews and 0% Negroes, the charge cannot be dismissed with silence.

We continue to defend clubs' right to select members as they please, and their members' right to hold any public office they seek, on the much-criticized theory that one man's "racism" may simply be another man's convenience.

But if club leaders shrug off the honest objections of those who disagree with their practices, they're damning those among them to which membership is simply a convenience, and not a pervasive life style.

Led by Brin and King, forty-seven Marbleheaders petitioned the State Alcoholic Beverages Control Commission on April 30 to overturn the selectmen's approval. Meanwhile, the controversy provoked a vigorous and sometimes heated letter exchange in the *Messenger*. Mr. and Mrs. George Cass, for example, on May 7 proposed to apply the yardstick that was ultimately wielded by the ABCC:

All of us who live in the suburbs are aware that golf clubs, yachting clubs, etc., that own the best (and sometimes the only) sports facilities, so arrange their memberships as to insure the exclusion or inclusion of specific religious and ethnic groups. . . . Where these organizations seek the protection of the State— i.e. incorporate, require zoning, licensing, the use of public facilities, . . . then they do involve the society at large, and they have an obligation to incorporate the applicable portions of the Constitution of the United States into the rules and regulations that guide their conduct.

At present, de facto segregation in clubs is immoral. We look forward to the day when a court decision, based perhaps on the challenge of a liquor license, will make it illegal, as has already occurred with schools and to a limited extent with housing. . . .

On May 14, twelve days before the ABCC's scheduled private hearing to determine if there were sufficient grounds for holding a public one, an official of the Boston Anti-Defamation League told the *Messenger*: "If it can be determined that no known Jewish members are in the Eastern Yacht Club, there may be a prima facie case, and it's the club's responsibility to prove that it doesn't discriminate."

Three days later, with its centennial season about to open and the very fount of celebration in the balance, the Club's predicament made the front page of the *Boston Sunday Globe* in a long article by Robert L. Levey.

... Since the end of World War II, a steady trickle of "new people" has produced a condition whereby Jews are the major minority group in the town. Most live in the Clifton area. Some are there by choice. Others moved there because of long-standing real estate patterns in the town which lead Jews seeking houses away from Old Town, Marblehead Neck and posh Peaches Point, which defends itself from "new elements" by formation of associations that get a crack at supervising the resale of property.

The "Gentlemen's Agreement" has gone on for a long time in Marblehead. It cuts both ways. Rabbi Robert Shapiro of Temple Emanu-el admits that many Marblehead Jews have gladly gone along with a "live and let live" attitude, never questioning or opposing the explicit residential and social separations in town. And the old families, many drawing their heritage from early American history, their incomes from law firms, banks and businesses and their faith from Christ, acted the same way.

Everyone knew that Jews couldn't get into the major yacht clubs, the Corinthian, the Eastern, or the Tedesco Golf Club. The issue was never challenged. It was tradition. Now the Jewish population and the other "new people" in town, the reform-minded professional people and generally younger citizens, amount to a decisive voting bloc.

Reporter Levey quoted Commodore John T.G. Nichols as stating that the Club's membership policy was based entirely on "compatibility and an interest in sailing."

Petitioners against Eastern point out that "compatibility" can cover a multitude of sins, including the presumption that Jews are automatically incompatible. Nichols has refused to either defend or explain the club's internal policies. Responding to an inquiry about whether there are Jewish members, he said first: "I don't personally know whether there are or there are not." When asked again he said, "Well, it's a semantic question what you mean by a Jew, isn't it?"

This was a reference to the fact that one or two Eastern members are reportedly of Jewish birth but are Episcopalian by religion.

The *Globe* man interviewed School Committeeman Nick Stone, whose membership in the Eastern and another private club had so enraged Louis Brin:

Stone said the stir of the Eastern license has "put off the time you'll see a representative number of Jews in these clubs." He regards the whole episode as "a great mistake" on the part of the petitioners and said that he feels the singling-out of his yacht club membership is a discriminatory act against him. Stone and his wife have been personally active in numerous liberal causes, and he said that if Eastern's policies need revision, he will work for them inside the club.

Rabbi Shapiro told the *Globe* he rejected the Club's claim of compatibility as the basis for admission, because any young people in town can join the Pleon and are considered "compatible" until they reach twenty-one, "but the Jewish members and their families would then be ineligible for Eastern. Mr. Shapiro said that he sees a typical pattern of historical anti-Semitism in the attitudes of some yacht club types who believe that the entrance of Jews will inevitably lead to a 'takeover.'"

Following its preliminary hearing, the Alcoholic Beverages Control Commission issued the Club a conditional liquor license and gave the petitioners until June 29 to file affidavits substantiating their claims of discrimination in admissions. On August 12 the ABCC decided:

> The petitioners' affidavits relate mostly to incidents of possible discrimination in the community of Marblehead and not to the licensee. The one affidavit relating directly to the yacht club comes from the wife of a former member. She says that the club apparently discriminates in the selection of its membership and that she "never saw a Jew on the premises.". . . We are unable to attribute any discrimination which may exist in the town of Marblehead to the Eastern Yacht Club.

However, the commission accepted the underlying rationale of the petitioners, cautioning that "we think it abundantly clear that it is not in the public interest to grant a liquor license to a person or organization that discriminates in the selection of its membership on the basis of race, creed or color."

The decision was reported to be the first under Governor Francis Sargent's order that all state agencies "actively utilize their authority" under his new antibias Code of Fair Practices.

The first Annual Regatta of the Eastern Yacht Club had been sailed on July 12, 1870, from an anchor start off Marblehead Rock to Minot's Ledge and back by fourteen schooners and sloops for prizes of $150 and $100, respectively. The entire fleet consisted of twenty-six yachts—namely, sixteen schooners, nine sloops, and one steamer.

A hundred years later minus nine days, thirty-six out of a fleet of 243 sailed the Centennial Regatta on July 3, 1970, in a flying start from Tinker's to The Graves to the Boston Lightship and back. Cash had long since given way to trophies, and Brad Noyes won the Club's oldest, the Puritan, for the fifth time with his *Tioga*, as well as the Charles Francis Adams Trophy in memory of the most famous helmsman ever to fly the Club burgee.

Twenty-two racing participants in the Centennial Cruise, led by Commodore Nichols, rendezvoused at Pocasset on July 5, in contrast to the first Annual Cruise, which departed Marblehead on July 25, 1870, and made the round trip to Mount Desert in a fortnight with the assistance of chart, compass, and taffrail log. The centennialists hailed into Newport for a lay day on July 11 in the middle of the America's Cup observation races between the new Twelves *Valiant* and *Heritage*, *Intrepid* and *Weatherly*; they raced back to Marion the next day and disbanded. Again it was Noyes and *Tioga* all the way, winning the Puritan-Genesta Decanter, and the Shepard Trophy for the third time.

Twelve days later, the New York Yacht Club Cruise rendezvoused at Newport. Again it was Ted Hood's turn, this time with his latest *Robin*, a 52-foot one-off fiberglass yawl of his own design, built in Holland. She had already won the Eastern's Lambert Ocean Race and finished second in the Bermuda Race and now carried off everything in the New York's Class II and the Una and the Cygnet cups. A Navy Challenge Cup was won by Arthur J. Santry, Jr.'s new *Pleione*, a big, 59-foot sloop designed by Aage Nielsen and built by Abeking & Rasmussen in Germany. In 1971 she would win the Puritan Cup, as her namesake had in 1953.

It was a matter of some regret in Marblehead that the New York Yacht Club decided to abandon its customary invitation to the Eastern during the Fifties and Sixties to join its Annual Cruise.

The Centennial Committee of Charles Pingree, Robert B.M. Barton, James Bowers, and John Wales had been at work, and the season culminated on Friday, August 7, in Dress Ship Day and the Centennial Dinner Dance in the clubhouse.

As if the dynastic burden of a hundred years reaching back to steamer days was more than could be borne, the Club's old

Race Committee boat gave notice of its retirement this centennial season. The ancient craft had served the Eastern since the 1930s, had served the Coast Guard cadets in the same capacity during the war, then went back to civilian service for twenty-five years. Since the formation of the Marblehead Racing Association, it had been serving quadruple duty with the other three clubs on the line. It owed the Club nothing, but when it was retired and sold, it just couldn't stay away: as the *Elizabeth M.*, moored in Little Harbor and still fitted with signal mast and yards, she now and then served on the line when called.

Race Chairman E. Denton Cook and others traveled to Maine and Rhode Island and found a design for a successor committee boat. His successor, John E. Searle, Jr., got Council approval and was about to go ahead at $30,000 when ex-Commodore Gifford Simonds suggested that the Marblehead YMCA was willing to sell its Children's Island Day Camp ferry *Y-Naut*, formerly a lobsterboat, the *Eleanor G.* The *Eleanor G.*, built around 1966 at the Webber's Cove Boat Yard in Blue Hill, Maine, was bought by Raymond W. Ellis of Marblehead, an Eastern member, and his son Melvin, and named for Mrs. Ellis. After the usual mishaps getting into service, the *Eleanor G.* helped Mel tend 120 pots between 1966 and 1968, when she sank at her mooring in Marblehead Harbor during a December northeaster and was acquired by the Y.

And that is how the handsome and unique "new" committee boat was rebuilt under the direction of Emerson Oliver and launched from Cloutman's Boat Yard in time for the 1971 season—at a cost of something less than $14,000.

If the Club was a little diffident, a bit make-do, a trifle Yankeeish about the observance of its hundredth anniversary, its peers were not, and on November 24, 1970, the Yacht Racing Union of Massachusetts Bay acclaimed it the Yacht Club of the Year "for its accomplishments in yachting for over a hundred years." Cited among them were its role in the defense of the America's Cup, in the early promotion of junior racing (including the inauguration of the Sears Cup in 1921), its contributions to the development of racing in boats of all sizes, its support of Marblehead Race Week, and, of course, its part in organizing the YRUMB.

Do centennials, like certain prophecies, provide their own occasions for fulfillment, for change, for the turning of the leaf? The Seventies, a decade of such altercation and alteration in the world, had commenced with a disturbing social confrontation for the Eastern, and there would be much further soul-searching before they passed into history.

In another of those periodic ebbs, the guard was changing. John Blodgett, whose lovely schooner *Mistral*, built in Saugus, had succeeded to the place of honor in the line of *Constellation* and *Pleione*, died on April 27, 1971, at the age of eighty-nine.

While *Mistral* often accompanied the Annual Cruise, her owner enjoyed equally exploring the coast on his own hook. The future Commodore Donald Blodgett was along on one such independent coasting expedition when his father had no alternative but to fire his professional skipper, who had communed once too often with the bottle, and ordered the transgressor ashore forthwith.

> This guy had a nice, big, beautiful radio—this was back in the days when they made them that way—and some other stuff, and he yelled as he was packing up, "If I'm leavin', nobody's gonna have my stuff!" And he hove it overboard, right out of the forward hatch.

The Centennial Dinner Dance of the Eastern Yacht Club, August 7, 1970.

Mistral was sold just prior to John Blodgett's death to a buyer who gave her to the U.S. Naval Academy, which sent her on a six-month cadet training cruise to Europe under a female skipper. After three or four years, she was sold by the Academy to a California party and was last heard of by Don Blodgett in Sausalito, still in excellent shape.

On July 27, former Commodore Chandler Hovey crossed the bar. He was ninety-one, patriarch of an internationally famous yachting clan, benefactor of Marblehead, a sportsman's sportsman, and almost singlehandedly responsible for the Club's reentry into the contention for the America's Cup—first with the J-boats in the 1930s, and then in the 1960s with the Twelves.

During the summer, the yachting world was shocked by the untimely death of Leonard M. Fowle, Jr., who had so ably succeeded his father at the *Boston Globe* and made his own name as one of the foremost reporters, writers, and general experts on the sport for which such a passion had run so powerfully in their family. Len Fowle's knowledge of every aspect of sailing and racing was encyclopedic; his loyalty to all the clubs and the Eastern in particular was unequivocal; and his legacy was as much in his advancement of the juniors and the teaching of the fundamentals of sailing, navigation, and sportsmanship as in the prodigious volume of notes, records, and scrapbooks— the life work of father and son—that he left to the Club archives and to the Peabody Museum of Salem.

Though the cup seemed suddenly in passage that summer, a dwindling handful was still at it. Gene Connolly in his *Leenane* won the Eugene T. Connolly Trophy, given in his own honor for the winner of the Club Championship Series in the Shields class. He was eighty-one.

And Frances Gilliland nearly bisected the span of the club to which she had given forty-seven years of her life running the front desk. At the general meeting on the evening of September 5, 1971, she was called from her command post to the head table by Commodore Nichols and named the first honorary woman associate member. "With it come responsibilities," postscripted Chairman Jack Searle. "The Race Committee appoints Frances an honorary member and puts her in charge of the wind and sun!" She recalled:

I was up near Commodore Nichols when he announced that I was made an honorary member, and when Mr. Barton escorted me down through the living room, they clapped. Evelyn Hurley was at the switchboard, and she said, "I thought they'd never stop clapping." And I said, "They should clap. I was made a member."

While the newest Honorary Member was practicing her recently bestowed powers with the wind and sun during the next off-season, the worst blizzard in years gave the waterfront a Washington's Birthday battering that cost the Club ninety feet of seawall and embankment, requiring repair or replacement as one of the first priorities of Commodore Charles W. Pingree's tour of duty in 1972. In the aftermath, the Council created the Storm Committee as a standby waterfront rescue squad. For the first time, the Club opened on April 15, with weekend service, and a chowder luncheon on April 19. Full service began on June 3.

A look at the classes assigned to the starting lines in 1971 reveals the extent of the ascendancy of technology and molded

---

Frances Gilliland, after 47 years at the front desk, was named the first honorary woman associate member of the Club on September 5, 1971.

fiberglass's conquest of wood, with the resultant uniformity, cost control, drysailability, lower maintenance, and versatility of storage. On the outside line were the Internationals, Shields, U.S. One-Designs, Solings, 210s, 110s, and Ensigns; on the high performance line were the Tempests, Jolly Boats, Lightnings, 505s and 420s; on the inside were the Rhodes, Day Sailers, Towns, Corinthians, Bullseyes, Herreshoffs, Widgeons, and Barnegats.

Nevertheless, Race Week entries had dropped from 331 to 313 in 1971, further evidence of a decline in interest that seemed to reflect the popularity of similar events in other ports. For 1972 it was decided by the Marblehead Racing Association to cut back from five days of one race per day to four days of two each, a change that paid off in 1973 when 341 boats started on July 27, and on July 28, 817 boats, including twenty-four ocean racers.

The big one-design news for 1972, and perhaps for the decade, at least as far as the Eastern was concerned, was the fadeout of the Solings in the wake of the whirlwind conquest of the Etchells 22s, of which a dozen or so locals were turning up on the starting line. This time Dave Curtis, an early bird in the Solings in 1969, was beaten to the line by the veteran Ben Smith of Annisquam, supposed die-hard Lightning sailor, who was the first to shift ships in 1971. Curtis:

The Etchells had been coming up from the Sound for Race Week, and the IODs and U.S. Ones were too proud to admit that this boat should start ahead of them, so it would start third and sail through all of them and finish fifteen minutes ahead. Most of the people who got into the Solings were winners in their own classes, and it was new and different; then I think they got discouraged because in one class they weren't all going to win. I went into the Etchells because I wanted to be competitive on a world level; it was easier as a sailmaker to make the sails faster, so evolution really hurt the old boats, and it was easier to go on to a new class. Some others went into Shields, and some went cruising.

We'd seen the Etchells year after year, seen how on a light-air day you'd be in an hour before the first Shields or IOD, before six o'clock, and not have to paddle. You didn't have to hike, which you do in a Soling; you're not even allowed to. The Etchells has twice as big a keel, is beamier and much more stable. The two look very similar, but the Soling is a thousand pounds, a third, lighter. So the Etchells is an excellent fleet racing boat; it doesn't make any difference how big you are, because it's got a skeg and isn't as sensitive to sail, and is powerful and stable. The average age in our fleet in 1987 is over fifty-five.

The competitive Curtis was accustomed to virtuoso performances, however, trying for the Olympics in the Solings in 1972, 1976, 1980, and 1984.

In recognition of his leading part in the revival of round-the-buoys racing, L. Pemberton Pleasants, Jr., who would succeed Jack Searle as chairman of the Race Committee that fall, was awarded the Fowle Trophy. This kept it in the family, since the previous season of 1972 the trophy had gone to his wife Betty, the second woman holder ever, for her outstanding performance in her Shields class *Lotus*. Betty had won the first of four straight Connolly Trophies and the E. Denton Cook Trophy, which had been given by Connolly and others in 1968 in tribute to the former Race Committee chairman, for the winner of the class Sunday Series.

In the hope of stimulating broader interest in small-boat racing among the regional clubs and the general public, the Eastern, the Pleon, and other Marblehead friends in 1972 organized the Leonard M. Fowle, Jr., Memorial Yacht Racing Foundation in furtherance of his special concerns with junior yachting. The foundation sponsored "Sail '73," the second annual parade of boats, on May 28, opening day.

In the television age, no longer was the Sunday night buffet supper and movie sufficient to satisfy the rest of the week's yen for entertainment. One who savored the Club's most popular social event, and the dances and partying that marked those decades from the early Thirties over a span of forty years, has nostalgic memories:

It was a sell-out every Sunday. Various groups took turns going to each other's homes for cocktails beforehand. The tables at the buffet were stretched the whole length of the porch, and there was great rivalry for the choice locations near the commodore, who had a big one in the bay at the head of the steps so that he didn't have to move for the movie.

The buffet would feature lots of clam broth or chilled vichyssoise, lobster tails, roast beef, ham, turkey, salads and so forth, and delicious desserts. Then for the movie, benches were set up on the lawn in front of the screen. The children got lollipops at the desk and sprawled down on the grass on blankets.

Most of the weekly dances were informal. The July Fourth, Race Week, and Labor Day dances were formal. George Henderson, who lived at the Club, would give a cocktail party Sunday noon after Labor Day, followed by a Dutch treat luncheon and the married couples tennis tournament, with a lot of people in costume—one of those things that started out as a fun idea but got too big and out of hand and was stopped. And of course there were the Tuesday family suppers that started in the late Fifties and tapered off in the Seventies.

But times changed. There was a weeknight show in 1972, and more social events were scheduled, such as the weekly family night, with a limited and less expensive menu to encourage more volume, a water show in the pool, the first overnight family cruise—to Gloucester—on August 5 and 6, and on August 15 the first annual Children's Show. And a quarter of the membership was so actively using the tennis courts that a junior program was suggested to relieve the pressure on them.

On May 29 a venerable Marblehead yachting tradition was revived (and formalized the following season as "Sail '73") with a parade of boats behind *Nefertiti* and the New Eagle Jazz Band aboard the Graves workboat, then the Internationals, the U.S. Ones, the new Etchells fleet, and on in single file in descending order of length past the reviewing officials of the Marblehead Racing Association. Back on the moorings, launches rounded up all hands for the Fowle Foundation benefit party at the Club. The night before the Fourth saw the resurrection of another grand and glorious tradition, the harbor illumination, with flares lit one by one every ten feet until the entire shore was aglow, topped off with a resounding display of fireworks.

And the 1972 season was extended at the other end as well, long beyond the yachting part of it, with a closing informal dinner dance on October 28.

The previous day, closing out his own extended season, his seventy-fifth with the Club, former Commodore B. Devereux Barker, Number One for nine years and a member since July 28, 1898, died at the age of ninety-four. The Grand Old Man of the Eastern was the last of the Old Guard whose official association stretched back into the nineteenth century, when the big schooner, the gaff rig, a deepwater sailing master, a proper paid crew, and plenty of brass and brightwork were taken for granted. It gave pause that Commodore Barker's successor as Number One was Nathaniel C. Nash, who was admitted fully eighteen years later, on July 12, 1916.

Ten years had elapsed since Barker responded a little ruefully in 1962 to the rhetorical question, "Do you want a yacht club or a casino?"—"Well, now we have a casino and a good one; but the hard core of interest is in boats and life afloat."

Less as a matter of deliberate policy than of gradual practice,

the Eastern Yacht Club was entering its second century with objects more diffuse and certainly more informal than the singleminded aims of 1871, which centered on the encouragement of yachtbuilding and naval architecture, and the cultivation of nautical science.

One can never tell what minor maneuver may get major matters out on the table. In 1971 it was China's invitation to come over and play ping-pong that began the thaw in relations with the United States. On Marblehead Neck that year and the next, it was the ardent desire of enthusiasts for the maxi form of the game, platform tennis, or "paddle," to hold court at the Eastern Yacht Club. This brought some festering divisions into the open, which was the first step toward their resolution.

Paddle is a winter variant of doubles on a wooden platform; the vogue swept into New England in the early 1970s by way of Connecticut and was introduced into the Eastern by B. Devereux Barker III, Charles C. Ives, and Benjamin A. Rowland, Jr.

The suggestion to the Council that the Club might benefit from an off-season platform tennis court, as had other leading yacht clubs, struck the traditionalists under the banner of Robert B.M. Barton as utter heresy, the final evidence that now even the hard nautical core of the old Eastern was being threatened by a sort of rectangular Horse of Troy. And innocent as it was, the proposal came at a time when sailing was clearly not the sole preoccupation of the membership, perhaps a little less so every year, hence the battleground symbolism of the landbound paddle court.

Since the extent of interest had not been demonstrated beyond a few, the Council in 1973 approved the construction of one instead of the two proposed platforms. Charles Ives, one of the initial paddle buffs in 1971, outlined the stipulations in a letter dated June 26, 1974, to Bob Barton, the principal dissident in the matter:

The Council agreed that the use of the court should be given to those members who advanced a special activity fee (five years in advance) so that the construction costs were covered in full, in large measure from the initial group of 35 sponsors, and in part by a portion of a bequest from the late former Commodore B. Devereux Barker. The Club actually has title to the court, and the Council members selected the site and placed control of the facility under the House Committee. It was further stipulated that all playing privileges for the initial sponsors would expire in 1979, providing the Club with a $15,000 capital asset at NO cost to the membership-at-large.

A proposal for a second paddle court was presented to the Council for action at their June 3 meeting, after a survey was made of the membership-at-large. The results showed an additional group of twenty-six members who indicated their interest in the game—in addition to the original thirty-five members who wanted to see a two-court facility. The Council, however, decided to refer this matter to the Long-Range Planning Committee for further study.

Could the Eastern really ride two horses, Trojan or otherwise? Could it be both yacht club and casino? The facilities were getting "tatty," as one member put it, and, more bluntly, "membership was declining in quantity and quality." Budgetary pressures were increasing (the Council okayed a minimum monthly restaurant charge of thirty dollars a member in an effort to legislate usage). George Henderson, the Boston hotelier who for years was a seasonal resident in the House, died in 1973 and left the Club $50,000, which begged the question: in which direction was it to be spent?

Vice Commodore Garrett D. Bowne III had succeeded Charles Pingree as commodore at the end of the 1973 season, and one of his first official acts in January 1974 was to appoint a Long-Range Planning Committee, with Pingree as chairman, comprised of Thomas G. Brown, Jr., Edward D. Cook, Robert C. Harding, Nils P. Peterson, L. Pemberton Pleasants, Jr., Joseph C. Roper, Jr., and Jonathan C. Wales. Subcommittees were organized on waterfront, clubhouse, court activities, and financing.

At this juncture, Bob Barton learned that an outstanding Shields class racing man and his wife, who had moved to Marblehead from Larchmont and met the membership requirements, had been advised not to apply because a tennis player had filled the quota. So the Shields racer had joined the Corinthian.

So I started a movement, abetted by Jon Wales, to change the bylaws so that a yachtsman in the true sense of the word, regardless of whether he owned a cruising boat, would go to the top of the list. The Admissions Committee would be compelled to give all yachtsmen priority.

I also felt that if taking in tennis and paddle tennis players and swimmers ahead of yachtsmen continued, the Nominating Committee might well be appointed in their favor, and we would lose control of the Club. So I wanted to have the bylaw changed to make it four out of five on the Nominating Committee to be yachtsmen.

That May, the Long-Range Planning Committee drew up a Statement of Purpose, which was adopted by the Council on August 5:

The Eastern Yacht Club was incorporated in 1871 "for the purpose of encouraging yacht building and naval architecture, and the cultivation of nautical science," as written in the charter. This statement of purpose has become and remains today the principal tradition of the club. Out of this declaration, the Eastern Yacht Club has become one of the best known yachting organizations in North America. This reputation has been earned through the efforts of hundreds of our club's yachtsmen, racing and cruising under the colors of the Eastern Yacht Club, and participating in virtually every major yachting competition throughout the more than 100-year history of the club. This long tradition is our greatest asset, and while our members are the beneficiaries of that tradition, we are also charged with the responsibility to carry it on. This important background must be the guide to the future of the Eastern Yacht Club.

However, due to changes in social and economic conditions over the years, significant changes have occurred in the requirements of the membership. There is a trend toward the increasing use of club facilities as the focal point of a family's leisure activities, not only during the summer, but extending into the other seasons. This trend is reflected in the growth of our tennis, including platform tennis, and swimming programs. These facilities are not inconsistent with the yachting character of the club, and serve to maximize the use of the grounds, as well as to supplement waterfront activities to produce a well-balanced recreational facility for the membership.

With the above considerations in mind, the Long Range Planning Committee, appointed by the Commodore, will review all proposed projects in light of their potential utility to the greatest number of members, consistent with the original statement of purpose noted in the first paragraph.

In the meantime, Barton pressed on, and, at the second general meeting on June 25, 1974, moved:

1. That the Council immediately rescind all and any special rights and privileges that it has heretofore granted to any one or more club members and that it be empowered to take all necessary legal and financial action to accomplish this directive.
2. That the Council take immediate action to formulate a broad policy directive for our Admissions Committee which will assure that the overwhelming majority of new members are yachtsmen or persons whose main interest is yachting and blue water sailing, regardless of yacht ownership.
3. That all nominating committees appointed by the Club's

Commodore contain no more than one club member who is not a yachtsman or blue water sailor or whose primary interest is not in yachting and sailing in general.

4. That the Council be empowered to accept the resignation of any club member who is in disagreement with this club directing its energies and money mainly towards yachting and to pay to that member so resigning the full amount of the initiation fee he or she paid at the time of admission.

The Barton motion was debated all summer, and then the Council recommended to the general meeting on August 27 that it be rejected. The mover recalls telling Commodore Bowne, "I'm going to propose we do it in spite of your recommendation, and I think I'm going to win because the younger members are all in favor of this." He continues:

That night the place was packed. I got up and said, "I'm sorry to go against the Council's recommendation, but again I move that yachtsmen be given priority over non-yachtsmen regardless of boat ownership and that the Nominating Committee always have four out of five members yachtsmen." Both proposals were seconded; both were put to a vote and overwhelmingly carried.

The meeting raised the dues, added a new article of paddle rules, and amended the bylaws governing admissions as follows:

Whenever the Club has a total of 500 or more active members, there shall be no further elections, unless a candidate (a) has been a junior member for at least two years, has reached the age of 21 and has timely filed his application for regular membership; (b) is a widow of a former member; (c) is the sole owner of a yacht which is sixteen feet or over on the waterline and is fully decked (reasonable cockpits excepted) and which shall by design, construction and fittings be well able to accompany the squadron on a cruise, subject to the approval of the Race Committee; or (d) has, in the judgment of the Committee on Admissions, demonstrated outstanding participation and interest in yachting.

Few would disagree that Bob Barton, in his fortieth season as a member, had set the Eastern on a course of soul-searching back more than a century to the purposes for which it was founded.

For all the furor, floats and courts had been coexisting at the Eastern for longer than anyone could remember. Traditionally, New England yachtsmen and women have resorted to the ri-

gors of tennis as a contrast to the confines of the cockpit, and the game was pursued in a leisurely way on the Club's clay courts, with an annual tournament, into the early 1960s. A shoreside feature of Race Week in the Thirties and Forties was the invitational that drew first-rate players from the North Shore and Boston, always watched with interest from the porch and steps by sailors in from racing.

The craze for the sport that swept the country in the late Fifties and Sixties necessarily gave it a new emphasis at the Club, with more specific attention to the encouragement of ladies' tennis, under the leadership of Joyce Baker Brown and Charles Newhall. There was pressure for what amounted to tennis memberships; the courts were crowded and hard-surface courts were added; a pro shop appeared; matches were arranged with Essex County, Manchester Bath & Tennis, and Myopia; new club tournaments sprang up; and whites were ruled de rigeur.

The existing low-key junior program was beefed up on the initiative of Joyce Brown, Sally Clark, and Carol Nash with a North Shore tourney attracting as many as eighty youngsters while the courts were more available during the Annual Cruise.

By the 1970s, five to ten doubles teams represented the Eastern in the tennis interclubs, and draws exceeding thirty-two teams were not uncommon for member-guest and club tournaments. With their arrival in Marblehead from Gloucester, the sailing Sides family—Bob, Kate, Bucky, and Kitty Sides Flather—dominated the courts in the mid-Seventies and early Eighties, as they accounted themselves afloat.

The mid-Eighties saw some abatement of the national frenzy, but the sport remains a firm fixture at the Club, with the member-guest tournaments, the club championships, the Newhall Cup with the Corinthian, and the popular "Three Blind Mice," a blind mixed-doubles draw with the Corinthian and the Beach Club involving as many as sixty teams, followed by a dinner-dance at the Eastern.

John Silsbee Lawrence, one of the last of the Old Guard, died on December 14, 1973, at ninety-five. He started sailing in the 1880s, joined the Eastern in 1905, four years after his graduation from Harvard and seven years after Devereux Barker, although they were classmates and nearly the same age. He was a retired partner in Lawrence & Company, founded by his great-grandfather, among the largest textile distributors in the world. Almost half a century had elapsed since this quintes-

The aluminum Twelve-meter *Independence*, designed by Ted Hood, runs with the spirit of '76 off Marblehead. Polly Brown photos.

Left: Dr. Louis Pocharski's *Spirit,* on the wind.

Below: Commodore Connolly's flagship *Taygeta*.

Right: A striking sunflower blooms in New Meadows Basin during the Annual Cruise to Maine on July 7, 1981. Clockwise from *Tioga*, the largest, at 7, are *Qaudrille, Palmyra, Andiamo, Elsinore, Vija, Off Call, Eastward, Alamar, Free Spirit, Arion, Katama, Sunup, Glass Slipper, Capella, Sirocco, Gurnet, Manticore, Pibroch, Jubilee, Watermelon, Celebration* and Commodore Steve Connolly's flagship *Taygeta*.

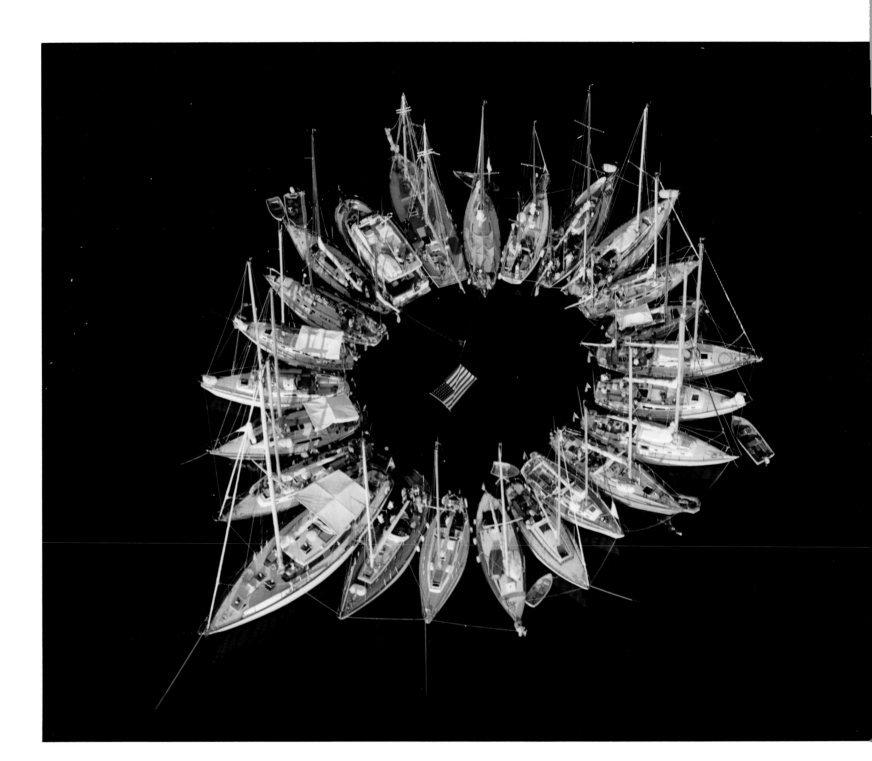

Neither fog nor flat daunted the 1982 Annual Cruise, which took
to the tenders and materialized on a Maine island for a discussion of both.

The Annual Cruise visits the mirrorlike waters of Mystic Seaport, Connecticut, and a pine-girt cove on the coast of Maine.

Classical clipper bows, handsome lines and traditional rigs distinguish John Blodgett's schooner *Mistral* (*left*) and John P. Chase's Friendship sloop *Hostess*, smallest boat on cruise (*below*).

Don Blodgett's *Sirocco* (*left*) and Weston Adams's *Stampede* (*below*) exemplify the advance of design and technology that revolutionized the Eastern fleet after World War II.

Dr. Clarke Staples is not on call when he's on *Off Call*.

Passing the plate in Maplejuice Cove during the 1967 Annual Cruise.

The Shields class provided slick sailing in the 1970s. Polly Brown photo.

The essence of the elegant Etchells, racing machine of the Eighties. Polly Brown photo.

George Lowden's *Dark Horse* doesn't look the part, galloping to weather on a racy day.

A shower of Stars vies for the first magnitude during the Worlds hosted by the Eastern in 1981. Jim Brown photo.

Above: Bradley Noyes's first Hood designed *Tioga* shows her stuff.

Below: Making hardly a ripple, Sargent Goodchild's *Manxman* meanders along in midsummer.

The clubhouse in spring dress, 1987.

To colors! And another opening of the Club as the grand old flags are raised.

(*Overleaf*): The Eastern Yacht Club.

sential Yankee yachtsman introduced the staysail schooner with *Advance*.

They went and they came, but Frances Gilliland remained, in her friendly fortress behind the front desk. Fifty years of it in 1974 called for a testimonial dinner on June 14.

I knew about the party because they couldn't keep it from me, but I didn't know anything about the money. It was ten thousand dollars. It was a beautiful night, and they had a nice orchestra, and there were about three hundred and nineteen there. I had all my family up. We were out on the lawn. They had four bars, so they must have been thinking I drink a lot. But I told them they didn't have my drink. I drink hard cider. Mister G.K. Simonds was my master of ceremonies, and he was very fine.

And while on the subject of testimonials, another mark in the course of Ted Hood's remarkable career was rounded in 1974. His *Revaluation* in 1972 and most recent *Robin* in 1973 won for him his sixth and seventh Puritan Cups and fifth and sixth Charles Francis Adams Memorial Trophies. He had designed and sailed *Nefertiti* and cut sails for the Twelves since 1958, until he was all but the official sailmaker for the Cup contenders; but the helm in an actual defense eluded him until 1974, when the aluminum *Courageous* had only been able to even it out with the older, wooden *Intrepid*, and there was one sudden-death race to go. Her owners in desperation turned her over to the modest man from Marblehead, who on September 2 sailed *Courageous* to victory in the trials and then, four straight over the Australian Alan Bond's *Southern Cross*, to one more successful defense.

Back again in Marblehead, Ted was appropriately awarded the Puritan-Genesta Trophy by the Eastern and congratulated by all three clubs at a joint dinner at the Corinthian on October 25. But for him, laurels were neither to be worn nor rested upon. He sailed his latest *Robin* to win her class and place fifth overall in the Southern Circuit, was the unanimous selection as Martini & Rossi's Racing Sailor of the Year, and was picked for the three-boat U.S. Admiral's Cup team to go to England in 1975.

For ten years, Hood had enjoyed an ideal relationship with the Maas yard in the Netherlands, which had produced a succession of Airex-core ocean racers for him. At the same time, he was extending his textile and sailmaking operations worldwide and getting into various ancillary activities of the boat business.

We'd just send Maas the plans, didn't even ask the price; halfway through, they'd say it's gonna cost so much, and we'd say, that's fine. No deposit or anything. They were getting to be one of the top one-off yards, and then they tried to go into big production when in the early Seventies the recession hit, and they went bankrupt.

But not before Brad Noyes made one of the most heartrending decisions for a traditionalist—to forsake wood for fiberglass. He sold his last wood *Tioga* (now *Elskov*) to Hope and Walter Smith, which meant a fond parting of those particular ways with Aage Nielsen:

I went to Ted for the 60-foot boat I built in '73 for my first fiberglass. Aage had no experience with glass, didn't want to do it, and almost refused to get involved with it. Well, with the Airex core this was a great boat, a wonderful boat, a watermelon upside down. Not a racer, but we took her in the first Marion-to-Bermuda race and got first in our class and third in the fleet. I loved her. She'd go to weather faster than she'd reach. Unbelievable. I kept her fourteen years, sold her last year, and Ted's now [1987] building me a Little Harbor 46.

Two more of the Old Guard died before the opening of the 1975 season—J. Amory Jeffries, Honorary Member, loyal member since 1929, former chairman of the Race Committee and treasurer, former president of the NAYRU, who had paraded so gloriously off the Parker float one July evening of 1949; and George E. McQuesten, Number Two member, Life Member, and former rear commodore, who joined in 1919. His family affiliation went back to 1890. A rather reserved bachelor, McQuesten lived in one of the largest houses on the Neck, owned a fine yacht, enjoyed tennis, and occasionally put on a cocktail party at which his female guests were presented corsages before the Sunday night pre-movie buffet. His principal license plate is remembered as number 4. He drove a Rolls on Sundays, a Cadillac to Boston, a Chrysler around town, and a sports car and a motorcycle when so inclined.

The atmosphere of the Club's second-century identity crisis and the backward/forward-looking preparations for the United States Bicentennial inspired L. Pemberton Pleasants to propose the creation of the Historical Committee, which was approved by the Council in February 1975. In the same spirit of institutional self-awareness, the first issue of the first newsletter, *The Easterner*, appeared in May.

Maybe because patriotism was back in fashion, 1974 and

1975 were star-spangled-banner years for racing in anything that floated, be it alongshore, out on the deep—with one soggy exception—or off Newport, Rhode Island.

Among the one-designs, Stephen Wales won the World Championship in the Internationals off Larchmont in 1974, as brother Jonathan had in 1968 at Marblehead (where the Eastern hosted them again in 1971), and as Steve would for the third time for the family at Edinburgh in 1975. The new class of Lasers appeared in the harbor, where there were now twenty-nine E-22s in which David Curtis was emerging as a top helmsman, and nineteen Internationals. In the Shields, Frank Scully won five straight and the Fowle Trophy in the 1975 Race Week, then placed third in the nationals at Monterey, California.

For the offshore racers, Race Committee Chairman Pem Pleasants had the idea in 1974 of reviving various retired awards for the Eastern Yacht Club Trophy Series to stimulate team competition among the cruising-type yachts of USYRU-affiliated clubs. The Club put up the IOR (International Offshore Rule) Compass, NER (New England Rule) Chronometer, and MORC (Massachusetts Ocean Racing Circuit) Anemometer trophies, which were supplemented by the Tioga Trophy, offered by Bradley Noyes to the Eastern yacht skippered by the Eastern member with the lowest accumulated point score for those classes.

Other individual trophies in the series were offered in 1974 and 1975 for ocean-racing events to be determined by the Race Committee: the Pleione, by Mrs. Joseph Santry and her daughter, Mrs. Henri W. Emmet; the Hornet, retired by former Commodore B. Devereux Barker in 1928 and put up by his son, former Commodore B. Devereux Barker, Jr.; and the John G. Alden, by his daughter, Mrs. Chester M. Sawtelle. The Haze and the Gracie trophies, dating back to 1871, were revived by the Club. The Frank C. Paine Bowl was given by Mrs. Frank C. Paine in memory of her husband. The Periwinkle Trophy was offered by Frances Pitcher Copeland, who with her *Periwinkle* had retired it as the first three-time winner of the Shepard Trophy. It was to be a permanent award for competition, preferably among members and between yachts eligible for the Annual Cruise, initially in the Lambert Ocean Race.

Measurement rules and their effect on racing—and, more significantly, on design—were becoming the subject of ever-hotter debate in the 1970s. Not that they weren't always. At

The International One-designs run for it during the 1975 Race Week.

L. Pemberton (Pem) Pleasants, Jr., long-time House and Race Committee chairman

Yacht Club or Casino?

Eastern Yacht Club trophies: Cleopatra's Barge Cup, Puritan-Genesta Decanter, Lambert Trophy. Marshall Henrichs photos.

the center of the storm was the International Offshore Rule: was the IOR promoting speed at the expense of that old-fashioned concept, wholesomeness? Writing in 1977, Professor Evers Burtner had this to say on the matter after half a century of measuring:

The IOR, CCA Rule, the Offsoundings Rule and several local rules give credit for beam greater than the base beam. Naturally, this encourages maximum beam. . . . Auxiliary powered racing cruisers of various rigs replaced the custom-built and designed larger weekend open class racing yachts shortly after World War II. These modern yachts often are built to measure in at a maximum rating. Many show the effect of local measurements specified by the International Offshore Rule.

Thus, deck plans show no convexity exists at the rail near the forward girth station, i.e., the deck breadth has been pulled in or pinched here, giving a sharp wedge at the bow. Also, the midship beam is rather locally increased, producing the effect of a bustle. Such features show the weak points of the Rule.

In both the International and the International Offshore Rules credit is given for freeboard. All the above illustrates how rating rules affect hull dimensions and form. . . . Undeniably, the greater beam of many modern cruising yachts does provide more deck space and accommodations. On the other hand, ex-

cessive beam undoubtedly has greatly contributed to the reported knockdowns and lack of control while racing under rugged conditions.

We must avoid this in cruising yachts. It will be most interesting to note future trends in sailing yacht beam, hull form and sail plan, also the changes that will be made in the rules. . . . This together with a handicapping approach allowing for weather, wind, and relative length of windward, reaching, and downwind legs should place racing on more even terms.

Such considerations as beam, freeboard, and susceptibility to knockdown somehow did not seem to matter so much during the forgettable, and yet not quite forgotten, interim between July 7 and July 12—designated in the records as the 1975 Annual Cruise. In the words of Commodore Garrett Bowne:

The fleet proceeded to Boothbay at will on July 7th, bypassing Quahog Bay. On the 9th the fleet followed the committee boat in thick fog to the John's River, where Mr. and Mrs. Robert B.M. Barton graciously entertained all at a cocktail party at their summer home. The following morning the only race of the cruise was started as scheduled, but there were no finishers due to fog and light air.

On the next day, July 11th, the fleet awoke to another foggy, showery morning. After receiving the weather report which forecast more of the same for the following several days, it was decided to proceed directly to Camden, thus bypassing two scheduled harbors, Pulpit and Castine. Part of the fleet (about seven boats including the Vice and Rear Commodores and Fleet Captain) headed back towards Marblehead. En route to Camden the Commodore's *Endymion* developed engine problems and was towed by the committee boat the rest of the way.

Twenty-six yachts arrived safely at Camden and were entertained by the Race Committee for cocktails at the Camden Yacht Club the following evening, July 12, after another cloudy day. The 1975 cruise was disbanded at evening colors, just as it started to clear. None of the six races scheduled was completed, possibly an all-time record.

Back on the Neck, the dining room service and relations with the kitchen staff had been unsatisfactory for several seasons. On the eve of the visit of the New York Yacht Club Cruise, it was learned that a walk-out was planned just before a combined dinner dance on August 2. Unable to reach Commodore Bowne, who was still cruising, or to get the Council together in time, Vice Commodore Albert Parker fired the manager and the kitchen help, brought in a caterer, talked the Board of Health into allowing the Club to survive the emergency "change of management," and the show went on. The New Yorkers had their dinner dance and the Club got through the rest of the season.

After more than a year of study involving a questionnaire to members that yielded a 40 percent response, the Long-Range Planning Committee submitted its report, adopted by the Council on August 7, 1975. Attention was first directed to the waterfront.

> With the increasing number of class boats that are owned by members, nonexisting mooring space, the trend toward more yachtsmen amongst the membership and the regattas that are being hosted by the Club, the Committee feels our waterfront should be seriously updated.
>
> In many instances it is an honor to be selected to hold special regattas, and it shows that different sailing organizations regard the judgment and efficiency of our Race Committee and the Club as hosts to be one of the best. If we fail to have the facilities that are needed to make a smooth operation, not only will we lose the chance to uphold our reputation, but all that goes with it.

The committee recommended that the Club finally make up its mind to raze the Samoset, which was inefficiently used and in need of major repairs, relocate the existing paddle tennis court there (releasing needed parking space), and add a second

The coming generation at the pier house rail, 1972: Josh and Nate Burke and Sam Paige.

court to accommodate the rising pressure for prime weekend and evening time and tournaments.

The major portion of the area occupied by the Samoset, about 20,000 square feet, or two-thirds, would be assigned to drysailing. To meet the increasing interest in drysailing and to keep pace with hauling and launching needs generally, the committee proposed widening the existing ramp from 15 to 24 feet; lengthening and gradualizing it almost to low water, about 50 feet; and installing a new hoist with a substantially greater capacity than its current two tons, a limitation that excluded the Shields and other heavier classes.

Yacht Club or Casino?

Three years ago, permission was granted to use the area behind the Samoset for dry-sailing, and at that time we had a dozen or so boats. This past season, there was an average of 35 boats crammed into this space on any given day. The Committee sees no expectation that this figure should decrease, but believes with the added protection of fencing and improved launching and hauling facilities that the numbers will increase.

Turning to the clubhouse, the committee proposed a dining/function room to obviate interruption of the Club's routine by meetings and special events and dinners. This would be achieved by extending the porch about 15 feet toward the harbor over the Galley Grille, adding picture windows, and enclosing the new area to seat at least 125.

Proposals included a new, octagonal lounge with an open porch around its perimeter as an addition to the northerly end of the existing porch; facilities and shower rooms for visiting yachtsmen in the basement, with access from the waterfront; renovation of rooms on the second and third floors to accommodate housing pressure from the razing of the Samoset; and removal of part of the barracks-garage, for easy access to the parking lot from the front door of the clubhouse and for launch storage on the ground level via the installation of large doors at the shortened end.

Of the options for financing, the committee recommended

an annual assessment of approximately 20 percent of dues to "eliminate the element of surprise or dismay which has accompanied the disclosures in the past of significant capital repairs."

The grand design would be implemented in three phases, the first of which would involve the dining/function room, razing of the Samoset, creation of the drysailing and paddle tennis area, and purchase of a new hoist. The second, $16,850 paddle tennis court would be fully amortized by the users, the Club bearing the $4,400 cost of moving the original to the Samoset site. The George Henderson bequest of $50,000, with accrued interest of $7,000, would largely cover the $65,000 cost of the new dining/function room in his memory. The waterfront package would cost $23,371. The whole projected cost of Phase I would be $109,721.

It is of interest that the Club sailed through the 1975 season safely in the black; income of $411,838, including $202,000 in dues, exceeded expenses of $361,961 by $49,877.

Vice Commodore Parker had succeeded Garrett Bowne as commodore and presided at a special membership meeting on December 15, 1975, during which it was estimated that the entire long-range plan would come to about $200,000 and require an annual assessment of $100 for as many as five years. The following January the members gave the go-ahead for Phase I of the Club's future.

Rounding the Mark

Chapter 19   **Rounding the Mark**   *1976–1979*

Fortunately for the Club's second century, by the year of the United States Bicentennial, the women had surged forth from their dining room bridgehead and along the piazza and into the house, forcing the retreating gents into the bar and reading room. By then, Corinthianism had broken the Victorian grip of those founding Bostonians of wealth and high character and their scions and turned sailing into a participatory sport. The day of the yachtswoman was at hand.

New England's last resort for gentlemanly maritime pursuits was forced, as we have seen, to offer something more than a flowing sea and Dramamine to a changing membership. And though such aberrations as paddle and a pool dismayed the purists, they were tolerated or taken up by a consensus that regarded a wooden boat as an antediluvian ark and drysailed in what the dwindling traditionalists ridiculed as Clorox bottles not much bigger than *Constellation*'s gig.

But every sail has two surfaces. One-designs cloned to the last gram and centimeter know no language barriers. Seventy-five years after Chairman Howard guided the Club to the summit of small-boat competition in the Sonders, the Eastern was back on top in the Etchells, Internationals, and Shields.

Phase I of the long-range planning initiated under Commodore Bowne was implemented early in 1976 by his successor, Albert C. Parker, whose father, former Commodore James P. Parker, a member since 1927 with a special interest in the Club's history, died soon after the son took office. The main floor of the clubhouse was decorated. After years of pulling and hauling, the Samoset House was razed, and the site was graded, surfaced, and landscaped for drysailed boat storage.

The demolition of the old summer boardinghouse made it possible to relocate the paddle operation. The original plat-

form in the parking lot had been so mislocated that the late afternoon sun simply went to sleep on top of the net; the court was repositioned properly near the Samoset site, and its companion was built alongside. In 1981 the players erected a warming hut from which they could watch the play and take refreshment.

Some sixty families currently support this off-season club-within-the-club, paying dues of $100 in addition to their regular dues. They are split about fifty-fifty in their primary interest between paddles and tillers, enjoying monthly scrambles and matches, such as with the Essex County Club players. The season begins in October and concludes in April, when awards for the men's, women's, and mixed doubles championships are presented at a banquet the night before the Club opens .

The Club formally opened on May 8 with "Sail '76" for the benefit of the Fowle Foundation. Some claim could have been made that this was the first shot of the maritime Bicentennial from the birthplace of the American Navy. A few weeks later, the stirring spectacle of Operation Sail brought most of the world's biggest windships to Boston for the celebration of the Battle of Bunker Hill on June 17, the first major engagement of the American Revolution. Many members of the Eastern were there, by boat when possible.

The birthday party continued with a fireworks display from Riverhead Beach on the weekend of the Fourth that illuminated a harbor solid with boats. To the Annual Regatta Ted Hood brought his own rocket, named *Robin*, with which he orbited with the Puritan Cup for the ninth time.

Race Week in this two-hundredth year of independence was started off with 340 boats, convoyed by a total of thirty-one sharks by actual count (including a pair said to be twelve feet long), and consigned to history with the awarding of the Fowle Trophy to Eugene Connolly, the Eastern's Grand Old Man at the tiller at eighty-five, who sailed in his first Race Week sixty-four years earlier.

Because Stephen Wales had won the Internationals World Championship in Edinburgh in 1975, the Club was host to the Worlds in 1976. This time brother Jonathan was first again, trading off with Steve, who placed third. And Robert W. Sides, with David A. Curtis and Peter Q. McKee, won the Manhasset Bay Challenge Cup.

With a somewhat restructured Phase I of the Long-Range Plan completed on schedule, the members at the general meeting on January 11, 1977, approved a four-year plan for Phases II and III submitted by the Facilities Planning Committee under Richard Robie.

Phase II, to begin in the spring, involved two new projects: a wood and steel pier 18 feet wide and 48 feet long, projecting at the level of the Old Stone Wharf and equipped with a 4-ton crane above three and a half feet of water at mean low; and an additional tennis court next to court number 2 near the old bangboard. Total cost: $84,000.

Phase III would be the new and enlarged Henderson Dining Room, with major kitchen improvements, from plans by architect David Mehlin, with the assistance of House Chairman Pemberton Pleasants. Cost: $94,000.

The $178,000 cost of Phases II and III would be financed by an annual assessment of $100 per member for four years, generating approximately $128,000, and by bank loans.

The committee projected that Phase IV would close in the ground floor and improve the sailors' lounge there, install showers, modernize the Galley Grille, and create a large locker room for sails and gear.

After some delay in getting started, the Historical Committee formally organized at the beginning of 1977, Eugene Connolly in the chair, with the object of bringing C.H.W. Foster's *Ditty Box* up to date from 1900, establishing an archival library in the clubhouse (for which a room on the second floor was designated the following year), and getting on with a series of taped interviews with longtime members and staff.

The post-Bicentennial was also the year of the franchise for the non-boatowning members. The bylaws were amended to eliminate the ownership qualification, which in 107 years had been lowered by degrees from 30 feet on the water to 16, and henceforth all regular members of the Club were eligible to vote for flag officers. Women associates, nevertheless, remained beyond this particular pale.

This was another America's Cup year, and Ted Hood, who had sailed the Olin Stephens Twelve Meter *Courageous* to victory in 1974, had been preparing more or less ever since then. He had the option of skippering her again but agreed with Lee Loomis, who was handling the business side of their sponsoring Kings Point Fund syndicate, that it would not be wise without a proper trial horse. Old *Intrepid* being unavailable, they made the decision to build their own, *Independence*, much along the lines of *Courageous* but with fuller bow, narrower quarter, and less displacement, Hood acting as designer and sailmaker gratis. The aluminum *Independence* was built by Minneford at City Island, New York, launched in July, and

Dry sailing—and wet sailors (Josh Burke and Craig Huff) come of age. Hauling out the 420s, 1976.

outfitted by Hood's yard at Little Harbor. Meanwhile, *Enterprise*, another near-clone of his *Courageous*, had been designed by Olin Stephens.

Toward the end of the 1976 season and well into the fall, *Independence* and *Courageous* got in some almost-daily jousting off Marblehead that suggested a good match. They were hauled by Hood, who shortened the cupholder's waterline and added some displacement, among other changes. Ted Turner, the versatile and brash international sailor and owner of the Atlanta Braves, who was talking up his reputation as the self-proclaimed "Mouth from the South," was picked to skipper *Courageous*. Lowell North, the West coast sailmaker, was given *Enterprise*. It was shaping up into a contest between sailmakers as well as designers, builders, skippers, and crew.

A contest from which Marblehead might have been eliminated without ever setting sail. A severe, unpredicted storm with winds up to 50 miles an hour swept the coast on May 9, 1977, two days after the Club opened. More than twenty-five boats were torn from their moorings, some damaging others as they barged through the fleet. The havoc among the yachts was the worst in a decade, with estimates ranging from $200,000 to $1,000,000. Fortunately, *Courageous* and *Independence* were on the heaviest moorings in the harbor and had out 90-pound Danforths besides. Even so, the water was waist-deep in *Courageous* at the worst of it, and their crews pumped both Twelves for hours when they weren't out helping to rescue loose boats such as Hood's Gulfstar 50, which was saved a hundred yards from the beach. The Club's old wooden launch and a float were wrecked.

Within three weeks, on May 27 and 28, the Eastern had recovered enough to sponsor three races between *Courageous* and *Independence* off Marblehead. For this it dusted off the Charles P. Curtis Cup (not to be confused with the Curtis Cup for the North Shore Junior Championship) originally put up by the late commodore for a similar series in 1930 between contending American J-boats off Newport in 1930 and won by the first *Enterprise*.

Independence, with Hood at the helm, was leading toward the end of the first race when *Courageous* parted her mainsheet, and Turner withdrew. The new Twelve won the second race and the Curtis Cup in light airs by 20 seconds. *Courageous* took the third in a southeast breeze by a minute and 20 seconds. Some saw a paradox in the presence as sail trimmer on *Courageous* of the Eastern's Robert E. (Robbie) Doyle—single-

hander, Olympic racer, SORC winner, and vice president of Hood Sailmakers—but it was Hood's policy to follow through wherever it took him with his magic weaves, which happened to fly on both boats in his syndicate.

Robbie Doyle is a case of a phoenix arisen out of early burnout. He was sailing at six in 1956; as he grew, he owed much to the tutelage of his older brother Richard. He first won the Sears Cup for the Corinthian in 1964 at the age of fourteen; Richard was second. He won again in 1965.

I had always wanted to go into the Olympics. I tried swimming and basketball when I was young, then decided the Finns were my best chance. I got invited by the Olympic committee to teach Finn sailing. From there I went to the Olympic trials in 1968—more for the sake of the Olympics than for the sailing—and ended up second when I was seventeen. Then at Harvard I went into intercollegiate racing in the dinghies, where the competition is intense. I sailed so intensely that I burned out and got tired of it. I expected to win every time and was frustrated when I didn't, and I had lost interest when I was eighteen or nineteen.

I was out in a Finn one day, suffering and aching, and saw Ted Hood come reaching in and decided that was an easier way. By the time I finished college in '72 I was involved with Ted in the design and sailmaking of *Dynamite* for the Canada Cup, and in the competition as tactician. I was planning to go to medical school but decided to take a year out and just sail. I met Ted Turner and sailed with him in the supposedly favored Twelve *Mariner* in the '74 America's Cup, which turned out to be the biggest dog ever.

I ended up virtually running Ted Hood's company at twenty-three, which seemed more exciting than med school; he hadn't really developed people under him, so there was no one between him and myself. I stayed with him ten years until I left and started my own company, Doyle Sailmakers.

Doyle joined the Eastern in 1975 and two years later was back in the Cup fray with Turner, who reassembled his *Mariner* crew when he bought *Courageous*, for whose winning program he credits Hood.

In the 1977 trials *Independence* got off to a bad start, hampered by a foul bottom and gear failures. But as the jockeying between the three contenders for the defense seesawed during the summer, the Marblehead Twelve's troubles seemed to come down to crew inexperience. In the end, Turner's drive, his luck, and his superior backup prevailed. The NYYC Selection Committee ruled out *Independence*, and then *Enterprise*, dogged by bad fortune. It was *Courageous* again, this time versus *Australia*, and the Cup stayed put.

What happened with *Independence*? In 1987 Hood had the benefit of a decade of hindsight:

The tank led us astray again, giving us credit for sail area. We knew *Courageous* was a good boat, and we said, let's not do two boats equal, so we sort of went half way between *Intrepid* and *Courageous*. We had a little bit shorter boat with a lot more sail area, because the tank said adding length to your main boom made the boat go faster, and it didn't. We proved that when we took the little mainsail off *Courageous* and put it on *Independence*, and took the big main off *Independence* and put it on *Courageous*, and it made no difference. She went just as fast with the small sail.

And he concedes that his crew discipline has always been pretty laid back, which can make a difference when the outcome depends on a few seconds.

It's one of my weaknesses. It might not have mattered ten years ago, but it does now [1987]. Now everyone's got hot-shot crews. They go out training, and racing's a different game. If you don't do it that way you're not gonna win. You've got to take it very seriously or don't bother. The cheapest you can do the Southern Circuit in the smallest boat is $20,000. In the old days you used to take the boat down, race it, then go cruising. No one cruises in those boats any more.

To which may be added a footnote from Brad Noyes, who decided to quit racing in 1975 except as occasional crew for his old friend, with whom he subsequently won a Bermuda Race in one of the *Robins* and sailed on six or seven Southern Circuits:

Back when Ted Hood was getting into the designing bit himself, and I was going on the Southern Circuit in *Tioga*, he said I could do a lot better if I'd cut my boom down and lower my rating, because it won't slow the boat. I said, yeah, but she wouldn't be as nice-looking, so I went down with her the way Aage and I had her. We were more into the aesthetics, what we thought was wholesome. I guess most of my competitive streak would come out when I got out on the water and the starting gun went off.

A number of Etchells sailors eager for team racing in the class—including Peter Godfrey, Rick Howard, and Dave Curtis of the Eastern—worked up a series between Marblehead and Bermuda that first came off in 1976, when Marblehead swept at home in August and on the island in October. The following year, each team won on its own water. The series has continued, almost annually, without further losses for the

Shields Nationals, 1977. Skipper Francis P. Scully, Ernest Godschalk, and John Francis.

'Headers. One notable win went to the Yanks because the commodore of the Royal Bermuda Yacht Club performed an "unseamanlike rounding of the leeward mark" when his lowering spinnaker wrapped itself around the shroud of a Marblehead boat that must have been a bit close aboard.

In August 1977, as the winner of the Manhasset Cup in 1976, the Eastern hosted the series, and Bob Sides and crew retained the cup against fifteen Etchells. In September the Three-quarter-ton North American Championships were held by the Eastern. Twenty-three in the Shields class competed out of the Club in the Nationals, won by Frank Scully in his *Aeolus*.

The J-24s (24 feet overall) debuted during Block Island Race Week and spread slowly at first to Marblehead, which had one in 1977 but forty by 1982 after a siege of super promotion that represented the class as an all-round performer. The fleet has settled down to about ten, of which three were in the top four of the J-24 Worlds by the mid-1980s.

Nineteen seventy-eight was off to a slowed-down start for Commodore Garlan Morse and everyone else who lived along the New England coast, which was smacked on February 6 and 7 with the worst blizzard in memory. Winds gusting to 80 dumped as much as thirty inches of snow and escalated already-high moon tides by six and seven feet.

The Causeway was inundated by waves crashing in from

both directions, shutting off the Neck, where a Marblehead fire engine had foresightedly been stationed. The Eastern put up the four firemen for thirty hours until the waters receded. They left a note: "Hi! Thanks for your hospitality. We spent the storm in your office and may have messed up your pillows and blankets. Thanks for the shelter. Marblehead Fire Dept." And the department designated the Club henceforth as its command post on the Neck for future emergencies.

The pier house and 150 feet of seawall were washed away, and it was later discovered that some of the columns had been unseated. The surge filled the pool with sand and boulders and eroded the retaining wall. The Club secured a $110,000 loan from the Small Business Administration to reinforce the main pier with new concrete foundations, build a new pier house, repair the seawall, and rebuild the pool retaining wall.

In addition, thirty-seven new members helped to fill the breech, raising the total from 484 to 521.

The Club succeeded in opening on April 29. The front hall, living room, and ballroom had been redecorated, and on June 23 the new enclosed Henderson Dining Room was dedicated. Designed to seat 127 in all weather for an extended season, it enabled the ballroom to double as another function room, with a new service bar adjoining the kitchen. Nine members of the late donor's family and many of his old porch cronies were on hand, and Frances Henderson presented the portrait of her brother that presides from the wall.

The foundation under the new area was reinforced and the Galley Grille enlarged and upscaled into the Samoset Lounge.

Faced with more diverse activities and broader responsibilities ashore, and a constantly expanding schedule of racing, the Council adopted a reorganization that split the old Race Committee into One-Design and Ocean Racing committees and created Planning, Waterfront, Pool, Finance, and Racquet committees, the last subdivided further into Tennis and Paddle committees.

The Ocean Racing Committee opened the offshore season by running for the first time one of the three races of the New England Ocean Racing Circuit Spring Series on May 21, with twenty-one entries. Besides the usual events, the Eastern in 1978 hosted and won the second match with the Bermudians, in July, this time in the E-22s—likewise the Beverly Yacht

The Great Blizzard of February 6 and 7, 1978, washed away the pier house and 150 feet of seawall.

Club's Shields Challenge Trophy, the Roosevelt Bowl dating back to 1934.

Northeast winds ranging up to 50 and 60, with great lumpy seas, dogged the Fourth of July Annual Regatta—and the Ocean Racing Committee, which borrowed the old committee boat, a notorious roller. Thirty-nine yachts sailed around the course, while aboard the roller the fuel tank ruptured into the slopping bilge, with predictable gastric consequences for the passengers. Lou Pocharski's *Spirit* rolled in with the Puritan Cup.

Forty boats sailed off on the Annual Cruise, during which a great piece of crew work was witnessed by the committee boat taking a shortcut through Deer Island Thorofare to the finish line of the second race. Class B was reaching under spinnakers past Stonington when hit by northwest winds in gusts of 38 miles an hour. Knight Alexander's *Windsong* lost her spinnaker sheet and was being pressed by Thomas Barrows's *Windrush* when the latter was hit and spun out on a knockdown, only to be struck again as she rose, and then again, and again. *Windrush* took four knockdowns, gaining enough on her rival to pull it out and overtake *Windsong* in an upwind finish that earned Tom Shepard's grandson the Shepard Trophy.

Continuing its work of fine-tuning the buoys circuits, the Marblehead Racing Association in 1978 redistributed the twenty-two racing marks into an Olympic circle for each of the three starting lines. Much care was taken to assign classes according to size, challenge, and the need for sea room, starting with the smallest west of Cat Island and nearest the harbor for safety reasons. Two races an afternoon were run for the younger skippers, over shorter courses for more sailhandling. The whole was designed around a natural progression encouraging the juniors to aspire to greater challenges and higher rewards. Many classes were starting an average of twenty boats, and the Saturday afternoon training ground for future skippers in Marblehead was looking like Race Week elsewhere.

At the same time, the Ladies Sailing Program, which had been first organized in the 1950s and then lapsed, was brought back to life, mainly on the initiative of Nancy Godfrey. Based at the Pleon, and employing Pleon instructors and Widgeons, the revived program set off initially on a Wednesday afternoon series in racing techniques and was open to members of all three clubs.

For individual performance, this was again Dave Curtis's year. In January, two Eastern teams flew to Australia for the Etchells Worlds, hosted by the Royal Prince Albert Yacht Club at Sydney. With Twig Burke as crew, Curtis was the best of the Americans and finished eighth out of forty-one, while Bob Sides, with son Bucky, finished fourteenth, in winds of 20-to-25 and rough, rolling seas. In April, Curtis won the Soling North American Championship in Miami, finally prevailing over his nemesis of ten years, Buddy Melges, in the last race. Curtis sailed through the fleet of twenty-five to knock Melges so far out of first place that the EYC sailor, going into the finale in second, emerged the champion even though he finished third.

Three Eastern boats and crews traveled to Newport Beach, California, in August for the forty-boat Etchells Worlds. Two of the boats were trailered by the skippers' wives, Joanne Curtis and Nancy Godfrey, and they came in one, two, three. Dave Curtis and Bob McCann co-captained *Close Encounters* for the championship, followed by Rick Howard in *Meltemi* and Peter Godfrey in *Jaundice*.

In September, Curtis won the North American Etchells Championships in Larchmont, with David Gundy second, while Stephen Wales finished second and Charles Hamlin third in the IOD Worlds hosted by the American Yacht Club in Rye.

C. Raymond Hunt died during the summer of 1978 at the age of seventy. His lifelong connection with the Eastern dated back to 1923, when at fifteen he led his Duxbury Yacht Club crew to his first Sears Cup, a victory that he repeated in 1925. His contributions to boat design are still being assessed. The more prominent include the 110 and 210, the Concordia yawl, the Boston Whaler, his revolutionary 5.5 Meter *Quixotic*, the deep V-bottomed powerboat, and the beautiful if flawed Twelve Meter *Easterner*, whose model is a centerpiece of the Club's living room. In 1963, at fifty-five, he won the 5.5 Worlds in *Chaje II*, his own design, and was so far ahead after the fifth race that he sat out the sixth.

Tradition held no veils over the eyes of Ray Hunt. Some of the original 110s were still competitive after forty years. He really *had* invented a better mousetrap.

In mid-August, 1979, the year after the designer's death, the Eastern co-hosted the fortieth anniversary International 110 Class Nationals, with the Pleon and Marblehead's Fleet Number 1. A northeast gale passed through, bringing with it plenty of air for the six races and thirty entries, six of them from the Club. Mark O'Connor of Marblehead, the national champion in 1970, finished 1, 12, 1, 1, 1, and 2, with his father Bob as crew. Tacking in 25 knots in the second race, their jib sheet jammed and they went over. Father and son stood on the keel, righted her, and, bailing furiously, raced through most of the fleet to that twelfth-place finish, which turned out to be their throw-out race. It was the first national win by a fiberglass 110; of the top ten, four were glass and six were still wood. The addition of the hiking harness to the 110's allowable gear sparked the national racing revival of the venerable double-ended wedge.

The year 1978 was a big one for Marblehead, the Eastern, and Race Committee Chairman P. Tapley (Tap) Stephenson, who doubled as chairman of the Marblehead Racing Association and initiated many of the season's innovations. In November, for the second time in the decade, the fifty-member Yacht Racing Union of Massachusetts Bay conferred its annual Leonard M. Fowle, Jr., Yacht Club of the Year Award on the Eastern.

Long before the end of its first season, the new crane had proven itself, and the Club was able to provide winter storage at $100 a boat and a spar loft under the porch. Members of the new Marblehead Frostbite Association were welcomed to keep their boats in the parking lot and to use the stone pier ramp for launching and hauling, and the Samoset Lounge for fortifying and thawing out. Fireflies were sailed by the frostbiters when they were first bitten in the fifties; later they used the Interclub Dinghies.

Paddle played counterpoint to the tennis craze then current, and the day after the Great February Blizzard, forty men, women, and children were observed digging the courts out from under 6-to-10-foot drifts—not waves, but drifts.

Garlan Morse chose to serve only one year as commodore and was succeeded after the 1978 season by Vice Commodore W. Gardner Barker, a cousin of former Commodore B. Devereux Barker, Jr.

The Club lost its Number One since 1973, Nathaniel Cushing (Cush) Nash, a member since 1916. Next in line was Robert E. Peabody, who joined in 1919.

And the staff lost Don Peterson, who died on July 14; he was sixty-four and only two months away from retirement after twenty years. As a versatile and energetic craftsman and some-time bartender, he had left his mark, inside and out, but most enduringly on the hearts of the members. On the other hand, Frances Gilliland remained on the job after fifty-five years of it.

The 1979 season opened on April 28 with the traditional flag-raising and chowder. A new, 26-foot diesel, Fortier fiberglass launch, with a twenty-eight-passenger capacity, supplemented the Club's pair of overworked workboats. It was to be a summer of resurgent celebration, the 350th anniversary of the old fishing settlement of Marblehead, kicked off on the water with the annual harbor parade, Sail '79, benefitting the Fowle Foundation, on May 27.

June 17 was the first Eastern Yacht Club "R&R Day," as described by an interested celebrant:

Whether defined as race and racquets, rest and relaxation, or reveling and rejoicing, R&R Day was designed to bring old and new, young and not so young, sailor, tennis player, swimmer and porch sitter together to participate in a fun day of sporting, spectatoring, and socializing. Each participant was given a visor with a handsomely embroidered R&R Day emblem.

Blessed with weather of the most spectacular summer variety, the activities began with games of croquet, tennis, volleyball (played on the paddle courts), followed by a chowder luncheon. The afternoon offered "The Crazy Race," a fox-and-hounds-style race where members were assigned to one of over twenty-five cruising boats. Finally, cocktails and a steak cookout were held on the lawn for 187 hungry participants.

On June 23, Marblehead officially celebrated its 350th anniversary. Commodore and Mrs. Barker represented the Eastern at the reception at the Boston Yacht Club. The day was topped off with another of those spectacular harbor illuminations and fireworks displays from the Causeway for which the old town has long been famous.

Six more days into this already busy season, the Club co-sponsored, with the Cruising Club of America, the Transatlantic Race to Ireland in observance of the fiftieth anniversary of the Irish Cruising Club (and put up the Puritan-Genesta Cup for the winner). Prerace cocktail parties and dinners were given at the Club, one by the CCA and the Irish Tourist Board, the other by the Eastern. On June 29, scores of spectator boats gathered near Tinker's gong for the noon start of the fifteen yachts from Ireland, the United States, Canada, Great Britain, and Sweden on the 2,638 miles to Cork.

Under favorable conditions, the 79-foot sloop *Kialoa*, owned by John B. Kilroy of El Segundo, California, one of three maxis in the race, reached Cork in 11 days, 23 hours, 28 minutes, and 59 seconds—considered a record passage. The overall winner on corrected time was the 54-foot *Alliance*, sponsored by the

U.S. Naval Academy and skippered by Captain Edwin A. Shuman, who grew up in Marblehead and was the son of Arthur Shuman, outstanding Eastern helmsman and amateur designer who taught sailing at Annapolis. Upon arrival, many of the contestants joined the cruise of the Royal Cork Yacht Club (founded in 1720 and oldest in the world) in celebration of their Cruising Club's fiftieth.

Right after the Annual Regatta on the Fourth of July (part of the new, week-long Massachusetts Bay Regatta), Commodore Barker in his flagship *Star Song* took the Annual Cruise down east on a two-part extended voyage east of Schoodic Point to Machias Seal Island, just short of Grand Manan. From the rendezvous at South Freeport on July 7 they visited Love's Cove in Ebenecook Harbor, Maple Juice Cove, Seal Bay on the northeast side of Vinalhaven, Pretty Marsh, Northeast Harbor, and Somes Sound. Allie (Mrs. Donald) Blodgett kept an informal log:

> The race from Seal Bay to Pretty Marsh was the fourth and last of the cruise and included a spinnaker run through Deer Island Thorofare. It was a beautiful day, bright and clear, with the wind shifting off the land, causing constant spinnaker adjustments and course alterations. The six yachts in the lead entered the Thorofare practically abreast. The next four miles were a constant juggling of positions as all six struggled for the lead. The tide and wind gave first one the advantage, and then another. Those in close proximity to the Vice Commodore got a big chuckle when, at one point, he lost the lead. As everyone seemed to be passing him to weather, he became so frustrated he grabbed his cap off his head and threw it down the companionway.
>
> Pretty Marsh Harbor, on the western side of Mount Desert Island, is one of the most beautiful anchorages in Blue Hill Bay. The cruise was invited ashore to a BYOB [Bring Your Own Bottle] cocktail party. One captain suffered the mishap of missing his dinghy as he stepped from the dock. A handsome pair of white trousers suddenly became covered with mud.

The Club took over Abel's Lobster Restaurant at the head of Somes Sound for a cocktail party and cookout—an excellent evening in spite of a power outage that forced the chef to cook with the help of a flashlight as the waitresses stumbled over roots trying to serve outside until the power company arrived with a new transformer.

The formal cruise ended in Somes Sound. Vice Commodore Stephen J. Connolly III, in the 41-foot Aage Nielsen sloop *Tay-*

Jazzing it up for Sail '79, featuring George Poor on the trumpet.

geta, built in 1964, won the racing class and Shepard Trophy, and George R. Poor in *Tinavire* won the cruising class and the MacPherson Bowl. (Poor's soulful trumpet is remembered from the nights when the Club's family cruise used to anchor off Raymond's Beach and the author's home on Eastern Point.)

On July 14, twenty-six boats took on supplies and fuel at Northeast Harbor and sailed on to Winter Harbor. Next day was Sunday, fogbound, and *Taygeta* heard three Maydays on the radio from boats, not EYC, on the rocks. Nevertheless, nine ventured forth behind *Tioga* for Bunker Harbor, off Roque Island. The rest huddled in the fog, grateful for the hospitality of the Winter Harbor Yacht Club, all Monday until Tuesday, when the captains' meeting decided to follow the leader through the thick behind radar-equipped *Star Song* to The Cow Yard, on the south shore of Head Harbor Island, where it slowly lifted.

Wednesday, July 18, dawned a perfect day for the excursion to Machias Seal Island arranged by Donald and Beverly Seamans. The rocky, twenty-acre birder's paradise lies fifteen miles offshore, due east of Head Harbor Island, and is unoccupied save by the lighthouse that Canada has maintained since 1832 as a foothold for its claim of sovereignty. Allie Blodgett's log continues:

At 8 o'clock two lobster boats from Jonesport, both freshly painted for the occasion, came alongside to pick up the thirty-four captains, crews and guests who had signed up for this never-to-be-forgotten trip. The sea was as smooth as glass, the sun shone, and the three-hour run was uneventful. Even with smooth waters, the landing at Machias Seal was a real feat. The group was rowed ashore by fours in small rowboats and then required to make a huge jump onto slippery rocks.

The Canadian wildlife guide welcomed all, but he was visibly upset that there were so many visitors. Only a hundred are allowed ashore in the entire year, and in that one day a third of the quota came. The Arctic terns were nesting, and some of the little chicks were already unsteadily walking on the paths. Their parents, audibly upset, divebombed every visitor, pecking at their heads. It was a four-star day, seeing at intimate range razor-billed auks, Arctic terns and ivory gulls. The trip back to The Cow Yard was placid. Immediately each yacht weighed anchor and motored to Roque Island, where once again fog awaited.

Thursday was fog again, and after the usual captains' meeting the yachts lined up for follow-the-radar-leader Barker. The destination was Winter Harbor; the passage was wet, rough and long. More of the same on Friday, but at last the cruise reached Northeast Harbor, where it disbanded. Walter Smith, the fleet captain for the cruise, returned home to find his mooring occupied by a ketch called *Dominique*, allegedly involved in illegal drug traffic.

Since he had to represent a club to qualify, and Charlie Hamlin was already sailing for the Eastern, Jon Wales won the Manhasset Bay Challenge in the IODs in September under the Pleon's burgee. Likewise, Ann Mayer of the Pleon, with her crew, Suze Connolly and Sharon Grinnell, daughters of Eastern members, and Debbie Rice, represented the Pleon in a quest for the Ladies National Sailing Championship, the Adams Cup; they won the North Shore, Massachusetts Bay, and New England rounds, then traveled across the country to Monterey, where they came in second for the top U.S. women's trophy.

For the first time since 1957, the Club in 1979 hosted the Men's National Senior Sailing Championship for the Mallory Cup, September 13 through 15. The boats were borrowed E-22s. Glenn Darden of the Fort Worth, Texas, Boat Club, with

no experience in the Etchells, successfully defended his title in the 15-to-20-knot backlash of Hurricane Frederick. Peter Godfrey, the Eastern's would-be entry in the finals, had the bad luck to be squeezed out of the semifinals at Bristol, Rhode Island, at the last minute by a shortage of boats.

This was another Etchells year for Dave Curtis, spiced with a dash of Soling. Co-skippering with Bob McCann and Peter Warren, he won the New England Championship in June. Switching to the Solings, he won five out of six and a gold medal for the United States at the Pan American Games in Puerto Rico. Back again in the E-22s, he and Bob McCann won five out of six in Race Week and the Fowle Memorial Trophy. In August, the three were defending world champions in Toronto but lost to John Savage of Australia; of the six Eastern boats out of a fleet of fifty-five, four finished in the top ten.

Curtis received the Distinguished Service to Yachting award at the YRUMB annual dinner in November, the sixth Eastern member so honored. Between the Etchells and the Soling, he had them coming and going.

The International One-Design loyalists, with hearts of iron and boats of wood, chafed at the attention-getting upstarts and their molded racing machines. In the early 1960s, the IOD was an endangered species, down to four or five in Marblehead. In 1965 William Widnall, then a member of the Corinthian, bought one, followed by David Smith in 1966 and Jon Wales in 1967. Under such catalytic influence, the fleet was up to fourteen by 1968, when Wales won the first IOD Worlds in Marblehead. Team races with Larchmont started up about that time and continued into the early Eighties, when scheduling difficulties and Larchmont's dwindling fleet called it quits. Team racing was extended to Bermuda in the mid-1970s.

By 1979, the class was at its peak, with twenty-five IODs out of Marblehead alone. The Corinthian Race Committee had been doing a slow burn over the notoriously fast starts of the E-22s—so early that during Race Week it would finally be provoked to cancel one of their matches after two recalls for gun-jumps. The IODs, too, were burning to show the E-22s a thing or two.

So on July 15 the Corinthian offered to settle once and for all the racy rivalry between these top classes with a pair of sudden-death races, five versus five in Internationals, and five versus five in Etchells. The IOD sailors carried the day, inspiring the Eastern's poet laureate for the occasion, Charlie Hamlin, to scribble a triumphant snatch of doggerel for *The Easterner*:

Top Eastern skippers of the IODs include Robert McCann, Peter Warren, William Widnall and Jonathan Wales.

THE ETCHELLS AND THE I.O.D.s
WITH APOLOGIES TO LEWIS CARROLL

The Etchells crew, a motley lot,
Surfeit with impudence,
All felt they were without peer
In sailing skills and sense;
And this they often touted loud
With little reverence.

One day these blokes with misplaced pride
Regaled the I.O.D.'s;
They claimed that none were quite so fast
As those that sailed the "E's."
"Let's show them what this game's about,"
They crowed in scornful glee.

The I.O.D.'s were seasoned men,
Old Marblehead's elite,
And known throughout the racing world
As cunning, shrewd and fleet;
And this was hardly odd because
They were so hard to beat.

"The time has come," the Etchells jeered,
"To find who's fast and slow;

We'll race a team of I.O.D.'s
To see who eats the crow;
And who shall rule the porch supreme
For all the Club to know!"

The I.O.D.'s, in calm resolve,
Took on that vaunting crew.
"It's time we taught those boys to sail
The Etchells Twenty-two."
And so they picked the best to fight
Amidst the foggy dew.

The races came and two were held,
A fair and even test;
The Etchells battled fitfully
The I.O.D.'s to best.
But pride was not enough to put
The better team to rest.

So Badly Beaten were the "E's,"
They lost in every race,
That home to port they had to go
In humble pie disgrace;
The I.O.D.'s in nonchalence
Had Etchells' pride erased.

A pall now hangs o'er Eastern's porch;
It hangs with awful weight,
To think of their sad state.
And this is odd because they knew
Before the race, their fate.

A fortnight later, Charlie Hamlin put his money where his poetry was and, with Jud Smith as co-skipper, won the IOD Worlds at Edinburgh over three-time and defending champion Bill Widnall of the Corinthian and a fleet of international finalists. The seven-race series in early August 1979 was hosted by the Royal Firth Yacht Club. The 16-to-17-foot tides running at 2½ knots back and forth through the Firth of Forth were not unfamiliar to Eastern helmsmen, who had been there before. In the auld Scots tradition of "ye take th' high road, an' I'll take th' low," the races had to be run at the slack or the full, and at the mercy of the shiftiest of winds—to make it all the more interesting.

Winding up the IOD season September 21 to 23, Jon Wales won the Manhasset Bay Challenge Cup at Marblehead, representing the Pleon, with the Eastern team of Hamlin/Smith second.

Chapter 20 *Aurae Vela Vocant* *1980–1985*

Never before in yachting history had anything approached the competitive pressures of the 1980s. Neither boat ownership, yacht club membership, nor access to the shore was any longer the special privilege of those who could afford summer homes. Yachts were mass-produced, and sailing was a popular sport, one of a cluster of family activities that had turned the clubs perforce into the new social centers for a summer season that gave less way each year to the old bounds of spring, fall, and central heating.

Having traveled the worldly Etchells circuit, Dave Curtis had a perspective on the mid-Eighties larger than most. What had started in Marblehead had spread around the globe; now the old town was another yachting center—though never *just*, no longer *the* capital of the sport:

> We do much less one-design racing here than everywhere else where they're doing it. We have a very short season. Weekends in October right up into November at Annapolis you'd think it was the busiest Race Week you ever saw. Or Long Island Sound. There aren't many people like Bob Sides or Ben Smith who just want to go out and race every Saturday. Instead, people will sail two or three races on a weekend and then do something else for two or three weeks. They're busier and have so much else to do. Cruising has cut into it, but not much. The number of boats in the harbor that don't leave the mooring more than five times a year is staggering.
>
> And I find Marblehead the hardest place to sail. Unpredictable, and I think there's less wind than there used to be. When you go out to the line it's invariably from the southeast or within thirty degrees of it, and you never know from one week to the next, even though the conditions are the same, whether you're going to sail to the right or the left on the first leg. As the thermal breeze in the early afternoon starts to fill in and build,

it will swing one way or the other, but it won't swing back, so if you're going out to the left side of the course and the breeze goes to the left, you're going to be two hundred yards ahead of the people that went the other way—or behind, if you do it backwards. But once that first shift sets in, it doesn't give you a chance to get back if you went the wrong way, because that's what you're going to have the rest of the day. Of course it's equally difficult for everybody else. It was better in the old days, starting later in the afternoon when the breeze had already settled in.

> Prior to the mid- or late Sixties, sailing hadn't caught on to the degree that it was popular here. Now the pendulum has swung the other way. We haven't had that many go on to be world class. Florida, Texas, and California are where the good sailors are coming from. The clubs in Texas are rolling in dough, and they'll send the kids wherever they want to go. These kids of twelve know more than I did at twenty, and when that happens, they all get better faster.

For all that, a recap of the 1985 season confirms that Eastern one-design skippers were right up there in the national and international running. They sailed and were usually high in the standings in North American, national, and midwinter regattas in Massachusetts (seven), Florida (seven), Maryland (two), Wisconsin (two), California (two), Maine, Connecticut, Tennessee, Georgia, Montana, Colorado, Virginia, Nebraska, and Ohio, as well as world meets twice each in Australia and Japan, Bermuda, West Germany, Italy, and France.

Everyone of course agreed that Marblehead was no longer *the* capital of yachting. In 1982 John Ahern of the *Boston Globe* paused in the middle of Race Week to lament its decline and thought he saw some other reasons:

What made this the great regatta it used to be were the fleets that came from other ports. They arrived here in droves from Boston Harbor clubs, from Quincy, Hingham, Cohasset and Hull. They came from Lynn, Swampscott, Manchester, Nahant, Conomo, Beverly, Ipswich, Annisquam, Eastern Point and Sandy Bay. They came from faraway places like Long Island Sound and, once in a while, from the inland lakes.

They don't come any more and the reasons are many. The economy has something to do with it. But not as much as you might think. This was a resort place, and that brought many sailors. There were hotels, motels, restaurants, boarding and rooming houses. A yachtsman could settle in for a week. That luxury is gone. This is a bedroom town now. The hotels and rooming houses are no more. Nor are the restaurants, for a great part. There is a scarcity of parking spaces. There is a shortage of moorings. So why come?

The way we use our leisure as a society is symptomatic of what's going on beneath the surface. No doubt about it: yachting was undergoing a sea change in the 1980s. Take design alone. One who had seen it all, and been responsible for plenty of it himself, was Ted Hood:

We did the first center cockpit which you could walk under with headroom in a heavy-displacement boat for the depth. Going back to my training in house design, I always cram a lot into a small space and work on the details of the creature comforts. No matter the size of the boat, the human being's the same. Make sure the seats are comfortable, back rests and bunk length are right, there's room to spread out, elbow and head room, don't bump your shoulders on things.

Hood deplored the trendy maxim that lighter is better and cheaper. He pointed to a half-model of a 90-foot maxi (defined as having a 70-foot or longer IOR rating) with only a 6-foot draft, of his design, unpurchased because it didn't look right without a keel.

That boat can go anywhere. It has lots of ballast and displacement, and with the centerboard has more stability and is much more seaworthy than a keel boat. And the heavier mast, we've found, is better than a light one because the wave has gone by before the weight aloft can react, since it takes longer.

Light's fast, so they're building lighter and lighter. We just dented a hull that we didn't build, lifting it in the slings. That's what they're racing today. The only thing that's gonna stop it is if the crew says, I'll lose my life on it, it's too dangerous. You can't have racing boats without scantlings; the old timers proved that.

And the IMS [International Measurement System, an attempt at a common rating for cruising and racing boats] is allowing wing keels and full-length battens. Maybe the full-length batten is all right in cruising, but they said, "We can rate the guy racing," and I said, "You wait till the experts get hold of full-length battens and see what they do with 'em. You won't know where you are, because you know they're faster." Everyone's gonna be frustrated if they allow wing keels. IOR forbids it, but not the IMS, the cruising rule. There's no way they're gonna be able to rate 'em, and the poor guys with their ordinary boats are gonna get cleaned up on, and it'll take years to clear it up.

After the Maas yard in Holland went bankrupt in the early 1970s, Ted returned to the United States, where a few years of inflation, high costs, and customer resistance sent him back to the Far East. By 1980 he had leased a yard in Taiwan. (By 1987 he had sold off his sailmaking operations and his outgrown Little Harbor yard in Marblehead and relocated in Bristol, Rhode Island. And he had a fine-tuned facility in Taiwan with eighty-eight employees, including half a dozen Taiwanese graduates in naval architecture, overseen by son Teddy and turning out stock 42-, 44-, 46-, 50-, 53-, and 63-foot hulls with optional interiors.)

The New England Rule adopted in 1972 gave way to the Performance Handicap Rating Formula (PHRF), based on past performance, which governed most racing in Massachusetts Bay. (The Club had applied the NER to Class A on the Annual Cruise and the Eastern Cruising Canvas to Class B, as it had for some time.) In a sense, it was a reaction against the anticruising "tunnel vision" imposed on design by the narrower parameters of the IOR, a throwback to the Yankee pragmatism that governed the Club's regattas a couple of generations before high technology got into the measuring act.

The first PHRF races were hosted by the Boston Yacht Club in 1977. By 1980, the other Marblehead clubs were offering PHRF starts in all their weekend regattas, and by the mid-Eighties the new measurement virtually ruled all local ocean racing.

A degree of pragmatism (some would call it merely common sense) had returned to measurement, and, ultimately, to design. The PHRF was welcomed in an advertisement by Hinckley, the respected Southwest Harbor (Maine) boatbuilder, which reminded yachtsmen that with the ascendance of the IOR in the early Seventies after its adoption in 1970, the yard quit building for competition "rather than chase the mythical 'cruiser/racer' which so often proved to be neither." Now, with the shift in the mid-Eighties toward the more Corinthian PHRF and the International Measurement System (a computerized speed-prediction refinement of the MHS designed to bring older and cruising boats into competition), Hinckley was back with "safe and sensible" offshore sailers that could also win races.

Dave Breed was an early Marblehead and Eastern PHRF standout in his *Gambit*, which wound up as Class C Boat of the Year in 1980, 1981, and 1982. Sargent Goodchild's *Manxman* topped Class A in 1984, George Lowden and Rich Hill's *Dark Horse* in 1985. Jack Wells's *Pique Dame* and Tim Jenkins's *Crocodile* won Class B in 1983 and 1985, with Peter Schwarzenbach's *Ra* the 1985 Class D Boat of the Year.

The outcome of the 1980 Indy of the blue-water faction, the Bermuda Race, suggested that there might be something in the old verities after all. Among the entries, for the second time since 1970, was John J. Wilson's 42.6-foot ketch *Holger Danske*, under his son Richard, an old and old-fashioned boat competing in an old and new-fashioned race against million-dollar machines put together for the express purpose of winning it. Rich recorded in the *Cruising Club News* the latest chapter of the saga after it had taken its place in the modern folklore of the ocean, the CCA, and the Eastern:

The first idea to enter the Bermuda Race came during a transatlantic crossing from the Canaries to Barbados in the fall of 1978. A flat, bullet-proof spinnaker tacked to the bowsprit and sheeted at the end of the wung-out main boom and occasionally a twin jib poled out on the other side provided the front-wheel drive to pull us along at seven knots for three straight weeks in only Force three to four breezes. The motion was so easy and the speed so consistently fast that I began to ponder what *Holger Danske* might do with a hot-shot crew, a little intensity and some good fortune in weather.

My father had skippered *Holger Danske* in the 1970 Bermuda Race. A disadvantageous rating under the still-developing IOR rule and many hours of calm had placed us well down in the fleet. Since *Holger Danske* is the antithesis of an IOR boat, we had not bothered again. Instead, *Holger Danske* had logged well over 50,000 miles in cruising three laps around the North Atlantic and the Caribbean plus a Mediterranean cruise [in 1968/69, 1972/73, and 1977/78].

Now [1980], with the MHS handicapping hulls and rigs from first principles of hydro- and aerodynamics, we felt we could enter and at least have a shot at doing well. I spruced up our

instrumentation and electronics with a Loran set and a digital speedometer and log. Our apparent wind indicator remained our faithful windsock sewn by my sister two transatlantic passages back; our anemometer was the traditional, highly calibrated wet finger.

In assembling the crew, my objective was to create a synergistic blend of one-design expertise and deep water experience. I knew Aage Nielsen had designed a very fast and sea-kindly boat and that she was ready to go to sea. The weather always contains some measure of luck, so the only controllable variable was the crew. A stellar boat performance would be a function of their efforts.

Of the ten, six had made at least one transatlantic passage aboard *Holger Danske* and thus knew the boat well. Believing that in a long-distance race, the helmsmen were the critical factor, another subset of six had considerable one-design success on their resumes. With several aspiring to be comedians, the combination proved safe, fast and hilarious. [Eastern members, besides Rich Wilson as skipper and navigator, were leading one-design sailors William C. (Twig) Burke III and Peter Warren, who shared command responsibilities with him.]. . .

Recruiting small-boat helmsmen clearly proved correct. Early on, in our worst conditions of going to windward in a steep chop, they hung on to our class leaders. Now, on a more favorable point of sail [averaging 8½ knots going into the first evening], they wouldn't let the Class C or D boats pass. We saw no more F or E boats until we were docked at the Royal Bermuda Yacht Club. Helmsmen switched every fifteen to thirty minutes for maximum concentration and effect. The competition to log the highest speed was fierce. The on-deck chiding, jeering and cheering was endless and infectious.

Months of poring over NOAA Gulf Stream data and weather forecasts primed Wilson to chart three points of passage that his Loran enabled him to hold on course and hit with astounding accuracy. The start was Friday, June 20.

For example, if our course was 155 degrees magnetic and the 25000 Series line was slowly decreasing by tenths of microseconds, the helmsman was tending to the east of the course. In a minute or two this trend was discernible on the Loran, and the preferred course for that individual would be revised, say to 157 degrees. Thus he would tend, ever so slightly more, to steer our intended route.

The combined effect of our expert helmsmen and this correction method was stunning as shown by a post-race analysis of

Holger Danske, driven to a brilliant dark-horse win of the 1980 Bermuda Race by owner John Wilson's son Rich, and his crew. Edwin A. Hills photo.

our chart. Indeed, from the time when the wind freed up on Friday until our entrance into the Gulf Stream 184 miles later, our hourly Loran fixes show maximum deviation from a perfect rhumb line between these two endpoints of less than one nautical mile. Aided by the boosts from the warm eddy and southside back loop, our log registered only 650 miles at the finish of this 625-mile race.

In short, *Holger Danske* and her crew did rather well by each other, and when it was all over were actually given permission to tie up alongside the sleek earlier finishers at the Royal Bermuda Yacht Club.

Although it was only 7:30 A.M., the bar was doing a booming business. Rumors abounded, and our crew was jubilant. Showers, a couple or three drinks, wash the decks, and suddenly Commodore Cooper appeared at our gangway requesting permission to come aboard.

"Congratulations, Skipper, *Holger Danske* is the official winner of the 1980 Bermuda Race!"

My fantastic crew wrestled me up to the foredeck and threw me in the water (giving the *Bermuda Sun* a fabulous picture of a crazed man being dragged away to go with their headline "Sex Attack Man Jailed").

Floating momentarily beneath Hamilton Harbor, I hardly cared whether I surfaced or not.

Holger Danske beat all the other twenty-one boats in Class F on elapsed time, twenty-six of the twenty-eight in E, twenty-five of the thirty-five in D, and six of the thirty-six in C. Of the twenty Newport-Bermuda Races since 1936, her time of 63 hours and 43 minutes bettered that of all other overall winners except four, of which three were A and one B.

Twig Burke's version of the triumph might be entitled "Sixty-three Hours Before the Mast," had he not been co-skipper. He wrote, in part:

Two hours after the start, after a lot of the bigger boats sailed through us, a front came through. The wind started to go aft, and *Holger* started to pick up speed. We had three-hour watches, and we decided to have a little contest. We called it Miles for Mopeds. Whichever team logged the most miles on the watch would be bought mopeds by the rest of the guys when we got to the island. [Burke's watch won.] We ended up sailing her like a dinghy, constantly changing sails. Who could get the boat going the fastest on the digital speedo? 10.93 was the winner, a three-way tie. I still can't believe three people got the same number. We almost had two 200-mile days—one at 212, the other at 186. When we finished we all toasted our-

selves with two bottles of champagne at four in the morning. When we got to the dock, we were told we had won by six hours.

On a more pedestrian plane, the loose ends of Phase IV of the Long-Range Plan were tied up early in 1980. The barracks was razed, leaving the garage section on Harbor Avenue, which diminished the fire hazard and improved the looks. The ancient original tennis court in front of the clubhouse, plagued by drainage problems, was rebuilt. The ground level of the house was remodeled for men's and ladies' rooms, with showers. And a second-floor bedroom and bath were remodeled as the Parker Suite, in memory of Commodore James P. Parker, by his four children and their spouses. This was the first of two to be renovated, bringing to thirteen the number of doubles for rent as the result of eliminating housing for employees—with the exception of Frances Gilliland and the tennis pro.

On the waterfront, activity was increasing at a rate that now required a supervisor, and overtime regulations dictated raising the staff from four launchmen to seven launchpersons, including the Club's first woman driver.

As if to balance off the frostbiters between November and April, a group of female sailboarders organized the Flying Mums, many on boards that matched their bathing suits. This mad water sport was gripping the more lithe and limber on and in the frigid waters of the North Shore. They must have taken some of their inspiration from a 'surfer who made it around the course, with numerous spills, in the 1979 Chowder Race and was awarded an EYC pool towel for his persistence. One addict had her board forwarded to Florida so she could get a winter's jump on the other Mums.

The goings-on at the once-staid Eastern Yacht Club, as the 1980s dawned, would have astounded the founders, who frowned on a round of croquet as an effete distraction from matters of serious yachting and sail-watching.

Now, besides frostbiting and sailboarding, there were shore-side paddle platforms that occasionally had to be shoveled as prelude to the play, and of course racquet tennis as a distraction of longer standing. Having achieved tournament status, and the committees and trophies to stamp their legitimacy, both were a permanent part of the Eastern's sporting picture. The pool was host to swimming meets, an annual water ballet

---

The clubhouse in 1988. Clive Russ photos.

Aurae Vela Vocant

show, and, in this summer of 1980, a harbor seal named Salisbury, loaned by the New England Aquarium for the event. Salisbury not only refused to perform but would not return to his cage until the next day, requiring his trainer to sleep in her wetsuit at poolside for fear he would succumb to the call of the nearby mother waters, waddle out during the night, and be gone.

No longer a simple operation for the summer sailors, the Club opened in 1980 on April 26 with the chowder luncheon and an evening dance and closed exactly twenty-six weeks later on October 26, with the Oktoberfest, featuring dinner, a German band, and Bavarian costumes.

In between were the Mother's Day brunch; Sail '80 (canceled on May 25 due to high winds); Tall Ships Night on May 30, the day the windjammers returned for Boston's 350th; the EYC Olympics on June 15, torched off by Giff Simonds running up the stairs to light the flame, followed by a barrage of balloons, fun and games, steak cookout, and awards; the third EYC All-Star Night of softball and buffet; the Fourth of July dance, swimfest, and pig roast; and the return of the Great Rubber Band, with 280 for dinner and more than 500 jammed into the clubhouse for the evening.

Commenting on the similarly full season a couple of years earlier, a member of the Historical Committee observed a little wistfully:

As the full membership utilizes the facilities, there is obviously increased hustle, bustle, and confusion. This is, no doubt, a pleasure for many, but perhaps there are a few who look longingly beyond the harbor, wishing to be at sea where the only sounds are the screech of a seagull and the lapping of the waves against the sleek hull of a yacht as it slips quietly through the water.

Forty-eight sleek hulls slipped along not so quietly behind Commodore Barker's *Star Song* for the start of the 1980 Annual Cruise on Sunday, July 6, at Marion. Again, Allie Blodgett kept her log. The wind was gusting up to 50 from the northwest. One captain lost his power in the Canal; trying to sail into Marion, he hit a rock and ripped his mainsail pulling it down. The next day twenty boats raced to Hadley's Harbor in a 30-knot southwesterly.

On Tuesday, twenty-two raced to Edgartown, finishing in rain with 35 knots of wind. Wednesday opened with light air and was blowing 12 by the time the fleet reached Nantucket.

Star Song developed engine trouble and was towed in by the Connollys' powerboat *Celaeno* (like their *Taygeta*, one of the Pleiades). Former Commodore and Mrs. B. Devereux Barker, Jr., entertained the fleet at their home overlooking the harbor.

From Nantucket, they proceeded to Stage Harbor, Chatham, at will, as there was no wind. Departing with the fleet for Osterville on Saturday, Fleet Surgeon William E. Johnson in *Elsinore* lost his steerage in the narrow Stage Harbor channel. The Coast Guard was called and, upon arrival, its vessel started to sink. More help was called, and a Coast Guard cutter came up, towed the sinking boat into the harbor, and returned to tow *Elsinore*, which had been anchored patiently in the channel.

The race to Osterville, like Stage Harbor a new port for the Annual Cruise, was a close reach with wind gusting up to 35. From the North Bay anchorage, all were ferried down to Crosby's Boat Yard for cocktails and a chicken barbecue. The last race started off Osterville, with no air and a strong adverse current, and ended off Woods Hole in a dead beat with winds up to 25.

The weather and five races had cut the fleet down from thirty-three to seventeen, besides which, one out of every five boats had a mechanical problem, leading one member to remark, "We have a fleet captain and a fleet surgeon, but what we really need is a fleet mechanic."

The last night was spent at Quissett, where it was announced during the party aboard the *Empress*, the chartered committee boat, that Vice Commodore Steve Connolly in *Taygeta* won the Shepard Trophy and Brad Noyes in *Tioga* won the MacPherson Bowl. Various whimsical awards followed in the first Annual Cruise Roasting.

In an attempt to relieve the pressure of afternoon starts treading on morning finishes, the Marblehead Racing Association reinstituted a one-a-day, seven-day Race Week in 1980. In his 1972 *Robin*, Ted Hood won his class in the Southern Ocean Racing Circuit, as he had the previous year, and his class in the New York Yacht Club Cruise in August with six firsts and a second. Mary Lou Grinnell, with Joanne Curtis in her crew, finished second in the Wakeman, won the Colt Trophy for the New England Championship, then went on to New Orleans to represent the Eastern—first time in nineteen years—in the USYRU Women's Championship.

Dave Curtis was busier than a one-man afterguard. With Bob

McCann as crew, he finished second in the Etchells Worlds in Australia. In Puerto Rico he came in eighth in the Soling Worlds, although he was in first place after four of the seven races. With Jamie Hardenbergh crewing, he was second in the Soling Nationals in Florida, won the Etchells North American Championship in Chicago and the Soling Atlantic Coast Championship, and finished second in the J-24 Districts in Marblehead. In the Newport trials for the Moscow Olympics, boycotted by the United States, Curtis and Rick Howard placed fifth and eleventh, respectively. For good measure, Curtis wound up first in four and second in three major Lightning regattas.

The International One-Design World Championship was hosted by the Eastern, beginning September 7, because the defending champions were members Charlie Hamlin and Jud Smith. Qualifying were sixteen boats from the United States, Scotland, Bermuda, Norway, and Sweden—four of them from Marblehead, including three from the Eastern: Jon Wales/Ted Cook, Steve Wales, and Hamlin/Smith. The conclusion of this best-of-seven series was Friendly Fratricide in the most brotherly Wales tradition, as described by one who was there:

It all came down to the last race. Just as it did in 1976. It came down to the same two skippers. Just as it did in 1976. The tactical situation, the yacht club, the conditions—all were the same. The irony even carried to the boats sailed by the vying skippers. Steve Wales sailed his brother's boat, *Saga,* and Jon Wales sailed *Dubious,* one of the fastest in the fleet. Number 51 versus number 15. Brother against brother for the title of 1980 world champion of the International One-Design class.

Going to the starting line, Steve Wales held the lead precariously by one and a quarter points over his brother. Wales/Cook had to put a boat between themselves and Steve to win. They also had the tactical option of driving Steve to the bottom of the fleet. If both boats finished worse than ninth, Wales/Cook would win by forcing Steve to score an earlier, very poor finish.

The race was further complicated by the battle for third place between Bill Widnall and the Hamlin/Smith crew.

The whole regatta came to a dramatic close in the last leg. Wales/Cook, having chosen to race their own race, sailed superbly and led all the way around the course. But the race was far from over, and the results of the regatta a long way from being settled.

Steve got off to a bad start and had boat speed problems early in the race, despite the fact that he was sailing his brother's boat, a boat that had won the season's championship. Going into the last leg, the positions were Wales/Cook, Widnall, Hamlin/Smith, Marshall Napier, Fraser Mills, and Steve Wales. Steve had to finish second to win.

Halfway up the last leg, Widnall, Hamlin/Smith, and Napier were tightly bunched on the left-hand side of the course, well ahead of Mills and Steve, who were on the right-hand side. Widnall, needing to put a boat between himself and Hamlin/Smith, made a bold play to slow down his group, for if he could put either Steve or Mills between himself and Hamlin/Smith, he would win third place. A fierce tacking duel ensued as both Napier and Hamlin/Smith tried to break Widnall's cover.

On the opposite side of the course, Steve and Mills were in a close and similar battle as Steve tried to break Mills's cover. Both were gaining rapidly on Widnall, Hamlin/Smith, and Napier. Wales/Cook in the lead watched with bated breath as their sure regatta win came closer and closer by a hair's breadth, if a win at all.

Widnall miscalculated by one boat length. Mills closed the door on the starboard tack at the pin end of the finish line, and Widnall had to take his stern. Hamlin/Smith crossed fourth. Steve Wales, unable to break Mills's cover, finished fifth, 21 seconds out of second and a regatta victory.

The final results were: 1. Jon Wales/Teddy Cook; 2. Steve Wales; 3. Charlie Hamlin/Jud Smith.

Vice Commodore Stephen J. Connolly III succeeded Gardner Barker as commodore and led twenty-five boats on the 1981 Annual Cruise in *Taygeta* from the Portland rendezvous as far as Camden, where his flagship won another Shepard Trophy; John Kells's *Celebration* won the MacPherson Bowl. Among the cozy cul-de-sacs visited en route was The Basin, off the New Meadows River, where the horticulturally inclined arranged their craft as petals of a convivial sunflower raft around Brad Noyes's *Tioga.*

Twenty-two boats (minus the disappointed Connollys, who had organized the informal sequel but were unable at the last minute to participate), sailed forth from Northeast Harbor under the guidance of Sam Batchelder and Sherman Morss from the Manchester Yacht Club—both steeped in local knowledge from previous cruises—for eight days in the Saint John River in New Brunswick, the farthest east ever ventured by even a semiofficial EYC Annual Cruise. Wrote Joseph C. Roper, Jr.:

At Chance, Canada, the fleet was met by Jerry Peer of the Royal Kennebecasis Yacht Club who guided the yachts to the city of Saint John in the Bay of Fundy. At the appropriate time the crossing of the Reversing Falls was made, putting the fleet in fresh water for a delightful stay in fog-free sunshine exploring the many miles of the river with its coves, lakes and pleasant anchorages. There is no current, good sailing and few boats.

The Reversing Falls at Saint John gets its name because at low tide the ocean is ten or fifteen feet lower than the river, whereas at high tide it is six to ten feet higher. Thus the current runs hard in one direction, reversing itself every six hours. No boat could pass through the rapids and over the rocks that make up the falls except during slack or nearly slack water, a period of less than an hour.

The Eastern squadron was regally entertained by members of the Royal Kennebecasis Yacht Club, whose races were traditionally started by a woman firing a shotgun out of a second-story window.

Former Commodore Wells Morss sailed his last Bermuda Race—actually a cruising race from Marion to the Patch—in 1981, which marked his forty-fourth season of Eastern membership. His ocean-racing record was something to contemplate. He had sailed in fifteen regular Bermuda Races, twelve of them in his own boat, since his first in the fabled *Grenadier* in 1934 (after voyaging to England in her for the Fastnet the previous year). He had sailed in twelve Halifax Races since 1939, when *Grenadier* won the schooner class, and in 1969 won Class B in the only custom boat he ever owned, the 44-foot Sparkman & Stephens sloop *Carillon*. He completed Southern Circuits in his latest *Legend*, a Swan 48, and *Errant* in 1973 and 1975 and portions of two others when he chartered. He sailed in seventeen of the Portland Yacht Club's Monhegan Races, usually in his own boat, took home silver more than half the time, and won overall twice.

Besides a few other miscellaneous ocean races here and there, Commodore Morss sailed across the Atlantic six times, including the round trip in *Legend*, and once on the return in *Holger Danske*. And in 1972 he raced from Bermuda to Bayona, Spain, in a brand-new boat, running into a bad storm that required repairs on arrival, after which they joined the Cruising Club for a jaunt to Cape Finisterre.

Race Week's Fowle Trophy Award for 1981 went to the quartet of Eastern members who for a decade had patrolled the courses in their "scatboats," putting out race marks, rescuing, towing, keeping in radio contact, and generally making it all work. Powerboaters Tom Brown, Donald Cahoon, Marion Kirkpatrick, and Jim Reiley, who shared the honor, are the "real-life guardians of the hundreds who sail in the area," John Ahern wrote on August 3 in the *Boston Globe*:

During Race Week, the four would meet before noon and decide which area would be patrolled by whom. One would go to the outside line. Another would stick with Brimbles line boats. The other two would oversee the little boats on the inside line. They were in touch with each other and with each race committee boat by radio. They kept all hands apprised of trouble spots.

A week ago today, for instance, an Etchells was in trouble in the heavy northwesterly going. It broke down near the leeward mark well out to the southeast. Reiley was contacted and headed for the area, not knowing that the boat, under jury rig, had headed for Gloucester. Reiley got halfway to Provincetown, and the search was fruitful. He picked up another yacht that had broken down well out to sea and might have drifted unspotted through the night. . . .

The satisfaction of knowing they are performing a vital service is their only reward, and many times, there's not even a thank you for a job so perfectly done.

The high point at the end of the 1981 season was the almost back-to-back Worlds hosted by the Club in September: the Etchells between September 5 and 12, which survived to thrive after an early northeaster, and the International Stars from September 19 through 26, which did the same. A nice touch was the presence at the latter event of its all-time star husband-and-wife team, and the inventors of the former, Skip and Mary Etchells.

The Eastern's Peter Godfrey and Alan Bell were co-chairmen of the Etchells show, with Charlie Pickering chairman of the regatta Race Committee and Nancy Godfrey running the social end. And when it was all over on September 12, John Ahern gave a blow-by-blow summary in the *Boston Globe* of Dave Curtis-and-crew's triumph:

For about an hour after they got ashore last night, the crew of *Whip* sat around, sipped champagne and asked anybody who came by to pinch each one of them—and pinch hard.

That was one way to find out if they were dreaming. After a lot of friends and foes had inflicted the punishment, Dave Curtis, Bobby McCann and Jamie Hardenbergh knew that what they were hoping was true—they had won the Etchells Class World's Championship, beating 68 other entries from seven other nations in a regatta that was second to none.

They wrapped up the title—the third time for Curtis—by finishing fifth in yesterday's race that was won by this port's [and the Eastern's] Rick Howard, the only skipper in the entire show to win twice. It was life and death getting that fifth, but all was saved as Poddy O'Donnell, the defender from Australia, finished eighth and Don Bever, from Newport Beach, Calif., was third. [Bob Sides and Jud Smith of the Eastern also placed in the top ten.]. . .

The day before it all began, *Whip* was rammed in a practice race. Half the transom was torn away in the accident and there was talk of changing the name to *Whipped*. That night the three of them worked for eight straight hours putting the yacht back together and the job was so professional that nary a scar shows. Then came Sad Sunday, the day the winds turned into a carousel. They shifted so much that Curtis thought there should have been abandonment of the race. He felt so strongly that he withdrew and protested. That was not upheld [although forty skippers petitioned for the scratch]. He had to take last-place points. That meant he had no further flexibility in the series. It meant he had to excel in every race if he were to win. That's exactly what he did, although yesterday was a nail-biter.

The problem was brought about by himself. Fifteen minutes before the start, the easterly began piping up. It went from 10 knots to 17 very quickly. Thinking it would get even more muscular, Curtis called for a sail change. He wanted and got a flatter mains'l. Then the breeze settled in at 15 knots. From there it was a struggle to get that fifth and the title, a prize that is worth more than all others he has won.

The acceptance by the Star organization in 1979 of the invitation of House Chairman Pem Pleasants was a special tribute to the Club. The Star World Championship had never before been held in a port without a home fleet, and the class never at all at Marblehead except during Race Week. This was because drysailing facilities had only recently become available with Eastern's lift, and because the absence of spinnaker work and the need for an extra-heavy crew to keep the boat upright did not suit local custom. In fact, the Star people even agreed to wetsail the series (since eighty-five boats couldn't possibly be hauled and put back twice a day from the Eastern wharf), with the proviso that each was allowed a single haulout in case of a problem, with the approval of the Race Committee.

In laying the groundwork, Pleasants had the special assistance of Ralph DeLuca and Jeff Foster, who had experience in Stars. Rear Commodore Don Blodgett was appointed chairman, and his committee met monthly for the first year and more frequently as the event drew nigh. Charles Pickering was again chairman of the special Race Committee, aided by Eastern Race Chairman John Coolidge, using Charles and John Pin-

Dave Curtis and his crew of Jamie Hardenbergh and Bobby McCann, Etchells World Champions in *Whip*, September 1981.

gree's boats to set up the lines and run the course for two races a day. James and Mary Lou Grinnell managed the measuring, feeding the eighty-five boats that had been shipped in through six stations that finished with a stamp affixed to each approved stern.

Patty Kehoe had charge of finding housing for the world influx of 250; completion of the third-floor renovations made accommodations available for as many as fifty-two in the club-house, whose hospitality was augmented by the new informal dining area on the northerly end of the porch adjacent to the men's bar. James Bowers was treasurer. Members and families pitched in mightily with housing and ferrying to and from the boats. There were five regular Club launchmen as well as launches from the Corinthian and the Boston. Francis Markey handled liaison. Betty Pleasants, Hazel Oliver, Dee Cushman, and Peg Reiley organized the entertainment, reception, and banquet.

A cold and rainy northeaster on the opening day, September 19, failed to dampen ceremonial salutes from the Marblehead Artillery, the band, the hoisting of colors, and the greetings of Commodore Connolly and other dignitaries. The Star Worlds were on, running six days through September 26 and the banquet.

Among the contestants was an Australian crew that had competed a few days earlier in a borrowed E-22, then bought a brand new Star and raced *it* with an exuberance that left its overhead mark on the big tent, which had become a fixture on the lawn, when one of their number raced on and around *it* by foot.

"The racing was excellent," Chairman Blodgett remembers. "There were all types of conditions, excellent courses, and only one bulge that got restarted. The rule was in effect that anyone over had to go back around either buoy or boat. No more bulges. Treasurer Jim Bowers was very tough on Dee Cushman, who defined the expenses of the banquet to the half cent. Because of this close fiscal responsibility, the event donated a speaker system and $3,000 to the Club."

Alex Hagen of West Germany, the youngest skipper to win the Star Worlds since 1945, and crew Vincent Hoesch nosed out Peter Wright of Chicago in very nearly a photo finish and won the trophy, which had to be air-expressed from San Francisco after defending champion Tom Blackaller forgot it—or perhaps in supreme self-confidence hadn't bothered to pack it. Blackaller finished fourth.

"And the setting could not have been better than the Eastern Yacht Club," bread-and-buttered *Starlights*, the class publication. "With a name that smacks of Yankee Establishment, the Eastern is one of the warmest, friendliest and most enjoyable yacht clubs in the world. Can you imagine a yacht club with no Star fleet putting on such a traditional extravaganza as the Gold Star? This one did."

Eugene T. Connolly, the Nestor of Eastern and Marblehead yachtsmen in direct line of succession to Tom Shepard and the two Charlies, Adams and Foster, and Commodore Steve Connolly's uncle, died on April 22, 1982, at ninety, working almost to the last on the chronology of the Club.

Gene Connolly was born in Beverly Farms and learned to sail as a boy in the 23-foot-waterline, plumb-stemmed sloop *Nixie*, designed as a keel cat by Edward Burgess in 1885 for Alexander Cochran of the Eastern, who appears to have sold her to the Connollys around 1898. At the age of 100, she awaits restoration at Mystic Seaport, in whose *Log* John Gardner passed along the partially apocryphal yarn about a premature fate she barely escaped at the "obsessively neat" hands of the man Cochran sold her to, presumably Gene's sire:

Stepping aboard *Nixie* one day, as the story goes, and finding what must have been a monumental mess, the result of a riotous feed of clams that his children had neglected to clean up, he became so incensed [he must have had a temper to match the mess] that he straightaway took *Nixie* to Tom White's yard in Manchester, where he ordered that she be smashed up. Demolition started with the removal of her rig and lead keel, but was held up when the owner of the yard died.

A good yarn, but Commodore Steve Connolly had a better twist, straight from the horse's mouth, as delivered in a corrective note to the next issue of *The Log of Mystic Seaport*:

My grandfather, Stephen J. Connolly, had *Nixie* outfitted and at her mooring in Manchester for his sons, Gregory P. Connolly II, my father, and Eugene T. Connolly for their return from Exeter in perhaps 1908 or 1909. . . . [He] did not order *Nixie* smashed up. He did have her hauled and she fell from her cradle when a team of horses, frightened by a train, (the Gloucester branch passed through the White yard) struck the cradle. The lead keel was removed by Captain [Charlton] Smith, brought to Marblehead on a truck, and the *Nixie*, minus her keel, was towed to Marblehead. My father, brother and I watched Captain Smith rebuild *Nixie* in the mid 1930s.

Aurae Vela Vocant

Eugene T. (Gene) Connolly.

Charmed her life must have been, for years later she was indeed rescued by Cap Smith, the sailor/boatbuilder/story-teller/all-round Marblehead character (from whose Front Street boatshop the first Brutal Beasts had emerged), and re-launched probably in 1937. And what a crew was aboard! Besides Smith, they were Richard D. Sears, Jr., (Alexander Cochran's grand-nephew), B.B. Crowninshield, Francis Herreshoff, and Howard Chapelle. The designer's son, Starling Burgess, had hoped to make it but couldn't.

And to round it out rather nicely, Edward Burgess's grandson, Frederic Tudor, found old *Nixie* in much-reduced circum-

stances in Rhode Island in 1973, bought her, and presented her to Mystic as a memorial to his grandfather.

Gene Connolly learned to sail in *Nixie* and then raced in the 31-foot Bar Harbor class around World War I and in the Bird class out of Annisquam. After graduating from Yale University and Harvard Law School, he practiced in Boston until his retirement in 1970. While living in Swampscott in the 1930s, he owned the M-B *Taira*. In 1941 he moved with his family to Marblehead for the sailing. In 1946 he got Carl Alberg to line off the U.S. One-Design, in which he excelled. He was a founder and first president of the Yacht Racing Union of Massachusetts Bay. In 1967, when he was seventy-five, he helped Frank Scully introduce the Shields class locally and raced successfully in his *Leenane* until 1978, when he injured his back and sold her. Of him it was written:

> This was the ultimate skipper, the man to admire and emulate. He sailed well. He sailed to win. If he did win, there was a very gracious salute to the losers. If he lost, and that fate befell him as it does to all good skippers, there was an even more gracious salute to the winner. This was a man among men.

Seven Eastern yachts were entered in the biennial Bermuda Race in 1982. Up front were Ted Hood's *Robin*, fifth in Class B and sixth in the fleet, and F.D. Winder's *Katrinka*, second in Class F and ninth in the fleet. Spread over the course were Rich Wilson's 1980 winner *Holger Danske*, Weston Adams's *Stampede*, Jeffrey Foster's chartered *Thorfinn*, Robert Hood's *Nathaniel Bowditch*, and Dave Smith's *Drummer Boy*. Westy Adams, New England ocean racing champion in 1977, 1978, and 1980, had been making the Bermuda run since the early 1970s, besides participating in numerous Halifax and Monhegan races.

Commodore Connolly again took the 1982 Annual Cruise, thirty boats strong, to Camden. Again a smaller contingent (twelve yachts) sailed to Northeast Harbor and continued east, this time to Passamaquoddy and Grand Manan, pausing at Roque Island and then going on to Campobello—amid strange waters, strong tides, fog, rain, and blustery winds—for a tour of the Roosevelt retreat there.

As so much of the racing around the buoys and the tennis courts at the Club had been since they moved to Marblehead from Gloucester, Race Week this year was a Sides family affair. Bob won the Etchells in *Sidekick II* while grandson Charles R. Flather (brother of granddaughter Kate, Fowle Award winner

Robert Sides, veteran 210 champion, turned to the Etchells and won both Atlantic Coast and Race Week in the class in 1972.

in 1980) was winning the Widgeons with crew Hugh Hallowell in *Topsides*. The same day Charlie's father, Charles Flather, won the Stone Horse Race in Manchester's Crocker Regatta.

Steve Connolly was succeeded as commodore by Vice Commodore Donald W. Blodgett. The sailing world was saddened by the death on April 28, 1983, of John Ahern, Jr., who had ably succeeded Leonard Fowle, Jr., as the yachting writer for the *Boston Globe*. Contrariwise, Dave Curtis for the second time since 1979 was recognized with the Distinguished Service to Yachting Award of the Yacht Racing Union of Massachusetts Bay. And Frances Gilliland and the members celebrated her sixtieth year behind the front desk at her Club.

Commodore Blodgett took the Annual Cruise behind his *Sirocco*, in which he won the Puritan Cup in 1982, as far to the westward as Fishers Island. Following the recent precedent set by his predecessor, he won his class, only to lose his flagship back in Marblehead on August 11 when a storm broke her loose from her mooring onto Bowden Point, where she was damaged beyond repair. Undaunted, Blodgett was determined to replace her, which he did before the following season.

Robert E. Peabody, a member since 1919 and Number One since 1979, died at ninety-seven on January 20, 1984. After graduating from Harvard in 1909, he got a job as a purser with the Mallory Line to the West Indies, making thirty-seven trips to Cuba over the next several years. He further acted out his family heritage when as a young man he organized a syndicate and built the three-master *Grand Turk* (after the spice ships of his great-grandfather Elias Haskett Derby, builder of Derby Wharf in Salem), which traded lumber and coal for molasses and sugar in the West Indies until she was lost in a storm off the Yucatan. In 1932 he was cofounder of the Boston steamship agency of Peabody and Lane.

A man of diverse interests, Peabody wrote several valuable historical works on maritime Salem and a history of Peach's Point, where he summered most of his life, engaged in his pastime as a watercolorist, and sailed to his heart's content. "He never said a bad word about anyone," a nephew said of Robert Peabody. "I never heard him swear, and he never smoked. Everyone in his eyes was an equal."

Another particular loss for the Eastern in 1984 was the death of Joseph T. Ballard, owner since 1951 of the beautiful schooner *Ellida*, at 62 feet overall the largest yacht in the fleet for several years since the departure of *Mistral*. She was designed by John Alden in 1922 for Dr. Austin Riggs, owner of an earlier schooner of the same name. After the testing of a six-foot scale model in the Concord River, she was framed at the Charles W. Morse yard in Thomaston, Maine, of oak cut from the nearby woods; some of the yellow pine used in her was 40 feet long.

After the death of Dr. Riggs, *Ellida* was purchased by Henry L. Shattuck of Boston and enrolled in the Eastern fleet. She served on patrol in Maine during World War II and on her discharge from the service was returned to Marblehead and restored to her original condition by Shattuck before she was acquired by the Ballards. They threw a fiftieth birthday party for her at the Club dock in 1972. Mrs. Ballard became a member in her own right in 1984 and kept the mistress of the fleet on the rolls.

Outside of Ted Hood's ninth win of the Puritan Cup since 1961, with his latest *Robin*, the peak of the 1984 season was the Eastern's capture of the new U.S. Challenge Cup in California. The object of this first-time national invitational was to come up with the top crew from eleven clubs selected on the basis of strength in ocean, one-design, and junior racing, as well as for their social programs. Robbie Doyle was the Eastern's skipper:

The U.S. Challenge came out of a discussion among some Eastern and New York people and others of a *New York Times* article claiming that the New York Yacht Club had the best sailors in the world. Somebody from the St. Francis [of San Francisco] took issue, pointing out the number of St. Francis and California people in different events and in the America's Cup itself. So somebody from the Newport Harbor Yacht Club [Newport Beach, California] proposed a regatta there of yacht clubs in the home boats, New York Thirty-Sixes, rotating, to see who really has the best sailors.

There was no time for eliminations, and I was asked to represent the Eastern. I had Juddy Smith, Buddy Duncan, Charlie Hamlin, Henry Brauer and Alan Bell. I decided I was better off as tactician, with Juddy on sail trim and Buddy steering, and though I was skipper I'd start the boat, and as soon as we were clear of the line, Buddy would drive.

We won comfortably, because the boat we had to beat got into a collision at the start and did horribly. But there were two or three going into the end that could have won. St. Francis was second.

A stellar addition to the roster in 1984 was Gerald B. Braun, a former Pleon standout who had risen rapidly in the national, world, and Olympic circles of team racing in the high-performance 420s, 470s, and 505s. In 1985, "J.B." moved into the Flying Dutchman as well and was a member of the U.S. Olympic Flying Dutchman and U.S. 505 World Championship (for the third year) teams.

Vice Commodore Francis U. Paige succeeded Donald Blodgett as commodore for 1985. Former Commodore Garlan Morse died on May 26. Two clay tennis courts and the pool were rebuilt. The House Committee permitted ladies to use the bar, which caused some grumbling among the men. Commodore Paige in *Gurnet* took the Annual Cruise south, where Walter J. Cairns and *Nixie* led twenty-one competitors over six courses in Class B for the MacPherson Bowl and former Commodore Steve Connolly and *Taygeta* in Class A copped their fifth Shepard Trophy in seven years.

And Dr. Louis A. Pocharski, Jr., a veteran ocean racer, won his third Puritan Cup (the others were in 1976 and 1978) in his 35-foot sloop *Spirit*. The Pocharski record was impressive: Lightning class world champion; winner of several Patton

Ellida, Mr. and Mrs. Joseph Ballard's 1922, 62-foot Alden schooner was Queen of the Eastern fleet until 1988. Norman Fortier photo.

Bowls and Hovey Races; New England ocean racing champion; Massachusetts Bay champion in 1982, 1984, and 1985; participant in the One-Ton Nationals and Worlds; and numerous other ocean racing events.

The Yacht Racing Union of Massachusetts Bay presented its 1985 Distinguished Service to Yachting Award to L. Pemberton Pleasants, Jr., Race Committee chairman since 1984 (and before that in 1974–75) and House Committee chairman from 1976 to 1981. He was the seventh recipient of the eighth award (Dave Curtis won it in both 1979 and 1983) representing the Eastern, and the eighth member including Leonard Fowle, who represented the Pleon in 1964, a roster unmatched by any other club. His citation:

The 1984 Race Committee: (front) Arthur I. Strang, Chairman L. Pemberton Pleasants, James H. Ballou, Ralph H. Magoon, Pendleton C. Keiler, Henry W. Cook, Jr.; (rear) John W. Coolidge, Jr., Thornton Jenkins, Wesley E. Bevins, E. John DeBeer, John F. Koopman, Emerson T. Oliver, Thomas M. Brennan, Francis H. Markey. Tom Naylor photo.

The recipient of this award has distinguished himself by his race management and organizational skills which have contributed to the success of numerous One Design and Ocean Racing Regattas.

He has served on the New England Ocean Racing Circuit Committee, and is now Chairman of the Race Committee for the Eastern Yacht Club and was head of the Marblehead Racing Association. He has assisted and volunteered his time to organize and run such events as the Carroll Trophy for YRUMB and the Area A Match Racing Championships of 1985. In addition, both the 1985 Etchells and J 22 North American Championships were sponsored under his direction.

During this past summer, his innovative style led to the creation of an Ocean Racing Clinic involving classroom discussion and critique, with on-the-water-racing including video applications. His plans for 1986 include events for YRUMB as well as the Finn North Americans and IOD Worlds.

The Yacht Racing Union of Massachusetts Bay is proud to recognize this individual who has contributed so much to make the sport of sailboat racing such a success for those of us who participate at all levels.

If Pem Pleasants left his mark on the Eastern as a nonhelmsman, Jeffrey C. Foster had been making his as a helmsman but nonowner. In 1985 he skippered the Twelve Meter trial horse *Defender* and was helmsman on *Courageous*, and winning helmsman in the Patton Bowl and Fort Lauderdale-Key West races. In 1984 he was, as far as he knew, the youngest skipper to complete five Bermuda Races (1976, 1978, 1980, 1982, and 1984—navigator as well in 1982 and 1984). And in his first year as an Eastern member, 1975, he skippered the United States Southern Cross team in the Halifax and Lambert Cup races, and was the only known Eastern member to skipper in the Sidney-Hobart Race, Down Under.

"Ocean racing has changed so much from the days when I started," Jeff Foster has written, "that it's hard to assess what's important and what isn't. Today the helmsman, tactician and navigator are no more wrapped up in the skipper role. Many of us have found that we can sail and fulfill important functions without the burden of ownership. And PHRF has watered down the competition, with many side effects, mainly the desire to avoid overnight racing at any cost."

In 1985 the Eastern joined the million-dollar-yacht-club club under the pressures of growth and inflation. By the 1985–86 season, income totaled $1,376,643, against expenses of

$1,327,420—more than a threefold increase in ten years. The staff required to carry on an operation consistent with what may be assumed would have been the expectations of the founders stood at eighty—only thirty fewer than the number of founders—about equally divided between full time and part time.

A. Wentworth Erickson, Jr., who had joined on June 29, 1928, was Number One in 1985, followed by Lincoln Davis, Jr., Henry A. Morss, Jr., B. Devereux Barker, Jr., and Robert B.M. Barton. All five had been members for fifty years or more, and the fathers of four of them had been members. Not a bad record of continuity after 115 years.

Fierce guardian of the treasury, defiant defender of the old ways, raconteur supreme, Bob Barton remained first and foremost a devoted yachtsman from the moment he joined the Eastern on May 3, 1934, and thereby launched himself on his sailing career. He marked fifty years of membership in the summer of 1984 with his third cruise to the Saint John River in New Brunswick in *Sally V*, a Hinckley 50, the latest of the dynasty of boats honoring Mrs. Barton. They spent part of each summer in their house on Foster Island in Maine's St. John River. On the North Shore or down east, his greatest pleasure, fair weather or foul, was daysailing, virtually daily and frequently with no companion but his professional skipper.

From the start, getting out on the water, the sail, the race, the cruise, have been the thing. For 110 years, the Great Committee up there has been tinkering with the course, the boats, the crews, the weather, and certainly the rules. But the water is as wet as ever, and as salty. *Aurae vela vocant*. An apt Club motto. "The winds call to the sails."

It all began sedately enough up on deck, if uproariously down below, and by 1880, when the new house was rising on the recently purchased Marblehead Neck property, the Club had 240 male members of wealth and character who among them owned sixty-nine substantial yachts. The forty-one schooners outnumbered the sloops almost two-to-one. Not one measured under 30 feet on the water, and virtually all were professionally sailed.

Fifty years passed, and in the shaky year of 1930, the membership hovered at 624, the fleet at 362, more than a fivefold increase. Of the 236 over 30 feet waterline, fifty were schoon-

ers and seventy-two were sloops, yawls, and ketches. There were ten steam yachts, one barque, and one brig; another 125 were under 30 feet. Of course the roster and the fleet were swelled by members from a distance who joined to avail themselves of privileges while cruising.

The Club remained almost wholly preoccupied with sailing in 1930. Corinthianism now held sway, although the pros continued to run the big boats. And the overwhelming majority of the fleet was still built of wood—hand-built like violins, no two exactly alike, even when crafted from one design.

A sure sign of the times was the gradual but relentless erosion of the big boat/small boat chalk line from 30 feet to nothing. In 1980 the fleet was essentially unchanged, at 262 (only seven more than in 1935, the bottom of the Depression), of which 203 were over 20 feet on the waterline and fifty-nine under. Only four sailboats and one powerboat exceeded 50 feet. Eighty-three were one-designs.

Few were not fiberglass, and the gentle caress of wavelets against countless counters on a windless June evening 'neath the brooding guardianship of Fort Sewall had been drowned out by the metallic chorus of a thousand stainless halyards slapping a thousand aluminum masts. With the exception of the Internationals and the U.S. Ones, the one-designs in top competition were universally glass. Almost obsessively, strict design and construction standards—made possible by computers, molding, and quantity production of hulls, sails, rigging, hardware, and surface compounds—imposed a degree of uniformity and a common language that reduced "character" to a matter of class distinction and put the utmost emphasis on the character of the sailor.

And that, when you got right down to it, was what son, father, and great-grandfather had been trying for since the first crude handicapping of the old rule-o'-thumb gaff-riggers.

Times had certainly changed since Charlie Foster evoked the early years of the Club before the turn of the century with his frontispiece photograph in *The Ditty Box* of a hard-handed old professional skipper, walrus mustache and all, gripping the mahogany wheel of one of those grand varnished yachts of the fathers and grandfathers. But the joy of it was the same, forever there, somewhere, anywhere, beyond Marblehead Rock. With Fostery enthusiasm, the first historian burst forth for all time, and for all sailors:

Aurae Vela Vocant

Oh, the Joy of It!

Look at him! Isn't he the embodiment of nautical happiness? Every inch the old sailor, as you can tell by his pose at the wheel. Been aloft and below on square-riggers around the Horn; been fishing and yachting, and just adores a scrap either with another boat or with Nature as he meets it in its angry moods. But it is his experience with the latter that has taught him to appreciate to its fullest extent the conditions as we see them in our picture.

Now, my readers, just put yourself in his place and mentally get some of the thrill. On board the famous *Puritan*, broad of deck, all spic and span, a new and fine-setting suit of sails, trimmed in, but with a good full, and a speed of say 9 knots, though with the wind in your face it seems like 20. Just see how she heels to the breeze and rushes along—but a spoke now and then is all she needs. It is along the Maine coast, through reach and thoroughfare, with a crisp offshore breeze laden with the Maine woods' piney fragrance. Anchor down in some little cove for lunch, then on again until sundown in harbor under the hills—and what a glorious sunset in back of them! And what a night to sleep, hatches and skylights open! Does not the thought of it thrill you?

Aurae Vela Vocant
The Winds Call to the Sails

Bibliography

Note: Sources marked as EYC are in the Historical Committee room at the clubhouse.

[Anon.]. Letter to C.H.W. Foster (Cruise of the *Vashti*), June 20, 1932. EYC.

Baker, William A. "The Original Knockabouts." *WoodenBoat*, January/February 1976.

Barker, B. Devereux. "The Eastern Yacht Club Story 1900-1962." Typescript dated October 22, 1962. EYC.

Barker, B. Devereux, III. "Ray Hunt." *Yachting*, July 1964.

Blanchard, Fessenden S. *The Sailboat Classes of America*. New York, 1968.

Blumenson, Martin. *The Patton Papers 1885–1940*. Boston, 1972.

Boardman, Edwin A. *The Small Yacht: Its Management and Handling for Racing and Sailing*. Boston, 1909.

Bolger, Philip C. "L. Francis Herreshoff." *Nautical Quarterly*, no. 9, 1980.

Burtner, Evers. *The Golden Age of Open Class Racing at Marblehead, 1906–1940*. Plaistow, NH, 1977.

———. Letter to Commodore James Parker, January 24, 1963. EYC.

———. Miscellaneous typewritten notes. EYC.

Carrick, Robert W., and Richard Henderson. *John G. Alden and His Yacht Designs*. Camden, Maine, 1983.

Carter, Robert. *A Summer Cruise on the Coast of New England*. 1864. Reprinted as *Carter's Coast of New England*. Somersworth, NH. 1969.

Chapelle, Howard I. *The American Fishing Schooners 1825–1935*. New York, 1973.

Connolly, Eugene T. *U.S. One Design Class History*. 1959. Spiral bound.

Connolly, James T. Letter to Suzanne S. Connolly, undated.

Connolly, Stephen J., III. Letter in *The Log of Mystic Seaport*. Mystic, CT, Summer 1981.

Crockett, Mary Elizabeth. "Winning a Race from FDR." *Down East*, September 1979.

Crowninshield, Francis B. *The Log of Cleopatra's Barge, 1928–1942*. Boston, 1948.

Cruising Club of America 50th Anniversary Yearbook.

Curtis, Greely. Manuscript journal.

Cushman, Rufus C. Scrapbook.

Davis, Lincoln, Jr. Scrapbooks.

Day, Thomas Fleming. "Ocean Races to Bermuda." *The Rudder*, July 1907.

Duncan, Roger F., and Fessenden S. Blanchard. *A Cruising Guide to the New England Coast*. New York, 1959.

Eastern Yacht Club. Committee reports.
    Council minutes.
    Historical Committee Annual Reviews, 1901–1985.
    Regatta Committee minutes, 1871–1888.
    Regatta Committee records, 1907–1926.
    Supplement, 1976.
    Yearbooks.

"Eastern Yacht Club, The." *Yachts and Yachting*, 1911.

Eaton, William S. Letter to C.H.W. Foster, July 6, 1932. EYC.

Farwell, Edith Foster. "Our 419-Ton Summer House." *Yankee*, May 1964.

Ferguson, David L. *Cleopatra's Barge: The Crowninshield Story*. Boston, 1976.

First Grand International Yachting Festival at Marblehead Monday, September 3, 1906. Souvenir booklet.

Foley, James P. "Searching for *Edna's* Past." *WoodenBoat*, September/October 1974.

Foster, Charles H.W. *The Eastern Yacht Club Ditty Box 1870–1900.* Norwood, MA, 1932.

———. Notes on the Boats Owned & Sailed by C.H.W. Foster. Undated typescript. EYC.

———. Recollections of boats, 1875–1933. Undated typescript. EYC.

———. Yachts owned by C.H.W. Foster. Typescript with penciled additions to 1946. EYC.

Fowle, Leonard M., Jr. "He Had Ideas, and Designers Set Them Down." (about C.H.W. Foster). *Boston Globe*, December 31, 1933.

———. "Foster Exemplified the Best in Yachting." *Boston Globe*, September 25, 1955.

———. Obituary (of C.H.W. Foster) in *Yachting*, November 1955.

———. "Marblehead: A Nation's Yachting Capital." In: *Marblehead Tercentenary Booklet 1649–1949.* Marblehead, 1949.

Gardner, John. "Nixie." *The Log of Mystic Seaport.* Mystic, CT, Spring 1981.

Garland, Joseph E. *Boston's North Shore 1823–1890.* Boston, 1978.

———. *Boston's Gold Coast 1890–1929.* Boston, 1981.

———. *Down to the Sea.* Boston, 1983.

———. *Eastern Point.* Dublin, NH, 1971.

Gribbins, J. Patrick. "Ray Hunt—New England Archimedes." *Nautical Quarterly*, Spring 1984.

Haskell, Rebecca Benson. Recollections of Marblehead Neck 1912–1932. Manuscript.

Haskins, Sturgis. "Searching for *Edna's* Past, Part II." *WoodenBoat*, March/April 1975.

Herreshoff, L. Francis. *Capt. Nat Herreshoff: The Wizard of Bristol.* New York, 1953.

———. *The Common Sense of Yacht Design.* Jamaica, NY, 1966.

Herreshoff, Nathanael G. Correspondence with C.H.W. Foster. EYC.

History of the Boston Yacht Club. Boston, 1891.

Homans, George C. "Sailing with Uncle Charlie." *Atlantic Monthly*, July 1965.

Hovey, Charles F. Letter to Eugene T. Connolly, March 13, 1979.

Howard, Henry. *Charting My Life.* Boston, 1948.

———. "History of the International Sonder Class Races Held Under the Joint Auspices of the Eastern Yacht Club at Marblehead and the Kaiserlicher Yacht Club of Kiel, Germany." Submitted to the Council of the Eastern Yacht Club, December 5, 1907. Typescript. EYC.

Howland, Llewellyn, III. "The Burgess Legacy." *WoodenBoat*, July/August, September/October, November/December 1986, January/February 1987.

Kimball, F.R. *Handbook of Marblehead Neck.* Boston, 1882.

Lawrence, John S. Account of cruise, to C.H.W. Foster, April 22, 1932. EYC.

———. Account of cruise of *Indian* for Foster. (undated). EYC.

Levey, Robert L. "The Currents of Controversy." *Boston Globe*, May 17, 1960.

Lord, Priscilla S., and Virginia C. Gamage. *Marblehead: The Spirit of '76 Lives Here.* Philadelphia, 1972.

Loring, Caleb, Jr. Letter to author, July 6, 1987.

McNamara, John, Jr. "Maritime Marblehead 1929–1979." In: *Marblehead 350th Anniversary Booklet.* Marblehead, 1979.

McQuesten, Frank B. Account of *Gitana* cruise of 1898. Typescript. EYC.

Morison, Samuel Eliot. *The Story of Mt. Desert Island.* Boston, 1960.

Mount Desert Reading Room Club Rules

Noyes, Bradley P. Scrapbooks.

O'Neil, Gladys. "The Mount Desert Reading Room, from Club House to Hotel in 63 Years." Undated typescript.

Parkinson, John, Jr. *The History of the New York Yacht Club.* 2 vols. New York, 1975.

Peabody, Robert E. "Peach's Point, Marblehead." *Essex Institute Historical Collections*, January 1966.

Phillips, James D. "Commuting to Salem and Its Summer Resorts Fifty Years Ago." *Essex Institute Historical Collections*, April 1944.

Poor, George R. Scrapbooks.

Robinson, W.E. Profile of Charles Francis Adams. *The Rudder*, May 1898.

Roosevelt, James, and Paul D. Rust, Jr. "The President Goes Cruising." *Yachting*, August 1933.

Rosenfeld, Morris and Stanley. *A Century Under Sail.* Reading, MA, 1984.

Sailing Regulations (1870–1931). Typescript in James P. Parker notebook. EYC.

Sears, Herbert M. "Cruise of the *Constellation* to the West Indies, Winter of 1916." Bound typescript.

Shanabrook, Paul E. *The Boston (A History of the Boston Yacht Club) 1866–1979.* Boston, 1979.

Shepard, Timothy. *Peaches Point.* New York, 1976.

Stephens, William P. *American Yachting.* New York, 1904.

———. *Traditions and Memories of American Yachting.* New York, 1942.

———. Letters to C.H.W. Foster. EYC.

Story, Dana. *Frame-Up!* Barre, MA, 1964.

Swan, William U. "A Century of Yachting at Marblehead." In: Joseph S. Robinson, *The Story of Marblehead.* Salem, MA, 1936.

———. Profile of Charles Francis Adams. *Boston Transcript,* July 3, 1920.

———. Profile of Adams. *American Sportsman,* 1931.

———. "Fifty Years Young" (*Constellation*). *Yachting,* June 1938.

Taggard, Henry. Typed notes for C.H.W. Foster. EYC.

Testimonial to Charles J. Paine and Edward Burgess from the City of Boston for Their Successful Defence of the America's Cup. Boston, 1887.

Thompson, Winfield M. "German-American Match." *The Rudder,* August 1906.

———. "Germany vs. America." Ibid., October 1906.

———. "The Third German-American Match." Ibid., October 1909.

———. "Marblehead to Halifax." Ibid., November 1905.

———, William P. Stephens, and William U. Swan. *The Yacht "America."* Boston, 1925.

Wilson, John. "Flirting with Brenda." In *Far Horizons: Adventures in Cruising by Members of the Cruising Club of America.* Cruising Club of America, 1971.

Wilson, Richard B. "The Dane Awakes. *Holger Danske* Wins the Bermuda Race." *Cruising Club News,* January 1981.

OTHER SOURCES

Boston Globe, Boston Herald, Boston Transcript, Brooklyn Citizen, Gloucester Times, Halifax Chronicle, Lynn Item, The (Marblehead) *Mainsheet, Marblehead Mercury, Marblehead Messenger, Marblehead Reporter, Miami News, Mount Desert Herald, New York Times, North Shore Breeze, Queensborough* (N.Y.), *Dispatch.*

The Easterner (newsletter of the Eastern Yacht Club), *New England Yachtsman, New England Yachting News, The Rudder, Yachting.*

Bar Harbor Historical Society, Essex Institute, Harvard University Archives, Marblehead Historical Society, Peabody Museum of Salem.

INTERVIEWS

Herbert N. Baldwin, Robert B.M. Barton, Donald W. Blodgett, Garrett D. Bowne III, David A. Curtis, Frances Gilliland, Francis Lee Higginson, Frederick E. Hood, Francis H. Markey, Elizabeth Hovey Morss, Henry A. Morss, Jr., Nathaniel Cushing Nash, Jr., Bradley P. Noyes, Albert C. Parker, L. Pemberton Pleasants, Jr., Arthur P. Poor, George R. Poor, Eugene Stetson.

ACKNOWLEDGMENTS

James C. Ayer, Thomas S. Barrows, Lloyd Bergeson, David Breed, Walter J. Cairns, Edward D. Cook, Jr., Mrs. Catherine T. Farlow, Thomas Halsted, Charles F. Hovey, George L. Hubbell, Betty Iacono, Mrs. Henry A. Morss, Jr., Gladys O'Neil, Dorothy Osborn, Asa E. Phillips, Jr., the late Gordon C. Prince, Robert W. Sides, Samuel Vaughan.

Photo Credits

Except as noted below, photographs are from the Eastern Yacht Club collection.

Text

Color Section

Index